Washington, D.C., from A to Z

From *The City Guide Series*, books that offer travel information to exciting destinations arranged alphabetically. Other titles include:

New York from A to Z: The Traveler's Look-Up Source for the Big Apple by Paul Wasserman

Also by Paul Wasserman

Information for Administrators. Cornell University Press. 1956.
Sources of Commodity Prices. Special Libraries Association. 1960.
The Librarian and the Machine. Gale Research Company. 1965.
Encyclopedia of Business Information Sources. Gale Research Company. 1971.
The New Librarianship. R. R. Bowker Company. 1972.
Consumer Sourcebook. Gale Research Company. 1974.
Speakers and Lecturers: How to Find Them. Gale Research Company. 1979.
Encyclopedia of Health Information Sources. Gale Research Company. 1987.
Encyclopedia of Legal Information Sources. Gale Research Company. 1988.
The Best of Times: A Personal Odyssey and Occupational Odyssey. Omnigraphics. 2000.
New York from A to Z: The Traveler's Look-Up Source for the Big Apple. Capital Books, 2002.

WASHINGTON, D.C.
FROM A to Z

The Traveler's Look-Up Source
for the Nation's Capital

Paul Wasserman
and
Don Hausrath

CAPITAL
BOOKS, INC.
Sterling, Virginia

Capital Books, Inc.
P.O. Box 605
Herndon, Virginia 20172-0605

ISBN 1-931868-07-7 (alk.paper)

Library of Congress Cataloging-in-Publication Data
Wasserman, Paul
    Washington, DC from A to Z : the traveler's look-up source for the
nation's capital / Paul Wasserman and Don Hausrath.—1st ed.
        p.   cm. — (The city guide series)
    Includes bibliographical references.
        ISBN 1-931868-07-7 (alk. paper)
        1. Washington (D.C.)—Guidebooks.   2. Washington (D.C.)—Directories.
I. Hausrath, Don.   II. Title.   III. Series.

    F192.3.W36   2003
    917.5304'42—dc21   2003000006

Printed in the United States of America on acid-free paper that meets the American National Standards Institute Z39-48 Standard.

First Edition

10   9   8   7   6   5   4   3   2   1

Contents

Acknowledgments   vii

Foreword   ix

Introduction: How to Use This Book   xi

What Is Included and Not Included   xiii

Abbreviations Used in This Book   xv

Washington, D.C., from A to Z   1

Acknowledgments

The authors wish to express their grateful appreciation to the many individuals, organizations, government agencies, and private organizations who, while un-named here because of their sheer numbers, graciously responded to requests for information about their activities and functions. In a work of this scope the accuracy of the content is inextricably dependent on such cooperation and for this invaluable assistance we extend our heartfelt thanks. Important research assistance was provided by Yu Hsiu Wang and Karen Patterson of the library of the College of Information Studies of the University of Maryland. Peggy Barrett performed diligently and intelligently the task of word processing the manuscript in her cheerful, consistent, and painstaking style. Dorothy Drennen aided in countless ways all during the manuscript's preparation stages.

Foreword

The major effort in preparing this book took place during 2002. Since this was a time soon after the events of September 11, 2001, in New York and at the Pentagon just across the Potomac from Washington, the effects were then and are still being felt in many ways in the nation's capital. In particular, a number of traditionally open and accessible government and public buildings in some instances have been made less available or have been closed to the public. We have sought to include details about public access to these sites as of late fall 2002. However, there continue to be changes in the terms and conditions of visitor access to government installations most sensitive to security concerns. The reader will find it advisable to call in advance of visiting to ensure that the details provided in this volume have not been modified.

Introduction: How to Use This Book

The idea underlying this book's content is to offer its users an arrangement and specific descriptive details in the simplest and most accessible form with precise information on what they seek rather than lengthy descriptive accounts. It is an easy-to-use tool arranged alphabetically. To find information, turn directly to the entry where the basic details are provided.

Example: To learn about Ford's Theatre and Lincoln Museum turn to the entry under F:

Ford's Theatre and Lincoln Museum 511 10th St. NW btw E and F Sts. (202) 347-4833 www.fordstheatre.org

This site where Abraham Lincoln was fatally wounded has been painstakingly restored to its 1860s appearance. It is open daily 9 a.m.–5 p.m., except when there are rehearsals or matinee performances in the theater. Admission is free and there is a self-directed tour and a 15-minute narrative on the Washington scene during the Civil War and of the assassination. The museum in the basement lays out the details of the assassination and displays the pistol John Wilkes Booth used and other artifacts. The theater is an active venue for live musical and theatrical performances. Metro: Metro Center.

For information by category, look for it in the alphabetical listings under the subject sought.

Example: To learn about HISTORIC HOUSES AND BUILDINGS, simply turn to that entry under H for a listing of all the specific entries included in the book. Then turn to the specific HISTORIC HOUSE, for example Old Stone House. Turn to the entry Old Stone House for the details:

Old Stone House 3051 M St. NW btw 30th and 31st Sts. (202) 426-6851 www.nps.gov/rocr/oldstonehouse

This historic cottage in Georgetown is probably the oldest pre-Revolutionary building still surviving in the city. It has been restored and contains Colonial furnishings in its small rooms. The house and its lovely gardens in the rear are maintained by the National Park Service. Open Wed–Sun noon–5 p.m. Admission free. Metro: Foggy Bottom-GWU, then 30, 32, 34, 35, or 36 Bus.

Note also that the alphabetical listings offer innumerable references to redirect the user: Example: Friendship Archway *see* Chinatown Friendship Archway; Hamilton Statue *see* Alexander Hamilton Statue. Similarly, cross-references will lead the user from an entry where the information is not given, to the precise designation under which it can be found. For example: Gymnasiums *see* Fitness Centers.

What Is Included and Not Included

Washington, D.C., from A to Z contains some 2,100 entries across the entire range of features and attractions of the capital city and its nearby suburbs in Virginia and Maryland. Some categories, such as hotels, restaurants, retail stores, night clubs, and bars, because they literally number in the thousands, have been screened to incorporate a selective listing. Hotel accommodations included in the book have been carefully chosen to provide descriptive details of establishments across a wide range of locations and price levels. Restaurants have been selected from the entire metropolitan Washington area to offer the widest possible range of culinary and ethnic specialties with varying cost categories. Bars and night clubs listed offer a broad sweep of types of ambiance, entertainment forms, and price variations. We provide all but comprehensive coverage of major shopping malls and selectively list principal department stores plus the most outstanding, unusual, or popular retail outlets.

For every other category we are extremely inclusive, providing entries for the city's attractions, activities, and places of interest. Entries reach back to the city's Colonial days, and serve as a quick reference for sites associated with major figures in the history of the city and the nation. These sites include homes, monuments, and sculptures. The creators of buildings, bridges, and monuments are listed along with comments regarding their historic significance. Included as well are details about the area's museums, entertainment centers, public attractions, theaters, concert halls, farmers markets, fairs, festivals, parks, tourist services, and many other visitor destinations.

Two features of this book are particularly useful to newcomers and tourists. First, we provide current Web site information for many of the entries. Second, we offer an extensive listing of events, including a monthly checklist of festivals, parades, celebrations, and other activities drawing thousands of participants each year.

Listed Web sites bring together current information on such disparate subjects as the week's blues offerings, children's events, restaurant reviews, line dancing, late-night pub crawling, architectural street surveys, concerts, hiking trails, bike outings, and historic neighborhood walks. Other sites provide a remarkable depth of information, illustrations, and hyperlinks to related topics. The National Park Service, for example, offers details about the area's monuments, parks, and historic sites and provides downloadable brochures. The White House; Georgetown, D.C.;

Art Museum of the Americas; and the U.K. Embassy sites, among others, include striking virtual tours. Other sites suggest ways children can make the most of their visit to a museum or historic site or explain how to get about Washington and the suburbs using public transportation. While some sites are notoriously dated, most provide useful up-to-the-minute information, including recent changes in visiting hours and public access regulations.

Abbreviations Used in This Book

ATM = automated teller machine
Ave. = Avenue
Blvd. = Boulevard
btw = between
DJ = Disc Jockey
Dr. = Drive
E = East
ext = extension
Fri = Friday
Hwy. = Highway
Mon = Monday
N = North
NE = Northeast
NW = Northwest
Pkwy. = Parkway
Pl. = Place
Rd. = Road
Rte. = Route
S = South
SE = Southeast
Sat = Saturday
St. = Saint
St. = Street
Sun = Sunday
Tues = Tuesday
Thurs = Thursday
U.S. = United States
W = West
Wed = Wednesday

ADC Map and Travel Center 1636 I St. NW (202) 628-2608 www.adcmap.com
The store in Washington for every conceivable map, atlas, globe, and travel guidebook for the intrepid world traveler, as well as comprehensive information on Washington and its environs. Metro system maps for bus and train routes and books featuring day trips to suburban locations around the city are also available. Open Mon–Thurs 9 a.m.–6:30 p.m., Fri 9 a.m.–5:30 p.m., Sat 11 a.m.–5 p.m. Metro: Farragut West.

AMC Mazza Gallerie 5300 Wisconsin Ave. NW at Western Ave. (202) 537-9953
Located on the top floor of an upscale shopping center where northwest D.C. meets Maryland, this recently constructed seven-screen film complex shows current Hollywood releases. Metro: Friendship Heights.

AMC Union Station 50 Massachusetts Ave. NE (703) 998-4AMC
Located on the lower level of the train station, this nine-theater movie complex features popular current film fare. Metro: Union Station.

ATM Locations
Both Visa and MasterCard offer ATM location services on their Web sites with maps showing machine locations in metropolitan Washington or anywhere else on the planet. You can use the service to locate 24-hour ATMs, locate machines by zip code, or by entering a specific address and finding the nearest location. The site for Visa is www.visa.com, and the MasterCard site is www.mastercard.com.

A. V. Ristorante Italiano 607 New York Ave. NW (202) 737-0550
An old-fashioned legendary family restaurant featuring everything Italian from pizza to pastas to meat dishes, all served in casual style in a cozy ambiance at quite modest prices. Open Mon–Fri for lunch and dinner, Sat dinner. Metro: Mount Vernon Square.

A. Philip Randolph Statue at Union Station 50 Massachusetts Ave. NE
Located within the station near Gate C, this is a larger-than-life bronze memo-

rial to the founder of the Sleeping Car Porters Union and civil rights activist who helped organize the 1963 March on Washington. Metro: Union Station.

Aangan Indian Restaurant 4920 St. Elmo Ave., Bethesda (301) 657-1262
This modest-priced dining spot offers what must be the most tranquil ambiance in Bethesda. The pleasant service and tasty daily buffet lunch and brunch as well as the succulent daily dinners make a visit here a treat in every sense. Metro: Bethesda.

Aatish 609 Pennsylvania Ave. SE (202) 544-0931
Tandoori clay-oven-prepared breads, vegetables, and succulent meat and seafood dishes are served in a relaxed environment in this inexpensive Indian/Pakistani-style restaurant. Lunch and dinner Mon–Sat. Metro: Eastern Market.

Abraham Lincoln Birthday Celebration Lincoln Memorial, 23rd St. and Independence Ave. NW (202) 619-7222
The reading of the Gettysburg Address and a wreath-laying ceremony highlight this birthday event on February 12 at the site of one of the city's most cherished monuments. Metro: Foggy Bottom or Smithsonian.

Abraham Lincoln Memorial *see* Lincoln Memorial.

Abraham Lincoln Statue *see* Lincoln Statue.

Accommodations in Washington, D.C. *see* Bed-and-Breakfasts, Bed-and-Breakfast Rental Agencies, Budget Hotels, Deluxe Hotels, First-Class Hotels, Guest Houses, Hostels, Hotel Reservation Agencies, Middle-Range Hotels, YMCA of Metropolitan Washington, YWCA.

Active Sports Activity *see* Bicycling, Boating, Bowling, Climbing, Golf, Hiking, Horseback Riding, Ice-skating, In-line Skating, Pool, Racquetball, Running, Squash, Swimming, Tennis.

Adams Inn 1744 Lanier Pl. NW btw Calvert St. and Ontario Rd. (202) 745-3600 or (800) 578-6807, fax (202) 319-7598 www.adamsinn.com
Located on a quiet residential street in three older buildings, this is a modestly priced bed-and-breakfast offering clean, simply furnished rooms, many with shared bath and free breakfast. There is no TV or room phone, but there is access to coffee, the common lounge, washer-dryer, and a lobby pay phone. Metro: Woodley Park-Zoo, then 90, 91, 92, 93, 96 Bus.

Adams Memorial In Rock Creek Cemetery at Rock Creek Church Rd. and Webster St. NW
Created by celebrated American sculptor Augustus Saint-Gaudens and architect Stanford White, this 1891 monument to the wife of Henry Adams is the best-known memorial in this tranquil burial ground. A map of the cemetery is available at the office next to the main gate. Metro: Brookland-CUA, then H8 Bus toward Mount Pleasant.

Adams Morgan www.adamsmorgan.net
The city's liveliest and trendiest multi-ethnic neighborhood is transformed after dark from a quiet area into a vibrant, crowded, social, and cultural center. Bounded by Euclid St. on the north, 15th St. on the east, T St. on the south, and 19th St. on

the west, the epicenter is the intersection of Columbia Rd. and 18th St. The area is also where many fine old brownstones, townhouses, and classy older apartment buildings are home to young white upward mobiles who comprise a distinct element living alongside a large population of residents from Latin America, the Caribbean, Africa, and Asia. Along Greenwich Village–style 18th St. visitors will discover a colorful plethora of ethnic restaurants, cafés, bars, nightclubs, boutiques, and more. Metro: Dupont Circle, then L2 Bus, or Woodley Park-Zoo then 90, 91, 92, 93, or 96 Bus.

Adams Morgan Day www.adamsmorganday.org

This great ethnic festival is celebrated with enormous participation from musicians, craftspeople, and food vendors along 18th St. between Columbia Rd. and Florida Ave. NW, usually on the second Sunday in September. It's one of the most popular attractions in the city's most culturally diverse community. Details at (202) 789-7000 or www.adamsmorganday.org. Metro: Woodley Park-Zoo, then 90, 91, 92, 93, or 96 Bus.

Adams Morgan Farmers Market (301) 587-2248

This small, lively open-air market of local growers is open 8 a.m.–4 p.m. on Saturdays from May to December at 18th St. and Columbia Rd. NW in this multicultural neighborhood. Metro: Woodley Park-Zoo, then 90, 91, 92, 93, or 96 Bus.

Adamson Gallery *see* David Adamson Gallery/Editions.

Adas Israel Congregation 2850 Quebec St. NW (202) 362-4433 www.adas israel.org

The largest conservative Jewish synagogue membership in the city has been at its present site since 1951 but has a history dating from the mid-nineteenth century when it was located at an earlier site. Set back from Connecticut Ave. on a triangular lot bordered by Porter and Quebec Sts., the granite-faced structure has five massive bronze doors and a giant-sized menorah facing out on Connecticut Ave. Metro: Cleveland Park.

Addie's 11120 Rockville Pike, Rockville, MD (301) 881-0081

The quirky furnishings at this suburban frame house flavor the ambiance at this smart and trendy restaurant serving excellent American-style food at moderate to expensive prices. Lunch Mon-Sat, dinner daily. Metro: Grovesnor-Strathmore or White Flint.

Addis Ababa 2106 18th St. NW (202) 232-6092

This inexpensive Adams Morgan restaurant serves bountiful and tasty food that is just as popular with Ethiopians as with its other customers. Lunch and dinner daily. Metro: Woodley Park-Zoo, then 90, 91, 92, 93, or 96 Bus; or Dupont Circle then L2 Bus.

Addisu Gebeya 2202 18th St. NW, btw Wyoming Ave. and Kalorama Rd. (202) 986-6013

This Adams Morgan Ethiopian market sells various spicy vegetables, spongy *injera* bread, flour, cookbooks, records, and tapes. Open daily from 9 a.m. on. Metro: Woodley Park-Zoo, then 90, 91, 92, 93, or 96 Bus.

Aditi 3299 M St, NW at 33rd St. (202) 625-6825

This moderately priced Indian restaurant in Georgetown features tandoori and curry dishes for both meat and vegetable fanciers and is open for lunch and dinner daily. Metro: Foggy Bottom-GWU, then 30, 32, 34, 35, or 36 Bus.

Admiral David G. Farragut Sculpture *see* Farragut Sculpture.

Adventure Theater Glen Echo Park, 7300 MacArthur Blvd. (301) 320-5331 www .nps.gov/glec/adtheat.htm

The Washington area's longest running performance center for children features plays designed for kids from about 4 to 12, which dramatize fairy tales, fables, and classic stories on Saturday and Sunday at 1:30 and 3:30 p.m. Tickets are $6 per person of any age. *See also* Glen Echo Park.

Affrica 2010 R St. at Connecticut Ave. NW (202) 745-7272 www.affrica.com

Begun some 25 years ago, this Dupont Circle gallery features traditional artworks from Africa including masks, textiles, pottery, furniture, and carvings. Open Tues 2 p.m.–6 p.m., Wed to Sat noon–6 p.m., and other times by appointment. Metro: Dupont Circle.

Afghan Restaurants *see* Faryab, Panjshir. *See also* www.dcpages.com, www.wash ingtonpost.com, www.restaurant.com, www.opentable.com.

African American Civil War Memorial 10th and U Sts. NW (202) 667-2667 www.afroamcivilwar.org/museum.html

This stone and bronze 11-foot statue with figures of three soldiers and a sailor on one side and a family on the other honors the 200,000 or so African-Americans and their white officers who fought for the Union in the Civil War. Bas reliefs bear the names of the soldiers. The African American Civil War Memorial Museum is located in the True Reformer Building at 1200 U St., 3 blocks away, which offers a database of information on the military groups' members and battles. Open Mon–Fri 9 a.m.–5 p.m., weekends 2 p.m.–5 p.m. Metro: U St.-Cardozo. *See also* www .commuterpage.com/venues/memorials.htm.

African American Heritage Tour (202) 636-9203 www.dcheritage.org

This 3-hour bus tour visits the Frederick Douglass Historic Site and other Washington locations of importance in African-American history. Adult tickets are $20 with a reduced price for children under 12.

African American Women's Resource Center at Sisterspace and Books 1515 U St. NW (202) 332-6561

This educational and cultural group seeks to advance projects and activities that inform, educate, and celebrate African-American girls and women. It sponsors an evening walking tour of the U St. neighborhood, notable for its rich history and recent rebirth as the Broadway of Black Americans. Metro: U St.-Cardozo.

African Heritage Center for Dance 4018 Minnesota Ave. NE (202) 399-5252 www.ahdd.org/history.html

This group has been in operation for 45 years performing in its own center and throughout the region. Its specialty is traditional West African dance, and it offers classes for children and adults. Metro: Minnesota Ave.

African Restaurants *see* Harambee Café, Songhai. *See also* Ethiopian Restaurants, www.dcpages.com, www.restaurant.com, www.washingtonpost.com, www.open table.com.

Agriculture Department *see* U.S. Department of Agriculture Visitor's Center.

Air Force Band Summer Concerts www.nps.gov/ncro/PublicAffairs/Summerin theCity.htm

The U.S. Air Force Band and Singing Sergeants offer five concerts during summer months on Tuesday evenings on the east side of the Capitol and Friday evenings at the Washington Monument. All year long the band and its members perform at many sites in and around the city. Schedule information at (202) 767-5658.

Air Force Memorial

The only branch of the nation's military services without a memorial in the capital city area to its some 53,000 battle casualties is planning for construction in the foreseeable future. The memorial is expected to be situated at the promontory point overlooking the Pentagon from the southwest. The design was to have been resolved by the end of 2002, and the fund-raising efforts to speed the project to conclusion are being carried out by the Air Force Memorial Foundation. Details on the effort's status are available at (703) 247-5808 or www.airforcememorial.org.

Airport Transportation

Washington is served by three airports: Reagan National Airport, Dulles Airport, and Baltimore-Washington Airport. *See also* www.shop.viator.com.

Reagan National Airport (703) 417-8000 www.metwashairports.com/national

This is the closest airport to the city and is served by the Metro subway system. Follow the signs in the terminal or use the free shuttle bus to the Metro station. It is about a 20-minute ride to downtown and the fare depends on the time of day, running no more than $1.50. Taxicabs to downtown should cost under $12 depending upon traffic. The Super Shuttle (800-BLUEVAN, www.supershuttle.com) offers shared-ride door-to-door service 5:30 a.m.–12:30 a.m. for about $10 to downtown.

Dulles Airport (703) 417-8000 www.washairports.com

This airport is located in the countryside in Virginia some 26 miles from the city center. The Super Shuttle (800-BLUEVAN, www.supershuttle.com) provides shared-ride door-to-door service 5:30 a.m.–12:30 a.m. for about $24. A taxi ride from Dulles will cost around $50. The Washington Flyer Bus (888-WASHFLY) runs every ½ hour 5:20 a.m.–around 11 p.m. (every hour on weekends) and goes to a city center location for about $18 one way with a slightly reduced price for a round-trip ticket. A recently begun Metrobus 5A to Dulles runs every half hour daily from L'Enfant Plaza. It takes 55 minutes. For information about this route and schedule call (202) 637-7700 or check the Web site: www.metroopensdoors.com. There's also a regularly scheduled Metro bus that brings riders to the Metro stop that goes downtown.

Baltimore-Washington Airport (800) 435-9294 or (410) 859-7111 www.bwiair port.com

Cheaper fares sometimes attract people to use this airport, which is some 35 miles northwest of D.C., but getting to Washington from here can be more time consuming and expensive. The lowest-cost option entails taking the free shuttle bus marked BWI Rail from the terminal to the train station. From there take a MARC or Amtrak train south to Union Station in Washington, D.C. (the Amtrak fare is about $12 compared to around $6 for the MARC train). The ride is about 20 minutes to Union Station where one can take the Metro or a taxi to the final destination. Taxi fare from Baltimore-Washington Airport to Washington can run around $60. *See also* Baltimore-Washington Airport.

Airports *see* Baltimore-Washington Airport, Dulles Airport, Reagan National Airport.

Al Tiramisu *see* Al Tiramisu under T.

Aladdin's Lamp Children's Books 126 W Broad St., Falls Church, VA (703) 241-8281

This independent bookstore is still operating after 15 years and contains a large selection of titles and a range of programs for kids from story hours to author appearances. It is open until 6 p.m. most evenings, but until 8 p.m. on one or two nights each week. Metro: East Falls Church, then about a 25-minute walk.

Albania Embassy 2100 S St. NW (202) 223-4942 www.embassy.org/embassies/al .html

Embassy of the Republic of Albania.

Albert Einstein Memorial (202) 334-2000 www.capcomgroup.com/einstein.html

This 12-foot-high seated bronze statue of the scientist holding a notebook containing his equations is located in the garden of the National Academy of Sciences at 2101 Constitution Ave. NW. A map of the solar system is spread out at the feet of the statue. Visible daily 24 hours. Metro: Foggy Bottom-GWU.

Albert Gallatin Statue www.nps.gov/whho/Statues

Located at North Plaza, Pennsylvania Ave., and 15th St. NW in the Lafayette Square area, this monument celebrates the American secretary of the treasury, congressman, senator, and ambassador to England and France. Metro: Farragut North or McPherson Square. *See also* Sewall-Belmont House, U.S. Treasury Department.

Albert Pike Statue

Located at 3rd and D Sts. NW in the downtown neighborhood, this is the sole monument in D.C. to a Confederate Army general, although it is said to have been sculpted to honor Pike as the leader of the Scottish Rite of Freemasonry during the latter part of the nineteenth century. Metro: Judiciary Square.

Alexander Graham Bell Association for the Deaf 1537 35th St. NW (202) 337-5220 www.agbell.org

Located in the Volta Laboratory and Bureau Building, a National Historic Landmark, this Roman temple–style construction in the Georgetown area functions as a clearing center for information on new development for the hearing impaired. There is also a small monument to Bell in the building and a little museum of the inventor's family memorabilia and exhibits of hearing devices. Open Mon–Fri 9 a.m.–3:30 p.m.

Alexander Hamilton Statue
This bronze monument to America's first secretary of the treasury can be found in the south entrance to the U.S. Treasury Department building between 15th St. and East Executive Ave. NW. Metro: Metro Center.

Alexander Pushkin Statue *see* Pushkin Statue.

Alexandria http://ci.alexandria.va.us/
This 16-square-mile attractive and colorful northern Virginia city is a basic element of the Washington metropolitan area and has its eastern border on the Potomac River. Its principal tourist destination is the well-maintained historic district, Old Town. Strolling here is rewarded by views of the picturesque waterfront area, an endless array of restaurants and cafés, fine galleries, boutiques and shops, attractive brick sidewalks, cobblestone streets and alleys, and the occasional glimpse of gas-lamp street lighting. Many Alexandria streets seem little changed from the way they were 200 years ago with more than 1,000 homes and buildings still inhabited that date from the eighteenth and nineteenth centuries. Alexandria is just a short Metro ride from downtown D.C. Metro: King Street, then a 20-minute walk to Old Town, or use the free shuttle bus on Friday night, Saturday, and Sunday to various locations in Old Town.

Alexandria African American Heritage Park Duke St. on Holland Lane, Alexandria (703) 838-4356
This 8-acre memorial park is maintained by the Alexandria Black History Resource Center and can be entered at Duke St. on Holland Lane. One section is a preserved nineteenth-century cemetery with a few burial sites at their original location with the headstones intact. The park also contains a wetlands area with wildlife in their natural habitats. Metro: King Street. *See also* www.commuterpage.com/ venues/sightseeing_VA.htm.

Alexandria Archaeology Museum Torpedo Factory Art Center, Studio 327, 105 N Union St. btw King and Cameron Sts., Alexandria (703) 838-4399 http://oha.ci .alexandria.va.us/archaeology/
Professionals and volunteers work in this city-run center, which carries out programs focused on the study, preservation, and interpretation of artifacts from Alexandria's history, some of which are on display. Open Tues–Fri 10 a.m.–3 p.m., Sat 10 a.m.–5 p.m., Sun 1 p.m.–5 p.m. Admission charge. Metro: King Street, then exit station and take the DAT5 DASH Bus toward Braddock Road Metro to the stop at N Fairfax St. and King St., walk 1 block east on King St. to N Union St. Or take Metrobus 28B toward Royal and Pendleton to the stop at King St. and Royal St. and walk 2 blocks east on King St. to N Union St.

Alexandria Black History Resource Center 638 N Alfred St., Alexandria (703) 838-4356 http://oha.ci.alexandria.va.us/bhrc/

For 20 years now the center has featured exhibits recounting the history of African-Americans in Alexandria and Virginia from the mid-eighteenth century to the present. Staff members offer lectures, conduct guided tours (reservations are necessary), and maintain a library. Open Tues–Sat 10 a.m.–4 p.m., Sun 1 p.m.– 5 p.m. Admission free. Metro: Braddock Road, exit the station and walk 3 blocks on Wythe St., turn right on N Alfred St., and walk 1 block south. *See also* www .commuterpage.com/venues/sightseeing_VA.htm.

Alexandria Christmas Tree Lighting

This ceremony takes place at 7 p.m. on the Friday after Thanksgiving in Market Square to the accompaniment of choir music, dance, and puppetry performances along with the appearance of Santa Claus and his entourage of elves. As the tree is lighted, hundreds of little lights go on at the same time along King St. Details at (703) 838-4200. Metro: King Street, then free shuttle bus.

Alexandria Convention and Visitor Association 221 King St. at N Fairfax St. (703) 838-4200 or (800) 388-9119 www.funside.com

Located in several rooms of the historic Ramsey House, this center is open daily 9 a.m.–5 p.m. providing free maps, brochures, hotel reservations, and reduced-rate tickets to some of the city's most popular sites, and other tourist information. Metro: King Street, then free shuttle bus on Friday night, Saturday, and Sunday, or a 20-minute walk. *See also* Ramsey House.

Alexandria Farmers Market 301 King St., Market Square at City Hall, Alexandria (703) 370-8723

This year-round operation is open every Saturday 5 p.m.–10 p.m. Metro: King Street.

Alexandria Garden Tour

In mid to late April each year, a ticket to this event provides admission to some seven private gardens and other historic sites in this historic city. Details at (703) 838-4200.

Alexandria National Cemetery 1450 Wilkes St., Alexandria www.cem.va.gov/pdf/ AlexVA.pdf

This burial site contains the graves of around 3,500 Civil War soldiers. It was dedicated in 1862 by President Abraham Lincoln and includes men who served as the U.S. Colored Troops. Metro: Braddock Road, exit the station and take the DAT3 DASH Bus toward Old Town to the stop at West and King Sts. Walk 3 blocks south on S West St., turn right on Wilkes St., and walk 1 block west. *See also* www .commuterpage.com/venues/sightseeing_VA.htm.

Alexandria Old Town *see* Old Town Alexandria.

Alexandria Red Cross Waterfront Festival www.waterfrontfestival.org

On a weekend in early June this annual family event celebrates Alexandria's maritime heritage with tall ships available for visits, various types of arts and crafts displays, entertainment, a running event, and a blessing of the fleet. Admission charge. Details at (703) 549-8300.

Alexandria Seaport Foundation Seaport Center just south of Founders Park at the end of Cameron St. (703) 549-7978 www.alexandriaseaport.org/
This organization concentrates on boat building in what can best be described as an operating museum and library with a marine laboratory. Open daily 9 a.m.–4 p.m. Metro: King Street, then DAT5 DASH Bus to Old Town to corner of King and Fairfax Sts. *See also* Seaport Center.

Alexandria Suites Hotel 420 N Van Dorn St., Alexandria, VA (703) 370-1000 www.ohwy.com/va/a/aaiihlxr.htm
Located in northern Virginia some 5 miles west of Old Town, this hotel offers 186 budget-priced suites containing kitchens in the west end of Alexandria near the Landmark Shopping Mall and close to Hwy. 395.

Algeria Embassy 2137 Wyoming Ave. NW (202) 265-2800 www.algeria-us.org
Embassy of the People's Democratic Republic of Algeria. Metro: Dupont Circle.

Algonkian Regional Park 47001 Fairway Dr., Sterling, VA (703) 450-4655 www.nvrpa.org
This park administered by the Northern Virginia Regional Park Authority in eastern Loudoun County along the Potomac River boasts an outdoor pool, a nature trail, and riverfront cabins available for rental year-round. There is also an 18-hole golf course in the park.

All Souls Unitarian Church 2935 16th St. NW at Harvard St. (202) 332-5266 www.all-souls.org
This integrated and politically active church was built in 1924 and modeled after St. Martin-in-the-Fields in London. Metro: Metro Center, then S2 or S4 Bus toward Silver Spring.

Allen Lee Hotel 2224 F St. NW at 23rd St. (202) 331-1224 or (800) 462-0186, fax (202) 296-3518 www.allenleehotel.com
This basic and cheap Foggy Bottom hotel on the George Washington University campus appeals to young and international visitors. Most of the spartan rooms have shared bathrooms but do have air-conditioning, phones, and TV. Metro: Foggy Bottom-GWU.

Alliance Française 2142 Wyoming Ave. NW (202) 234-7911 www.francedc.org
The Washington branch of this worldwide organization sponsors language courses, lectures, concerts, films, exhibitions, museum tours, and receptions for Francophiles. It features an extensive library and video collection and a newsletter, for a modest membership fee, which chronicles special events. Metro: Dupont Circle.

Alma Thomas House 1530 15th St. NW www.cr.nps.gov/nr/travel/wash/dc61.htm
This 1875 structure and its front yard inspired many of the artistic efforts of the celebrated African-American artist, whose works hang in widely known museums and who graduated in 1924 from Howard University and taught for many years at Shaw Junior High School. The building is not open to visitors. Metro: U St.-Cardozo.

Almas Temple 1315 K St. NW (202) 898-1688

This striking Moorish construction is home to the local Scottish Rite of Free-masonry chapter. Metro: McPherson Square.

Al's Magic Shop 1012 Vermont Ave. NW (202) 789-2800 www.tobias.cc/alsmagic/

The place in Washington since 1936 for everything in magic and disguise with a very competent staff to assist customers. Open Mon–Sat 9 a.m.–5 p.m., closing somewhat earlier on Saturday. Metro: McPherson Square.

Alternative Music *see* Rock, Alternative, and Ethnic Music.

Alvin Mason Lothrop House *see* Russia Embassy.

America 50 Massachusetts Ave. NE inside Union Station (202) 682-9555

Open daily for lunch and dinner, this affordable four-level eatery in the station's West Hall offers more than 200 dishes featuring specialties from virtually every state. A table on the balcony provides a view of the busy main hall of Union Station while the 4th-floor window tables look out at the Capitol. There's a second location at Tysons Corner Center. Metro: Union Station.

American Century Theater P.O. Box 6313, Arlington, VA (703) 553-8782 www.americancentury.org

One of the growing number of smaller theater companies in the D.C. area, this one has been consistently mounting fine performances at various venues. The group publishes a periodic newsletter, *Subtext*, describing these offerings. Details about current productions on the Web site. *See also* www.commuterpage.com/venues/venue-en.htm.

American College Theater Festival at the Kennedy Center for the Performing Arts, New Hampshire Ave. at Rock Creek Pkwy. NW (202) 467-4600 www.kennedycenter.org/education/actf/

In mid to late April a number of award-winning plays by college student writers are performed with tickets available at a nominal price. Metro: Foggy Bottom-GWU.

American Film Institute at the Kennedy Center for the Performing Arts, New Hampshire Ave. at Rock Creek Pkwy. NW (202) 785-4600 www.afi.com

The institute is a membership organization for film buffs and is home to AFI's 224-seat theater where classic film fare from across a spectrum of silent films to avant-garde works is presented. It features, as well, festival films and premier show-ings. Metro: Foggy Bottom-GWU. A second facility, the AFI Silver Theater, is slated to open in 2003 after completion of renovation and expansion of the former Silver Theater in Silver Spring at 8619 Colesville Rd. btw Georgia Ave. and Fenton St. Metro: Silver Spring.

American Indian Heritage Month

Every November the Smithsonian Institution schedules a range of programs and exhibitions on this theme at a number of the museums and publishes a catalog of these events available to those interested. Details at (202) 786-2403.

American Inn of Bethesda 8130 Wisconsin Ave., Bethesda (301) 656-9300 or (800) 323-7081 www.american-inn.com

Situated about midway between the National Institutes of Health and the Metro station, this moderate-priced basic hotel is within easy walking distance to Bethesda's popular restaurant row and provides guests access to its swimming pool during the warmer months. Metro: Bethesda.

American Institute of Architects 1735 New York Ave. NW (202) 626-7492 www.aiaonline.com

The 1973 headquarters of this society offers architectural exhibits in its lobby and sits behind the Octagon. Its shop carries works on architectural topics and there is also a library. The building is open during normal business hours Mon–Fri. Metro: Foggy Bottom-GWU.

American Legion Bridge crosses the Potomac on I-495

Opened in 1962, the structure is the northern I-495 (the Beltway) crossing of the Potomac, entering Fairfax County, Virginia, from Montgomery County, Maryland, between Little Falls and Great Falls.

American Pharmaceutical Association Building 2215 Constitution Ave. NW (202) 628-4410 www.aphanet.org

Designed in 1934 by John Russell Pope, who was responsible for the National Gallery of Art's West Wing and the Lincoln Memorial, this white marble structure is home to some 3,000 trade and professional organizations, which makes the site the epicenter of a great volume of congressional lobbying efforts. Metro: Foggy Bottom.

American Red Cross Headquarters Building 1730 E St. NW (202) 639-3300 www.redcross.org

The finest example in Washington of 10-foot-high Louis Comfort Tiffany stained glass windows, which have adorned the Board of Governors Hall on the 2nd floor since it opened in 1917, the building is open to the public weekdays 9 a.m.–4 p.m. Metro: Farragut West.

American Red Cross Museum 1730 E St. NW (202) 639-3300 www.redcross.org

Devoted to describing and explaining the Red Cross heritage, the History and Education Center located in the national headquarters building mounted its first exhibition in 1995. Its features include online viewing of objects and arts reflecting the organization's past and present as well as a registry that pays tribute to those who have contributed to its history. Open Mon–Fri 9 a.m.–4 p.m. Metro: Farragut West.

American Restaurants *see* Addie's, America, Andale, Ardeo, Bistro Bistro, Café Deluxe, Capital Grille, Carlyle Grand Café, Cashion's Eat Place, Chadwicks, Citronelle, Clyde's of Georgetown, Coeur de Lion, Colonnade at the Washington Monarch Hotel, D.C. Coast, Elysium, Equinox, Greenwood Restaurant, Hard Rock Café, Hard Times Café, Houston's, Kinkead's, M & S Grill, McCormick and Schmick's, Melrose, Mercury Grill, Mr. Smith's, Monocle, Morrison-Clark Inn Restaurant, New Heights, Nora, Old Angler's Inn, Old Dominion Brewing Company, Old Ebbitt Grill, Old Glory, Persimmon, Planet Hollywood, Rainforest Café, Roof Terrace Restaurant, Ruppers, Sam and Harry's, Seasons, Sequoia, 1789 Restaurant, Tabard Inn, Tahoga, Tom Sarris' Orleans House, Two Quail, Willard Room. *See also* Contemporary Restaurants, Web sites: www.dcpages.com, www.restaurant.com, www.washingtonpost.com, www.opentable.com.

American University 4400 Massachusetts Ave. NW at Nebraska Ave. (202) 885-1000 www.american.edu

Located in a beautiful residential area in the upper northwest corner of the city, this institution sprawls over 80 acres and its 11,000 graduate and undergraduate students are offered a wide range of academic specialties. Its FM station, WAMU, broadcasts National Public Radio offerings, and there is a strong law library. Guided tours of the campus area available by appointment. Metro: Tenleytown-AU, then M4 Bus.

American University Basketball www.aueagles.com

The Eagles are not the basketball powerhouses that the University of Maryland Terrapins or the Georgetown Hoyas are, but tickets are more readily available at modest prices for their games at Bender Arena on the campus. Ticket details at (202) 885-3267.

American University Bender Library 4400 Massachusetts Ave. NW at Nebraska Ave. (202) 885-3200 www.library.american.edu/

This is one of Washington's major university libraries with particular strength in the social sciences, public and international affairs, and the sciences. Hours of opening vary on different days but normally it opens early and closes late. Metro: Tenleytown-AU, then M4 Bus.

American University Department of Performing Arts 4400 Massachusetts Ave. NW at Nebraska Ave. www.american.edu/academic.depts/cas/perarts/

Concerts, orchestra programs, and theatrical performances are offered during fall and spring semesters at the McDonald Recital Hall in the Kreeger Building, the Experimental Theater, and the Kay Spiritual Life Center. Details at (202) 885-2787 or (202) 885-2431. Metro: Tenleytown-AU, then M4 Bus.

American University Park Neighborhood

On the edges of American University in upper northwest D.C. and bounded on the north by Western Ave., on the east by Wisconsin Ave., south by Garfield St., and west by Canal Rd., this community has a suburban flavor with many tree-lined streets, large private homes, townhouses, and upscale high-rise apartment complexes. Access to downtown is provided by Metrobus and Metro from the Tenleytown-AU station. The blocks nearest to the university tend to be somewhat more modest than some of the older more established streets, and the appeal of the academic atmosphere draws faculty and grad students to the neighborhood's rental housing market.

Americana Market 8541 Piney Branch Rd., Silver Spring, MD (301) 495-0864

This expanding grocery operation features food and specialty products directed at Latin American consumers and operates at two other Maryland locations: 4900 Annapolis Rd. in Bladensburg (301) 864-4870, and 1500 University Blvd. E in

Langley Park (301) 434-8922. In Virginia there's a store at 6128 Columbia Pike in Falls Church (703) 671-9625.

Americans at Work Statue Federal Trade Commission, Pennsylvania and Constitution Aves. btw 6th and 7th Sts. NW

This panel adjoining the Apex Building is made of limestone and was constructed in 1937 by four sculptors to offer reliefs of four different aspects of work in America—shopping, industry, agriculture, and international trade. Metro: Archives-Navy Memorial.

Ames 514 Rhode Island Ave. NE at 4th St. (202) 635-6022

Rock-bottom prices are the lure at this discount department store offering bargains in clothing, shoes, household goods, and appliances. Open daily, hours vary. Metro: Rhode Island Ave.

Amma Vegetarian Kitchen 3291 M St. NW (202) 625-6625

This Georgetown 2nd-floor Indian restaurant is open daily for lunch and dinner and serves well-prepared and imaginative vegetable concoctions and curries, which are tasty, filling, and inexpensive. Metro: Foggy Bottom-GWU, then 30, 32, 34, 35, or 36 Bus.

Anacostia

This black residential area contains sections of nineteenth-century historic buildings, but in the main it suffers from poor housing, underfunding, unemployment, and high crime rates. But it is the location of Cedar Hill, the home of the celebrated nineteenth-century abolitionist Frederick Douglass, and the Anacostia Museum and Center for African American History and Culture. Best to come by tour bus rather than public transport. The neighborhood lies east of the Anacostia River. The historic district runs from about Martin Luther King Ave. on the west, Good Hope Rd. on the north, Tindall St. on the east, and Bangor St. on the south.

Anacostia Farmers Market (703) 543-3063

On Fridays from around 9 a.m. to 1 p.m. between May and November fresh produce is sold by growers in the parking lot of the Union Temple Baptist Church, 1225 W St. SE.

Anacostia Museum and Center for African American History and Culture 1901 Fort Pl. SE at Martin Luther King Jr. Ave. near Fort Stanton Park (202) 357-2700 http://anacostia.si.edu/

Reopened in February 2002 after considerable renovation, this Smithsonian branch concentrates its changing exhibitions on themes that highlight African-American artists, history, and culture. It functions also as a key community resource featuring timely local concerns and a program of lectures, workshops, and films. Open daily 10 a.m.–5 p.m. Admission free. Metro: Anacostia, then Fort Stanton W-1 or W-2 bus. *See also* www.commuterpage.com/venues/museums-si .htm#AnacostiaMuseum.

Anacostia Park Fairlawn Ave. SE btw 16th St. and Pennsylvania Ave. (202) 472-3873 www.nps.gov/anac/

Straddling both sides of the Anacostia River, this 1,200-acre area is as much a natural preserve as a typical park. It contains Kenilworth Aquatic Gardens, a swimming pool run by the city's Recreation Department, a large roller skating rink, ball fields, tennis courts, and the Langston Golf Course. Open daily 6 a.m.–dusk. Metro: Anacostia.

Anatolia Turkish Café 633 Pennsylvania Ave. SE (202) 544-4753

This modest-priced family-run restaurant offers the full range of tasty appetizers and kebabs in a quiet pleasing ambiance and is open for dinner Mon–Sat, lunch Mon–Fri. Metro: Eastern Market.

Andale 401 7th St. NW at D St. (202) 783-3133 www.andaledc.com

Formerly The Mark, this restaurant still offers innovative American cuisine and a lively ambiance in this old Victorian building in the thriving new art gallery and entertainment neighborhood of downtown D.C. This highly popular, moderately expensive spot is open for lunch and dinner Mon–Sat, and reservations are usually necessary. Metro: Archives-Navy Memorial.

Andalucia 9431 Elm St. (301) 907-0052 www.andaluciarestaurant.com

Excellent southern Spanish food is offered at both branches of this moderately expensive restaurant where the zesty dishes are served with style in an attractive setting. The Rockville location is open for lunch and dinner daily except Mon. In Bethesda lunch is served Mon–Fri, dinner nightly. Rockville: 12300 Wisconsin Ave. off Parklawn Dr. (301) 770-1880. Metro: Twinbrook. Bethesda: 9431 Elm St. (301) 907-0052. Metro: Bethesda.

Anderson Cottage at the Soldiers' and Airmen's Home, Rock Creek Church Rd. and Upshur Dr. NW (301) 722-3000 http://showcase.netins.net/web/creative/lincoln/news/anderson.htm

Once a summer retreat for several U.S. presidents, including Abraham Lincoln, this Victorian Gothic 14-room structure was built around 1842 and remains one of the structures of this veterans' home. Call ahead about possibility of tour. Metro: Brookland-CUA, then H8 or H9 Bus toward Mount Pleasant.

Anderson House *see* Society of the Cincinnati of Anderson House.

André Chreky 1604 K St. NW (202) 293-9393 http://andrechreky.com/

This full-service salon and spa is open daily in a lovely townhouse offering all the rejuvenation options for enhancing appearance and glamour at reasonable prices. Metro: Farragut North.

Andrew Jackson Statue

This equestrian bronze memorial depicting the general reviewing his troops at the final battle of the War of 1812 in New Orleans dates from 1853 and was created by an American sculptor, Clark Mills. It is located at the center of Lafayette Park on Pennsylvania Ave. NW between Jackson Pl. and Madison Pl. Metro: McPherson Square.

Andrew W. Mellon Memorial Fountain located in the triangle bounded by Pennsylvania Ave., Constitution Ave., and 6th St. NW

Consisting of three tiers of bronze basins, this circular fountain was built in

1952. There is a stone bench with shade nearby from which to enjoy the view of the cascading water. Metro: Judiciary Square.

Andrews Air Force Base Open House Andrews Air Force Base, Camp Springs, MD (301) 981-4424

This has become a one-day, mid-May event for displaying at no charge to the public American military air prowess featuring bombers, fighter craft, and precision formation flying. Transportation to the viewing location is available from the Branch Ave. Metro station and FedEx Field from which buses transport visitors.

Anecdotal History Walks (301) 294-9514 www.tours.com/sightseeing/washington_dc/wash_dc_tours. php

Author and engaging tour guide Anthony Pitch leads a number of highly entertaining and informative tours of Adams Morgan, Georgetown, the White House to the Capitol, homes of the presidents, and more, by appointment and at scheduled times.

Angola Embassy 2101 16th St. NW (202) 785-1156 www.angola.org

Embassy of the Republic of Angola. Metro: U St.-Cardozo.

Annandale Farmers Market Madison District Park, Columbia Pike, Annandale, VA (703) 941-7987

On Thursdays 8 a.m.–12:30 p.m. from early May to early November producers sell their farm products.

Annual Capital Area Auto Show Washington Convention Center, 900 9th St. NW (800) 697-7574 www.washingtonautoshow.com

Every year from December 26 to January 1 this is the place to see the new car models and preview the concept cars that may someday come to fruition, all graced by sleek models draped across the car bodies. Admission charge. Metro: Gallery Pl.-Chinatown or Metro Center.

Annual Seafaring Celebration (202) 433-6897 www.history.navy.mil/branches/seafaring.htm

Sponsored by the Navy Museum, in Building 76 of the Washington Navy Yard at 9th and M Sts. SE, this annual family event celebrates the American maritime heritage in early November each year with entertainment, arts and crafts, and food. (At the time of this writing, the museum was contemplating relocating to a prospective new site nearby, but outside the Navy Yard's military perimeter.) Metro: Eastern Market or Navy Yard.

Antigua and Barbuda Embassy 3216 New Mexico Ave. NW (202) 362-5211 www.embassy.org/embassies/ag.html

Metro: Tenleytown-AU.

Antiques Fair *see* D.C. Armory Antiques Fair.

Anton Gallery 2108 R St. NW btw Florida and Connecticut Aves. NW (202) 328-0828 www.antongallery.com

Featuring works by artists from Washington and elsewhere working in various media this active gallery is open Tues–Sat, noon–5 p.m. or by appointment. Metro: Dupont Circle.

Apartment Buildings *see* The Broadmoor, The Cairo, The Chastleton, Kennedy-Warren, Marriott Wardman-Park Hotel, Tilden Gardens, Woodward Apartments.

Apex Building 625-633 Pennsylvania Ave. NW

Located at the eastern edge of the Federal Triangle and containing the offices of the Federal Trade Commission, this unusual structure combines three different buildings constructed at different times, and its twin towers serve as the secretariat of the National Council of Negro Women. Metro: Archives-Navy Memorial.

Appetizing Stores *See* Specialty Food Stores and Bakeries.

Aquarelle in the Swissôtel Washington-The Watergate, 2650 Virginia Ave. NW (202) 298-4455

Serving breakfast, lunch, and dinner daily, this luxurious restaurant featuring American and continental dishes is close to the Kennedy Center. More casual before evening, at dinner a jacket is obligatory. When reserving, request a window table looking out on the Potomac, and choosing the pre-theater prix-fixe dinner might well heighten the evening's pleasure. Metro: Foggy Bottom-GWU.

Arboretum *see* National Arboretum.

Ardeo 3311 Connecticut Ave. at Macomb St. NW (202) 244-6750 www .ardeorestaurant.com/

Located in upper northwest Cleveland Park, this artistically designed restaurant features classic dishes and excellent wine selections with gracious and attentive service for dinner daily at moderately expensive prices. Metro: Cleveland Park.

Arena Stage 1101 6th St. at Maine Ave. SW (202) 488-3300 www.arenastage.com

The most prestigious Washington repertory company offers contemporary and classic productions in three theaters: the Fichandler, a theater-in-the-round, accommodates some 800; the Kreeger offers a 500-seat proscenium stage; and the Old Vat Room is a more cabaret-style theater. Productions range from experimental works to children's theatrical offerings to musicals, and showcases talented locals as well as imported performers. Metro: Waterfront-SEU. *See also* www.com puterpage.com/venues/venue-en.htm.

Argentina Embassy 1600 New Hampshire Ave. NW (202) 238-6400 www.em bassyofargentina-usa.org

Embassy of the Argentine Republic. Metro: Dupont Circle.

Argentinean Restaurants *see* Latin American Restaurants.

Arlan D. Williams Jr. Memorial Bridge *see* 14th Street Bridges.

Arlington

Located directly across the Potomac River, this is a distinctive northern Virginia suburb of the city with a population of some 185,000 affluent professionals who commute and a sizable group of Latinos and South Asians. It is a small county containing offices and hotel complexes like Rosslyn, Pentagon City, Crystal City, residential clusters, and high-rise structures, as well as Arlington National Cemetery, the Pentagon, and Reagan National Airport. Its boundaries are Williamsburg Blvd. and N Glebe Rd. on the north, the Potomac River on the east, Rte. 395 and Rte. 7 on the south, and Rte. 7 on the west. Rosslyn, the downtown area where the Rosslyn Metro station can be found, is within walking distance of Georgetown across the Key Bridge.

Arlington Arts Center 3550 Wilson Blvd. at Monroe St., Arlington, VA (703) 524-1494 www.arlingtonarts.org/

Closed for renovation until late in 2003, this not-for-profit center of visual arts located in a historic one-time school building, offers studio space for artists and mounts exhibitions, workshops, and sponsors lectures and tours. Metro: Virginia Square-GMU, exit the station and walk 1 block southeast on N Lincoln St. *See also* www.commuterpage.com/venues/sightseeing_VA.htm.

Arlington Cemetery *see* Arlington National Cemetery.

Arlington Cinema and Draft House 2903 Columbia Pike, Arlington, VA (703) 486-2345

Located ¼ mile from Leesburg Pike this much frequented restaurant serves light foods, pizza, beer, and wine while showing popular films that are a bit past their first run. Movie tickets are about half the price of regular theaters and the films are shown on a big screen. Call for show time and the current feature.

Arlington Convention and Visitors Service 735 S 18th St. at Hayes St., Arlington, VA (800) 677-6267 or (703) 228-0888 www.co.arlington.va.us

Open daily 9 a.m.–5 p.m. Metro: Pentagon City.

Arlington County Cultural Affairs Division 3700 S Four Mile Run, Arlington, VA (703) 228-1850 www.arlingtonarts.org

This government body coordinates countless summer concerts at parks around the county, performances at theaters, visual arts exhibitions, and much more. Details are provided on its Web site.

Arlington Farmers Market N Courthouse Rd. and N 14th St., Arlington, VA (703) 228-6400 www.arlingtonfarmersmarket.com

This producers' market sells its wares Saturdays 8 a.m.–noon from mid-April to mid-December. Metro: Courthouse Square.

Arlington Historical Society and Museum 1805 S Arlington Ridge Rd., Arlington, VA (703) 892-4204 www.arlingtonhistory.org

This society's membership focuses upon the county's past in arts, literature, and buildings; sponsors meetings and other events at locations in the region; and maintains the museum in an old brick schoolhouse structure, which is open Sat–Sun 1 p.m.–4 p.m. and by appointment. Admission free. Metro: Pentagon, exit the station to the Pentagon Transit Center (Upper Level Bay 12) and take Metrobus 10A toward Hunting Towers to the stop at S Arlington Ridge Rd. and S 23rd St. Walk 1 block west on 23rd St. S, turn right on S Arlington Ridge Rd. and walk 4 blocks north.

Arlington House, the Robert E. Lee Memorial in Arlington National Cemetery, Memorial Dr., Arlington, VA (703) 557-0613 www.nps.gov/arho

Located on a rise overlooking the Potomac River, the National Park Service administers this building, which has been restored to its 1861 appearance and contains some of the original family furnishings. It is open daily 9:30 a.m.–4:30 p.m. Admission free. The portico in front offers a panoramic view of Washington. The memorial is accessible by shuttle bus or by a 10-minute walk from the Arlington National Cemetery Visitor Center/parking area.

Arlington Memorial Bridge www.nps.gov/gwmp/memorial_bridge.htm
This picturesque structure spans the Potomac River from Arlington National Cemetery to Rock Creek Pkwy. near the Lincoln Memorial. It is judged Washington's finest with its graceful arches and lovely carvings. Metro: Arlington Cemetery.

Arlington National Cemetery Memorial Dr., Arlington, VA (703) 607-8052 www
.mdw.army.mil/cemetery.htm
This 600-acre sylvan setting is the nation's most revered burial ground and the resting place for more than 200,000 veterans. It is open daily 8 a.m.–5 p.m. October through March, and 8 a.m.–7 p.m. April through September. A highly informative narrated Tourmobile with a modest charge permits getting off and reboarding at major sites and leaves often from the visitors center. Metro: Arlington Cemetery, exit the station and walk 2 blocks northeast on Memorial Dr., turn right on state Hwy. 110 and walk 1 block southeast. *See also* Tomb of the Unknowns, www.com muterpage.com/venues/memorials.htm.

Arlington National Cemetery Tour *see* Washington/Arlington National Cemetery Tour.

Arlington Symphony 4238 Wilson Blvd., Arlington, VA (703) 528-1817 www
.arlingtonsymphony.org
This symphony comprising some 75 professional and semi-professional musicians has been performing for almost 60 years. The season runs from September to May in a new concert hall on the campus of Northern Virginia Community College in Alexandria. Details by phone or on the Web site.

Armed Forces Concerts www.nps.gov/ncro/PublicAffairs/SummerintheCity.htm
During the summer months the bands of all of the military branches perform free concerts on the East Terrace of the Capitol and at the Sylvan Theater on the grounds of the Washington Monument. During the year the bands perform frequently at various area locations. Call for information: Air Force (202) 767-5658; Army (703) 696-3718; Navy (202) 433-2525; Marines (202) 433-4011. *See also* Air Force Band Summer Concerts, Army Band Summer Concerts, Marine Band Summer Concerts, Navy Band Summer Concerts, United States Marine Band.

Armed Forces Medical Museum *see* National Museum of Health and Medicine.

Armenia Embassy 2225 R St. NW (202) 319-1976 www.armeniaemb.org
Embassy of the Republic of Armenia.

Army Band Summer Concerts www.nps.gov/ncro/PublicAffairs/Summerinthe City.htm
From June to August the U.S. Army Band offers free concerts on the Capitol grounds and at the Washington Monument. Details at (703) 696-3718.

Art and Design Museums *see* Art Museum of the Americas, Arthur N. Sackler Gallery, Arts and Industries Building, Corcoran Gallery of Art, Daughters of the American Revolution Museum and Constitution Hall, Dumbarton Oaks Research Library and Collections, Freer Gallery of Art, Hirshhorn Museum, National Gallery of Art, National Museum of African Art, National Museum of American Art, National Museum of Women in the Arts, National Portrait Gallery, Phillips Collection, Renwick Gallery of the National Museum of American Art. *See also* Ethnic and Community Museums, Historical Museums, Major Museums, Media Museums, Military Museums, Museums of Particular Interest to Children, Science and Technology Museums, Smithsonian Institution Museums, Specialized Museums, www.washingtonpost.com.

Art Galleries *See* Affrica, Anton Gallery, Arlington Arts Center, The Art League, Artists' Museum, Capitol Hill Art League Gallery, Creative Partners Gallery, David Adamson Gallery/Editions, District of Columbia Arts Center, Ellipse Arts Center, Fairfax Art League Gallery, Foundry Gallery, Fraser Gallery, Gallery K, Gallery 10 Ltd., Govinda Gallery, Greater Reston Arts Center, Howard University Blackburn Center Gallery, Indian Craft Shop, Kathleen Ewing Gallery, Marsha Mateyka Gallery, McLean Project for the Arts, Millennium Arts Center, Montpelier Mansion and Cultural Arts Center, Numark Gallery, Prince Royal Gallery, Robert Brown Gallery, Rockville Arts Place, St. Luke's Gallery, Signal 66, Spectrum Gallery, Strathmore Hall Arts Center, Susan Conway Gallery, Torpedo Factory Art Center, Touchstone Gallery, Troyer Gallery, Washington Printmakers Gallery, Washington Project for the Arts, Washington Studio School, Zenith Gallery. *See also* www.washingtonpost.com.

The Art League in the Torpedo Factory, 105 N Union St., Alexandria, VA (703) 683-1780 www.theartleague.org

Members' works are shown after juried selection in the league's main gallery every month. The gallery is open Mon–Sat 10 a.m.–5 p.m., Sun noon–5 p.m. Metro: King Street, exit station and take the DAT2 or DAT5 DASH bus to the stop at King and Fairfax Sts., walk 2 blocks east on King St. to N Union St. *See also* Torpedo Factory Art Center, www.commuterpage.com/venues/sightseeing_VA.htm.

Art Museum of the Americas 201 18th St. NW (behind the Organization of American States building) (202) 458-6016 www.museum.oas.org

Established in 1976, the museum is located in the former residence of the secretaries general of the Organization of American States, a Spanish Colonial–style structure designed by Paul Cret, designer of the Folger Shakespeare Library. The building was completed in 1912. The permanent collection of Latin American and Caribbean artists includes outstanding examples from 1900 onward. There are, as well, major exhibitions drawn from the museum's client countries' artists. The virtual gallery on the Web site offers several exhibits each year, providing background information about the artists and representative works. Museum admission free. Open Tues–Sun 10 a.m.–5 p.m. Closed Monday, federal holidays, Good Friday. Metro: Farragut West, then a 6-block walk.

Arthur M. Sackler Gallery 1050 Independence Ave. SW btw 11th and 12th Sts.
(202) 357-1300 www.si.edu/asia

This Smithsonian museum is located in a three-level building, which, except for its entrance area, is underground. It features a permanent collection of art from China, the Near East, and south and Southeast Asia. Exhibitions offer changing showings of paintings, sculpture, bronzes, jade, and other forms drawn from Asian cultures. It is open daily 10 a.m.–5:30 p.m. Admission free. Guided tours are offered and there are frequently free events like concerts, dance performances, and film showings, as well as a hands-on art program for children. Metro: Smithsonian. *See also* www.commuterpage.com/venues/museums-si.htm.

Artifactory 641 Indiana Ave. off 7th St. NW (202) 393-2727

This unusual shop offers selections of choice handicrafts from Africa and Southeast Asia ranging from puppets to masks to carved wooden art constructions and statuary. Open Mon–Sat 10 a.m.–6 p.m. Metro: Archives-Navy Memorial.

Artigas Statue

This 9-foot-high bronze statue of General José Artigas, the father of Uruguayan independence, is located at Constitution Ave. and 18th St. NW. Metro: Farragut West.

The Artisans 1366 Chain Bridge Rd., McLean, VA (703) 506-0158 www
.artisansofmclean.com/

Genuine craftwork and design are featured in this specialty store offering unique wearable art, jewelry, sculpted stone and glass objects, as well as unusual costume jewelry and housewares, all at relatively high prices for the fine workmanship. Open Mon–Sat 10 a.m.–6 p.m.

Artists' Museum 406 7th St. NW (202) 638-7001 www.artistsmuseum.com

This well-regarded gallery showcases prints, paintings, and other art forms. Open Wed–Fri 11 a.m.–5 p.m., Sat and Sun noon–5 p.m. Metro: Gallery Pl.-Chinatown.

Arts and Industries Building 900 Jefferson Dr. SW btw 7th St. and Independence Ave. and the Mall and Tidal Basin (202) 357-2700 www.si.edu/ai

This 1881 building holds selections from the 1876 Philadelphia Centennial Exhibition including steam engines, printing presses, and other late nineteenth-century artifacts as well as changing exhibits and the popular Discovery Theater, which offers performances for children (202) 357-1500. Open daily 10 a.m.–5:30 p.m. Admission free. Metro: Smithsonian. *See also* Smithsonian Discovery Theater, www.commuterpage.com/venues/museums-si.htm.

Arts Centers *see* Art Galleries.

Arts Club of Washington 2017 I St. NW btw 20th and 21st Sts. (202) 331-7282 www.artsclubofwashington.org

This membership organization of local enthusiasts drawn from the fine arts as well as architecture, dance, drama, music, and literature, sponsors a continuing series of free exhibitions in its gallery space and the adjoining house. Open Tues–Fri 10 a.m.–5 p.m., Sat 10 a.m.–2 p.m. Metro: Farragut West.

Arts Organizations *see* Arlington County Cultural Affairs Division, The Art League, Arts Club of Washington, Athenaeum, District of Columbia Arts Center, Jewish Community Center of Greater Washington, McLean Project for the Arts, Millennium Arts Center, Montpelier Mansion and Cultural Arts Center, Rockville Arts Place, Smithsonian Associates, Strathmore Hall Arts Center, Torpedo Factory Art Center, Vocal Arts Society, Washington Performing Arts Society, Washington Project for the Arts, Wolf Trap Farm Park for the Performing Arts.

Asbury United Methodist Church 926 11th St. NW at K St. (202) 628-0009 www.asburyumcdc.org

This influential African-American church has been located at this site since 1836 and is in the National Registry of Historic Places. It is celebrated for its wide range of community programs and the significance of some of its congregants' contributions to the African-American heritage. Metro: Metro Center.

Asia Nora 2213 M St. NW btw 22nd and 23rd Sts. (202) 797-4860 www.noras.com

This small strikingly attractive dining room features fresh vegetables and fish dishes in a Pan-Asian style all imaginatively concocted and tasty. Open for dinner Mon–Sat. Fairly expensive with reservations a good idea. Metro: Foggy Bottom-GWU or Dupont Circle.

Asia Society Washington Center, 1800 K St. NW, Suite 1102 (202) 833-2742 www.asiasociety.org/worldwide/washington/

This is the local chapter of the organization and sponsors a wide range of educational, cultural, and historical programs. Activities include lectures, performances, seminars, film offerings, and special events. The Web site has links to the D.C. branch and provides details of activities. Metro: Farragut North.

Asian Foods 2301 University Blvd. E, Wheaton, MD (301) 933-6071

This food market selling Thai foods is open daily. Metro: Wheaton.

Asian Restaurants *See* Asia Nora, Burma, East St. Café, Oodles Noodles, Perry's, Raku, Spices, Teaism, Yanyu. *See also* Chinese Restaurants, Indian Restaurants, Japanese Restaurants, Korean Restaurants, Thai Restaurants, Vietnamese Restaurants. *See also* Web sites: www.dcpages.com, www.restaurant.com, www.washingtonpost.com, www.opentable.com.

Associates of American Foreign Service Worldwide 5125 MacArthur Blvd. NW (202) 362-6514 www.aafsw.org

With strong links to the State Department, this organization serves as a resource for Foreign Service families and is open Mon–Fri 10 a.m.–2 p.m.

Atami 3155 Wilson Blvd. at Henderson Rd., Arlington, VA (703) 522-4787

This restaurant has a relaxed ambiance with moderate prices and serves sushi with the Japanese orientation tempered somewhat by Southeast Asian–style dishes as well. The most popular choice is the all-you-can-eat sushi. Open daily for lunch and dinner except on Sunday when only dinner is served. Metro: Clarendon.

Athenaeum 201 Prince St. in Old Town Alexandria (703) 548-0038

In this 150-year-old structure the Northern Virginia Fine Arts Association carries out a diverse program of art exhibitions, lectures, theater productions, and dance classes. Art exhibitions are free. Open Wed–Sun, hours vary. Metro: King Street.

Athenian Plaka *see* Café Plaka.

Athletics *see* Active Sports Activity, Fitness Centers, Spectator Sports.

Atlantic Canoe and Kayak (703) 838-9072 www.atlantickayak.com

This company offers aquatic tours on local waterways starting on the Alexandria and Georgetown waterfronts. Guides do the paddling and treat cultural, natural, and historic themes along the way.

Atomic Billiards 3427 Connecticut Ave. NW (202) 363-7665 http://atomic-billiards.com/atomicbilliards.html

This downstairs pool hall is as much a neighborhood bar as a billiard parlor. It opens at 4 p.m. daily with late-night closing hours varying by the day. There are a limited number of tables, but the comfortable atmosphere where mostly beer and wine are served make it a pleasant spot where both sexes seem to enjoy hanging out while waiting for a free table. Metro: Cleveland Park.

Atomic Grounds 1555 Wilson Blvd. btw N Pierce and N Oak Sts., Arlington, VA (703) 524-2157 www.atomicgrounds.micronpcweb.com/

This is a friendly cybercafé in Rosslyn where bagels, soups, and sandwiches serve as the accompaniment when using the computers for surfing or e-mail. Open Mon–Fri 6:30 a.m.–6:30 p.m. with more limited hours on Sat and Sun. Metro: Rosslyn.

Au Bon Pain 1701 Pennsylvania Ave. NW at 17th St. (202) 887-9331 www.aubonpain.com

This store serving the area around the White House is only one of some dozen D.C. outlets for this chain where squeezed orange juice, freshly brewed coffee, and the accompaniments are served. This location open Mon–Fri 6:30 a.m.–6 p.m. Only cash is accepted at any of the stores. See phone directory for the other locations, some of which are open evenings and weekends. Metro: Farragut West.

Au Pied de Cochon 1335 Wisconsin Ave. NW at Dumbarton St. (202) 337-6400

This moderate-priced French bistro is open daily 24 hours serving fare like omelets, quiches, and soups, making it popular around the clock. An outdoor patio is glass enclosed during the colder season.

L'Auberge Chez François 332 Springvale Rd., Great Falls, VA (703) 759-3800 www.laubergechezfrancois.com

Perhaps the most charming and romantic French country inn in the D.C. area, the Alsatian fare here is succulent and bountiful. Accessible only after a drive ending in a winding road in the woods, this family-owned-and-run place is open for dinner Tues–Sat from 5:30 p.m., and Sun from 1:30 p.m. The cuisine is outstanding, choices often include seasonal fish and game, a wide range of imported and domestic wines, and there's a splendid prix-fixe dinner at this deservedly expensive spot where reservations, particularly on weekends, are essential far in advance.

Audubon Bookshop 8940 Jones Mill Rd., Chevy Chase, MD (301) 652-3606
www.audubonnaturalist.org

Located at the Central Atlantic States headquarters of the Audubon Naturalist Society this bookstore is very strong in materials on natural science for adults and children. Open Mon–Fri 10 a.m.–5 p.m., Sat 9 a.m.–5 p.m. Because it's on the grounds of the society's nature preserve, a walk along the nature trail might be combined with the bookstore visit. Metro: Medical Center, then quite a long walk or a cab ride.

Audubon Naturalist Society of the Central Atlantic States, Inc. 8940 Jones Mill Rd., Chevy Chase, MD (301) 652-9188 www.audubonnaturalist.org

The site of this 40-acre estate home known as Woodend is a wildlife sanctuary of meadows, woodland, and a ³/₄-mile nature trail. There are several bird watching programs sponsored by the society of which the regularly scheduled weekly bird walks are the most popular. Metro: Medical Center, then quite a long walk or a cab ride.

Austin Grill 2404 Wisconsin Ave. NW btw Hall Pl. and Calvert St. (202) 337-8080 www.austingrill.com

This popular Tex-Mex spot serves the full range of south of the border specialties and drinks and has a following of families as well as young people. Inexpensive but often crowded with no reservations accepted. Open for lunch and dinner daily. Metro: Foggy Bottom-GWU, then 30, 32, 34, 35, or 36 Bus. Other branches with varying days and hours of service are downtown at 750 E St. NW (202) 393-3776; Old Town Alexandria at 801 King St. (703) 684-8969; in the Virginia suburbs at 8430-A Old Keene Mill Rd. (Old Keene Mill Center) in West Springfield (703) 644-3111; and in Bethesda, Maryland, at 7278 Woodmont Ave. (301) 656-1366.

Australia Embassy 1601 Massachusetts Ave. NW (202) 797-3000 www .austemb.org

Located in Scott Circle, the product of Australian architect Bates Smart Mc-Cutcheon, this building was completed in 1965. The embassy is often the venue for Down Under art.

Austria Embassy 3524 International Court NW (202) 895-6700 www.austria.org/
Metro: Van Ness-UDC

Avalon Movie Theater 5612 Connecticut Ave. NW (202) 966-2600 www.the avalon.org

This refurbished Art Moderne structure with two screens is the city's largest continuously operating movie theater, begun in 1922. It features important American and foreign films. Metro: Friendship Heights, then about a 20-minute walk.

The Awakening

Located at Hains Point at the edge of East Potomac Park SW, this giant sculpture by Seward Johnson of a bearded man half buried and emerging from the ground is particularly appealing to children who delight in climbing on it.

Awash 2218 18th St. NW btw Wyoming Ave. and Kalorama Rd. (202) 588-8181

This popular and inexpensive Ethiopian restaurant in Adams Morgan is open daily for lunch and dinner serving well-prepared and filling East African dishes. Metro: Dupont Circle, then L2 Bus.

Azerbaijan Embassy 2741 34th St. NW (202) 337-3500 www.azembassy.com
Embassy of the Republic of Azerbaijan. Metro: Cleveland Park.

Aztec Garden 201 18th St. at Virginia Ave. NW
Situated between the Organization of American States and the Art Museum of the Americas, this garden displays sculptures by Hispanic American artists and a statue of the Aztec god of flowers, Xochipili. A reflecting pool lies in the center of the garden. Open 10 a.m.–5 p.m. Tues–Sun, except on holidays. Metro: Farragut West.

BWI *see* Baltimore-Washington Airport.

B. Smith's Massachusetts Ave. NE in Union Station (202) 289-6188 http://bsmith
.com/shop/shop_restaurants.shtml

This expensive restaurant situated in the one-time Presidential Suite of the station is elegant and stylish and offers a full range of creative Southern-style dishes designed to attract an upscale multi-ethnic clientele. Open Mon–Fri for lunch and dinner, with brunch and dinner served on Sat and Sun. Metro: Union Station.

Babe's Billiards 4600 Wisconsin Ave. NW (202) 966-0082

Located in Tenleytown, this well-appointed pool parlor has a good number of tables, serves a wide selection of draft beers, as well as good food accompaniments in the café portion of the place. The atmosphere is congenial, the open hours start at 11 a.m. and run to 4 a.m., and all of the prices are in the moderate range. Metro: Tenleytown-AU.

Baby-sitting *see* Mothers' Aides Inc., White House Nannies, Inc.

Bacchus 1827 Jefferson Pl. NW at M St. (202) 785-0734

This Lebanese restaurant is located in a pleasant downtown basement where diners may select from the Middle Eastern main courses or make a meal from a choice of several tasty appetizers. Open for lunch and dinner Mon–Fri, dinner only on Sat. Metro: Dupont Circle or Farragut North. The second location, in Bethesda at 7945 Norfolk Ave. between Cordell and Del Ray Aves. (301) 657-1722, is open for lunch Mon–Fri, dinner nightly. Metro: Bethesda. The food is succulent and the prices moderate at both branches.

Bach Marathon

On a Sunday in mid-March each year, Johann Sebastian Bach's birthday is celebrated 1 p.m.–6 p.m. at the Chevy Chase Presbyterian Church at 1 Chevy Chase Circle NW. Ten organists play the pipe organ and the day's events conclude with a German dinner celebration. Details at (202) 363-2202.

Badlands 1415 22nd St. NW at P St. (202) 296-0505

This is a popular gay dance spot with a huge dance floor open Tues and Thurs–Sat from 9 p.m. on. Cover charge varies, but no credit cards are accepted and some nights the admission lines lengthen as the night progresses. Metro: Dupont Circle.

Bahamas Embassy 2220 Massachusetts Ave. NW (202) 319-2660 www.emb.com/bs.shtml

Embassy of the Commonwealth of the Bahamas.

Bahrain Embassy 3502 International Dr. NW (202) 342-0741 www.bahrainembassy.org

Embassy of the Kingdom of Bahrain. Metro: Van Ness-UDC.

Bailiwick Inn 4023 Chain Bridge Rd., Fairfax, VA (703) 691-2266 www.bailiwickinn.com

This fairly expensive bed-and-breakfast has 14 well-appointed rooms with feather beds, and some rooms include fireplaces and Jacuzzis. It is well located in Fairfax City's historic district not far from George Mason University and dishes up a splendid breakfast. Metro: Vienna/Fairfax-GMU, then Q Bus.

Bakeries *see* Specialty Food Stores and Bakeries.

Ball-Sellers House 5620 3rd St. S, Arlington, VA (703) 379-2123

The logwood section of this house was constructed in the mid-eighteenth century and may well be the oldest surviving building in Arlington County. The Victorian farmhouse is adjoined. Open Sundays 1 p.m.–4 p.m. April through October. Admission free. Metro: Rosslyn, exit the station and take Metrobus 4B toward Seven Corners to the stop at Arlington Blvd. Service Roadway and N Carlin Springs Rd. Walk 1 block west on S Carlin Springs Rd., then 1 block south on S Carlin Springs Rd. Turn left on 1st St. S, walk 2 blocks east, turn right on S Kensington St., walk 1 block south, turn left on 3rd St. S, and walk 1 block east. *See also* www.commuterpage.com/venues/sightseeing_VA.htm.

Ballet *see* Dance, Kirov Academy.

Ballooning *see* Balloons Unlimited, Fantasy Flights.

Balloons Unlimited 2946-O Chain Bridge Rd., Oakton, VA (703) 281-2300 www.balloonsunlimited.com

The store is located at the intersection of Hunter Mill Rd. and Rte. 23, but the balloon rides go up from Middleburg and rise above the Shenandoah area. Weather permitting, arrangements can be made for soaring aloft at around sunrise or sunset any day of the week from spring to fall for $150 per passenger.

Ballston

This suburban Virginia enclave, a convenient commute from downtown D.C., has many high-rise apartment buildings and townhouses that appeal principally to childless singles or couples, unlike the more family-attracting Alexandria or Arlington. The Ballston Metro stop is near many of the apartment sites. Its boundaries are roughly N Glebe Rd. on the west and south, Quincey St. on the east, and W Washington Blvd. on the north. Metro: Ballston-MU.

Ballston Common 4238 Wilson Blvd. at N Glebe Rd., Arlington, VA (703) 243-8088 www.ballston-common.com

This shopping mall is only a block away from the Metro stop and offers access to more than 100 retail stores and specialty shops, a wide range of restaurants, and multiple movie screens. Metro: Ballston-MU. *See also* www.commuterpage.com/venues/venue-shop.htm.

Baltimore-Washington Airport Anne Arundel County, MD (301) 261-1000 or (800) I-FLY-BWI www.bwiairport.com

Located some 28 miles north of downtown D.C., BWI is the region's number three airport. A free shuttle bus runs between the airport and the train station where riders can take Amtrak or MARC commuter trains to Union Station in northeast Washington. *See also* Airport Transportation.

Banana Café 500 8th St. NE at E St. (202) 543-5906

This Capitol Hill spot features a variety of well-prepared Caribbean and Mexican dishes at modest prices. Lunch is served weekdays, dinner nightly, and a very popular brunch is offered on Sundays. The lively upstairs piano bar is open nightly. Metro: Eastern Market.

Bangkok Bistro 3251 Prospect St. NW off Wisconsin Ave. (202) 337-2424

This moderate-priced stylish Thai restaurant close to the main center of Georgetown offers savory dishes, curries, and all the other Southeast Asian specialties in an exotic setting, with an attractive outside courtyard accessible in mild weather. Open daily for lunch and dinner. Metro: Foggy Bottom-GWU, then 30, 32, 34, 35, or 36 Bus.

Bangkok Garden 4906 St. Elmo Ave., Bethesda, MD (301) 951-0670

This friendly inexpensive Thai restaurant, chock full of colorful animal statuary and an imposing Buddha, features a full array of well-prepared choices and is popular with many regular diners from both the Thai and non-Thai communities. Open daily for lunch and dinner. Metro: Bethesda.

Bangladesh Embassy 3510 International Dr. NW (202) 244-2745 www.bangladoot.org

Embassy of the People's Republic of Bangladesh. Metro: Van Ness-UDC.

Banneker Circle and Fountain

This commemorative memorial to the African-American scientist Benjamin Banneker, who worked with Pierre L'Enfant on the capital city's design in 1791, is located in this circular park at 10th and G Sts. SW at the edge of the L'Enfant Promenade overlooking the waterfront. Metro: L'Enfant Plaza.

Banks *see* ATM Locations.

Bar Nun 1326 U St. NW btw 13th and 14th Sts. (202) 667-6680

This dance club featuring DJs playing an eclectic array of music forms is open nightly. Cover charge varies. Special events are sometimes booked here, so calling ahead is a good idea. Metro: U St.-Cardozo.

Barbados Embassy 2144 Wyoming Ave. NW (202) 939-9200

Metro: Dupont Circle.

Barbecue and Ribs Restaurants *see* Carpool, Florida Avenue Grill, Kenny's Bar-B-Que, O'Brien's Pit Barbeque, Old Glory, Red Hot and Blue, Rocklands. *See also* Southern Restaurants.

Barbuda Embassy *see* Antigua and Barbuda Embassy.

Barcelo Hotel Radisson *see* Radisson Barcelo Hotel.

Bardia's New Orleans Café 2412 18th St. NW at Columbus Rd. (202) 234-0420
Open every day but Monday for lunch and dinner, this comfortable and inexpensive spot features Creole-style fare from beignets to red beans and rice to coffee with chicory and more. The brunch on Saturday and Sunday is a popular attraction. Metro: Woodley Park-Zoo.

Barge Rides *see* C&O Canal Barge Rides.

Barnes & Noble 3040 M St. NW corner of Jefferson St. (202) 965-9880 www .bn.com
This quality chain outlet is situated on 3 floors in a former warehouse building in Georgetown. It is well stocked, has lots of comfortable seats, includes an espresso coffee bar, and schedules frequent literary and music events. Open daily 9 a.m.–11 p.m. Metro: Foggy Bottom-GWU. There are a number of other branches in the suburbs. The one in Bethesda at 4801 Bethesda Ave., corner of Woodmont, (301) 986-1761 near the Bethesda Metro station, is open the same hours and is an equally spacious, lively, and popular center.

The Barns at Wolf Trap 1635 Trap Rd., Vienna, VA (703) 938-2404 www.wolf trap.org
Just about ½ mile south of Wolf Trap Farm Park in Virginia off the Dulles toll road, this intimate 350-seat theater is made up of two eighteenth-century barns in which dance, music, and opera productions take place from fall to spring. Details on programs at (703) 938-2404.

Barolo 223 Pennsylvania Ave. SE (202) 547-5011
This fine Italian restaurant specializes in dishes from the Piedmont region. It is open for dinner Mon–Sat, lunch Mon–Fri. The dishes are fairly expensive but the food is very well prepared and pleasantly served. Metro: Capitol South.

Barry Statue *see* Commodore John Barry Statue.

Bars *see* B. Smith's, Badlands, The Big Hunt, Billy Martin's Tavern, Black Rooster, Bottom Line, Brickskeller, Bullfeathers, Butlers, the Cigar Bar, Capitol City Brewing Company, Capitol Lounge, Champions, Chi-Cha Lounge, Crush, Dan's Café, Dave and Buster's, District Chop House and Brewery, Dr. Dremo's Taphouse, Dragonfly, Dubliner, 18th Street Lounge, Fadó Irish Pub, Fast Eddie's, Fish Market, Fox and Hounds, Grand Slam, Guards, Hawk and Dove, Hung Jury, Ireland's Four Provinces, J. Paul's, Kelly's Irish Times, Lulu's Club Mardi Gras, Mr. Smith's, Murphy's Irish Pub and Restaurant, My Brother's Place Bar and Grill, Nanny O'Brien's Irish Pub, Nathan's, Off the Record, Old Ebbitt Grill, Ozio, Pharmacy Bar, Politiki, Post Pub, Rock Sports Bar and Restaurant, Round Robin Bar, Sign of the Whale, Sky Terrace, State of the Union, Tortilla Coast, Tryst, Tune Inn, Xando Cosi, Yacht Club. *See also* www.frommers.com, www.washingtonpost.com.

Bartholdi Fountain in Bartholdi Park at 1st and Independence Sts. SW www.aoc
.gov/USBG/bartholdi.htm

Located in the center of Bartholdi Park, this 25-foot-high cast-iron construction
was created by Frédéric Auguste Bartholdi, sculptor of the more celebrated Statue
of Liberty. It features sea monsters, nymphs, and lighted globes, and was created
for the Philadelphia Centennial Exhibition in 1876. Metro: Federal Center SW.

Bartholdi Park Independence Ave. btw 1st St. and Washington State Ave. SW
www.usbg.gov/virtual-tour/bartholdi-park.cfm

This park is a 2-acre extension of the U.S. Botanic Garden and is open to visitors
daily. The Bartholdi Fountain is at the center of the park surrounded by a number
of themed gardens. Metro: Federal Center SW.

Baseball *see* Bowie Bay Sox, Frederick Keys, Potomac Cannons.

Basil Thai 1608 Wisconsin Ave. NW at Q St. (202) 944-8660

This attractive upper-Georgetown restaurant offers well-prepared and zesty
dishes at moderate prices. Open for lunch Mon–Sat, dinner daily. Metro: Foggy
Bottom-GWU, then 30, 32, 34, 35, or 36 Bus.

Basilica of the National Shrine of the Immaculate Conception Michigan Ave. at
4th St. NE (202) 526-8300 www.nationalshrine.com

Featuring a lofty bell tower, this huge Roman Catholic Church is the largest in
the country and one of the biggest in the world. It was dedicated in 1959 and blends
Byzantine and Roman styles. Self-directed tours lead visitors through the great treasures including stained glass art, sculptures, mosaics, and more than fifty chapels
celebrating visions of Mary. The building is open daily April to October 7 a.m.–
7 p.m., 7 a.m.–6 p.m. the rest of the year. Free 1-hour guided tours are offered in
the morning and afternoon Mon–Sat, and afternoons on Sun. There are scheduled
recitals on the fifty-six-bell carillon in the tower as well as free organ recitals.
Metro: Brookland-CUA.

Basin Street Lounge 219 King St., Alexandria, VA (703) 549-1141

The sounds of live jazz Tues–Sat evenings reverberate from the aged rafters supporting the Two-Nineteen Restaurant upstairs. Considered one of the best Old
Town Alexandria bars, Basin Street starts the music at 8 p.m. Tues and Thurs, and
9 p.m. Fri and Sat. Closes at 1 a.m. on Fri and Sat, otherwise midnight. Cover
charge Fri and Sat. Metro: King Street, then DAT5 DASH Bus toward Braddock
Road Metro to the stop at King and Washington Sts.

Basketball *see* American University Basketball, George Mason University Patriots,
George Washington University Colonials, Georgetown University Hoyas, Howard
University Bison, MCI Center, University of Maryland Terrapins, Washington
Mystics, Washington Wizards.

Basketball Season

Professional basketball home games for the men's Washington Wizards run November to May, and for the women's Washington Mystics, June to August. Both
teams play at the MCI Center in Washington at 601 F St. NW (202) 628-3200.
Metro: Gallery Pl.-Chinatown.

Bastille Day
On July 14 Washington celebrates French Independence Day with live entertainment and a competition by waiters and waitresses who race, balancing trays, from 12th St. and Pennsylvania Ave. to the Capitol and back. Sponsored by Les Halles Restaurant with details at (202) 347-8648. Metro: Federal Triangle.

Battery-Kemble Park www.nps.gov/rocr/ftcircle/kemble.htm
This small park in northwest D.C., running 1 mile long and ⅛-mile wide, is bounded by Chain Bridge Rd., MacArthur Blvd., 49th St., and Nebraska Ave. It is a thick woodland area surrounding a rocky narrow gorge with a path winding through a shady ravine and over the small stream that flows through the park. Home to a wide range of tree species, it attracts a variety of birds and is a favorite place for picnics and summer frolics. Open daily throughout the year. Details at (202) 426-6829.

Battleground National Cemetery 6625 Georgia Ave. NW www.nps.gov/batt
This is the country's smallest national cemetery where forty-one soldiers who defended Fort Stevens during the only Confederate attack on Washington during the Civil War are buried. Open dawn to dusk. Metro: Silver Spring, then 70 or 71 Bus to Aspen St.

Bead Museum and Learning Center 400 7th St. NW corner of D St. (202) 624-4500 www.thebeadmuseum.org
Changing exhibitions of glass beads and ornamented jewelry from the United States and many other regions of the world can be found here, as well as educational programs on bead-making craftsmanship and traditions. Open Mon, Wed, Fri 11 a.m.–4 p.m.; Sat noon–5 p.m.; Sun 1 p.m.–4 p.m. Admission free. Metro: Archives-Navy Memorial.

Beall-Dawson House 103 W Montgomery Ave. at N Adams St., Rockville, MD (301) 762-1492 www.montgomeryhistory.org
Owned by the Montgomery County Historical Society, this is a completely restored 1815 brick house furnished in the period's Federal style. Open Tues–Sun noon–4 p.m. Tours until 3:30 p.m. Admission $3, seniors and students $2. Metro: Rockville, then 20-minute walk.

Beauty Salons *see* Beauty Spas and Salons.

Beauty Spas and Salons *see* André Chreky, Elizabeth Arden Red Door Salon and Spa, Georgette Klinger, Jacques Dessange, Jolie, Lillian Laurence Ltd., Petra's Skin Spa, S/p/alon, Victoria's Day Spa, Washington Institute for Skin Care.

Bed and Breakfast Accommodations Ltd. (202) 328-3510 www.bedandbreakfast.com
Offers a selection of private guesthouses, small inns, and self-hosted furnished apartments including some historic properties in popular District neighborhoods as well as the Maryland and Virginia suburbs. Price range is modest to expensive.

Bed and Breakfast League *see* Bed and Breakfast/Sweet Dreams and Toast.

Bed and Breakfast/Sweet Dreams and Toast (202) 363-5542
This rental agency handles a wide range of accommodations at different prices

in the Capitol Hill, Dupont Circle, Cleveland Park, and North Cleveland Park sections of the city.

Bed-and-Breakfast Rental Agencies *see* Bed-and-Breakfast Accommodations Ltd., Bed and Breakfast/Sweet Dreams and Toast.

Bed-and-Breakfasts *see* Adams Inn, Bed and Breakfast Accommodations Ltd., Bailiwick Inn, Bull Moose Bed and Breakfast, H. H. Leonard's Mansion, Hereford House, Kalorama Guest House, Norris House Inn, Princely Bed and Breakfast Ltd., Shipman House Bed and Breakfast, Swann House, Taft Bridge Inn. *See also* Guest Houses, Hostels.

Bedrock Billiards 1841 Columbia Rd. btw 18th St. and Belmont Rd. (202) 667-7765 www.bedrockbilliards.com

This is a low-key Adams Morgan area pool parlor and games room with the walls covered with Flintstone cave drawings. Opens 4 p.m. Mon–Fri, 1 p.m. Sat and Sun, remaining open until 1 a.m. or 2 a.m. depending on the day. Hourly rates vary by number of players, day, and time. Beers of various kinds are available as is espresso and cappuccino. Metro: Dupont Circle, then 42 Bus.

Beduci 2100 P St. NW (202) 223-3824 www.beduci.com

The name is an acronym formed from the first two letters of Below Dupont Circle, and the accent at this moderately expensive restaurant is French, Spanish, and Italian with a wide choice of wines from the same countries. Open for lunch Mon–Sat, dinner daily. Metro: Dupont Circle.

Bee Won Secret Garden 6678 Arlington Blvd., Falls Church, VA (703) 553-1004 www.fallschurchwebsite.com/BeeWonRestaurant.htm

This may be the oldest Korean restaurant in metropolitan Washington, having opened in 1980. With its light wood tables and glass-fronted sushi bar, it looks more Japanese than Korean, except for the gas grills sunk into some of the tables. The sushi is fresh and served on traditional wooden platters. The extensive Korean menu includes the highly regarded seafood pancakes and barbecued short ribs. Inexpensive. Open daily 11 a.m.–11 p.m. Metro: Ballston-MU, then Metrobus IC Fair Oaks Hospital to Arlington Blvd.

Belarus Embassy 1619 New Hampshire Ave. NW (202) 986-1606 www.belarus embassy.org

Embassy of the Republic of Belarus.

Belgium Embassy 3330 Garfield St. NW (202) 333-6900 www.diplobel.us/

Metro: Woodley Park-Zoo, then a 20-minute walk.

Belize Embassy 2535 Massachusetts Ave. NW (202) 332-9636 www.embassyof belize.org

Embassy of the Republic of Belize.

Belle Haven Marina 1 Bell Haven Rd., Alexandria, VA (703) 768-0018 www.sail dc.com

Located off the George Washington Pkwy. just south of the Wilson Bridge in

Alexandria, this place rents sailboats and other types of boats for a minimum of 2 hours for use on the Potomac River.

Bellevue Neighborhood

This is a community located on the east side of the Anacostia River in the farthermost corner of southwest D.C. From this southernmost point in the city there are excellent views of the Potomac River and Fort Carroll. Accessible only by automobile.

Belmont Mansion www.easternstar.org/temple/home.html

Located at the intersection of 18th St. and New Hampshire Ave. NW is one of the city's most striking buildings. This is a massive, heavily ornamented 54-room mansion built in 1909 for a U.S. congressman and ambassador to Spain, Perry Belmont. This spectacular Beaux Arts building is on the National Registry and is now owned and occupied by the Order of the Eastern Star and is open only to members and their guests. Metro: Dupont Circle.

The Beltway

This circumferential roadway (I-495/I-95) encircles Washington, D.C., and is traveled by some 200,000 vehicles a day. It loops widely for 67 miles around the city and was designed as a bypass for traffic around and into the city. The term "inside the Beltway" has come to mean that this is where political discourse affecting the nation takes place. The Beltway's inner loop is the set of clockwise travel lanes around the city; the outer loop carries traffic in the opposite direction, outside the inner loop. The Beltway cuts through Fairfax County and Alexandria in northern Virginia and Prince George's and Montgomery Counties in Maryland.

Beltway Plaza 600 Greenbelt Rd., Greenbelt, MD (301) 345-1500 www.beltway plazacenter.com

This shopping mall in Prince George's County offers more than 100 fashion, specialty and food stores, a workout gym, and multiple movie theaters. Metro: Prince George's Plaza. *See also* www.commuterpage.com/venues/venue-shop.htm.

Ben Davis House 7112 Cedar Ave., Takoma Park, MD

This striking Queen Anne–style house was built in 1888. It is designed asymmetrically with a steep decorated multi-gable roof and a wide railed porch. It is not open to tourists. Metro: Takoma.

Bender Arena Sports Center American University, 4400 Massachusetts Ave. NW (202) 885-3032 www.american.edu/athletics

Built in 1988, the arena seats 5,000 for sports events and 6,000 for concerts. It is the venue for varsity basketball—the AU Eagles and volleyball. Metro: Tenleytown-AU, then take Metrobus N2 toward Farragut Square to Ward Circle and Nebraska Ave. NW. Walk east on Ward Circle, turn left on Massachusetts Ave. at the entrance to American University. Turn left to Bender Sports Arena. *See also* American University Basketball.

Benin Embassy 2124 Kalorama Rd. NW (202) 232-6656 www.embassy.org/em bassies/bj.html

Embassy of the Republic of Benin. Metro: Dupont Circle.

Benito Juárez Statue *see* Juárez Statue.

Benjamin Banneker Memorial Circle and Fountain *see* Banneker Circle and Fountain.

Benjamin Franklin Statue Pennsylvania Ave. at 10th St. NW

In the courtyard of the Old Post Office Building this 1889 sculpture by Jacques Jouvenal celebrates America's well-loved statesman, inventor, postmaster, and patriot. Metro: Federal Triangle.

Benjarong 855C Rockville Pike, Rockville, MD (301) 424-5533

Located about midway between the Twinbrook and Rockville Metro stations in the Wintergreen Plaza, this restaurant is open for lunch Mon–Sat, dinner daily. It features an extensive menu of well-prepared southern Thai cooking spiced to individual taste, with hospitable service and modest prices.

Benning Road Bridge Benning Rd. across the Anacostia River

The present structure of concrete-cased steel was built in 1934. The original bridge on the site was completed in about 1800 and was known as Ewell's Bridge. It was burned in 1814 to slow the invading British troops. Rebuilt in 1820 and sold 3 years later to William Benning, he replaced it in 1830 with a new wooden toll bridge. It survived a flood in 1840 and the Civil War but was finally replaced with a steel bridge in 1892. Metro: Minnesota Ave.

Ben's Chili Bowl 1213 U St. NW btw 12th and 13th Sts. (202) 667-0909 www .benschilibowl.com/index2.shtml

This neighborhood hangout has become a Washington institution. Specialties are chili dishes—plain, on burgers, chilidogs, or half smokes. Big Southern-style breakfasts are a favorite. Open daily from 6 a.m., except on Sunday at noon, and it stays open well past midnight except on Sunday. No credit cards, but very inexpensive. Metro: U St.-Cardozo.

La Bergerie 218 N Lee St., 1 block from King St. and Torpedo Factory, Alexandria, VA (703) 683-1007 www.labergerie.com

Elegantly prepared dishes and gracious service are the hallmark at this restaurant, which features Basque cuisine as well as traditional French fare. Moderately expensive. Open for lunch Mon–Sat, dinner nightly. Metro: King Street, then free shuttle bus on Friday night and Saturday and Sunday, or 20-minute walk.

Best Western Pentagon 2480 S Glebe Rd., Arlington, VA 22206 (703) 979-4400 or (800) 426-6886, fax (703) 685-0051 www.bestwestern.com/prop_09101

This moderately priced close-to-downtown hotel has shuttle service from Reagan National Airport and to nearby Metro stops. It offers more than 300 nicely furnished rooms, a pool, and an exercise room.

Bethesda Area

Just beyond Chevy Chase in the Maryland suburbs, this community is at the southern end of Montgomery County. Downtown Bethesda, accessible by the Bethesda Metro stop, is a high-rise commercial and business center as well as a very popular dining destination with its Woodmont Triangle area boasting innumerable restaurants of every kind from budget to deluxe. Still an important and affluent residential enclave, Bethesda contains many gracious, tree-lined streets and lovely family homes with landscaped gardens as well as high-rise apartments and town-houses. To the north, the world-famous National Institutes of Health is at the Medical Center Metro station.

Bethesda Crab House 4958 Bethesda Ave., Bethesda, MD (301) 652-3382

Open daily for lunch and dinner until midnight, this is a popular spot for de-vouring fresh Chesapeake Bay crabs after cracking them open with a hammer, al-though other seafood choices are available. Inexpensive and very informal. Metro: Bethesda, then about a 15-minute walk.

Bethesda Farm Women's Cooperative Market 71515 Wisconsin Ave. at Bethesda Ave., Bethesda, MD (301) 652-2291

This year-round operation is open Wednesdays and Saturdays 7 a.m.–3 p.m. Metro: Bethesda.

Bethesda Literary Festival Bethesda, MD (301) 215-6660 www.bethesda.org/specialevents/literaryfestival.htm

This four-day April event takes place throughout downtown Bethesda's book-stores, art galleries, restaurants, and at the Writers Center. Experience a poetry slam or meet poets, journalists, novelists, children's authors, and nonfiction writers in a variety of programs. Metro: Bethesda.

Bethesda Marriott 5151 Pooks Hill Rd., Bethesda, MD (301) 897-9400 www .marriott.com

Situated on a hill off Wisconsin Ave. just south of the Washington Beltway in Bethesda, this 400-room luxury facility has many dining facilities, indoor and out-door pools, and an exercise room. Free weekday morning and evening shuttle ser-vice is provided to the Medical Center Metro station.

Bethesda Ramada 8400 Wisconsin Ave. at Woodmont Ave., Bethesda, MD (301) 654-1000 or (800) 272-6232 www.fourpoints.com

This is an inexpensive hotel with 160 or so rooms located at the far north end of the Bethesda Wisconsin Ave. business district. There is an exercise room and pool and it is located 15 minutes from the Medical Center Metro stop.

Bethesda Row Cinema 7235 Woodmont Ave., Bethesda, MD (301) 652-7273 www.landmarktheaters.com

Located in the landmark Bethesda Row, this recently opened movie showplace offers eight screens and features art, foreign, and independent films for viewers seeking other than conventional mainstream cinema offerings. Metro: Bethesda.

Bethune House *see* Mary McLeod Bethune House.

Bicycle Rentals *see* Big Wheel Bikes, Bike the Sites Tours, City Bikes, Fletcher's Boat House, Thompson's Boat Center, Washington Sailing Marina

Bicycle Tours *see* Bike the Sites Tours.

Bicycle Trails *see* C&O Canal Towpath, Capital Crescent Trail, Mount Vernon Trail, Rock Creek Trail, Washington and Old Dominion Railroad Regional Park,

Washington Area Bicyclist Association. *See also* www.trails.com, www.washington post.com.

Bicycling *see* Bicycle Rentals, Bicycle Trails, Washington Area Bicyclist Association.

The Big Hunt 1345 Connecticut Ave. btw Dupont Circle and N St. (202) 785-2333
Best known for its jungle décor ambiance and its innumerable moderate-priced choices of beer, this cavernous casual spot is open Mon–Thurs 4 p.m.–2 a.m., 5 p.m.–2 a.m. or 3 a.m. on weekends. Metro: Dupont Circle.

Big Wheel Bikes www.bigwheelbikes.com
This firm has four locations where traditional bicycles and mountain bikes for adults and children can be rented by the hour or the day. Locations are in George-town near the C&O Canal Towpath at 1034 33rd St. NW (202) 337-0254; Old Town Alexandria near the Mount Vernon Trail at 2 Prince St. on the Potomac (703) 739-2300; Arlington at 3119 Lee Hwy. (703) 522-1110; and Bethesda at 6917 Arlington Rd. (301) 652-0192. Store hours vary but all are open daily 10 a.m. or 11 a.m.–evening.

Bike Rentals *see* Bicycle Rentals.

Bike the Sites Tours (202) 966-8662 www.bikethesites.com
Knowledgeable guides lead bike tours to many landmark historic and architec-tural sites, a number of which are not accessible by other means. Bicycles and hel-mets can be provided. Details at (202) 966-8662.

Billiards *see* Pool.

Billy Martin's Tavern 1264 Wisconsin Ave. NW at N St. (202) 333-7370 www .billymartinstavern.com
This old-fashioned Irish-American Georgetown pub has been around since 1933 and is a warm and comfortable quiet place that has the feel of a private club. It's less a bar than a restaurant serving three meals a day with weekend brunch at moderate prices. Open Mon–Thurs 10 a.m.–11 p.m., Fri 10 a.m.–1 a.m., Sat–Sun 8 a.m.–11 p.m. Metro: Foggy Bottom-GWU, then 30, 32, 34, 35, or 36 Bus.

Biltmore Street
Located in the Adams Morgan district, this is one of Washington's loveliest resi-dential streets. Starting from Cliffbourne Pl. each of the row houses has its own unique façade, then the duplex building with its unusual roof, and near the other end of the street at 1940 is the Biltmore building with its graceful roof and cornices. Metro: Woodley Park-Zoo, then 90, 91, 92, 93, or 96 Bus.

Birchmere 3701 Mount Vernon Ave. btw Glebe Rd. and S Glebe Rd., Alexandria, VA (703) 549-7500 www.birchmere.com
Half night club, half concert hall, this is one of the region's finest spots for country, bluegrass, folk, pop, blues, and other types of live musical entertainment. It draws top national names as well as talented local performers. Schedule and ad-mission charge varies with each show. Metro: Braddock Road, then 10A, 10B, or 10C Bus. *See also* www.commuterpage.com/venues/venue-en.htm.

Bird-In-Hand Bookstore and Gallery 323 7th St. SE at Pennsylvania Ave. (202) 543-0744

This Capitol Hill store specializes in books on art, design, and architecture and also carries exhibition catalogs of museum shows. Open Tues 11 a.m.–4 p.m., Thurs 3:30 p.m.–6 p.m., Fri 11 a.m.–4 p.m., Sat 11 a.m.–6 p.m. Closed Wed. Metro: Eastern Market.

Bird Watching *see* Audubon Naturalist Society of the Central Atlantic States Inc., Fairfax Audubon Society.

Bis in Hotel George, 15 E St. btw N Capitol and New Jersey Ave. (202) 661-2700

This sleek dining spot with zinc bar and visible kitchen offers classic bistro dishes with an American flair attractively concocted and pleasantly served. It's very popular and quite expensive. Lunch and dinner reservations are advisable. Open for breakfast daily, lunch Mon–Fri, brunch Sat and Sun, dinner nightly. Metro: Union Station.

Bishop John Carroll Statue

Located at 37th and O Sts. in Georgetown, this sculpture by Jerome Connor memorializes the founder of Georgetown University and is also the university's symbol.

Bishop William Pinckney Statue

At the rear of the gatehouse to the Oak Hill Cemetery at 30th and R Sts. NW in Georgetown, this marble human-sized statue memorializes this notable church personality.

Bishop's Garden (202) 364-6616 www.cathedral.org

Located on the grounds of the grand Washington National Cathedral at Massachusetts and Wisconsin Aves. NW, this secluded garden of medieval design contains lovely stone paths and foliage, and serves as an ideal place for quiet thought and contemplation. Open daily 10 a.m.–5 p.m. Metro: Tenleytown, then 30, 32, 34, or 36 Bus to Woodley St.

Bison Bridge 23rd and Q Sts. NW

This bridge stretching across Rock Creek Park and Pkwy. is officially known as the Dumbarton Bridge and it is sometimes called the Buffalo Bridge. It was designed to link the Dupont Circle area to Georgetown. The four 8-feet-high bronze statues that adorn the eastern and western approaches to the bridge were designed in 1914 by the sculptor A. Phimister Proctor. The sides of the bridge, which can be seen from underneath the bridge, are decorated with busts of American Indians. The bridge architects were Glenn and Bedford Brown. Metro: Dupont Circle.

Bistro Bistro 4021 S 28th St. btw S Quincy and S Randolph Sts., Arlington, VA (703) 379-0300

This restaurant, easily accessible only by automobile off Hwy. 395, may well be worth the trip since it is a lovely two-level, elegantly appointed dining room serving excellent French/American dishes. Open Mon–Sat for lunch and dinner, brunch and dinner Sun. Prices are moderately expensive and reservations are suggested.

Bistro Français 3128 M St. NW btw 31st St. and Wisconsin Ave. (202) 338-3830

This is a long-standing Georgetown favorite offering fine fixed-price lunch and pre-theater menus. Its specialties are fresh fish and southern French dishes. Open for lunch and dinner daily, staying open until the wee hours with prices that are quite moderate considering how good the food is. Dinner reservations are a good idea. Metro: Foggy Bottom-GWU, then 30, 32, 34, 35, or 36 Bus.

Bistrot Lépic 1736 Wisconsin Ave. at S St. (202) 333-0111 www.bistrotlepic.com

This is a classic family-run bistro serving authentic French food in a small storefront with lunch and dinner Tues–Sun. Meal and wine prices are reasonable. The cozy atmosphere is enhanced by the colorful Left Bank wall mural, and reservations are essential.

Black Cat 1831 14th St. NW btw S and T Sts. (202) 667-7960 www.blackcatdc.com

Open nightly, this is an eclectic bar-club that showcases local and visiting performers in a cavernous space featuring different kinds of alternative music styles. Admission prices vary depending on the entertainment and no credit cards are accepted. To learn what's on which nights call for the schedule (202) 667-7960 or check the Web site. Metro: U St.-Cardozo.

Black Family Reunion

The National Council of Negro Women sponsors this annual weekend event in early September on the grounds of the Washington Monument to celebrate the African-American family with music, art, storytelling, food, and performances. Details at (202) 737-0120.

Black Fashion Museum 2007 Vermont Ave. NW btw U and V Sts. (202) 667-0744 www.bfmcd.org

Committed to displaying African-American contributions to design and fashion, this small exhibit area features rotating shows of lovely designs drawn from the museum's extensive collection. Open by appointment only. Suggested $2 donation. Metro: U St.-Cardozo.

Black Hill Regional Park 20930 Lake Ridge Dr., Boyds, MD (301) 972-3476 www .mncppc.org

This lovely park is operated on some 1,900 acres by the Maryland National Capital Park and Planning Commission and is open daily 6 a.m.–sunset. It appeals to trail hikers, boaters, and fishermen. Canoes and rowboats can be rented on Little Seneca Lake. The visitor center features wildlife exhibits and is in the midst of natural gardens. There are also playgrounds and picnic places. Modest admission charge. Instructions on reaching the park from Washington, D.C., by car at (301) 972-3476.

Black History Month

During February each year many events are held throughout the city. The Smithsonian Institution holds special exhibitions, cultural programs, and other activities at its museums throughout the period reflecting African-American history and culture. Details at (202) 357-1300. For information on additional activities call the Martin Luther King Memorial Library (202) 727-1126.

Black History National Recreational Trail
Started in 1988 during Black History Month, this trail was designed to be followed by driving, walking, or biking. It incorporates many Washington locations and sites from the period of early slavery in the United States to the 1930s. There is no fixed route, but the places to be seen include historic houses, statues of important figures, and more. Three of the sites included are maintained by the National Park Service. Others are privately owned and maintained. For a brochure that describes the history and details of all the stops on the trail call (202) 619-7222.

Black History Resource Center 638 N Alfred St., Alexandria, VA (703) 838-4356 www.alexblackhistory.org
Open Tues–Sun 10 a.m.–5 p.m., this museum exhibits materials celebrating the contributions of African-Americans to Alexandria and Virginia history from the mid-eighteenth century to the present. Admission free. Metro: Braddock Road.

Black Patriots Memorial (202) 452-1776 www.blackpatriots.org
Slated for construction at a site in Constitution Gardens not far from the Vietnam War Memorial, this commemorative structure will honor the estimated 5,000 African-American soldiers and sailors who served in the Revolutionary War. The design by Edward Dwight Jr. features two curving and rising walls. One wall will depict men, women, and children performing heroic wartime acts. The other will contain quotations from black patriots. Funds are being raised through private donations by the Black Patriots Foundation. Information on the project's status is available by calling (202) 452-1776 or at the Web site.

Black Revolutionary War Patriots Memorial *see* Black Patriots Memorial.

Black Rooster 1919 L St. NW (202) 659-4431
This is a very popular and friendly place with the flavor of a British pub. Drink prices are modest and there are even a couple of dartboards at the front of the bar. Open Mon–Fri 11:30 a.m.–2 a.m. or 2:30 a.m., Sat 7 p.m.–2:30 a.m. Closed Sun Metro: Farragut North.

Blackie's House of Beef 1217 22nd St. NW off M St. (202) 333-1100 www.blackies dc.com
This New Orleans–style landmark building houses a restaurant that has been dishing out thick steaks, onion soup, and baked potatoes at moderate prices since 1946 to a clientele with hearty appetites. Open for lunch Mon–Fri, dinner daily. Metro: Foggy Bottom-GWU.

Blaine Mansion 2000 Massachusetts Ave. NW
This building, constructed in 1881, is the oldest surviving great house in the Dupont Circle area. It was built by the architect John Fraser as the residence of James Blaine, one of the Republican Party's founders and a failed presidential candidate. The dark brick structure, altered over the years, combines Victorian, Gothic, Romanesque, and Renaissance features with towers, multiple chimneys and skylights, and an elaborate porch entrance. Not open to the public. Metro: Dupont Circle.

Blair House 1651–53 Pennsylvania Ave. NW btw Jackson Pl. and 17th St.

Blair House was built in 1858 and is connected to the Lee House next to it built in 1824. Restoration and enlargement took place in 1988. It serves as the guest residence for high foreign officials and heads of state and is a National Historic Landmark. The building is not open to the public. Metro: Farragut West.

Bliss House *see* Dr. E. B. Bliss House.

Bloomingdale's

This department store has two locations in the Washington suburbs. White Flint Mall in Kensington, MD (301) 984-4600, open Mon–Sat 10 a.m.–9:30 p.m., Sun noon–6 p.m. By car take Exit 34 Rockville off the Beltway (I-495) and go north 1½ miles to the mall on the right. In Virginia the store is located in the Tysons Corner Center in McLean (703) 556-4600, Mon–Sat 10 a.m.–9:30 p.m., Sun 11 a.m.–6 p.m. To reach this store by car take Exit 103 off the Beltway (I-495) and go north ¼ mile to the mall on the right.

Blues Alley 1073 Wisconsin Ave. NW below M St. (202) 337-4141 www.blues alley.com

This legendary Georgetown night club showcases world-class artists, serves Creole cooking, charges a fairly steep entertainment charge (it varies with the talent), and is the preeminent Washington spot for jazz. Shows at 8 p.m. and 10 p.m. nightly with a midnight show added usually on Fri and Sat. Dinner starts at 6 p.m. Acoustics are excellent and the club is small so reserving early is essential. Metro: Foggy Bottom-GWU, then 30, 32, 34, 35, or 36 Bus. *See also* www.commuter page.com/venues/venue-en.htm.

Blues Music *see* Jazz Spots.

B'nai B'rith Klutznick National Jewish Museum 2020 K St. NW at 20th St. (202) 857-6600 www.bnaibrith.org

What was since 1957 a major museum of archaeological Jewish artifacts as well as of work by Jewish artists has been replaced with a smaller gallery accessible only by appointment. This was necessitated by the move of B'nai B'rith to only 1 floor of a corporate building in July 2002 from its former decades-long occupancy of its headquarters building at 1640 Rhode Island Ave. NW. Parts of the museum's collection are designated to become traveling exhibits, while others are to be lent to other institutions. The Philip Klutznick exhibit, which documents the life of one of the twentieth century's most influential businessmen, has been shipped to Omaha. This leaves visitors to the city with just the U.S. Holocaust Museum as the only site that highlights one aspect of Jewish history. Metro: Farragut North. *See also* www.commuterpage.com/venues/museums.htm.

Boat Rentals *see* Atlantic Canoe and Kayak, Belle Haven Marina, Fletcher's Boat House, Jack's Boats, Springriver, Swain's Lock Boat House, Thompson's Boat Center, Tidal Basin Boathouse, Washington Sailing Marina.

Boat Tours *see* Atlantic Canoe and Kayak, C&O Canal Barge Rides, Capitol River Cruises, Dandy Restaurant Cruises, Duck Tours, Odyssey Cruises, Potomac Riverboat Company, Potomac Spirit, Shore Shot Cruises.

Boating *see* Atlantic Canoe and Kayak, Belle Haven Marina, Black Hill Regional Park, Burke Lake Park, Capital Yacht Club, Fletcher's Boat House, Jack's Boats, Lake Accotink Park, Paddle Boats at the Tidal Basin, Pohick Bay Regional Park, Potomac River, Potomac Riverboat Company, Riverbend Park, Rock Creek Regional Park, Seaport Center, Springriver, Swain's Lock Boat House, Thompson Boat Center, Tidal Basin Boathouse, Washington Sailing Marina, White's Ferry. *See also* Boat Rentals, Potomac.

Bobby Van's Steakhouse 809 15th St. NW btw H and I Sts. (202) 589-0060 http://bobbyvans.citysearch.com

This expensive restaurant is consistent in always serving great porterhouse steaks and top selected prime beef, long aged and tender. There are the requisite accompaniments as well as other dishes, but here it's the steak that lures the customers. Open for lunch Mon–Fri, dinner Mon–Sat Metro: McPherson Square.

Bodisco House 3322 O St. NW

This famous Georgetown house was built in 1815 by Clement Smith but gained fame later in the mid-nineteenth century as the place where the aging Baron de Bodisco, Russian ambassador to the United States, and his native Georgetown 16-year-old bride made their home. The building has been beautifully restored and is a fine example of Federal-style architecture with its graceful wrought iron staircase railings and lovely window above the entry door. Metro: Foggy Bottom-GWU.

Bohemian Caverns 2003 11th St. NW at U St. (202) 299-0800 www.bohemiancaverns.com

This was one of the most celebrated cabarets and jazz clubs that flourished in the heyday of Black Broadway in Washington. After a major renovation it recently reopened and is open Tues–Sun nights with live jazz every Fri. Entertainment and cover charge varies, so call or check the Web site for details about what's on tap. Metro: U St.-Cardozo. *See also* www.commuterpage.com/venues/venue-sp.htm.

Bolívar Statue

Situated on 18th St. at C St. and Virginia Aves. NW in Foggy Bottom, this 27-foot-high bronze monument to Gen. Simón Bolívar is on a base of black marble, beside a marble walk and six fountains, and was sculpted by Felix W. de Weldon who also created the Iwo Jima Memorial at Arlington Cemetery. This is one of the largest equestrian statues in the United States and was a gift from Venezuela in 1959. Metro: Foggy Bottom-GWU.

Bolivia Embassy 3014 Massachusetts Ave. NW (202) 483-4410

Embassy of the Republic of Bolivia. Metro: Dupont Circle.

Bombay Bistro 98 W Montgomery Ave., Rockville, MD (301) 762-8798; and 3570 Chain Bridge Rd., Fairfax, VA (703) 359-5310 www.bombaybistro.com

Open daily for lunch and dinner, at both branches the food is excellent, filling, and with a very wide selection of tandoori chicken, tandoori salmon, many fine vegetarian offerings, and much, much more. Service is casual, prices are inexpensive. The all-you-can-eat lunch buffet is served at both spots, is very popular, and attracts a large satisfied clientele of Indians and everyone else. For Rockville, Metro:

Rockville. For Fairfax, Metro: Vienna, then a 1-mile walk; or by car to Chain Bridge Rd. at Lee Hwy.

Bombay Club 815 Connecticut Ave. NW btw H and I Sts. (202) 659-3727 www .bombayclubdc.com

This has to be the classiest Indian restaurant in town with its British colonial ceiling fans and wicker chairs and its elegant dishes and splendid service. Open Mon–Fri for lunch and dinner, Sat dinner, Sun brunch and dinner. It is fairly expensive, jacket and tie are suggested, and reservations are recommended. Metro: Farragut West.

Bonifant Books 11240 Georgia Ave., Wheaton, MD

Located just 1 block north of the Metro stop, this well-stocked used bookstore carries a very good wide-ranging collection on many subjects. Open Mon–Fri 10 a.m.–8 p.m., Sat 10 a.m.–6 p.m., Sun 11 a.m.–6 p.m. Metro: Wheaton.

Boo at the Zoo National Zoo, entrance in the 3000 block of Connecticut Ave. NW on Harvard St. and on Beach Dr. www.fonz.org/events.htm

On the weekend before Halloween, usually on Fri and Sat, the zoo stays open late for special tours of haunted trails, some of the animal houses, and trick-or-treat stops along the way where strangely attired volunteers give out treats for kids between 5:30 p.m. and 8 p.m. Admission fee for children and adults and the event is popular enough to get tickets early. Details at (202) 673-4800. Metro: Woodley Park-Zoo.

Book and Poetry Readings see Bar Nun, Borders Books and Music, Caravan Books, Chapters Literary Bookstore, Folger Shakespeare Library and Theater, Joaquin Miller Cabin Poetry Series, Kramer Books and Afterwords Café, Lambda Rising, Library of Congress, Martin Luther King Jr. Memorial Library, National Archives, Politics and Prose, Red Circle of Washington, SoHo Tea and Coffee. See also Public Lectures.

Booked Up 1204 31st St. at M St. (202) 965-3244

Upstairs at this Georgetown store is an antiquarian bookshop that exudes the flavor of England past with its striking walnut shelving and rows of first editions and vintage travel guides among its bibliophilic treasures. Open Mon–Fri 11 a.m.– 3 p.m., 10 a.m.–12:30 p.m. Sat. Metro: Foggy Bottom-GWU, then 30, 32, 34, 35, or 36 Bus.

Bookstores See ADC Map and Travel Center, Aladdin's Lamp Children's Books, Audubon Book Shop, Barnes & Noble, Bird-In-Hand Bookstore and Gallery, Bonifant Books, Booked Up, Borders Books and Music, Bridge St. Books, Bryn Mawr Lantern Bookshop, Capitol Hill Books, Chapters Literary Bookstore, Cleveland Park Bookshop, Franz Bader Bookshop, Government Printing Office Bookstores, Idle Time Books, International Language Center, J. F. Ptak Science Books, Kramer Books and Afterwords Café, Lamda Rising, Luna Books and Coffee Shop, Olsson's Books and Records, Once Upon A Time, Politics and Prose, Reiters, Reprint Bookshop, Second Story Books, Sisterspace and Books, Trover Books, Vertigo Books, Yawa Books and Gifts.

Borders Books and Music 1800 L St. NW (202) 466-4999 www.borders.com

This store spreads over 2 stories providing access to a very extensive selection of obscure titles, as well as current popular fiction and nonfiction, CDs, a wide choice of magazines and newspapers, a café espresso bar, comfortable seating for browsing, and a range of book-related and entertainment events scheduled through the week. Open Mon–Thurs 8 a.m.–9 p.m., Fri 8 a.m.–10 p.m., Sat 10 a.m.–9 p.m., Sun 10 a.m.–6 p.m. There's another downtown store at 600 14th St. NW (202) 737-1385, and branches at a number of locations in the Virginia and Maryland suburbs. Check phone book for addresses and phone numbers. Metro: Farragut West or Farragut North.

Bosnia and Herzegovina Embassy 2109 E St. NW (202) 337-1500 www.bosnian embassy.org

Embassy of the Republic of Bosnia and Herzegovina. Metro: Foggy Bottom-GWU.

Botanic Garden *see* U.S. Botanic Garden.

Botswana Embassy 1531–3 New Hampshire Ave. NW (202) 244-4990 www .embassy.org/embassies/bw.html

Embassy of the Republic of Botswana. Metro: Dupont Circle.

Bottom Line 1716 I St. NW (202) 298-8488 www.thebottomlinedc.com

This is a comfortable basement saloon offering a friendly neighborhood bar feel and a stylish ambiance along with moderate prices. Open Mon–Thurs 11:30 a.m.– 2 a.m., Fri–Sat 11:30 a.m.–3 a.m. Metro: Farragut West.

Bowie

This Maryland suburban town is situated on Rte. 50 about halfway between downtown Washington and Annapolis. It is primarily a bedroom community, but it is also home to Bowie State University (301) 860-3435, www.bowiestate.edu, which forms an important feature of the community's cultural life.

Bowie Baysox Prince George's Stadium, 4101 NE Crain Hwy., Bowie, MD (301) 805-6000 www.theorioles.com

Since Washington is without its own major league baseball team, the Bay Sox, a Baltimore Orioles Class-AA team, seeks to fill the void with its games at this 10,000-seat stadium 45 minutes from downtown D.C. just off Rtes. 50 and 301 in Bowie. Tickets are inexpensively priced and there are lots of discounts and special events, an amusement area for kids, and low-priced things to eat and drink.

Bowie Farmers Market Gallant Fox Lane and Rte. 197, Bowie, MD (301) 809-3076 www.localharvest.org/farms/M2415

From mid-May to late October on Sundays 8 a.m.–noon producers bring their products to sell.

Bowie State University 14000 Jericho Park Rd., Bowie, MD (301) 860-3435 www .bowiestate.edu

The undergraduate and graduate enrollment of more than 5,000 at this institution is predominantly black, but the student population includes international and multicultural elements as well. The grounds spread out over some 300 acres and in addition to a strong intercollegiate sports program there is an art gallery and radio and TV stations. Access to the campus other than by car is with the MARC commuter rail line with a stop close by.

Boy Scout Memorial

Located near the Ellipse at 15th St. between Constitution Ave. and E St. NW, this bronze sculpture by Donald DeLue depicts a uniformed Boy Scout next to a male figure symbolizing patriotism and a female figure bearing the light of faith. Metro: McPherson Square.

Boyhood Home of Robert E. Lee *see* Robert E. Lee Boyhood Home.

La Brasserie 239 Massachusetts Ave. NE btw 3rd and D Sts. (202) 546-9154 www.labrasserie.com/

Situated in two connected townhouses with outdoor dining in the milder season, this charming French restaurant serves classic country dishes as well as nouvelle fare at moderate to fairly expensive prices. Open Mon for breakfast and lunch; Tues–Fri breakfast, lunch, and dinner; Sat dinner; Sun brunch and dinner. Reservations suggested, particularly on weekends. Metro: Union Station.

Bravo! Bravo! 1001 Connecticut Ave. NW near K St. (202) 223-5330 www.just salsa.com/washingtondc/clubs/bravobravo

Down a flight of stairs into this cavernous space, the night club beat here is Latin, with salsa and merengue very popular. The music and dancing takes place Wed 10 p.m.–3 a.m., Sat 10 p.m.–4 a.m. Modest entrance charge. Lunch is served Mon–Thurs here in the bar. Metro: Farragut North.

Braxton Hotel 1440 Rhode Island Ave. NW at 14th St. (202) 232-7800 or (800) 350-5759 www.braxtonhotel.com

This budget hotel is popular with young travelers because the rates are very low and each room, even if quite small, has its own bathroom and cable TV and includes a continental breakfast. Metro: McPherson Square or Dupont Circle.

Brazil Embassy 3006 Massachusetts Ave. NW (202) 238-2700 www.brasilemb.org

Described as "a translucent crystal box," the building appears to be suspended in air. Designed by Brazilian architect Olavo Redig de Campos, it was completed in 1971 and houses the embassy's chancery. Next door at 3000 Massachusetts Ave. the ambassador lives in a less revealing edifice: a sturdy Italianate palace designed by John Russell Pope, creator of the Jefferson Memorial, among others. This building was completed in 1909 and acquired by the Brazilian government in 1934. Metro: Dupont Circle.

Brazilian-American Cultural Institute 4103 Connecticut Ave. NW at Upton St. (202) 362-8334 www.bacidc.org

Located in a townhouse along the Connecticut Ave. corridor, this center is given over to numerous Brazilian cultural offerings including art exhibitions, musical performances, lectures, film and video showings, and an extensive library containing English and Portuguese books, magazines and newspapers, videos and records.

Portuguese language instruction is also available. Open Mon–Fri 9 a.m.–5 p.m., except for scheduled evening events. Metro: Van Ness-UDC.

Brazilian Restaurants *see* Grill from Ipanema. *See also* www.dcpages.com, www.washingtonpost.com, www.restaurant.com, www.opentable.com.

Bread and Chocolate

This café serving excellent specialty coffees, delicious pastries, tarts, crepes, sandwiches, and soups is open daily for breakfast, lunch, and dinner. Branches are located at 2301 M St. with the entrance on 23rd St. (202) 833-8360, Metro: Foggy Bottom-GWU; 616 Pennsylvania Ave. SE at 7th St. (202) 547-2875, Metro: Eastern Market; and 5542 Connecticut Ave. NW between Morrison and McKinley Sts. (202) 966-7413, Metro: Friendship Heights.

Bread Line 1751 Pennsylvania Ave. NW btw 17th and 18th Sts. (202) 822-8900

Between 7:30 a.m. and 3:30 p.m. Mon–Fri, this is the place for tasty food products made with fine ingredients. Menu includes French toast, bagels, pizzas, empanadas, focaccia, and innumerable other baked goods and creative sandwiches. Metro: Farragut West.

Breads Unlimited 6914 Arlington Rd., Bethesda, MD (301) 656-2340

More than twenty-five different types of bread without cholesterol or fat are painstakingly prepared daily at this fine bakery open 7 a.m.–7 p.m. An affiliated branch is the New Yorker Bakery at 9443 Georgia Ave. at Seminary Rd. in Silver Spring, MD (301) 585-2875, which is open daily 7 a.m.–3 p.m. Metro: Bethesda.

Brickskeller 1523 22nd St. NW btw P and Q Sts. (202) 293-1885 www.thebrickskeller.com

This spot is billed as a dining place and saloon, but the accent is on the latter. Pub food is available, but the draw is the choice from more than 900 beer brands from everywhere imaginable in the world. Open Mon–Thurs 11:30 a.m.–2 a.m., Fri 11:30 a.m.–3 a.m., Sat 6 p.m.–3 a.m., Sun 6 p.m.–2 a.m. Metro: Dupont Circle, then G2 Bus.

Brickskeller Inn 1523 22nd St. NW btw P and Q Sts. (202) 293-1885 www.thebrickskeller.com

This no-frills 40-room hotel is cheap and clean and some rooms have private baths, TV, and air-conditioning. It sits above the bar and is conveniently located near Rock Creek Park. Metro: Dupont Circle, then G2 Bus.

Bridge Street Books 2814 Pennsylvania Ave. NW near 28th St. (202) 965-5200

This bookstore at the edge of Georgetown caters thoughtfully to client needs, particularly in such topical areas as philosophy, literature, politics, cultural affairs, history, and poetry. Open Mon–Thurs 11 a.m.–10 p.m., Fri–Sat 11 a.m.–11 p.m., and Sun noon–6 p.m. Metro: Foggy Bottom-GWU, then a 10-minute walk.

Bridges *see* American Legion Bridge, Arlington Memorial Bridge, Bison Bridge, Cabin John Aqueduct Bridge, Chain Bridge, Connecticut Avenue Bridge, Duke Ellington Memorial Bridge, 11th Street Bridge, 14th Street Bridges, Frederick Douglass Memorial Bridge, Harvard Street Bridges, High Street Bridge, K Street

Bridge, Key Bridge, Klingle Valley Bridge, M Street NW Bridge, Massachusetts Avenue NW Bridge, P Street NW Bridge, Pennsylvania Avenue NW Bridge, Potomac Railroad Bridge, 16th Street NW Bridge, Spout Run Bridge, Taft Bridge, Theodore Roosevelt Memorial Bridge, Whitney M. Young Jr. Memorial Bridge, Wisconsin Avenue Bridge, Woodrow Wilson Memorial Bridge.

British Embassy *see* United Kingdom Embassy.

The Broadmoor

Situated at 3601 Connecticut Ave., this apartment building is the tallest structure in its neighborhood. Designed in impressive Gothic Revival style in 1929 by architect Joseph Abel, it is surrounded by lovely grounds. Throughout its history it has been the domicile of a number of Washington notables and is now a condominium. Not open to the public. Metro: Cleveland Park.

Brookings Institution 1775 Massachusetts Ave. NW (202) 797-6000 www.brookings.edu

Housed in an architecturally undistinguished building, this celebrated public policy research organization's some 75 resident scholars produce weighty studies and analytical monographs on economics, foreign affairs, education, health services, and legislative issues. Metro: Dupont Circle.

Brookland

This neighborhood in northeast Washington is the site of Catholic University of America, Trinity University, the Franciscan Monastery, and the Basilica of the Shrine of the Immaculate Conception. It is bounded by Brentwood Rd. and Michigan and Rhode Island Aves. The district is populated by predominantly middle-class residents living in detached dwellings constructed in various architectural styles. Metro: Brookland-CUA.

Brookside Gardens 1500 Glenallan Ave. btw Kemp Mill and Randolph Rds., Wheaton, MD (301) 949-8230 www.brooksidegardens.org

This lush 50-acre parkland is administered by the Maryland National Park and Planning Commission and features two conservatories, thematic and seasonal gardens, a wide range of educational programs, guided tours, and horticultural information services. Grounds are open daily 9 a.m.–dusk and the conservatories 10 a.m.–5 p.m. Admission free. Its library is open Mon–Sat noon–5 p.m. By car from the Beltway (I-495), take Exit 31N Georgia Ave., then drive 3 miles to Randolph Rd., turn right or east and go 2 blocks, and then south about 3/4 mile on Glenallan Ave. *See also* www.commuterpage.com/venues/gardens.htm.

Brookside Nature Center 1400 Glenallan Ave. btw Kemp Mill and Randolph Rds., Wheaton, MD (301) 946-9071 www.mc-mncppc.org/parks/facilities/brookside_nature.shtm

This center focuses on natural history and includes animal displays, a hands-on learning place for children, films, and slide shows. Guided tours are available by appointment. There are also hiking trails through wooded areas and picnic grounds. The center is open Tues–Sat 9 a.m.–5 p.m., Sun 1 p.m.–5 p.m. The trails are open from dawn to dusk. Free admission. By car from the Beltway (I-495) take

Exit 31N Georgia Ave., then go about 3 miles to Randolph Rd., turn right or east and go 2 blocks, then south about ¾ mile on Glenallan Ave.

Brunei Embassy 3520 International Court NW (202) 237-1838 www.brunei embassy.org

Embassy of Brunei Darussalam. Metro: Van Ness-UDC.

Bryn Mawr Lantern Bookshop 3241 P St. NW off Wisconsin Ave. (202) 333-3222 www.his.com/~lantern/

This volunteer-managed store selling used books in upper Georgetown supports scholarships at Bryn Mawr College, is inexpensive, and offers a very broad selection of topics. Open Mon–Fri 11 a.m.–4 p.m., Sat 11 a.m.–5 p.m., Sun noon–4 p.m.

Bua 1635 P St. NW btw 16th and 17th Sts. (202) 265-0828

This is good Thai cooking in an attractive and comfortable restaurant featuring an upstairs terrace and tasty and inexpensive lunch specials. Open daily for lunch and dinner. Metro: Dupont Circle.

Buca di Beppo 1825 Connecticut Ave. NW (202) 232-8466 www.bucadibeppo.com

Located just 3 blocks north of the Metro stop, this restaurant features large portions of southern Italian food including huge pizzas and pasta dishes, as well as other standards that are filling and moderately priced. Open for dinner daily, with lunch and dinner on Sun. Metro: Dupont Circle.

Buchanan Memorial *see* James Buchanan Memorial.

Budget Hotels *see* Alexandria Suites Hotel, Allen Lee Hotel, American Inn of Bethesda, Best Western Pentagon, Bethesda Ramada, Brickskeller Inn, Embassy Square, Braxton Hotel, Channel Inn, Days Inn Connecticut Avenue, Days Inn Crystal City, Days Inn Silver Spring, Econo Lodge Metro, Embassy Inn, Embassy Square, Holiday Inn Silver Spring, Hotel Harrington, Park Inn International, Quality Inn Courthouse Plaza, Quality Inn Iwo Jima, Red Roof Inn, Tabard Inn, Travelodge Cherry Blossom Motel, Windsor Inn, Windsor Park Hotel. *See also* www.hostels.com, www.frommers.com.

Buffalo Billiards 1330 19th St. NW at Dupont Circle (202) 331-7665 www.buf falobilliards.com

This below-ground pool emporium boasts some thirty good tables, dartboards, a snooker table, a cigar bar, a restaurant with a Southwestern menu, and moderate-priced drinks. Playing charges vary 1 p.m.–3 a.m. Sat and Sun, with no entry charge. Metro: Dupont Circle.

Buffalo Bridge *see* Bison Bridge

Bukom Café 2442 18th St. NW (202) 265-4600 www.bukomcafe.com

This relaxed Adams Morgan restaurant/bar offers tasty African dishes and beers as well as live music daily 4 p.m.–2 a.m. at moderate prices with no cover charge. Metro: Dupont Circle, then L2 Bus.

Bulgaria Embassy 1621 22nd St. NW (202) 387-0174 www.bulgaria-embassy.org

Embassy of the Republic of Bulgaria. Metro: Dupont Circle.

Bull Moose Bed and Breakfast 101 5th St. NE (202) 547-1050 or (800) 261-2768
www.bullmoose-b-and-b.com

This 18-guestroom hostelry in a Victorian building with tall ceilings and
wooden panels offers singles and doubles with private or shared baths at moderate
prices. The rooms have themes inspired by Teddy Roosevelt and his family. It is
located about 5 blocks from the Capitol. Metro: Union Station or Capitol South.

Bull Run Regional Park 7700 Bull Run Dr. off Route 28, Centreville, VA (703)
631-0550 www.nvrpa.org/bullrunpark.html

The principal park area remains untouched wilderness with a range of eco-
systems, from swampland to meadow to two creeks and glorious wildflowers. It is
open from mid-March through November and is not very far from the Manassas
National Battlefield Park. Its several thousand acres contain 150 campsites, a large
outdoor swimming pool, miniature golf, skeet and trap shooting, indoor archery,
lovely nature trails, and a concert amphitheater. Nonresidents of the area pay a
moderate entrance fee. For details about park facilities and special events call or
check the Web site.

Bullfeathers 410 1st St. SE btw N Carolina Ave. and D St. (202) 543-5005 www
.bullfeathersofcapitolhill.com

This is a comfortable Capitol Hill Victorian-style pub with an outdoor patio
offering well-prepared American-style food and drink at reasonable prices. Open
Mon–Sat lunch and dinner, Sun brunch and dinner. Metro: Capitol South.

Bureau of Engraving and Printing 14th St. and C St. SW 1 block south of the Mall
(202) 874-3019 www.moneyfactory.com

This is where the government designs, engraves, and prints paper money,
bonds, and postage stamps and provides a visitors center featuring related exhibits.
Admission is free and hours are 9 a.m.–2 p.m. Mon–Fri, and June to August
5 p.m.–7 p.m. as well. There is a fascinating 40-minute guided tour (no self-
conducted allowed). Tour tickets to this very popular government plant are available from 8 a.m. at the Raoul Wallenberg Pl. (15th St.) entrance. Metro: Smithsonian.

Burke Centre Farmers Market 5671 Roberts Pkwy. in VRE parking lot, Burke
Centre, VA (703) 941-7987

On Saturdays 8 a.m.–noon between early May and the end of October producers sell fruit and vegetables.

Burke Lake Golf Course 7315 Ox Rd., Fairfax Station, VA (703) 323-1641

This popular golf course is one of a number of Fairfax County Park Authority
courses. It is next to Burke Lake Park and has 18 holes and is 2,500 or so yards long
in a picturesque lakeside area. It has a putting green, clubhouse, and driving range.
Call for details on fees, subscriptions, location directions, and tee times.

Burke Lake Park 7315 Ox Rd., Fairfax Station, VA (703) 323-6600 www.fairfaxco
.gov/parks

This 900-acre Fairfax County park contains a 218-acre lake where rowboats can
be rented and visitors can take a guided tour of the lake on a pontoon boat, miles

of hiking trails, a campground, play areas, picnicking places, and an amphitheater. Next to the park is the Burke Lake Golf Course. The park is south of Washington. Take I-95 to Exit 123N, then drive 9 or 10 miles to the park.

Burke Memorial *see* Edward Burke Memorial.

Burkino Faso Embassy 2340 Massachusetts Ave. NW (202) 332-5577 www.burkina embassy-usa.org
    Metro: Dupont Circle.

Burma Embassy (Myanmar) 2300 S St. NW (202) 332-9044 www.embassy.org/ embassies/mm.html
    Architect Appleton P. Clark Jr. designed this building, completed in 1902. It was the home of Herbert Hoover twice, first in 1921 when he served as secretary of Commerce, and again when Franklin Delano Roosevelt ousted him from his Pennsylvania Ave. residence. Pearl Mesta, the inspiration of the musical *Call Me Madam*, lived here in the 1960s. Metro: Dupont Circle.

Burma Restaurant 740 6th St. NW btw G and H Sts. (202) 638-1280
    This upstairs spot features tasty dishes, inexpensive prices, a casual ambiance, friendly service, and unusual Asian cuisine including excellent noodle and vegetarian entrees. Open for lunch Mon–Fri, dinner daily. Metro: Gallery Pl.-Chinatown.

Burmese Restaurants *see* Asian Restaurants.

The Burro 1621 Connecticut Ave. at R St. (202) 483-6861
    Fresh, cheap, tasty, and filling Tex-Mex fast-food choices are served in this no-frills dining spot that's open daily for lunch and dinner. A second location at 2000 Pennsylvania Ave. in Foggy Bottom (202) 293-9449. Metro: Dupont Circle.

Burundi Embassy 2233 Wisconsin Ave. NW, Suite 212 (202) 342-2574 www .embassy.org/embassies/bi.html
    Embassy of the Republic of Burundi. Metro: Tenleytown-AU.

Bus Tours *see* Duck Tours, Frederick Douglass Tour, Gray Line Bus Tours, Interiors of Public Buildings Tours, Li'l Red Trolley All-Day Tour, Mount Vernon and Alexandria Tour, Tourmobile Sightseeing Inc., Washington/Arlington National Cemetery Tour, Washington Embassy and Arlington Cemetery Tours, Washington Old Town Trolley Tours. *See also* Special Interest Tours, www.shop.viator.com.

Busara 2340 Wisconsin Ave. NW btw Hall Pl. and Calvert St. (202) 337-2340
    The sleek décor at this brightly lit restaurant in Glover Park is the setting for well-presented and zestfully prepared Thai fare from seafood to pork to curries to Asian bouillabaisse, at moderate prices. Open daily for lunch and dinner. There is a clone of this place at Tysons Corner in the Virginia suburbs at 8142 Watson St., McLean (703) 356-2288.

Buses
    Metrobus runs to all areas of the city and much of the outlying suburban areas in Maryland and Virginia. There are some 5,000 bus stops in and around the city. Riders need the exact change for the fare and dollar bills are not accepted. There are no transfers from bus to subway, but there are transfers from bus to another

bus with free transfers from the driver requested on boarding. Metrorail to bus transfers can be bought from a machine in the station when entering the Metrorail. The bus is the only public transportation to Georgetown and Adams Morgan since neither is served by Metrorail. Washington's bus routing system is complicated, and the best way to learn about routes, schedules, and fares to any destination is to phone Metrorail/Metrobus information at (202) 637-7000 or use the Web site: www.metroopensdoors.com. *See also* Georgetown Shuttle Bus, www.commuter page.com.

Butlers, the Cigar Bar in the Grand Hyatt Hotel, 1000 H St. NW (202) 637-4765

The place in town for cigars and martinis or whatever other drink appeals. Its comfortable Art Deco ambiance evokes the flavor of pre-Castro Havana, except here the ventilation process keeps the place from smelling like the proverbial smoke-filled room. Low-level background jazz adds to the elegance of this classy place near the old Convention Center. Open 5 p.m.–1 a.m. every night but Sunday. Metro: Gallery Pl.-Chinatown or Metro Center.

Butt-Millet Memorial Fountain www.encyclopedia-titanica.org/documents/ butt_aw_memorial. shtml

This limestone and marble fountain erected in 1913 by sculptor Daniel Chester French commemorates two men, Archibald W. Butt and Francis D. Millet, who perished in the Titanic disaster in April 1912. It is located on the Ellipse, below the White House, at Ellipse Dr. and Executive Ave. NW. Metro: Federal Triangle.

Byrd Stadium University of Maryland, Field House Drive, College Park, MD http://umterps.ocsn.com

This home of the champions (national champion in football and men's and women's lacrosse) was built in 1950 and renovated in 1995. It now can seat up to 62,000 fans. The stadium is named for H. C. "Curley" Byrd, a former football coach turned college president at the University of Maryland. It has been the site of more than 50 Atlantic Coast Conference track and field championships. Metro: West Hyattsville, then take Metrobus F6 toward New Carrollton Station to the stop at Campus Drive and Library Lane, then a 4-block walk.

C

C&O Canal

Built in the middle of the nineteenth century to carry lumber, coal, and other cargo from western Maryland and Pennsylvania all the way to Washington, D.C., this 184-mile waterway from Cumberland, Maryland, to Georgetown operated until 1924. It employed more than 70 locks and a huge tunnel carved through the mountains of western Maryland. Today it is a National Historic Park with jogging paths and walking trails along most of its length. A very attractive short stretch between Thomas Jefferson St. and 31st St. in Georgetown features picturesque houses that have been restored as private homes, shops, and offices. The canal is reached by walking downhill from M St. in Georgetown. Details from the Visitors Center at (202) 653-5190 or the Web site: www.nps.gov/choh.

C&O Canal Barge Rides

From April through October mule-drawn barge trips along the canal in Georgetown are led by guides from the National Park Service in nineteenth-century costumes. The excursion starts between Thomas Jefferson and 30th Sts., 1 block below M St. in Georgetown. The 70-minute ride on a replica of a nineteenth-century canal boat goes through one lock and along ½ mile and back through the old historic district, with the tour guide explaining the canal's history in stories and song. Tickets are sold at the Visitors Center at 1057 Thomas Jefferson St. NW with discounts for seniors and children. The rides take place two or three times each day except Mon and Tues. Details at (202) 653-5190 or www.nps.gov/choh.

C&O Canal National Historic Park *see* Chesapeake and Ohio Canal National Historical Park.

C&O Canal Towpath www.nps.gov/choh

This pathway once trod by mules has become a favorite scenic place for Washingtonians to hike, jog, and bicycle along the hard-packed gravel and dirt trail. It starts in Georgetown and runs the length of the canal past the 70 locks to Cumberland, Maryland. The canal and the towpath have been designated and maintained as a national park for more than 30 years.

C&O National Historical Park *see* Chesapeake and Ohio National Historical Park.

C. C. Huntley House 1601 16th St. NW www.cr.nps.gov/nr/travel/wash/dc53.htm
Built in 1876 for Huntley, a major landowner on 16th St., this stucco house with its stable is among the earliest examples of the brick row houses along this street. Metro: Dupont Circle.

Cabaret *see* Comedy Clubs, Night Clubs.

Cabin John Aqueduct Bridge Off the Clara Barton Freeway in Cabin John, MD www.nps.gov/choh/co_aqua.htm
Spanning Cabin John Creek, construction started in 1857 when the builder, the U.S. Army Corps of Engineers, reported to Secretary of War Jefferson Davis, who resigned to become president of the Confederacy and was not around when the bridge was completed in 1863. This historic structure held the record as the longest stone masonry arch in the world—220 feet—until 1903. The corps continues to maintain the structure, which supports a torrent of water under the roadway, millions of gallons a day piped in a 9-foot-diameter, cast-iron, lined masonry conduit to Washington and environs.

Cabin John Regional Park 7700 Tuckerman Lane, Rockville, MD (301) 299-1971 www.mncppc.org
Located in Montgomery County between Old Georgetown Rd. and Seven Locks Rd., this 500-acre park offers ice-skating, outdoor tennis and handball courts, hiking trails, summer concerts, a nature center, picnic tables, an attractive children's playground, and a miniature train ride that traverses more than a mile through the woods. Fees for ice-skating, tennis, and train rides. Call for details.

Cabs *see* Taxis.

Cactus Cantina 3300 Wisconsin Ave. NW at Macomb St. (202) 686-7222
Near the National Cathedral in upper-northwest D.C., this extremely popular and bustling Tex-Mex spot serves up portions that are generous, high quality, delicious, and inexpensive. Open daily for lunch and dinner. Metro: Cleveland Park.

Cada Vez 1438 U St. NW near 14th St. (202) 667-0785 www.cadavezonline.com
One of the newer restaurant/dance bars featuring live music some nights, typically Latin sounds. Open Tues–Sat from 5 p.m. on beginning with early dinner and then casual dining with drinks, once the entertainment and dancing begins. No cover charge. Menu and entertainment details are on the Web site. Metro: U St.-Cardozo.

Cadillac Grand Prix
This event takes place on three days in July over a weekend when racing cars, motorcycles, and trucks take part in daredevil competitions and other special activities at RFK Stadium. Details at (202) 546-8352 or www.cadillacgrandprix.com.

Cady Lee Mansion www.cadyleemansion.com
On the corner of Eastern Ave. and Piney Branch Rd. in Takoma Park right on the border between D.C. and Maryland, this National Register of Historic Places house with 22 rooms was built in 1887. The architect was Leon Dessez, a celebrated

builder of the period. It is the only remaining private residence constructed in Queen Anne Victorian style in this area. After renovation, the building was sold in 2002 for more than a million dollars. Metro: Takoma.

Café Atlantico 405 8th St. NW btw D and E Sts. (202) 393-0812 www.cafeatlan ticodc.com

The accent here is on South American and Caribbean dishes in this multi-level, colorful, lively, and bustling upscale restaurant/night club. The dazzling range of dining choices are imaginatively and elegantly prepared. Open for lunch and dinner daily, with a fixed-price Latin brunch on Sat. Moderately expensive. Metro: Archives-Navy Memorial.

Café Berlin 322 Massachusetts Ave. NE btw 3rd and 4th Sts. www.cafeberlin dc.com/

A comfortable lower townhouse setting helps evoke the old-world European atmosphere and flavor for the hearty German dishes served inside and outside on the terrace at this restaurant 3 blocks from Union Station. Open Mon–Sat for lunch and dinner, Sun dinner only. Moderate prices. Metro: Union Station.

Café Dalat 3143 Wilson Blvd. btw Herndon and N Hudson Sts., Arlington, VA (703) 276-0935

Low prices and friendly service are features of this plain but pleasant Vietnamese restaurant in a neighborhood filled with Asian places. It is open daily for lunch and dinner, and Mon–Fri there's a very popular lunch buffet. Metro: Clarendon.

Café Deluxe 3228 Wisconsin Ave. btw Woodley Rd. and Macomb St. (202) 686-2233

Always busy and lively, the American-style food in this plain and simple place is a great favorite and is moderately priced so there's often a line waiting for indoor or outdoor tables. Mon–Sat lunch and dinner, Sun brunch and dinner. Metro: Cleveland Park.

Café des Amis du Café 1020 19th St. NW btw K and L Sts.

This busy place is open only Mon–Friday 7 a.m.–4 p.m. and provides only counter seating, but the sandwiches and salads are fresh and inexpensive and the coffee is good, too. Cash only. Metro: Farragut North or Farragut West.

Café La Ruche 1039 31st St. NW off M St. toward the river (202) 965-2684 www .cafelaruche.com

Café-style food is served at inexpensive prices in Georgetown's oldest French restaurant. Open Mon–Sat for lunch and dinner, prix-fixe brunch and dinner Sat and Sun. Tables in the garden, weather cooperating, make for a tranquil, charming setting. Metro: Foggy Bottom-GWU, then 30, 32, 34, 35, or 36 Bus.

Café Milano 3251 Prospect St. NW at Wisconsin Ave. (202) 333-6183

Specializing in northern Italian food this Georgetown restaurant serves good tasty dishes, pastas, and salads, at expensive prices and enjoys a reputation for being the place where the beautiful people dine or join in at the crowded bar later in the evening. Open for lunch and dinner daily. Metro: Foggy Bottom-GWU, then 30, 32, 34, 35, or 36 Bus.

Café Olé 4000 Wisconsin Ave. NW btw Rodman and Van Ness Sts. (202) 224-1330
    This popular Tenleytown storefront eatery is open daily for lunch and dinner offering a vast menu of small portions (mezes) of various kinds of international dishes that are delicious and exotic along with wines by the glass and all at very reasonable prices. There's an enclosed outdoor patio open year-round. Metro: Tenleytown-AU.

Café Plaka 7833 Woodmont Ave. btw Fairmont and St. Elmo Sts., Bethesda, MD (301) 986-1337
    This moderately priced Greek restaurant with sidewalk tables available in mild weather serves tasty and carefully prepared dishes featuring many classic choices as well as fresh seafood in season. Open daily for lunch and dinner. Metro: Bethesda.

Café Promenade in the Renaissance Mayflower Hotel, 1127 Connecticut Ave. NW (202) 347-2233
    This is a classy hotel coffee shop, which also serves Mediterranean dishes at moderately expensive prices. Open daily for breakfast, lunch, and dinner. Metro: Farragut North.

Café Saigon 1135 N Highland St. at Wilson Blvd., Arlington, VA
    This modest-looking spot serves excellently prepared seafood and meat dishes as well as typical Vietnamese fare, all at very inexpensive prices. Open daily for lunch and dinner. Metro: Clarendon.

Cafés *see* Atomic Grounds, Au Bon Pain, Borders Books and Music, Café des Amis du Café, Café Promenade, Corner Bakery Café, Footnotes a Café, Java House Coffeeshop, Jolt 'N Bolt Coffee and Tea House, Kramer Books and Afterwords Café, Mudd House, Sirius Coffee Company, Soho Tea and Coffee, Starbucks, Tryst, Xando Cosi. *See also* Coffee and Cakes, Tea Rooms, www.frommers.com, www.washingtonpost.com.

The Cairo 1615 Q St. NW near 17th St.
    This 14-story luxury apartment building was constructed by architect Thomas Franklin Schneider in 1894 and intended to be the city's largest nongovernment structure (165 feet high). The Moorish and Art Nouveau features of the façade and the carved elephants add to its impressive appearance. The building was renovated in 1972 and later became a condominium. It is not open to the public. Metro: Dupont Circle.

Cajun Restaurants *see* Bardia's New Orleans Café, Louisiana Express Company, Tunnicliffs, Two-Nineteen Restaurant, The Warehouse Bar and Grill. *See also* Southern Restaurants.

Calvary Baptist Church 755 8th St. NW btw G and H Sts. (202) 347-8355 www.calvarydc.com
    This is one of the oldest black churches in Washington, established in 1862. It served as a way station of the Underground Railroad. The original building was destroyed in a fire and the current structure dates from the late 1860s. Open only for services. Metro: Gallery Pl.-Chinatown.

Calvert St. Bridge *see* Duke Ellington Memorial Bridge.

Cambodia Embassy 4530 16th St. NW (202) 726-7742 www.embassy.org/cambodia
   Embassy of the Kingdom of Cambodia. Metro: Silver Spring and bus connection.

Cameron Run Regional Park 4001 Eisenhower Ave. btw Bluestone Rd. and Clermont Ave., Alexandria, VA (703) 960-0767 www.nvrpa.org
   This park is a haven during sticky weather with its Great Waves Water Park and its wave pool, tall water slides, and water playground to delight kids. There's also a batting cage and an attractive miniature golf course. Admission charge. Open daily 10 a.m.–8 p.m. from Memorial Day to Labor Day. Metro: Eisenhower Avenue.

Cameroon Embassy 2349 Massachusetts Ave. (202) 265-8790 www.embassy.org/embassies/cm.html
   This fanciful limestone mansion, built in 1906, was another Beaux Arts creation of architect George Oakley Totten Jr. Commissioned by Christian Hague, Norway's soon-to-die minister to the United States, his widow lived there for 19 years. Prior to its 1972 sale to the Cameroon government, it was the Czechoslovakian mission. Metro: Dupont Circle.

Canada Embassy 501 Pennsylvania Ave. NW (202) 682-1740 www.canadianembassy.org
   Designed by Canada's gold-medallist architect Arthur Erickson, this 6-story post-modern structure opened in 1989. Details of the periodic exhibits and concerts are on the Web site. Metro: Judiciary Square.

Canal Barge Ride *see* C&O Canal Barge Rides.

La Cantanita's Havana Café 3100 Clarendon Blvd. btw Highland St. and Washington Blvd., Arlington, VA (703) 524-3611
   Genuine Cuban fare is served in this bright, cheery place located in the courtyard, where the dishes are zesty and filling and the prices moderate. Open for lunch Mon–Fri, dinner daily. Metro: Clarendon.

Cantate Chamber Singers P.O. Box 34070, Bethesda, MD (301) 986-1779 www.cantate.org
   This choral ensemble based in Montgomery County has been operating for almost 20 years and has a reputation for adventuresome programming, for performing a cappella and accompanied choral works spanning five centuries, as well as for its commitment to twentieth-century music and to commissioning and premiering new works. It performs at various locations in the Washington area and conducts a biennial contest for young composers.

Cape Verde Embassy 3415 Massachusetts Ave. (202) 965-6820 http://virtualcapeverde.net
   Embassy of the Republic of Cape Verde. Metro: Dupont Circle.

Capital Beltway *see* The Beltway.

Capital Children's Museum 800 3rd St. NE at H St. (202) 675-4120 www.ccm.org
   This sprawling 3-floor hands-on interactive learning laboratory is designed for

kids 2 to 12 and is one of the country's oldest and largest. The place is just 3 blocks from Union Station and is replete with enticing exhibits and creative experiences from craft making to an ice-age cave to a fire station to a chemical science center. Open daily 10 a.m.–5 p.m. Modest admission charge. Metro: Union Station.

Capital Classic www.jordancapitalclassic.com/home.html

Each year in early April, high school basketball stars from all over the United States play in this all-star competition. For tickets and dates call TicketMaster at (202) 432-7328 or MCI Center (202) 628-3200.

Capital Crescent Trail www.cctrail.org

This car-free trail for hikers and bicyclists runs along an 11-mile path from K St. in Georgetown to Bethesda and Rock Creek Park and to Silver Spring. It is on the former right-of-way of the Baltimore & Ohio Railroad's Georgetown spur. From Bethesda to Silver Spring, unlike the path from Georgetown to Bethesda, which is paved, the trail is a gravel surface. At the Web site there is a map of the trail's completed and still uncompleted sections as well as the historic background, parking locations, and other details. For recorded information call the Coalition for the Capital Crescent Trail at (202) 234-4834.

Capital Grille 601 Pennsylvania Ave. NW at 6th St. (202) 737-6200

This trendy restaurant in the Federal Triangle area exudes a club-like flavor with its classic dark wood paneling. Well-aged steaks, fresh lobsters, baked potatoes, and huge salads are the typical choices. Open for lunch Mon–Fri, dinner daily at this expensive dining spot where reservations are recommended. Metro: Archives-Navy Memorial.

Capital Hilton 1001 16th St. NW at K St. (202) 393-1000 or (800) 445-8667, fax (202) 639-5780 www.hilton.com

This centrally located 12-floor hotel with some 500 rooms, underwent a major overhaul and provides all the expected amenities of a very expensive hostelry. Metro: Farragut North, Farragut West, or McPherson Square.

Capital Jazz Fest

For more than 10 years this annual outdoor music event has been the place for hearing and viewing some of the country's finest contemporary jazz musicians. It takes place on a weekend early in June at different locations in the greater Washington, D.C., area. Information at (301) 218-0404 or www.capitaljazz.com.

Capital Price Fest *see* Gay Pride Celebration.

Capital Spotlight 4920 3rd St. NW (202) 745-7858

This is a free weekly newspaper centered on news and features oriented toward the interests of the community's African-American population. It is available on Thursdays in schools, community centers, churches, and libraries all through the city.

Capital Yacht Club 1000 Water St. SW near 9th St. and Maine Ave. (202) 488-8110 www.capitalyachtclub.com

In existence since 1892, the club provides berths for many transient boats of all sizes up to 250 feet during the season. It sponsors a number of annual community events of which the Blessing of the Fleet is probably the best known. Metro: L'Enfant Plaza.

The Capitol *see* U.S. Capitol.

Capitol City Brewing Company 1100 New York Ave. NW at 11th St. (202) 628-2222 www.capcitybrew.com/

The reason many people come here is for the beer, and there are all kinds, although reasonably good moderately priced food is served at lunch and dinner amid the din of the thirsty and voluble beer-guzzling crowds. Open 11 a.m.–midnight, and a little later on some nights. There are now two branches in D.C. and two in the suburbs. This one is a converted Greyhound bus station. Metro: Metro Center. The other, at 2 Massachusetts Ave. NE at N Capitol St. and Union Station (202) 842-2337, is in what was once the office of the postmaster general. Suburban locations are at 7735 Old Georgetown Rd. in Bethesda (301) 652-2282, and 4001 S 28th St. in Arlington (703) 578-3888.

Capitol College 11301 Springfield Rd. off Hwy. 197, Laurel, MD (301) 369-2800 www.capitol-college.edu

Since 1927 this private college on a sizable campus in Prince George's County has been preparing students for careers in technology. It offers associate and bachelor's degrees in engineering and communications with specializations in computers, electronics, and telecommunications.

Capitol Country Dancin' (Web site) www.countrydancin.com

This remarkable site provides a comprehensive, current guide to Country Western dance in the Metropolitan Washington and Baltimore area. It provides current information on West Coast Swing, Country Western, and Hustle dancing and will update you with a weekly e-mail. The site allows you to search by regularly scheduled dances, by day of the week, by club, bar or dance hall, other Country Western dance sites, as well as regional competitions. There is, as well, an interactive map of locations.

Capitol East Natatorium 635 North Carolina Ave. SE at Pennsylvania Ave. (202) 724-4495

One of the better-equipped indoor pools in the city. It is open year-round Mon–Fri 6:30 a.m.–9 p.m., Sat–Sun 10 a.m.–5 p.m. Admission free. Metro: Eastern Market.

Capitol Entertainment Services (202) 636-9203 www.washington-dc-tours.com/contact.htm

This organization runs tours centered on black history focusing on Capitol Hill, the Mall, and other sites for groups throughout the year, but during the summer months it picks up families and individuals.

Capitol Guided Tours www.aoc.gov/visit/visit_overview.htm

The Capitol is open to visitors Mon–Sat 9 a.m.–4:30 p.m., including national holidays, but is not open on Sun. Guided tours begin outside the main entrance of the building, which faces the Library of Congress and the Supreme Court. All visitors must have a ticket and distribution of tickets starts at 8 a.m. Only the Rotunda, Statuary Hall, and the crypt are included in the 30-minute tour. For a detailed message describing the aspects of the visit to the Capitol call (202) 225-6827.

Capitol Hill

This section of the city clearly includes the U.S. Capitol and the nearby Library of Congress, Supreme Court, Senate and House Office Buildings, and the Folger Shakespeare Library, but it is much more than the center of the government. It is also a mix of many restored and attractive residential tree-shaded streets of Victorian row houses, cafés, restaurants, galleries, boutiques, lovely small parks, and the old-style Eastern Market. It is also home to a population of predominantly younger neighborhood residents who serve as staff members in the offices of congressmen and senators, as well as in other federal offices. They also serve as strong civic activists who work strenuously to prevent the residential character of the area from being transformed through inappropriate development.

Capitol Hill Art League Gallery 545 7th St. SE btw E and G Sts. (202) 547-6839 www.chaw.org

A changing program of exhibits of Capitol Hill artists' paintings, photos, and other media are shown here, and there are also gallery lectures and discussions about the works. Open Mon–Thurs 9 a.m.–6 p.m., Fri 9 a.m.–8 p.m., Sat 9:30 a.m.–2 p.m. Metro: Eastern Market.

Capitol Hill Books 657 C St. SE at 7th St. (202) 544-1621 www.capitolhillbooks-dc.com

An eclectic mix of used books are for sale in this lively shop loaded with titles from first editions to time-worn and like-new works. Open Mon–Fri 11:30 a.m.–6 p.m., Sat and Sun 9 a.m.–6 p.m. Metro: Eastern Market.

Capitol Hill Guest House *see* Bull Moose Guest House.

Capitol Hill Historic District

Bounded roughly by H St. NE on the north, 13th St. on the east, the Southeast Freeway on the south, and N Capitol St. and S Capitol St. on the west, this is one of the oldest and most architecturally diverse neighborhoods in the city. Many restored nineteenth-century row houses on long blocks with interesting façades as well as many with plain frame construction are part of its charm. Homeowners and residents represent a mix of congressional staff workers, bureaucrats, lobbyists, and professionals in this racially balanced community where new construction is rare but renovation is ubiquitous. The district can be entered from Metro stops at Capitol South, Eastern Market, and Union Station.

Capitol Hill Restoration Society House and Garden Tour *see* Mother's Day Tour.

Capitol Hill Suites 200 C St. SE at 2nd St. (202) 543-6000 or (800) 424-9165 www.capitolhillsuites.com

Located on a quiet street in a lovely neighborhood very close to the Capitol, Supreme Court, and Library of Congress, this all-suite hotel rents its remodeled 152 suites, studios, and efficiencies daily, weekly, or by the month at middle-range rates. Light continental breakfast and daily newspaper are part of the amenities. Metro: Capitol South.

Capitol Lounge 229 Pennsylvania Ave. SE btw 2nd and 3rd Sts. (202) 547-2098

This is a very popular saloon much favored by Capitol Hill staff members at the front bar or in the downstairs cigar lounge. Lots of TVs going, different special events on different nights, and a raucous decibel level are all part of the lively ambiance. Open midafternoon during the week, at 11 a.m. on Sat and Sun, and closing at 2 a.m. or 3 a.m. Metro: Capitol South.

Capitol Reflecting Pool *see* Reflecting Pool.

Capitol Reservations (202) 452-1270 or (800) 847-4832 www.capitolreservations .com/listings.htm

This agency centers its efforts in booking hotel rooms and arranging tour packages for travelers in the Washington, D.C., area.

Capitol River Cruises Washington Harbour, 3050 K St. NW at 31st St. (301) 460-7447 or (800) 405-5511 www.capitolrivercruises.com

Passengers can board the 65-foot *Nightingale* from its departure point every hour at the Georgetown waterfront noon–8 p.m. for a 50-minute narrated tour of the Potomac offering views of the Kennedy Center, Watergate, the Capitol, and various monuments. No reservations are necessary and tickets are less expensive for children.

Capitol Rotunda

In this space one stands at the very center of the city in an area 180 feet high and 96 feet across. The fresco inside the dome took Constantino Brumidi, an Italian immigrant, 1 year to complete, and he worked from 1855 to 1880 in executing the massive frieze around the Rotunda, which portrays 400 years of American history. The eight large paintings on the walls depict idealized representations of events in American history. Four are the work of John Turnbull and are based on events from the American Revolution. Statues of American leaders encircle the room.

Capitol Statuary Hall

To the right of the Rotunda, the House of Representatives met in this room until 1857. Each state was later asked to send statues of two distinguished citizens for display here. Several had to be moved elsewhere because the weight of the marble was too excessive for the floor to bear. But a considerable number of these great stone figures still remain in this room of tile and drapery.

Capitol Steps (703) 683-8330 www.capsteps.com

This musical political satire and parody group of ex-congressional staffers performs at various locations around the city and elsewhere. To learn where you can catch their highly entertaining lampooning routines call or check the Web site.

Caravan Books 6053 Oxon Hill Rd., Oxon Hill, MD (301) 567-8234

This bookshop features African-American literature and holds book-signing events with popular black authors and regular storytelling programs for children. Open Mon–Sat 10 a.m.–9 p.m., Sun 12–6 p.m. The location is in the Rivertown Shopping Center off St. Barnabus Rd.

Carberry House

Located at 423 6th St. SE, this building, constructed around 1813, is part of a group of houses along 6th St. to G St., which are among the oldest houses in the Capitol Hill neighborhood. Metro: Eastern Market.

Caribbean Carnival (202) 726-2204 www.dccaribbeancarnival.com

This annual festival runs on a weekend in the second half of June culminating in a lively parade on Georgia Ave. in which participants are lavishly and colorfully costumed, and many bands also participate. Call or check the Web site for information.

Caribbean Restaurants *see* Latin American Restaurants.

Carlyle Grand Café 4000 S 28th St. at S Quincy St. just off I-395, Shirlington, VA (703) 931-0777

Open daily for lunch and dinner this large restaurant serving new American cuisine has a simple décor with Art Deco wall posters and excellent food. The downstairs part, where the bar is, is noisier. Upstairs it's more tranquil. The moderately priced dishes are equally enticing in both parts. Metro: Pentagon, then take a bus to 1775 S Quincy St.

Carlyle House 121 N Fairfax St. btw King and Cameron Sts., Alexandria, VA (703) 549-2997 www.carlylehouse.org

Built in 1753, this large Georgian stone manor house was constructed as the home for a Scottish merchant and his family. The 2-story building and its rooms have been renovated and are furnished and decorated in authentic eighteenth-century style. Open Tues–Sat 10 a.m.–4:30 p.m., Sun noon–4:30 p.m. Admission charge is nominal and guided tours of the mansion are conducted every half hour. Metro: King Street, exit the station and take the DAT5 DASH Bus toward Braddock Road Metro to the stop at N Fairfax and King Sts. Walk north on N Fairfax St.

Carlyle Suites 1731 New Hampshire Ave. NW at S St. (202) 234-3200 www .carlylesuites.com

Located 2 blocks from Dupont Circle in a quiet residential street, this Art Deco hotel features fully equipped kitchens and dining areas and is particularly popular with families. Rates are in the mid-price range and guests have free entry to a neighborhood health club and access to a limited number of free parking spaces. Metro: Dupont Circle.

Carnegie Institution of Washington 1530 P St. NW at 16th St. (202) 387-6400 www.ciw.edu

Located in a grand structure built between 1908 and 1910 by architects Carrère and Hastings, this internationally recognized organization is dedicated to advancing scientific knowledge. The building has an extraordinary interior with a lovely rotunda and attractive auditorium. The institution sponsors regular lectures by outstanding scientists and researchers, which are open to the public. Details by phone or on the Web site. Metro: Dupont Circle.

Carousel on the Mall *see* Smithsonian Carousel.

Carpool 4000 Fairfax Dr. btw Randolph and Quincy Sts., Ballston, VA (703) 532-7665 www.nts95.com/carpool/default.htm

The décor at this classy billiard parlor and rib spot screams of cars and pool with its innumerable furnishing features. The barbecued chicken and ribs are good, and the 16 pool tables are in good condition, and there's a good selection of beers at reasonable prices. Some tables are reserved for nonsmokers. Open Mon–Thurs 4 p.m.–2 a.m., Fri 3 p.m.–2 a.m., Sat–Sun noon–2 a.m. Busiest times are weekend nights. Metro: Ballston-MU.

Carter Barron Amphitheater in Rock Creek Park, 16th St. and Colorado Ave. NW (202) 426-6837 (summer and fall); (202) 619-7222 (winter and spring) www.nps .gov/rocr/cbarron.htm

This outdoor performance site seating 4,250 is run by the National Park Service and offers a summer festival featuring rock, jazz, and classical concerts. Its free summer performances by the Washington Shakespeare Theater are another of the highly popular regular summer events. There is free parking at the site and it can also be reached by Bus S1. Details on summer and fall programs at the phone numbers or the Web site.

Casa Fiesta 4910 Wisconsin Ave. NW at Tenley Circle, NW (202) 244-8888

At this Salvadoran restaurant in upper-northwest D.C. you'll see locals grabbing a bite, tourists getting a good inexpensive meal, and native Spanish speakers coming in for some authentic fare. Look to the Spanish section of the menu for the best *yucca con chicharron* (deep fried yucca and pork) in town. Don't skip on the *curdito* (a spicy, tangy slaw) and the homey *pupusas* (pork- or cheese-stuffed corn pancakes). Formerly called El Tamarindo, the name has changed, but the owners and menu are the same. Open daily for lunch and dinner. Metro: Tenleytown-AU.

Cashion's Eat Place 1819 Columbia Rd. NW btw Mintwood Pl. and Baltimore St. (202) 797-1819

Imaginative new American cuisine and a frequently changing menu are features of this attractive Adams Morgan restaurant that appeals to a wide-ranging clientele for the food, drink, and casual bistro flavor. Open for dinner Tues–Sun, brunch Sun. Booking a table in advance, particularly in the warmer months when the outdoor patio is much in demand, is recommended. Prices are moderately expensive. Metro: Dupont Circle, then L2 bus.

The Castle *see* Smithsonian Institution Building (The Castle).

Cathedral Heights

This relatively small, quiet residential area takes its name from its major landmark institution, the Washington National Cathedral. Cathedral Heights is up Wisconsin Ave. north of Georgetown and is roughly bounded by Wisconsin Ave. on the east, Fulton St. on the south, and Glover Archbold Park on the west. The neighborhood has many Tudor and Colonial private homes, primarily on the side streets off Wisconsin Ave., while apartment buildings tend to cluster on Wisconsin Ave. and the side streets off it to the west.

Cathedral of St. Peter and St. Paul *see* Washington National Cathedral.

Catholic University of America 620 Michigan Ave. NE btw John McCormick and Harewood Rds. (202) 319-5000 www.cua.edu

Begun more than a century ago, this Gothic-style national university of the Catholic church located on 144 acres has more than 6,000 graduate and undergraduate students. Only a portion pursue the religious studies curriculum; the rest study philosophy, law, arts and sciences, engineering, social services, nursing, music, librarianship, or architecture and planning. Free guided campus tours may be arranged by appointment in advance by calling (202) 319-5305. Metro: Brookland-CUA.

Catholic University of America Mullen Memorial Library 620 Michigan Ave. NE on the university campus (202) 319-5070 http://libraries.cua.edu/welcome.html

Unlike many private academic institution libraries, this marbled Romanesque library building is open to members of the public with suitable identification. Its holdings of rare books and manuscripts, works on American Catholic issues, philosophy, and labor movement history are very fine. The university's law library, located at 3600 John McCormick Rd. NE at Michigan Ave. (202) 319-5155, is outstanding for legal research resources. Metro: Brookland-CUA.

Catholic University Hartke Theatre *see* Hartke Theatre at Catholic University.

Cedar Hill *see* Frederick Douglass National Historic Site.

Celebrate Fairfax

For three days in June each year Fairfax County, Virginia, sponsors a great many entertainment attractions, musical events, a technology fair, carnival, and other crowd-pleasing activities at the Fairfax County Government Center, 12000 Government Center Pkwy. in Fairfax. For details call (703) 324-3247 or check the Web site at www.celebratefairfax.com.

Celebrity Washington Tours http://dcregistry.com/users/celebrity/index.html

For those interested in seeing and learning about the homes of Washington's famous people, where they hang out, and the locations where movies have been made in the city, this guided tour is ideal. It is led by Jan Pottker, author of *Celebrity Washington*. Details at (301) 762-3049.

Cemeteries *see* Alexandria African American Heritage Park, Alexandria National Cemetery, Arlington National Cemetery, Battleground National Cemetery, Confederate Cemetery, Congressional Cemetery, Fairfax City Cemetery, Glenwood Cemetery, Mount Zion Cemetery, National Memorial Park, Oak Hill Cemetery, Rock Creek Cemetery, Union Burial Society of Georgetown Cemetery, U.S. Soldiers' and Airmen's Home National Cemetery, Woodlawn Cemetery.

Center for the Study of Services *see* Washington Consumers' Checkbook.

Central African Republic Embassy 1618 22nd St. NW (202) 483-7800 www .embassy.org/embassies/cf.html

Metro: Dupont Circle.

Chad Embassy 2002 R St. NW (202) 462-4009 www.chadembassy.org

Embassy of the Republic of Chad. Metro: Dupont Circle.

Chadwick's 3205 K St. NW at Wisconsin Ave. under the Whitehurst Freeway (202) 333-2565

This Georgetown restaurant/saloon is open for lunch and dinner daily and also serves Sunday brunch. The bar is very busy on weekends and the menu features quite tasty hamburgers as well as other hearty fare all at moderate prices. Two other locations: Chadwicks-Old Town at 203 S Strand St. in Alexandria (703) 836-4442, and Chadwicks-Friendship Heights at 5247 Wisconsin Ave. NW (202) 362-8040.

Chain Bridge Chain Bridge Rd. crossing the Potomac into Virginia www.weta.org/ potomac/regions/region7/detail6.html

Built in 1939 for $339,000—the 1870 piers were recycled—this is the eighth bridge built at this site. The first was built in 1797 with a toll of 3 cents for a pedestrian and 50 cents for a four-wheeled vehicle; George Washington records shelling out to cross. The first collapsed in 1804; the second washed away the same year; the third, completed in 1810, was a chain bridge suspended from stone towers. It washed away in 1812; the fourth was damaged by floods in 1815; the fifth, built in 1840, was lost to flooding; the sixth, built in the 1850s, was not washed away until 1870. A 1936 flood took care of the seventh. Metro: Tenleytown-AU, then take M4 (Sibley Hospital) Bus to MacArthur Blvd. and Manning Pl.

Chamber Music *see* Corcoran Gallery of Art Musical Evenings Series, Folger Shakespeare Library Folger Consort, Library of Congress Coolidge Auditorium, National Academy of Sciences Music Programs, National Chamber Orchestra, Phillips Collection Sunday Chamber Music Concerts. *See also* Choral Music, Classical Music.

Champion Billiards 2620 S Shirlington Rd., Arlington, VA (703) 521-3800 www .championbilliards.com

To reach this place out in the wilds of Shirlington, take I-395 south to Exit 7 Glebe/Shirlington and then continue on Shirlington for a short way. Open daily 11 a.m.–1 a.m. or 2 a.m. This is the spot for serious pool players with plenty of fine tables, but it's also a casual relaxed setting serving inexpensive beer and light food fare.

Champions 1206 Wisconsin Ave. NW (202) 965-4005

This is a big lively and hugely popular sports bar, which attracts lots of Georgetown and George Washington University students at its alleyway location close to the main intersection at Wisconsin Ave. and M St. in Georgetown. It serves saloon food and beverages, mostly beer, and the walls are filled with sports memorabilia and autographed photos. Open nightly until 2 a.m. or 3 a.m., no cover charge, with the biggest crowds on weekends. Metro: Foggy Bottom-GWU, then 30, 32, 34, 35, or 36 Bus.

Channel Inn 650 Water St., SW (202) 554-2400 or (800) 368-5668 www.channel inn.com

This moderate-priced hotel with free parking on the southwest waterfront offers views of the marina nearby and the Potomac River. There's a pool, the Pier 7 Restaurant, and it's close to Arena Stage Theater and within walking distance of the Mall. Metro: Waterfront-SEU.

Channel Promenade *see* Washington Channel Promenade

Chapters Literary Bookstore 1512 K St. NW btw 15th and 16th Sts. (202) 347-5495 www.chaptersliterary.com

This independent bookshop is committed to the serious reader, with its emphasis on literary criticism, poetry, biography, and the broadest range of publications of quality as well as personal service to its clients. It is a well-attended venue for readings, lectures, and poetry with book-signing events by acclaimed contemporary authors. Open Mon–Fri 10 a.m.–6:30 p.m. (later on evenings when events are scheduled), Sat 11 a.m.–5 p.m. Metro: McPherson Square.

Charles E. Smith Center George Washington University, 600 22nd St. NW (202) 994-6650 http://gwsports.ocsn.com/

Built in 1978, and renovated in 1996, this handsome 3-story building covers an entire city block. The complex houses the university's Department of Athletics and Recreation, extensive recreational facilities, an eight-lane competitive pool, and the center's main area, the home of the Colonials: GW men's and women's basketball, volleyball, and gymnastics teams. Metro: Foggy Bottom-GWU.

Charles Sumner School Museum and Archives 1201 17th St. NW at M St. (202) 442-6060 www.k12.us

This historic red brick structure with its handsome central clock tower was designed by Adolph Cluss in 1872 and was the city's first school for black children. It is named for the senator who was physically beaten in the Senate by a Southern congressman after his speech against slavery. Beautifully restored in 1986, the building is now home to the D.C. Public School Archives as well as exhibitions on local history, Martin Luther King Jr., Frederick Douglass, and Charles Sumner. The building is used principally as a conference center, but the exhibits are available for viewing Tues–Sat 10 a.m.–5 p.m. Metro: Farragut North or Farragut West.

The Chastleton 1701 16th St. NW

Built in 1920 with Philip Jullien as its architect, this Gothic Revival apartment building with its ornate façade ranks among the most striking structures in the city. It is not open to the public. Metro: U St.-Cardozo.

La Chaumière 2813 M St. NW near 28th St. (202) 338-1784 www.lachaumiere.com

This old-fashioned restaurant has the flavor and charm of a French country inn serving delicious meals in which fresh seafood, venison, and couscous are some of the standouts. Its daily special attracts a loyal following on the nights when customers' favorites are on the menu. Prices are moderately expensive. Open for lunch Mon–Fri, and dinner Mon–Sat. Closed Sun. Metro: Foggy Bottom-GWU.

Cherry Blossom Festival

Beginning usually in late March or early April, this two-week-long celebration of arts and culture opens with a Japanese lantern lighting ceremony and culminates in a parade extravaganza honoring the blooming of the city's more than 6,000 Japanese cherry trees planted around the Tidal Basin. Events take place at various parks and locations near the Mall. Details at (202) 547-1500 or www.nationalcherry blossomfestival.org.

Cherry Hill Farmhouse 312 Park Ave., Falls Church, VA (703) 248-5171 www.ci
.falls-church.va.us/history/gfc8.htm
The house was constructed around 1845 and the timber-frame barn was built
in the 1850s. The farm was worked from around 1856 to 1868. The outbuildings
were renovated in 1975 and the house was restored in 1976. The house is furnished
in the fashion of the mid-nineteenth century and the site is open to the public Mon–
Thurs 10 a.m.–3 p.m., Sat 10 a.m.–1 p.m. Metro: Rosslyn, exit the station and take
Metrobus 3B toward Tysons Corner to the stop at W Broad St. and N Little Falls
St. Walk 1 block northeast on Little Falls St., turn left on Park Ave., and walk 1 block
northwest.

Chesapeake and Ohio Canal *See* C&O Canal.

Chesapeake and Ohio Canal National Historical Park
This park is operated by the National Park Service and extends from Georgetown in Washington, D.C., running 185 miles along the shore of the Potomac River
to Cumberland in Western Maryland. The canal has 70 lift locks, 11 aqueducts, and
a number of historic lock houses are still standing. The park operates a visitors
center at 1057 Thomas Jefferson St., NW in Georgetown (202) 653-5190, www.nps
.gov/choh. *See also* C&O Canal, C&O Canal Barge Rides.

Chevy Chase Area
This neighborhood is at the border between the District and Maryland. Much
of it is vintage suburbia with expensive large Victorian and Colonial private homes
with a sprinkling of apartment complexes and groups of townhouses. Old Chevy
Chase is home to lovely trees, stately houses, and exclusive clubs like the Chevy
Chase Club. Historic Chevy Chase, D.C., has been working for a dozen years to
study and document the community and its features and to encourage the neighborhood's preservation. It sponsors a number of lectures, walking tours of the
community, and house and garden tours during the year. Details at www.hccdc
.org. *See also* Bethesda Area.

Chevy Chase Pavilion 5335 Wisconsin Ave. NW at Western Ave., Chevy Chase
(202) 686-5335 www.ccpavilion.com/
Located at the very north end of the city at the Maryland line this low-key, classy
mall has more than fifty boutiques; salons; houseware, gourmet, and other specialty
stores; and restaurants on three levels around an atrium. Metro: Friendship
Heights.

Chi-Cha Lounge 1624 U St. at 17th St. (202) 234-8400 www.chi-cha.com
The setting here is comfortable lounge furniture, Latin jazz sounds in the background, no ties or suits, smoking of whatever is legal, *tapas* from the Andes, and a
lively chic ambiance nightly. No cover charge. Metro: U St.-Cardozo.

Children in Washington D.C. *see* Baby-sitting, Museums of Particular Interest to
Children, Parks and Playgrounds in Washington D.C., Places That Appeal to Children and Teens

Children's Concierge www.shopdcmetro.com/washington_dc/toy_and_games/
This is a custom-designed program for families with kids that lays out plans,

itineraries, or other helpful packages specifically oriented to the particular needs of the particular child or children. It does not conduct tours or baby-sit, but works to shape a useful and meaningful plan that the family then executes. Cost varies based upon the requirements of each client. The group operates in six different cities including Washington, D.C. For information about the service and charges call (301) 948-3312, or check the Web site: www.childrensconcierge.com.

Children's Festival at Wolf Trap Theater

This festival in Vienna, Virginia, consists of performances by entertainers for kids, including clowns and puppet shows for two days in mid-September each year. The entrance payment covers the costs of the day's amusements. Details at (703) 642-0862 or www.artsfairfax.com.

Children's Theater at Thomas Jefferson Community Theater, 125 S Old Glebe Rd., Arlington, VA (703) 548-1154 www.potomacstages.com/ChildrensArl.htm

This group offers plays by and for children and young adults and also lets kids work on theatrical productions. Shows feature young actors who are used as backstage crews. Performances are inexpensive for adults as well as for children. Call for details on programs, tickets, and participation.

Chile Embassy 1736 Massachusetts Ave. NW (202) 785-1746 www.chile-usa.org

Chili Championship Cook-Off www.kidneywdc.org

At this annual event held on a Saturday in May, more than 100 D.C. cooks compete for a chance to participate in the International Chili Society's national contest. It takes place from late morning until evening on Pennsylvania Ave. NW between 10th and 14th Sts., with live entertainment from several bands and food and beverages for purchase. The admission charge benefits the National Kidney Foundation. Information at (202) 244-7900.

Chili Restaurants *see* Austin Grill, Ben's Chili Bowl, Hard Times Café.

China Embassy 2300 Connecticut Ave. NW (202) 328-2500 www.china-embassy.org

Embassy of the People's Republic of China.

Chinatown

Running along G and H Sts. between 6th and 8th Sts. NW, this compact community lacks the scope and variety of San Francisco or New York, but it has a number of fine established restaurants featuring Cantonese, Hunan, Szechuan, and even Mongolian food, as well as many inexpensive choices. The Friendship Archway at 7th and H Sts. marks the entry to Chinatown. The most interesting shops are the traditional pharmacies, which sell unusual folk medicines and herbs thought to foster long life, good health, and potency. Metro: Gallery Pl.-Chinatown.

Chinatown Friendship Archway

Designed by Alfred Liu for the governments of Beijing and Washington, D.C., this giant gilded gold and red arch straddles the entrance to Chinatown at 7th and H Sts. The wooden structure features seven roofs. Metro: Gallery Pl.-Chinatown.

Chinese New Year Celebration

Beginning on the first day of the Chinese New Year and the days following, usually in February each year, residents of Chinatown put on a colorful display of fireworks, dragon dancers, and a celebratory parade, while the neighborhood restaurants offer special menus to usher in the new year. Details at (202) 789-7000 or (202) 638-1041.

Chinese Restaurants *see* City Lights of China, Full Kee, Go Lo's, Good Fortune, Hope Key, Hunan Chinatown, Li Ho, Mr. K's, Mr. Yung's, Peking Gourmet Inn, Tony Cheng's, Vegetable Garden. *See also* www.dcpages.com, www.restaurant.com, www.washingtonpost.com, www.opentable.com.

Ching Ching Cha 1063 Wisconsin Ave. NW btw M and K Sts. (202) 333-8288

This traditional teahouse serves and sells every imaginable tea from China and Taiwan. It is a beautiful and tranquil setting with chair or pillow seating. Light "Tea Meals" are served at moderate prices, and the ambiance is blissfully serene, unlike anywhere else in Georgetown. Open from 11:30 a.m. daily except Mon. Metro: Foggy Bottom-GWU, then 30, 32, 34, 35, or 36 Bus.

Choral Arts Society of Washington 4321 Wisconsin Ave. NW (202) 244-3669 www .choralarts.org

This is a celebrated volunteer choral group begun in 1965, which performs regularly at the Kennedy Center Concert Hall and offers concerts at other locations and at special celebratory events. Call for details or check the Web site.

Choral Music *see* Basilica of the National Shrine of the Immaculate Conception, Cantate Chamber Singers, Cathedral Choral Society, Choral Arts Society of Washington, Gay Men's Chorus of Washington D.C., Master Chorale of Washington, Vocal Arts Society, The Washington Kantorei, The Washington Sängerbund.

Chreky *see* André Chreky.

Christ Church (Alexandria) 118 N Washington St. at Cameron St., Arlington, VA (703) 549-1450 www.historicchristchurch.org/

Built by John Carlyle, the founder of Arlington in 1773, this Episcopal English country-style structure has been in service ever since. Its panels are inscribed by James Wren with the Lord's Prayer and the Ten Commandments. Plaques mark the pews where George Washington and Robert E. Lee worshipped regularly. Open Mon–Sat 9 a.m.–4 p.m., Sun 2 p.m.–4 p.m. Docents offer 20-minute guided tours. Metro: Braddock Road, exit the station and take the DAT3 DASH Bus toward Old Town to the stop at King St. and Washington St. Walk 1 block north on Washington St.

Christ Church (Capitol Hill) 620 G St. SE (202) 547-9300

Often attributed to the important Washington architect Benjamin Latrobe, the actual architect was an unheralded assistant to him, Robert Alexander. The cornerstone was laid in 1798 and the church began to serve parishioners in 1806. Major renovations were made to this Episcopal church during the nineteenth century, and it is said to have been visited by several American presidents. There are two Louis Comfort Tiffany windows in the building. Open to visitors Mon–Thurs 9 a.m.–11:30 a.m. Metro: Eastern Market.

Christ Church (Georgetown) 31st and O Sts. NW (202) 333-6677 http://christ churchgeorgetown.org

The present Gothic-design structure of this Episcopal church organized in 1817 was built by the architects Cassell and Laws in 1885. It is open only for services. Metro: Foggy Bottom-GWU.

Christ, the Light of the World Statue

Built by sculptor Eugene Kormendi in 1949, this 22-foot bronze statue of the founder of the Christian faith was moved from its former location on Massachusetts Ave. in northwest Washington to its present site on the grounds of the U.S. Conference of Catholic Bishops down from the Basilica of the Shrine of the Immaculate Conception on 4th St. NE. Metro: Brookland-CUA.

Christmas Tree Lighting

On the Ellipse behind the White House in mid-December the president begins the holiday season by turning on the lights of the national Christmas tree to begin the Pageant of Peace. This is the site of nightly choral performances, a nativity scene, and display of lighted trees representing the states and territories of the United States. Details about tickets for the event (call six or eight weeks ahead) are available at (202) 619-7222.

Christopher Columbus Memorial Fountain *see* Columbus Memorial Fountain.

Christopher Columbus Monument *see* Columbus Monument.

Church of Jesus Christ of Latter-day Saints *see* Temple of the Church of Jesus Christ of Latter-day Saints.

Church of the Ascension and St. Agnes 1217 Massachusetts Ave. btw 12th and 13th Sts. (202) 347-7816 www.ascensionandsaintagnes.org

Built in 1874 by architects Dixon and Carson, this Episcopal worship center was constructed in High Victorian Gothic design and is well preserved. It contains a mural over the altar by Jan de Rosen, whose art can also be found at the Washington National Cathedral. It also has cast-iron columns, walnut pews, and the nave windows feature abstract designs. Open for services only. Metro: McPherson Square.

Church of the Epiphany 1317 G St. NW at 13th St. (202) 347-2635 www.epiph anydc.org

This Gothic Revival church was constructed in 1843 by architect John Harkness, with later additions in 1890 and 1922. The building is open only for services, but the garden is open to the public Mon–Fri during the daylight hours. The church sponsors a program of well-attended musical events. Metro: Metro Center.

Church of the Holy City 1611 16th St. NW at the southeast corner of 16th and Corcoran (btw Q and R Sts.) (202) 462-6734

This National Swedenborgian Church was constructed in 1896 by architect H. Langford Warren. It was built of limestone in English Country Gothic and French Gothic style with striking gargoyles, a lovely tower, and stained glass windows, including one by Louis Comfort Tiffany. It is open to visitors during daytime hours and in the evenings when public functions are held. Metro: Dupont Circle.

Church Street Theater 1742 Church St. NW btw 17th and 18th Sts. (202) 265-3748

This is one of the city's smaller performance venues, which makes its stage available to local companies. Tickets to its productions usually are priced much below the levels of the major D.C. performance houses. Metro: Dupont Circle.

Churches *see* All Souls Unitarian Church, Asbury United Methodist Church, Basilica of the National Shrine of the Immaculate Conception, Calvary Baptist Church, Christ Church (Alexandria), Christ Church (Capitol Hill), Christ Church (Georgetown), Church of the Ascension and St. Agnes, Church of the Epiphany, Church of the Holy City, Convent of Mercy, Falls Church Episcopal Church, First Baptist Church of the City of Washington, First Church of Christ Scientist, Foundry United Methodist Church, Georgetown Presbyterian Church, Grace Episcopal Church, Grace Reformed Church, Greater New Hope Baptist Church, Holy Rosary Church, Holy Trinity Catholic Church of Georgetown, Immaculate Conception Catholic Church, Luther Place Memorial Church, Metropolitan African Methodist Episcopal Church, Metropolitan Baptist Church, Mount Olivet Lutheran Church, Mount Vernon Place United Methodist Church, Mount Zion United Methodist Church, National Baptist Memorial Church, National City Christian Church, National Presbyterian Church and Center, New York Avenue Presbyterian Church, Old Presbyterian Meeting House, St. Aloysius Catholic Church, St. Augustine Catholic Church, St. Augustine's Episcopal Church, St. Dominic Church, St. John's Episcopal Church, St. Luke's Episcopal Church, St. Mark's Episcopal Church, St. Mary Mother of God Catholic Church, St. Mary's Catholic Church, St. Mary's Episcopal Church, St. Matthew's Cathedral, St. Patrick's Catholic Church, St. Paul's Episcopal Church, St. Sophia Greek Orthodox Cathedral, St. Teresa's Catholic Church, St. Thomas Episcopal Church, Shiloh Baptist Church, Shrine of the Sacred Heart, Takoma Park Presbyterian Church, Takoma Park Seventh-Day Adventist Church, Temple of the Church of Jesus Christ of Latter-day Saints, Turner Memorial A. M. E. Church, Unification Church, United Church, Universalist National Memorial Church, Vermont Avenue Baptist Church, Washington National Cathedral. *See also* Mosques, Synagogues.

Churchill Hotel 1914 Connecticut Ave. NW btw California Ave. and Leroy Pl. (202) 797-2000 or (800) 424-2464 www.thechurchillhotel.com

The former Sofitel on Connecticut Ave. opposite the Washington Hilton is now the Churchill Hotel, but it remains a first-class luxury hotel with large, comfortable rooms, excellent service, a health club, and a high elevation in a convenient part of the city. Upper-floor rooms feature excellent views of Washington. Metro: Dupont Circle, then 42 Bus.

Churchill Statue *see* Sir Winston Churchill Statue.

Churreria Madrid 2505 Champlain St. NW at Columbia Rd. (202) 483-4441

This Adams Morgan restaurant features inexpensive Latino dishes, but the favorite here is the *churro*, a concoction of fried dough sprinkled with sugar, which is consumed in large numbers by patrons. Open 11 a.m.–11 p.m. Tues–Sat. Metro: Woodley Park-Zoo, then 90, 91, 92, 93, or 96 Bus; or Dupont Circle, then L2 Bus.

Cinema *see* Foreign and Independent Films.

Cinema Arts Film Club 9650 Main St., Fairfax, VA (703) 978-6853 www.cinema artstheatre.com

Meets on Sunday mornings at 10 a.m. at the Cinema Arts Theatre for the purpose of exhibiting and critiquing independent or foreign films not yet released. Local film critics serve as panelists. To join buy the four-film series. See location directions under Cinema Arts Theatre.

Cinema Arts Theatre 9650 Main St., Fairfax, VA (703) 978-6853 www.cinemaarts theatre.com

Located in the Fair City Mall in Fairfax, Cinema Arts Theatre schedules a wide range of specialized films, including independent, foreign language, documentary, and "art" films. Open daily. Very comfortable seating, extensive snack menu. Provides weekly e-mailed newsletter to more than 5,000 film buffs. From I-495 (the Beltway) take the Little River Turnpike/Main St. Exit and go approximately 3 miles, then turn into the Fair City Mall shortly after the Picket Rd. intersection.

Cinema Groups *see* Film Groups.

Cineplex Odeon Avalon *see* Avalon Movie Theater.

Cineplex Odeon Cinema 5100 Wisconsin Ave. NW (202) 966-7248 or (800) 555-TELL

This is a modern six-screen complex in far upper-northwest D.C. Metro: Friendship Heights.

Cineplex Odeon Dupont Circle 1350 19th St. NW on M St. (202) 872-9555 or (800) 555-TELL

Multi-screen house. Metro: Dupont Circle.

Cineplex Odeon Inner Circle 2301 M St. NW at 23rd St. (800) 555-TELL

Located in Foggy Bottom with three screens. Metro: Foggy Bottom-GWU.

Cineplex Odeon Outer Circle 4849 Wisconsin Ave. NW at Ellicott St. (202) 244-3116 or (800) 555-TELL

This two-screen movie house in upper northwest usually shows non-Hollywood films. Metro: Tenleytown-AU.

Cineplex Odeon Shirlington 7 2772 S Randolph St., Arlington, VA (703) 671-0910

This theater screens many of the top-ranked art and independent films—unique in the area, but for its Virginia rival, Cinema Arts. The neighboring Village of Shirlington's strip of restaurants and bars makes this a popular dinner and show site. By car take I-395 to the Shirlington exit, park in main shopping area.

Cineplex Odeon Uptown Theater 3426 Connecticut Ave. btw Newark and Ordway Sts. (202) 966-5400 or (800) 555-TELL

This is the last of Washington's large one-screen Art Deco movie palaces, built in 1936 by John Jacob Zink and renovated in 1996. It shows current Hollywood films with seating in its comfortable lower level and spacious balcony. Metro: Cleveland Park.

Cineplex Odeon Wisconsin Avenue 4000 Wisconsin Ave. NW (202) 244-0880 or (800) 555-TELL

This is a six-screen house showing current Hollywood productions in a palatial interior. Metro: Tenleytown-AU, then walk 6 blocks south.

Cities 2424 18th St. NW btw Belmont and Columbia Rds. (202) 328-2100

This is a sophisticated and fairly expensive Adams Morgan restaurant serving continental fare that's as popular for the atmosphere and ambiance as for its excellent *tapas* and seafood and meat dishes. Open for dinner nightly. Reservations recommended. Metro: Woodley Park-Zoo.

Citronelle in the Latham Hotel, 3000 M St. NW at 30th St. (202) 625-2150 www .citronelledc.com

The hallmark of the celebrity chef's stylish touch in this very expensive restaurant, where customers flock perhaps as much to be seen as for the food, is the glass-front kitchen. Serious and sometimes whimsical concoctions of appetizers and main courses are the fare in the attractively designed area providing an exotic and comprehensive menu of American dishes. Open daily for breakfast and dinner, lunch Mon–Fri. Reservations recommended. Metro: Foggy Bottom-GWU.

City Bikes 2501 Champlain St. NW at Euclid St. (202) 265-1564 www.city bikes.com

This store in Adams Morgan not far from the Rock Creek bicycle path rents, sells, and services bikes and roller blades for children and adults. Open Mon–Wed and Fri–Sat 10 a.m.–7 p.m., Thurs 10 a.m.–9 p.m., Sun noon–5 p.m. Metro: Woodley Park-Zoo, then 90, 91, 92, 93, or 96 Bus; or Dupont Circle, then L2 Bus.

City Lights of China 1731 Connecticut Ave. NW btw R and S Sts. (202) 265-6688 www.citylightsofchina.com

Located in the basement of a townhouse in the Dupont Circle neighborhood, this moderately expensive place offers a wide range of fresh, filling, and typically succulent Chinese dishes, including many vegetarian offerings. Open for lunch and dinner daily. Metro: Dupont Circle.

City Museum of Washington, D.C.

This new museum opened in March 2003 in the restored building of the former Carnegie Public Library at Mount Vernon Square between 7th and 9th Sts. NW, just south of the new convention center. It is operated by the Historical Society of Washington, with permanent and changing exhibitions celebrating the city's neighborhoods, its history, and its people. A research library and theater, as well as a café, are among the institution's components. Details at www.hswdc.org or www .citymuseumdc.org or by calling (202) 785-2068. Metro: Mount Vernon Square-7th St. *See also* Old Central Public Library Building.

City of Rockville Farmers Market Rockville Town Center, Rockville, MD (301) 309-3335 www.ci.rockville.md.us/recreation/farmmark.htm

Open mid-May to October on Wednesdays 11 a.m.–2 p.m. and Sat 9 a.m.–1 p.m., producers offer their farm products here.

City Paper 2390 Champlain St. NW (202) 332-2100 www.washingtoncity
paper.com

Washington's alternative weekly tabloid newspaper is distributed free every
Thursday at Metro stations, community centers, street corner vending machines,
and many other locations around the city and nearby suburbs. It is interestingly
written and a good source of local news and all types of cultural events, particularly
concerts, films, museum exhibitions, and night life. It also carries critical reviews
and muckraking exposés of current newsworthy issues and innumerable personal
ads of every type imaginable.

City Paper (Web site) 2930 Champlain St. NW (202) 332-2100 www.washington
citypaper.com

This Web site posts not only the paper's latest cover stories, but its well-worth-
scanning announcements of music and arts and events. Movie and theater listings
include thoughtful reviews. The extensive listing of forthcoming poets' and writers'
talks, exhibits, and other events is well worth reviewing. Music events are broken
down into Blues, Cabaret, Classical, Country, Festivals, Folk, Go-Go, Hip-Hop,
Jazz, Opera, Rock, Techno, Vocal, and World. All the classified ads, with the exception of Adult Services, are also online.

City Place Mall 8661 Colesville Rd. at Fenton St., Silver Spring, MD (301) 589-
1091

This site is home to some sixty discount shops including such titans as Nordstrom Rack, Marshalls, and Burlington Coat Factory, all selling their wares at bargain prices. Open daily. Metro: Silver Spring.

City Tavern 3206 M St. NW near Wisconsin Ave. www.citytavernclub.org

This building is now a private club and not open to the public, but it was constructed in 1796 and is among the oldest structures in Georgetown. It was renovated in 1962 by architects Macomber and Peter. Metro: Foggy Bottom-GWU, then
30, 32, 34, 35, or 36 Bus.

City Tours *see* Boat Tours, Bus Tours, Special Interest Tours, Walking Tours.

Civil War Fort 330 Center St., Vienna, VA www.visitfairfax.org/civil_war_attract
.htm#civil

Located next to the American Legion Post this unusual star-shaped earth forti-
fication with a perimeter of 130 yards was used by both Confederate and Union
soldiers during the Civil War. Metro: East Falls Church, exit the station and take
Metrobus 2C toward Tysons Corner to the stop at Cottage St. and Elm St. Walk
1 block northeast on Elm St. SW, turn left on Center St. S, and walk a short distance
northwest.

Clara Barton National Historic Site 5801 Oxford Rd. beside Glen Echo Park parking lot off MacArthur Blvd., Glen Echo, MD (301) 492-6245 www.nps.gov/clba

This big yellow house on a hill is now a museum run by the National Park
Service. It began as a warehouse for Red Cross supplies and was later transformed
into the house of the woman who came to fame as the celebrated Civil War nurse
who founded the American Red Cross. The 1891 Victorian 36-room house has

been preserved as authentically as possible and contains many of the original furnishings as well as Clara Barton's personal artifacts. Open daily 10 a.m.–4 p.m. Admission free. Guided tours are offered every hour on the hour.

Clarence Moore House 1746 Massachusetts Ave. NW

This palatial structure was the home of an American mining tycoon who perished in the Titanic sinking of 1912. This Beaux Arts mansion was built in 1909 by a prominent architect of the period, Jules Henri de Sibour. Closed to the public. Metro: Dupont Circle.

Clarendon

This northern Virginia suburb is just up Wilson Blvd. from Arlington Courthouse. It is mostly a quiet residential neighborhood of older low-rise private homes with a plethora of ethnic restaurants. The community's central point is the square at the Clarendon Metro stop. A World War I monument in the middle of the square is overshadowed by the modern high-rise structures dominating its setting on Clarendon Blvd. The community's cultural transformation is reflected in the number of Asian restaurants, particularly the popular Vietnamese dining spots.

Clarice Smith Center for the Performing Arts *see* University of Maryland Clarice Smith Center for the Performing Arts.

Classical Music *see* Choral Arts Society, Columbia Flute Choir, Corcoran Gallery of Art Musical Evening Series, Dumbarton Concert Series, Folger Shakespeare Library Folger Consort, Kennedy Center for the Performing Arts Terrace Theater, Library of Congress Coolidge Auditorium, National Academy of Sciences Music Programs, National Musical Arts Chamber Society, National Academy of Sciences U.S. Marines Chamber Orchestra, National Chamber Orchestra, National Symphony Orchestra, Phillips Collection Sunday Chamber Music Concerts, United States Marine Band, Washington Chamber Symphony, The Washington Kantorei, Washington National Cathedral Choral Society, Washington Performing Arts Society, The Washington Sängerbund, Woodbridge Flute Choir. *See also* Chamber Music, Choral Music.

Claude Moore Colonial Farm at Turkey Run 6310 Georgetown Pike btw Dolley Madison Blvd. and Balls Hill Rd., McLean, VA (703) 442-7557 www.1771.org

Located about 2½ miles traveling east on SR 193 after taking Exit 13 off I-495 (the Beltway), this is the only privately run national park in the United States. Here one can observe a pre-Revolutionary War, poor farm family, including period-costumed "family" members, using the tools and performing the chores of eighteenth-century farm life. A dozen or so of the 100 acres here are cultivated with crops and an orchard. The third weekends in May, July, and October feature colonial farm fairs with special reenactments of a number of unique activities. Open Wed–Sat 10 a.m.–4:30 p.m. April to mid-December. Minimal admission charge. Metro: Rosslyn, exit the station and take the FX404 FX Bus toward George Mason University to the stop at Dolley Madison Blvd. and Ballantrae Lane. Walk 3 blocks north on Ballantrae Lane, turn right on Chain Bridge Rd., walk 2 blocks northeast, turn left on Georgetown Pike, and walk 2 blocks west.

Cleveland Park

This tree-lined community of brick sidewalks and large-frame housing is located between Woodley Park and the Van Ness/University of the District of Columbia area in northwest D.C. It is roughly bounded by Tilden St. on the north, Rock Creek Park on the east, Cathedral Ave. on the south, and Wisconsin Ave. on the west. The area features old Victorian houses of late nineteenth and early twentieth-century vintage, with wide porches and shady lawns. There are stores and restaurants along Connecticut Ave., but the side streets exude a suburban character and the community is home to many of the city's most affluent families. Metro: Cleveland Park and Van Ness-UDC.

Cleveland Park Bookshop 3416 Wisconsin Ave. NW btw Newark St. and Idaho Ave. (202) 363-1112 www.clevelandpark.com/clevelandparkbookshop

This is a quiet and helpful neighborhood bookshop, one of an unfortunately diminishing number in this time of mammoth chains. The bookshop offers a wide range of all categories and the staff will get for you whatever's not on the shelves. Special events include author book signings. Open Mon–Sat 10 a.m.–8 p.m., Sun 1 p.m.–6 p.m. Metro: Tenleytown-AU or Cleveland Park.

Cleveland Park Historical District

The Cleveland Park neighborhood's claim to a significant past stems from the time near the end of the nineteenth century when trolley lines on Connecticut and Wisconsin Aves. were extended north. An extraordinary growth then followed in the number of attractive and unique gracious private homes designed in many different architectural styles. Later on in the early part of the twentieth century came more residential construction accompanied by commercial buildings along Connecticut and Wisconsin Aves. The community represents a rich range of striking and attractive types of architecture reflecting the evolution of the neighborhood over more than a century.

Climbing *see* Sportrock I, II, and III.

Club Chaos 1633 Q St. NW at 17th St. (202) 232-4141 www.chaosdc.com

This night spot features different events and entertainment for a gay clientele on different nights ranging from bingo to music to drag shows. There's also food, drink, a dance floor, and sometimes a modest cover charge. Open Tues–Sun 4 p.m.–2 a.m. or 3 a.m.

Clubs *see* Arts Club of Washington, Capital Yacht Club, Cosmos Club, Friday Morning Music Club, Georgetown Polo Club, National Press Club, Sierra Club, Sulgrave Club, Washington Club, Women's National Democratic Club.

Clubs for Dancing *see* Dance Clubs.

Clyde's of Georgetown 3326 M St. NW btw Wisconsin Ave. and Potomac Rd. (202) 333-9180

Going since 1963 this popular pub serves moderately priced good food and drink with lots of dark wood and Americana. Fine place for chili, hamburgers, and fresh vegetables from local farms. Open for lunch and dinner Mon–Fri, brunch and dinner Sat and Sun. Metro: Foggy Bottom-GWU, then 30, 32, 34, or 36 Bus. A number of cloned branches have been opened in the suburbs. Meals served and hours vary. They are Chevy Chase, 70 Wisconsin Circle (btw Western and Wisconsin Aves.) (301) 951-9600; Reston, VA, 11905 Market St. in Town Center (703) 787-6601; Tysons Corner, VA, 8332 Leesburg Pike (btw Gallows and Chain Bridge Rds.) (703) 734-1900.

Coeur de Lion in the Henley-Park Hotel, 926 Massachusetts Ave. NW at 10th St. (202) 414-0500 www.henleypark.com

This is an elegant and charming downtown hotel restaurant with well-spaced tables and a romantic ambiance serving continental and American dishes at moderately expensive prices. Open Mon–Fri for breakfast, lunch, and dinner; Sat breakfast and brunch; Sun brunch. There is also a delightful tea service featuring scones and pastries 4 p.m.–6 p.m. Dinner reservations are suggested. Metro: Gallery Pl.-Chinatown or Metro Center.

Coffee and Cakes *see* Churreria Madrid, Firehook Bakery and Coffeehouse, Patisserie Poupon, Senses. *See also* Cafés, Tearooms.

Coffee Houses *see* Cafés.

College Park

Located in the Maryland suburbs this is home to the sprawling campus of the University of Maryland. It covers a wide expanse on the east side of Baltimore Ave. (U.S. Hwy. 1), the community's main thoroughfare. On the other side of Baltimore Ave. the older residential section of College Park has many 2-story Colonial houses and ranch-style homes, many retaining their late nineteenth-century appearance. Part of this older residential side of town is also home to multiple dwellings occupied by the more transient student population of the campus. Baltimore Ave. is replete with the restaurants, bars, and other businesses common to strip malls all over the country. Metro: College Park-U of MD.

College Park Aviation Museum 1985 Corporal Frank Scott Dr., College Park, MD (301) 864-6029 www.avialantic.com/collpark.html

This is a 27,000-square-foot center of interactive exhibitions, displays, artifacts, and memorabilia on aviation history. It is located 2 blocks from the Metro stop at the site of the world's oldest operating airport, which opened in 1909. The museum is open daily 10 a.m.–5 p.m., except holidays. Modest admission charge. Metro: College Park-U of MD.

College Park Farmers Market Linson Pool, 5211 Paint Branch Rd., College Park, MD (301) 262-8662 www.localharvest.org/farms/M2419

Open from early May to mid-November Saturdays 7 a.m.–noon.

Colleges *see* Universities and Colleges.

La Colline 400 N Capitol St. NW at D St. (202) 737-0400 www.restaurant.com/lacolline

Reputed to be one of the city's best French restaurants, this spot with its comfortable seating and quiet atmosphere offers county-style traditional fare that is delicious and fresh and features many seasonal choices. Service is excellent and prices moderately expensive. Open Mon–Fri for breakfast, lunch, and dinner; Sat dinner. Reservations for lunch or dinner are recommended. Metro: Union Station.

Collingwood Library and Museum on Americanism 8301 East Blvd. Dr. on the Potomac, Alexandria, VA (703) 765-1652 www.collingwoodlibrary.com

The building's oldest part has been here since 1783 when it was the home of the overseer for George Washington's River Farm. The library's collection is for reference use dealing exclusively with American history. The museum contains eclectic artifacts drawn from the country's past. Open Mon and Thurs–Sat 10 a.m.–4 p.m., Sun 1 p.m.–4 p.m. Admission free. Because the space is sometimes used for private events on weekends, calling in advance is suggested. The location is off the George Washington Pkwy. some 4³/₄ miles past Old Town and reached by turning left at Collingwood Rd. then proceeding ¹/₄ mile to E Boulevard Dr. to the Collingwood's location on the Potomac. Metro: Huntington, exit the station and take the FX101 FX Bus toward Mount Vernon and Cunningham Dr. to the stop at Fort Hunt Rd. and Collingwood Rd. Walk 5 blocks east on Collingwood Rd., turn right on East Boulevard Dr., walk 2 blocks southeast on E Boulevard Dr.

Colombia Embassy 2118 Leroy Pl. NW (202) 387-8338 www.colombiaemb.org

Embassy of the Republic of Colombia. Metro: Dupont Circle.

Colonnade at the Washington Monarch Hotel, 2401 M St. NW at 24th St. (202) 457-5000 www.monarchdc.com

This expensive restaurant serving American food in a glass-enclosed dining space is open Mon–Sat for breakfast, lunch, and dinner. On Sun only brunch is available and it is this buffet meal that has gained acclaim for its excellent and bountiful array of delectable choices and enticing desserts. Metro: Foggy Bottom-GWU.

Columbia Flute Choir Administration: 115 Gresham Pl., Falls Church, VA (703) 532-6565 http://flute.net/cfc

This musical group has been performing in the Washington area since 1994. The ensemble plays a variety of classical pieces as well as modern works written for flute choirs. The group hosts a Flute Choir Festival each fall and performs at local churches and flute fairs and has appeared at the Kennedy Center and the White House.

Columbia Heights Community Marketplace 14th and Irving Pl. NW www.inner city.org/chcm

Fresh produce is sold here on Saturdays 8 a.m.–1 p.m. from mid-May to the end of October.

Columbia Pike Farmers Market Columbia Pike and S Walter Reed Dr., Arlington, VA (703) 892-2776 www.columbiapikepartnership.com/cprofarmersmarket.html

Producers set up here on Sundays 10 a.m.–2 p.m. from early May to mid-November.

Columbia Station 2325 18th St. NW btw Columbia and Kalorama Rds. (202) 462-6040

This Adams Morgan spot is a longtime favorite featuring good New Orleans-style food and nightly live jazz or blues with interesting art works adorning the walls. It all comes together to create a sophisticated, classy ambiance. Open Mon–Thurs 5 p.m.–1:30 a.m., Fri–Sun 5 p.m.–2:30 a.m. Metro: Dupont Circle, then L2 Bus.

Columbia Union College 7600 Flower Ave., Takoma Park, MD (301) 891-4080 or (800) 835-4212 www.cuc.edu

Located on a 20-acre campus this primarily commuter undergraduate college is affiliated with the Seventh-Day Adventist Church. It has a relatively small enrollment and offers a range of areas of study. Nursing and business are popular choices, along with spiritual studies and community service playing an important extracurricular role in the life of the institution. Metro: Silver Spring, then 12 Bus to Takoma Park.

Columbus Day Ceremonies

Every year on October 14 at the Columbus Memorial Plaza in front of Union Station there is a commemorative tribute celebration honoring Christopher Columbus. Details at (202) 619-7222. Metro: Union Station.

Columbus Memorial Fountain Union Station Plaza, Massachusetts and Delaware Aves., NE

This is a semicircular fountain ornamented with sculpted figures, lions, and flagpoles. At the center is a 45-foot-high shaft from which is projected a ship's prow with a winged figurehead representing discovery. It is the site of the marble statue of Christopher Columbus. Metro: Union Station.

Columbus Monument Union Station Plaza, Massachusetts and Delaware Aves. NE

Located in the plaza in front of Union Station is a 15-foot marble statue of Christopher Columbus designed by Lorado Taft in 1912 with an aged bearded figure representing old Europe on one side and an Indian brave representing the New World on Columbus's other side. Metro: Union Station.

Colvin Run Mill Historic Site 10017 Colvin Run Rd., btw Leesburg Pike and Walker St., Great Falls, VA (703) 759-2771 www.colvinrunmill.org

This restored early nineteenth-century water-powered gristmill still grinds cornmeal and whole wheat into flour. The miller's house and the barn contain historic exhibits. Open daily 11 a.m.–5 p.m. except Tuesday. Admission to the grounds is free, but entry to the house and the barn has a nominal charge, which covers the cost of the guided tour offered every hour. The site is also the location of frequent special events. Call for details or check the Web site. Located on SR 7, 7 miles west of the Washington Beltway (I-495). Metro: West Falls Church-VT/UVA, exit the station and take the FX905 FX Bus toward Reston Town Center to the stop at Reston Town Center at Explorer St. Terminal, then take the FX574 FX Bus toward Tysons Corner to the stop at Leesburg Turnpike and Colvin Run Rd. Walk 1 block northwest on Colvin Run Rd. *See also* www.commuterpage.com/venues/sightseeing_VA.htm.

Comedy Clubs *see* Capitol Steps, Gross National Product, Headliners, Improv. *See also* Night Clubs.

Commerce Department 409 15th St. NW btw 15th and 14th Sts. on the east and west, and btw Constitution Ave. and E St. on the north and south. (202) 482-2000 www.doc.gov

This building, constructed in 1931 as the largest government office building of its time, was designed by architect Louis Ayres. It is also known as the Herbert Hoover Building. It covers 17 acres of floor space and 8 miles of corridors. The building is open daily 9 a.m.–5 p.m. Attractions in this structure include the census clock in the lobby clicking off the country's estimated population every second, the seismograph machine that registers earthquake tremors, and the oldest aquarium in the United States, the National Aquarium (for details see National Aquarium). The building is also home to the White House Visitor Center with the entry at 15th and E Sts. (details under White House Visitor Center). Metro: Federal Triangle.

Commerce Department Library in the Commerce Department Building, 409 15th St. NW btw 15th and 14th Sts. on the east and west and btw Constitution Ave. and E St. on the north and south. (202) 248-5511 www.osec.doc.gov/lib/pquest.htm

This government special library has a strong collection treating foreign trade, corporations, and many other business subjects. It is open to government employees Mon–Fri 9 a.m.–4 p.m., and to the public Mon–Fri 1 p.m.–4 p.m. Metro: Federal Triangle.

Commission for Women Counseling and Career Center 255 Washington St. at Beall St., NationsBank Building, Rockville, MD (301) 279-1800 www.montgomery works.com/E/00024/Detail.cfm?ID = 10

Since 1972 this group has served as an advocate for equal rights for women in Montgomery County by functioning as a women's resource, counseling, and career center offering personal, career, and financial planning; seminars and workshops on personal development; and information on job openings. Appointments are required and workshops have modest charges. Metro: Rockville, then about a ¹/₂-mile walk.

Commodore John Barry Statue in Franklin Park, 14th St. btw I and K Sts. NW

This monument to the naval hero of the American Revolutionary War was sculpted by John J. Boyle in 1914. Metro: McPherson Square.

Commodore John Paul Jones Monument

This bronze and marble memorial to the most famous American naval hero of the Revolutionary War can be found in West Potomac Park at 17th St. and Independence Ave. SW. His celebrated battle cry is inscribed on the pedestal: "Surrender? I have not yet begun to fight." Metro: Smithsonian.

The Common Denominator 680 Rhode Island Ave. NE, Suite N (202) 635-6397 www.thecommondenominator.com

This biweekly, issued on alternative Mondays, bills itself "Washington's Independent Hometown Newspaper." It is sold by subscription, in vending boxes, and at CVS pharmacies. It provides an excellent public affairs calendar, covers the District's commercial and economic issues, churches and nonprofits, and offers innovative neighborhood and historical coverage and a host of columns and ward reports. Its Web site is a major source of D.C. civic and cultural information and includes classified ads. Metro: Rhode Island Ave. *See also* www.thecommondenomi nator.com.

Community Farmers Market Main and West Sts., Fairfax, VA (703) 404-8994

In Fairfax City from early May to late October local and regional growers sell their produce.

Concerts *see* Crampton Auditorium, Daughters of the American Revolution Museum and Constitution Hall, George Mason University, Kennedy Center for the Performing Arts, MCI Center, Lisner Auditorium of George Washington University, Smithsonian Institution, University of Maryland Clarice Smith Center for the Performing Arts, Wolf Trap Farm Park for the Performing Arts. *See also* Classical Music.

Confederate Cemetery Center St., Old Town, Manassas, VA

On an acre of land in the center of Manassas in Prince William County, 250 soldiers of the Confederacy have found their final repose. The burial ground's central feature is a red sandstone monument with a bronze statue rising above it inscribed, "At Rest."

Confederate Cemetery Monument *see* Fairfax City Cemetery. *See also* www.com muterpage.com/venues/sightseeing_VA.htm.

Confederate Memorial

Located in Arlington National Cemetery off McPherson Dr., this monument was constructed by the United Daughters of the Confederacy in 1914 to honor their dead. The graves of soldiers and veterans of the Confederacy who died in the Washington area are arranged around the monument in concentric circles. Metro: Arlington Cemetery.

Confederate Statue S Washington and Prince Sts., Alexandria, VA (703) 838-4554

This bronze monument dedicated in 1889 to the fallen men of the Confederacy, is a single unarmed soldier in an upright position facing south. The names of 100 Alexandria Confederate dead are carved on the base. It is located at a busy intersection about a 20-minute walk from the Metro stop. Metro: King Street, then walk toward the river turning left at S Washington St., and then to Prince St.

Congo Embassy 4891 Colorado Ave. NW (202) 726-5500 www.embassyof congo.org

Embassy of the Democratic Republic of Congo.

Congressional Cemetery 18th and E Sts. SE (202) 543-0539 www.congressional cemetery.org/Interment.html

This, the oldest national cemetery in the nation, was founded in 1807 on a 30-acre slope next to the Anacostia River at the southeast tip of the Capitol Hill neighborhood. There are 60,000 grave sites and among the American notables resting here are John Philip Sousa, Matthew Brady, and J. Edgar Hoover, as well as some eighty congressmen and nineteen senators. Open daily during daylight hours. Metro: Potomac Ave., then 96, B2, or D2 Bus.

Connecticut Avenue Bridge Crossing over Klingle Rd., NW btw Devonshire Pl. and Macomb St.

This single-arched steel bridge, designed by architect Paul Cret, crosses over wooded Klingle Valley. It was completed in 1931 at a cost of $458,951. Metro: Cleveland Park.

Connecticut Avenue Corridor

This long stretch in northwest D.C. from Taft Bridge at the southern end to Chevy Chase Circle on the north is one of the city's most important thoroughfares. The communities along the way are Woodley Park, then Van Ness, and finally Chevy Chase, D.C. The eastern edge is Rock Creek Pkwy. and Beach Dr., and at the western end 34th St. and Reno Rd. The essential characteristic of the corridor is a mix of apartment buildings and condominiums and smaller stores and restaurants lining Connecticut Ave., while the side streets have some high-rise residential structures near Connecticut Ave., but with mostly an eclectic mix of older and elegant private residences and smaller more modest middle-class homes. The entire region remains very attractive for its transportation convenience, handy shops, eateries, and old-fashioned charm.

Constitution Day Commemoration

The anniversary of the signing of the Constitution of the United States is celebrated on a day in mid-September each year. Events held include a naturalization ceremony, speakers, and musical entertainment. Details at (202) 501-5000.

Constitution Gardens Constitution Ave. NW btw 17th and 23rd Sts. (202) 426-6841 www.nps.gov/coga/index2.htm

Located near the Reflecting Pool, between the Washington Monument and the Lincoln Memorial, this 52-acre park contains a 6-acre lake and a garden covering 1 acre. The Vietnam Veterans Memorial is in the park. A wooden bridge leads to an island where Joseph E. Brown created a memorial in a semicircle of low granite stones containing the names of each of the fifty-six signers of the Declaration of Independence. There are also walking paths and bike trails and some 5,000 shade trees. Open daily during daylight hours. Metro: Foggy Bottom-GWU. *See also* www.commuterpage.com/venues/gardens.htm.

Constitution Hall *see* Daughters of the American Revolution Museum and Constitution Hall.

Contemporary Restaurants *see* Bread Line, Cashion's Eat Place, Citronelle, Coeur de Lion, D.C. Coast, Elysium, Felix, Inn at Little Washington, New Heights, Nora, Rupperts, 701 Pennsylvania Ave., U-Topia. *See also* American Restaurants, www .frommers.com, www.washingtonpost.com.

Continental Restaurants *see* Aquarelle, Coeur de Lion, Village Bistro. *See also* www.frommers.com, www.washingtonpost.com.

Convent of Mercy 3515 N St. NW off 35th St.

This, the old Holy Trinity Church, was constructed at the western end of Georgetown before the end of the eighteenth century and is the city's oldest Catholic church. It is open for services only. Metro: Foggy Bottom-GWU, then 30, 32, 34, 35, or 36 Bus.

Convention Center *see* Washington Convention Center.

Conway Gallery *see* Susan Conway Gallery.

Cooke's Row 3007-3029 Q St. NW

Built in 1868 by architects Starkweather and Plowman in Georgetown, this striking row of double houses was constructed in Second Empire and Italianate style. They bear the name of the District's wealthy governor, Henry D. Cooke, of that time.

Coolidge Auditorium of the Library of Congress *see* Library of Congress Coolidge Auditorium.

Coppi's 1414 U St. NW btw 14th and 15th Sts. (202) 319-7773

The walls are covered with bike gear, posters, and photos, and the oven-baked pizzas are delectable, sprinkled with imaginative toppings like fresh herbs and fine mushrooms. They are also fairly expensive. Open daily 4 p.m. or 5 p.m.–11 p.m. or midnight. Metro: U St.-Cardozo.

Corcoran Gallery of Art 17th St. NW btw E St. and New York Ave. (202) 639-1700 www.corcoran.org

This is Washington's oldest and largest private museum, begun in 1869 and based on the collection of one of the cofounders of Riggs Bank. Its greatest strength is its collection of nineteenth-century American art and sculpture. Numerous solo and group exhibitions by local, national, and international artists and photographers are held here as well. Open daily 10 a.m.–5:30 p.m. except Tues, Thurs evenings until 9 p.m. Modest suggested donation. The Corcoran also sponsors a school of art as a training center for area artists and is the city's only professional program in art and design. Metro: Farragut West.

Corcoran Gallery of Art Musical Evenings Series 17th St. NW btw E St. and New York Ave. (202) 639-1700 (Office of Special Events) www.corcoran.org

This very popular concert series featuring a wide range of music ensembles is held on eight Friday evenings from October to May. Tickets are often sold out well in advance of the season's beginning. Metro: Farragut West.

Corcoran School of Art 17th St. NW btw E St. and New York Ave. (202) 639-1814 www.corcoran.org

More than 300 students are regularly enrolled for full-time study at this, the city's only professional college program in art, design, and photography. In addition, the school's continuing education program offers many classes for children and adults each year. Metro: Farragut West.

Corner Bakery Café Union Station, 50 Massachusetts Ave. NE at N Capitol St. (202) 371-8811 www.cornerbakery.com

This is one of a chain of bistro-type bakery and café spots at a number of locations in and around the city. They serve very good European-style hearth-baked breads, pastas, sandwiches, and soups as well as coffee. Open 7 a.m. Mon–Fri,

8 a.m. Sat, and 9 a.m. Sun, remaining open until evening. Metro: Union Station. Other locations in the city: National Press Building, 529 14th St. NW at F St (202) 662-7400; 5300 Wisconsin Ave. NW near Western Ave. (202) 237-2200. For locations in the Maryland and Virginia suburbs, check the telephone books or the Web site.

Cosmos Club 2121 Massachusetts Ave. NW btw Q St. and Florida Ave. (202) 387-7783 www.cosmos-club.org

Occupying a mansion constructed in 1901 by architects Carrère and Hastings for the railroad tycoon Richard Townsend, this club is one of the most influential and prestigious private clubs in Washington. Members form a roster of men and women of what the members term "distinction, character and sociability." Its roster has included presidents and Nobel laureates, and is composed of stellar figures in the arts, politics, science, and academic pursuits. Not open to the public. Metro: Dupont Circle.

Costa Rica Embassy 2114 S St. NW (202) 234-2945 or 46 http://costarica-embassy .org Metro: Dupont Circle.

La Côte d'Or Café 6876 Lee Hwy., Arlington, VA (703) 538-3033 www.lacotedor cafe.com

This moderately expensive Provençal restaurant is located in the suburbs just off Hwy. I-66 in an attractive townhouse with a romantic interior décor featuring comfortable seating and floral arrangements. The food is country French, hearty and zestful, with fine sauces. It is open daily for lunch and dinner, and reservations are suggested.

Cottonwood Café 4844 Cordell Ave. near Woodmont Ave. and Old Georgetown Rd., Bethesda, MD (301) 656-4844 www.cottonwoodcafe.com

This restaurant offers a blend of dishes indigenous to the American Southwest using an open grill to prepare their dishes seasoned liberally with spices and herbs. It's an upscale popular eatery with moderately expensive prices. Open for lunch Mon–Sat, dinner nightly. Metro: Bethesda.

Council House *see* Mary McLeod Bethune House.

Counter Spy Shop 1027 Connecticut Ave. NW btw K and L Sts. (202) 887-1717 www.spyzone.com

James Bond would be in his element at this store, which sells a wide range of gadgetry for clandestine and undercover operations from wiretap detectors to disguised and concealed video cameras. Open Mon–Fri 9 a.m.–6 p.m., Sat 10 a.m.–3 p.m. Metro: Farragut North.

Country Music *see* Folk and Country Music.

Courtyard by Marriott 1900 Connecticut Ave. NW at Leroy Pl. (202) 332-9300 or (800) 842-4211 http://www.marriott.com

Located in a convenient part of town this moderately priced 147-room hotel offers an outdoor pool and a fitness center among its amenities. Lower weekend rates are an added inducement. Metro: Dupont Circle. Other locations in town of this chain are 900 F St. NW (202) 638-4600; 1600 Rhode Island Ave. NW (202) 293-8000.

Cowboy Café North 4792 Lee Hwy. btw N Glebe Rd. and Columbus St., Arlington, VA (703) 243-8010

This is a friendly, comfortable, and casual place to go for decent food, drink, and country and western music, some nights live, with no cover charge and reasonable prices. Open Mon–Fri from 11 a.m., Sat–Sun from 9 a.m. Metro: Ballston-MU, then 22F, 23A, or 23B Bus. A sister spot offers the same fare at Cowboy Café South, 2421 Columbus Pike at Adams Square in Arlington (703) 486-3467.

Cox Row 3327-3339 N St. NW btw 33rd and 34th Sts.

This group of five row houses built in 1817 in Georgetown is named for Col. John Cox, Georgetown's first mayor and the builder-owner of these Federal-style houses. The doorways and dormers are particularly handsome in this fine series of distinctive homes. Not open to the public. Metro: Foggy Bottom-GWU, then 30, 32, 34, 35, or 36 Bus.

Crampton Auditorium 2455 6th St. NW on Howard University campus across from the Business School (202) 806-7198

This Howard University auditorium seats 1,500 and is frequently the venue for jazz, gospel, and other musical and special events. Metro: Shaw-Howard University.

Creative Partners Gallery 4600 E West Hwy. entrance on Waverly Pl., Suite 120, Bethesda, MD (301) 951-9441 www.creativepartnersart.com

This gallery, open Tues–Sat 11 a.m.–5 p.m., showcases new works by members of the artists' collective in painting, sculpture, photography, ceramics, pottery, and jewelry. Metro: Bethesda.

Creole Restaurants *see* Cajun Restaurants.

Crisfield 8012 Georgia Ave. btw E West Hwy and Blair Mill Rd., Silver Spring, MD (301) 589-1306

Looking like a 1930s barbershop this restaurant has been attracting diners for some 50 years with an unchanging menu of fresh and authentic seafood dishes. The decor may be utilitarian but the prices are fairly high, which doesn't seem to deter the long lines of customers. It's open for lunch Tues–Fri, dinner Tues–Sun. Metro: Silver Spring. A second location in Silver Spring at 8606 Colesville Rd. in Lee Plaza (301) 588-1572, is a newer, fancier but less picturesque alternative. Open for lunch Mon–Fri, dinner nightly. Metro: Silver Spring.

Croatia Embassy 2343 Massachusetts Ave. NW (202) 588-5899 www.croatia emb.org

The first Embassy of the Republic of Croatia in the United States opened in 1964 at a former Austrian Embassy site. A bronze statue of St. Jerome, sculpted by Ivan Mestrovic, Croatia's most famous sculptor, stands in front of the embassy. Mestrovic became a U.S. citizen in 1954, the year the piece was cast. Metro: Dupont Circle.

Crush 2323 18th St. NW in Adams Morgan (202) 319-1111

This dance spot is open Fri–Sat 6 p.m.–3 a.m. From 9:30 p.m. on there is DJ music, and 6 p.m.–10 p.m. a very inexpensive bountiful buffet includes two drinks. Metro: Dupont Circle, then L2 Bus; or Woodley Park-Zoo, then 90, 91, 92, 93, or 96 Bus.

Crystal City

This is a big complex of towering office buildings, hotels, apartments, and condominiums very close to Reagan National Airport in Virginia. Lining both sides of Jefferson Davis Hwy. (Rte. 1) are some of the Virginia suburbs' largest high-rises filled with renters and condo owners. There are some single-family homes on the west side of the Jefferson Davis Hwy. Compensation for the neighborhood's density and airplane noise is its close-in location to downtown and the Crystal City Underground Shopping Center located beneath the highway between 15th and 23rd Sts. Metro: Crystal City.

Crystal City Marriott 1999 Jefferson Davis Hwy. at S 20th St., Arlington, VA (703) 413-5500 or (800) 228-9290 www.marriotthotels.com

Close to Reagan National Airport and the Pentagon this 336-room hotel offers a luxurious lobby, a fitness room, airport shuttle service, comfortable but unexceptional accommodations, and moderately expensive rates. It is connected to the Crystal City Underground Shopping Center and the Metro station—a 15-minute ride to downtown D.C. Metro: Crystal City.

Crystal City Underground Shopping Center Jefferson Davis Hwy. btw 15th and 23rd Sts., Arlington, VA www.crystalcity.com/cc_shops.htm

The Underground shops are between 15th and 18th Sts. on Crystal Dr. and the Plaza shops are located at the corner of Crystal Dr. and 23rd St. More than 125 specialty stores, restaurants, and cafes are located in these subterranean temperature-controlled consumer-enticing places. It's all linked to the Metro stop at 18th St. and Jefferson Davis Hwy. Metro: Crystal City.

Crystal Gateway Marriott 1700 Jefferson Davis Hwy. btw S 15th and S 18th Sts., Arlington, VA (703) 920-3230 or (800) 228-9290 www.marriotthotels.com

This is the second and larger of the two Crystal City Marriotts. This one has 697 rooms. It, too, is connected to the Underground shops and the Metro and provides airport shuttle service. It offers indoor and outdoor pools, concierge service, an exercise facility, several restaurants, and somewhat more expensive room rates. Metro: Crystal City.

Cuban Restaurants *see* Latin American Restaurants.

Cultural Alliance of Greater Washington 1436 U St. NW, Suite 103 (202) 638-2406 www.cultural-alliance.org

This nonprofit organization supports the cultural arts community in the area with a variety of services and programs and more than 330 organizational members. Online articles from its trade publication *Arts Washington* highlight important cultural events, exhibits, and programs. Its online Job Bank is a free service for employers and people looking for a job in the arts. A number of publications related to marketing and organizing cultural events are available for purchase, and they provide specialized workshops for writers, artists, and cultural organizations. A calendar of events lists forthcoming CAGW events. Particularly useful are its links to other arts organizations and Washington and local events sites such as Art Calendar Online, Culture Finder, On Stage, Washington City Paper Events Calendar, Arts Edge, and some local embassy cultural sites.

Cyprus Embassy 2211 R St. NW (202) 462-5772 www.cyprusembassy.net
Embassy of the Republic of Cyprus. Metro: Dupont Circle.

Czech Republic Embassy 3900 Spring of Freedom St. NW (202) 274-9100 http://transport911.com/Embassies/cs.htm
Metro: Cleveland Park or Van Ness-UDC.

DAR Museum and Constitution Hall *see* Daughters of the American Revolution Museum and Constitution Hall.

DCAC *see* District of Columbia Arts Center.

D.C. Armory *see* RFK Stadium.

D.C. Armory Antiques Fair 2001 E Capitol St. SE (202) 547-9077

Each spring in May, and each fall in October and December, this widely attended event features artifacts displayed by some 200 dealers from around the United States and foreign countries. Furniture, oriental rugs, porcelain objects, and various other kinds of treasures that make the collector's heart beat faster are on offer. Admission charge. Details at (202) 547-9077.

D.C. Blues Festival

In early September blues concerts are held at various venues around town. For information call (202) 828-3028 or check the Web site, www.dcblues.org.

D.C. Blues Hotline

This is information central for details about forthcoming concerts, jam sessions, and festivals in Washington and the suburbs. This group also publishes a regular newsletter. Information at (202) 828-3028 or the Web site: www.dcblues.org.

D.C. Blues Society (Web site) www.dcblues.org

This Web site maintained by an all-volunteer organization provides timely and comprehensive coverage of what's happening in blues music in the Washington, D.C., area. It includes news and events related to the society, a daily event calendar, links, and e-mail addresses of local bands and musicians, blues Web sites, a bulletin board, membership information, CD releases, radio and TV blues broadcast schedules, photos from recent events and the group's meetings, and news of the annual Blues Festival.

D.C. Chamber of Commerce Visitor Information Center in the Ronald Reagan Building (Wilson Plaza entrance), 1300 Pennsylvania Ave. NW, 1 block from the Mall (202) 328-4748 www.dcvisit.com

This is the place for information on the city—maps, tours, performance tickets, hotels, restaurants, brochures, and a staff prepared to help with specific questions. It is open Mon–Fri 8 a.m.–6 p.m., Sat 9 a.m.–5 p.m. Metro: Federal Triangle.

D.C. Coast 1401 K St. at 14th St. (202) 216-5988 www.dccoast.com

Located in the Tower Building, this 2-floor airy, Art Deco, sophisticated and quite expensive restaurant that is far from any water specializes in excellent seafood from waterways like the Atlantic, Pacific, Gulf of Mexico, and Chesapeake Bay. Open for lunch Mon–Fri, dinner Mon–Sat. Reservations are essential. Metro: Mc-Pherson Square.

DCDanceNet (Web site) www.dcdancenet.com

Founded in 1996, this dance information conglomerate now receives more than 2,500 hits a week, and demonstrates how varied and vital dance opportunities are in the metropolitan Washington area. Coverage includes notices about dances classed as Ballroom, Swing, Hustle, Latin/Salsa, Shag, Argentine Tango, Clogging, Square Dancing, Tap, and Country and Western. Classes, events, and dance news are included. The heavily illustrated site provides advertisements and notices for dances, special party events, workshops, dance camps, cruises, and dance vacations.

D.C. Department of Parks and Recreation http://dpr.dc.gov/index.asp

The city has fifty-seven locations for its 130 tennis courts available on a first-come, first-served basis for 1-hour intervals, unless a permit has been issued for extended use. About twenty-five courts are lighted for night use. Questions regarding regulations, lessons, tournaments, or other matters can be answered by the Sports Office (202) 645-3944.

D.C. Department of Parks and Recreation, Aquatics Division

The city operates six public indoor pools, some twenty large outdoor pools, and another fifteen pools suitable for small children. Information about them from the Aquatics Division of D.C. Parks and Recreation at (202) 282-0728 or http://dpr.dc.gov/services/program_guide.asp.

D.C. Duck Tours *see* Duck Tours.

D.C. Eagle 639 New York Ave. btw 6th and 7th Sts. (202) 347-6025 www.dceagle.com

The city's only leather bar offers billiards and pinball games downstairs, and upstairs the music resounds to a techno beat and the expensively priced beer flows. Lots of special events with discount drinks at different times. For details phone or check the Web site. Open from 4 p.m. daily. Metro: Mount Vernon Square-UDC.

D.C. Farmers Market 1309 5th St. NE at Neal Pl. (202) 547-3142 www.ams.usda.gov/farmersmarkets/states/dc.htm

Open year-round Tues–Thurs 7 a.m.–5:30 p.m., Fri–Sat 7 a.m.–6:30 p.m., Sun 7 a.m.–2 p.m.

D.C. Heritage Tourism Coalition 1250 H St. NW, Suite 850 (202) 332-7103

Established in 1996, this nonprofit organization of various cultural and neighborhood organizations promotes Washington tourism and appreciation for local history through its publications, historic heritage trails, organizing tours, and establishing themed itineraries to often overlooked city attractions. Information and services are accessed primarily through the Web site, which also provides information on how to acquire the coalition's publication of the city's "heritage and cultural inventory." Metro: Metro Center.

D.C. Heritage Tourism Coalition (Web site) www.dcheritage.org

This Web site offers the visitor a city beyond the monuments, from historic homes to ethnic heritage, from parks and gardens to art at notable small museums. It provides a directory of links, from information about programs and performances to hotels, restaurants and visitor sites, an itinerary planner, an interactive calendar of events, discussions of historic neighborhoods, a remarkably comprehensive "heritage and cultural inventory" of the city, and listings of the coalition's programs, including topical bus and walking tours.

D.C. Heritage Walking Tours

The D.C. Heritage Tourism Coalition provides details about a number of walking tours in many of the city's unique neighborhoods. Consult the menu of possibilities by calling (202) 828-9255 or check the Web site at www.dcheritage.org.

D.C. Jewish Community Center 1529 16th St. NW at Q St. (202) 518-9400 www .dcjcc.org

Located in a limestone landmark structure built in 1925 and renovated in the 1990s, the center provides a wide range of programs for seniors of all faiths, an art gallery, and a 250-seat theater where year-round musical, literary, and film events are held. The exercise facilities include a gym, a pool, exercise equipment, and racquetball and squash courts. Day memberships offer access to all the fitness facilities. Metro: Dupont Circle.

D.C. Open-Air Farmers Market (202) 678-0610

Located in RFK Stadium Parking Lot 6 at Oklahoma Ave. and Benning Rd. NE, this fresh produce market is open all year on Thursdays and Saturdays 7 a.m.–5 p.m. and on Tuesdays also July–November. Metro: Stadium-Armory.

DCpages.com (Web site) 9813 Belhaven Rd., Bethesda, MD (301) 493-9273 www .dcpages.com

Founded in a basement in 1994, DCpages.com grew into a prize-winning community resource receiving more than 7,000 hits a day. This nonprofit organization provides a directory of Web sites on D.C.'s activities and offerings: business, attractions, entertainment, community resources, transportation, sports, travel, jobs, tourist information, lodging, museums, history, restaurants, and more. Listings include 24 main categories with 1,900 subcategories, with popular and new sites appearing first.

D.C. Preservation League 1815 Pennsylvania Ave. NW near 18th St., Suite 200 (202) 955-5616 www.dcpreservation.org

This nonprofit's activities include walking tours, historic home and building visits, and a Web site providing thumbnails of Washington's most endangered places. Its many activities aim to preserve, protect and enhance the historic environment of Washington, D.C. through advocacy and education. Metro: Farragut W.

dcregistry.com (Web site) www.dcregistry.com

A diverse one-stop source of Web sites of local businesses, organizations, and services, including classified ads, discussion forums on various topics, free home pages, a chat room, and listings of local galleries (www.dcregistry.com/art.html), museums, bands, and theaters.

D.C. United (703) 478-6600 www.dcunited.com

This is Washington's home team in the relatively new major league soccer competition. The season runs from April through October with the local team, including some player imports from Latin America, meeting its opponents at RFK Stadium, 22nd and E Capitol Sts. Metro: Stadium-Armory.

D.C. War Memorial

Located in W Potomac Park south of the Reflecting Pool and just north of Independence Ave. is this classical monument recognizing Washington, D.C.'s citizens who served during the First World War. It was dedicated in 1931 and the designer was Frederick H. Brooke. Metro: Smithsonian.

Da Hua Market 623 H St. NW at 7th St. (202) 371-8888

This is the place for authentic Asian shopping for fresh produce, meat and fish, seasonings, packaged goods, teas, and other staples of Oriental meal preparation. Open daily 10 a.m.–7:30 p.m. Metro: Gallery Pl.-Chinatown.

Dacor-Bacon House *see* Ringgold-Carroll House.

Dance *see* Arthur M. Sackler Gallery, Athenaeum, Dance Place, dcflamenco.com, Gala Hispanic Theatre, George Mason University Center for the Arts, Joy of Motion, Kankouran West African Dance Company, Kennedy Center for the Performing Arts Opera House, Lisner Auditorium of George Washington University, Liz Lerman Dance Exchange, Montpelier Mansion and Cultural Arts Center, National Theater, University of Maryland Clarice Smith Center for the Performing Arts, Washington Ballet, Washington Performing Arts Society, Wolf Trap Farm Park for the Performing Arts. *See also* Dance Clubs, www.washingtonpost.com.

Dance Africa–D.C.

This festival runs for two days sometime in early June each year celebrating African and African-American dance and music. Admission is free but some of the performances bear an admission price. It all happens at Dance Place, 3225 8th St. NE at Monroe St. Details at (202) 269-1600 or at the Web site, www.danceplace .org. Metro: Brookland-CUA.

Dance Clubs *see* Badlands, Bar Nun, Bravo! Bravo!, Cada Vez, Crush, Diversité, 18th Street Lounge, Glen Echo Park Spanish Ballroom, Heaven and Hell, Hung Jury, Latin Jazz Alley, Lulu's Club Mardi Gras, Metro Café, Nation Nightclub, 9:30 Club, Polly Esther's, Red, Ritz, Rumors, State of the Union, Zanzibar on the Waterfront. *See also* Night Clubs, Capitol Country Dancin', Dancer's Corner, DC-DanceNet.

Dance Place 3225 8th St. NE at Monroe St. (202) 269-1600 www.danceplace.org

This is a nonprofit center for dance instruction, which also hosts Washington's most renowned non-ballet modern and avant-garde dance performances on weekends. In the 200-seat theater some of the finest resident, national, and international dance companies are showcased. Call for information or check the Web site. Metro: Brookland-CUA. *See also* www.commuterpage.com/venues/venue-en.htm.

The Dancer's Corner (Web site) www.ppgi.com/dancers.htm

The Dancer's Corner offers a remarkably comprehensive calendar of forthcoming dances in the metropolitan Washington area. Its catalog of dance types includes West/East Coast Swing, Disco, Hustle, DC Hand Dance, Cajun/Zydeco, Lindy, Free Style Rock & Roll, and Shag Dancing. For each dance style, the site lists dates, venues, and band information. The site provides links to related sites involving other dance organizations, group or individual lessons, and home pages of local musical groups.

Dancing Crab 4611 Wisconsin Ave. NW at Brandywine St. (202) 244-1882 www.dancingcrab.com/

This is a casual place for devouring all-you-can-eat crabs by smashing them open with mallets on paper-covered tables and drinking beer along with it. When crabs are out of season, there's other seafood to consume. Open daily for lunch and dinner at moderate prices but reservations are suggested for busy times in the evening. Metro: Tenleytown-AU.

Dandy Restaurant Cruises Prince St. btw Duke and King Sts., Old Town, Alexandria, VA (703) 683-6076 www.dandydinnerboat.com

This enclosed boat cruises on the Potomac providing views of some of Washington's important sights on the way. There are lunch, brunch, and dinner cruises daily and in the evening there is dancing as well. Reservations are strongly suggested. Call or check the Web site for complete details and reservations. Metro: King Street, then take a bus to the Potomac.

Daniel Webster Statue

Located at Scott Circle, Massachusetts Ave., and 16th St. NW, this 12-foot bronze statue of the famous American statesman and orator was created by Gaetano Trentanove in 1900. Metro: Dupont Circle.

Dan's Café 2315 18th St. NW (202) 265-9241

This Adams Morgan bar is a throwback to the days when a bar was smoker-friendly. This one still is. In the middle is a pool table. Beers are what people usually drink here and the range covers only the standard brands and two or three imported kinds, and prices are moderate. Naturally the place is as laid back and casual as can be. Open daily 7 p.m.–midnight, until 2:30 a.m. on Fri and Sat. Metro: Dupont Circle, then L2 Bus, or Woodley Park-Zoo, then 90, 91, 92, 93, or 96 Bus.

Dante Statue

This monument of the renowned poet and diplomat Dante Alighieri of the Middle Ages stands at 16th St. and Florida Ave. NW. The architect Ettore Ximenes constructed it in 1920.

Darlington Fountain

In Judiciary Square at 5th and D Sts. NW this Art Deco sculpture commissioned by colleagues of Joseph Darlington honors this celebrated barrister of the early twentieth century. It was designed by Carl Jennewin in 1920. The sculpture's nymph and fawn raised some eyebrows when it was first erected. Metro: Judiciary Square.

Daruma 6931 Arlington Rd., behind CVS Pharmacy off Bradley Rd., Bethesda, MD (301) 654-8832

This shop sells food products and packaged goods that appeal to Japanese consumers and others looking for a wide array of Oriental home staples. Metro: Bethesda.

Daughters of the American Revolution Museum and Constitution Hall 1776 D St. NW btw 17th and 18th Sts., entrance on D St. (202) 879-3241 www.dar.org

This free museum is located in Memorial Continental Hall, a 1910 Georgian Revival building designed by architect Edward Pearce Caseys. It consists of 33 period rooms decorated in the style of various states and furnished with decorative art, paintings, ceramics, silver, and other materials used in early American history. There are two galleries. One displays a permanent collection, the other rotates exhibitions. Guided tours are offered by docents. Open Mon–Fri 8:30 a.m.–4 p.m., Sat 9 a.m.–5 p.m. Constitution Hall is next to the museum at 18th and D Sts. (202) 628-4780. It is a 3,746-seat auditorium where concerts, lectures, meetings, and other events take place. It was built in 1910 in neoclassic style by architect John Russell Pope. There is also a notable genealogical library maintained by the DAR with a collection of more than 100,000 books, court, church, Bible, and census records, as well as family histories. There is a modest fee for use of the library. Hours are Mon–Fri 8:30 a.m.–4 p.m., Sat 9 a.m.–5 p.m. Metro: Farragut West. *See also* www.commuterpage.com/venues/museums.htm.

Dave and Buster's White Flint Shopping Center, 11301 Rockville Pike, Rockville, MD (301) 230-5151 www.daveandbusters.com

This is a bar, restaurant, and carnival of games. It's open for lunch and dinner daily from 11 a.m. on. The interactive sports simulations, small billiard tables, pinball and video games, and casino fun are all part of the frenetic scene that seems to appeal to children of all ages. Style is casual and there's no cover charge except late on Fri and Sat, when there's a special show. Food consists of giant portions of suburban fare of considerable variety. Metro: White Flint.

David Adamson Gallery/Editions 406 7th St. NW btw D and E Sts. (202) 628-0257

In concert with the adjoining printmaking studio, this gallery features traditional paintings and avant-garde print exhibitions of work by well-regarded local and national artists. Open Tues–Sat 11 a.m.–5 p.m. Metro: Gallery Pl.-Chinatown.

Davis House *see* Ben Davis House.

Days Inn Connecticut Avenue 4400 Connecticut Ave. NW (202) 244-5600 or (800) 329-7466 www.daysinn-washingtondc.com

This upper-northwest hotel offers 155 reasonably priced, modest-sized rooms with free parking two blocks from the Metro in a residential and university neighborhood that is conveniently located near the zoo and many restaurants and shops. Metro: Van Ness-UDC.

Days Inn Crystal City 2000 Jefferson Davis Hwy. (Rt. 1), Arlington, VA (703) 920-8600 www.daysinncrystal.com

This hotel offers free parking, an exercise room, restaurant, airport shuttle, and more than 200 rooms on 8 floors, located between the Pentagon and Reagan National Airport. It's also very close to the Crystal City Underground complex of shops and restaurants and the Metro stop. This is one of the classier hostelries of the chain. Metro: Crystal City.

Days Inn Silver Spring 8040 13th St. off Georgia Ave., Silver Spring, MD (301) 588-4400 www.daysinn.com

This is an economic hotel choice about a mile north of Walter Reed Hospital, which is about the same distance from downtown Silver Spring, and close to Takoma Park to the east.

dcflamenco.com (Web site) www.dcflamenco.com

This electronic kiosk lists present and forthcoming weekly flamenco shows in metropolitan Washington restaurants and clubs and one-time special events such as concerts in theaters, workshops, and lectures. Venues, show times, and nearest Metro stops are provided. The site offers FAQs about flamenco matters: teachers, recommended recordings, photos of performers, and current happenings in the local flamenco scene.

Dean & DeLuca 3276 M St. NW at Potomac St. (202) 342-2500 www.deandeluca .com

Located in the historic old Georgetown Market House just across from the Georgetown Park Shopping Mall, this is a branch of the celebrated New York City gourmet food shop. It's a very popular stop for meats, fish, cheeses, fresh produce, and baked goods. There's also a self-service café counter with a limited but tasty menu of pasta, salads, sandwiches, small pizzas, and espresso at somewhat inflated prices. Open daily from 10 a.m.–evening. Metro: Foggy Bottom-GWU, then 30, 32, 34, 35, or 36 Bus. There's a second café location downtown at 1299 Pennsylvania Ave. NW at 13th St. (202) 628-8155 between two Metro stops: Federal Triangle or Metro Center.

Decatur House 748 Jackson Pl. NW, corner of H St. on Lafayette Square (202) 842-0920 www.decaturhouse.org

Designed by Benjamin Latrobe, a pioneer of Early American architecture, for War of 1812 naval hero Commodore Stephen Decatur and built in 1819, this elegant red brick Federal-style structure is one of Washington's oldest surviving buildings. It now functions as a museum where tour guides conduct visitors every half hour through the rooms decorated with period furnishings and describe what life was like almost two centuries ago for the city's elite. Admission free. Open Tues–Fri 10 a.m.–3 p.m., Sat and Sun noon–4 p.m. Metro: Farragut West.

Decatur Terrace Steps and Fountain

Located at 22nd St. NW between Decatur Pl. and S St., this street in the form of a staircase connects Decatur to the much higher-level S St. in an attractive and imaginative construction built in 1912, which is little known to most Washingtonians. Metro: Dupont Circle.

Del Ray Farmers Market Mount Vernon and Custiss Aves., Alexandria, VA (703) 683-2570 www.radiodelray.com/drfm

Producers sell their fresh produce here on Saturdays 8 a.m.–noon from late April to December.

Delano Monument *see* Jane A. Delano Monument.

Delhi Dhaba 2424 Wilson Blvd. at Barton St., Arlington, VA (703) 524-0008

This rock-bottom-priced, cafeteria-style Indian eatery offers succulent meat and vegetarian dishes that are satisfying and filling. Open daily for lunch and dinner. Metro: Court House. There's another branch at 7236 Woodmont Ave. in Bethesda (301) 718-0008. Metro: Bethesda.

Delicatessens *see* Heidelberg Pastry Shop, Krupins, Vace.

Delights of the Garden 2616 Georgia Ave. NW btw Euclid and Fairmont Sts. (202) 319-8747

Located opposite Howard University, this vegetarian restaurant serves dishes that are natural and uncooked in very creative ways to make ingredients like raw nuts, fruits, sprouts, and mushrooms passed once through the blender or food processor very appetizing. Open daily for lunch and dinner. No alcohol and no credit cards. Metro: U St.-Cardozo.

Deluxe Hotels *see* Bethesda Marriott, Churchill Hotel, Four Seasons, The Hay-Adams Hotel, Hilton McLean at Tysons Corner, Hilton Washington Embassy Row, Hotel Monaco, Hyatt Regency Capitol Hill, Loew's L'Enfant Plaza, Madison Hotel, Monarch Hotel, Omni Shoreham Hotel, Park Hyatt Washington, Phoenix Park Hotel, Renaissance Mayflower Hotel, Ritz Carlton Pentagon City, Ritz Carlton Tysons Corner, St. Regis, Sheraton Premiere at Tysons Corner, Swissôtel Washington-The Watergate, Washington Court Hotel, Westfield Marriott, Willard Inter-Continental Hotel. *See also* www.frommers.com.

Denmark Embassy 3200 Whitehaven St. NW (202) 234-4300 www.denmark emb.org

The Royal Danish Embassy. Metro: Dupont Circle, then transfer to Massachusetts Ave. Bus.

Department of Agriculture *see* U.S. Department of Agriculture.

Department of Commerce *see* Commerce Department.

Department of Housing and Urban Development 451 7th St. SW adjacent to the Southwest Freeway www.hud.gov

This building and its plaza were designed by architects Marcel Breuer and Herbert Beckhard in 1968 as one of the first structures following President Kennedy's mandate to improve the aesthetics of federal construction. Its curvilinear shape is intended to provide maximum natural light for the greatest number of offices. The plaza feature was designed to relate the building to the nearby Mall. Metro: L'Enfant Plaza.

Department of Labor Building *see* Francis Perkins Department of Labor Building.

Department of State *see* State Department.

Department of the Interior 1849 C St. NW btw 18th and 19th Sts. www.doi.gov
Constructed in 1937 and designed by Waddy B. Wood, this was the period's most modern government structure complete with escalators and air-conditioning, both rarities in the 1930s. The two-block square exterior is undistinguished but on the interior there are great murals by WPA artists featuring 1930s-style realism in frescoes and statues of Indian life, national parks, and the pioneers' westward trek. Located in the building are an Indian crafts shop, National Park Service Information Office, and the Interior Department Museum. Metro: Farragut West.

Department of the Interior Museum 1849 C St. NW at 19th St. (202) 208-4743 www.doi.gov/museum
Most of the Interior Department's bureaus have gallery space in the museum with exhibits of artifacts, drawings, photos, and paintings. Dioramas depict American historic scenes and the Native Indian section shows pottery and baskets. Open Mon–Fri 8:30 a.m.–4:30 p.m. Hour-long guided tours are available, which include wall murals in restricted areas of the building, but reservations must be made weeks ahead of time. The Indian Craft Shop, one of the city's finest specialty stores in the building opposite the museum (202) 208-4056 has enticing authentic American Indian arts and crafts for sale and is open the same hours as the museum. Metro: Farragut West.

Department of the Treasury *see* U.S. Treasury Department.

Department Stores *see* Bloomingdale's, Filene's Basement, Hecht's, Lord & Taylor, Macy's, Neiman Marcus, Nordstrom, Saks Fifth Avenue. *See also* Shopping Malls.

Diners *see* Florida Avenue Grill, Tastee Diner.

Disabled Services http://dc.about.com/cs/disabledresources
Washington D.C. is one of the most accessible cities in the world for physically challenged travelers. Most museums, monuments, and memorials are accessible to visitors riding wheelchairs, as are a great many restaurants in and around the city. The Smithsonian Institution distributes a free brochure completely detailing accessibility features at all of its affiliated agencies. It is entitled "Smithsonian Access" and is available in various formats at Smithsonian museum information desks, by calling (202) 357-2000, or by writing Smithsonian Information Center, SI Building 153, Washington, D.C. 20560-0010. The Washington, D.C. Metro transportation system offers discount fares on its subways and buses to the handicapped and to seniors and has elevators at stations and lift mechanisms on buses. For information about Metro phone (202) 962-1245. For details on the National Parks Service special services for the disabled at their sites call (202) 619-7222, or write to the National Park Service, Office of Public Inquiries, 1849 C St. NW, Washington, D.C.

20240 for a copy of the "National Park Service System Map and Guide" and the pamphlet "Federal Recreation Pass Programs."

Discount Stores and Factory Outlets *see* Ames, City Place Mall, Leesburg Corner Premium Outlets, Potomac Mills.

Discovery Creek Children's Museum at Glen Echo Park, 4954 MacArthur Blvd., Glen Echo, MD (202) 364-3111 www.discoverycreek.org

Located in the last of the area's one-room red-brick schoolhouses (it was built in 1864), this museum and activity center for small children provides the opportunity to learn about and experience the natural environment and geography through interactive activities. Open Sat 10 a.m.–3 p.m., Sun 11 a.m.–3 p.m. Modest admission charge for children.

Discovery Theater *see* Smithsonian Discovery Theater.

Discovery Zone *see* Kidzone.

Diskobolos of Myron

This copy of the statue of the famous discus thrower cast in Greece some 2,500 years ago, which no longer exists, came to Washington in 1956 as a gift from the Italian people in gratitude to the United States for the return of Italian art stolen by the Germans during World War II. The 5-foot-high bronze nude athlete ready to let loose of the disc is perched above a column in Foggy Bottom in Kelly Park at Virginia Ave. and 21st St. NW. Metro: Foggy Bottom-GWU.

Distinctive Bookbinding and Stationery 1150 Connecticut Ave. NW entrance at 18th and M Sts. (202) 466-4866

This is the place in the city to find the finest quality papers and writing equipment and to arrange for restoring and rebinding treasured volumes. Open Mon–Fri 10 a.m.–6 p.m. Metro: Farragut North.

District Building *see* John A. Wilson Building.

District Chop House and Brewery 509 7th St. NW btw E and F Sts. (202) 347-3434 www.districtchophouse.com

Located in a late nineteenth-century bank building with cast iron, granite, and metal on the outside, and the inside looking like a 1920s speakeasy complete with pool tables from the period, this moderate-priced brewpub serves giant platters of meat and fish, marvelous salads, and oceans of beer. Open for lunch Mon–Fri, dinner daily. Reservations recommended when events are taking place at MCI Center. Metro: Gallery Pl.-Chinatown.

District Curators

This organization presents musical performances of top-flight jazz artists at various venues around the city. Information at (202) 723-7500 or at www.jazzarts.org.

District of Columbia Arts Center 2438 18th St. NW btw Columbia and Belmont Rds. (202) 462-7833 www.dcartscenter.org

This is a visual and performance arts center in Adams Morgan that presents avant-garde theatrical programs and offbeat performance art in a 50-seat theater and exhibits local and other artists in the gallery space. Admission to the gallery is free and it is open Wed–Sun 2 p.m.–7 p.m. and later, until around 10 p.m., on performance nights, usually Fri and Sat. Metro: Woodley Park-Zoo, then 90, 91, 92, 93, or 96 Bus.

District of Columbia Government (Web site) www.dc.gov

This local government Web site provides information on citizen services, business services, city facts, figures and finances, and forthcoming city government events.

District of Columbia War Memorial *see* D.C. War Memorial.

Diversité 1526 14th St. NW at U St. (202) 234-5740 www.salsaweb.com/dc/diversite1.htm

This elegant and popular supper and dance club is open for dinner from 4 p.m. every night. It is one part Italian-style restaurant and another part Latin music headquarters for salsa and merengue on Fri and Sat nights, tango on Mon and Thurs. The food and drink is fairly priced, and there's lots of dancing space in this one-time auto showroom and repair space. Call for changes in the schedule. Metro: U St.-Cardozo.

Djibouti Embassy 1156 15th St. NW, Suite 515 (202) 331-0270

Embassy of the Republic of Djibouti. Metro: McPherson Square.

Dr. Dremo's Tap House 2001 Clarendon Blvd., Arlington, VA (703) 528-4660 www.drdremo.com

This billiard place boasts forty-four pool tables and a wide range of different beers with a schedule of events and entertainment offered on different nights of the week. Open from 5 p.m. every night but Mon. Metro: Court House.

Dr. E. B. Bliss House 7116 Maple Ave., Takoma Park, MD

This Italianate mansion was constructed in the 1880s. Some of its more interesting features include the square tower well above the roofline, the gabled wings, tall narrow windows, and strangely cut porch rails. Even though it looks like a brick and stone house, it is actually built of wood. Not open to tourists. Metro: Takoma.

Doctor John Witherspoon Statue *see* Witherspoon Statue.

Dominica Embassy 3216 New Mexico Ave. NW (202) 364-6781 www.embassy.org/embassies/dm.html

Embassy of the Commonwealth of Dominica.

Dominican Republic Embassy 1715 22nd St. NW (202) 332-6280 www.domrep.org

Metro: Dupont Circle.

Donatello 2514 L St. NW btw Pennsylvania Ave. and 26th St. (202) 333-1485 http://donatello-dc.com/homepage.htm

In a 2-floor renovated townhouse with brick walls and an outdoor patio for warmer weather, this moderately priced Italian restaurant offers fine veal and pasta dishes in a romantic ambiance. Open for lunch Mon–Fri, dinner daily. Metro: Foggy Bottom-GWU.

Doorways to Old Virginia

Costumed tour guides in Colonial garb lead one-hour evening walking tours of Old Town Alexandria from April through October. Details at (703) 548-0100.

Doubletree Guest Suites 801 New Hampshire Ave. NW at H St. (202) 785-2000 www.doubletree.com

There are 101 suites at this location, each offering a living room, dining area, and fully equipped kitchen and large bedroom. There is no restaurant but there is a small swimming pool on the roof. Rates are moderately expensive and parking is additional. It is 1 block from the Metro. Metro: Foggy Bottom-GWU. Another Guest Suites in town is located at 2500 Pennsylvania Ave. at 25th St. (202) 333-8060.

Doubletree Hotel–National Airport 300 Army Navy Dr. at Jefferson Davis Hwy. (Rt. 1), Arlington, VA (703) 416-4100 www.doubletree.com

There are 632 rooms including 152 suites at this fairly expensive place located near the Pentagon City shopping mall. Amenities include two restaurants, exercise room, and enclosed rooftop swimming pool. There's also shuttle service to the Pentagon and Reagan National Airport. Metro: Pentagon City.

Doubletree Park Terrace Hotel 1515 Rhode Island Ave. NW btw 15th and 16th Sts. (202) 232-7000 or (800) 222-8733

Conveniently located at Scott Circle, this mid-priced hotel with humdrum rooms does have an exercise room. Metro: Dupont Circle or McPherson Square.

Douglass Memorial Bridge *see* Frederick Douglass Memorial Bridge.

Douglass National Historic Site *see* Frederick Douglass National Historic Site.

Downtown Civil War Tour www.dcheritage.org

This downtown walking tour is led by a costumed tour guide, who describes events taking place in the 1860s during the war period. Details at (202) 661-7576 or www.dcheritage.org.

Downtown Historic District

The oldest and most eclectic and diverse section of the city during the late-eighteenth century to the 1930s, this area is roughly bounded by F St. NE to the north, the Southeast Freeway to the south, the area around the Capitol on the west, and 13th St. NE and SE on the east. The earliest homes in southeast D.C. were around the Navy Yard and extended to the Capitol. In the nineteenth century many more row houses came into existence. Commercial buildings and institutional structures can be found along Pennsylvania Ave. The styles of architecture run the gamut from Federal to Classical Revival to many, many other forms.

Doyle Normandy 2118 Wyoming Ave. NW btw Connecticut Ave. and 23rd St. (202) 483-1350 or (800) 424-3729 www.jurysdoyle.com

This recently renovated, moderately priced 75-room hotel has a distinct European flavor and is located in a quiet residential and embassy neighborhood. Underground parking and continental breakfast are among its amenities. Metro: Dupont Circle, then L1 Bus.

Doyle Washington *see* Jury's Washington Hotel.

Dragonfly 1215 Connecticut Ave. NW btw M and N Sts. (202) 331-1775
This place has been transformed from a sushi restaurant into a very in bar with video scenes projected on the white walls to the beat of music playing on into the late hours. Open Mon–Fri 5:30 p.m.–2 a.m., Sat and Sun 6 p.m.–1:30 a.m. Metro: Farragut North, then 42 Bus.

Drug Enforcement Administration Museum and Visitors Bureau 700 Army-Navy Drive opposite Macy's at Pentagon City Shopping Mall, Arlington, VA (202) 307-3463 www.usdoj.gov/dea/deamuseum/home.htm
The museum highlights the long history of the country's ties to the illegal traffic in drugs. In a relatively small space, the displays and photos provide an informative and interesting perspective on the problems connected with drug use. Open Tues–Fri 10 a.m.–4 p.m. with self-guided tours of about 45 minutes, which require reservations. Metro: Pentagon City.

Duangrat's 5878 Leesburg Pike at Glen Forest Dr., Bailey's Crossroads, Falls Church, VA (703) 820-5775
Reputed to be one of the area's finest Thai restaurants, this place is open daily for lunch and dinner featuring beautifully clad waitresses serving excellent Thai specialties, which are interestingly prepared and varied. On Saturday nights colorfully costumed Thai dancers perform in the upstairs dining room.

Dubliner in the Phoenix Park Hotel, 520 N Capitol St. at Massachusetts Ave. (202) 773-3773 www.dublinerdc.com
Serving from breakfast on at 7 a.m. daily and open for food and drink until 2 a.m. or 3 a.m., this classic Irish pub/restaurant boasts paneled rooms, a clubby ambiance, and live and lively Celtic music nightly to go with the Guinness on draft. Metro: Union Station.

Duck Tours (202) 832-9800 www.historictours.com/washington/dcducks.htm
This firm offers a 1½-hour narrated tour from April through October of monuments and museums around the Mall and then the vehicle switches to amphibious mode and continues on the Potomac. Information at (202) 832-9800 or www.dcducks.com.

Duke Ellington Memorial Bridge Calvert St. NW btw Woodley Pl. and 24th St.
Completed in 1935, this three-arched concrete bridge towering above Rock Creek features a crisp, unadorned design by architect Paul Cret. Originally called Calvert Street Bridge, it was renamed to honor Washington's master musician Duke Ellington. The central arch would need about 20 feet under the roadway to make a full circle. Metro: Woodley Park-Zoo.

Duke Ellington Mural
Located in Ellington's native Shaw neighborhood at 1214 U St. NW, attached to the side wall of the Mood Indigo building, this larger-than-life-sized representation of the jazz virtuoso was created by the white mural artist Byron Pick and painted from a photo of the Duke. Metro: U St.-Cardozo.

Duke Ellington School of the Arts 1698 35th St. at R St. NW (202) 282-0123

Located in the former Western High School this neoclassical structure has served as a magnet high school since 1974 for some 500 or so of the city's most gifted youngsters, who pursue college preparatory courses plus classes in music, dance, theater, visual arts, voice, and museum studies. A very high proportion continues on to college and goes on to careers in performance or the arts.

Duke Ellington's D.C. Tours

During the summer months this tour group takes visitors on foot and by bus through Duke Ellington's childhood haunts around the Shaw neighborhood, to museum exhibitions, and to a number of historic sites associated with African-American history and culture in the city. Information at (202) 636-9203.

Duke Ellington's Home

The childhood home of Washington's native son and incomparable jazz composer and performer is located in the Shaw neighborhood at 1212 T St. NW at the intersection of 12th and T Sts. Edward Kennedy Ellington first played his music in nightspots, theaters, and dance halls in this neighborhood. The house is not open to tourists. Metro: U St.-Cardozo.

Dulles Airport Chantilly, VA (703) 417-8000 www.metwashairports.com/Dulles

Located 26 miles from D.C. (50 minutes from downtown, longer during rush hour), this domestic and international flight hub is situated on the border between Loudoun and Fairfax, close to residential neighborhoods and a thriving business corridor, which keeps expanding into the surrounding meadows and forests. For details on transportation to the city, see Airport Transportation.

Dulles Airport Marriott 45020 Aviation Dr. at Dulles Access Rd. (703) 471-9500 or (800) 462-9671 www.marriott.com

This mid-range-priced hotel is the closest to the airport and operates a shuttle bus every 15 minutes. The amenities at this 360-room hostelry include indoor and outdoor pools, exercise and weight room, outdoor tennis court, and a restaurant serving breakfast, lunch, and dinner. A regularly scheduled Metrobus connects to the Metro station for travel on to downtown D.C.

Dulles Town Center 21100 Dulles Town Circle, Dulles, VA (703) 404-7120 www .shopdullestowncenter.com

This, the region's most recently constructed shopping mall, is a large two-level complex offering more than 100 shops, eateries, and entertainment places. To reach the mall from the Beltway (I-495) take Rte. 7 Leesburg Pike W to Rte. 28 Sully Rd. N. The shopping center is at the intersection of Rt. 7 and Rt. 28.

Dumbarton Bridge *see* Bison Bridge.

Dumbarton Concert Series 3133 Dumbarton St. NW off Wisconsin Ave. (202) 965-2000 www.dumbartonconcerts.org

From October through April a variety of musical entertainment programs are offered in the Dumbarton Concert Gallery in Georgetown, ranging from chamber music to jazz to Renaissance music to Christmas events. Tickets are available by subscription or single performances. Call or check the Web site for information. Metro: Foggy Bottom-GWU, then 30, 32, 34, 35 or 36 Bus.

Dumbarton House 2715 Q St. NW btw 27th and 28th Sts. (202) 337-2288 www
.dumbartonhouse.org
This brick Federal-style building in Georgetown (not to be confused with
Dumbarton Oaks), was built around 1800 and restored in 1928 by Fiske Kimball
and Horace Peaslee. It is now a museum and headquarters of the National Society
of the Colonial Dames of America. It contains period furnishings, silver, Persian
rugs, porcelain, early prints of the city, and portraits. It is open for tours at 10:15
a.m., 11:15 a.m., and 12:15 p.m. Tues–Sat from September through July. A modest
donation is suggested. Metro: Dupont Circle, then D1, D2, or D6 Bus on Q St.

Dumbarton Oaks Park http://dumbartonoakspark.org
This 27-acre area is a lovely woodland in upper Georgetown, open daily with
no entrance fee from 9 a.m. to dusk. It is accessible only on foot by way of Lovers
Lane near 31st and R Sts. NW. It was a gift to the city from the Bliss family and is
seen at its most beautiful in spring with its profusion of wildflowers.

Dumbarton Oaks Research Library and Collections 1703 32nd St. NW btw R and
S Sts. (202) 339-6400 www.doaks.org
Located in a nineteenth-century Federal-style brick building with an addition
designed by architect Philip Johnson, the museum and gardens are the property of
Harvard University through a bequest by Robert Bliss and his wife in 1940. It is
now a research center and showplace for the Byzantine and pre-Columbian art,
sculpture, carvings, textiles, and jewelry collections beautifully displayed in eight
circular glass pavilions bathed in natural light. The 10-acre terraced garden is reputed to be one of the finest in the United States. Suggested donation for the museum. Open Tues–Sun 2 p.m.–5 p.m. The gardens, accessible from the entrance at
31st and R Sts., are open daily except on holidays. Modest admission charge.
Metro: Dupont Circle, then 30, 32, 34, or 36 Bus.

Duncanson Cranch House 468 N St. SW www.dcheritage.org
Built near the end of the eighteenth century and attributed to architect William
Lovering, this Federal-style property was built by James Greenleaf, Robert Morris,
the Philadelphia financier, and John Nicholson. It functions now as townhouses in
the Harbour Square community. Metro: Waterfront-SEU.

Dupont at the Circle 1606 19th St. NW at Q St. (202) 332-5251 www.dupontat
thecircle.com
This bed-and-breakfast in a Victorian townhouse less than a block from the
Metro stop offers only a small number of high-ceiling rooms. They are all elegantly
appointed with full baths, and continental breakfast and the daily newspaper are
provided. It is situated on a tree-lined residential street and its rates are moderate.
Metro: Dupont Circle.

Dupont Circle
Massachusetts, New Hampshire, and Connecticut Aves. converge at this large
traffic island located in northwest D.C. with a marble fountain at its center. The
lawns and benches here are one of the city's most popular neighborhood hangouts
with chess playing at the tables in the middle of the circle, which is surrounded by

a bustling plethora of shops, restaurants, bookstores, and galleries within a few minutes' walk. The area is a lively, sometimes frenetic community with a great diversity of cultural interests and lifestyles, popular with students, professionals, and gays. There are Metro entrances to the north and south of the circle. Metro: Dupont Circle.

Dupont Circle Freshfarm Market (202) 331-7300, ext. 3010 www.farmland.org

Every Sunday 9 a.m.–1 p.m. from April to mid-December this producers' market sets up in the parking area behind the bank building off the circle at 20th St. NW between Q St. and Massachusetts Ave. Metro: Dupont Circle.

Dupont Circle Historic Homes Tour

This tour takes place each year in mid-October. For details and registration information phone (202) 265-3222.

Dupont Circle Memorial Park

This is the name of the green area within the traffic circle where Massachusetts, Connecticut, and New Hampshire Aves. intersect in northwest D.C. The central 17-foot-high white marble fountain built in 1921 was designed by Daniel Chester French, who also designed the Lincoln Memorial. Metro: Dupont Circle.

Dupont Italian Kitchen 1637 17th St. NW at R St. (202) 328-3222

This casual spot is open for lunch and dinner daily, offering moderate-priced traditional Italian food and drink and ample space for observing the scene along 17th St. The upstairs bar, which attracts mainly gay men, is open from 4 p.m. daily. Metro: Dupont Circle.

Dupont-Kalorama Museum Walk Day www.dkmuseums.com/walk.html

On a Saturday early in June each year some ten museums at various locations in this artistic region of the city open their doors to the public for free. For full details about locations and hours call (202) 667-0441.

Dupont Memorial Fountain www.dcheritage.org

Located in Dupont Circle at the intersection of Connecticut, Massachusetts, and New Hampshire Aves., this 17-foot-high white marble fountain was sculpted in 1921 by Daniel Chester French, who also constructed the Lincoln Memorial. Metro: Dupont Circle.

Dyke Marsh www.nps.gov/gwmp/dyke-marsh.htm

This is a wetlands area with walking trails under the jurisdiction of the National Park Service in Alexandria, Virginia, since 1956. It is approached by driving about 3 miles toward Mount Vernon on the George Washington Memorial Pkwy. south of Old Town, where a National Park Service sign designates the turnoff to the crossover bridge to reach the trail entrance. The extensive range of this protected region runs along between the Potomac River and the George Washington Memorial Pkwy. Information at (202) 619-7222.

E Travel DC (Web site) www.etraveldc.com

This Web site, maintained by a twelve-hotel Washington conglomerate, offers useful, albeit sometimes outdated, recommendations on what to do and see in Washington. It offers suggestions for vacations in Washington sorted by the number of days of the visit, suggestions for getting around, books on D.C., D.C. for kids, hotel special offers, and the like. They offer, as well, a number of links to other sources.

East Capitol St. Bridge *see* Whitney M. Young Jr. Memorial Bridge.

East Capitol St. Row Houses 512–516 E Capitol St. SE btw 5th and 6th Sts.

These row houses constructed in brick and trimmed with wood and cast iron were built in the late nineteenth century and their height and similarity contrast sharply with the mix of various other types of architectural styles around them on this section of E Capitol St. Metro: Capital South.

East Potomac Golf Course 972 Ohio Dr. SW at Hains Point in East Potomac Park (202) 554-7660

Among the city's public courses, this one located south of the Franklin D. Roosevelt Memorial doubtless offers the greatest views of Washington's monuments from the course and is certainly the busiest. There are two 9-hole courses, one 18-hole course, and an 18-hole miniature course. Metro: Smithsonian.

East Potomac Park Ohio Dr. SW south of Independence Ave. (202) 727-6523

Located south and east of the Jefferson Memorial in southwest Washington is this 300-acre island between the Washington Channel on the east and the Potomac River to the west. It includes playgrounds, picnic tables, swimming pools, golf courses, and tennis courts. There are bike paths and waterfront walking trails as well. Metro: Smithsonian.

East Potomac Tennis Center 1090 Ohio Dr. SW at Hains Point (202) 554-5962

The city has a number of public outdoor courts. This location offers fifteen courts and three are lit at night. Courts can be reserved and the easiest time to get a court is on weekdays from mid-morning to 3 p.m. Information at (202) 554-5962. Metro: Smithsonian.

East Street Café 50 Massachusetts Ave. NE in Union Station (202) 371-6788

Located on the mezzanine level of Union Station, this lively spot features dishes from a good number of Asian countries like curries, tempura, and rice and noodle dishes. Service is pleasant and prices are moderate. Open daily for lunch and dinner. Metro: Union Station.

Easter Egg Hunt for Blind Children

A special egg hunt for blind kids is held Easter Sunday at the Washington Monument grounds of the Mall where the children hunt for eggs that make a beeping sound that they can trade for prizes. Information at (202) 619-7222.

Easter Sunrise Service Arlington National Cemetery, Memorial Dr., Arlington, VA (703) 607-8052

A service is conducted each year by Washington clergy at the Memorial Amphitheater for worship at daybreak. Metro: Arlington Cemetery.

Eastern Market 225 7th St. SE btw C St. and North Carolina Ave. (202) 546-2698 www.easternmarket.net

Since 1802 a farmers market has been located here in the Capitol Hill neighborhood. One historic and brick building from 1873, whose architect was Adolf Cluss, still stands. It contains produce, meat, and fish stalls and a popular unpretentious spot for eating, Market Lunch, and a choice of restaurants across the street. On weekends the market overflows to outdoors as well with a flea market, arts and crafts, and fresh food and flowers. Hours are Tues–Sat 7 a.m.–6 p.m., Sun 9 a.m.–4 p.m. Metro: Eastern Market.

Eastern Market Flea Market 7th St. SE btw Pennsylvania and North Carolina Aves. (703) 534-7612 www.easternmarket.net

Every Sunday 10 a.m.–5 p.m. between March and the end of the year an international market featuring vendors of ethnic handicrafts, old furniture, assorted bric-a-brac, old records, wearable art, and much, much more set up their stalls here to negotiate prices for their wares with an eclectic flock of treasure-seeking consumers. Metro: Eastern Market.

Eastern Market Outdoor Farmers Market 225 7th St. SE btw Pennsylvania and North Carolina Aves.

All year-round on Saturdays and Sundays from 8 a.m. until selling out, local growers market their fresh produce here. Metro: Eastern Market.

Ebbitt Grill *see* Old Ebbitt Grill.

Ebenezer United Methodist Church 400 D St. SE corner of 4th St. (202) 544-1415

This is the oldest church on Capitol Hill for blacks and the first public school for blacks in the city was started at this site in 1863. Originally built in 1838, the building was reconstructed at this location in 1897 by architects Crump and Palmer in Romanesque Revival style. Metro: Capitol South.

Econo Lodge Metro 6800 Lee Hwy., Arlington, VA (703) 538-5300 or (800) 78LODGE www.econometro.com

This 47-room budget motel is located at the point where I-66 and Lee Hwy. come together and has the reputation for being one of the best in the entire chain. It is a short walk to the Metro station. Metro: East Falls Church.

Economist.com (Web site) www.economist.com

This Web site offers an insightful look at Washington. Its pull-down windows include information on selected hotels, restaurants, sightseeing, shopping, nightlife, a brief history of the city and news events, basic facts, "insider tips," as well as an illustrated cultural calendar highlighting the best of gallery exhibits and other events. It also suggests the best books on Washington and the best surfing sites that are well organized and current.

Ecuador Embassy 2535 15th St. NW (202) 234-7200 www.ecuador.org

Eden Supermarket 6763 Wilson Blvd., Falls Church, VA (703) 532-4950

This specialized market stocks all the food and household staples that appeal to customers seeking Vietnamese products. Open daily 9:30 a.m.–8:30 p.m. Metro: East Falls Church, then a 20-minute walk.

Edmund Burke Memorial Massachusetts Ave. and 11th St. NW

This bronze statue sculpted by J. Howard Thomas in 1922 memorializes the British statesman who eloquently defended the cause of the American colonies in England's Parliament. Metro: Metro Center.

Edward Simon Lewis House 456 N St. SW

Constructed around 1817 in the typical brick building style of the period, the single-family house was converted for apartment use in the 1920s. Renovated in the 1960s as part of the Harbour Square development it has become a single-family townhouse. Metro: Waterfront-SEU.

Egypt Embassy 3521 International Court NW (202) 895-5400 www.embassyof egyptwashingtondc.org

The residence of the Ambassador of the Arab Republic of Egypt is located at 2301 Massachusetts Ave. at R St. on Sheridan Circle. The secretary of the American Institute of Architects from 1899 to 1913, Glen Brown, designed this limestone and stucco mansion for Joseph Beale in 1907. It is considered his residential master-piece. In 1928 Egypt purchased the property. Metro: Embassy: Van Ness-UDC; Residence: Dupont Circle.

18th Street Lounge 1212 18th St. NW btw Jefferson Pl. and M St. (202) 466-3922 www.eslmusic.com/lounge/lounge.html

As one of the city's livelier dance clubs that ranks high for being in, it's necessary to wait in line to get in, particularly as it gets later in the evening. Drinks are fairly expensive. Admission charge. Opens Tues–Wed 9:30 p.m., Thurs–Fri 6 p.m., Sat–Sun 9:30 p.m., staying open until around 2:30 a.m. Jazz music live on Fri and Sat, DJs on other nights. Metro: Farragut North or Dupont Circle.

Einstein Memorial *see* Albert Einstein Memorial.

Eisenhower Theater *see* Kennedy Center for the Performing Arts Eisenhower The-ater.

Eko Food Market 6507 Annapolis Rd., Landover Hills, MD (301) 341-5050

This store stocks food products that are in demand by people looking for West African produce and selections. Open Mon–Fri 10 a.m.–6 p.m., Sat–Sun 10 a.m.–6 p.m. Metro: New Carrolton, then Bus T-18.

El Salvador Embassy 2308 California St. NW (202) 265-9671 www.elsalvador.org

11th Street Bridge

Running across the Anacostia River at 11th St., or I-295, the first bridge was constructed in 1800, with the current bridge dating from 1960. Metro: Navy Yard.

Elizabeth Arden Red Door Salon and Spa 5225 Wisconsin Ave. NW near Jennifer St. (202) 362-9890 www.reddoorsalons.com

Open daily from 8 a.m. until evening, except Sunday from 10 a.m. until evening, this mecca of feminine splendor in upper-northwest D.C. offers all manner of loveliness-treatment rites individually or in all-day combination packages at moderately expensive prices. Metro: Friendship Heights.

Ellington Memorial Bridge *see* Duke Ellington Memorial Bridge.

The Ellipse

Bounded by 15th and 17th Sts. NW and Constitution Ave. and E St., this 50-acre oval grassy expanse south of the White House functions frequently as ceremonial grounds for the White House, for pageants, and sometimes for large demonstrations. The rest of the time its chief features include chess enthusiasts, ball players, street vendors, and strolling tourists. Metro: Farragut West or McPherson Square.

Ellipse Arts Center 4350 N Fairfax Dr., Arlington, VA (703) 228-7710 www.arlingtonarts.org

The Arlington Cultural Affairs Division shows exhibitions here of various types of visual arts by local, national, and international artists in changing shows throughout the year. Open Tues–Fri 10 a.m.–6 p.m., Sat 11 a.m.– 5 p.m. Metro: Ballston-MU, exit the station and walk one block west on N Fairfax Dr. *See also* www.commuterpage.com/venues/sightseeing_VA.htm.

Elysium 116 S Alfred St., btw King and Prince Sts., Alexandria, VA (703) 838-8000 www.morrisonhouse.com

Located in the handsome Morrison House hotel in Old Town Alexandria this elegant and expensive restaurant features a rotating menu with the chef discussing the choices with the clients. The chef draws upon seasonal game and stylish American, classic French, and Southwestern influences in fashioning the imaginative culinary creations. Open for dinner Tues–Sat. Reservations are necessary well ahead for Fri and Sat. Metro: King Street, then a 7-block walk.

Emancipation Statue www.cr.nps.gov/nr/travel/wash/dc87.htm

Located at the west end of Lincoln Park at E Capitol St. between 11th and 13th Sts., this bronze statue depicts Arthur Alexander, the last slave captured under the Fugitive Slave Law, being freed by Abraham Lincoln. It was sculpted by Thomas Ball in 1876 with Frederick Douglass delivering the keynote address at the dedication ceremony. Metro: Eastern Market.

Embassies *see* Albania, Algeria, Angola, Antigua and Barbuda, Argentina, Armenia, Australia, Austria, Azerbaijan, Bahamas, Bahrain, Bangladesh, Barbados, Belarus, Belgium, Belize, Benin, Bolivia, Bosnia and Herzegovina, Botswana, Brazil, Brunei, Bulgaria, Burkina Faso, Burma, Burundi, Cambodia, Cameroon, Canada, Cape Verde, Central African Republic, Chad, Chile, China, Colombia, Congo, Costa Rica, Croatia, Cyprus, Czech Republic, Denmark, Djibouti, Dominica, Dominican Republic, Ecuador, Egypt, El Salvador, Equatorial Guinea, Eritrea, Estonia, Ethiopia, Fiji, Finland, France, Gabon, Gambia, Georgia, Germany, Ghana, Greece, Grenada, Guatemala, Guinea, Guinea Bissau, Guyana, Haiti, Holy See, Honduras, Hungary, Iceland, India, Indonesia, Ireland, Israel, Italy, Ivory Coast, Jamaica, Japan, Jordan, Kazakhstan, Kenya, Kuwait, Kyrgyzstan, Laos, Latvia, Lebanon, Lesotho, Liberia, Lithuania, Luxembourg, Macedonia, Madagascar, Malawi, Malaysia, Mali, Malta, Marshall Islands, Mauritania, Mauritius, Mexico, Micronesia, Moldova, Mongolia, Morocco, Mozambique, Namibia, Nepal, Netherlands, New Zealand, Nicaragua, Niger, Nigeria, Norway, Oman, Pakistan, Panama, Papua New Guinea, Paraguay, Peru, Philippines, Poland, Portugal, Qatar, Romania, Russia, Rwanda, St. Kitts and Nevis, St. Lucia, St. Vincent and the Grenadines, Saudi Arabia, Senegal, Sierra Leone, Singapore, Slovakia, Slovenia, South Africa, South Korea, Sri Lanka, Sudan, Suriname, Swaziland, Sweden, Switzerland, Syria, Tanzania, Thailand, Togo, Trinidad and Tobago, Tunisia, Turkey, Turkmenistan, Uganda, Ukraine, United Arab Emirates, United Kingdom, Uruguay, Uzbekistan, Venezuela, Vietnam, Yemen, Yugoslavia, Zambia, Zimbabwe.

Embassy Annual Goodwill Tour

On the second Saturday in May some of the city's most splendid embassy buildings and residences are open to tour 10 a.m.–5 p.m. in which shuttle buses transport those who have purchased tickets around the city to visit these notable structures and their resplendent interiors. For information and to order tickets phone (202) 636-4225.

Embassy Events

While the receptions held at foreign embassies are limited to those invited, many of the diplomatic cultural activities welcome public participation. They range from film showings to lectures, theatrical performances, concerts, and exhibitions of art. Normally these events showcase the work of specialists, musicians, and artists from the country represented and many of these programs, which are scheduled at art and cultural centers, museums, and the embassies are free. Information about these activities is available by telephoning the embassies, many of which will add the interested inquirer to the mailing list of their cultural offerings. *See also The Party Digest, Washington Diplomat.*

Embassy Inn 1627 16th St. NW btw Q and R Sts. (202) 234-7800 or (800) 423-9111 www.bedandbreakfast.com

This is a modestly priced 38-room hotel in a 4-story townhouse with no elevators situated on a pleasant street amid older homes and churches. The rooms are small but the atmosphere is friendly, and continental breakfast and evening sherry are among the amenities. Metro: Dupont Circle.

ular description of the 2-mile stretch of Massachusetts Ave. NW Observatory Circles. Many of the city's foreign chancelleries and dences are found with flags fluttering in front of the Beaux Arts-style structures, which in earlier years were privately owned mansions of Washington's most illustrious socialites, politicians, diplomats, tycoons, and high-ranking military officers.

Embassy Row Hilton 2015 Massachusetts Ave. NW (202) 265-1600 or (800) 445-8667 www.hilton.com

Located one block from Dupont Circle at the entryway to Embassy Row, this renovated 193-room expensive hostelry features a rooftop pool, fitness room, marble bathrooms, and complimentary daily newspaper among its amenities. Metro: Dupont Circle.

Embassy Square 2000 N St. NW at 20th St. (202) 659-9000 or (800) 424-2999 www.staydc.com

This 278-suite Summerfield Suites Hotel located 1½ blocks from the Metro offers a range of choices at fairly expensive rates from efficiencies to larger apartments designed to meet the needs of families relocating to the D.C. area or those on business assignments. There's a swimming pool, guest access to a nearby health club, and continental breakfast. Metro: Dupont Circle.

Embassy Suites at Tysons Corner 8517 Leesburg Pike btw Chain Bridge and Dulles Access Rds. (703) 883-0707 or (800) EMBASSY www.embassy-suites.com

Very close to Tysons Corner Center, this showy hotel contains 232 two-room suites, an indoor pool, Jacuzzi and sauna, complimentary breakfast, and shuttle service in a 5-mile radius.

Embassy Suites Downtown 1250 22nd St. NW btw M and N Sts. (202) 857-3388 or (800) EMBASSY www.embassy-suites.com

This modern structure has a sky-lit picturesque atrium and each of the 318 two-room suites in this upscale and expensive residence is equipped with all the latest features and amenities. There is an indoor swimming pool and exercise room and a complimentary cooked breakfast and evening cocktail hour. Metro: Foggy Bottom-GWU or Dupont Circle.

Embassy Suites Hotel at Chevy Chase Pavilion 4300 Military Rd. NW at 43rd St. (202) 362-9300 or (800) EMBASSY www.embassy-suites.com

Located right at the upscale shopping mall that is just between northwest D.C. and Maryland, this 198-suite expensive hotel includes complimentary breakfast and happy hour, health club, and indoor pool among its attractions and is only 15 minutes by Metro to downtown D.C. Metro: Friendship Heights.

Embassy Suites Old Town Alexandria 1900 Diagonal Rd., Alexandria, VA (703) 684-8902 or (800) EMBASSY www.embassy-suites.com

Located about 100 yards from the Metro station, this expensive, modern 2-room suites hotel offers an indoor pool, exercise room, and complimentary breakfast and evening cocktail reception among its features. Metro: King Street.

Emergencies

As in virtually everywhere in the United States, dial 911 (free from public phones) for emergencies of any kind—police, fire, or accident. Other more specific crisis response numbers are: Poison Control (202) 625-3333; 24-hour hospital emergency rooms: George Washington University Medical Center at 23rd St. and Pennsylvania Ave. NW (202) 715-4911; Georgetown University Medical Center at 3800 Reservoir Rd. NW (202) 784-2119; Rape Crisis Hotline (202) 333-7273; Police (non-emergency) (202) 727-1010.

Emmett Statue *see* Robert Emmett Statue.

Engine Company 21 1763 Lanier Place NW www.dcfdhistory.com/e21hist.htm

Built in 1908 on a residential street not far from Adams Morgan by Appleton P. Clark Jr., this quaint-looking stuccoed red brick building with its tower resembles a Spanish mission more than it does a firehouse. Metro: Dupont Circle, then L2 Bus.

Enid A. Haupt Garden 10th and Independence Ave. NW (202) 357-2700 http://gardens.si.edu/

This 4-acre garden, which opened in 1987, is surrounded by the National Museum of African Art, the Smithsonian Castle, the Sackler/Freer Galleries, and the Arts and Industries Building of the Smithsonian complex. Actually, it is a garden on the roof of the building that lies beneath it. It is a lovely contemplative setting containing antique benches, nineteenth-century lampposts, brick walkways, and changing seasonal plantings. From Memorial Day to the end of September it is open 7 a.m.–8 p.m., and October to May 7 a.m.–5:45 p.m. Metro: Smithsonian.

Enriqueta's 2811 M St. NW, btw 28th and 29th Sts. (202) 338-7772

This moderate-priced Georgetown landmark features authentic Mexican fare rather than Tex-Mex. It is a charming yet casual place with tasty servings of prepared dishes of pork, chicken, beef, and seafood. Open for lunch Mon–Fri, dinner nightly. Metro: Foggy Bottom-GWU, then 30, 32, 34, 35, or 36 Bus.

Enterprise 2802 Enterprise Rd., Mitchellville, MD (301) 249-2040

This is one of the best-maintained public golf courses in Washington's close-by suburbs. It is a 6,200-yard par 72, 18-hole course with exceedingly well-landscaped grounds. It is located some 30 minutes from center city off the Beltway in Prince George's County. Turn off at Exit 17A to second light, turn left, and at the next light turn left onto 193 and go ½ mile. Information and details at (301) 249-2040.

Environmental Film Festival

For one week in mid-March this noteworthy film event is held at various locations around the city. Details at (202) 342-2564 or at www.dcenvironmentalfilm fest.org.

Equatorial Guinea Embassy 2020 16th St. NW (202) 518-5700 www.embassy.org/embassies/gq.html

Metro: Dupont Circle or Columbia Heights.

Equinox 818 Connecticut Ave. NW btw H and I Sts. (202) 331-8118 www.equinoxrestaurant.com

Serving American bistro fare, this moderately priced restaurant has found a loyal following for its simple yet imaginative culinary concoctions. Open for lunch Mon–Fri, dinner nightly. Metro: Farragut West.

Eritrea Embassy 1708 New Hampshire Ave. NW (202) 319-1991 www.embassy .org/embassies/er.html

Estonia Embassy 2131 Massachusetts Ave. NW (202) 588-0101 www.estemb.org

Ethiopia Embassy 3506 International Dr. NW (202) 364-1200 www.ethiopian embassy.org
Metro: Van Ness-UDC.

Ethiopian Restaurants *see* Addis Ababa, Awash, Harambee Café, Meskerem, Red Sea, Zed's Ethiopian Cuisine. *See also* African Restaurants, www.dcpages.com, www .restaurant.com, www.washingtonpost.com, www.opentable.com.

Ethnic and Community Museums *see* Alexandria Archeology Museum, Alexandria Black History Resources Center, Anacostia Museum and Center for African American History and Culture, B'nai B'rith Klutznick National Jewish Museum, Charles Sumner School Museum and Archives, Jewish Historical Society of Greater Washington, Lillian and Albert Small Jewish Museum, National Museum of African Art, National Museum of American Jewish Military History. *See also* Art and Design Museums, Historical Museums.

Ethnic Foods *see* Specialty Food Stores and Bakeries.

Ethnic Music *see* Rock, Alternative, and Ethnic Music.

Etrusco 1606 20th St. NW (202) 667-0047
This restaurant offers a limited menu of delicious Tuscan dishes. Try the minestrone or the *ragù* of duck or the braised veal shank. Hours Mon–Sat 5:30 p.m.–10:30 p.m. Moderate prices. Metro: Dupont Circle.

Events in Washington D.C. and Environs *see* Abraham Lincoln Birthday Celebration, Adams Morgan Day, Air Force Band Summer Concerts, Alexandria Christmas Tree Lighting, Alexandria Garden Tour, Alexandria Red Cross Waterfront Festival, American College Theater Festival, American Indian Heritage Month, Andrews Air Force Base Open House, Annual Capital Area Auto Show, Annual Seafaring Celebration, Bach Marathon, Bastille Day, Bethesda Literary Festival, Black Family Reunion, Black History Month, Boo at the Zoo, Cadillac Grand Prix, Capital Classic, Capital Jazz Fest, Caribbean Carnival, Celebrate Fairfax, Cherry Blossom Festival, Children's Festival at Wolf Trap Theater, Chili Championship Cook-Off, Chinese New Year's Celebration, Christmas Tree Lighting, Columbus Day Ceremonies, Constitution Day Commemoration, D.C. Armory Antiques Fair, D.C. Blues Festival, Dance Africa D.C., Dupont Circle Historic Homes Tour, Dupont-Kalorama Museum Walk Day, Easter Egg Hunt for Blind Children, Easter Sunrise Service, Embassy Annual Goodwill Tour, Environmental Film Festival, Festival of Lights, Filmfest D.C., Frederick Douglass Birthday Celebration, Gay Pride Celebration, George Washington Birthday Celebration, Georgetown Annual Garden Tour, Georgetown House Tour, Georgia Avenue Day, German American Day, Greek Fall

Festival, Greek Spring Festival, Halloween High Heel Race, Halloween Monster Bash at the Capital Children's Museum, Independence Day Celebrations, International Children's Festival, International Jewish Film Festival, Jefferson's Birthday, Jewish Film Festival, Kalorama Embassy and House Tour, Kemper Open, Kennedy Center for the Performing Arts Open House, Labor Day Weekend Concert, Latino Festival, Legg Mason Tennis Classic, Marine Band Summer Concerts, Marine Corps Marathon, Martin Luther King Birthday Celebrations, Mary McLeod Bethune Celebration, Maryland Renaissance Festival, Memorial Day Celebrations and Ceremonies, Memorial Day Jazz Festival, Menorah Lighting, Mostly Mozart Music Festival, Mother's Day Tour, Mount Pleasant Festival, Mount Vernon Holiday Tours, Mount Vernon Wine Festival, National Capital Barbecue Battle, National Law Enforcement Officers Candlelight Vigil, National Race for the Cure, Navy Band Summer Concerts, New Year's Eve Celebrations, Old Town Arts and Crafts Fair, Reel Affirmations, Robert E. Lee Birthday Celebration, Rock Creek Park Day, St. Patrick's Day Parade, Scottish Christmas Walk, Shakespeare Theatre in the Park, Smithsonian Annual Kite Festival, Smithsonian Asian Pacific American Heritage Month, Smithsonian Craft Show, Smithsonian Folklife Festival, Soap Box Derby, Sugarloaf Crafts Festival, Takoma Park Folk Festival, Takoma Park JazzFest, Taste of Arlington, Taste of Bethesda, Taste of D.C., Taste of the Nation, Taste of Wheaton, Theodore Roosevelt Birthday, Twilight Tattoo, UNIFEST, U.S. Navy Birthday, Vienna Halloween Parade, Virginia Scottish Games, Washington Antiques Show, Washington Boat Show, Washington Craft Show, Washington Home and Garden Show, Washington International Horse Show, Washington National Cathedral Christmas Celebration, Washington National Cathedral Flower Mart, Washington National Cathedral Open House, Washington National Cathedral Summer Music Festival, Washington Tennis Classic, Washington Theatre Festival, White House Easter Egg Roll, White House Fall House and Garden Tour, White House Spring Garden and Grounds Tour, William Shakespeare's Birthday.

Events in Washington D.C. by Month

January *see* Martin Luther King Birthday Celebrations, Robert E. Lee Birthday Celebration, Washington Antiques Show.

February *see* Abraham Lincoln Birthday Celebration, Black History Month, Chinese New York Celebration, Frederick Douglass Birthday Celebration, George Washington Birthday Celebration, Sugarloaf Crafts Festival, Washington Boat Show.

March *see* Bach Marathon, Cherry Blossom Festival, D.C. Armory Antiques Fair, Environmental Film Festival, St. Patrick's Day Parade, Smithsonian Annual Kite Festival, Washington Home and Garden Show.

April *see* Alexandria Garden Tour, American College Theater Festival, Bethesda Literary Festival, Capital Classic, Easter Egg Hunt for Blind Children, Easter Sunrise Service, Filmfest D.C., Georgetown House Tour, International Jewish Film Festival, Jefferson's Birthday, Smithsonian Craft Show, Sugarloaf Crafts Festival, Taste of the Nation, Washington National Cathedral Flower Mart, White House Easter Egg Roll, White House Spring Garden and Grounds Tours, William Shakespeare's Birthday.

May *see* Air Force Band Summer Concerts, Andrews Air Force Base Open House, Army Band Summer Concerts, Chili Championship Cook-Off, D.C. Armory Antiques Fair, Embassy Annual Goodwill Tour, Georgetown Annual Garden Tour, Greek Spring Festival, International Jewish Film Festival, Memorial Day Celebrations and Ceremonies, Memorial Day Jazz Festival, Mother's Day Tour, Mount Vernon Wine Festival, National Law Enforcement Officers Candlelight Vigil, Navy Band Summer Concerts, Old Town Arts and Crafts Fair, Smithsonian Annual Kite Festival, Smithsonian Asian Pacific American Heritage Month, Takoma Park JazzFest, Taste of Arlington, Taste of Wheaton, Twilight Tattoo, Washington National Cathedral Flower Mart.

June *see* Alexandria Red Cross Waterfront Festival, Capital Jazz Fest, Caribbean Carnival, Celebrate Fairfax, Dance Africa–D.C., Dupont-Kalorama Museum Walk Day, Gay Pride Celebration, Kemper Open, Marine Band Summer Concerts, Mostly Mozart Music Festival, Mount Pleasant Festival, National Capital District Barbecue Battle, National Race for the Cure, Shakespeare Theatre in the Park, Smithsonian Folklife Festival, UNIFEST, Washington National Cathedral Summer Music Festival.

July *see* Air Force Band Summer Concerts, Bastille Day, Cadillac Grand Prix, Children's Festival at Wolf Trap Theater, Independence Day Celebrations, Mary McLeod Bethune Celebration, Latino Festival, Legg Mason Tennis Classic, Soap Box Derby, Virginia Scottish Games, Washington Theater Festival.

August *see* Andrews Air Force Base Open House, Georgia Avenue Day, Legg Mason Tennis Classic, Maryland Renaissance Festival, Washington Tennis Classic.

September *see* Adams Morgan Day, Black Family Reunion, Children's Festival at Wolf Trap Theater, Constitution Day Commemoration, D.C. Blues Festival, German American Day, Greek Fall Festival, International Children's Festival, Kalorama Embassy and House Tour, Kennedy Center for the Performing Arts Open House, Labor Day Weekend Concert, Rock Creek Park Day, Sugarloaf Crafts Festival, Takoma Park Folk Festival, Washington National Cathedral Open House.

October *see* Alexandria Home and Arts Festival, Boo at the Zoo, Columbus Day Ceremonies, D.C. Armory Antiques Fair, Dupont Circle Historic Homes Tour, Halloween High Heel Race, Halloween Monster Bash at the Capital Children's Museum, Marine Marathon, Reel Affirmations, Taste of Bethesda, Taste of D.C., Theodore Roosevelt Birthday, U.S. Navy Birthday, Vienna Halloween Parade, Washington International Horse Show, White House Fall House and Garden Tour.

November *see* Alexandria Christmas Tree Lighting, American Indian Heritage Month Ceremonies, Annual Seafaring Celebration, Sugarloaf Crafts Festival, Veterans Day Ceremonies, Washington Craft Show.

December *see* Annual Capital Area Auto Show, Christmas Tree Lighting, D.C. Armory Antiques Fair, Festival of Lights, Jewish Film Festival, Menorah Lighting, Mount Vernon Holiday Tours, New Year's Eve Celebrations, Scottish Christmas Walk, Washington National Cathedral Christmas Celebration.

Everett House *see* Turkey Embassy.

Evermay 1623 28th St. NW btw Q and R Sts. www.cr.nps.gov/nr/travel/wash/dc15.htm

This elegant 2½-story manor house is one of Georgetown's showplaces. It was built in 1801 by Nicholas Hedges for a Scot, Samuel Davidson, and restored in the 1920s to its original splendor. The house, which boasts a lovely garden of boxwood, azaleas, and magnolias, is not open to the public except on special occasions.

Ewing Gallery *see* Kathleen Ewing Gallery.

Executive Club Suites Alexandria 610 Bashford La., Alexandria, VA (703) 739-2582 or (800) 535-2582 www.dcexeclub.com

Located at the north side of Old Town, this all-suites hotel has comfortable elegantly decorated living rooms, bedrooms, and well-equipped kitchens. This moderately expensive hostelry provides complimentary continental breakfast and evening reception, health club, outdoor pool, and convenient shuttle service to National Airport Metro station.

Executive Office Building *see* Old Executive Office Building.

Exercise *see* Fitness Centers, Participatory Sports Activity.

Exorcist Steps

Located opposite the old barn on M St. at 36th and Prospect Sts. in Georgetown, this very steep staircase achieved fame and notoriety for its use in the last scene of the movie *The Exorcist*. Metro: Foggy Bottom-GWU, then 30, 32, 34, 35, or 36 Bus.

FBI Building *see* J. Edgar Hoover FBI Building.

F. Scott Fitzgerald Grave Site
The grave sites of F. Scott Fitzgerald and his wife, Zelda, can be found at the cemetery of St. Mary's Catholic Church (301) 424-5550, located at 520 Viers Mills Rd. between Stonestreet Ave. and Hungerford Dr. in Rockville, Maryland. Their remains were moved here in 1975 from their original graves in Rockville Cemetery. Zelda was born in Rockville. Metro: Rockville.

F. Scott Fitzgerald Theatre Rockville Civic Center Park, Baltimore Rd. at Edmonston Rd., Rockville, MD, box office (240) 314-8690 www.ci.rockville.md.us/arts/theater.htm
This 500-seat theater, named for Rockville's noted author, is used by the Rockville Musical Theatre, Rockville Little Theatre, Rockville Civic Ballet, Victorian Lyric Opera Company, the National Chamber Orchestra, and the Musical Theatre Center. It is located in the Rockville Civic Center Park. Box office hours: Tues–Sat 2 p.m.–7 p.m., and two hours prior to performances. By car from Rte. 28 and I-270, proceed east on Rte. 28, cross Rte. 355, and follow Rte. 28 east (turns left at first light beyond Rte. 355). Travel 4 blocks to Baltimore Rd., turn right, go 3 blocks to Edmonston Dr., turn left, and Civic Center Park entrance is immediately on the right.

F Street Neighborhood
This area on F St. NW between 10th and 15th Sts. is the heart of the old downtown district, which flourished well into the post–World War II period. It has lost its luster, but the neighborhood still contains the National Theater, Ford's Theater, the Warner Theatre, and the Shops at National Place. It is only a few blocks above the Mall, where many of Washington's popular museums are. Metro: Metro Center.

Faccia Luna 2400 Wisconsin Ave. NW btw Calvert St. and Hall Pl. (202) 337-3132 www.faccialuna.com

Pizzas here are considered among the best in the city with their thin, chewy crusts and more than twenty different toppings baked in a brick oven. The subs are also a treat. Prices are modest. Open for lunch and dinner Mon–Sat, dinner only on Sun. Metro: Foggy Bottom-GWU, then 30, 32, 34, 35, or 36 Bus. Other locations in Virginia are in Arlington at 2909 Wilson Blvd. (703) 276-3099; and Old Town Alexandria at 823 S Washington St. (703) 838-5998.

Factory Outlets *see* Discount Stores and Factory Outlets.

Fadó Irish Pub 808 7th St. NW btw H and I Sts. (202) 789-0066

Designed to resemble a true Irish ambiance with its interesting decorative touches in the drinking areas, the food here includes the staples of Irish fare and some other dishes as well as a great selection of beers and whiskies. Food and drink are quite reasonably priced. Open daily 11:30 a.m.–2 a.m. or 3 a.m. Metro: Gallery Pl.-Chinatown.

Fahrney's Pens 1317 F St. NW near 13th St. (202) 628-2116 www.fahrneyspens .com

This firm has been selling writing instruments since early in the twentieth century and carries as complete a selection of all the brands as can be found in the city. Open Mon–Fri 9:30 a.m.–6 p.m., Sat 10 a.m.–5 p.m. Metro: Metro Center.

Fair Oaks Mall at intersection of I-66 and Hwy. 50, Fairfax, VA (703) 359-8300 www.shopfairoaksmall.com

This very large shopping center includes more than 200 shops, boutiques, and services, including some major specialty and department stores in the mix. By car take the I-66 West Exit off the Beltway (I-495) to Hwy. 50 West. *See also* www.com muterpage.com/venues/venue-shop.htm.

Fairfax Art League Gallery Old Town Hall, 3999 University Dr., Fairfax, VA (703) 273-2377 www.fairfaxartleague.org

This cooperative represents more than 100 local artists. Works include oils, watercolors, photography, and mixed media. Open Tues and Fri 10 a.m.–5 p.m., Wed–Thurs 10 a.m.–3 p.m. Metro: Vienna/Fairfax-GMU, exit station and take the QGO1 CUE Bus toward Gold 1 to the stop at University Dr. and Main St. Walk south on University Dr. *See also* www.commuterpage.venues/sightseeing_VA.htm.

Fairfax Audubon Society 4022 Hummer Rd., Annandale, VA (703) 256-6895 www .fairfaxaudubon.org

This is a very active organization that arranges frequent educational programs and bird walks. Information at (703) 256-6895 or www.fairfaxaudubon.org.

Fairfax City www.ci.fairfax.va.us

This place goes back to pre–Revolutionary War days, offering traces of the past in the Historic District where a number of buildings and homes from that early era can still be found. While downtown Fairfax retains its town-like flavor with its small houses and restaurants, the surrounding area is like the rest of the burgeoning Washington suburbs with malls and housing developments. Fairfax is home to one of the largest academic institutions in the state's higher-education system—George

Mason University. The Metro serves the area with a station at Vienna/Fairfax-GMU.

Fairfax City Cemetery 10561 Main St., Fairfax, VA (703) 385-8414 www.ci.fair fax.va.us

This is the final resting place of some 200 unknown Confederate War dead with a granite obelisk marking their graves. Metro: Vienna/Fairfax-GMU, exit the station and take the QGR1 CUE Bus toward Green 1 to the stop at University Dr. and Main St. and walk west on Main St.

Fairfax County Convention and Visitors Bureau 8300 Boone Blvd. at Tysons Corner, Vienna, VA (703) 790-3329 www.visitfairfax.org

This source of information for tourists is open Mon–Fri 8:30 a.m.–5 p.m. For information, call or check the Web site.

Fairfax Farmers Market Van Dyke Park on Old Lee Hwy. (Rte. 237), Fairfax, VA (703) 941-7987 www.washingtonfamilies.com/guides/market.htm

Open Tues 8 a.m.–12:30 p.m. from early May to late October; vegetables and fruit are sold by farm producers.

Fairfax Ice Arena 3779 Pickett Rd., Fairfax, VA (703) 323-1131 or (703) 323-1132 www.fairfaxicearena.com

A very popular indoor skating facility with a variable schedule of open hours. Skates can be rented for a modest charge. Hockey games take place here as well. Best to call for current schedule or check the Web site. Metro: Vienna/Fairfax-GMU, then take Fairfax City Q Bus to stop at Hwy. 236 and Pickett Rd.

Fairfax Museum and Visitor Center 10209 Main St., Fairfax, VA (703) 385-8414 or (800) 545-7950 www.ci.fairfax.va.us/CityHistory/VisitorCenter_and_Museum .htm

This museum is open daily 9 a.m.–5 p.m. and admission is free. It features exhibits of local history and sponsors programs relating to the region's past, including the Civil War period. It also provides informative brochures on the area and a self-guided walking tour map of Old Town Fairfax sites. Metro: Vienna/Fairfax-GMU, exit the station and take the QGO1 CUE Bus toward Gold 1 to the stop at Old Lee Hwy. and North St. Walk 1 block on Old Lee Hwy., turn left on Main St. and walk 4 blocks east. *See also* www.commuterpage.com.venues/sightseeing_VA.htm.

Falls Church www.ci.falls-church.va.us

This community began with a church in 1733 when the original wooden church was erected. The church and its cemetery remain as important historic landmarks. The church is now a brick building that was completely renovated in 1959. Falls Church is an independent municipality, which retains its small-town flavor with a mix of handsome older Victorian homes and newer townhouse developments. While the City of Falls Church covers only 2 square miles, the Falls Church region embraces a much wider area in Virginia. Much of the area between northern Arlington and McLean are part of it. East Falls Church encompasses the area between Arlington Blvd. and the East Falls Church Metro station. West Falls Church is an area of mostly private homes except for some apartment complexes situated between the West Falls Church Metro station and Tysons Corner.

Falls Church Episcopal Church 115 E Fairfax St. on U.S. Hwy. 29 btw E Broad St. and S Washington St., Falls Church, VA (703) 532-7600 www.thefallschurch.org

Constructed in 1733 near a road leading to the falls on the Potomac River, the building was replaced in 1769 at the same site. Complete renovation took place in 1959. It was a recruiting station during the American Revolution, and in the Civil War it became a hospital and stable. Services continue to be conducted here, and now fully restored to its early appearance, the church contains a small museum of historical artifacts. Open Mon–Fri 9 a.m.–5 p.m. Admission free. Metro: East Falls Church, then a 20-minute walk.

Falls Church Farmers Market 300 Park Ave., Falls Church, VA (703) 248-5077 www.localharvest.org/farms/M1109

Operating in the City Hall parking lot on Saturdays 8 a.m.–noon, from early May to before Thanksgiving, producers of farm products sell their wares here.

Family Tree of Life Statue www.thedistrict.com/thingsto/tourism/monmem.htm

Adjacent to the Carter Barron Amphitheater in Rock Creek Park at 16th and Colorado Sts. NW, the 15-foot-tall red oak totem monument by Dennis Stoy Jr. is designed to represent an African-American family. There is free parking at the Carter Barron Amphitheater site and it can also be reached by Bus S1.

Fantasy Flights (301) 417-0000 www.huseonica.org/fantasyflights

The owner/pilot of this company has been taking people up in 1-hour to 1½-hour flights in a five-person balloon since the early 1980s. They begin at sunrise and soar over Sugarloaf Mountain in the area between Gaithersburg and Frederick in the Maryland countryside, subject, of course, to suitable weather conditions. It costs $200 per person, includes no more than four passengers, and reservations and deposit well in advance are required. Fuller details at (301) 417-0000.

Farmers Markets *see* Adams Morgan Farmers Market, Alexandria Farmers Market, Anacostia Farmers Market, Annandale Farmers Market, Arlington Farmers Market, Bethesda Farm Women's Cooperative Market, Bowie Farmers Market, Burke Centre Farmers Market, City of Rockville Farmers Market, College Park Farmers Market, Columbia Pike Farmers Market, Community Farmers Market, D.C. Open Air Farmers Market, Del Ray Farmers Market, Dupont Circle Freshfarm Market, Eastern Market, Eastern Market Outdoor Farmers Market, Fairfax Farmers Market, Falls Church Farmers Market, Frying Pan Park Farmers Market, Gaithersburg Farmers Market, Gaithersburg Main Street Pavilion Farmers Market, Herndon Farmers Market, Montgomery County Farm Women's Market, Mount Vernon Farmers Market, Old Town Fairfax Farmers Market, Prince George's County Farmers Market, Reston Farmers Market, Rockville Farmers Market, Silver Spring Farmers Market, Takoma Park Farmers Market, Union Market (Florida Avenue Market), Wheaton Farmers Market. *See also* www.washingtonpost.com.

Farragut Sculpture in Farragut Square, K St. btw 16th and 17th Sts. NW

This 10-foot-high erect statue of America's first admiral, David G. Farragut, was sculpted by Vinnie Ream Hoxie in 1881. She also created the marble statue of Lincoln in the Capitol Rotunda. Metro: Farragut North.

Farragut Square K St. btw 16th and K Sts. NW

This may be the most heavily used park in the city. It is very popular with brown-baggers enjoying their lunches while watching the passing parade or the spontaneous or scheduled events that take place here. The statue of Adm. David G. Farragut of Civil War fame, who uttered the cry, "Damn the torpedoes! Full steam ahead!" is the centerpiece of this attractive urban park. Metro: Farragut North.

Faryab 4917 Cordell Ave. btw Old Georgetown Rd. and Norfolk St., Bethesda, MD (301) 951-3484

This is a moderately priced Afghan restaurant serving all the specialty dishes of that region of the world like sautéed pumpkin, *boulani*, and *aushak*, the centerpiece of any Afghanistan bill of fare. Open for lunch Tues–Fri, dinner Tues–Sun. Metro: Bethesda.

Fashion Center at Pentagon City 1100 S Hayes St. at Army-Navy Dr. and I-395, Arlington, VA (703) 415-2400 www.fashioncentrepentagon.com

This is one of the area's most elegant malls boasting a glass atrium containing some 160 or so retail shops, department stores including Macy's, and specialty boutiques, a food court, and movie theaters located on its four levels. It is situated at its own Metro stop some 15 minutes from downtown. Metro: Pentagon City. *See also* www.commuterpage.com/venues/venue-shop.htm.

Fast Eddie's 1520 K St. NW near 15th St. (202) 638-6800 www.fasteddies.com

This place started out as Fanatics Sports and Billiards. It's got lots of TVs, five pool tables, and dart games and is open daily 11:30 a.m.–2 a.m. or so. Lunch and dinner are served as well as virtually every kind of beer. Metro: McPherson Square or Farragut North.

Federal Bureau of Investigation *see* J. Edgar Hoover FBI Building.

Federal Gateway (Web site) www.fedgate.org

A supermarket (except it's free) of government online publications and information, be it national, state, or local, allowing you to compile needed information by topic rather than contacting the issuing organization. You can browse through "U.S. Historical Documents" or "Cool Fed Sites of the Week" listing such resources as "Federal Forms" and "U.S. Consumer Gateway."

Federal Judiciary Building *see* Thurgood Marshall Federal Judiciary Building.

Federal Reserve Board C St. btw 20th and 21st Sts. NW (202) 452-3149 www .federalreserve.gov

Located in an imposing marble Art Deco structure with pillared entrance hallways designed by architect Paul Cret in 1937 and with a 1-acre garden fashioned by landscape architects Wolfgang Oehme and James van Sweden, this building is the site of the Federal Reserve Board operations. Its gallery shows nineteenth and twentieth-century paintings, sculpture, and works on paper. The gallery has customarily been open to visitors and a weekly tour of the structure was possible, but as of summer 2002 the building has not been accessible to tourists. The current status of visits is accessible by calling or checking the Web site.

Federal Trade Commission *see* Apex Building.

Federal Triangle washington-landmarks.com/federal.html
   This section of the city is formed by the intersection of Constitution Ave. with the diagonal Pennsylvania Ave., bounded on the west side by 15th St. NW and on the east by 6th St. NW. The area consists of a mass of government Classical Revival buildings erected principally between 1929 and 1938. The most recent structure is the 1997 Ronald Reagan International Trade Building, completed in 1997 on the last available site. It's a remarkably uniform line of structures except for the Old Post Office and the District Building, which were saved from successive efforts at demolition over the years. Different architects worked on the buildings, but they all are very similar with their granite façades, stone reliefs, columns, and virtuous inscriptions on their walls. Metro: Federal Triangle on the west side, Archives-Navy Memorial on the east side.

FedEx Field Arena Dr. off Lottsford Rd., Landover, MD (301) 276-6050 www .justrt.com/index.htm
   This 80,000-seat colossus in a close-in Maryland suburb was constructed in 1997 as the home of the Washington Redskins. The problem is getting tickets to games since seats are sold out years in advance and the waiting list for season tickets is huge. A better prospect is the occasional summer music concerts scheduled here. Information at (301) 276-5000. Metro: Cheverly, Landover, or Addison Road, then take a shuttle bus directly to FedEx Field. Buses go to and from the stadium every 15 minutes. During regular season games, buses begin 3 hours before game time and end 1 hour after the game. For Monday night games, the shuttle runs from 5 p.m. until 1 a.m. *See also* Washington Redskins.

Felix 2406 18th St. NW btw Belmont and Columbia Rds. (202) 483-3549 www .thefelix.com
   This lively and moderately expensive Adams Morgan spot is a blend of restaurant and lounge with mammoth martinis, renowned matzo ball soup, and imaginative other food creations. Open for dinner every day. Metro: Dupont Circle, then 62 Bus.

La Ferme 7101 Brookville Rd. off East-West Hwy., Chevy Chase, MD (301) 986-5255 www.lafermerestaurant.com
   This expensive restaurant enjoys a reputation for the quality of its well-prepared meat and fish dishes. It is located in a residential suburban area and the décor inside this place is reminiscent of a French country inn. Open for lunch Tues–Fri, dinner Tues–Sun, and brunch on Sun. To reach the restaurant turn off East-West Hwy. on to Rte. 186 (which is Brookville Rd.) and the restaurant is on the left side before the second stoplight.

Festival of Lights Washington Mormon Temple, Visitors' Center, 9900 Stoneybrook Dr., Kensington, MD (301) 587-0144 www.mormonstoday.com
   During the Christmas season hundreds of lights are strung on the grounds of

this imposing temple, and inside the visitors' center the trees are decorated with ornaments from many parts of the world. To reach the site, take Exit 33 Connecticut Ave. off the Beltway (I-495) and go north toward Kensington. Turn right on Beach Dr., which is very close to the turnoff and drive a short distance to the Temple on Stoneybrook Dr.

Festivals *see* Events in Washington D.C. and Environs, Events in Washington D.C. by Month.

57 N Arts Complex 57 N St. NW near 1st St. (202) 234-6451 www.superbig cool.com

This quaint 1890 stable building serves as a creative center for a collective of artists working in various media. Four shows a year are scheduled in the upstairs gallery. Twice a year there are open studios, which include exhibits, demonstrations, and entertainment. Call for information or check the Web site. Metro: Mount Vernon Square.

Fiji Embassy 2233 Wisconsin Ave. NW, Suite 240 (202) 337-8320
Metro: Tenleytown-AU.

Filene's Basement 5300 Wisconsin Ave. NW in Mazza Gallerie (202) 996-0208 http://washington.dc.retailguide.com/data/s101059.htm

Right at the edge of the city in an upscale shopping mall is this mecca for bargain seekers looking for steep savings on designer men and women's clothing, shoes, and accessories. Metro: Friendship Heights. Other locations in the city are 529 14th St. NW (202) 638-4110; 1133 Connecticut Ave. NW (202) 872-8430.

Film Festivals *see* Events in Washington D.C., Events in Washington D.C. by Month.

Film Groups *see* American Film Institute, Cinema Arts Film Club.

Film Revivals *see* Foreign and Independent Films.

Filmfest D.C. (202) 274-6810 www.filmfestdc.org

During a two-week period starting in mid- or late April the city hosts some 75 carefully selected international and American films, some of them shown in premiere performances. The venues are movie theaters, embassies, and museums around town and the screenings are sometimes linked with discussions with filmmakers and receptions. Some showings are free, most are priced. Call or visit the Web site for details.

Films *see* Foreign and Independent Films, Movie Theaters.

Finland Embassy 3301 Massachusetts Ave. NW (202) 298-5800 www.finland.org
Metro: Dupont Circle.

Firehook Bakery and Coffeehouse 1909 Q St. NW at Connecticut Ave. (202) 588-9296 www.firehook.com

A fine place for wonderful breads, muffins, and cookies, tasty and thick sandwiches, and pies and cakes. Open from 7 a.m. weekdays and 9 a.m. Sat and Sun. Metro: Dupont Circle. Other locations are downtown, 912 17th St. NW (202) 429-

2253; Cleveland Park, 3411 Connecticut Ave. NW (202) 362-2253; Old Town Alexandria, 105 S Union St. (703) 519-8021.

First Baptist Church of the City of Washington 1328 16th St. NW at O St. (202) 387-2206 www.firstbaptistdc.org

This striking neo-Gothic structure was designed by architect Harold Waggoner in 1955 on the same site as an earlier church built in a fundamentally different style. The stained glass windows are among the church's most attractive embellishments. Metro: Dupont Circle.

First Church of Christ, Scientist 1770 Euclid St., ½ block east of 18th St. and Columbus Rd. (202) 265-1390

Constructed in 1911 by architectural firm Marsh & Peter and E. D. Ryerson, this brick and limestone building was built in classical style with an entrance porch colonnade. Services are scheduled here regularly in Spanish. Metro: Woodley Park-Zoo, then 90, 91, 92, 93, or 96 Bus; or Dupont Circle, then L2 Bus.

First-Class Hotels *see* Capital Hilton, Crystal Gateway Marriott, Doubletree Hotel-National Airport, Embassy Row Hilton, Embassy Suite at Tysons Corner, Embassy Suites Downtown, Embassy Suites Hotel at Chevy Chase Pavilion, Embassy Suites Old Town Alexandria, Executive Club Suites Alexandria, Georgetown Suites, Grand Hyatt Washington, Greenbelt Marriott, Holiday Inn Bethesda, Holiday Inn National Airport, Hotel George, Hotel Sofitel, Hotel Washington, Hyatt Arlington, Hyatt Regency Bethesda, Hyatt Regency Crystal City, J. W. Marriott Hotel, Jefferson Hotel, Key Bridge Marriott, Loew's L'Enfant Plaza, Marriott Bethesda, Marriott Wardman Park Hotel, Monticello Hotel, Morrison-Clark Inn, Morrison House, Omni Shoreham Hotel, Radisson Barcelo Hotel, Radisson Plaza Hotel, Renaissance Mayflower Hotel, Sheraton National, Sheraton Suites Alexandria, Topaz Hotel, Washington Hilton and Towers, Washington Suites Hotel, Westin Fairfax, Wyndham Washington Hotel. *See also* www.frommers.com.

First Division Monument in President's Park South, State Pl. and 17th St. NW www.bigredone.org/about/monuments.cfm

This memorial 90-foot statue was designed by sculptor Daniel Chester French in 1924. It is a winged-victory monument of gilded bronze and granite dedicated to the heroic soldiers who died fighting in this unit in World Wars I and II. Metro: Farragut West or Farragut North.

Fish Market 105 King St. btw N Union and N Lee Sts., Alexandria, VA (703) 836-5676 www.fishmarketoldtown.com

This is a multi-level and multi-room spot that doubles as a boisterous saloon featuring huge-sized beer containers and song and revelry and/or as a busy seafood restaurant featuring more conventional dining and drinking at moderate prices. Open daily for lunch and dinner with the bar open until 2 a.m. Metro: King Street.

Fish Restaurants *see* Seafood and Fish Restaurants.

Fish Wharf

Located at 1100 Maine Ave. SW along the waterfront, this is a favorite for viewing, buying, and eating at the city's prime depot for seafood from the waterways of the region and beyond, and is perhaps best known for its supply of Maryland blue and soft-shell crabs from Chesapeake Bay. Metro: Waterfront-SEU.

Fitness Centers *see* D.C. Jewish Community Center, Fitness Company West End, Gold's Gym, Jewish Community Center of Greater Washington, Jewish Community Center of Northern Virginia, Jewish Community Center of the District of Columbia, National Capital YMCA, Results the Gym, Washington Sports Clubs, YMCA of Metropolitan Washington, YWCA.

Fitness Company West End in the Monarch Hotel, 2401 M St. NW at 24th St. (202) 457-5070 www.thefitnesscompany.com

Guests identifying themselves with a room key from any local hotel can take advantage of a day membership at this exercise facility at a reduced rate. A full range of weights and aerobic equipment, including rowing, cycling, and stair-climbing machines, is available. Metro: Foggy Bottom-GWU.

Fitzhugh Residence *see* Turkey Embassy.

Flamenco *see* dcflamenco.com.

Flea Markets *see* Eastern Market Flea Market, Georgetown Flea Market. *See also* Markets.

Fletcher's Boat House 4940 Canal Rd. NW just north of Reservoir Rd. (202) 224-0461 www.fletchersboathouse.com

Three miles up the C&O Canal in upper-northwest D.C., this old stone building is the one-stop headquarters for renting rowboats, canoes, and bicycles. It is open from mid-March to mid-November from 7:30 a.m. to dusk every day except during foul weather. They also sell fishing bait, tackle, and licenses. The spot can be reached on foot or by D4 Bus.

The Floral Library

Located near the Tidal Basin and opposite the Holocaust Museum, this living library of lovely flowers was established in 1969 by the National Park Service. Its season starts in April with glorious tulips and goes on through the summer months with other extraordinarily attractive arrangements of blooming beauty. Details at (202) 619-7222. Metro: Smithsonian.

Florida Ave. Grill 1100 Florida Ave. NW at 11th St. (202) 265-1586

For more than 50 years this classic diner with counter and stools plus a few booths has been dishing out down-home Southern cooking and barbecue at budget prices. Open Tues–Sat 6:30 a.m.–9 p.m. Soul foods are the specialty and the corn muffins are a real treat. Metro: U St.-Cardozo.

Florida Avenue Market *see* Union Market (Florida Avenue Market).

Foggy Bottom www.dcheritage.org/information2550/information.htm?area = 2525

This neighborhood earned its name from the swampland on which it was built. It is bounded by Pennsylvania Ave. on the north, 17th St. on the east, E St. on the south and the Potomac River on the west. It is home to great diversity including large government agencies, embassies, numerous apartment houses, and nineteenth-century row houses on tree-lined quiet residential streets. Probably its most known tourist sites are the State Department, the John F. Kennedy Center for the Performing Arts, George Washington University (which sprawls across much of the neighborhood), and the notorious and luxurious Watergate office and residential complex. Metro: Foggy Bottom-GWU.

Folger Consort *see* Folger Shakespeare Library Folger Consort.

Folger Shakespeare Library and Theatre 201 E Capitol St. SE, east of the Library of Congress (202) 544-7077 www.folger.edu
   This world-renowned research library and research center is located in a handsome Art Deco structure designed by architect Paul Cret, who also created the Duke Ellington Memorial Bridge. Through its program of exhibitions, concerts, readings, and theatrical performances, it celebrates the cultural traditions of Elizabethan England and the Renaissance and features changing exhibits of Shakespearean artifacts including rare books and manuscripts, works of art, and other extraordinary treasures in the Tudor Great Hall. Open Mon–Sat 10 a.m.–4 p.m. Admission is free and 90-minute tours are available at 11 a.m. Mon–Sat as well as at 1 p.m. on Saturday. Metro: Capitol South. *See also* www.commuterpage.com/venues/venue-enhtm.

Folger Shakespeare Library Folger Consort
   The resident Renaissance ensemble presents musical programs of baroque, Renaissance, and medieval instrumental and vocal performances in the Folger's Elizabethan Theater during its October to May season. Details at (202) 544-7077 or the Web site: www.folger.edu.

Folk and Country Music *see* Birchmere, Cowboy Café North, Lewie's, St. Elmo's Coffee Pub, Soho Tea and Coffee.

Folklife Festival *see* Smithsonian Folklife Festival.

Fondo del Sol Visual Arts Center 2112 R St. NW btw Florida Ave. and 21st St. (202) 483-2777 www.dkmuseums.com/fondo.html
   This artist-managed nonprofit museum is centered on the cultural heritage and arts of the Americas. Its changing exhibition includes works by current Latin American, Native American, and Caribbean artists, and its permanent collection features pre-Columbian artifacts, santos (carved wooden saints), folk, and contemporary art. The museum also carries out a program of lectures, concerts, poetry readings, and an outdoor annual summer Caribbean Festival. Suggested donation. Open Wed–Sat 12:30 p.m.–5:30 p.m. Metro: Dupont Circle.

Food Specialties *see* Specialty Food Stores and Bakeries.

Football *see* FedEx Field, Howard University Bison, University of Maryland Football, Washington Redskins. *See also* www.commuterpage.com/venues/venue-sp.htm.

Footnotes, a Café in Olsson's Books and Records, 418 7th St. NW btw D and E Sts. (202) 638-4882
   This small café features sandwiches and salads in a club-like setting frequented by the bookstore and gallery visitors in this heavily visited downtown neighbor-

hood. Open Mon 9 a.m.–4:30 p.m., Tues–Sat 9 a.m.–7 p.m. Metro: Gallery Pl.-Chinatown.

Ford's Theatre and Lincoln Museum 511 10th St. NW btw E and F Sts. (202) 347-4833 www.fordstheatre.org

The site where Abraham Lincoln was fatally wounded has been painstakingly restored to its 1860s appearance. It is open daily 9 a.m.–5 p.m., except when there are rehearsals or matinee performances in the theater. Admission is free and there is a self-directed tour and a 15-minute narrative on the Washington scene during the Civil War and of the assassination. The museum in the basement lays out the details of the assassination and displays the pistol John Wilkes Booth used and other artifacts. The theater is an active venue for live musical and theatrical performances. Metro: Metro Center. *See also* www.commuterpage.com/venues/venuenhtm.

Foreign and Independent Films *see* American Film Institute, Arlington Cinema and Draft House, Bethesda Row Cinema, Cinema Arts Theater, Cineplex Odeon Cinema, Cineplex Odeon Inner Circle, Cineplex Odeon Outer Circle, Cineplex Odeon Uptown Theater, Cineplex Odeon Wisconsin Ave., Filmfest DC, Freer Gallery of Art Film Program, French Embassy Film Showings, Hirshhorn Museum and Sculpture Garden Film Program, International Jewish Film Festival, Library of Congress Film Program, National Gallery of Art Film Showings, National Geographic Society, National Museum of Women in the Arts Film Showings, Visions Cinema Bistro Lounge. *See also Washington Diplomat.*

Foreign Embassy Events *see* Embassy Events.

Forrest-Marbury House *see* Ukraine Embassy.

Fort Dupont Ice Arena in Fort Dupont Park at 3779 Ely Rd. SE off Minnesota Ave. (202) 584-5007 www.fdia.org

This year-round indoor ice rink is run by a nonprofit group and is open Fri noon–2 p.m., Sat and Sun 2:30 p.m.–4:30 p.m. Children under 12 pay $5 for admission and the loan of skates, and adults pay $6. Metro: Benning Rd., then U6 Bus.

Fort Dupont Park Minnesota Ave. and Randle Circle SE (202) 426-7723 www.nps .gov/fodu

This is one of the city's largest parks, covering 375 acres of woodland and serving as a site for picnics, bike paths, trail hiking, nature study, and outdoor sports. It is east of the Anacostia River on the site of one of the Union Army's many forts and gun batteries that ringed the city. The park is open daily from light until dusk. Metro: Benning Road, then U6 Bus. *See also* www.commuterpage.com/venues/gardens.htm.

Fort Lesley J. McNair 103 3rd Ave. SW at P St. (202) 685-4645 www.mdw .army.mil/fs-i04.htm

Located on the Potomac, this is one of the oldest military posts in the United States and situated in one of the most beautiful parts of the city. It contains broad lawns and lovely Beaux Arts buildings on its 98-acre site, as well as the prestigious

National Defense University. The fort is named for the commander of Army ground forces during World War II, who was killed in Normandy by friendly fire in 1944. The post is open to visitors on foot or upon presentation of suitable photo identification and an examination of the vehicle. Metro: Waterfront-SEU.

Fort Myer-the Old Guard Museum 249 Sheridan Ave. at Macomb St., Fort Myer, VA (703) 696-6670 www.mdw.army.mil/fs-g11.htm

This site next to Arlington National Cemetery has been a military post since 1863 and is home to the Third Infantry (the Old Guard), which is responsible for carrying out military ceremonies for foreign officials and conducting military funerals, standing guard at the Tomb of the Unknowns, and serving as presidential escorts. The museum exhibits include a media presentation on military ceremonies and the flag and a display of the fort and the division's history. Admission free. Open Mon–Sat 9 a.m.–4 p.m., Sun 1 p.m.–4 p.m. Metro: Rosslyn, then 4A Bus to entry gate. *See also* www.commuterpage.com/venues/sightseeing_VA.htm.

Fort Stevens 13th and Quackenbos St. NW just off Georgia Ave. www.nps.gov/rocr/ftcircle/stevens.htm

Now a grassy park, the fort has been partially reconstructed with its earthen works and cannon in place. This site is where the Confederate Army came nearest to capturing the city in the only military battle that ever took place in Washington. The fort was built in 1861 and the battle took place in 1864. The park is open from light to dusk. Metro: Silver Spring, then 70 or 71 Bus.

Fort Ward Museum and Historic Site 4301 W Braddock Rd., east of I-395 btw King St. and Seminary Rd. (703) 838-4848 http://oha.ci.alexandria.va.us/fortward/

This was one of the forts around Washington forming a defensive ring during the Civil War. Most of the ramparts remain and the northwest bastion has been restored to its 1864 condition. The museum features a large collection of Civil War artifacts and photographs. A self-guided walking tour of the site takes about 45 minutes. Museum admission is free and it is open Tues–Sat 9 a.m.–5 p.m., Sun noon–5 p.m. The 40-acre park contains picnic facilities and is open daily 9 a.m.–dusk. Metro: King Street, then take the DAT5 DASH Bus toward Landmark to the stop in front of Fort Ward. *See also* www.commuterpage.com/venues/sightseeing_VA.htm.

Fort Washington Park 13551 Fort Washington Rd., Fort Washington, MD (301) 763-4600 www.nps.gov/fowa

This 340-acre national park in Prince George's County, Maryland, is located on the Potomac River and features lovely distant views of the city and Mount Vernon. There are several trails leading to picnic areas in the historical site surrounding the fort, which was built originally to protect Washington during the War of 1812 and served later as a lookout position for the Union during the Civil War. Modest admission charge for vehicles and pedestrians. The grounds are open daily 8 a.m.–dusk and the visitor center, which features an exhibit area and film showing, is open 9 a.m.–5 p.m. To reach the fort, exit the Beltway (I-495) at Exit 3 (Indian Head Hwy., Rte. 210) south and drive about 4½ miles.

The Foundry 1055 Thomas Jefferson St. NW below M St. in Georgetown

This red brick construction designed by Arthur Cotton Moore preserves and adapts the original old foundry landmark building located at this Georgetown site on the C&O Canal. It is home to numerous shops and galleries. Metro: Foggy Bottom-GWU, then 30, 32, 34, 35, or 36 Bus.

Foundry Gallery 9 Hillyer Court NW behind the Phillips Collection at 21st and O Sts. (202) 387-0203 www.foundry-gallery.org

This artists' cooperative has been showing abstract, representational, and experimental art exhibitions for some 30 years in the Dupont Circle galleries district. Its hours are Wed–Sat 11 a.m.–5 p.m., Sun 1 p.m.–5 p.m. Metro: Dupont Circle.

Foundry United Methodist Church 1500 16th St. NW at P St. (202) 332-4010 www.foundryumc.org

Built in 1904 from architect Appleton Clark's plans, this Gothic Revival structure of rustic gray granite with a low dome is celebrated for its splendid acoustics. It was founded by Henry Foxall, operator of a Georgetown foundry, and is known for its activist urban congregation. Metro: Dupont Circle.

Four Seasons 2800 Pennsylvania Ave. NW btw 28th and 29th Sts. (202) 342-0444 or (800) 332-3442 www.fourseasons.com

Overlooking the C&O Canal and Rock Creek Park in Georgetown, this classy and upscale high-luxury hostelry attracts the rich and the famously rich. Its 260 rooms are bright and spacious with all manner of amenities, while the hotel's outstanding services run the full gamut from fitness facility to business and conference centers. Service here is superb and the restaurant is one of the city's finest and a popular favorite for Sunday brunch. Metro: Foggy Bottom-GWU, then 30, 32, 34, 35, or 36 Bus.

La Fourchette 2429 18th St. NW btw Belmont and Columbia Rds. (202) 332-3077

This venerable bistro offers all the French classic dishes at reasonable prices in a casual ambiance with attractive murals of café scenes adorning the walls. Its sidewalk café is another plus at this heavily frequented Adams Morgan spot. Open Mon–Fri for lunch and dinner, Sat–Sun brunch and dinner. Metro: Dupont Circle, then L2 Bus or Woodley Park-Zoo, then 90, 91, 92, 93, or 96 Bus.

14th Street Bridges I-395 btw the Jefferson Memorial and the Pentagon over the Potomac River

There are two 14th Street bridges. The first, completed in 1950, was dedicated to Comte de Rochambeau, and the other span, which opened in 1962, honors Bill of Rights author George Mason. In 1982, an Air Florida plane struck the bridge during a snowstorm. The Rochambeau span was renamed in 1982 honoring Arland D. William Jr., who perished saving others from the freezing Potomac below. Metro: Smithsonian.

Fourth of July Celebrations _see_ Independence Day Celebrations.

Fox and Hounds 1533 17th St. NW btw P and Q Sts. (202) 232-6307

This relaxed neighborhood watering hole serves basic bar food and large-sized donuts at moderate prices. The outdoor patio is a popular spot in mild weather for observing the colorful life on this busy street. Open Mon–Fri, 11 a.m.–1:30 a.m., Sat–Sun 10 a.m.–2:30 a.m. Metro: Dupont Circle.

Foxhall Neighborhood

This district in upper northwest comprises the neighborhood of Foxhall and the lesser-known Foxhall Village and Wesley Heights. The area extends roughly from 44th St. on the south to Battery Kemble Park and Nebraska Ave. on the north, Canal Rd. on the west and Glover Archbold Park and Massachusetts Ave. on the east. A good portion of the region is home to wealthier residents residing in large houses situated on spacious grounds. This section of the city is also home to American University and Mount Vernon College, now affiliated with George Washington University. The whole area is considered to be a very fashionable corner of the city. Accessed by D5 and D6 Buses.

Foxhall Square Mall 3301 New Mexico Ave. NW btw Cathedral Ave. and Embassy Park Dr. (202) 363-0027 www.foxhallsquare.com

This smaller-scale mall in upper-northwest D.C. incorporates some 25 shops and boutiques. Metro: Tenleytown.

France Embassy 4101 Reservoir Rd. NW (202) 944-6000 www.ambafrance-us.org

Frances Perkins Department of Labor Building 200 Constitution Ave. NW at 3rd St. (202) 371-6422

The point of interest in this massive government structure named for the first female American cabinet member is the building's Labor Hall of Fame. Artifacts from many who came to fame by embracing the union movement are on display here, along with an exhibit about Perkins, who was Franklin D. Roosevelt's secretary of labor from 1933 to 1945. The building is open Mon–Fri 8:15 a.m.–4:45 p.m. to those who present photo identification. Metro: Judiciary Square.

Francis Pool 25th and N Sts. NW (202) 727-3285

This city-run outdoor pool is a popular family aquatic recreation center. It is open from early June to early September, Mon and Wed–Fri 1 p.m.–8 p.m., Sat–Sun noon–7 p.m. Closed Tues. Very minimal admission charge. Metro: Dupont Circle.

Francis Scott Key Bridge *see* Key Bridge.

Francis Scott Key Memorial

In the center of the plaza of the park that bears his name, a bronze bust by Betty Dunston, a Georgetown sculptor, is a memorial to the author of the national anthem. A flag displaying the 15 stars and stripes it contained in 1814, the year Francis Scott Key wrote the anthem, flies from a 60-foot-high lighted flagpole 24 hours a day. The memorial is known also as the Star Spangled Banner Monument. The park is on M St. NW in Georgetown at the east entrance to Key Bridge. Metro: Foggy Bottom-GWU, then 30, 32, 34, 35, or 36 Bus.

Francis Scott Key Memorial Park

Located on M St. NW in Georgetown at the east entrance to Key Bridge, which crosses the Potomac to Rosslyn, Virginia, this small noisy park contains a circular colonnaded brick plaza behind a rose garden. The centerpiece is the bronze memorial bust of Francis Scott Key and the tall lighted flagpole flying a replica of the 1814 American flag, which inspired Key to write the national anthem. Metro: Foggy Bottom-GWU, then 30, 32, 34, 35, or 36 Bus.

Franciscan Monastery 1400 Quincy St. NE at 14th St. (202) 526-6800 www.myfranciscan.com

Located not far from the National Shrine of the Immaculate Conception this Byzantine-style monastery offers a serene setting and beautiful grounds and a fascinating view of replicas of shrines from the Holy Land, such as the Grotto of Bethlehem and Jerusalem's Holy Sepulchre. Reproductions of the Roman catacombs are underground. Church and gardens are open daily 9 a.m.–5 p.m. Admission is free. Tours are offered on the hour 9 a.m.–4 p.m. (except noon) Mon–Sat, 1 p.m.–4 p.m. Sun. Metro: Brookland-CUA.

Frank Lloyd Wright's Pope-Leighey House 900 Richmond Hwy., Mount Vernon, Virginia (703) 780-4000 www.nationaltrust.org

This cypress, brick and glass structure was built in 1940 by Wright at another Virginia location and was moved here to Woodlawn Plantation in the early 1990s. It is what the architect termed "Usonian" architecture, well-designed housing for middle-income families. The building contains original furnishings, which were also designed by Wright. From March to December it is open daily 10 a.m.–5 p.m. It is closed January and February. Visits are by guided tour only. Modest admission charge. It is most easily reached by car using the George Washington Memorial Pkwy. and is located 3 miles past Mount Vernon. *See also* www.commuterpage.com/venues/sightseeing_VA.htm.

Franklin Delano Roosevelt Memorial

Since 1997, on a $7^1/_2$-acre site in West Potomac Park along the Tidal Basin between the Jefferson and Lincoln Memorials, this park-like space features waterfalls and reflecting pools and four outdoor gallery rooms (one for each of Roosevelt's four presidential terms) as well as ten bronze sculptures. The design was by Lawrence Halperin. The granite walls are inscribed with memorable excerpts from FDR's speeches. In one room statues of hungry men wait for a handout during the depression; in another a man listens to a fireside address on the radio; in the third room a 9-foot statue shows Roosevelt seated with his dog, Fala; in the last a statue depicts Eleanor Roosevelt as champion of human rights and first lady. Open daily 24 hours, staffed 8 a.m.–midnight. Metro: Smithsonian, then about a $^1/_2$-mile walk. Information at the Web site: www.nps.gov/fdrm/index2.htm. *See also* www.commuterpage.com/venues/memorials.htm.

Franklin Park

Located between I and K Sts. NW and 13th and 14th Sts., this downtown city park features a central fountain, lovely old trees, pleasant walkways, and numerous benches in the shade where innumerable office workers take their lunch breaks. Metro: McPherson Square.

Franklin's Coffee House Café 2000 18th St. NW at Vernon St. (202) 319-1800
   This popular daytime spot for coffee is open Mon and Wed–Fri 8 a.m.–3 p.m., Sat–Sun 9 a.m.–4 p.m. Closed Tues. Metro: Dupont Circle or U St.-Cardozo.

Franz Bader Bookshop 1911 I St. NW at 19th St. (202) 337-5440
   This store's focus is upon the visual arts—graphics, photography, design, and architecture. The books on sale here are attractive and many are replete with lovely pictures. Open Mon–Sat 10 a.m.–6 p.m. Metro: Farragut West.

Fraser Gallery 1054 31st St. NW (202) 298-6450 www.thefrasergallery.com
   This Georgetown gallery showcases eclectic selections from lesser-known as well as established artists working in various media. Open Tues–Fri, noon–3 p.m., Sat noon–6 p.m. Metro: Foggy Bottom-GWU, then 30, 32, 34, 35, or 36 Bus.

Frederick Douglass Birthday Celebration
   On the birthday of this famed figure in American history on February 12 a wreath-laying ceremony is held at Cedar Hill, the Frederick Douglass National Historic Site at 1411 W St. SE at 14th St. There are performances and other special activities throughout the day. Information on the celebration at (202) 619-7222 or (202) 426-5961. Metro: Anacostia, then B2 Bus.

Frederick Douglass Memorial Bridge carries S Capitol St. across the Anacostia River into Anacostia
   Planned in 1942, World War II held up construction. It opened in 1949 and was dedicated in 1965 to abolitionist leader Frederick Douglass. His home, Cedar Hill, is nearby in Anacostia. The bridge, elevated at both ends, boasts one of the world's longest swing spans, 386 feet, allowing large ships to enter the neighboring Washington Navy Yard. Metro: Anacostia.

Frederick Douglass Museum and Hall of Fame for Caring Americans 320 A St. NE btw 3rd and 4th Sts. (202) 547-4273 www.caringinstitute.org
   Situated in a restored building where Frederick Douglass lived for a period on Capitol Hill, this small museum houses exhibits and artifacts of memorabilia from Douglass's fascinating life. It is also a memorial site for American individuals who are celebrated for having contributed to the betterment of human lives. Visits can be arranged by appointment. Metro: Union Station.

Frederick Douglass National Historic Site 1411 W St. SE at 14th St. (202) 426-5960 www.nps.gov/frdo
   The 21-room beautifully restored home (known popularly as Cedar Hill) of the celebrated former slave, abolitionist, and orator contains a vast collection of artifacts, his comprehensive library, and most of the original nineteenth-century Victorian furnishings. The house is maintained by the National Park Service as a museum to his memory. On the grounds is a life-size statue of Douglass executed by Ed Dwight. The visitor center features a 30-minute film on Douglass's life and times. The house site also provides a wonderful view of the city across the Anacostia River. Open daily 9 a.m.–5 p.m. Reservations are needed in advance for the guided tour and are accepted long in advance. Modest admission charge. Metro: Anacostia, then B2 Bus.

Frederick Douglass Tour

From June 15 to Labor Day this 2½-hour bus tour departs from Washington Monument and Arlington National Cemetery at noon daily. It includes Capitol Hill landmarks, the Frederick Douglass National Historic Site (Cedar Hill), the Mary McLeod Bethune Memorial, and Lincoln Park. Reservations in person required at least 30 minutes before departure at Arlington National Cemetery or Washington Monument ticket booths. Details at (202) 554-5100.

Frederick Keys Harry Grove Stadium, 6201 New Design Rd., Frederick, MD (301) 662-0013 www.frederickkeys.com

Even though Frederick is outside this book's radius, baseball enthusiasts might find the trek worthwhile. This is a Baltimore Orioles Class-A team playing a full season in the Carolina league. Minor league baseball is popular, very inexpensive, and this historic town loves its players, some of whom move up to become big-league stars. The stadium can be reached from the Market St. exit from Rte. 70 or Rte. 270 in Frederick.

Freedom Forum Journalists Memorial www.freedomforum.org/templates/docu ment.asp?documentID = 4000

The world's first monument to journalists killed in carrying out their reporting roles is located at the highest point in Freedom Park in Arlington, Virginia, on the overpass between 1100 and 1101 Wilson Blvd. On a 24-foot-high stainless steel structure glass panels are inscribed with the names of the 1,200 or so journalists who died since 1812 while carrying out their duties. Each year new names are selected by the Committee to Protect Journalists for addition to the distinguished roster. Metro: Rosslyn.

Freedom Park

Located over the Key Bridge in Arlington, Virginia, on an overpass between 1100 and 1101 Wilson Blvd., this small area contains a number of artifacts celebrating aspects of freedom—sections of the Berlin Wall, a bronze cast of Martin Luther King's jailhouse door, a toppled Lenin statue, a ballot box from South Africa—all leading to the park's main attraction, the Freedom Forum Journalists Memorial to those slain in the performance of their duties. The park is open daily from daylight to dusk. Metro: Rosslyn.

Freedom Plaza Pennsylvania Ave. btw 13th and 14th Sts. NW

Located across from the National Theater, this concrete stretch was named to honor Martin Luther King Jr., who delivered his "I Have a Dream" speech at his celebrated freedom rally. It's used mostly by rollerbladers and skateboarders and for the occasional outdoor concert or other public event. Metro: Federal Triangle or Metro Center. *See also* www.commuterpage.com/venues/gardens.htm.

Freedom Statue

This 19-foot construction atop the U.S. Capitol dome was made from a plaster model created by sculptor Thomas Crawford in Rome and shipped by sea. It was erected as the finishing touch above the dome in late 1863 to symbolize the continuity of the Federal Union.

Freeman House Museum 131 Church St., Vienna, VA (703) 938-5187 www.visit fairfax.org/museums.htm

This historic house was used at different times in its past as a residence, store, Civil War hospital, railroad station, post office, and fire department. Nowadays it is a museum and old-time general store. It is open to the public Sat noon–4 p.m., Sun 1 p.m.–5 p.m. Closed January and February. Metro: Dunn Loring/Merrifield, exit the station and take Metrobus 2C toward Tysons Corner to the stop at Maple Ave. and Center St. Walk 1 block northwest on Center St. N, turn right on Church St. NE, and walk 1 block northeast. *See also* www.commuterpage.com/venues/gardens.htm.

Freer Gallery of Art Jefferson Dr. at 12th St. SW (202) 357-2700 www.si.edu/asia

This must be one of the world's greatest collections of Asian art, but it also holds an important group of American works. The gallery is located in an Italian Renaissance-style structure and is part of the Smithsonian Institution. Among its more notable holdings are paintings by James Whistler. The Peacock Room, designed by Whistler, is the most heavily visited part of the building and contains a permanent installation that was transported in its entirety from England early in the twentieth century. There are tours of the gallery scheduled during the day. Open daily 10 a.m.–5:30 p.m. Admission free. Metro: Smithsonian. *See also* www .commuterpage.com/venues/museums-si.htm.

Freer Gallery of Art Film Program

A unique program of cinema screenings of films originating in the countries of Asia and the Middle East is an integral element of the Freer's regular schedule. Showings are usually offered during evening hours or on weekend afternoons in the Meyer Auditorium. Admission is free but the popularity of the movies draws a large audience. Call (202) 357-2700 for features and times of performances. Metro: Smithsonian.

French Embassy Film Showings

The cultural program of the French Embassy offers French-language films throughout the year at the embassy and other Washington venues. The embassy also sponsors music and art events frequently, many of which are free. Details at (202) 944-6022.

French Restaurants *see* Au Pied du Cochon, L'Auberge Chez François, La Bergerie, Bis, Bistro Français, Bistrot Lépic, La Brasserie, Café La Ruche, La Chaumière, Citronelle, La Colline, La Côte d'Or Café, La Ferme, La Fourchette, Le Gaulois, Gerard's Place, Hermitage Inn Restaurant, Jean-Michel, Lavandou, Marcel's, La Miche, La Provence, Le Rivage, Senses, Tempo, Le Vieux Logis. *See also* Web sites: www.dcpages.com, www.restaurant.com, www.washingtonpost.com, www.opentable.com.

Fresh Fields Whole Foods Market

Since opening its first store in Washington in 1996 in Tenleytown in upper-northwest D.C. at 4530 40th St. NW, (202) 237-5800, a number of other outlets of this swiftly growing supermarket chain have started up at a number of other locations in the city and the Maryland and Virginia suburbs. They specialize in healthy foods including organic produce, meat, seafood, dairy products, vegetables, gourmet preparations, and natural health care products. Check the D.C. and suburban telephone books for the numerous store branches.

Freshfarm Market *see* Dupont Circle Freshfarm Market.

Friday Morning Music Club (202) 333-2075 http://fmmc.org/orchestra/2002

Since the late nineteenth century this very active organization has worked to promote musical culture among its some 800 members and in the larger community. Its members include nonperforming music enthusiasts as well as singers, composers, conductors, and instrumentalists. The club sponsors its own chorale and orchestra and offers free concerts at a number of locations in the city and suburbs. Telephone for details.

Friendship Archway *see* Chinatown Friendship Archway.

Friendship Firehouse 107 S Alfred St. btw King and Prince Sts. (703) 838-3891 http://oha.ci.alexandria.va.us/friendship/ff-museum.html

Begun in 1774, this volunteer citizens fire brigade included George Washington among its members. The current brick building was erected in 1855. It features an exhibit room where early hand-drawn fire engines and firefighting equipment like leather buckets and speaking trumpets are displayed. Admission free. Open Fri–Sat 10 a.m.–4 p.m., Sun 1 p.m.–4 p.m. Metro: King Street, then either the DAT7 DASH Bus toward Old Town, or the DAT5 DASH Bus toward Braddock Road Metro, to the stop at King St. and South Alfred St. *See also* www.commuterpage.com/venues/sightseeing_VA.htm.

Friendship Heights

This neighborhood at the dividing line between northwest D.C. and Maryland is a small community of large luxury apartment structures and upscale stores. It is accessible from the Friendship Heights Metro stop at the intersection of Wisconsin and Western Aves., right on the border of the city. The Chevy Chase Pavilion and Mazza Gallerie, two distinctly upbeat shopping malls are located on either side of Wisconsin Ave., and American University is easily accessible.

Friendship House *see* Maples House.

Friendship House Settlement *see* Maples House.

Frying Pan Park Farmers Market 2709 W Ox Rd., Herndon, VA (703) 941-7987 www.springfield.va.us/living/activities/farmers_market/living_ activities_farmers .cfm

This market is open from early May to the end of October Wednesdays 8 a.m.–12:30 p.m., with producers selling fruit and vegetables.

Full Kee 509 H St. NW btw 5th and 6th Sts. (202) 371-2233

One of the best Chinese restaurants in town dispenses no alcohol and accepts only cash. It's a great popular favorite with Chinatown residents and other locals. Even though the ambiance is dreary, the authentic well-prepared dishes and the budget prices have enormous appeal. Open for lunch and dinner daily. Metro: Gallery Pl.-Chinatown.

G

Gabon Embassy 2034 20th St. NW (202) 797-1000 www.embassy.org/embassies/ga.html
Embassy of the Gabonese Republic. Metro: Dupont Circle.

Gabriel in the Radisson Barceló Hotel, 2121 P St. NW near 21st St. (202) 956-6690
This upscale and moderately expensive restaurant is popular for its *tapas* and innovative Latin American and Spanish dishes. It is probably best known for its sumptuous Sunday brunch buffet (reservations are recommended), which features breakfast items and a full gamut of specialty dishes and desserts. Open for breakfast daily, dinner Mon–Sat, Sun brunch. Metro: Dupont Circle.

Gadsby's Tavern Museum 134 N Royal St. btw King and Cameron Sts. (703) 838-4242 http://oha.ci.alexandria.va.us/gadsby/
This tavern, which functions as a museum, comprises the original 1770 tavern and the 1792 City Hotel. The older building preserves the condition of a late eighteenth-century American hostelry. The Tavern Restaurant next door at 138 N Royal St. (703) 548-8288, serves lunch and dinner daily at moderate prices. The museum is closed on Mon, open Tues–Sat 10 a.m.–5 p.m., Sun 1 p.m.–5 p.m. Tours are given 15 minutes before the hour and 15 minutes after the hour. Modest admission charge. Metro: King Street, exit the station and take the DAT7 DASH Bus toward Old Town to the stop at King and Royal Sts., walk north on Royal St. *See also* www.commuterpage.com/venues/sightseeing_VA.htm.

Gaithersburg www.ci.gaithersburg.md.us
About 20 miles from D.C. using I-270 or Rockville Pike (the extension of Wisconsin Ave.), this Maryland suburban region is bounded on the north by Goshen Rd., east by Georgia Ave., south by Shady Grove Rd., and west by Rte. 28, Darnestown Rd. The community retains some of its earlier character in the Old Town district (Gaithersburg was incorporated in 1878), but much of the development in various types of single-family housing is because of its proximity to the I-270 corridor, a commercial stretch along which many technology and bio-tech firms have

been located. It is one of the fastest growing regions on the East Coast. Residents can commute to the city by Metro or MARC trains, which run to Union Station. Metro: Shady Grove.

Gaithersburg Farmers Market off Rte. 355 at E Cedar and S Frederick Aves., Gaithersburg, MD (301) 590-2823 www.farmerlink.com

On Thursdays 2 p.m.–6 p.m. from early June to the end of October this Montgomery County market operates in the Gaithersburg Old Town area next to the commuter parking lot, selling the produce of local growers.

Gaithersburg Main Street Pavilion Farmers Market (301) 258-6350 ext. 123 www .communityharvestdc.org/markets.htm

At the corner of Main and Hart Sts. in Gaithersburg fresh farm produce is sold 9 a.m.–1 p.m. on Saturdays from early June to the end of September.

Gala Hispanic Theatre 1021 7th St. NW (202) 234-7174 www.galatheatre.org

For almost 30 years this company has been producing classic and contemporary plays in Spanish, English, or Spanish with English by Latin American and Spanish playwrights as well as other music and dance productions celebrating Hispanic culture. Tickets are moderately priced and performances are offered usually on weekend nights or matinees. Metro: Gallery Pl.-Chinatown. *See also* www.com muterpage.com/venues/venue-enhtm.

Galaxy Hut 2711 Wilson Blvd. btw Danville and Edgewood Sts., Arlington, VA (703) 525-8646 www.galaxyhut.com

This is a tiny spot that has a wide range of beers and an assortment of zesty dishes to go with the drink, a younger clientele, and live music Sat–Mon from 9:45 p.m. Open Mon–Fri 5 p.m.–2 a.m., Sat–Sun 7 p.m.–2 a.m. There is no cover charge, but beers are moderately expensive at this very in club. Metro: Clarendon or Court House.

Gales–Hoover House *see* Burma Embassy.

Galileo 1110 21st St. NW btw L and M Sts. (202) 293-7191 www.robertodonna .com

This lovely and celebrated dining spot requires reservations and has some of the city's finest Italian dishes at some of the city's most astronomical prices. It is open for lunch Mon–Fri, dinner nightly. Metro: Foggy Bottom-GWU or Farragut North.

Gallatin Statue *see* Albert Gallatin Statue.

Gallaudet University 800 Florida Ave. NE btw 6th St. and West Virginia Ave. (202) 651-5000 www.gallaudet.edu

The world's only university for the hearing impaired developed from a small school begun in 1856. Its enrollment numbers some 2,000 students working toward bachelor's and master's degrees in a wide range of disciplines. The campus is made up of a splendid group of Victorian Gothic and Queen Anne buildings surrounding the mall with grounds and garden designed by Frederick Law Olmstead of New York City Central Park fame. The visitors center is open Mon–Fri 9 a.m.–5 p.m. and offers tours. For details, call (202) 651-5050. To reach the campus from downtown use the D2, D4, or D6 Bus.

Galleria at Tysons II 2001 International Dr. btw Chain Bridge Rd. and Westpark Dr., McLean VA (703) 827-7700 www.shoptysonsgalleria.com/MallInfo.asp

This is a considerably more classy mélange of some 100 stores and boutiques than the much larger Tysons Corner Mall across the way. Saks, Neiman Marcus, and Macy's as well as countless other upscale specialty shops can be found here. Open Mon–Sat 10 a.m.–9 p.m., Sun noon–6 p.m. By car from the Beltway (I-495), take exit 46A, and at the second light make a right turn.

Galleries *see* Art Galleries.

Gallery K 2010 R St. NW at Connecticut Ave. (202) 234-0339 www.galleryk.com

This highly regarded showplace for important local as well as national and international artists is open Tues–Sat 11 a.m.–5 p.m. or by appointment. Metro: Dupont Circle.

Gallery Place Area

This section of the city is in the process of a major renovation and revival of its artistic character. It includes the blocks between E and H Sts. and 4th and 9th Sts. NW. This district is home to the National Museum of American Art, the National Portrait Gallery, the MCI Arena, the Shakespeare Theatre, and numerous galleries, restaurants and fashionable boutiques. Metro: Gallery Pl.-Chinatown.

Gallery Row

Following the renovation of the façades of several buildings dating from the mid-nineteenth century by architects Hartman and Cox in 1985, this building bringing together a number of galleries of art and photography was brought into being at 409 7th St. between D and E Sts. in downtown D.C. This was one of the earliest steps in the dramatic renaissance of the artistic character of this neighborhood. Metro: Gallery Pl.-Chinatown.

Gallery 10 Ltd. 1519 Connecticut Ave. NW at Q St. (202) 232-3326 www.gallery10dc.com

This gallery showcases artistic works by promising as well as established, local and imported, talented creators. Open Wed–Sat 11 a.m.–5 p.m. Metro: Dupont Circle.

Gambia Embassy 1155 15th St. NW, Suite 1000 (202) 785-1399 www.gambia.com/index.html

Gandhi Monument

This memorial to the celebrated Indian political passive resistance hero Mohandas K. Gandhi (commonly known as Mahatma Gandhi) can be found at Massachusetts Ave. where 21st and Q Sts. NW come together, opposite the Indian Embassy. Metro: Dupont Circle.

Garber Preservation, Restoration, and Storage Facility 3904 Old Silver Hill Rd. at St. Barnabas Rd., Suitland, MD (202) 357-1400 www.nasm.si.edu/nasm/garber/Garber.html.

This multi-building facility houses more stored and restored aircraft than the National Air and Space Museum. Some 160 air vehicles can be viewed up close, running the gamut from a Soviet MiG from the Korean War to a World War II Battle of Britain Hawker Hurricane. Guided-tour reservations must be made well in advance. They last 3 hours and take place Mon–Fri 10 a.m., and Sat and Sun 10 a.m. and 1 p.m. By car take Exit 4B off Hwy. I-95, then go 3 miles east on State Rd. 414 to the intersection of Old Silver Hill and St. Barnabas Rds.

Gardens *see* Audubon Naturalist Society of the Central Atlantic States Inc., Aztec Garden, Bishop's Garden, Brookside Gardens, Constitution Gardens, Dumbarton Oaks Research Library and Collections, Enid A. Haupt Garden, Federal Reserve Board, The Floral Library, Folger Shakespeare Library and Theatre, Franciscan Monastery, Hillwood Museum and Gardens, Historical Society of Washington, Kenilworth Aquatic Gardens, Meadowlark Gardens Regional Park, Meridian International Center, Mount Vernon, National Arboretum, Old Stone House, Organization of American States, Red Cross Square, River Farm, Society of the Cincinnati at Anderson House, Textile Museum, Tudor Place, U.S. Botanic Garden, Washington National Cathedral, The White House.

Garfield Memorial

Located near the Grant Monument and the U.S. Botanic Garden at 1st St. and Maryland Ave. SW, this bronze statue of the assassinated twentieth American president standing on a pedestal is situated with three other figures seated around it, each of them bearing a tablet inscribed "Law," "Justice," or "Prosperity." Metro: Federal Center.

Garrett's 3003 M St. NW at 30th St. (202) 333-1033 www.garrettsdc.com

This restaurant located in a historic Georgetown Colonial house has a lot of restored memorabilia to look at while enjoying a meal. It includes a glass-enclosed rooftop dining area on the 2nd floor. Prices are moderate and it's a pleasant place to take kids. Open for lunch and dinner daily. Metro: Foggy Bottom-GWU, then 30, 32, 34, 35, or 36 Bus.

Le Gaulois 1106 King St. btw S Henry and S Fayette Sts., Alexandria, VA (703) 739-9494

This popular bistro in Old Town serves excellent French country-style dishes prepared creatively at moderate prices in a comfortable, quiet, and welcoming ambiance. Open Mon–Sat for lunch and dinner. Metro: King Street

Gay Men's Chorus of Washington D.C.

This highly regarded choral group performs concerts throughout the year at various locations around the city. Details at (202) 338-7464 or at www.gmcw.org.

Gay Pride Celebration

The Washington area gay, lesbian, bisexual, and transgender community holds this annual celebration on a weekend in June. On Saturday there is a parade with floats and entertainment that starts at 24th and N Sts. and ends on 17th and P Sts. Metro: Dupont Circle. On Sunday a street festival from midday until evening on Pennsylvania Ave. between 3rd and 7th Sts. NW features music and theatrical performances. Metro: Archives-Navy Memorial. These events are free and attract hundreds of spectators. Information at (202) 789-7000.

Gelman Library *see* George Washington University Library.

Gen. Andrew Jackson Statue *see* Andrew Jackson Statue.

Gen. Comte Jean de Rochambeau Statue *see* Rochambeau Statue.

Gen. Comte Jean de Rochambeau Bridge *see* 14th Street Bridges.

Gen. George H. Thomas Statue *see* Thomas Statue.

Gen. James B. McPherson Statue www.hq.usace.army.mil/history/vignettes/vignette_23.htm

This Civil War hero of the Battle of Atlanta sits astride his horse in a bronze statue monument constructed in 1876 from what is said to have been a captured Confederate cannon. It is located in McPherson Square, 15th St. between K and I Sts. NW. Metro: McPherson Square.

Gen. John A. Logan Statue *see* Logan Statue.

Gen. John J. Pershing Memorial *see* Pershing Memorial.

Gen. McClellan Statue *see* McClellan Statue.

Gen. Philip H. Sheridan Statue *see* Sheridan Statue.

Gen. Winfield Scott Hancock Statue *see* Winfield Scott Hancock Statue.

Gen. Winfield Scott Statue *see* Winfield Scott Statue.

Generous George's Positive Pizza 3006 Duke St., Alexandria, VA (703) 370-4303 www.generousgeorge.com

The claim to fame is the huge size of the portions offered at this very popular budget-priced pizza parlor. The toppings are fresh and of excellent quality and the place is a fun spot, especially for kids with big appetites. Open Mon–Fri 11 a.m.–10 p.m., Sat–Sun 11 a.m.–midnight. The nearest Metro stop is King Street, but it's 3 miles away, so the best way is by car.

George Hotel *see* Hotel George.

George Mason Monument

This is the city's most recently placed memorial, dedicated in April 2002. The bronze larger-than-life seated statue of the author of the Virginia Declaration of Rights in 1776 was supported by private donations and executed by sculptor Wendy Ross. It can be found on Ohio Dr. near the Tidal Basin between the Franklin D. Roosevelt and Jefferson Memorials. Metro: Smithsonian, and then a good walk.

George Mason University 4400 University Dr., Fairfax, VA (703) 993-1000 www .gmu.edu

The second largest public university in the state has some 24,000 undergraduate and graduate students attending classes at the campus just outside Fairfax City. The range of study programs is extensive, but the major emphases are the humanities, technology, and public policy. Concerts and theater and dance performances are held at the Center for the Arts. The Patriot Center is where sporting events and concerts take place. To reach the campus from the Washington Beltway (I-495) take Exit 54B and go approximately 6 miles on Braddock Rd. W. Metro: Vienna, then CUE Bus. *See also* Patriot Center.

George Mason University Center for the Arts Va. Rte. 123 and Braddock Rd., Fairfax, VA (703) 993-8888 www.gmu.edu/cfa

This complex for artistic productions opened in 1988 and includes three theaters. There is a concert hall seating 1,900; the 500-seat Harris Theater showcasing ballet, dance, and theatrical performances; and the smaller Black Box Theater where the university's resident theatrical company, Theater of the First Amendment, performs innovative dramatic works and performance art. By car from the Washington Beltway (I-495) take Exit 54B and go approximately 6 miles on Braddock Rd. W. Metro: Vienna, then CUE Bus. *See also* www.commuterpage.com/venues/venue-en.htm.

George Mason University Libraries http://library.gmu.edu/

The two major library sites are the Fenwick Library, 4400 University Drive, Fairfax, VA (703) 993-2250, and the Johnson Center Library—an undergraduate library, an innovative media center, and food court complex near the Fenwick Library. The Johnson Center's information desk is (703) 993-9000. These open-stack collections with more than a million volumes include, as well, access to more than 300 databases covering a range of formats. Non-students may purchase "Friends of the Library" cards allowing them to borrow circulating materials. By car from the Washington Beltway (I-495) take Exit 60 at Rte. 123 S, Chain Bridge Rd. Follow Rte. 123 through the City of Fairfax and turn left at University Dr. Take the first right at Occoquan River Lane. Turn right at the stop sign onto Patriot Circle. At the pond, bear left to stay on Patriot Circle. Take the first left on Mason Pond Dr. to the Parking Deck, the last building on your right. An information kiosk is located outside the third level of the deck to help visitors navigate the campus.

George Mason University Patriot Center *see* Patriot Center.

George Mason University Patriots http://gmusports.ocsn.com/

The basketball team of the University plays its home games at the 10,000-seat Patriot Center on the campus in Fairfax, Virginia. Information at (703) 993-3000 or www.sports.gmu.edu.

George Washington Birthday Celebration

The country's largest and most colorful parade honoring the nation's first president and native son is held every year in mid-February and passes through Old Town Alexandria's historic buildings and homes ending at Gadsby's Tavern. Following the parade an open house with free admission is held at Mount Vernon where costumed historic figures, musical entertainment, and food add to the day's lustrous events. Information at (703) 838-4200.

George Washington Equestrian Statue *see* Washington Equestrian Statue.

George Washington Gristmill Historical State Park *see* Washington's Gristmill Historical State Park.

George Washington Masonic National Memorial 101 Callahan Dr. btw King and Duke Sts., Arlington, VA (703) 683-2007 www.gwmemorial.org

This 333-foot landmark stands just outside Old Town. The museum displays memorabilia of Washington's efforts on behalf of the Masons. Family possessions and the Washington family Bible are also on exhibit. From the 9th-floor observatory there is a spectacular view of the area with D.C. in the distance. Open daily 9 a.m.–5 p.m. Admission free. Guided tours of the building and observation deck are offered throughout the day. Metro: King Street, walk 1 one block southwest to Diagonal Rd., right on Duke, 1 block west to Callahan Dr. *See also* www.commuter page.com/venues/sightseeing_VA.htm.

George Washington Memorial Parkway (703) 285-2598 www.nps.gov/gwmp

This parkway was constructed in the 1930s and was modeled after the Bronx River Pkwy. in New York City. It runs along the Potomac River in Virginia, and adjacent to it, the Mount Vernon Trail provides lovely riverside hiking and biking trails that run from the riverbanks opposite Theodore Roosevelt Island south for some 19 miles all the way to Mount Vernon. Off the highway a number of pull-offs, especially south of Old Town Alexandria, provide space to park and then walk or bike.

George Washington Monument *see* Washington Monument.

George Washington Statue

In Washington Circle, at the intersection of New Hampshire and Pennsylvania Aves. NW, just north of George Washington University Hospital in Foggy Bottom, this monument was executed in 1860 by Clark Mills depicting General Washington at the Battle of Princeton in 1776 trying to move his reluctant horse forward in the face of heavy cannon fire. Metro: Foggy Bottom-GWU.

George Washington University 2121 I St. NW btw 21st and 22nd Sts. (202) 994-1000 www.gwu.edu

This private independent university with some 17,000 undergraduate and graduate students occupies an urban campus between G St. and K St. NW from 20th to 24th Sts. After the federal government, it is the city's second largest landowner. Much of its reputation stems from its excellent schools of law and medicine and the highly regarded George Washington University Hospital, but the academic programs here span a very wide range of liberal arts, social sciences, business, international affairs, and technical studies. There are some 80 doctoral and 180 master's degree programs. The Lisner Auditorium's 1,500 seats are the site of dance, music, and theatrical performances. Many of the university activities are centered in nineteenth-century row houses, some of which have been designated as historic sites. Metro: Foggy Bottom-GWU.

George Washington University Colonials http://gwsports.ocsn.com

Among the city's major college basketball lineup, both the men's and women's teams have recently emerged as stalwart competitors. They play their home games at the comfortable Smith Center on the campus at 600 22nd St. NW. Information at (202) 994-6650.

George Washington University Inn 824 New Hampshire Ave. NW btw I and H Sts. (202) 337-6620 or (800) 426-4455 www.gwuin.com

This former apartment building was converted into a hotel and later renovated. It is now a nicely furnished 95-room-and-suites hostelry. The location on a residential street in Foggy Bottom is near the Kennedy Center, the State Department, and convenient to campus activities. Guests can make use of the university's exercise facilities, and rates are in the mid-price range. The Zuki Moon restaurant is part of the premises and is designed like a Japanese tea garden specializing in Japanese food. Metro: Foggy Bottom-GWU.

George Washington University Library 2130 H St. NW (202) 994-6558 www .gwu.edu/gelman

A strong collection and full range of information services are available at the university's Melvin Gelman Library located on the campus. Metro: Foggy Bottom-GWU.

George Washington University Mount Vernon College *see* Mount Vernon College of George Washington University.

George Washington's River Farm

Located on the Potomac River 4 miles south of Old Town Alexandria off George Washington Memorial Pkwy., this 27-acre property was bought by George Washington in 1760. Since the 1970s it has been owned and operated by the American Horticulture Society, which displays gardens at the site. The main house dates from the 1750s and contains furnishings from that era. There are picnic facilities at the site and the society schedules lectures and other programs here. Admission free. Open Mon–Fri 8:30 a.m.–5 p.m., Sat 9 a.m.–1 p.m. Information at (703) 768-5700, (800) 777-7931, or www.ahs.org/river_farm/history.htm

Georgetown

The most colorful and choice neighborhood in the city is bordered by the Potomac River on the south, Rock Creek on the east, Georgetown University on the west, and Burleith, a residential area on the north. It is urban, cosmopolitan, trendy, and stylish. It contains smart shops, historic residences, lively street life, bars, restaurants, cafés, crowds, congestion, and traffic-jammed streets. Its epicenter is Wisconsin Ave. and M St. Georgetown is also the district's wealthiest area and contains numerous quiet tree-shaded residential streets with brick sidewalks, lovely old Federal houses, and choice gardens. Montrose Park and Dumbarton Oaks on the north side provide serene green spaces. The C&O Canal on the south, with the path at its side, permits leisurely strolling alongside shops, galleries, and historic houses. The commercial streets of M St. and Wisconsin Ave. are where the bustling crowds come to see and be seen and where innumerable restaurants of all kinds, street vendors, and specialty shops all compete for the eye of the countless pedestrians drawn to the city's most popular visitor destination. Metro: Foggy Bottom-GWU, then 30, 32, 34, 35, or 36 Bus.

Georgetown Annual Garden Tour

On the second Saturday in May, Christ Church at 31st and O Sts. NW sponsors this self-guided walking tour of more than a dozen of Georgetown's loveliest private gardens. The price of the ticket usually includes light fare. Information at (202) 333-6677.

Georgetown Bar and Billiards 3251 Prospect St. NW btw M and N Sts. off Wisconsin Ave. (202) 965-7665 www.georgetownbarandbilliards.com

This popular spot offers nineteen pool tables in good condition and reasonably priced beer and food. It is open daily 6 p.m.–2 a.m. The busiest hours are on weekends and after 9 p.m. weeknights. Metro: Foggy Bottom-GWU, then 30, 32, 34, 35, or 36 Bus.

Georgetown Connection *see* Georgetown Shuttle Bus.

Georgetown Custom House and Post Office 1215 31st St. NW btw M and N Sts. (202) 842-2487 www.cr.nps.gov/nr/travel/wash/dc16.htm

Before the Civil War this splendid structure served as a customs house. Its interior has been restored and it now serves as a post office in Georgetown. Metro: Foggy Bottom-GWU, then 30, 32, 34, 35, or 36 Bus.

Georgetown DC (Web site) www.georgetowndc.com

Sponsored by two Georgetown business associations and a local software company, this Web site is useful for almost any Georgetown activity. It provides a historical overview and virtual tour of Georgetown, lists major attractions, tours and operators, shows you where you can park, how to use public transportation, lists new business openings and sales, local events, shopping information, entertainment sites, schools, and even a local bulletin board. It links to the online version of *The Georgetowner*, a weekly free newspaper with Georgetown coverage and listings of shops, restaurants, and events.

Georgetown Flea Market www.georgetownfleamarket.com

Located at Wisconsin Ave. between S and T Sts. on weekends 9 a.m.–5 p.m. from spring through December more than 100 stalls with furniture, books, rugs, antiques, silver, art, jewelry, clothing, and more can be examined and haggled over.

Georgetown Historic District www.cr.nps.gov/nr/travel/wash/dc15.htm

This region of Washington began as a port town in the mid-eighteenth century before the city was established. Later it was annexed to the city. Its boundaries are roughly Dumbarton Oaks and Reservoir Pkwy. on the north, Rock Creek Park on the east, the Potomac River on the south, and Glover-Archbold Park on the west. The structures in the region are an eclectic mix from different periods of history. Homes range from simple houses to large estates and run the gamut of architectural styles with some 4,000 structures included in this National Historic Landmark community.

Georgetown House Tour

During April each year on a Saturday and Sunday some of the most splendid residences in Georgetown open their doors to visitors. Six homes can be viewed on Saturday, six more on Sunday. Arrangements are made by St. John's Episcopal Church Georgetown Parish at 3240 O St. With the price of the ticket on each day, a lovely tea service is provided. Information at (202) 338-1796 or www.georgetown housetour.com.

Georgetown Information Center www.nps.gov/choh/pphtml/facilities.html

This visitors center operated by the National Park Service is located at 1057 Thomas Jefferson St., 1 block below M St. on the C&O Canal. Open Wed–Sun 9 a.m.–4:30 p.m. from April to mid-November. Tickets are sold here for the 90-minute barge ride on the C&O Canal. Free maps are also available here from National Park Service rangers. Information at (202) 653-5190. Metro: Foggy Bottom-GWU, then 30, 32, 34, 35, or 36 Bus.

Georgetown Inn 1310 Wisconsin Ave. NW btw N and O Sts. (202) 333-8900 or (800) 424-2979 www.georgetowninn.com

Smack in the midst of bustling Georgetown this Federal-era red brick hostelry features Colonial-style décor in its tastefully furnished rooms. The ambiance and the services are all excellent, only befitting such an expensive address. Metro: Foggy Bottom-GWU, then 30, 32, 34, 35, or 36 Bus.

Georgetown Market 3276 M St. NW at Potomac St. www.cr.nps.gov/nr/travel/wash/dc18.htm

This is one of the rare market buildings still standing, which dates from the nineteenth century. Unlike the Eastern Market in the Capitol Hill neighborhood, which is still an active market at the original site, this building has been transformed into a food emporium operated by the Dean & DeLuca gourmet chain. Metro: Foggy Bottom-GWU, then 30, 32, 34, 35, or 36 Bus.

Georgetown Metro Connection *see* Georgetown Shuttle Bus.

The Georgetown Newspaper 1410 Wisconsin Ave. NW (202) 338-4833 www .georgetown.com

For some 50 years this paper has been distributed free in and around Georgetown once every two weeks with its content exclusively centered on news, features, events scheduled, and the like on this lively city neighborhood.

Georgetown Park 3222 M St. NW btw Market House and Wisconsin Ave. (202) 298-5577 www.shopsatgeorgetownpark.com

On the site of what was once a tobacco warehouse and later a horse-drawn trolley and then electric streetcar station, this mall retains the exterior façades with a multiple-level, neo-Victorian skylighted interior surrounded by more than 100 elegant shops, cafés, and dining places. There's even a small museum, open daily, of historical artifacts discovered during excavations at the site of the structure. This is a very upscale shoppers' playing ground, but it is also a rather interesting place in its own right as a unique and imaginative example of reconstruction architecture. Metro: Foggy Bottom-GWU, then 30, 32, 34, 35, or 36 Bus.

Georgetown Park Shops *see* Shops at Georgetown Park.

Georgetown Polo Club

During a season that normally runs on weekends from sometime in June to early September, free polo matches can be seen at West Potomac Park near the Lincoln Memorial. For information call (202) 619-7222. Metro: Foggy Bottom-GWU or Smithsonian, then a good walk.

Georgetown Pool 34th and Volta Sts. NW (202) 282-2366

This free outdoor pool operated by the D.C. Park and Recreation Department in upper Georgetown is open Tues–Fri 1 p.m.–8 p.m., Sat–Sun noon–7 p.m. from the end of May to the beginning of September.

Georgetown Presbyterian Church 3115 P St. NW at 31st St. (202) 338-1644 www .gtownpres.org

Originally built at M and 30th Sts. early in the nineteenth century, the church frequented by the Georgetown Scottish population was moved to its present site in 1873 and rebuilt in Victorian style. In 1956 the building was restored to its earlier Colonial style by Lorenzo Winslow. Metro: Foggy Bottom-GWU, then 30, 32, 34, 35, or 36 Bus.

Georgetown Seafood Grill 1200 19th St. NW at M St. (202) 530-4430 www.gsgrill .com

This long-standing seafood favorite moved here from Georgetown some five years ago. It still serves fine crab cakes in season as well as other succulent fish dishes at moderately expensive prices. Open for lunch Mon–Fri, and dinner daily. Metro: Dupont Circle.

Georgetown Shuttle Bus

While there is no Metro stop in Georgetown, two shuttle bus routes provide easy access day and night. The Georgetown Metro Connection runs between Georgetown and the Rosslyn, Foggy Bottom-GWU, and Dupont Circle Metro stations. Route 1, the Wisconsin Ave. Line, travels between Georgetown and Foggy Bottom-GWU Metro station via Wisconsin Ave. NW, the Georgetown Waterfront, and K St. NW. Route 2, the M St. Line, travels between the Rosslyn Metro station, Georgetown and 19th St., and Sunderland Place, NW ($^{1}/_{2}$ block south of the Dupont Circle Metro station) via Key Bridge, M St., Pennsylvania Ave., L St. and New Hampshire Ave. NW. The fare is inexpensive and is cut in half if you have a Metro transfer. Buses run every 10 minutes daily. Hours of operation: Mon–Thurs 7 a.m.–12 p.m., Fri 7 a.m.–2 a.m., Sat 8 a.m.–2 a.m., Sun 8 a.m.–midnight. Detailed bus stop locations are available at the Web site: www.georgetowndc.com/shut tle.php

Georgetown Suites 1111 30th St. NW at M St. (202) 298-7800 or (800) 348-7203 www.georgetownsuites.com

This is a well-located hostelry with more than 200 accommodations designed for longer stays on a quiet street near the main Georgetown scene. The suites contain good-sized rooms and well-equipped kitchens. Among the amenities at this fairly expensive place are an exercise facility, complimentary continental breakfast, and daily newspaper. Metro: Foggy Bottom-GWU, then 30, 32, 34, 35, or 36 Bus.

Georgetown Symphony Orchestra www.georgetownsymphony.org

This musical ensemble performs its concerts during the fall to spring season on the Georgetown University campus in Gaston Hall. The group includes professionals and well-qualified amateur musicians. Information on the concert schedule at (202) 298-1094.

Georgetown University entrance at 37th and O Sts. NW (202) 687-0100 www
.georgetown.edu

Established in 1789, this Jesuit institution, open to all faiths since its founding,
is the oldest Catholic higher-education university in the nation. Some 12,000 undergraduate and graduate students are attracted to this splendid 104-acre urban
campus for its programs in public administration, foreign affairs, liberal arts, law,
business, and medicine, including a first-rate teaching hospital. With its shady cobblestone streets and fortresslike structures, the grounds and buildings make an attractive tourist destination. Tours can be arranged by calling the admissions office
several weeks in advance at (202) 687-3600.

Georgetown University Hoyas www.guhoyas.com

This strong men's basketball team plays its home games at the MCI Center at
601 F St. NW, close to the Gallery Pl.-Chinatown Metro station. Information about
the schedule at the Web site. Tickets are sold through TicketMaster at (202) 432-
SEAT or www.TicketMaster.com.

Georgetown University Lauinger Memorial Library 1421 37th St. NW at N St.
(202) 687-7452 www.georgetown.edu/home/libraries.html

This modern structure, unlike the other campus buildings, houses the university's comprehensive collections. It was built in 1970 by architect John Carl War-
necke to honor Georgetown's first graduate to die in Vietnam, Joseph Mark
Lauinger. Other important libraries on the campus are the law and medical libraries.

Georgetown Visitation Preparatory School and Monastery 1500 35th St. NW at
P St. (202) 337-3350 www.visi.org

This is the first Catholic school for girls in the American colonies. The Gothic
chapel was built in 1821. The section of the red brick corner building facing 35th
St. was constructed in the 1830s and the part looking at P St. was erected in the
1850s. The academy building in Italianate style with a mansard roof dates from
1873. Its architect was Norris Starkweather.

Georgetown Walking Tours (301) 589-8999 www.tourdc.com

The specialty here is the history, culture, and other lore of one of the city's most
colorful and glamorous neighborhoods. Call for details or check the Web site.

Georgetowner 1054 Potomac St. NW (202) 338-4833 www.georgetowner.com

This is a weekly free newspaper—now more than 50 years old—with rich
Georgetown coverage and citywide articles as well on some topics, and listings of
shops, restaurants, and events. Drop points are throughout Georgetown hotels,
coffee shops, banks, groceries, book stores, and farther afield in Metro-area stores
of Borders, Barnes & Noble, and Fresh Fields.

Georgetowner (Web site) www.georgetowner.com

This venerable local paper has an online version including a guide to the area.
It locates stores, historic sites, and night spots. Updated at least weekly, its sections
are a calendar of events, dining, table-hopping, performances, visual arts, social,
haute and cool, movies, and body and soul.

Georgette Klinger 5345 Wisconsin Ave. NW at Military Rd. (202) 686-8880

Located in upper-northwest D.C. this thriving branch of this fashionable national skin-care and beauty treatment chain specializes in facials, and men are being attracted in growing numbers. Open Mon–Sat from 9 a.m., Sun 10 a.m., with evening hours on Tues and Thurs. Metro: Friendship Heights.

Georgia Avenue Day

On a weekend in late August, the city's longest business street holds a celebration centered around Banneker Community Center, 2500 Georgia Ave. NW with live music, children's carnival rides, food, and a parade in a mélange of Caribbean, African, and American Southern tradition and influences. Information at (202) 673-7624.

Georgia Brown's 950 15th St. NW btw I and K Sts. (202) 393-4499 www.gbrowns .com

Low-country Southern cooking with innovative variations can be found at this airy dining spot that's a favorite with many local bigwigs. The menu's down home, but the prices are upscale. Open Mon–Fri for lunch and dinner, Sat dinner, and Sun brunch and dinner. Reservations recommended for Sunday brunch and weekend dinner. Metro: McPherson Square.

Georgia Embassy 1615 New Hampshire Ave. NW, Suite 300 (202) 387-2390, fax (202) 393-4537 www.georgiaemb.org

Gerard's Place 915 15th St. NW btw I and K Sts. (202) 737-4445

This is the place for gourmets seeking innovative French cuisine prepared in intriguing yet simple ways by one of the city's master chefs. It's very expensive but the discriminating diners in D.C. keep returning. Open Mon–Fri for lunch and dinner, Sat for dinner. Recommendations are necessary. Metro: McPherson Square.

German American Day www.geocities.com/agas_dc

Every year on a Sunday at the end of September or early October this celebration takes place on the grounds near the Washington Monument around midday featuring food, entertainment, speeches, and fraternal spirit. Information at (202) 467-5000 or (202) 554-2664.

German Cultural Center *see* Goethe Institut.

German Gourmet 7185 Lee Hwy., Falls Church, VA (703) 534-1908 http://area guides.com/german-gourmet

This specialty store features all manner of German food choices and is open Mon and Sat 9 a.m.–6 p.m., Tues–Thurs 9 a.m.–7 p.m. Open on Sun also only in December. Metro: East Falls Church, then the Lee Hwy. Bus or a 15-minute walk.

German Restaurants *see* Café Berlin, Old Europe. *See also* Heidelberg Pastry Shop.

Germany Embassy 4645 Reservoir Rd. NW (202) 298-4000 www.germany-info.org

Ghana Embassy 3512 International Dr. NW (202) 686-4520 www.ghana-embassy .org

Glen Echo Park 7300 MacArthur Blvd. near Goldsboro Rd., Glen Echo, MD (301) 492-6282 or (301) 492-6229 www.nps.gov/glec

Located near the Potomac this historic park is now administered by Montgomery County in a partnership with the National Park Service as a center for art, theater, and dance as well as an amusement site. Historic buildings contain studios for glassmakers, quilters, and metal workers, and some of their creations are displayed in an art gallery. An old-time carousel usually operates on some days of the week from April to October. Adventure Theater presents fairy tales and children's stories on weekends and the Puppet Company performs several times a week. Also located here is the Discovery Creek Children's Museum. Picnic facilities are also available. The park is open Mon–Thurs 9 a.m.–5 p.m., Fri–Sat 9 a.m.–midnight, Sun 9 a.m.–6 p.m. There is free parking close by. Information on the park's programs and activities at (301) 492-6282 or (301) 492-6229 or on the Web site. Metro: Tenleytown-AU, then Ride-On 29 Bus. *See also* Adventure Theater, Discovery Creek Children's Museum, Puppet Company Playhouse.

Glen Echo Park Spanish Ballroom 7300 MacArthur Blvd. near Goldsboro Rd., Glen Echo, MD (301) 492-6282 or (301) 492-6229 www.nps.gov/glec

This is a 70-year-old mission-style building with 7,500 square feet of wood floor space given over to various types of ballroom, swing, and square dancing without smoking or drinking. Operates usually on weekends from spring to fall. Call for schedule information or check the Web site. Metro: Tenleytown-AU, then Ride-On 29 Bus.

Glenview Mansion 603 Edmonston Dr., Rockville, MD (240) 314-8660 www.ci .rockville.md.us/glenview

This 25-room mansion, built in 1838 and renovated in 1926, is situated in what is now Rockville Civic Center Park. Surrounding the mansion are Italianate terraced gardens installed in 1927. The mansion is rented for balls, business functions, and weddings, and docents are sometimes available for tours. An art gallery also is located at the site. By car from Rte. 28 and I-270, proceed east on Rte. 28, cross Rte. 355 and follow Rte. 28 east (turns left at first light beyond Rte. 355). Travel 4 blocks to Baltimore Rd., turn right, go 3 blocks to Edmonston Drive, turn left, and Civic Center Park entrance is immediately on the right.

Glenwood Cemetery 2219 Lincoln Rd. NE off 4th St. (202) 667-1016

Many illustrious local residents can be found in this tranquil burial site near Catholic University including Constantino Brumidi, who painted the frescoes on the interior of the Capitol dome, and Emanuel Leutze, the artist who did the famous painting *Washington Crossing the Delaware*. There are also a number of unusual and dramatic memorial tombs of less renowned people to be found here. Open dawn to dusk. Metro: Brookland-CUA, then walk on Michigan Ave. to the Basilica of the Shrine of the Immaculate Conception and turn left on 4th St. and walk to Lincoln Rd.

Glover Archbold Park Van Ness St. NW btw Wisconsin and Nebraska Aves. (202) 426-6829

This is a 183-acre park passing through some of the finest neighborhoods in northwest D.C. It contains a 3^1/$_2$-mile nature trail suitable for strolling or running through scenic woodlands of oak and elm trees. Metro: Tenleytown-AU, then walk south on Wisconsin Ave. to Van Ness St., then right 1 block to a sign on the left marking the park's north entrance.

Glover Park

This residential neighborhood is just above Georgetown bordering the Washington National Cathedral and bounded by Wisconsin Ave. and Glover and Whitehaven Parks. Homes here are an eclectic mix of single-family houses, brownstones, and townhouses. Many homes sport comfortable front porches. There are also high-rise and garden-style apartment buildings in the area. There are a number of restaurants and retail shops along Wisconsin Ave. Metro: Tenleytown-AU, then walk north on Wisconsin Ave.

Goddard Space Flight Center *see* NASA Goddard Visitor Center.

Goethe Institut 814 7th St. NW btw H and I Sts. (202) 289-1200 www.goethe.de/ Washington

This German cultural and language center offers a wide program of art exhibitions, lectures, films, and language courses. Open Mon–Thurs 9 a.m.–5 p.m., Fri 9 a.m.–3 p.m. Metro: Gallery Pl.-Chinatown.

Gold Line/Gray Line Bus Tours *see* Gray Line Bus Tours.

Goldoni 1909 K St. NW btw 19th and 20th Sts. (202) 955-9494 www.teatrogoldoni .com

This restaurant features Venetian-style imaginative Italian cooking with fine sauces and well-flavored pasta dishes. Prices are moderate. Open for lunch Mon–Fri, dinner Mon–Sat. Metro: Farragut North.

Gold's Gym 408 4th St., SW btw D and E Sts. (202) 554-4653 www.goldsgym.com

This national chain fitness facility operates here and at a number of other venues in D.C. and the Virginia and Maryland suburbs. Daily and weekly rates are offered. Memberships in other places are good for limited periods of use by visitors. For other locations in and around the city, check the phone books. Metro: Federal Center SW.

Golf *see* Kemper Open.

Golf (Participatory Sports Activity) *see* Algonkian Regional Park, Anacostia Park, Burke Lake Golf Course, East Potomac Golf Course, Enterprise, Langston Golf Course, Needwood Golf Course, Northwest Park Golf Course, Penderbrook, Pleasant Valley Golfers Club, Pohick Bay Regional Park Golf Course, Potomac Park, Raspberry Falls Golf and Hunt Club, Reston National Golf Course, Rock Creek Golf Course, Seneca Creek State Park, South Riding, Trotters Glen Family Golf Center, U.S. Soldiers' and Airmen's Home

Go Lo's 604 H St. NW near 6th St. (202) 437-4656

The site occupied by this Chinese restaurant is the building in which Mary Surratt operated a boardinghouse in which John Wilkes Booth and fellow conspirators allegedly met to plot the assassination of Abraham Lincoln. There's a landmark plaque on the building. The food here is a blend of Szechuan and Cantonese styles.

Service is cordial, prices inexpensive. Open daily for lunch and dinner. Metro: Gallery Pl.-Chinatown.

Gompers Memorial *see* Samuel Gompers Memorial.

Good Fortune 2646 University Blvd. W btw Georgia Ave. and Viers Mill Rd., Wheaton, MD (301) 929-8818

A roomy, comfortable restaurant serving dim sum every day at lunch and offering a very extensive selection of well-prepared Cantonese-style dishes at very inexpensive prices. Open daily for lunch and dinner. Metro: Wheaton.

Government Printing Office 710 N Capitol St. NW btw G and H Sts. http://book store.gpo.gov

The central building of the largest printing establishment in the world covers 1 city block and is a massive Romanesque Revival structure built entirely of brick. More than a billion items are published here each year for the three branches of government, and innumerable publications of consumer and citizen interest. Some 5,000 government employees work for this agency and use extraordinary amounts of paper annually. The printing plant is closed to the public, but the retail bookstore at this site sells government-published books, pamphlets, and manuals about countless subjects. Metro: Union Station.

Government Printing Office Bookstore 710 N Capitol St. NW btw G and H Sts. (202) 512-0132 www.bookstore.gpo.gov

This retail outlet for government publications stocks an inventory of some 3,000 titles including guides, statistical compilations, policy studies, manuals, self-help pamphlets, and titles dealing with innumerable special topics. Open Mon–Fri 8 a.m.–4 p.m. Metro: Union Station.

Governor's House Hotel 1615 Rhode Island Ave. NW at 17th St. (202) 296-2100 or (800) 821-4367 www.governorshousewdc.com

This is a moderate-priced renovated hotel with large well-furnished rooms and some kitchen-equipped suites. Access to a nearby YMCA fitness facility and a large outdoor pool are among the amenities. Metro: Dupont Circle or Farragut North.

Govinda Gallery 1227 34th St. NW at Prospect St. (202) 333-1180 www.govinda gallery.com

This Georgetown Gallery specializes in exhibiting photography dealing with pop music stars and themes. Open 11 a.m.–6 p.m. Tues–Sun Metro: Foggy Bottom-GWU, then 30, 32, 34, 35, or 36 Bus.

Grace Episcopal Church 1041 Wisconsin Ave. btw South St. and the C&O Canal (202) 333-7100 www.gracedc.org

This is a community-involved activist church constructed of stone in Gothic Revival style with a gabled roof. It is also the venue for concerts and performances of area theatrical companies. Metro: Foggy Bottom-GWU, then 30, 32, 34, 35, or 36 Bus.

Grace Reformed Church 1405 15th St. NW btw O and P Sts. (202) 387-3131

President Theodore Roosevelt laid the foundation stone of this church in 1903 and attended services here regularly. The church was established in the mid-nineteenth century and located at this site in 1880. Metro: Dupont Circle.

Grand Army of the Republic Memorial 7th and C Sts. NW

This monument by sculptor John M. Rhind was constructed in 1909 as a memorial to the founder of the Grand Army of the Republic, Dr. Benjamin Stephenson, who served with the Union army as a surgeon during the Civil War. Metro: Archives-Navy Memorial.

Grand Hyatt Washington 1000 H St. NW btw 10th and 11th Sts. (202) 582-1234 or (800) 233-1234 www.washingtonhyatt.com

This is a top-class 900-room high-rise built around a natural lagoon with an atrium glass roof above. It features a swimming pool, a health facility, several restaurants, and other luxury hotel amenities. The downtown location puts it close to the MCI Center, theaters, and shops and near the Metro. Metro: Metro Center.

Grand Slam in the Grand Hyatt Hotel 1000 H St. NW btw 10th and 11th Sts. (202) 637-4789

This may be the city's best sports bar with two huge TV screens, a dozen regular TVs, a pool table, a number of games, and amiable service. It is comfortable, roomy, clean, and well designed for drinking and watching games, very different from the typical sports bar. A wide range of different types of customers frequent this spot. Open daily from 11 a.m.–2 a.m. Metro: Metro Center.

Grant Memorial Union Square, 1st St. NW btw Pennsylvania and Maryland Aves. www.kittytours.org/thatman2/search.asp?subject = 17

This 252-foot-long monument in front of the Capitol Reflecting Pool, the largest equestrian statue in the United States, was sculpted by Henry Merwin Shrady in 1922. The bronze figure of Gen. Ulysses S. Grant is on horseback adjacent to Union cavalry troops and artillery in a dramatic battle depiction. Metro: Federal Center.

Grave of John F. Kennedy www.arlingtoncemetery.org/visitor_information/JFK.html

This memorial is marked by an eternal flame and selections from the former president's inaugural speech. The simple marble terrace offers a sweeping view of the city from this site in Arlington National Cemetery. Jacqueline Kennedy is buried beside him. Metro: Arlington Cemetery.

Gray Line Bus Tours Terminal at Union Station, 50 Massachusetts Ave. NE (202) 289-1995 www.graylinedc.com

This well-known tour company runs a wide selection of tour routes to popular sites in and around the city offering guided excursions in air-conditioned buses of varying lengths of time from 3 to 9 hours, morning, afternoon, and evening. Call for information or check the Web site.

Great Britain Embassy *see* United Kingdom Embassy.

Great Falls *see* McLean/Great Falls.

Great Falls and Riverbend Parks Old Dominion Dr. at Georgetown Pike, Great Falls, VA Great Falls Park: (703) 285-2966 www.nps.gov/gwmp.grfa; Riverbend Park: (703) 759-9018 www.co.fairfax.va.us/parks

These two parks, one administered by the National Park Service and the other by Fairfax County, are on the Virginia side of the Potomac River some 10 miles northwest of the city. Great Falls is where the river courses through large and dramatic boulders and the park offers well-marked trails, picnic facilities, and a visitor center with geological displays. The park is open daily from 9 a.m. to dark. Admission charge. Riverbend is a less-developed park but it does have miles of paths ideal for nature walks. Driving on the Beltway (I-495) take Exit 13 to Rte. 193. The entrance to the parks, which are adjacent to each other, is 6 miles west on Rte. 193.

Greater New Hope Baptist Church 816 8th St. NW at H St. (202) 842-1036

This church was constructed in 1898 by architects Stutz and Pease as a synagogue for the Washington Hebrew Congregation. The structure is an impressive Byzantine-style building with a minaret at the top. The present church occupants have kept the window on the south side with the Star of David. This is one of several churches in the city's downtown area that were begun as Jewish places of worship. Metro: Gallery Pl.-Chinatown.

Greater Reston Arts Center 11911 Freedom Dr., SR 110, Reston, VA (703) 471-9242 www.restonart.com

This community arts center shows rotating exhibitions of contemporary visual art. It also sponsors an annual fine arts festival and offers art classes as part of its continuing program to support and encourage artistic achievement.

Greece Embassy 2221 Massachusetts Ave. NW (202) 939-5800 www.greekembassy .org

Greek Fall Festival

The Sts. Constantine and Helen Greek Orthodox Church at 4115 16th St. NW at Upshur St. holds a three-day weekend celebration in mid-September of Greek culture and food. Information at (202) 829-2910.

Greek Restaurants *see* Café Plaka, Mykonos, Taverna the Greek Islands, Yanni's Greek Taverna, Zorba's Café. *See also* Middle Eastern Restaurants, Web sites: www .dcpages.com, www.restaurant.com, www.washingtonpost.com, www.opentable .com.

Greek Spring Festival

St. Sophia Greek Orthodox Cathedral, 36th St. and Massachusetts Ave. NW (1 block from Washington Cathedral) holds its annual festival on a Friday, Saturday, and Sunday in mid-May from noon to 9 p.m. This festival is held rain or shine and features Greek food and drink, arts and crafts, and live Greek music and dancing. Details at (202) 333-4730. Metro: Tenleytown-AU, then bus on Wisconsin Ave. toward D.C.

Green Spring Gardens Park 4603 Green Spring Rd., Alexandria, VA (703) 642-5173 www.co.fairfax.va.us/parks

This is the ideal park for those who enjoy walking along paths beside beautifully tended demonstration gardens. It is open dawn to dusk. Metro: King Street, then 29N Bus.

Greenbelt www.ci.greenbelt.md.us

This is a suburban Maryland community that was conceived in the 1930s as a planned garden city with Depression-era federal funds under the New Deal of the Roosevelt administration. It is located where major roads come together—the Beltway (I-495), Baltimore Washington Pkwy., Kenilworth Ave., and Rte. 1. Downtown D.C. is some 15 miles away. Much of the original housing is still being used and the community maintains a museum at 10B Crescent Rd. in one of the original buildings. The community is home to many academics and engineers employed at the NASA/Goddard Space Flight Center and the University of Maryland and it remains the center for many cooperative and activist efforts derived from its original character. Metro: Greenbelt.

Greenbelt Marriott 6400 Ivy Lane, Greenbelt, MD (301) 441-3700 www.marriott .com

This moderately expensive hotel is one of the better accommodations located near the NASA/Goddard Space Flight Center and the University of Maryland. It features indoor and outdoor pools, an exercise facility, tennis courts, and restaurants as well as free parking. Shuttle service is provided to the Greenbelt Metro station. By car on the Beltway (I-495), take Exit 23N and drive on Rte. 201 less than 1/2 mile to Ivy Lane and turn left.

Greenbelt Park 6565 Greenbelt Rd. btw Baltimore Washington Pkwy. and Kenilworth Ave., Greenbelt, MD (301) 344-3948 www.nps.gov/gree

Some 12 miles from the center of the city is this 1,100-acre forest with streams, deer, and foxes, numerous walking trails and picnic areas as well as campsites. Open dawn to dusk. By car exit the Beltway (I-495) at Exit 23 on Kenilworth Ave. to Greenbelt Rd. (Rte. 193) and go left a short distance to the park entrance.

Greenwood Restaurant 5031 Connecticut Ave. NW at Nebraska Ave. (202) 364-4444 www.greenwoodrestaurant.com

The nearest appellation for the food here might be California style. Everything is organized on the dish to look appetizing using the best possible ingredients that are fresh and seasonal. Salads and vegetables are attractive creations, and the fish and meat dishes are imaginatively and tastefully prepared. Prices are moderate and dinner is served Tues–Sun. Metro: Van Ness-UDC.

Grenada Embassy 1701 New Hampshire Ave. NW (202) 265-2561 www.embassy .org/embassies/gd.html

Grill From Ipanema 1858 Columbia Rd. NW at Kalorama Rd. (202) 986-0757 www.thegrillfromipanema.com

Brazilian beverages and food from *feijoada* (black bean stew) to grilled meats and fish to other hearty fare are served here at inexpensive prices. Open for dinner Mon–Fri, Sat and Sun brunch and dinner. Metro: Woodley Park-Zoo.

Grillfish 1200 New Hampshire Ave. NW at M St. (202) 331-7310 www.grill fish.com

This large relaxed restaurant serves modestly priced, well-prepared seafood and fish dishes for lunch Mon–Fri, Sat dinner, and Sun brunch and dinner. Metro: Foggy Bottom-GWU.

Grist Mill Historical State Park 5514 Mount Vernon Memorial Hwy., just east of Richmond Hwy. (Rte. 1) (703) 780-3383 or (703) 550-0960 www.dcr.state.va.us/index.htm

George Washington built a mill at this site in 1770 and used it throughout his life to grind flour. By 1850 it had fallen into ruins, but in 1932, the bicentennial of Washington's birthday, it was reconstructed and restored. Tours are offered for a nominal fee, and archaeologists continue to work at the site regularly. Open daily 10 a.m.–5 p.m. By car the park is reached by taking Rte. 235 west from Mount Vernon 3 miles.

Grog and Tankard 2408 Wisconsin Ave. NW btw Hall Pl. and Calvert St. (202) 333-3114

This is a small, crowded night club/bar filled with young people who come here for the scene as well as the loud rock music by local and imported bands on some nights. On those nights there is a cover charge. Call for information about performers, entry fee, and times.

Gross National Product (202) 783-7212 www.gnpcomedy.com

This is a local troupe that spoofs the nation's political foibles and fumblers. They perform at various venues in town and around the country on tour with their irreverent sketches of government machinations and *maladroits*. Call for information or check the Web site.

The Guards 2915 M St. NW btw 29th and 30th Sts. (202) 965-2350

This restaurant and bar is a favorite Georgetown place for its congenial, elegant atmosphere, which attracts regulars and tourists of different ages for the drink and the food. Open 11:30 a.m.–2 a.m. or 3 a.m. every day but Mon. Metro: Foggy Bottom-GWU, then 30, 32, 34, 35 or 36 Bus.

Guatemala Embassy 2220 R St. NW (202) 745-4952 www.guatemala-embassy.org

Guest Houses *see* Adams Inn, Kalorama Guest House. *See also* Bed-and-Breakfasts.

Guinea Embassy 2112 Leroy Pl. NW www.embassy.org/embassies/gn.html
Embassy of the Republic of Guinea.

Guinea-Bissau Embassy 15929 Yukon La., Rockville, MD (301) 947-3958 www.embassy.org/embassies/gw.html
Embassy of the Republic of Guinea-Bissau.

Gum Springs Museum and Cultural Center 8100 Fordson Rd., Alexandria, VA (703) 799-1198 www.gshsfcva.org/gshs05.htm

Gum Springs was founded by West Ford, a former slave of George Washington's family, who acquired the property in 1833. Gum Springs became a place to live for runaways and recently freed slaves. Helped by Quakers, freed slaves worked in the trades they had learned as estate slaves. The Gum Springs Historical Society's Museum and Cultural Center's many activities and exhibits celebrate the long continuity of this historic black community. Today, Gum Springs has more than 2,500 residents, and as many as 500 are descendants of the original families. The center is open Mon–Fri 6 p.m.–8 p.m., and Sat and Tues 1 p.m.–3 p.m. Metro: Huntington Ave., exit the station and take the FX105 FX Bus toward Woodlawn-IMP to the stop at Sherwood Hall Lane and Fordson Rd. Walk 3 blocks south on Fordson Rd.

Gunston Hall 10709 Gunston Rd., southeast of Rte. 1, Mason Neck, VA (703) 550-9220 or (800) 811-6966 www.gunstonhall.org

This is a splendid estate in southeastern Fairfax County built in the mid-eighteenth century by George Mason, who was an influential figure in the adoption of the American Bill of Rights. The mansion is open to visitors by guided tour only daily 9:30 a.m.–5 p.m. Modest admission charge. The interior of the brick building contains beautifully restored carved woodwork, and the rooms are filled with furniture from the Colonial period, some of which was owned by the family. The spacious grounds include a schoolhouse and a formal garden as well as a nature trail. The visitor center presents an orientation film. By car take the George Washington Memorial Pkwy. to Mount Vernon. Then take the Mount Vernon Memorial Hwy. to Richmond Hwy. (Rte. 1), and on Rte. 1 drive south about 5 miles beyond Woodlawn Plantation to Gunston Rd. and Gunston Hall. *See also* Frank Lloyd Wright's Pope Leighey House.

Guyana Embassy 2490 Tracy Pl. NW (202) 265-6900 www.guyana.org/embassy .htm.

Gymnasiums *see* Fitness Centers.

H. H. Leonard's Mansion 2020 O St. NW near 20th St. (202) 496-2000 www .omansion.com

This very small bed-and-breakfast is an exceptional lodging in an old brownstone featuring attractively decorated unique rooms, an exercise room, and an outdoor pool. Accommodations are fairly steep, but the place is very charming and well located. Metro: Dupont Circle.

HR 57 Center for Preservation of Jazz and Blues 1610 14th St. NW (202) 667-3700 www.hr57.org

Founded in 1993, this nonprofit organization celebrates "a rare and valuable national treasure" through jazz and blues performances, seminars, discussions, an Internet radio station, recording and practice studios, and an active outreach program to local schools. The quoted material comes from a House of Representatives 1987 resolution on the subject, as does the name (H. Con Res 57). HR 57 hosts jazz jam sessions on Wednesday starting about 8:30 p.m. until midnight, and Fri and Sat 9 p.m.–midnight or later. Thursdays could be a big band or even a house quartet, playing 8 p.m.–midnight. Modest fees for jazz performances; membership discounts. You can bring your own alcoholic beverages. Metro: Dupont Circle.

Haad Thai 1100 New York Ave. NW at 11th St. (202) 682-1111 www.haadthai.com

This is a popular conveniently located downtown restaurant, which provides a great variety of choices of Thai specialties at moderate prices. Open for lunch Mon–Sat, dinner nightly. Metro: Metro Center.

Hahnemann Memorial www.nlm.nih.gov/hmd/medtour/hahnemann.html

Located in the triangle east of Scott Circle at the intersection of Rhode Island Ave., Massachusetts Ave., and 16th St. NW, this bronze, granite, and mosaic monument was designed by architect Charles Henry Niehaus. It was built in 1900 to honor the German doctor who founded homeopathic medicine, Dr. Samuel C. F. Hahnemann. Metro: Dupont Circle.

Hains Point

This is the southernmost point of the peninsula created by the Washington

Channel, at the bottom of East Potomac Park in southwest D.C. It provides beautiful views of the city, but automobile traffic here is frequently restricted or heavily congested. It is the site of the giant sculpture *The Awakening. See also* The Awakening.

Haiti Embassy 2311 Massachusetts Ave. NW (202) 332-4090 www.haiti.org

Halcyon House 3400 Prospect St. NW at 34th St. www.cr.nps.gov/nr/travel/wash/dc15.htm

This house at the edge of Georgetown was constructed in 1787 by Benjamin Stoddart, the first American secretary of the navy. It has undergone innumerable renovations and additions over the years so that it is now an eclectic mix of architectural styles, but the views of the river and beyond are unrivaled. It is privately owned and not open to tourists.

Hall of Fame for Caring Americans *see* Frederick Douglass Museum and Hall of Fame for Caring Americans.

Halloween High Heel Race

This event takes place every year on 17th St. NW between S and P Sts. on or around October 31. The contest enlists the participation of some of the best-looking drag racers in town and attracts a big crowd to watch the short-lived frolic. Information at (202) 328-0090. Metro: Dupont Circle.

Halloween Monster Bash at the Capital Children's Museum

Almost every year on or around October 31 this festive and spooky event for kids 2 to 12 takes place at the museum at 3rd and H Sts. NE, located behind the parking lot of Union Station. Information at (202) 675-4125. Metro: Union Station.

Hamburgers *see* Hard Rock Café, Stoneys.

Hamilton Crowne Plaza 14th and K Sts. NW (202) 682-0111 or (800) 637-3788 www.hamiltoncrowneplazawashingtondc.com/

This 318-room hotel with attractive modest-sized accommodations is conveniently located downtown in a Beaux Arts structure on Franklin Square. An exercise room at this mid-range establishment is among the amenities. Metro: McPherson Square.

Hamilton Statue *see* Alexander Hamilton Statue.

Handicapped Services *see* Disabled Services.

Harambee Café 1771 U St. NW at 18th St. (202) 332-6435

This family restaurant in Adams Morgan is open every day for lunch and dinner serving simple but filling African dishes of chicken, beef, lamb, and vegetables on spongy *injera* bread at budget prices. Metro: Dupont Circle, then L2 Bus; or Woodley Park-Zoo, then 90, 91, 92, 93, or 96 Bus.

Harbour Square

Located in the southwest and bounded by 4th, N St., O St., and the waterfront, this complex was designed in 1966 by architect Chlothiel Woodward Smith. It incorporates modern high-rise buildings and townhouses but also includes three surviving early nineteenth-century structures. At the center of this large development are a fountain and gardens. Metro: Waterfront-SEU.

Hard Rock Café 999 E St. NW at 10th St. (202) 737-7625 www.hardrock.com

Like all the other branches of this enormously successful international chain, this spot is a mecca for rock and roll memorabilia enthusiasts. The moderately priced hamburgers, barbecue, and nachos are pretty good, too. Open 11 a.m.–late night daily. Metro: Metro Center or Gallery Pl.-Chinatown.

Hard Times Café 1404 King St. btw South West and South Peyton Sts., Arlington, VA (703) 683-5340

This is where chili reigns supreme in all three popular manifestations—vegetarian, Texas style, and Cincinnati style. There are other good cheap dishes here that come in big portions and all kinds of beers and an easygoing down-home ambiance to go with the country music on the jukebox. Open daily for lunch and dinner. Metro: King Street. Other locations at 3028 Wilson Blvd., Arlington, VA (703) 528-2233; 6362 Springfield Plaza, Springfield, VA (703) 913-5600; 428 Elden St., Herndon, VA (703) 318-8941; 4738 Cherry Hill Rd., College Park, MD (301) 474-8880.

Harrington Hotel *see* Hotel Harrington.

Hartke Theater at Catholic University 3801 Harewood Rd. NE near the Basilica (202) 319-4000

This group is part of the university drama department and showcases experimental, musical, and classical theatrical performances from fall to spring. Metro: Brookland-CUA.

Harvard Street Bridges Harvard St. NW at the National Zoo entrance

Two side-by-side Harvard St. bridges cross Rock Creek at the entrance to the National Zoological Park. Both state-of-the-art designs in their day, the older, which is low and spans only the creek, was completed in 1901 and employed a self-supporting steel-beam grid to reinforce the concrete. The other, built in 1965, and contrasting with more traditional structures in the park, is one of the few bridges in the world employing a concrete box girder. Metro: Woodley Park-Zoo.

Hauge House *see* Cameroon Embassy.

Haupt Garden *see* Enid A. Haupt Garden.

Havana Breeze 1401 K St. NW at 14th St. (202) 789-1470

This two-level relaxed spot offers counter service downstairs featuring inexpensive Cuban sandwiches and all the specialty dishes. Upstairs there is table service and a bar. Open Mon–Fri for lunch and dinner, Sat dinner only. Metro: Farragut North.

Hawk and Dove 329 Pennsylvania Ave. SE btw 3rd and 4th Sts. (202) 543-3300

With decor looking more like a hunting lodge than a watering hole, the clientele here is a mix of young and older Capitol Hill types and local residents here for the drinks, the sandwiches and hamburgers, and the friendly ambiance. Open Mon–Thurs and Sun 10 a.m.–2 a.m., Fri and Sat 10 a.m.–3 a.m. Metro: Capitol South.

The Hay-Adams Hotel 1 Lafayette Square NW at 16th and H Sts. (202) 638-6600 or (800) 424-5054 www.hayadams.com

This is one of the city's grandest hotels. Located in an Italian Renaissance structure created in 1928 on the site of the former homes of John Jay and Henry Adams, it has ever since been the epitome of luxury. Its guest list is a roster of the world's elite and no service is spared in making the occupants of the lodging's 143 rooms and suites feel comfortably at home. The Lafayette dining room features American dishes and the afternoon tea service ranks with the city's most pleasurable. Metro: McPherson Square or Farragut West.

Headliners

This is a booking outfit for bringing seasoned comedy performers to a venue in the Maryland suburbs for shows on Friday and Saturday nights during much of the year. Information at (301) 929-8686 or the Web site: www.headlinerscomedy.com.

Heaven and Hell 2327 18th St. NW opposite Belmont St. (202) 667-4355 or (703) 522-HELL (4227)

Upstairs naturally is Heaven, and Hell is down below where it's darker and creepier. This Adams Morgan nightspot with the split personality is a place for dancing and drinking. Different hours and open days in the two locations. Some nights it takes a cover charge to get into Heaven. Best to call ahead for program details. Event information at (703) 522-4227. Club line (202) 677-HELL. Metro: Woodley Park-Zoo, then 90, 91, 92, 93, or 96 Bus.

Hecht's G and 12th Sts. NW (202) 628-6661

This is the sole surviving classic department store in the city center with the full range of clothing and home furnishings on the premises. There are branches of this and the other stores of its type in the suburban shopping malls in the Virginia and Maryland suburbs. Metro: Metro Center.

Hee Been 6231 Little River Turnpike, Alexandria, VA (703) 941-3737

A favorite spot for moderate-priced Korean dishes for local Koreans as well as the rest of its devoted clientele where the barbecues and the succulent soups are top selections. Open daily for lunch and dinner.

Heidelberg Pastry Shop Lee Hwy. and N Culpepper St., Arlington, VA (703) 527-8394

The specialty is German baked goods including tasty strudels and marzipan pastries, but there are also meats, sausages, and cheeses available in the delicatessen. Open Mon–Fri 6:30 a.m.–evening, Sat 8 a.m.–5 p.m., Sun 8 a.m.–1 p.m. Metro: Ballston-MU, then bus.

Heller's 3221 Mount Pleasant St. btw Lamont St. and Park Rd. (202) 265-1190

This bakery has been preparing excellent pastry, breads, croissants, and different types of delectable cakes for 75 years. Open Mon–Sat 6:30 a.m.–6:30 p.m., Sun 6:30 a.m.–2 p.m. Metro: Columbia Heights.

Hemphill Fine Arts 1027 23rd St. NW at M St. (202) 342-5610 www.hemphill finearts.com

This Georgetown gallery has been showing contemporary art in original and novel exhibitions featuring some of Washington's more established as well as emergent artists for some 10 years. Open Tues–Sat 10 a.m.–6 p.m. Metro: Foggy Bottom-GWU, then 30, 32, 34, 35, or 36 Bus.

Henley Park Hotel 926 Massachusetts Ave. NW btw 9th and 10th Sts. (202) 638-5200 or (800) 222-8474 www.cchotels.com

This European-type hotel located in a converted 1918 Tudor-style apartment building has 79 rooms and 17 suites furnished comfortably in English country house fashion. The downtown location near the Mall is convenient, the romantic Coeur de Lion is one of the city's better restaurants, and the room rates are quite expensive. Metro: Metro Center or Gallery Pl.-Chinatown.

Henry Wadsworth Longfellow Statue www.kittytours.org/thatman2/search.asp? subject = 33

This bronze memorial to the country's famous nineteenth-century poet can be found at Connecticut Ave. and M St. NW. It was executed by sculptors Thomas Ball and William Couper in 1909. Metro: Farragut North.

Hereford House 604 S Carolina Ave. SE (202) 543-0102 www.bbonline.com/de/hereford

This charming brick townhouse with bright rooms and small garden has only 4 rooms with a shared bath for each 2 rooms and features a cooked breakfast included in the modest rates. It is located on Capitol Hill only 1 block from the Metro. Metro: Eastern Market.

Heritage India 2400 Wisconsin Ave. NW at Calvert St. (202) 333-3120 www.heritageindia.biz

This is a comfortably relaxed Indian place serving very well-prepared and tastefully flavored dishes for meat enthusiasts as well as vegetarians at moderate prices. Open for lunch Sun–Fri, dinner nightly. Metro: Foggy Bottom-GWU, then 30, 32, 34, 35, or 36 Bus.

Hermitage Inn Restaurant 7134 Main St., Clifton, VA (703) 266-1623 www.hermitageinnrestaurant.com

This "destination restaurant" is well known for its French Mediterranean cuisine, good service and romantic settings, as well as its numerous celebrations and wedding parties at the site. A beautifully restored historic building, it is a former hotel visited by rusticating Presidents Grant, Hayes, and Theodore Roosevelt. Meals are prix fixe and somewhat expensive, but there is moderately priced Sunday brunch. Open for dinner Wed–Sun from 5:30 p.m., Sun brunch 11:30 a.m.–2:30 p.m. By car take Hwy. 66 W to Exit 55, then take Rte. 7100 Exit, Fairfax Country Pkwy. S, onto Rte. 29, Lee Hwy. and go south, left onto Clifton Rd.

Herndon www.town.herndon.va.us

This Virginia suburban community near Reston was once a small village. It grew as a consequence of the growth in the region spawned by the construction of Dulles Toll Rd. and the concomitant business development along the Dulles Airport corridor. The town has been affected by the inflow of these businesses and the residents who came with them. The old historic town center, now restored, still has something of its former village flavor with its small, old train station still situated in the middle of town. Near the center can be found renovated older homes with the newer houses spreading out toward the edges of this community, which is only a bit over 4 square miles in all. It can be reached by bus from the West Falls Church-VT/UVA Metro station.

Herndon Farmers Market Eldon and Spring Sts. (next to the Red Caboose), Herndon, VA (703) 941-7987 www.localharvest.org/farms/M1114

Producers sell their vegetables and fruit Thursdays from early May to the end of October 8:30 a.m.–12:30 p.m.

Heurich House Museum *see* Historical Society of Washington.

High Street Bridge

There were once five bridges over the C&O Canal in Georgetown, but this is the only surviving one. It was built in 1831 and crosses the canal at Wisconsin Ave. On the bridge a marble commemorative obelisk dates from 1850. Metro: Foggy Bottom-GWU, then 30, 32, 34, 35, or 36 Bus.

The Hiker *see* United Spanish War Veteran's Memorial.

Hiking *See* Audubon Naturalist Society, Black History National Recreational Trail, Capital Crescent Trail, Chesapeake and Ohio Canal National Historical Park, Dumbarton Oaks Park, Huntley Meadows Park, Mount Vernon Trail, National Arboretum Walking Trail, National Park Service (Web site), Rock Creek Park Trail, Sligo Creek Parkway, Theodore Roosevelt Island Hiking Path, www.trails.com

The Hill 735 15th St. NW (202) 628-8500 www.hillnews.com

For 10 years this weekly paper has been featuring coverage of what is actually going on in the congressional staff offices. It is available on Washington newsstands and by subscription.

Hill Rag 224 7th St. SE (202) 543-8300 www.hillrag.com

This free newspaper is issued monthly and covers the scene on Capitol Hill. It includes news of interest to those who reside or work on Capitol Hill and incorporates editorial commentary and reviews of books and films. It is widely available in public places in the neighborhood.

Hillwood Museum and Gardens 4155 Linnean Ave. NW btw Tilden and Upton Sts. (202) 686-8507 www.hillwoodmuseum.org

This 25-acre estate and 40-room Georgian mansion located beside the Rock Creek Park has recently undergone restoration. The building is filled with Russian and French decorative art collected by Washington socialite Marjorie Merriweather Post. The collection includes Russian icons, cases filled with elaborate miniature boxes, period rooms lavishly decorated, striking eighteenth and nineteenth-century portraits, Fabergé eggs, Sèvres porcelain, Beauvais tapestries, and more. The grounds feature 18 acres of beautifully sculpted gardens, including one in Japanese and another in French style. Open Tues–Sat 9 a.m.–5 p.m. Admission free but reservations are required for tours. Metro: Van Ness-UDC. *See also* www.commuterpage.com/venues/museums.htm.

Hilton McLean at Tysons Corner 7920 Jones Branch Dr., McLean, VA (703) 847-5000 or (800) 445-8667 www.hilton.com

Very close to the two giant malls this striking structure has a glass-domed atrium and 458 guest rooms. Amenities include an indoor pool, exercise facility, restaurant, and all the usual other accompaniments to be found at a luxury hostelry. It is accessible off the Beltway (I-495) by taking Exit 43A on to Rte. 123 Chain Bridge Rd., and it is off Gallery Dr.

Hilton Washington Embassy Row 2015 Massachusetts Ave. NW at 20th St. (202) 265-1600 or (800) 445-8667 www.hilton.com

This fine well-located hotel with a rooftop pool and exercise facility features 193 comfortably appointed rooms at expensive rates. Metro: Dupont Circle.

Hirshhorn Museum and Sculpture Garden 7th St. and Independence Ave., SW (202) 357-1300 www.si.edu/hirshhorn

This extraordinary-looking modern structure erected along the Mall in 1974 holds a collection of European and American art including paintings and sculpture from the late nineteenth century to date. Just north of the building is the Sunken Sculpture Garden with stone, bronze, and other metal works by such giants as Moore, Matisse, and Rodin. Guided tours are offered. Open daily 10:30 a.m.–5:30 p.m. Free admission. Garden open 7:30 a.m.–dusk. Metro: L'Enfant Plaza. *See also* www.commuterpage.com/venues/museums-si.htm.

Hirshhorn Museum and Sculpture Garden Film Program 7th St. and Independence Ave., SW (202) 357-2700

Experimental and avant-garde cinema offerings, drawn from some of the best from world film festivals, are shown free usually on Thursday and Friday evenings. Call for information. Metro: L'Enfant Plaza.

Hispanic Festival *see* Latino Festival.

Historic Brookland Farmers Market at the Brookland Metro station

This producers' market is located east of the Metro stop and is open from early June to late October on Sun 10 a.m.–1 p.m., and Tues 4 p.m.–7 p.m.

Historic Buildings *see* Historic Houses and Buildings.

Historic Districts *see* Anacostia, Capitol Hill Historic District, Cleveland Park Historic District, Downtown Historic District, Georgetown Historic District, Lafayette Square Historic District, Woodley Park Historic District.

Historic Downtown D.C. Walking Tour

This 1½-hour guided tour is offered on weekends and begins from 7th and F Sts. NW at the Gallery Pl.-Chinatown Metro station. Details at (202) 828-WALK or at the Web site: www.dcheritage.org.

Historic Georgetown Tour

Follow an experienced guide on an informative 90-minute walking tour on the weekend to some of the city's most interesting sites. Call (301) 588-8999 or check the Web site: www.tourdc.com for details.

Historic Houses and Buildings *see* Alexander Graham Bell Association for the Deaf, Alma Thomas House, Anderson Cottage, Apex Building, Arlington House the Robert E. Lee Memorial, Ball-Sellers House, Belmont Mansion, Ben Davis House, Blaine Mansion, Bodisco House, C. C. Huntley House, Cady Lee Mansion, The Cairo, Carberry House, Carlyle House, Charles Sumner School Museum and Archives, Cherry Hill Farmhouse, City Tavern, Clara Barton National Historic Site, Clarence Moore House, Claude Moore Colonial Farm at Turkey Run, Colvin Run Mill Historic Site, Cooke's Row, Cox Row, Dr. E. B. Bliss House, Duke Ellington's Home, Dumbarton House, Duncanson Cranch House, East Capitol Street Row Houses, Edward Simon Lewis House, Evermay, Frank Lloyd Wright's Pope-Leighy House, Frederick Douglass National Historic Site, Glenview Mansion, Friendship Firehouse, George Washington's River Farm, Georgetown Custom House and Post Office, Georgetown Visitation Preparatory School and Monastery, Gunston Hall, Halcyon House, Historic Sully, Indonesia Embassy, Industrial Bank, John A. Wilson Building, Justice Brown House, Lee-Fendall House Museum, Lindens, Lloyd House, Maples House, Mary McLeod Bethune House, Mount Vernon, Mountjoy Bayly House, Oatlands, The Octagon, Old Central Public Library Building, Old Stone House, Petersen House, Pierce Mill, Pohick Church, Prospect House, Queen Anne Row Houses, Ramsey House, Ringgold-Carroll House, Russian Consulate, Scott-Grant House, Scottish Rite Masonic Temple, Sewall-Belmont House, Smith Row, Society of the Cincinnati at Anderson House, Stoddert House, Sulgrave Club, Sully Historic Site, Thomas Law House, Thomas-Siegler House and Gardens, Tudor Place, Vigilant Fire Department Building, Warder-Totten House, Washington Club, Wheat Row, White-Meyer House, Women's National Democratic Club, Woodlawn Plantation, Woodrow Wilson House. *See also* D.C. Preservation League, National Park Service (Web site).

Historic Sully across from Washington Dulles Airport on Rte. 28, Chantilly, VA (703) 437-1794 www.co.fairfax.va.us/parks/sully/
   This plantation owned by northern Virginia's first congressman, Richard Bland Lee, was built in 1794 and has been restored. The house is furnished with antiques from the Federal period, and tours are offered of the building, the dairy, and the smokehouse. Modest admission charge. Open 11 a.m.–4 p.m. daily except Tues.

Historical Museums *see* Alexandria Archaeology Museum, Anacostia Museum and Center for African-American History and Culture, Arlington Historical Society and Museum, Collingwood Library and Museum of Americanism, Daughters of the American Revolution Museum and Constitution Hall, Dumbarton House, Fairfax Museum and Visitor Center, Gadsby's Tavern Museum, Historical Society of Washington, Jewish Historical Society of Greater Washington, Loudoun Museum, The Lyceum Museum, Manassas Museum, National Museum of American History, National Museum of American Jewish Military History, Old Stone House, Stabler-Leadbeater Apothecary Shop Museum, Surratt House Museum, U.S. Holocaust Memorial Museum. *See also* Art and Design Museums, Ethic and Community Museums, Major Museums, Media Museums, Military Museums, Museums of Particular Interest to Children, Science and Technology Museums, Smithsonian Institution Museums, Specialized Museums, www.washingtonpost.com.

Historical Society of Washington 1307 New Hampshire Ave. NW btw 20th St. and Dupont Circle (202) 785-2068 www.hswdc.org

Until 2003 the society occupied the Heurich Mansion, a 31-room Grand Victorian brownstone built in 1894 along Romanesque Revival lines for a German immigrant beer tycoon by architect John Granville Meyers. The building furnishings include original pieces from the early home. In March 2003 the society was to relocate its office, archives, library, and special collections to the site of the restored Carnegie Public Library building at Mount Vernon Square between 7th and 9th Sts. NW just south of the new convention center, which has become the City Museum of Washington, D.C. The Heurich Mansion remains under the direction of the historical society and following renovation it will be open to the public. For information about open hours and tours call or check the Web site. Metro: Dupont Circle.

Hitching Post 200 Upshur St. NW opposite the gate of the Soldiers Home on Rock Creek Church Rd. (202) 726-1511

This small unpretentious neighborhood restaurant is a find for those seeking authentic Southern-style cooking at its best—fried chicken, crab cakes, baked ham, or lamb chops at very moderate prices. Open for lunch and dinner Tues–Sat Metro: Brookland-CUA, then H8 Bus.

Hockey *see* Ice Hockey.

Hogate's 800 Water St. off Maine Ave. SW (202) 484-6300

For more than 65 years this large casual restaurant on the waterfront with its nautical décor and choice river views from some locations has been serving all kinds of seafood dishes at moderate to expensive prices. It's busiest during tourist traffic seasons when reservations may be useful. Metro: L'Enfant Plaza or Waterfront-SEU.

Holiday Inn Arlington at Ballston 4610 Fairfax Dr. btw N Glebe Rd. and N Buchanan St., Arlington, VA (202) 243-9800 or (800) HOLIDAY www.hiarlington.com

This is a 221-room moderately priced hotel, which offers an exercise room and outdoor pool among its features. There's a jogging trail close by and the hotel is 3 blocks from the Metro. Metro: Ballston.

Holiday Inn Bethesda 8120 Wisconsin Ave. btw Cordell Ave. and Battery Lane., Bethesda, MD (301) 652-2000 or (800) HOLIDAY www.holiday-inn.com/bethesdamd

Located near the National Institutes of Health and the Bethesda Naval Hospital, this mid-range-priced hotel offers guests free shuttle service to the Metro. Metro: Medical Center.

Holiday Inn Capitol 555 C St. SW (202) 479-4000 or (800) 465-4329 www.holidayinncapitol.com

This 259-room-and-suites hostelry is within easy walking distance of all the

Mall museums. There's a rooftop pool, an exercise facility, and underground parking at this mid-range hotel that appeals to families and tour groups because of its ideal location. Metro: L'Enfant Plaza.

Holiday Inn Chevy Chase 5520 Wisconsin Ave., Chevy Chase, MD (301) 365-1500 or (800) 465-4329 www.holiday-inn.com

Situated just 3 blocks north of the dividing line from D.C./Western Ave., this comfortable mid-range hotel is right in the midst of the Chevy Chase district's upscale shopping area. There is a pool and free parking available to guests at this moderate-priced facility convenient to the Metro. Metro: Friendship Heights.

Holiday Inn Downtown 1155 14th St. NW at Thomas Circle (202) 737-1200 or (800) 465-4329 www.holiday-inn.com

This mid-priced 14-story structure features a family-friendly atmosphere, a pool on the roof, a next-door fitness center, and a handy location. Metro: McPherson Square.

Holiday Inn Dulles Airport 1000 Sully Rd. at Dulles Access Rd. (703) 471-7411 or (800) HOLIDAY www.holiday-inn.com

Situated right at the airport, this moderate-priced hotel offers comfortable accommodations plus indoor pool, sauna, and whirlpool.

Holiday Inn Georgetown 2101 Wisconsin Ave. NW (202) 338-4600 or (800) HOLIDAY www.higeorgetown.com

Located at the upper end of Georgetown some 10 blocks above M St. this moderate-priced hotel has a pool and exercise room with parking for an added charge.

Holiday Inn National Airport 2650 Jefferson Davis Hwy., Arlington, VA (703) 684-7200 or (800) HOLIDAY www.holiday-inn.com

This motel close to Crystal City shopping is near Reagan National Airport and has undergone extensive renovations. Prices are fairly expensive, but there is free parking, a pool, an exercise facility, and free shuttle service to the airport and National Airport Metro station.

Holiday Inn Old Town 480 King St. at Pitt St., Alexandria, VA (703) 549-6080 or (800) HOLIDAY www.axe-oldtown.hiselect.com

Located behind Colonial brick walls at one of the choicest locations in Old Town, this 227-room high-priced hostelry ranks with the very best that this chain offers anywhere in the country. Amenities include indoor pool, indoor parking, exercise facility, and complimentary shuttle service to Reagan National Airport and the Metro. Metro: King Street.

Holiday Inn on the Hill 415 New Jersey Ave. NW btw D and E Sts. (202) 638-1616 or (800) HOLIDAY www.holiday-inn.com

This is a family-oriented hotel with many incentives and attractions for bringing kids along. It is located near the Mall and Union Station and offers a pool, exercise facility, sauna, parking for a fee, and mid-range prices. Metro: Union Station.

Holiday Day Inn Rosslyn Westpark 1900 N Fort Myer Dr., Arlington, VA (703) 807-2000 or (800) HOLIDAY www.holiday-inn.com

This well-located moderate-priced establishment is 2 blocks from the Metro and just a pleasant walk across Key Bridge to Georgetown. There is an indoor pool, exercise facility, free parking, and spectacular views of Washington from its Vantage Point Restaurant's windows. Metro: Rosslyn.

Holiday Inn Silver Spring 8777 Georgia Ave. near Spring St., Silver Spring, MD (301) 589-0800 or (800) HOLIDAY www.holiday-inn.com

This recently refurbished 231-room hotel is located in an established suburban neighborhood and near the Silver Spring renaissance, which is under way downtown. Prices are moderate and there is indoor parking. The Metro is within easy walking distance. Metro: Silver Spring.

Holy Rosary Church 595 3rd St. NW at F St. (202) 638-0165 www.holyrosary churchdc.org

This simple church was built in 1913 by Italian immigrants in what was then an Italian neighborhood. Services are conducted in Italian and English. Still attached to the church at 595½ 3rd St. is the Casa Italiana Language School, which offers courses in Italian. Information at (202) 638-1348 or the Web site: www.CasaItali anaSchool.org. Metro: Judiciary Square.

Holy See Embassy the Apostolic Nunciature, 3339 Massachusetts Ave. NW (202) 333-7121 www.embassy.org/embassies/va.html

Holy Trinity Catholic Church of Georgetown 36th and O Sts. NW (202) 337-2840 www.holytrinitydc.org

When it was first begun in the late eighteenth century, this was the first Catholic Church in Washington. The original church building at 3525 N St. serves as the parish center. The current church building at 3513 N St. was built in the mid-nineteenth century and was renovated in 1979. John F. Kennedy and his family have been among its worshippers. Metro: Foggy Bottom-GWU, then 30, 32, 34, 35, or 36 Bus.

Honduras Embassy 3007 Tilden St. NW, Suite 4M (202) 966-7702 www.honduras emb.org

Hoover FBI Building *see* J. Edgar Hoover FBI Building.

Hope Key 3131 Wilson Blvd. at Highland St., Arlington, VA (703) 243-8388

This bustling Chinese restaurant is open for lunch and dinner daily until 1 a.m. or 2 a.m. The menu is extensive, the dishes are tasty and filling, and the prices are very moderate. Metro: Clarendon.

Horse Racing *see* Laurel Park Race Course, Pimlico Race Course, Rosecroft Raceway.

Horseback Riding *see* Meadowbrook Stable, Riverbend Park, Rock Creek Park Horse Center, Washington and Old Dominion Railroad Regional Park, Wheaton Park Stables.

Hostelling International-AYH Hostel 1009 11th St. NW (202) 737-2333, fax (202) 737-1508 www.hiayh.org

Formerly the Washington International AYH-Hostel, this youth hostel provides low-cost dormitory lodging for 270 usually college-age travelers. Bunk beds, without private bathrooms, but families are given their own room if there is space. Clean bathrooms and kitchen, laundry facilities. Central location. Metro: Metro Center.

Hostels *see* Hostelling International-AYH Hostel, India House Too, International Guest House, International Student House, Thompson-Markwood Hall. *See also* YMCA of Metropolitan Washington, YWCA, www.hostels.com.

Hotel Accommodations *see* Deluxe Hotels, First-Class Hotels, Middle-Range Hotels, Budget Hotels.

Hotel George 15 E St. NW btw N Capitol St. and New Jersey Ave. (202) 347-4200 or (800) 576-8331 www.hotelgeorge.com

The old Bellevue after renovation has metamorphosed into a sleek new 139-room hostelry with large rooms, ultramodern décor, and a fitness and billiard room among its amenities. The bistro-style Bis restaurant/bar is another chic addition. Rates are moderately expensive. Metro: Union Station.

Hotel Harrington 436 11th St. NW at E St. (202) 628-8140 or (800) 424-8532 www.hotel-harrington.com

This popular budget hostelry offers clean basic rooms with bath and air-conditioning, without frills. Its choice downtown location not far from the Mall appeals to families, tour groups, and foreign travelers. Metro: Metro Center.

Hotel Jefferson *see* Jefferson Hotel.

Hotel Latham *see* Latham Hotel.

Hotel Lombardy 2019 I St. NW at Pennsylvania Ave. (202) 828-2600 or (800) 424-5486 www.hotellombardy.com

This quaint Foggy Bottom place offers 127 rooms and suites in a former apartment building with good-sized rooms, many with kitchen areas, at moderate prices. Its foreign guests lend the place its international flavor. Metro: Foggy Bottom or Farragut West.

Hotel Monaco 700 F St. NW at 7th St. (202) 628-7177 or (877) 202-5411 www.monaco-dc.com

Located on a property site designated as a National Historic Landmark in the building earlier known as the Tariff Building, this new luxury hotel opened in July 2002. It features 200 beautifully decorated guest rooms and suites, a high-tech fitness center, complimentary wine hour, morning coffee, and many of the other amenities expected to be found in a contemporary deluxe hostelry. It is conveniently located in the Downtown Historic District near many of the city's principal tourist attractions. Metro: Gallery Pl.-Chinatown.

Hotel Reservation Agencies

A number of organizations provide information on hotel and bed-and-breakfast accommodations in and around the city. Some serve as booking agents, sometimes at a discounted price. Frequently they are easily accessible at their Web sites. Among the best agencies and sources for Washington, D.C., are:

- Washington D.C. Accommodations (202) 289-2220 or (800) 554-2220 www
  .dcaccommodations.com
    This company has knowledgeable hotel reservation specialists on the local
  area.

- www.washington.org
    This searchable hotel listing service is prepared by the Washington, D.C.,
  Convention and Visitors Association and is based on location and price for
  hotels and bed-and-breakfasts. It provides information on weekend rates as
  well.

- www.washingtonpost.com
    This site locates hotels in the city arranged by neighborhood and price.

Hotel Sofitel 806 15th St. NW at H St. (202) 639-2044 or (800) 763-4835 www
.hotel-chains.dovehotels.com/sofitel-hotels-1.html
    This hotel opened in 2002 after a multimillion-dollar conversion of a former
office building into a 237-room luxury hotel. It was designed by Pierre-Yves Ro-
chan, who conceived the Carlton Hotel in Cannes and the Essex House in New
York. Everything one might expect to find in the finest imaginable French-managed
hostelry is here, including the very steep room rates. The location is excellent, too,
with the American Bar Association headquarters across the street. Metro: McPherson Square.

Hotel Washington 515 15th St. NW at Pennsylvania Ave. (202) 638-5900 or (800)
424-9540 www.hotelwashington.com
    This elegant and venerable hotel (built in 1918) features handsomely furnished
Edwardian rooms and a comfortable lobby and is quite near the White House. The
rooftop restaurant/bar offers some of the most breathtaking views in town. There
is an exercise facility with saunas. Rates are quite high. Metro: Metro Center or
Federal Triangle.

House and Senate Office Buildings *see* Senate and House Office Buildings.

House of the Temple Library/Museum 1733 16th St. NW btw R and S Sts. (202)
232-3579 www.bessel.org/maslibs.htm
    This is home to the Supreme Council of the 33rd Degree of the Ancient and
Accepted Scottish Rite of Freemasonry, Southern Jurisdiction U.S.A. It is a neoclas-
sical structure modeled after a famous tomb in Asia Minor. There is a museum of
Masonic memorabilia as well as works about the poet Robert Burns on display. A
research library and archives are located here as well. Open Mon–Fri 8 a.m.–2 p.m.
Tours are offered, which last about 1½ hours. Admission free. Metro: Dupont
Circle.

Houston's 7715 Woodmont Ave. off Wisconsin Ave., Bethesda, MD (301) 656-
9755
    The menu here is simply hamburgers, seafood, ribs, grilled chicken, and salads,
but the casual ambiance and moderate prices at this Texas-style dining spot cap-
tures a large flock of eager customers all the time. Open for lunch and dinner daily.

Metro: Bethesda. There is another location in suburban Maryland at 12256 Rockville Pike, Rockville, MD (301) 468-3535.

Howard Johnson Plaza Hotel and Suites 1430 Rhode Island Ave. NW btw 14th and 15th Sts. (202) 462-7777 or (800) 368-5690 www.hojo.com

This is one of the best of this chain's accommodations in the area, conveniently located off Scott Circle and not far from two Metro stations. There's a rooftop pool and underground parking. Rooms are sizable and rates are moderate. Metro: Dupont Circle or McPherson Square.

Howard Theater 624 T St. NW at 7th St.

In its prime this was the site in the city for watching the finest performances by black musicians and artists. It was built in 1910 and was the epicenter of Washington's Black Broadway—an Italian Renaissance Beaux Arts auditorium seating 1,200 with a balcony and box seats. It closed in 1970, but renovation plans for a reopening as a restored modern cultural institution are said to be in progress. Metro: U St.-Cardozo.

Howard University 2400 6th St. NW btw W and Fairmont Sts. (202) 806-6100 www.howard.edu

Situated on an 89-acre campus is the nation's oldest and most respected higher-education institution committed to educating African-Americans and other disenfranchised groups. More than 10,000 students study medicine, engineering, social work, dentistry, communications, and the liberal arts. Its alumni form a roster of distinguished Americans in fields as varied as law and entertainment, and the student body is drawn from everywhere in the United States and more than 100 foreign lands. Metro: Shaw-Howard University.

Howard University Bison box office (202) 806-7198 www.bisonmania.com

Much of the intercollegiate athletic interest at the university centers on the football team, which plays home games at Greene Stadium. Ticket information is available at the box office in Crampton Auditorium.

Howard University Blackburn Center Gallery Blackburn Center on the Howard University Campus, 2455 6th St. NW btw W and Fairmont Sts. (202) 806-5983 http://138.238.64.46/Student_Affairs/Blackburn.html

The Armour J. Blackburn Center Gallery features a permanent display of African arts and offers changing exhibitions of works by outstanding African-American painters and sculptors. Open Mon–Fri 10 a.m.–9 p.m. Admission free. Metro: Shaw-Howard University.

Howard University Founders Library 500 Howard Pl. btw Rankin Chapel and the Undergraduate Library on the Howard University campus (202) 806-7250 www.howard.edu/library

This Colonial Revival structure was built in 1937. The architectural design by Louis E. Fry Sr. was based roughly on Independence Hall in Philadelphia. It is home to the Moorland-Spingarn Research Center, a celebrated collection of historical materials documenting the culture of black people, as well as the University Library, which supports the curriculum and research programs on the campus.

Open daily, hours vary. Metro: Shaw-Howard University. *See also* Howard University Moorland-Spingarn Research Center.

Howard University James Herring Gallery of Art 2455 6th St. NW btw W and Fairmont Sts. (202) 806-7070 www.howard.edu/library/art@Howard/GoA/general info.htm

Open Mon–Fri 9:30 a.m.–5 p.m. during the academic year from late August to mid-April, this art gallery showcases work by faculty and students and offers special exhibitions as well. Metro: Shaw-Howard University.

Howard University Moorland-Spingarn Research Center in Founders Library, 500 Howard Pl. btw Rankin Chapel and the Undergraduate Library on the Howard University campus (202) 806-7239

This collection is the nation's largest and finest for materials relating to the history and culture of the people of African origin living in the countries of the Western hemisphere. It is open to the public and widely used by scholars, film makers, journalists, and historians as well as university faculty and students. Open Mon–Fri 9 a.m.–4:30 p.m. The manuscript and archives collections are open only by appointment. Metro: Shaw-Howard University. *See also* Howard University Founders Library.

Hubert Humphrey Federal Office Building Independence Ave. SW btw 2nd and 3rd Sts.

This structure was erected in 1976 to span part of the Southwest Freeway, which runs beneath it. Designed by architects Marcel Breuer and Herbert Beckhard, this is a rectangular building of 6 stories. It is not open to the public. Metro: Federal Center SW.

Hunan Chinatown 624 H St. NW btw 6th and 7th Sts. (202) 783-5858

First-class Szechuan and Hunan dishes are served in this white-tablecloth restaurant where the service and fine ingredients are a notch above most of its Chinatown competitors. Open for lunch and dinner daily with moderate prices. Metro: Gallery Pl.-Chinatown.

Hung Jury 1819 H St. NW at Pennsylvania Ave. (202) 785-8181

Open Fri and Sat 9 p.m.–4 a.m., this predominately lesbian dance bar has a modest admission charge and inexpensive drinks. It is reputed to be the oldest women's bar in the country, in operation for some 20 years. The women here are mostly younger, of college age, with a few somewhat older part of the mix. Metro: Farragut West.

Hungary Embassy 3910 Shoemaker St. NW (202) 362-6730 www.huembwas.org

Huntley House *see* C. C. Huntley House.

Huntley Meadows Park 3701 Lockheed Blvd., Alexandria, VA (703) 768-2525 www.co.fairfax.va.us/parks

This 1,400-acre park is the delight of nature lovers. Birds of every kind can be found here. Much of the area is wetlands and is inhabited by deer, beavers, and waterfowl. A boardwalk circles through a marsh and there are miles of trails through the park. Admission is free and the park is open from dawn to dusk. The visitor center is open from spring to fall during varying hours, but typically it is available Mon and Wed–Fri 9 a.m.–5 p.m. Closed Tues. To reach the park by car take the Beltway (I-495) to Exit 177A, then follow Rte. 1 S (Richmond Hwy.) 3½ miles to Lockheed Blvd., turn right, and go ½ mile to entrance.

Hyatt Arlington 1325 Wilson Blvd. btw Fort Myer Dr. and N Nash St. (703) 525-1234 or (800) 233-1234 www.hyatt.com

This is a 302-room establishment with a European flavor that offers an exercise facility, restaurants, and lounges, and is within walking distance to Georgetown across the Key Bridge. Rates are moderately high. Metro: Rosslyn.

Hyatt Regency Bethesda 1 Bethesda Metro Center on the 7400 block of Wisconsin Ave., Bethesda, MD (301) 657-1234 or (800) 233-1234 www.hyatt.com

Located beside the Bethesda Metro stop is this elegant 381-room hostelry with atrium lobby, glass elevator, nicely furnished rooms, indoor pool, and exercise facility. All the usual first-class hotel features are here and the room rates reflect this. The location is convenient to Bethesda's many restaurants and businesses, and downtown D.C. is only 20 minutes away by Metro.

Hyatt Regency Capitol Hill 400 New Jersey Ave. NW at D St. (202) 737-1234 or (800) 233-1234 www.hyatt.com

Located just 2 blocks from the Capitol and 2 blocks from Union Station, this 11-story hotel has 834 rooms and 31 suites. Classy features like an atrium, glass elevators, indoor pool, and fitness facility are included. The room rates befit the luxury nature of the hostelry. Metro: Union Station.

Hyatt Regency Crystal City 2799 Jefferson Davis Hwy at Crystal Dr. (703) 418-1234 or (800) 223-1234 www.hyatt.com

Boasting all the usual amenities of a luxury-class hotel, this 685-room place includes an outdoor pool, a health facility with a whirlpool, and a rooftop restaurant with fine views of the city. It is close to Reagan National Airport and Crystal City and offers complimentary shuttle service to both. Rates are quite expensive. Metro: Crystal City.

Hyattsville

This is a small residential community in the Maryland suburbs inside the Washington Beltway in Prince George's County. It was established in 1742 and incorporated in 1854. The area is made up principally of older, single-family homes and has been the scene of a good deal of effort in recent years to renovate and refurbish the houses. The town is about midway between the city and the University of Maryland, each of which is less than 5 miles away. Many residents work in Washington as federal employees and a good many others on the campus at the University of Maryland. The area is served by the Metro with stations at Hyattsville and Prince George's Plaza, and bus transportation traveling along U.S. Hwy. 1 (Baltimore Ave.) north and south.

IMF Center *see* International Monetary Fund Center.

I Matti 2436 18th St. NW btw Belmont and Columbia Rds. (202) 462-8844

This Adams Morgan Italian restaurant is a bright, casual place featuring excellent pizzas and pastas and well-prepared meat and fish dishes at moderate prices. It offers fine values and is open for lunch Sat and Sun, dinner nightly. Metro: Woodley Park-Zoo, then 90, 91, 92, 93, or 96 Bus.

I Ricchi 1220 19th St. NW btw M and N Sts. (202) 835-0459 www.iricchi.net

Tuscan food is featured in this classy restaurant with its lovely stone and tile décor and a menu that varies with the seasons and its always-succulent grilled specialties. Open for lunch Mon–Fri, dinner Mon–Sat. Fairly expensive and reservations are suggested. Metro: Dupont Circle.

Ice Hockey *see* MCI Center, Washington Capitals. *See also* www.commuterpage.com/venues/venue-sp.htm.

Ice Hockey Season www.washingtoncaps.com

The Washington Capitals play their home games from October through April at the MCI Center, 601 F St. NW. Information on the schedule at (202) 628-3200. For tickets call (202) 432-7328 or (800) 551-7328.

Ice-skating *see* Cabin John Regional Park, Fairfax Ice Arena, Fort Dupont Ice Arena, Mount Vernon Recreation Center, Pershing Park Ice Rink, Reflecting Pool, Sculpture Gardens Outdoor Rink, Wheaton Regional Park.

Iceland Embassy 1156 15th St. NW, Suite 1200 (202) 265-6653 www.iceland.org

Idle Time Books 2410 18th St. NW btw Belmont and Columbia Rds. (202) 232-4774

This spacious used bookstore in Adams Morgan offers a wide selection of genuine bargain books. Open daily 11 a.m.–10 p.m. Metro: Woodley Park-Zoo, then 90, 91, 92, 93, or 96 Bus.

Il Radicchio 223 Pennsylvania Ave. SE btw 2nd and 3rd Sts. (202) 547-5114

This trattoria serves spaghetti and sauce in a gimmicky way but it adds up to very ample, tasty fare at bargain prices. There's also fine wood-fired pizza and a variety of other choices. This is a very busy place that accepts no reservations so there may well be a wait. Open for lunch Mon–Sat, dinner daily. Metro: Capitol South. There's another location in the Virginia suburbs at 1801 Clarendon Blvd., Arlington (703) 276-2627.

Imagination Stage White Flint Mall, on the second level, 11301 Rockville Pike, Rockville, MD (301) 881-5106 www.imaginationstage.org

The Bethesda Academy of Performing Arts offers performances of children's favorites by professional actors on weekend afternoons at this suburban mall. Call for details on what's on, show times, and ticket prices or check the Web site.

Immaculate Conception Catholic Church 1315 8th St. NW at N St. (202) 332-8888

This church was constructed in 1870 with the tower added some 30 years later. Next to it at 711 N St. is the Immaculate Conception School, which started offering classes in 1865. Metro: Shaw-Howard University.

Improv 1140 Connecticut Ave. NW btw L and M Sts. (202) 296-7008 www.dc improv.com

The D.C. branch of a national chain showcases local and national comic talent, often recognizable from TV programs. The bigger the name, the more difficult to get seats in this spot, so advance reservation well ahead for top comedians makes sense. There is an admission charge and dinner reservations may improve prospects for getting a good seat. Metro: Farragut North. *See also* www.commuterpage.com/venues/venue-en.htm.

Independence Day Celebrations

The Fourth of July weekend is when the city hosts hordes of tourists and locals. There is a reading at 10 a.m. of the Declaration of Independence and Colonial military maneuvers at the National Archives. Usually at noon a huge parade with floats and countless marching bands strut down Constitution Ave. There is entertainment at the Sylvan Theater at the Washington Monument in the evening. The National Symphony Orchestra performs on the Capitol's west lawn at 8 p.m., and spectacular fireworks explode over the Washington Monument at sunset (around 9:15 p.m.). Other smaller celebrations are held at various sites around the city and in the suburbs, which are announced in the media. For information on D.C. events call (202) 619-7222.

Independent Films *see* Foreign and Independent Films.

India Embassy 2107 Massachusetts Ave. NW (202) 939-7000 www.indianembassy .org

India House Too 300 Carvel St. NW (202) 291-1195

This large brick house just up the hill on the right from the Metro stop in Takoma Park is a great favorite with backpacking young people 18 or older. It is a casual hostel with modest sleeping accommodations with shared baths, but there's a kitchen, cable TV, parking, and a deck and garden. Rates are about the cheapest in the city for such a pleasant, safe place, and it's some 15 minutes by Metro from Union Station. Metro: Takoma.

Indian Craft Shop in the Department of Interior Building, 1849 C St. NW btw 18th and 19th Sts. (202) 737-4381

Ever since 1938 some of the finest examples of Native American handicrafts—sculptures, beads, sand paintings, fetishes, and more from some 40 tribal areas have been sold here. Open Mon–Fri 8:30 a.m.–4:30 p.m., and on the third Saturday each month from 10 a.m.–4 p.m. Metro: Farragut West.

Indian Restaurants *see* Aangan, Aatish, Aditi, Amma Vegetarian Kitchen, Bombay Bistro, Bombay Club, Delhi Dhaba, Heritage India, Langley Park, Taj Mahal, Tiffin, Udupi Palace, Woodlands. *See also* Web sites: www.dcpages.com, www.washing tonpost.com, www.restaurant.com, www.opentable.com

Indian Spices and Gifts 3901 Wilson Blvd. at Pollard, Arlington, VA (703) 522-0149

This shop specializes in international groceries and is open Mon–Sat 11 a.m.–8:30 p.m., Sun 11 a.m.–7 p.m. Metro: Virginia Square-GMU or Ballston-MU.

Indonesia Embassy 2020 Massachusetts Ave. NW (202) 775-5200 www.embassy ofindonesia.org

This 60-room Beaux Arts mansion was built by architect Henry Anderson in 1902 for Thomas F. Walsh, a penniless immigrant who was transformed into a multimillionaire by striking gold in 1896 in Colorado. Evalyn Walsh McLean, of Hope diamond fame, inherited the house from her mother in 1932. Since 1951, it has served as the Indonesian Embassy. Metro: Dupont Circle.

Indonesian Restaurants *see* Asia Nora, Ivy's Place, Sabang, Satay Sarinah. *See also* Web sites: www.dcpages.com, www.washingtonpost.com, www.restaurant.com, www.opentable.com

Industrial Bank 2002 11th St. NW at U St. (202) 722-2050 www.industrial-bank .com

The oldest black-owned bank in the city was begun as the Industrial Building and Loan Association. The architect of the structure in 1909 was Isaiah T. Hatton. It is one of the neighborhood's oldest buildings financed, conceived, and constructed by blacks. Metro: U St.-Cardozo.

Information for Tourists *see* Tourist Information.

In-line Skating

A major source of information on this topic is the nonprofit Washington Area Roadskaters (202) 466-5005. Founded in 1987, they have a membership of several thousand men and women who share their passion for in-line skating. The Web site, www.skatedc.org, provides links to classes in in-line skating, venues, group skates, rentals, and skating sites. Another organization, American Inline Skating, provides private and group instruction in the area for beginner through advanced, as well as roller hockey courses. This group is located at 4329 Runabout Lane, Fairfax, VA (703) 803-7100 and the Web site, www.his.com/americaninline/index.html, provides additional information regarding in-line skating opportunities, summer camps, and roller hockey leagues. Skate shops in the area that offer equipment, training, and rentals include Caravan Skate Shop, 10766 Tucker St, Beltsville, MD (301) 937-0066 and 18707-C N Frederick Rd. (Rte. 355), Gaithersburg, MD (301) 921-0066; City Bikes, 2501 Champlain St. NW (Adams Morgan) (202) 265-1564; Ski Chalet, 203 Muddy Branch Rd., Gaithersburg, MD (301) 948-5200; Skater's Paradise, 1602 Belleview Blvd., Alexandria, VA (703) 660-6525, and 2704 Columbia Pike, Arlington, VA (703) 521-1700, and 8338 Leesburg Pike, Tysons Corner, VA (703) 761-3040; Ski & Skate, 3036 Annandale Rd. (Corner Rte. 50) Falls Church, VA (703) 533-7200.

Inn at Foggy Bottom *See* George Washington University Inn.

Inn at Little Washington Middle and Main Sts., Washington, VA (540) 675-3800
   This restaurant is somewhat beyond the parameters of inclusion in this book, but because it is such a celebrated place for Washingtonians looking for an extraordinary dining experience, we have included it. Located about a 90-minute drive away from D.C. through the rolling hills and small farms of the Virginia countryside, this inn is easily recognized by its splendid English country-manor décor. The menu is prix fixe for the multi-course gourmet meal, and the price is astronomical, but then this is reputed to be one of the world's ten best restaurants. The fare is New American cuisine, the ingredients are fresh and seasonal, the service is impeccable, and the sum of the experience makes for the fondest of memories. Dinner daily except Tues. Reserve several weeks ahead for the restaurant and for rooms.

Inner Circle Movie House *see* Cineplex Odeon Inner Circle.

Intelstat 3400 International Dr. NW at Van Ness St. (202) 944-7500 www.intelsat.com
   This is the 110-nation cooperative that owns and operates communications satellites. The building (designed by John Andrews International) is set on 18 acres, and the square atrium, flanked by steel and glass block towers, shines like a spaceship. Octagonal office pods are protected from the sun by louvered gray glass to maximize solar energy and natural cooling. Informative tours of about 45 minutes describing Intelstat, its history and operations, and some of the satellites on display, can be arranged by making reservations two weeks in advance by calling (202) 944-7584 or (202) 944-6902. Metro Van Ness-UDC.

InterAmerican Development Bank Cultural Center 1300 New York Ave. NW at 13th St. (202) 623-3774 www.iadb.org
   This international bank finances economic and social development in Latin America and the Caribbean. The center features changing exhibitions of artifacts, paintings, and sculpture from countries south of the North American border, and also sponsors performance programs by artists from the region. Open Mon–Fri 11 a.m.–6 p.m. Admission free. Metro: Metro Center.

Interior Department *see* Department of the Interior.

Interiors of Public Buildings Tour
   This 9-hour tour operates Mon–Sat starting at 8:30 a.m. from Union Station.

Stops are made at Ford's Theatre, Jefferson Memorial, National Museum of American History, and other locations in the city. For details call (301) 386-8300.

International Broadcasting Bureau (Voice of America) 330 Independence Ave. SW (202) 619-3919 www.ibb.gov

Getting the word out abroad—news, features, and policy issues—has been the task of the Voice of America since its first broadcast in 1942. The International Broadcasting Bureau hosts the "Voice" as well as WORLDNET Television and Film Service, Radio Sawa, and Radio and TV Martí (Office of Cuba Broadcasting). The Voice of America tour tells the story of how it broadcasts to millions in fifty-three languages around the clock allowing access to what America is thinking and doing, including the policies of the United States. A free tour of the studios is offered Mon–Fri at 10:30 a.m., 1:30 p.m., and 2:30 p.m. Call in advance for reservations. Metro: Federal Center.

International Children's Festival

Each year on a weekend in mid-September this outdoor event celebrating the arts takes place at the Wolf Trap Farm Park for the Performing Arts in Vienna, Virginia. Its sponsor is the Fairfax County Arts Council and it includes performances and programs by groups drawn from the region, around the country, and the world. Many of the performers are children. Admission charge. Information at (703) 642-0862 or (703) 255-1900.

International Eastern Star Temple 1618 New Hampshire Ave. NW at Corcoran St.

This building, sometimes called the Perry Belmont house, was built in 1909 and designed by Etienne Sanson and Horace Trumbull. Since 1935 it has been occupied by the Order of the Eastern Star, the women's affiliate of the Masons. The building served in its earlier history as one of the major social centers in the city and for short periods housed diplomatic missions. It was constructed in eighteenth-century French style. Metro: Dupont Circle.

International Guest House 1441 Kennedy St. NW at 16th St. (202) 726-5808 www.bedandbreakfast.com

This very modest guest hostel located 4 miles by bus from downtown offers neat and clean rooms with two beds and shared bath at very minimal rates. There are curfew limits and smoking and drinking are taboo. It is reached by taking the S2 or S4 Bus up 16th St. to Kennedy St.

International Jewish Film Festival Jewish Community Center of Northern Virginia, 8900 Little River Turnpike, Fairfax, VA (703) 323-0880 www.jccnv.org

Established in 2001, this annual event in late April or early May offers fifteen to twenty outstanding films from around the world with Jewish or immigrant themes. The films are screened at the nearby Cinema Arts Theater, Fair City Mall in Fairfax, and at George Mason University. Phone for venues and prices or check out this information on the Web site.

International Language Center 1803 Connecticut Ave. NW btw Florida Ave. and S St. (202) 332-2894

This spot is open daily 7 a.m.–9 p.m. and sells books, videos, newspapers, and magazines in some 200 languages. Metro: Dupont Circle.

International Monetary Fund Center 720 19th St. NW btw G and H Sts. (202) 623-6869 www.imf.org

There is an exhibit here on "Money Matters" and international finance, which highlight the work of this 182-nation organization. Changing shows are offered as well as a display of the coins and currency of the member countries. Admission free. Open 10 a.m.–4:30 p.m. Mon–Fri. Metro: Farragut West.

International Spy Museum F St. NW near 7th St. next door to Hotel Monaco (202) 393-7798 www.spymuseum.org

Opened in July 2002 with a collection of 600 intriguing artifacts at a site in the entertainment hub around the MCI Center, this is the place to see memorabilia of the world of clandestine activity. It spans spy sagas from the CIA to the KGB, from Nathan Hale to Robert Hanssen. There's even a February 1777 letter from George Washington to a New Yorker authorizing him to build a spy network and promising to pay $50 for his efforts. This place is as much a for-profit attraction as a genuine museum with its innumerable interactive gadgetry. Open daily 10 a.m.–6 p.m. April to October, 10 a.m.–6 p.m. November to March. Admission charge. Metro: Gallery Pl.-Chinatown. *See also* www.commuterpage.com/venues/museums .htm.

International Student House 1825 R St. at 18th St. (202) 387-6445

This lodging facility for over-21-year-olds requires long-term stays during the summer and its 90 guests typically remain for the academic year. Moderate rates include breakfast and dinner for shared rooms, more for single rooms, and more for single room with private bath or parking. Reservations long in advance are essential. Metro: Dupont Circle.

International Trade Center *see* Ronald Reagan Building and International Trade Center.

International Visitors Information Center *see* Meridian International Center.

Internet Resources on Washington, D.C. *see* Web Sites about Washington, D.C.

Iota Café 2832 Wilson Blvd. at Filmore St., Arlington, VA (703) 522-8340 www .iotaclubandcafe.com

This is a music spot in a warehouse-type space that is easygoing and pleasant, attracting a loyal audience for the local and national folk and blues performers. The bar and restaurant have the look of an old-fashioned diner with some living-room furniture mixed in. Open daily 11 a.m.–2 a.m. Metro: Clarendon.

Ireland Embassy 2234 Massachusetts Ave. NW (202) 462-3939 www.ireland emb.org

Ireland's Four Provinces 3412 Connecticut Ave. NW (202) 244-0860 www.ire landsfourprovinces.com

This very popular and authentic Irish watering place enjoys a cheery rollicking crowd for the light food, the drink, the friendly good cheer, and the music. It's located 3 blocks north of the National Zoo and is open daily at 5 p.m. until the wee hours with the music starting every night at 9 p.m. Metro: Cleveland Park.

Irish Restaurants *see* Dubliner, Fadó Irish Pub, Ireland's Four Provinces, Kelly's Irish Times, Murphy's Irish Pub and Restaurant, Nanny O'Brien's Irish Pub. *See also* www.dcpages.com, www.restaurant.com, www.washingtonpost.com.

Islamic Center 2551 Massachusetts Ave. at Belmont Rd. (202) 332-9343 www.irshad.org/pages/worship.htm

This mosque is a house of worship, culture, and education. The long white limestone building is surmounted by a minaret some 16 feet high and is filled with splendid craftworks by artisans from the Muslim world. There is an ebony pulpit, Persian rugs, and stained glass windows. Open daily 10 a.m.–5 p.m. Proper dress is required when entering—arms and legs must be covered, shoes removed, and women's heads covered. Metro: Dupont Circle.

The Islander 1201 U St. NW at 12th St. (202) 234-4955

This is the place to experience authentic Caribbean food specialties and drink in a casual and friendly restaurant/lounge. The dishes use fresh vegetables, fish, chicken, sauces, and more, to reflect the African and Indian origins of the culinary styles. Open for lunch and dinner daily except Mon. Metro: Shaw-Howard University

Israel Embassy 3514 International Dr. NW (202) 364-5500 www.israelemb.org

Italian Cultural Society of Washington, D.C. 5480 Wisconsin Ave. near Friendship Heights Metro station, Chevy Chase, MD (301) 215-7885 www.italianculturalsociety.org

The society sponsors language instruction classes and group gatherings for those interested in practicing Italian in social situations. Details at (202) 215-7885. Metro: Friendship Heights.

Italian Restaurants *see* A.V. Ristorante Italiano, Barolo, Buca di Beppo, Café Milano, Coppi's, Diversité, Donatello, Dupont Italian Kitchen, Galileo, Goldoni, I Matti, I Ricchi, Ledo, Il Radicchio, Luigino, Luigi's, Obelisk, Paolo's, Pasta Mia, Pine's of Rome, Positano, Primi Piatti, Sesto Senso, Tempo, Al Tiramisu, Tragara, Trattoria Alberto, Tuscana West, Vace. *See also* Litteri's, Web sites: www.dcpages.com, www.restaurant.com, www.washingtonpost.com, www.opentable.com.

Italy Embassy 3000 Whitehaven St. NW (202) 612-4400 www.italyemb.org

Ivory Coast Embassy 3421 Massachusetts Ave. NW (202) 797-0300
Embassy of Côte d'Ivoire (Ivory Coast).

Ivy's Place 3520 Connecticut Ave. NW btw Porter and Ordway Sts. (202) 363-7802

This is a modestly priced Southeast Asian dining location serving a mélange of tasty Indonesian and Thai food specialties. Open daily for lunch and dinner, except Mon. Metro: Cleveland Park.

Iwo Jima Memorial *see* Marine Corps War Memorial.

J. Edgar Hoover FBI Building on E St. NW btw 9th and 10th Sts. (202) 324-3447
www.fbi.gov

This building occupying a whole city block has traditionally been one of the city's prime tourist destinations. Most recently it has been closed to any except those on group tours or individuals who have had arrangements made by their congressman several weeks in advance for them to join a tour group. The tours are offered Mon–Fri from 9 a.m.–3 p.m. and take visitors on a one-hour visit offering an inside glimpse at the labs, technicians, firearms, history, and work of the government's intriguing police force. Metro: Metro Center.

J. F. Ptak Science Books 1531 33rd St. NW at Volta Pl. (202) 337-0945 www.the
sciencebookstore.com

This Georgetown shop is the city's premiere place dealing with the physical sciences. It has a very large book stock with a strong representation of works treating all aspects and histories of computers, mathematics, astrophysics, along with biographies of scientists. Early photographs, maps, and prints form another rich element of what's available here. Open Tues–Sat noon–5 p.m. Metro: Foggy Bottom-GWU, then 30, 32, 34, 35, or 36 Bus.

J. Paul's 3218 M St. NW btw Wisconsin Ave. and Warehouse Pl. (202) 333-3450
www.capitalrestaurantconcepts.com

This place is a worthy competitor to Clyde's and has been serving good food, especially raw shellfish and too many brands of Scotch whiskey to count, for many years. It's a busy spot with moderate prices and is open Mon–Fri for lunch and dinner, Sat–Sun brunch and dinner. It stays open 11:30 a.m.–1:30 a.m. or 2:30 a.m. daily. Metro: Foggy Bottom-GWU, then 30, 32, 34, 35, or 36 Bus.

JR's 1519 17th St. NW btw P and Q Sts. (202) 328-0090

This bar and grill is a popular place with the lively men's gay clientele who frequent it for the music, drinks, and light food. It attracts a crowd of 30-ish types who come here to meet and greet. Open midday–2 a.m. or 3 a.m. with the grill closing at 3 p.m. on Sun. Metro: Dupont Circle.

J. W. Marriott Hotel 1331 Pennsylvania Ave. NW at 14th St. (202) 393-2000 or (800) 228-9290 www.marriott.com

This chain's flagship D.C. hostelry is in a prime location near the Mall and close to everything in the city's center. It boasts 772 rooms and suites, an indoor pool, a health club, and connects with National Place, the shopping center featuring some eighty shops and restaurants. All the customary luxury hotel amenities are provided here and are reflected in the expensive room rates. Metro: Metro Center.

Jack's Boats 3500 K St. NW below the Key Bridge (202) 337-9642

This place is near the foot of Wisconsin Ave. in Georgetown and rents out rowboats, canoes, and kayaks for use on the Potomac. Open sunrise to sunset every day from April to November. Metro: Rosslyn, then walk across Key Bridge.

Jackson Statue *see* Andrew Jackson Statue.

Jacques Dessange 5410 Wisconsin Ave. btw Willard and Jennifer Sts., Chevy Chase, MD (301) 913-9373 www.jacques-dessange.com

This is a well-regarded, upscale, and fashionable salon offering the full range of ministrations to enhance feminine beauty. Open Mon–Sat, days and hours vary. Metro: Friendship Heights.

Jaleo 480 7th St. NW at E St. (202) 628-7949

This is a stylish and trendy Spanish *tapas* place with the constant bustle of ever arriving throngs. It's constantly filled for the flavor of the combination of zesty smaller portions and the buoyant ambiance. Lunch and dinner Mon–Sat, brunch and dinner Sun. Moderate prices. Metro: Gallery Pl.-Chinatown or Archives-Navy Memorial. Second location at 7255 Woodmont St. at Elm St. in Bethesda. Metro: Bethesda.

Jamaica Embassy 1520 New Hampshire Ave. NW (202) 452-0660 www.emjam -usa.org

James Buchanan Memorial www.kittytours.org/thatman2/search.asp?subject = 96

This bronze sculpture of the seated American diplomat and president was created by Hans Schuler in 1930 and can be found in the southeast section of Meridian Hill Park, also known as Malcolm X Park, at Florida Ave. and 16th St. NW. Metro: U St.-Cardozo.

James Garfield Memorial *see* Garfield Memorial.

James Herring Gallery of Art *see* Howard University James Herring Gallery of Art.

Jandara 2606 Connecticut Ave. NW near Calvert St. (202) 338-8876

The menu here features a long litany of standard Thai food choices at moderate prices served by an affable staff. Open daily for lunch and dinner. Metro: Woodley Park-Zoo. Another location at 4237 Wisconsin Ave. NW (202) 237-1570.

Jane A. Delano Monument www.kittytours.org/thatman2/search.asp?subject = 109

This bronze memorial celebrates the founder of the Red Cross nursing program and honors the nurses who died during the First World War. It can be found at Red Cross Square located between 17th and 18th Sts. and E and D Sts. NW. Metro: Farragut West.

Japan-American Society of Washington, D.C. 1020 19th St. NW (202) 833-2210
www.us-japan.org/dc
    This organization designed to promote understanding and friendship between
the two countries has a considerable membership in the area. It sponsors symposia,
lectures, and films treating various facets of Japan—cultural, economic, and political. Exhibits, workshops, and performances are also featured centering on Japanese
arts and crafts. These events are scheduled at various venues around the city. Call
for information or check the Web site.

Japan Embassy 2520 Massachusetts Ave. NW (202) 238-6700

Japan Information and Culture Center 1155 21st St. NW (202) 238-6949 www
.gwjapan.com
    This is an affiliate of the Japanese Embassy and schedules a regular program of
events on cultural themes by treating Japanese concerns in seminars, films, demonstrations, and other cultural activities. Exhibits of a wide range of Japanese artistic
works are showcased here as well. All the programs are free. Open Mon–Fri 9
a.m.–5 p.m. Call for information or check the Web site.

Japan Inn 1715 Wisconsin Ave. NW btw R and S Sts. (202) 337-3400 www.japan
inn.com
    For a good many years this unique restaurant in upper Georgetown has been
elegantly serving unequaled meals cooked on a tabletop grill in a tranquil setting.
One can celebrate the event even more dramatically by reserving a tatami room
upstairs where diners sit at a low table and experience an even more colorful preparation and service. Open for lunch Mon–Fri, dinner Mon–Sat. Reservations are recommended at this fairly expensive place.

Japanese Restaurants *see* Atami, Japan Inn, Kaz Sushi Bistro, Makato, Matuba,
Perry's, Sushi-ko, Sushi Taro, Tachibana, Tako Grill, Tono Sushi Japanese and
Asian Cuisine. *See also* www.dcpages.com, www.restaurant.com, www.washington
post.com, www.opentable.com.

Java House Coffeeshop 1645 Q St. NW at 17th St. (202) 387-6622
    More than seventy types of coffee beans are roasted and flavored right here and
the brew can be savored indoors or on the patio along with a sandwich or a bagel.
Open Sun–Thurs 7 a.m.–11 p.m., Fri–Sat 7 a.m.–midnight. Metro: Dupont Circle.

Jaxx 6355 Rolling Rd. at Old Keene Rd., Springfield, VA (703) 569-5940 www.jaxx
roxx.com
    This is a rock concert hall booking older and newer performance groups all
week long with the price of admission changing with the talent. Show times vary
so call or check the Web site. Metro: Franconia-Springfield and taxi the rest of the
way.

Jazz Spots *see* Basin Street Lounge, Blues Alley, Bohemian Caverns, Chi-Cha
Lounge, Columbia Station, 18th Street Lounge, HR-57 Center for Preservation of
Jazz and Blues, Kinkead's, Latin Jazz Alley, Mr. Henry's, Ortanique, Saloun, State
of the Union, Takoma Station, Twins Jazz, U-Topia, The Wharf, Whitey's. *See also*

Potomac River Jazz Club, D.C. Blues Hotline, D.C. Blues Society, D.C. Blues Society (Web site), U St. Corridor.

Jean-Michel 10223 Old Georgetown Rd. at intersection with Democracy Blvd., Bethesda, MD (301) 564-4910

Somewhat off the beaten track for a classy French place, this moderately expensive restaurant is found in a smaller cluster of shops near a busy traffic intersection. Yet the food and the lively ambiance merit a visit and the Gallic dishes are well prepared and tasty. Open for lunch Mon–Fri, dinner nightly.

Jefferson Hotel 1200 16th St. NW at M St. (202) 347-2200 or (800) 368-5966 www.loewshotels.com

This venerable hostelry offers gracious old-world character in what was a Beaux Arts–style mansion. A luxury accommodation abounding in antiques, busts, and paintings, there are only 100 rooms and suites, but all the amenities can be found here including access to a swimming pool and exercise facility at the nearby University Club. Metro: Farragut North.

Jefferson Memorial located across the Tidal Basin from the Washington Monument (202) 426-6821 www.nps.gov/thje

This classical-style monument in the city's southwest is a circular dome supported by fifty-four Ionic columns housing Rudolph Evans's 10-foot bronze statue of the author of the Declaration of Independence and the third U.S. president, surrounded by panels inscribed with Thomas Jefferson's most renowned writings. Since its dedication in 1943 it has been one of the more popular tourist sightseeing destinations in D.C. Open daily 8 a.m.–midnight. Metro: Smithsonian.

Jefferson's Birthday

On or around April 13 at the Thomas Jefferson Memorial across the Tidal Basin from the Washington Monument, military drills and a wreath-laying ceremony take place to commemorate and honor America's third president and author of the Declaration of Independence. Information at (202) 619-7222. Metro: Smithsonian.

Jewish Community Center of Greater Washington 6125 Montrose Rd., Rockville, MD (301) 881-0100 www.jccgw.org

This very active facility is a multipurpose agency sponsoring concerts, plays, art exhibitions, children's programs, senior activities, educational programs, sports, swimming, and access to fitness equipment among its range of offerings.

Jewish Community Center of Northern Virginia 8900 Little River Turnpike, Fairfax, VA (703) 323-0880 www.jccnv.org

Among the activities sponsored here are programs for children and seniors, entertainment, and cultural events. There is also a gymnasium, indoor pool, exercise facility, and a library. To reach the center by car take Exit 52A off the Beltway (I-495) and drive 1 1/2 miles west to the center on the right.

Jewish Community Center of the District of Columbia 1529 16th St. NW at Q St. (202) 518-9400 www.dcjcc.org

This classical limestone structure, designed by architect B. Stanley Simmons in 1910, was owned by the University of the District of Columbia for a number of years. In 1990 it was repurchased by a Jewish group. Presently it runs a full-scale program featuring activities in the arts, theater, dance, films, health and fitness, community services, and family programs. There is a library, a fine gym, and a swimming pool. Metro: Dupont Circle.

Jewish Community Center Symphony Orchestra 6125 Montrose Rd., Rockville, MD (301) 881-0100 www.jccso.org

This orchestra has a long tradition of performing several concerts a year for adults and children. Its membership spans a wide age range and has offered concerts with many distinguished artists at a number of different venues in the region. Call for information on program details, ext. 6740, or check the Web site.

Jewish Film Festival

For a week in December each year at the Jewish Community Center of the District of Columbia in the Cecile Goldman Theater at 1529 16th St. at Q St. NW, this international cinema event shows features, documentaries, and short films, often accompanied by discussions by authors and film producers. Information at (202) 518-9400, ext. 247, or the Web site: www.wjff.org.

Jewish Historical Society of Greater Washington 701 3rd St. NW at G St. (202) 789-0900 www.jewishhistoricalsoc.com

Located on the lower floor of what was the oldest synagogue in the city, built in 1876, the society now exhibits local Jewish historical artifacts in a setting that has preserved some of the original synagogue's elements. It also maintains archives, oral and video histories, and a library. Open Mon–Thurs 10 a.m.–4 p.m. Admission free, modest donation appreciated. Metro: Judiciary Square.

Jewish Restaurants *see* Krupin's, Loeb's. *See also* Delicatessens, Kosher Restaurants, www.washingtonpost.com.

Joan of Arc Statue www.kittytours.org/thatman2/search.asp?subject = 95

Located in Meridian Hill Park (Malcolm X Park) at 16th St. and Florida Ave. NW, this bronze equestrian monument was executed in 1922 by sculptor Paul Dubois and is the only statue of a woman astride a horse to be found in the city. Metro: 52 or 54 Bus on 16th St.

Joaquin Miller Cabin in Rock Creek Park, Grove 6 (Picnic Area 6), Beach Dr. and Military Rd. NW (202) 895-6070

This log cabin was built in the woods in the late nineteenth century by the poet Joaquin Miller, an eccentric and flamboyant individual, who sought escape from civilization by living here alone. It is not open and can only be viewed from the outside. Metro: Bus 52 or 54 on 16th St. to Military Rd.

Joaquin Miller Cabin Poetry Readings

Every summer at 7:30 p.m. on Thursdays in June and the first four Thursdays in July the Joaquin Miller Poetry Series is held outdoors near the Joaquin Miller cabin in Rock Creek Park, Grove 6 (Picnic Area 6) just north of Military Rd. on Beach Dr. Poets read from their work following a competition for this honor in which a committee chooses from the many poets who enter their works. The series has been sponsored for some 20 years by Word Works Press. Information about the series at (202) 726-0971. Metro: Bus 52 or 54 on 16th St. to Military Rd.

Jogging *see* Running.

John A. Wilson Building 1350 Pennsylvania Ave. NW at 14th St.

Formerly known as the District Building until it was renamed to honor the once city council chairman, this Beaux Arts classic structure located in Federal Triangle, was designed in 1908 by architects Cope and Stewardson. It is listed on the National Register of Historic Places and is where much of the city's government activity is centered. Metro: Federal Triangle.

John F. Kennedy Bust www.kennedy-center.org/about/gifts/bust.html

This very imposing 7-foot-high bronze sculptured representation of President Kennedy by Robert Berks is in the Grand Foyer of the John F. Kennedy Center for the Performing Arts, New Hampshire Ave. and Rock Creek Pkwy. NW. Metro: Foggy Bottom-GWU.

John F. Kennedy Center for the Performing Arts *see* Kennedy Center for the Performing Arts.

John F. Kennedy Grave *see* Grave of John F. Kennedy.

John Howard Payne Memorial *see* Payne Memorial.

John Marshall House *see* Ringgold-Carroll House.

John Marshall Park Pennsylvania Ave. and 4th St. NW

This small park connects the city's court district with Pennsylvania Ave. and is named for the Supreme Court Chief Justice John Marshall. Metro: Judiciary Square.

John Paul Jones Monument *see* Commodore John Paul Jones Monument.

John Philip Sousa Bridge Pennsylvania Ave. SE across the Anacostia River to Anacostia

The nearby Marine Corps Barracks played a part in the naming of this bridge. March king John Philip Sousa served as bandmaster there from 1880 to 1882 and an admiring Congress, when it opened in 1940, named the bridge in his honor. The first bridge on the site, a wooden structure built in 1804, was burned by the U.S. Navy in 1814 in a vain attempt to slow invading British troops. The steel plate, rivets, and girder construction seems appropriate. Metro: Potomac Ave.

Johnny's Half Shell 2002 P St. NW at 20th St. (202) 296-2021

Located in the heart of the Dupont Circle neighborhood, this very popular small restaurant specializes in all types of tasty fish choices. There may be a line, but the regulars insist it's worth it at this moderate-priced spot open for lunch and dinner every day but Sun. Metro: Dupont Circle.

Jolie 7200 Wisconsin Ave. at Bethesda Ave., Bethesda, MD (301) 986-9293

Billing itself as a day spa and hair-design center, this place offers the full range of beauty services as well as spa packages of up to a full day's ministrations. Open six days a week at 9 a.m., Sun at 10 a.m., with evening hours Wed and Thurs. Metro: Bethesda.

Jolt 'N Bolt Coffee and Tea House 1918 18th St. NW at M St. (202) 232-0077
This heavily frequented neighborhood place is popular for its coffee. Bagels are the preference of most. Open daily 7:30 a.m. until past midnight. Metro: Dupont Circle.

Jordan Embassy 3504 International Dr. NW (202) 966-2664 www.jordanembassy us.org
Embassy of the Hashemite Kingdom of Jordan.

Journalists Memorial *see* Freedom Forum Journalists Memorial.

Joy of Motion 5207 Wisconsin Ave. NW at Harrison St. (301) 362-3042 www.joy ofmotion.org
Since 1976 this nonprofit organization has been offering instruction in various types of dancing—jazz, tap, ballet, and modern dance. It also sponsors fitness classes like aerobics. Workshops, performances, and resident dance companies are some of the features. Call for details on the various offerings or check the Web site. Metro: Friendship Heights. Joy of Motion is at two other locations as well: 1643 Connecticut Ave. NW (202) 387-0911; and 7707 Woodmont Ave., Bethesda (301) 986-0016.

Juárez Statue
Located at New Hampshire and Virginia Aves. NW in Foggy Bottom this 12-foot bronze statue depicts the Zapotec Indian, Benito Juárez, who became Mexico's president in 1860. This copy of the original made in 1895 by sculptor Enrique Alciati was given by Mexico to the United States in exchange for a statue of Abraham Lincoln in 1969. Metro: Foggy Bottom-GWU.

Judiciary Square Area
Just across from the National Building Museum, east of 5th St. NW between E and F Sts., this section of the city has been the center of the city's judiciary activities for 200 years. This is considered the eastern end of downtown. It is home to the courts and other governmental offices. The U.S. Tax Court, the District of Columbia Court House, and the U.S. (Federal) Court House are nearby. Metro: Judiciary Square.

Julia's Empanadas 2452 18th St. NW at Columbia Rd. (202) 328-6232
All manner of baked Latin pie-like delicacies stuffed with succulent fillings that appeal to vegetarians as well as carnivores are sold at modest cash prices here from 10:30 a.m. until late at night daily. Metro: Woodley Park-Zoo, then 90, 91, 92, 93, or 96 Bus, or Dupont Circle, then L2 Bus. Other locations at 1221 Connecticut Ave. NW (202) 861-8828; 1410 U St. NW (202) 387-4100; and 1000 Vermont Ave. NW (202) 789-1878.

Julio's 1604 U St. at New Hampshire Ave. (202) 483-8500
Fine pizza, a roof deck with a pleasant view, and very popular all-you-can-eat Sunday brunch are the appeals of this inexpensive place. Open daily for lunch and dinner. Metro: U St.-Cardozo.

Jury's Washington Hotel 1500 New Hampshire Ave. NW (202) 483-3600 or (800) 423-6953 www.jurysdoyle.com

This 314-room hotel is located right on Dupont Circle, which makes it central to a lot of what goes on in Washington. Guest rooms are comfortably furnished and the service is very congenial at this mid-range hostelry. Metro: Dupont Circle.

Justice Brown House 1720 16th St. NW near Riggs Pl.

This mansion, constructed in the 1880s for Supreme Court Justice Henry B. Brown, with its interestingly designed building and attached carriage house features an unusual design for city structures of its period. Metro: Dupont Circle.

Justice William O. Douglas Statue www.kittytours.org/thatman2/search.asp?sub ject = 10

This memorial to the Supreme Court justice celebrated for his dedication to the outdoors and the environment is appropriately situated along the C&O Canal Towpath at 30th St. NW in Georgetown. Metro: Foggy Bottom-GWU, then 30, 32, 34, 35, or 36 Bus.

K Street Bridge K St. NW entering Whitehurst Freeway

This bridge, a multi-level concrete structure faced with squared blocks of building stone, crosses Rock Creek at two levels. Built in 1939, it replaced an 1869 bridge, which in turn replaced a bridge opened in 1792, upon whose arches were engraved the names of the original thirteen states. The center arch celebrated Pennsylvania, the Keystone State, from which the bridge derives its name. Metro: Foggy Bottom-GWU.

K Street Downtown

The district along K St. NW and the streets around it from around 12th to 21st Sts. constitutes one of the city's busiest with hordes of lawyers, lobbyists, and business firms located here. K St. itself is the setting for many restaurants, shops, hotels, and business services to meet the neighborhood's needs.

Kahlil Gibran Memorial Garden

This small city park was dedicated in 1991 to the celebrated Lebanese American poet and philosopher. It is located on Massachusetts Ave. NW between 30th and 34th Sts., across the street from the British Embassy. A bronze bust of Gibran looks upon a small marble pool and limestone benches are engraved with quotations from the poet. Open daily 24 hours.

Kalorama

Bounded by Rock Creek Pkwy. on the north, 22nd St. on the east, Massachusetts Ave. on the west and on the south, this neighborhood north of Sheridan Circle stretches from Taft Bridge on Calvert St. to Massachusetts Ave. in the city's northwest. It is a quiet, beautiful enclave of tree-lined streets, luxurious homes and gardens, elegant apartment buildings, and consulates, and has been a prime residential area for Washington's elite since the early years of the twentieth century. Kalorama, incidentally, is Greek for beautiful view. Metro: Woodley Park-Zoo.

Kalorama Embassy and House Tour

On the second Sunday in September from noon to 5 p.m. self-guided walking tours are offered each year under the sponsorship of the Woodrow Wilson House. Lovely nineteenth-century homes and gardens as well as embassies in the neighborhood are open to viewers. Details and ticket information at (202) 387-4062 or the Web site: www.woodrowwilsonhouse.org.

Kalorama Guest House 1854 Mintwood Pl. NW btw 19th St. and Columbia Rd. (202) 667-6369 www.washingtonpost.com/yp/kgh

This very conveniently located bed-and-breakfast near Adams Morgan but distant enough not to be noisy, offers various modestly priced accommodations, some with shared bath, some with bath, some suites. The rooms are charmingly appointed. There's an attractive garden, the only TV is in the communal room, and there is a phone in the lobby that can be used to make local calls. Metro: Woodley Park-Zoo, then 90, 92, 93, 94, or 96 Bus. There's another branch at 2700 Cathedral Ave. NW at 27th St., 3 blocks from the Metro at Woodley Park-Zoo, (202) 328-0860.

Kalorama Park

Located at Columbia Rd. NW at 19th St. between 18th St. and Connecticut Ave., this small urban park contains splendid old oak trees. It is the only remaining public space in an area that was only woodland and farms 200 years ago. Open daily dawn to dusk. Metro: Woodley Park-Zoo, then 90, 91, 92, 93, or 96 Bus.

Kankouran West African Dance Company www.kankouran.org

This is one of the city's finest African dance groups, which has public performances in the city and at other venues. Program details at (202) 737-4941 or at the Web site: www.kankouran@aol.com.

Kathleen Ewing Gallery 1609 Connecticut Ave. NW btw Q and R Sts., Suite 200 (202) 328-0955 www.kathleenewinggallery.com

This is the venue for perhaps the city's best rotating celebrations of vintage and contemporary photography. Open Wed–Sat noon–5 p.m. and by appointment. Metro: Dupont Circle.

Kaz Sushi Bistro 1915 I St. btw 19th and 20th Sts. (202) 530-5500 www.kazsushi .com

This much-frequented restaurant serves splendid sushi as well as Japanese cooked dishes at moderate prices. Open Mon–Fri for lunch, dinner daily except Sun. Metro: Farragut West.

Kazakhstan Embassy 1401 16th St. NW (202) 232-5488 www.kazakhstan-embassy-us.org

Kazan 6813 Redmond Dr. btw Chain Bridge and Beverly Rds., McLean, VA (703) 734-1960

This is a place for a fine Middle Eastern dining experience under a tinted ceiling with well-clad servers offering a full range of excellent traditional Turkish dishes at moderately expensive prices. Open Mon–Fri lunch and dinner, Sat dinner. It is located on a side street off Old Dominion Rd.

Kelly's Irish Times 14 F St. btw N Capitol St. and New Jersey Ave. (202) 543-5433 www.kellysirishtimes.com

This pub offers light foods until 10 p.m. but the bar, which is the center point here, opens at 11 a.m. daily and stays open until 2 a.m., and 3 a.m. on Fri and Sat. It's very popular with younger Capitol Hill staffers and collegiate types. Metro: Union Station.

Kemper Open

This major professional golf tournament takes place every year beginning in late May at the Tournament Players Club at Avenel, 10000 Oaklyn Drive in Potomac, Maryland. Details about tickets and shuttle bus transportation to and from the golf courses at the Tournament office (301) 469-3737 or at the Web site: www.kemper open.com.

Kenilworth Aquatic Gardens Anacostia Ave. and Douglas St. NE (202) 426-6905 www.nps.gov/nace/keag

Fourteen acres of water flora and fauna constitute Washington's last natural marshland of quiet floating gardens. It is an extraordinary place for bird watching and views of wildlife like turtles, bullfrogs, waterfowl, muskrats, and opossums. Open daily daylight until 4 p.m., visitor center open 8 a.m.–4 p.m. Admission free. Metro: Deanwood. See also www.commuterpage.com/venues/gardens.htm.

Kennedy Bust *see* John F. Kennedy Bust.

Kennedy Center for the Performing Arts New Hampshire Ave. NW at Rock Creek Pkwy (202) 467-4600 www.kennedy-center.org

Overlooking the Potomac River this living memorial structure to the late president, and one of the country's busiest arts facilities offers more than 3,000 performances a year to audiences of more than two million. Entertainment is provided in six theaters: the Eisenhower Theater, the Opera House, the Concert Hall, the Terrace Theater, the Theater Lab, and the American Film Institute Theater. The building's architect was Edward Durell Stone and the opening was in 1971. The center's Grand Foyer holds a 7-foot bronze bust of President Kennedy. The Hall of the States contains flags of every state and the Hall of the Nations displays flags of each nation recognized by the United States. The center is open daily 10 a.m.–11 p.m. (on performance days). Admission free. Tours are offered Mon–Fri 10 a.m.–5 p.m., Sat–Sun 10 a.m.–1 p.m. Metro: Foggy Bottom-GWU, then free shuttle bus.

Kennedy Center for the Performing Arts Concert Hall New Hampshire Ave. NW at Rock Creek Pkwy. (202) 467-4600 www.kennedy-center.org

Located at the southern end of the Grand Foyer, this performance space seats some 2,400. It was renovated in 1997 and is where the National Symphony Orchestra, the Washington Chamber Symphony, and the Choral Arts Society regularly perform. Metro: Foggy Bottom-GWU, then free shuttle bus.

Kennedy Center for the Performing Arts Eisenhower Theater New Hampshire Ave. NW at Rock Creek Pkwy. (202) 467-4600 www.kennedy-center.org

Dramatic and comedy productions are presented at this theater in a performance space that seats 1,100. Metro: Foggy Bottom-GWU, then free shuttle bus.

Kennedy Center for the Performing Arts Millennium Stage New Hampshire Ave. NW at Rock Creek Pkwy. (202) 467-4600 www.kennedy-center.org

The Grand Foyer is the venue where the Millennium Stage presents free performances at 6 p.m. with artists drawn from the worlds of jazz, folklore, college choirs, puppetry, and other popular entertainment forms on different nights. Metro: Foggy Bottom-GWU, then free shuttle bus.

Kennedy Center for the Performing Arts Open House New Hampshire Ave. NW at Rock Creek Pkwy. (202) 467-4600 www.kennedy-center.org

Each year on a Sunday in September free concerts and other types of performances are offered free of charge. Call for information or check the Web site. Metro: Foggy Bottom-GWU, then free shuttle bus.

Kennedy Center for the Performing Arts Opera House New Hampshire Ave. NW at Rock Creek Pkwy. (202) 467-4600 www.kennedy-center.org

This theater with its 2,300 seats is the second largest performance space at the Kennedy Center. Musicals, dance performances, operas, and ballet are presented here. Metro: Foggy Bottom-GWU, then free shuttle bus.

Kennedy Center for the Performing Arts Roof Terrace Restaurant *see* Roof Terrace Restaurant.

Kennedy Center for the Performing Arts Terrace Theater New Hampshire Ave. NW at Rock Creek Pkwy. (202) 467-4600 www.kennedy-center.org

This intimate theater seating 500 has a varied program of chamber music, revues, comedies, and solo artistic performances. Metro: Foggy Bottom-GWU, then free shuttle bus.

Kennedy Center for the Performing Arts Theater Lab New Hampshire Ave. NW at Rock Creek Pkwy. (202) 467-4600 www.kennedy-center.org

This is the venue for a variety of children's programs during the day while the audience-participation murder-mystery comedy *Shear Madness* takes the stage in the evening. Metro: Foggy Bottom-GWU, then free shuttle bus.

Kennedy-Warren 3133 Connecticut Ave. NW

This apartment building designed by Joseph Younger and constructed in 1931 is an Art Deco fancier's delight with its decorative aluminum panels, streamlined entrance, stone griffins under the pyramid copper roof, and the carved eagles in the driveway. Metro: Cleveland Park.

Kenny's Bar-B-Que 3060 Duke St., Alexandria, VA (703) 823-3330

It doesn't look like much and it's about a mile from the Metro station, but the pork, beef, and chicken are first rate and the beans, coleslaw, and other accompaniments are just as good, all at budget prices. Open daily from 7:30 a.m. through dinner except Sun. Metro: King Street.

Kensington www.tok.org

This small primarily residential community, which is not very far out beyond the Beltway on Connecticut Ave. in the Maryland suburbs, is not accessible by Metro. Its principal claim to fame is its Antique Row reputed to be one of the area's choicest spots for collectibles, with some 40 stores selling everything from furniture to vintage clothes to Art Deco souvenirs and much more. It's all on Howard Ave.

between Connecticut and Montgomery Aves. By car turn right on Howard Ave. at 10600 Connecticut Ave. (Rte. 185).

Kensington Farmers Market at the Train Station, Howard Ave., Kensington, MD (301) 949-2424

From early May until the end of October 8 a.m.–noon on Saturdays producers of fruits and vegetables sell their farm products.

Kenya Embassy 2249 R St. NW (202) 387-6101 www.kenyaembassy.com

Kesher Israel Congregation–Georgetown Synagogue 2801 N St. NW at 28th St. (202) 333-2337 www.kesher.org

This synagogue serving a Jewish Orthodox congregation was constructed in 1931. It is possible to visit and see its interior by calling to arrange it. Metro: Foggy Bottom-GWU, then 30, 32, 34, 35, or 36 Bus.

Key Bridge

This bridge named for Francis Scott Key, composer of the "Star Spangled Banner," was completed in 1923 with Nathan C. Wyeth as its architect. It is 1,650 feet long and is decorated with a colorful railing and lampposts. The Key Bridge crosses the Potomac from the edge of Georgetown to Rosslyn in Virginia and is used heavily by pedestrians as well as motorists. Metro: Rosslyn.

Key Bridge Marriott 1401 Lee Hwy. btw Key Bridge and N Oak St., Arlington, VA (703) 524-6400 or (800) 228-9290 www.marriott.com

This 585-room expensive hotel is located on the banks of the Potomac and as close to the city as you can get in Virginia. A short walk over the Key Bridge from Georgetown, only 2 blocks from the Metro, this hotel offers extraordinary views of the city and the river, particularly at night. There's an indoor as well as outdoor pool, an exercise facility, and all the other customary luxury hotel amenities. Metro: Rosslyn.

Key Sunday Cinema Club at the AMC Courthouse Theatre, 2150 Clarendon Blvd., Arlington, VA (202) 965-4401

On selected Sunday mornings throughout the year for more than 25 years, club members have been watching and then discussing new releases of independent and foreign films here. After each screening a well-qualified moderator, often accompanied by a guest speaker, film critic, or writer leads a 45-minute to 1-hour discussion of the movie. Details on the program and membership at (202) 965-4401. Metro: Court House.

Kidwell Farm at Frying Pan Park, 2709 W Ox Rd., Herndon, VA (703) 437-9101 www.co.fairfax.va.us/parks/fryingpanpark

This is a small working model farm with a barnyard full of animals for kids' delight. There are hayrides (nominal charge) and a range of special events. The schedule of activities is available at (703) 324-8588. Open daily 10 a.m.–6 p.m. with free admission. The park is located south of Herndon between Centerville Rd. and Fairfax County Pkwy.

Kidzone in White Flint Mall, 11301 Rockville Pike, 3rd floor, N Bethesda, MD (301) 231-0505 www.kidzone.biz

Calling itself the fun center, this indoor exercise and fitness facility provides tunnels, mats, padded cubes, and lots of other things that kids 12 and under can enjoy climbing, jumping, or running loose around, on, with, or however. Open Mon–Sat 10 a.m.–8 p.m., Sun 11 a.m.–7 p.m. Admission price is based upon the children's ages, the younger the less expensive. Metro: White Flint.

King Library *see* Martin Luther King Memorial Library.

King Memorial Library *see* Martin Luther King Memorial Library.

Kinkead's 2000 Pennsylvania Ave. NW btw 20th and 21st Sts. (202) 296-7700

This very expensive restaurant deserves its reputation as one of the city's finest. It is open for lunch Mon–Sat, Sun brunch, and dinner nightly. The lower floor is a spacious bar/lounge where there's fine jazz music some nights, and food is also served. The menu specialties in this popular casual place are excellently prepared fish and seafood. Reservations are a must. Metro: Foggy Bottom-GWU.

Kiplinger Collection 1729 H St. NW btw 17th and I Sts. (202) 887-6537

Located in a gallery off the lobby in the Kiplinger Building, selections from the more than 5,000 prints, photographs, and paintings of Washington, D.C., are on display. The collection grew from selections by the founder of the *Kiplinger Washington Newsletter*, W. M. Kiplinger, beginning in the early part of the twentieth century. Many of the elements of this unusual collection of Washingtoniana are hung all around this building, which houses the company. Appointments to visit the gallery, which is open Mon–Fri 9 a.m.–5 p.m., must be made in advance by calling (202) 887-2537. Metro: Farragut West.

Kirov Academy 4301 Harewood Rd. NE at N Capitol St. (202) 832-1087

Just like the Kirov Academy in St. Petersburg, the Washington center has become one of the foremost places in the city for classes in ballet dancing. It also offers public performances through the year. Metro: Brookland-CUA, then H8 Bus to N Capitol St.

Klingle Valley Bridge Connecticut Ave. NW south of Macomb St.

Washington architect Paul Cret built this bridge to replace an earlier one constructed in 1891. It runs across the forested area around the Klingle tributary to Rock Creek at the entrance to the Cleveland Park neighborhood just north of the bridge and is adorned with distinctive limestone urns and fluted glass lanterns. Metro: Cleveland Park.

Klutznick National Jewish Museum *see* B'nai B'rith Klutznick National Jewish Museum.

Komen Race for the Cure *see* National Race for the Cure.

Korea Embassy *see* South Korea Embassy.

Korean Restaurants *see* Bee Won Secret Garden, Hee Been, Sam Woo, Woo Lae Oak. *See also* www.dcpages.com, www.restaurant.com, www.washingtonpost.com, www.opentable.com.

Korean War Veterans Memorial in West Potomac Park south of the Lincoln Memorial Reflecting Pool btw 21st and 23rd Sts. (202) 426-6841 www.nps.gov/kwvm

This commemorative display sculpted by Frank Gaylord of 19-foot-tall poncho-covered foot soldiers on patrol in the rugged countryside of Korea was constructed in 1995 and celebrates the veterans of this almost forgotten war. The black granite wall nearby contains a mural blasted into the rock depicting support troops. The striking memorial is staffed 8 a.m.–midnight daily. Metro: Smithsonian or Foggy Bottom-GWU, then a long walk. *See also* www.commuterpage.com/venues/memo rials.htm.

Kosciuszko Memorial Statue www.kittytours.org/thatman2/search.asp?subject =28

This monument to Polish Gen. Thaddeus Kosciuszko, who fought in the American Revolutionary War and later for Polish Independence from Russia, was sculpted by Antoni Popiel in 1910. It can be found in the northeast corner of Lafayette Park, at Pennsylvania Ave. NW between Jackson Pl. and Madison Pl. Metro: Farragut West or Farragut North.

Kosher Restaurants *see* Loeb's, Royal Dragon. *See also* Delicatessens, Jewish Restaurants, www.shamash.org.

Kramer Books and Afterwords Café 1517 Connecticut Ave. NW at Q St. Bookstore: (202) 387-1400; Café: (202) 387-3825 www.kramers.com

Since the 1970s this has been a Washington favorite spot. It combines in one location a fine independent bookshop with a strong inventory and knowledgeable staff and a genuinely good restaurant, not just an afterthought. Open 7 a.m.–1 a.m. Mon–Thurs and Sun, 24 hours Fri and Sat. Live music in the café several nights a week. Metro: Dupont Circle.

Kreeger Museum 2401 Foxhall Rd. NW btw Dexter and W Sts. (202) 338-3552 www.kreegermuseum.com

Located in a heavily wooded area, combining classical and Renaissance styles, and designed in 1967 by architect Philip Johnson, this museum was once home to David Kreeger and his wife. It contains an extraordinary collection of nineteenth- and twentieth-century European and American works by celebrated artists as well as an unusual exhibition of African tribal masks and woodcarvings. Opened to the public in 1994, the striking architecture and the art complement each other. Visits are by guided tour only, which last 90 minutes, on Mon, Tues, and Sat at 10 a.m. and 1:30 p.m., for which reservations are required. There is a modest suggested contribution, and children under 12 are not admitted. The museum is not readily accessible by public transportation but there is free parking. By car drive north on Massachusetts Ave. to Nebraska Ave. At the circle exit Nebraska to the west and turn left on Foxhall Rd.

Kreeger Theater adjoins Arena Stage, 1101 6th St. at Maine Ave. SW (202) 488-3300 www.arenastage.com

This 3-story theater wraps around the administration building of the Arena Stage structure. Unlike the Arena's Fichandler theater-in-the-round, the Kreeger is conventionally fan-shaped, seats 500, and tends to be the venue for experimental plays and children's theater. Metro: Waterfront-SEU. *See also* Arena Stage.

Krupin's 4620 Wisconsin Ave. NW btw Brandywine and Chesapeake Sts. (202) 686-1989

This inexpensive New York–style diner and delicatessen serves all the Jewish specialties from blintzes to potato pancakes to stuffed cabbage to lox and bagels to overstuffed pastrami sandwiches to matzo ball soup. Open daily 8 a.m.–10 p.m. Metro: Tenleytown-AU.

Kuwait Embassy 2940 Tilden St. NW (202) 966-0702 www.embassy.org/embassies/kw.html

Kyrgyzstan Embassy 1732 Wisconsin Ave. NW (202) 338-5141 www.kyrgyzstan.org

LBJ Memorial Grove

Located on the Potomac in Lady Bird Johnson Park, in this area of white pines, flowering dogwood trees, and flowers, a large pink granite memorial to President Johnson is the focal point. The best way to reach this spot is by automobile. From East Potomac Park cross the George Mason Memorial Bridge (I-395), and after crossing over the George Washington Memorial Pkwy., continue to the Boundary Dr. exit. Turn right (north) and follow the signs to the parking lot. Along the George Washington Memorial Pkwy. exits from both directions are provided for pulling off to Lady Bird Johnson Park. *See also* Lady Bird Johnson Park.

La Cantinita's Havana Café *see* La Cantinita's under C.

La Ruche Restaurant *see* Café la Ruche.

Labor Day Weekend Concert

The summer season in Washington closes with the National Symphony Orchestra performing a free concert of stirring patriotic and classical selections in the evening on the Capitol's West Lawn before an audience of thousands of tourists and locals. Details at (202) 619-7222.

Labor Department Building *see* Frances Perkins Department of Labor Building.

Lady Bird Johnson Park www.nps.gov/lyba

The 121-acre man-made Columbia Island in the Potomac River was designated as the Lady Bird Johnson Park in 1968 to honor the wife of the late President Lyndon Johnson. It is planted with groups of trees and offers lovely views of the river and the Washington skyline. The 15-acre LBJ Memorial Grove occupies the park's south end. It is accessible only from Virginia, and a car is the best way of reaching the park. From East Potomac Park cross the George Mason Memorial Bridge (I-395), and after crossing over the George Washington Memorial Pkwy., continue to the Boundary Dr. exit. Turn right (north) and follow the signs to the parking lot. Along the George Washington Memorial Pkwy. exits from both directions are provided for pulling off to Lady Bird Johnson Park. *See also* LBJ Memorial Grove.

Lafayette Memorial

www.dcheritage.org/dch_tourism2608/dch_tourism_sh ow.htm?doc_id = 42702

In the southeast corner of Lafayette Park on Pennsylvania Ave. between Jackson and Madison Places NW, this statue of Maj. Gen. Marquis Gilbert de Lafayette was erected in 1891. The sculptors were Jean Falguière and Marius Mercie. In the monument a naked figure symbolizing the United States is handing the Revolutionary War hero a sword. Metro: McPherson Square.

Lafayette Park

www.dcheritage.org/dch_tourism2555/dch_tourism.htm?doc_id = 44165&area = 2524

Located directly north of the White House at 16th St. and Pennsylvania Ave. NW and designed by Pierre L'Enfant, this 7-acre plot of land is named for the Marquis de Lafayette. It was originally part of an 80-acre presidential park that was to surround the White House. The park's four corners feature monuments to four foreigners who distinguished themselves in serving the American cause during the Revolutionary War—the Comte de Rochambeau, Gen. Thaddeus Kosciuszko, Baron von Steuben, and the Marquis de Lafayette. In the center is an equestrian statue of Andrew Jackson made from a cannon he captured during the War of 1812. The park, situated just opposite the White House, is a prominent site for frequent public demonstrations. Metro: McPherson Square.

Lafayette Square www.dcheritage.org/information2550/information.htm?area = 2524

Known until the early nineteenth century as President's Square because it was lined with the homes of Cabinet members and other prominent figures, the square is bounded by Pennsylvania Ave. NW, Jackson Pl., H St., and Madison Dr. President Thomas Jefferson authorized the separation of the parkland for public use from the President's Park in which it had been included in Pierre L'Enfant's plan for the city of 1791. It is often the scene of public protests by demonstrators holding up their signs facing the White House. Metro: McPherson Square.

Lafayette Square Historic District www.cr.nps.gov/nr/travel/wash/dc30.htm

Lafayette Park, the centerpiece of this area of the city, was designed in the midnineteenth century and remains an urban park of distinction with flowers blossoming in different seasons under the care of the National Park Service. In this area extending along Pennsylvania Ave. NW with Jackson Pl., H St., and Madison Dr. as its boundaries, are some thirty buildings constructed between 1815 and the 1940s. Metro: McPherson Square.

Lake Accotink Park 7500 Accotink Park Rd. btw Old Keene Mill and Braddock Rds., Springfield, VA (703) 569-3464 www.co.fairfax.va.us/parks

This 479-acre lovely parkland offers streams, wetlands, a 65-acre lake where canoes, rowboats, and pedal boats are rented, a miniature golf course, playgrounds, ball fields, and a carousel. It is open April to October from dawn to dusk. Information at (703) 569-3464 or the Web site.

Lakeforest Mall 701 Russell Ave., Gaithersburg, MD (301) 840-5840

This very large suburban shopping mall in the center of Gaithersburg offers more than 200 stores, shops, restaurants, and movie theaters. It is located off I-270 at Exit 11, Montgomery Village Ave. *See also* www.commuterpage.com/venues/venue-shop.htm.

Lambda Rising 1625 Connecticut Ave. NW btw Q and R Sts. (202) 462-6969

This comprehensive bookstore with an informed and helpful staff carries most every title addressing gay and lesbian reading interests and has been information central for Dupont Circle's otherwise-oriented community since 1974. It sponsors frequent author readings and book signing events. Open Sun–Thurs 10 a.m.–10 p.m., Fri–Sat 10 a.m.–midnight. Metro: Dupont Circle.

Landmark Mall 5801 Duke St., Alexandria, VA (703) 941-2582 www.landmark mall.com

This three-level modern enclosed shopping mall offers more than 120 department stores, shops, and restaurants to choose from. It is accessible by driving on I-395 south from the city and taking Duke St. Exit 3A and proceeding east. *See also* www.commuterpage.com/venues/venue-shop.htm.

Langley Park

This very heavily populated neighborhood is located next to Takoma Park and is across the district line in Maryland and part of Prince George's County. It is a multi-ethnic community with a large concentration of Spanish-speaking residents who are the most numerous, but there has been a considerable recent influx of Asians, including a growing number of people from India. The area abounds with multiple-dwelling structures, but there are some excellent dining spots, particularly in and around the Langley Park crossroads at University Blvd. and New Hampshire Ave., where Udupi Palace and Woodlands, both excellent Indian vegetarian restaurants, are located.

Langston Golf Course 26th St. and Benning Rd. NE (202) 397-8638 www.golfdc .com/gc/lng/news.htm

This public 18-hole course and driving range is near RFK Stadium and runs along the Anacostia River. Call for details about green fees and start-up times. Metro: Stadium-Armory.

Lansburg Shakespeare Theatre *see* Shakespeare Theatre.

Lao Embassy 2222 S St. NW (202) 332-6416 www.laoembassy.com

Embassy of the Lao People's Democratic Republic.

Larz Anderson House *see* Society of the Cincinnati at Anderson House.

Latham Hotel 3000 M St. NW at 30th St. (202) 726-5000 or (800) 368-5922 www .thelatham.com

This well-situated Georgetown hotel is insulated from the bustling tumult and offers 143 rooms and 9 suites, a rooftop pool, and the elegant amenities usually found in a luxury establishment. Citronelle, one of the city's most acclaimed French restaurants, is here as well. Metro: Foggy Bottom-GWU, then 30, 32, 34, 35 or 36 Bus.

Latin American Restaurants *See* Banana Café, Café Atlantico, La Cantinita's Havana Café, Casa Fiesta, Chi-Cha Lounge, Gabriel, Havana Breeze, The Islander, Julia's Empanadas, Lauriol Plaza, Mexicali Blues. *See also* Brazilian Restaurants, Mexican Restaurants, www.dcpages.com, www.restaurant.com, www.washington post.com, www.opentable.com.

Latin Jazz Alley 1721 Columbia Rd. NW (202) 328-6190 www.latinjazz4u@cs.com

This newer Adams Morgan spot offers salsa and merengue dance music and gives classes for novices and intermediates before the serious dancing begins later in the evening. Some nights feature live music. Open Wed–Sat 7 p.m. until the wee hours. No cover charge. Metro: Dupont Circle, then L2 Bus; or Woodley Park-Zoo, then 90, 91, 92, 93 or 96 Bus.

Latino Festival

On the last weekend in July the city's considerable Latin American community celebrates exuberantly and colorfully with two days of music, dance, food, and performances culminating in a parade on Sunday. It takes place on Pennsylvania Ave. NW between 9th and 14th Sts. Information at (301) 588-8719 or (202) 789-7000.

Latvia Embassy 4325 17th St. NW (202) 726-8213 www.latvia-usa.org

Laurel www.laurel.md.us

This is a typical Prince George's County, Maryland, suburban community. It is bounded by Guilford Rd. on the north, Baltimore-Washington Pkwy. on the east, Laurel Fort Meade Rd. on the south, and I-95 on the west. The most interesting aspect of this town is Old Laurel with its venerable Victorian wooden frame houses, many of which have been beautifully restored. Laurel is situated almost as near to Baltimore as to downtown D.C.

Laurel Farmers Market Main St. in the 300 block, Laurel, MD (301) 854-2917 www.laurel.md.us/farmersmap.htm

From late June until the end of October on Thursdays 11 a.m.–3 p.m. growers sell their vegetables and fruit.

Laurel Park Race Course Rte. 198 and Laurel Racetrack Rd., Laurel, MD (301) 725-0400 www.laurelpark.com

Since 1911 this racetrack has offered a calendar of thoroughbred races from January through March, late June to late August, and October through December. The ponies usually run Wed–Sun. To drive to the track from Washington, take the Baltimore-Washington Pkwy. and exit at 33A to Rte. 198.

Lauriol Plaza 1801 18th St. NW at S St. (202) 387-0035

On the border between the Adams Morgan and Dupont Circle neighborhoods this pleasantly casual corner restaurant is very popular for its Latin American and Spanish dishes at modest prices. It's especially pleasurable dining at the outdoor tables in warm weather. Open daily for lunch and dinner. Metro: Dupont Circle.

Lavandou 3321 Connecticut Ave. NW btw Macomb and Ordway Sts. (202) 966-3002

A charming and comfortable French bistro serving hearty portions of Provençale dishes at moderate prices. Open for lunch and dinner daily. Reservations are recommended. Metro: Cleveland Park.

Layalina 5216 Wilson Blvd. btw N Frederick and N Greenbrier Sts., Arlington, VA (703) 525-1170

This pleasant and friendly Syrian restaurant serves lunch and dinner Tues–Sun offering well-prepared Middle Eastern appetizers and main courses at moderate prices. Metro: Ballston, then a 20-minute walk.

Lebanese Taverna 2641 Connecticut Ave. NW btw Calvert St. and Woodley Rd. (202) 265-8681 www.lebanesetaverna.com

The meze platters (made up of different appetizers) are very popular here but so are the tasty main dishes and delicious Lebanese breads. Prices are moderate and this elegantly appointed restaurant serves lunch Mon–Sat and dinner nightly. Metro: Woodley Park-Zoo. Another location in Arlington, VA, at 5900 Washington Blvd. (703) 241-8681.

Lebanon Embassy 2560 28th St. NW (202) 939-6300 www.lebanonembassy.org

Lectures *see* Public Lectures.

Ledo 2420 University Blvd. E btw West Park Dr. and 24th Ave., Adelphi, MD (301) 422-8622

This restaurant located in a small shopping strip just down the road from the University of Maryland has the reputation for creating some of the finest pizzas in the Maryland suburbs. It's open for lunch and dinner daily serving inexpensive Italian dishes, and it distributes Ledo pizzas to a number of other dining locations around town.

Le Droit Park

This historic district of the city is bounded by 2nd, 6th, 5th, U, and Elm Sts. NW and Florida and Rhode Island Aves. NW. Many of its buildings date from the 1870s, and some fifty are still standing on U St. in the 400 block and T St. in the 500 block. The region has long been home to distinguished black citizens. The neighborhood is just east of Howard University and has been traditionally associated with the intellectual life of the community. Metro: Shaw-Howard University.

Lee Boyhood Home *see* Robert E. Lee Boyhood Home.

Lee Family Homes *see* Robert E. Lee Boyhood Home and Lee-Fendall House Museum.

Lee-Fendall House Museum 614 Oronoco St. at N Washington St., Alexandria, VA (703) 548-8450 www.leefendallhouse.org

This was home to several generations of the celebrated Lee family of Virginia. The large clapboard structure contains family furnishings, records, and historic research materials. The Lee family lived in this Greek Revival mansion from 1785 until 1903. The children's room features an exhibit of dollhouses, miniature architecture, and other changing exhibits. The house is augmented by a large garden with a huge magnolia tree, chestnut trees, a rose garden, and boxwood paths. Open 10 a.m.–4 p.m. Tues–Sat, noon–4 p.m. Sun. Admission charge. Metro: Braddock Rd. then DAT4 DASH Bus toward Hunting Towers to the stop at Pendleton St. and St. Asaph St., then 1 block on N St. Asaph St. *See also* www.commuterpage.com/venues/sightseeing_VA.htm.

Leesburg Animal Park 19270 James Monroe Hwy., Leesburg, VA (703) 433-0002
www.leesburganimalpark.com

Formerly the Reston Animal Park, kids can pet and feed a variety of animals,
some barnyard such as chickens, cows, and sheep, and some more exotic such as
llamas, antelope, and emus. Kids can enjoy watching giant tortoises, lemurs, and
squirrel monkeys or catch a hayride, a pony ride, or a live animal show. Moderate
admission charge. Closed on Mondays. Open March through October. Summer
hours: Mon–Thurs 10 a.m.–3 p.m., Fri–Sun 10 a.m.–5 p.m. Fall hours after Labor
Day Fri–Sun 10 a.m.–5 p.m. By car from the Beltway (I-495), take Dulles Toll Rd./
267 W, exit at Rte. 7 W, take Rte. 15 S for 1 mile, exit Rte. 15 S toward Warrenton,
drive 1½ miles to the park.

Leesburg Corner Premium Outlets Rte. 7 and U.S. Hwy. 15, Leesburg, VA (703)
737-3071 www.chelseagca.com/location/leesburg/lees.html

More than sixty shops offer discount prices on designer clothing, housewares,
jewelry, children's playthings, and other popular consumer goods.

Leesylvania State Park 16236 Neabsco Rd., Woodbridge, VA (703) 670-0372 www
.state.va.us/~dcs/parks/leesylva.htm

There are 6 miles of hiking paths and a sandy beach along the Potomac River
here as well as picnic areas. The park covers some 500 acres in Prince William
County and is located off U.S. Hwy. 1. It is open from dawn to dusk. Call for details
about special activities.

Legal Seafoods 2020 K St. NW at 20th St. (202) 496-1111

This branch of a popular seafood chain offers a full range of nicely prepared
and pleasantly served fish dishes at upper-mid-range prices in an upscale ambiance.
Open for lunch and dinner Mon–Fri and Sun, dinner nightly. Reservations are suggested. Metro: Farragut North. Other branches can be found at: 707 7th St. NW
(202) 347-0047; and Tysons Galleria, 2001 International Dr., McLean, VA (703)
827-8900.

Legg Mason Tennis Classic (202) 721-9500 www.leggmasontennisclassic.com

For more than 35 years Washington has hosted this premiere men's professional
tennis competition. It takes place in August around the middle of the month and
runs from one weekend through the next at the Wilham H. G. Fitzgerald Tennis
Center at 16th and Kennedy Sts. NW. Shuttle buses transport spectators from the
Van Ness Metro station during the tournament. Call for details.

L'Enfant Plaza

This area lies between D St. SW, the ramp to the 12th St. Expressway, the 9th
St. Expressway, and the Southwest Freeway. It was developed during the urban renewal efforts of the 1960s. The surface area of the plaza is the city's sole paved
square, containing a landscaped central garden and surrounded by office buildings.
Underneath is a shopping mall and a large parking garage. Metro: L'Enfant Plaza.

Leonard's Mansion *see* H. H. Leonard's Mansion.

Lerman Dance Exchange *see* Liz Lerman Dance Exchange.

Les Halles 1201 Pennsylvania Ave. NW at 12th St. (202) 347-6848

The specialty in this Parisian brasserie-style restaurant is beef, usually accompanied by *frites* and preceded by a fine salad. But all the other choices are prepared just as succulently and an upstairs section is reserved just for cigar smokers. Like steak houses generally, this one is expensive. Open daily for lunch and dinner. Metro: Federal Triangle or Metro Center.

Lesotho Embassy 2511 Massachusetts Ave. NW (202) 797-5533 www.embassy.org/embassies/ls.html

Embassy of the Kingdom of Lesotho.

Levantes 1320 19th St. NW at Dupont Circle (202) 293-3244

The specialties here are the popular dishes of the Mediterranean east—grilled kebabs and the tasty appetizers that can just as easily be combined to become a main course. This attractive spot seats diners inside and out in fair weather. It's open daily for lunch and dinner with medium prices. Metro: Dupont Circle. There's a second location in Bethesda at 7262 Woodmont Ave. (301) 657-2441.

Levine School of Music 2801 Upton St. NW off 28th St. (202) 686-9772 www.levineschool.org

This is one of the largest community music schools in the country providing instruction and performances for people of all ages and abilities. Offerings include instrument and voice, musical theater, opera, jazz, composition, and early-childhood and senior programs. There are also recitals and master classes with celebrated artists. Activities are carried out at four regional sites in the area: northwest D.C. at Upton St.; southeast D.C. at Johnson Junior High School, 1400 Bruce St. SE (202) 610-2036; Maryland at St. Paul's United Methodist Church, 10401 Armory Ave., Kensington (301) 933-0229; and Virginia at Westover Baptist Church, 1125 N Patrick Henry Dr., Arlington (703) 237-5655. For information and program details call or check the Web site. Metro: Van Ness-UDC.

Lewie's 6845 Reed St. at Woodmont Ave. and Bethesda St. in a small triangle (301) 652-1600 www.lewies.com

This casual place for drinking, eating, and dancing with live music is open Wed–Sat from 8:30 p.m. on. Modest cover charge, varying depending on the band. The crowd is an eclectic mix of people who come to enjoy the lively sounds and the pleasant comradery of fellow celebrants. Metro: Bethesda.

Li Ho 501 H St. NW at 5th St. (202) 289-2059

Good bountiful Chinese dishes at lunch and dinner are served here at inexpensive prices in this modest restaurant with a large following. Open daily. Metro: Gallery Pl.-Chinatown.

Liberia Embassy 5303 Colorado Ave. NW (202) 723-0437 www.liberiaemb.org

Libraries *see* Alliance Française, American Institute of Architects, American University Bender Library, Brazilian-American Cultural Institute, Catholic University of America Mullen Memorial Library, City Museum of Washington D.C., Collingwood Library and Museum on Americanism, Commerce Department Library, Daughters of the American Revolution and Constitution Hall, Dumbarton Oaks Research Library and Collections, Folger Shakespeare Library and Theatre, George Mason University Libraries, George Washington University Library, Georgetown

University Lauinger Memorial Library, Historical Society of Washington, House of the Temple Library/Museum, Howard University Founders Library, Howard University Moorland-Springarn Research Center, Library of Congress, Marine Band Library and Archives, Martin Luther King Jr. Memorial Library, Museum of the National Guard, National Genealogical Society Library, National Library of Medicine, Scottish Rite Masonic Temple, Smithsonian Institution, Textile Museum, University of Maryland Clarice Smith Center for the Performing Arts, University of Maryland–College Park Libraries, Washington Navy Yard.

Library of Congress Jefferson Building, 1st St. and Independence Ave. SE (202) 707-5000 www.loc.gov

The Library of Congress comprises three huge structures—the Jefferson, Madison, and Adams buildings. The library's history goes back to 1800, but the first building constructed for its use in 1897 was the Thomas Jefferson Building, a richly ornamental Italian Renaissance structure with a façade reminiscent of the Paris Opera House. The visitor center is located in this building. On the other side of Independence Ave. is the huge James Madison Building, which opened in 1980. The John Adams Building is diagonally opposite it and was constructed in 1939. Visitors enter the library at the Jefferson Building's 1st St. entrance. The library is open Mon–Sat 10 a.m.–5:30 p.m. Very knowledgeable tour guides lead visitors four times a day through the beautiful Main Reading Room, one of the city's loveliest interiors. There's also a short video describing the role of the world's largest library, whose holdings number in the millions. The Library of Congress also sponsors innumerable exhibitions, concerts, lectures, and film programs. Call (202) 707-5458 for tour and visitor information, and (202) 707-5502 for concert information. Metro: Capitol South or Union Station.

Library of Congress Coolidge Auditorium Ground Level, Jefferson Building, 1st St. and Independence Ave. SE (202) 707-5502 www.loc.gov/rr/perform/concert

This is the setting for the celebrated chamber music concerts offered free by the library. Call for details about the program schedule and reservations. The Coolidge Auditorium is also the venue for the library's poetry and literature program. Metro: Capitol South or Union Station. *See also* Library of Congress Poetry and Literature Program.

Library of Congress Film Program

In the Mary Pickford Theater of the library's Madison Building at 1st and Independence Ave. SE, free screenings of movies that often follow a particular theme take place on weeknights at 7. The films are drawn from the library's extensive holdings of classic and memorable cinematic works. Information on upcoming screenings and reservations (which can be made up to one week in advance) can be obtained at (202) 707-5677. Metro: Capitol South or Union Station.

Library of Congress Poetry and Literature Program (202) 707-5394 www.loc .gov/poetry

This is the city's longest running series, which has been featuring outstanding literary figures since the 1930s. Distinguished poets and authors read from their works and participate in public discussions from October to June in the library's Coolidge Auditorium on the ground level of the Jefferson Building. Admission free. Details are provided in the library's monthly calendar of events available at the library or by calling (202) 707-2905, or by calling the Poetry and Literature Program at the number above. Metro: Capitol South or Union Station.

A Likely Story 1555 King St., Alexandria, VA (703) 836-2498 www.alikelystory books.com

This independent bookstore, less than 2 blocks from the Metro, schedules story times, author and illustrator talks, active programs for little kids, and events for parents. Books are also sold here! Many special events require advance registration. Open Mon–Sat 10 a.m.–6 p.m., Sun 1 p.m.–5 p.m. Metro: King Street.

Li'l Red Trolley All-Day Tour http://populartours.com/2890T-All-Day-Lil-Red-Trolley-Tour.htm

Offers hop-on and hop-off service on a half-hour schedule to some of Washington's chief tourist sites. The entire circuit lasts 2 hours and operates 9 a.m.–4:30 p.m. with pickup at many hotels around the city. More information and prices at Gray Line (202) 289-1995 or (800) 862-1400. *See also* Gray Line Bus Tours.

Lillian and Albert Small Jewish Museum in the Adas Israel Synagogue, 701 3rd St. NW at G St. (202) 789-0900 www.loc.gov/rr/main/religion/jhw.html

Within the oldest synagogue in the city, a modest red brick structure built in 1876, which is home to the Jewish Historical Society of Greater Washington, the museum displays Jewish history in Washington and offers special exhibits on Jewish themes. The building also houses a restored religious sanctuary. Open Sun–Thurs noon–4 p.m. Admission free. Small suggested donation. Metro: Judiciary Square. *See also* Adas Israel Congregation, Jewish Historical Society of Greater Washington, www.commuterpage.com/venues/museums.htm.

Lillian Laurence, Ltd. 2000 M St. NW at 20th St. (202) 876-0606

This salon offers the full range of beauty treatments in a pleasant ambiance at moderately expensive prices in a convenient midtown location. Open Tues–Sat 9 a.m.–6 p.m. Metro: Dupont Circle.

Lincoln Memorial West Potomac Park, 23rd St. NW btw Constitution and Independence Aves. (202) 426-6841 www.nps.gov/linc

This, one of the city's most cherished monuments, forms a line with the Capitol and the Washington Monument. The monument's designer Henry Bacon was influenced by Greek architecture, and the memorial was dedicated in 1922. It stands just before the approach to the Arlington Memorial Bridge. It is positioned with its main entrance overlooking the Mall. The marble structure has 36 columns, one for each state at the time of Lincoln's death. Daniel Chester French created the 20-foot-high powerful marble statue of the seated president. The words of the Gettysburg Address and Lincoln's Second Inaugural Address are carved on the north and south walls of the memorial. Open daily 8 a.m.–midnight. Metro: Smithsonian or Foggy Bottom-GWU, then a long walk from either station. *See also* www.commuter page.com/venues/memorials.htm.

Lincoln Park E Capitol St. btw 11th and 13th Sts.

This 7-acre park offers some pleasant shade, a playground, some open space, a sunken promenade, and two interesting statues. Thomas Ball's *Emancipation Statue* sculpted in 1876 shows a life-size Abraham Lincoln freeing a rising slave. A second completed in 1974 by sculptor Robert Berk depicts Mary McLeod Bethune, the celebrated black educator and adviser to Franklin D. Roosevelt, passing her legacy to the next generation. Metro: Eastern Market.

Lincoln Statue D St. NW btw 4th and 5th Sts. http://showcase.netins.net/web/crea tive/lincoln/art/judiciary.htm

Far less known than the Lincoln Memorial, or even the *Emancipation Statue*, this life-size granite structure by sculptor Lot Flannery erected in 1868 depicts the celebrated American statesman. Metro: Judiciary Square.

Lincoln Suites Downtown 1823 L St. NW btw 18th and 19th Sts. (202) 223-4320 or (800) 424-2970 www.lincolnhotels.com

This moderate-priced hostelry features 99 suite accommodations, many with full kitchens, and is located only 5 blocks from the White House, with the museums and the Metro conveniently nearby. Parking available in adjoining garage for an added charge. Metro: Farragut North.

Lincoln Theatre 1215 U St. NW btw 12th and 13th Sts. (202) 328-6000 www.the lincolntheatre.org

Built in 1922 as a movie and vaudeville house, this is the only remaining entertainment palace left from the U St. halcyon years when the area was known as Black Broadway. Restored in 1994, it is one of the city's loveliest interior spaces with much of its plush original features still intact including the elaborate chandeliers, the floor, and the ornate plasterwork. Today it presents various forms of entertainment including plays, concerts, dance, and film showings. Call for details or check the Web site. Metro: U St.-Cardozo.

Lindens 2401 Kalorama Rd. NW at Kalorama Circle

This extraordinary Georgian frame house was built in 1754 in Massachusetts and then transported in sections and recreated at this site. Thus, while it may be the oldest surviving home in Washington, it did not begin here. Metro: Dupont Circle.

Lisner Auditorium of George Washington University 730 21st St. NW at H St. (202) 994-1500 www.lisner.org

Situated on the university's campus in Foggy Bottom, this 1,500-seat theater in a classic modern structure was built in the 1940s. It is the showplace throughout the year for concerts, dance, comedy shows, international acts, and other forms of popular entertainment. Metro: Foggy Bottom-GWU. *See also* www.commuterpage .com/venues/venue-eNhtm.

Lithuania Embassy 2622 16th St. NW (202) 234-5860 www.ltembassyus.org

Litteri's 517 Morse St. NE close to the intersection of New York and Florida Aves. (202) 544-0183

The area's largest, oldest, and finest Italian grocery is situated in the Capital City Market district with its warehouses and loading docks. Brimming with mouthwatering things to see and smell and with a counter selling wonderful hero sandwiches, this is Italy's greatest outpost in Washington. Open Tues–Wed 8 a.m.–4 p.m., Thurs–Fri 8 a.m.–5 p.m., Sat 8 a.m.–3 p.m. Driving is the best way to get here, but the D2, D4, or D6 Bus will bring you here from downtown.

Little Theater of Alexandria 600 N Wolfe St., Alexandria, VA (202) 683-5778 www .thelittletheater.com

This is one of the D.C. area's longest-standing and most active theatrical companies. During a typical season it mounts productions ranging from comedy to drama to musicals at its Old Town Alexandria performance site. Classes in acting, directing, playwriting, dance, and children's courses are offered as well. Metro: King Street. See also www.commuterpage.com/venues/venue-en.htm.

Little Viet Garden 3012 Wilson Blvd. btw Highland and Garfield Sts., Arlington, VA (703) 522-9686

Located opposite the Metro stop is this attractive and popular inexpensive restaurant serving all the traditional zesty and tasty Vietnamese specialties. The lovely outdoor terrace in mild weather adds to the pleasure of the dining experience. Open for lunch and dinner daily. Metro: Clarendon.

Liz Lerman Dance Exchange 7117 Maple Ave. at Carroll Ave., Takoma Park, MD (301) 270-6700 www.danceexchange.org/llabout2.html

Since 1976 this organization has been offering professional dance classes and mounting performances locally and around the country. At its Takoma Park studio instruction runs the gamut from modern dance to ballet and includes courses for teenagers and seniors. Metro: Takoma.

Lloyd House 220 N Washington St. near Queen St., Alexandria, VA (703) 838-4577

This late Georgian brick house in Old Town was built around 1800 by the owner of Gadsby's Tavern. It was restored and decorated in Federal style in 1976 and became part of the Alexandria Public Library system as its main historical branch. The house contains research materials for scholars, genealogists, and historians and a splendid collection of Civil War material. Open Mon–Sat 9 a.m.–5 p.m. Metro: King Street.

Lockkeeper's House Constitution Ave. and 17th St. NW

This stone building was the home of the lockkeeper at the end of the C&O Canal extension from Georgetown. It was built in the 1830s and was used until the waterway was covered over in the 1870s. It is not open to visitors. Metro: Federal Triangle.

Loeb's 832 15th St. at I St. (202) 371-1150

This inexpensive storefront deli serves overstuffed corned beef and pastrami sandwiches, bagels and cream cheese, and other Kosher specialties. It is close to Lafayette Square and open Mon–Fri 6 a.m.–4 p.m. Metro: McPherson Square.

Loew's Cineplex Odeon Inner Circle *see* Cineplex Odeon Inner Circle.

Loew's Cineplex Odeon Outer Circle *see* Cineplex Odeon Outer Circle.

Loew's Cineplex Odeon Uptown Theater *see* Cineplex Odeon Uptown Theater.

Loew's L'Enfant Plaza 480 L'Enfant Plaza, SW at 7th and D Sts. (202) 484-1000 or (800) 635-5065 www.loewshotels.com

This luxury hotel is located directly above a Metro station and shopping promenade and is conveniently near the Mall. There is a rooftop pool and fitness center and all the customary amenities of a top-level establishment at this 370-room facility. Metro: L'Enfant Plaza.

Logan Circle www.cr.nps.gov/nr/travel/wash/dc64.htm

Located at the junction of Rhode Island and Vermont Aves. NW and 13th and R Sts., this circle is named for Civil War Gen. John A. Logan. It is surrounded by large late Victorian homes built in the 1870s and 1880s. The neighborhood fell into decline in the mid-twentieth century, but preservationists have in recent years stimulated the restoration of a number of the historic houses, and residents of the area around the circle are attempting to further the renaissance of the area. Metro: U St.-Cardozo, then a good walk.

Logan Statue www.logancircle.org/history/history6.asp

This bronze equestrian monument of Civil War Gen. John A. Logan was designed by sculptor Franklin Simmons in 1901 in collaboration with the architect Richard Morris Hunt. Logan, as a senator representing Illinois, sponsored the legislation establishing Memorial Day as a national holiday. The statue can be found in Logan Circle at the junction of Rhode Island and Vermont Aves. NW and 13th and R Sts. Metro: U St.-Cardozo, then a good walk.

Lombardy Hotel *see* Hotel Lombardy.

Longfellow Statue *see* Henry Wadsworth Longfellow Statue.

Lord & Taylor 5255 Western Ave. NW near Wisconsin Ave. (202) 362-9600

Located in Chevy Chase right on the district line bordering Maryland, this elegant department store features classic clothing for women, men, and children with celebrated designer labels as well as cosmetics and jewelry. Metro: Friendship Heights.

Lothrop Mansion *see* Russian Consulate.

Loudoun Museum 16 Loudoun St. SW, Leesburg, VA (703) 777-7427 www .loudounmuseum.org

This museum features exhibits of artifacts and memorabilia describing life in Loudoun County from earliest times to the modern era, including interesting Civil War materials. There are hands-on exhibits and an audiovisual presentation. Open Mon–Sat 10 a.m.–5 p.m., Sun 1 p.m.–5 p.m. Small admission charge. By car take the Dulles Toll Rd. to the end and continue by following the signs to downtown Leesburg.

Loudoun Tourism Council Leesburg, VA (703) 771-4682 www.visitloudoun.org

The visitor center is open from 9 a.m. to 5 p.m. and is a good source of information on the area. Information by phone or from the Web site.

Louisiana Express Company 4921 Bethesda Ave. off Arlington Rd., Bethesda, MD (301) 652-6945

This is where to find all the Cajun food specialties in a casual Southern atmosphere, all at inexpensive prices. Open for lunch Mon–Sat, dinner nightly, brunch on Sun. Metro: Bethesda.

Low-Budget Accommodations *see* Hostels, YMCA of Metropolitan Washington, YWCA.

Luigino 1100 New York Ave. at 11th St. (202) 371-0595 www.luigino.com

Well-prepared northern Italian dishes are featured in this busy attractive downtown spot with moderately expensive prices. Open for lunch Mon–Fri, dinner nightly. Metro: Metro Center.

Luigi's 1132 19th St. btw L and M Sts. (202) 331-7574 www.famousluigis.com

Fine crusty pizzas are served here with a great range of toppings to choose from in this popular, reasonably priced Italian restaurant where all the dishes are well prepared and tasty. Open daily for lunch and dinner. Metro: Farragut North or Farragut West.

Lulu's Club Mardi Gras 1217 22nd St. NW at M St. (202) 861-5858 www.lulus club.com

This spot is open every day of the year from 5 p.m. on except Sunday when it opens at 8 p.m. The ambiance seeks to recreate the sights and sounds of Bourbon St. Light food and drinks are the accompaniment of the music for dancing. Details on the live performance schedule at the Web site. Metro: Foggy Bottom-GWU or Dupont Circle.

Luna Books and Coffee Shop 1633 P St. NW near 16th St. (202) 387-4005 www .skewers-cafeluna.com

More than just a bookstore, this place serves as a social center where feminist concerns are the central theme. All sorts of events are staged here from discussions on the environment to multicultural concerns. People are drawn here for the fine oversized cookies and coffee as much as for looking for books and keeping up with lively community issues. Open Mon–Thurs 8 a.m.–11 p.m., Fri 8 a.m.–1:30 a.m., Sat–Sun 10 a.m.–1 p.m. Metro: Dupont Circle.

Luther Place Memorial Church 1226 Vermont Ave. NW btw Thomas Circle and N St. (202) 667-1377 http://members.aol.com/_ht_a/lutherplacemc/church/luther place.html

This 1874 structure was designed by architect Judson York and is a red sandstone neo-Gothic building that soars. It is home to an evangelical Lutheran congregation. Metro: McPherson Square.

Luxembourg Embassy 2200 Massachusetts Ave. NW (202) 265-4171 www.luxem bourg-usa.org

Luxury Hotels *see* Deluxe Hotels.

The Lyceum Museum 201 S Washington St. at Prince St., Alexandria, VA (703) 838-4994 www.alexandriahistory.org

Built in 1839 as a cultural center to house a lecture hall and library, this Greek Revival building was first known as the Alexandria Lyceum. Since 1985 it has served as Alexandria's history museum, providing exhibitions, lectures and concerts, and school programs. Exhibits seek to illuminate and interpret life and culture during northern Virginia's 300-year history. Open Mon–Sat 10 a.m.–5 p.m., Sun 1 p.m.–5 p.m. Admission free. Metro: King Street. *See also* www.commuterpage.com/venues/sightseeing_VA.htm.

Lyndon B. Johnson Memorial Grove *see* LBJ Memorial Grove.

M & S Grill 600 13th St. NW at F St. (202) 347-1500

This moderately priced affiliate of McCormick and Schmick's, the more upscale seafood specialty chain, is a less formal dining experience with more emphasis on meat dishes. The ambiance is late nineteenth-century Victorian with lots of wood paneling, chandeliers, and Tiffany-like glass. But the fish here is quite good as well. Open for lunch Mon–Fri, dinner nightly, with low-priced snacks and sandwiches during happy hour. Metro: Metro Center.

MCI Center 601 F St. NW at 7th St. (202) 628-3200 www.mcicenter.com

This 20,000-seat facility was built in 1997 as a downtown entertainment and sports arena. It is the site of home games of the men's National Basketball Association's Washington Wizards, the Women's National Basketball Association's Washington Mystics, and the National Hockey League's Washington Capitals. It also hosts shows, concerts, ice-skating, and other special events. There's a sports gallery here also with electronic interactive games and interesting sports memorabilia and photographs. Metro: Gallery Pl.-Chinatown. *See also* www.commuterpage.com/venues/venue-sp.htm.

M Street NW Bridge M St. NW btw 26th and 29th Sts.

Completed in 1929 for $185,000, this three-span bridge crosses Rock Creek on the site of several earlier structures. The first, completed in 1788, washed out in a storm, drowning those crossing in a coach. A second, built in 1800, also a drawbridge like the first, allowed navigation up Rock Creek. The third, a covered bridge, was judged unstable in 1870 and replaced the following year with a light iron truss bridge, which survived until condemned in 1928. Metro: Foggy Bottom-GWU.

MTA *see* Washington Metropolitan Area Transit Authority.

Macedonia Embassy 1101 30th St. NW, Suite 302 (202) 337-3063

Macy's www.macys.com

The celebrated department store cannot be found in the city but only at three malls in Washington's Virginia suburbs: the Galleria at Tysons II in McLean, Fashion Center at Pentagon City in Arlington, and Springfield Mall in Springfield.

Madagascar Embassy 2347 Massachusetts Ave. NW (202) 265-5525 www.embassy.org/madagascar

Madam's Organ Restaurant and Bar 2461 18th St. NW at Columbia Rd. (202) 667-5370 www.madamsorgan.com

This Adams Morgan spot offers some tasty, light soul food but most people aren't there to eat. It's open nightly featuring live blues, bluegrass, funk, and rock music for a casual audience with lots of audience involvement in a strange-looking place that adds to its aura. Cover charge some nights. Call or check the Web site for performance schedule information. Metro: Dupont Circle, then L2 Bus, or Woodley Park-Zoo, then 90, 91, 92, 93, or 96 Bus.

Made By You 3413 Connecticut Ave. NW opposite the Uptown Theater (202) 363-9590 www.madebyyou.com

This unique store offers children and adults the opportunity to choose from a large inventory of already-made ceramic pieces that customers paint to their liking, which the shop then glazes and fires in a few days. Prices vary depending upon the item chosen, from about $7 up. Open Mon–Sat 11 a.m.–9 p.m., Sun noon–6 p.m. Metro: Cleveland Park. Other locations at 2319 Wilson Blvd. in Arlington (703) 841-3533; 4923 Elm St. in Bethesda (301) 654-3206; and 209 Washington St. in Rockville (301) 610-5496.

Madison Hotel 1177 15th St. NW at M St. (202) 862-1600 or (800) 424-8577 www.themadisonhotel.net

This old very elegant hotel offers 353 rooms and suites, a lobby replete with lovely antiques from China and France, all the amenities of a luxury establishment including sauna, steam room, exercise facility, and much more at very steep rates. Metro: McPherson Square.

Magazines *see* Newspapers and Magazines.

Maine Avenue

This is the street that runs runs along the edge of Washington Channel in southwest Washington. It is home to the Maine Avenue Fish Market and a line of restaurants stretching out along the avenue, which have terraces for prime views of the various types of boats docked along the channel. Metro: Waterfront-SEU.

Maine Avenue Fish Market Maine Ave. at 8th St. SW

This off-the-beaten-path site is beneath the expressways on the Washington Channel. It's *the* place in the city for seeing a variety of fresh fish from near and far on sale and laid out on barges where vendors purvey their wares daily 7:30 a.m.–8 p.m. It draws consumer customers as well as chefs from area restaurants who choose from the widest choice imaginable. Metro: L'Enfant Plaza.

Major Museums *see* Arthur M. Sackler Gallery, Corcoran Gallery of Art, Freer Gallery of Art, Hirshhorn Museum and Sculpture Garden, National Air and Space Museum, National Gallery of Art, National Museum of American Art, National

Museum of Natural History, National Museum of Women in the Arts, Phillips Collection, United States Holocaust Memorial Museum. *See also* www.commuterpage.com/venues/museums.htm, www.washingtonpost.com.

Makato 4822 MacArthur Blvd. NW at Reservoir Rd. (202) 298-6866

This unusual and little-known restaurant promises an exceptional experience. It's difficult to find and small, and reservations are recommended. But when you cross the threshold, you remove your shoes and embark upon a delightful culinary adventure featuring beautifully prepared and gracefully served Japanese specialties. Dining here is moderately expensive. Open for lunch Tues–Sat, dinner Tues–Sun. Public transportation here is difficult and using a car or taxi is suggested.

Malawi Embassy 2408 Massachusetts Ave. NW (202) 797-1007 www.embassy.org/embassies/mw.html

Malaysia Embassy 3516 International Court, NW (202) 572-9700 www.embassy.org/embassies/my.html

Malaysian Restaurants *see* Straits of Malaya.

Malcolm X Park *see* Meridian Hill Park.

Mali Embassy 2130 R St. NW (202) 332-2249 www.maliembassy-usa.org

The Mall www.nps.gov/nama

The nation's Mall is the stretch of green parkland running between Constitution and Independence Aves. NW. At one side is the U.S. Capitol on the east, and some two miles to the west is the Lincoln Memorial. The grounds of the Washington Monument divide the Mall. To the east along the sides of the Mall are the Smithsonian museums. To the west are the Vietnam Memorial, Constitution Gardens, and the Reflecting Pool. The Mall itself is a tree-shaded esplanade some 800 feet wide, where countless visitors come to view the sights, jog, or stroll leisurely, to celebrate national events, to picnic, or just to relax at the country's epicenter. Metro: Smithsonian, with a stop on the south side right on the Mall.

Malls *see* Shopping Malls.

Malta Embassy 2017 Connecticut Ave. NW (202) 462-3611 www.foreign.gov.mt/ORG/ministry/missions/washington2.htm

Mama Ayesha's 1967 Calvert St. NW btw Adams Mill Rd. and Woodley Pl. (202) 232-5431

This is a modestly priced Middle Eastern favorite for all the standard dishes like lamb and chicken kebabs, fresh hot pita bread, and the tasteful appetizers, which in combination can easily substitute for a main course. Open for lunch and dinner daily. Metro: Woodley Park-Zoo.

Man Controlling Trade Statue

Sculptor Michael Lantz constructed this limestone monument in 1942, which shows a man controlling a horse as a symbolic representation of the manner in which the Federal Trade Commission controls monopoly businesses. It is situated at the eastern point of the Federal Trade Commission where 6th St. NW and Pennsylvania and Constitution Aves. come together. Metro: Federal Triangle.

Manassas Museum 9101 Prince William St. at Main St., Manassas, VA (703) 368-1873 www.manassasmuseum.org

In a modern building in downtown Manassas this museum portrays the culture and history of Manassas and the Piedmont area of northern Virginia by displaying Civil War and railroad artifacts, agricultural implements, photographs, quilts, nineteenth-century toys, and exhibits of African-American history. Video features depict the development of Manassas and its role in the Civil War. Open Tues–Sun 10 a.m.–5 p.m. Modest admission charge. By car from Washington take Rte. I-66 to Hwy. 28 and then south into downtown Manassas.

Manassas National Battlefield Park 6511 Sudley Rd., Manassas, VA, Visitor Center (703) 361-1339; Park Headquarters (703) 754-1861 www.nps.gov/mana

Thirty miles west of Washington this park is located on State Rd. 234 between I-66 and Hwy. 29, just north of the scene of two major battles of the Civil War, the first and second Battles of Manassas. There are walking trails around the battlefield, and at the visitor center there are graphic displays and a small museum with further information about these two fierce military engagements. Park grounds are open daily from dawn to dusk while the visitor center is open daily during the summer from 8:30 a.m.–6 p.m. Admission free.

Manuel's Grocery 1813 Columbia Rd. NW at 18th St. (202) 986-5680

All the food provisions that go into the preparation of Caribbean and Latin American dishes can be found in this Adams Morgan shop. Open daily 8:30 a.m.–10 p.m. Metro: Woodley Park-Zoo, then 90, 91, 92, 93, or 96 Bus.

Map Store *see* ADC Map and Travel Center.

Maples House

Now serving as Friendship House Settlement, this structure was built by architect William Lovering between 1795 and 1806 and has been considerably modified since then. It stands at 619 D St. SE and is one of the oldest buildings on Capitol Hill. The original entrance was on the South Carolina Ave. side, but when it was converted in 1936 to its present use the entrance was moved to the D St. side. Metro: Eastern Market.

Maps *see* ADC Map and Travel Center, www.smartraveler.com.

Mar de Plata 1410 14th St. NW near P St. (202) 234-2679

This cheery and bright restaurant offers a wide range of *tapas* as well as tasty Spanish entrees at moderate prices, all in a warm friendly environment. Open for lunch and dinner Tues–Sun Metro: U St.-Cardozo.

Marcel's 2401 Pennsylvania Ave. NW at 24th St. (202) 296-1166 www.marcelsdc .com

This somewhat expensive restaurant features French dishes with a Belgian touch adding distinctively to the culinary creations. It is a somewhat formal setting in a large dining area where the dining experience is often memorable. Open for dinner daily. Metro: Foggy Bottom-GWU.

Marine Band Library and Archives Marine Barracks at 8th and I Sts. SE (202) 433-4298 www.marineband.usmc.mil/edu_links.html

This is a fine collection of thousands of musical pieces ranging from music for orchestra, band, and chamber groups as well as video and audiotapes and periodicals. It is open to scholars and researchers only after arranging for a visit in advance by telephoning or writing. Metro: Eastern Market.

Marine Band Summer Concerts

From June through August the Marine Band offers free concerts on Wednesday and Sunday at 8 p.m. On Wednesday the performance is on the west terrace of the U.S. Capitol and on Sunday at the Sylvan Theatre on the Washington Monument grounds. Program details at (202) 433-4011. These programs are different from the other summer programs offered at the Marine Barracks and the Iwo Jima Memorial. See the next entry, Marine Barracks, for information about these other events.

Marine Barracks 8th and I Sts. SE www.mbw.usmc.mil

This is the country's oldest Marine Corps installation and home to the Marine Band. It is open only for the evening parade and the show of the drum and bugle corps, precision marching, and silent rifle drills on Fridays at 8:45 p.m. from early May to late August. Because this is an enormously popular free public event, reservations must be made well in advance, preferably a month or longer before the preferred day. Details about making reservations at (202) 433-6060. An abbreviated version of this parade takes place on Tuesdays at 7:30 p.m. from late May to mid-August at the Iwo Jima Memorial. Details at (202) 433-6060.

Marine Corps Air-Ground Museum at Quantico Marine Base off U.S. Hwy. 1 and I-95 in Quantico, VA (703) 784-2606

The Marine Corps Air-Ground Museum at Quantico was closed permanently on November 15, 2002. This is part of the transition to the National Museum of the Marine Corps, that will be opening in the near future.

Marine Corps Marathon (703) 784-2225 www.marinemarathon.com

This popular event takes place on a Sunday late in October when thousands participate in this world-class 26-mile run that begins and ends at the Iwo Jima Memorial in Arlington after passing through the streets of Washington. Call for information or check the Web site.

Marine Corps Museum in the Washington Navy Yard, Building 58, 9th and M Sts. SE (202) 433-3840 http://hqinet001.hqmc.usmc.mil/HD/Home_Page.htm

This collection offers a variety of artifacts that follow the story of the corps from its beginnings early in the late eighteenth century through Desert Storm. On display are uniforms, photographs, documents, and weapons showing the evolution of this combat branch throughout the nation's history. Open Mon, Wed–Fri 10 a.m.–4 p.m. Admission free. Metro: Eastern Market.

Marine Corps War Memorial www.mbw.usmc.mil/parades/mcwm_default.asp

This 100-ton 78-foot-high bronze statue is located on the Virginia side of the Memorial Bridge between the main entrance to Arlington National Cemetery and Arlington Blvd., on a promontory at the north end of the cemetery. It is popularly termed the Iwo Jima Memorial and is based upon the celebrated photograph by Joseph Rosenthal. The sculpture by Felix de Weldon depicts the five Marines and a

Navy corpsman raising the flag at the top of Mount Suribachi in February 1945. It is open daily year-round. Metro: Arlington Cemetery. *See also* www.commuterpage .com/venues/memorials.htm.

Markets *see* Eastern Market, Georgetown Market, Maine Avenue Fish Market, O Street Market. *See also* Farmers Markets, Flea Markets.

Marquis de Lafayette Monument *see* Lafayette Memorial.

Marrakesh 617 New York Ave. NW btw 6th and 7th Sts. (202) 393-9393

This restaurant establishes its exotic atmosphere by serving diners seated on low sofas with equally low tables, and providing no utensils. Customers use their hands with flat bread as the implement. The fixed-price modestly priced menu includes a full and authentic Moroccan dinner with belly dancing as the featured entertainment. The food is very good and pleasantly served, all making the evening quite pleasurable. Open for dinner nightly. Reservations are required and only cash or checks are accepted. Metro: Mount Vernon Square-UDC.

Marriott at Metro Center 775 12th St. NW off Pennsylvania Ave. (202) 737-2200 or (800) 228-9290 www.marriott.com

This very well-located 456-room hotel is near everything in the downtown area—museums, theaters, restaurants, shopping, the MCI Center, and the Mall. It boasts a health club, indoor pool, and the other amenities as befits an expensive hostelry. Metro: Metro Center.

Marriott Bethesda 5151 Pooks Hill Rd., west of Rockville Pike (Wisconsin Ave.), Bethesda, MD (301) 897-9400 www.marriott.com

This hotel in the Maryland suburbs just inside the Washington Beltway contains 407 rooms, outdoor and indoor pools, a fitness room, lighted tennis courts, and restaurants. It is moderately expensive and offers shuttle service during morning and evening hours to the Metro's Medical Center station.

Marriott Courtyard *see* Courtyard by Marriott.

Marriott Hotel *see* J. W. Marriott Hotel.

Marriott Key Bridge *see* Key Bridge Marriott.

Marriott Residence Inn Pentagon City 550 Army Navy Dr., Arlington, VA (703) 413-6630 or (800) 228-9290 www.marriott.com

Located next to the Pentagon this all-suites establishment is only a block away from the Fashion Center at Pentagon City with 150 shops, movie theaters, and Metro station. It offers 299 comfortably appointed and well-equipped accommodations, indoor pool, exercise facility, and a wide range of other expensive-hotel amenities. Metro: Pentagon City.

Marriott Wardman Park Hotel (Wardman Tower) 2600 Woodley Rd. NW (202) 328-2000 or (800) 228-9290 www.wardmanpark.com

In 1918, the developer of the Woodley Park area, Harry Wardman, built a 1,000-room hotel on an 18-acre site overlooking Connecticut Ave. Ten years later, Wardman Tower was added by architect Mihran Mesrobian. It became the Watergate Complex of its day, numbering among its residents through the years three presidents, three vice presidents, one chief justice, and several senators. The entire property was purchased by the Sheraton Corporation in 1953, and in 1998 Marriott acquired it. The former Wardman Tower apartments are now an integral part of what is now the largest convention and business hotel in the city. Metro: Woodley Park-Zoo.

Marsha Mateyka Gallery 2012 R St. NW btw R and 21st St. (202) 328-0088 www.marshamateykagallery.com

This gallery, in a brownstone building with very attractive interior features, showcases important contemporary European and American artists working in sculpture and paintings. Open Wed–Sat 11 a.m.–5 p.m. Metro: Dupont Circle.

Marshall Islands Embassy 2433 Massachusetts Ave. NW (202) 234-5414 www.rmiembassyus.org/usemb.html

Marshall Park *see* John Marshall Park.

Martin Luther King Jr. Birthday Celebrations

At the Lincoln Memorial where King delivered his inspiring "I Have A Dream" address in 1963, ceremonies, speeches, choir performances, and a color guard salute take place in January each year in observance of the civil rights leader's birthday. Performances, lectures, and concerts also take place as part of the commemorative events at various other sites around the city. Information at (202) 619-7222.

Martin Luther King Jr. Memorial Library 901 G St. NW at 9th St. (202) 727-1111 www.dclibrary.org

The central library of the D.C. Public Library was designed in 1972 by Ludwig Mies van der Rohe. It is home to the Washingtoniana Collection of materials on the history of the city and the Black Studies Collection focused on local and national African-American history. A powerful mural by Don Miller covering the lobby wall depicts the life and times of the slain hero of the civil rights movement. The library holds its collection of books, periodicals, reference and children's material on the 5 floors of the building. Theatrical performances, poetry readings, concerts, and children's programs are often held here. For reference service phone (202) 727-1126, for events information call (202) 727-1186. Customary hours are Mon–Thurs 10 a.m.–9 p.m., Fri–Sat 10 a.m.–5:30 p.m., Sun 1–5 p.m., except in summer. Metro: Metro Center or Gallery Pl.-Chinatown.

Martin Luther Statue

This monument was constructed in 1884 to commemorate Luther's birth 400 years earlier. It can be found at Thomas Circle, 14th St. and Massachusetts Ave. NW. Metro: Farragut North.

Martin's Tavern *see* Billy Martin's Tavern.

Marvelous Market 1511 Connecticut Ave. NW btw Dupont Circle and Q St. (202) 332-3690 www.marvelousmarket.com

This is one branch of a very popular chain selling its own tangy freshly baked breads and pastries as well as pasta, produce, homemade soup, sandwiches, and cheeses. Open Mon–Sat 8 a.m.–9 p.m., Sun 8:30 a.m.–7 p.m. Other outlets are spread around the city and in the Maryland and Virginia suburbs (see the telephone book for locations).

Mary McLeod Bethune Celebration

Every year on July 10 or thereabouts the birthday of the celebrated African-American educator and civil rights champion is commemorated at Lincoln Park, 12th St. NW and E Capitol St., at the site of her memorial, with a wreath-laying ceremony, guest speakers, and gospel choir performances. Information at (202) 619-7222 or (202) 673-2402. Metro: Eastern Market.

Mary McLeod Bethune House 1318 Vermont Ave. NW btw N St. and Logan Circle (202) 673-2402 www.nps.gov/mamc

This National Historic Site was the home from 1936 to 1949 of the distinguished African American educator, activist, and founder of the National Council of Negro Women. This splendidly restored townhouse served also as the headquarters of the organization from 1943 to 1966. Today the building serves as a museum featuring temporary exhibits and as a center housing the National Archives for Black Women's History, the country's largest collection of material on the subject. Open Mon–Sat 9 a.m.–5 p.m. Admission free. Metro: McPherson Square.

Mary McLeod Bethune Memorial www.dcheritage.org/dch_tourism2556/dch_tourism.htm?doc_id = 45642

At the east end of Lincoln Park at E Capitol and 12th Sts. NW, this bronze 17-foot-high sculpture by Robert Berks completed in 1974 depicts the celebrated educator handing on her legacy to two black children. On the base of the statue Bethune's own words are inscribed to inspire successive generations. This was Washington's earliest monument to an African-American, and the first memorial to an American woman in a public park. Metro: Eastern Market.

Marie Reed Recreation Center 2200 Champlain St. NW off Florida Ave. (202) 673-7771

This indoor pool is climate controlled and open year-round Mon–Fri 11 a.m.–7 p.m. The best means of transportation is by using the S2 or S4 Bus along 16th St. NW to the Florida Ave. stop.

Maryland College of Art and Design 10500 Georgia Ave., Silver Spring, MD (301) 649-4454 www.mcadmd.org

At this small college, focused on fine arts and graphic design, the students receive considerable instruction in studio efforts leading to a 2-year Fine Arts degree. Metro: Wheaton.

Maryland Renaissance Festival www.rennfest.com

This annual event usually runs from late August to early October and features medieval entertainment, crafts and foods, with costume-clad performers juggling, jousting, and generally transforming the large site into a magical community reflecting the colorful historical past. It takes place in Crownsville, Maryland, on Crownsville Rd. off Hwy. 450. Admission charge. Details at (410) 266-7304 or the Web site: www.rennfest.com.

Maryland University-College Park Library *see* University of Maryland-College Park Libraries.

Marymount University 2807 N Glebe Rd., Arlington, VA (703) 284-1500 www .marymount.edu

Since 1986 this has been a coeducational institution offering undergraduate and graduate instruction in liberal arts, education, psychology, business, nursing, and other areas. There are evening as well as daytime courses at this and other locations in northern Virginia. Metro: Ballston-MU, then shuttle bus to campus.

Masaryk Memorial

This 12-foot-high bronze statue of Tomas G. Mazaryk, the Czech champion of his country's independence from Austria, stands in a small triangular park in northwest Washington at Massachusetts Ave. at 22nd and Q Sts. The Czech sculptor Vincent Makovsky created the memorial in 1938, and it came to Washington in 2002 as a gift from the Czech Republic. Metro: Dupont Circle.

Mason Monument *see* George Mason Monument.

Massachusetts Avenue NW Bridge Massachusetts Ave. btw Belmont Rd. and Whitehaven St.

In 1940, Washington architect Louis Justement began designing this 420-foot-long, rough-faced stone bridge, the most massive structure spanning Rock Creek Park. A single half-circle arch sweeps upward 75 feet from the park below. Metro: Woodley Park-Zoo.

Master Chorale of Washington http://masterchorale.org

This highly regarded choral company sings during its annual performance season. Information on its program and prices at (202) 471-4050 or the Web site: www.masterchorale.org.

Mateyka Gallery *see* Marsha Mateyka Gallery.

Matti *see* I Matti under I.

Matuba 4918 Cordell Ave. btw Old Georgetown Rd. and Norfolk St., Bethesda, MD (301) 652-7449

This modest-looking restaurant offers excellent Japanese dining choices from sushi and sashimi to a variety of house specialties to traditional noodles and meat and fish dishes. Prices are quite inexpensive. Open for lunch Mon–Fri, dinner nightly. Metro: Bethesda. There's a second location in Arlington at 2915 Columbia Pike (703) 521-2811.

Mauritania Embassy 2129 Leroy Pl. NW (202) 232-5700 www.mauritaniaembassy -usa.org

Embassy of the Islamic Republic of Mauritania.

Mauritius Embassy 4301 Connecticut Ave. NW, Suite 441 (202) 244-1491 www .maurinet.com/embassydc.html

Maxim 1725 F St. NW (202) 962-0280

This delightful Russian restaurant, associated with the Russian Gourmet in McLean, offers classic Russian cuisine, with a tilt toward Georgian dishes. Try the chicken Kiev, stuffed salmon, or maybe a sturgeon filet. The extensive wine list includes Georgian wines, and there is an amazingly comprehensive collection of vodkas. Sometimes Russian folk songs on weekends. Open for lunch Mon–Fri 11:30 a.m.–2:30 p.m., dinner Mon–Thurs 5:30 p.m.–10:30 p.m. and Fri–Sat 5:30 p.m.–2 a.m. Metro: Farragut West.

Maxim Gourmet Oriental Market 460 Hungerford Dr., Rockville, MD (301) 279-0110

This grocery carries a full line of staples used in preparing Chinese dishes. Open daily 9:30 a.m.–8 p.m. Metro: Rockville. Another location at 640 University Blvd. E at Piney Branch Rd., Silver Spring, MD (301) 439-0100.

Mayflower Hotel *see* Renaissance Mayflower Hotel.

Mazza Gallerie 5300 Wisconsin Ave. NW at Western Ave. (202) 966-6114 www.mazzagallerie.net

This upscale mall, where uppermost northwest D.C. joins Chevy Chase, offers a range of stylish shops, boutiques, 11 movie screens, and a Neiman Marcus store among its customer inducements. Metro: Friendship Heights. *See also* www.commuterpage.com/venues/venue-shop.htm.

McClellan Statue www.kittytours.org/thatman2/search.asp?subject = 77

Frederick MacMonnies designed this bronze equestrian monument of the commander of the Civil War's Union Army of the Potomac, Gen. George B. McClellan in 1907. It is located at Connecticut Ave. and Columbia Rd. in northwest D.C. Metro: Dupont Circle.

McCormick and Schmick's 1652 K St. NW at 16th St. (202) 861-2233 www.mccormickandschmicks.com

This seafood house offers a wide variety of shellfish and grilled dishes in an attractive setting featuring linen tablecloths, chandeliers, stained glass lamps, and comfortable booths, at moderate prices. Open for lunch Mon–Fri, dinner nightly, and opens Sun at 2 p.m. Metro: Farragut North or McPherson Square. Other locations: 7401 Woodmont Ave., Bethesda, MD (301) 961-2626; 8484 Westport Dr., McLean, VA (703) 648-8000; 11920 Democracy Dr., Reston, VA (703) 481-6600.

McCormick Building *see* National Trust for Historic Preservation.

McDonough Arena Georgetown University, 37th and O Sts. NW www.guhoyas.com

McDonough Arena, built in 1951, hosts the university's Department of Intercollegiate Athletics and is the home court for the Hoyas—GU's men's and women's basketball teams. The men's team plays in both the arena and the MCI Center. Metro: Metro Center, then take Metrobus D6 toward Sibley Hospital to the stop at Q St. NW and 35th St. NW.

McLean Farmers Market Lewinsville Park, 1659 Chain Bridge Rd., McLean, VA (703) 941-7987 www.co.fairfax.va.us/parks/farm-mkt.htm

On Fridays from early May until late November this producers market is open 8:30 a.m.–12:30 p.m.

McLean/Great Falls

McLean is the southernmost part of northern Virginia, just a short way from the Washington area's biggest shopping mall—Tysons Corner. Great Falls is nearby and the two form one of the wealthiest suburban areas around the city. McLean is perhaps best known as the home of the Central Intelligence Agency and for the natural beauty of Great Falls National Park and the lovely river views. Together they serve as the bedroom retreat of many of Washington's elite. The region is bounded by the Potomac River on the north and east, Old Dominion Dr. on the south, and the Washington Dulles Access Rd. on the west.

The McLean Orchestra

This ninety-member community orchestra performs classical, popular, and opera music. It is made up of professional musicians and guest artists and performs at various public events and offers instructional and performing opportunities for members of its Youth Ensemble. Information at (703) 893-8646 or check the Web site: www.tmo.org.

McLean Project for the Arts McLean Community Center, 1234 Ingleside Ave., McLean, VA (703) 790-0123 www.mcleanart.org

This is a nonprofit center for the visual arts that maintains a gallery in the McLean Community Center, which mounts exhibitions of work by local and regional artists. It also offers gallery talks, lectures, film programs, and sponsors classes for adults and children. The gallery is open Tues noon–6 p.m., Wed and Fri noon–8 p.m., Thurs, noon–4 p.m.

McLean Symphony (703) 522-7187 www.mcleansymphony.com

This is a seventy-member volunteer musical ensemble that performs four times a year at the McLean Community Center. Call for information or check the Web site.

McPherson Statue *see* Gen. James B. McPherson Statue.

Meadowbrook Stable 8200 Meadowbrook Lane, Chevy Chase, MD (301) 598-9026 www.meadowbrookstable.com

This facility offers riding instruction in a series of lessons during different seasons. It also sponsors public shows several times a year that are open to the public at no charge. Call for information or check the Web site. Most easily accessible by car by turning off Connecticut Ave. east on E West Hwy. and going a short distance to Meadowbrook Lane and proceeding right to the stable at 8200.

Meadowlark Gardens Regional Park 9750 Meadowlark Gardens Court off Beulah Rd., Vienna, VA (703) 255-3631 www.nvrpa.com

This 95-acre parkland is one of the loveliest in northern Virginia. It contains trailways through its gardens, wooded areas, and three lakes. There is an atrium and a visitors center but no swimming or boating. Open daily from 10 a.m. until evening with modest admission charge from April to October, and free at other times. The gardens are located between Rtes. 7 and 123 and can be approached by taking the Tysons Corner exit from the Beltway (I-495) and traveling west about 5 miles.

Media Museums *see* Newseum. *See also* Art and Design Museums, Major Museums, Military Museums, Museums of Special Interest to Children, Science and Technology Museums, Smithsonian Institution Museums, Specialized Museums.

Mediterranean Bakery 352 S Pickett St., Alexandria, VA (703) 751-1702
This food store offers staples and baked goods for consumers looking for Middle Eastern groceries. It is quite near the Metro station and is open Mon–Sat 8 a.m.–8 p.m., Sun 9 a.m.–6 p.m. Metro: Van Dorn St.

Mediterranean Restaurants *see* Middle Eastern Restaurants.

Medium-Priced Hotels *see* Middle-Range Hotels.

Mellon Memorial Fountain *see* Andrew W. Mellon Memorial Fountain.

Melrose in the Park Hyatt Hotel, 1201 24th St. NW at M St. (202) 955-3899
This upscale restaurant in an elegant hotel offers a dining room with comfortable banquettes and splendid service as well as lovely floral arrangements and glass walls on two sides. In warm weather diners may enjoy a sunken terrace outdoors with a garden and fountain. The modern American dishes are tasty and expensive. On Saturday nights a band provides music for dancing. Dinner nightly and reservations are suggested. Metro: Foggy Bottom-GWU.

Melvin Gelman Library *see* George Washington University Library.

Memorial Day Celebrations and Ceremonies
On this weekend at the end of May various activities commemorating this patriotic holiday take place. At the Vietnam Veterans Memorial there is a wreath-laying ceremony, along with military bands and speeches. Information at (202) 619-7222. At Arlington National Cemetery activities include a wreath laying at the Tomb of the Unknowns, services at the Memorial Amphitheatre featuring military bands, and a public address. Details at (703) 607-8052. At the U.S. Navy Memorial there is a wreath-laying ceremony and an outdoor concert by the U.S. Navy Band. Information at (202) 619-7222. The National Symphony Orchestra inaugurates the summer season with a free performance on the U.S. Capitol West Lawn. Details at (202) 619-7222.

Memorial Day Jazz Festival
This event sponsored by the Alexandria Recreation Department is held at Fort Ward Park at 4301 W Braddock St. east of I-395 between King St. and Seminary Rd. It features a number of fine jazz artists performing from midday to 8 p.m. on Memorial Day with food stalls in place as part of the scene. Information at (703) 883-4686 or (703) 838-4844. Metro: King Street then take the DAT5 DASH Bus toward Landmark to the stop at Fort Ward.

Memorials *see* Monuments and Memorials.

Menorah Lighting
In mid-December each year on the Ellipse behind the White House, the giant candelabra associated with the Jewish Hanukkah holiday celebration is lit for the eight nights of the festivity. Details at (202) 619-7222.

Mercury Grill 1602 17th St. NW btw Q and R Sts. (202) 667-5937

This lively restaurant located in a row house serves contemporary American dishes, and fish is particularly good here. The service is first rate and prices are moderately expensive. Open for lunch Mon–Fri, dinner nightly. Metro: Dupont Circle.

Meridian Hill

Located in the northwest section of the city, this high ground around the neighborhood surrounding 16th St. NW and Florida Ave. was once home to many wealthy families and embassies. Some embassies remain, but the neighborhood has still to fully recover from its decline in the years following World War II. It is home to Meridian Hill Park (Malcolm X Park) located between 15th and 16th Sts. and north of W St. NW. Meridian Hill is not easily accessed by Metro, but S2 and S4 Buses along 16th St. come through the district.

Meridian Hill Park www.nps.gov/rocr/cultural/merid.htm

Also known as Malcolm X Park, this urban park is bounded on the west by 16th St. NW, on the east by 15th St., on the south by W St., and on the north by Euclid St. At the southern end of the green space covering 12 acres is a striking cascading water staircase formed by thirteen terraced waterfalls flowing into a large pool. The park is home as well to a number of impressive monuments—the equestrian *Joan of Arc Statue*, the statue *Serenity* honoring Col. William Henry Scheutze, the memorial figure of the Italian poet Dante, and the bronze seated statue of James Buchanan. The park is not easily reached by Metro, but S2 and S4 Buses running along 16th St. pass by.

Meridian House 1630 Crescent Place off 16th St. NW

Surrounded by a small forest of linden trees, this 18th-century French-style mansion was built in 1920 for a member of a wealthy steel family, Irwin Boyle Laughlin, who served in the American Foreign Service from 1912 to 1933. The 30-room structure features parquet floors, ornamental iron grills, period furniture, and lovely tapestries. Since 1960 it has served as an international center and in 1992 it became the Meridian International Center. Next door to this building at 1624 and built in 1911 is the George White-Meyer House constructed for Henry White, who had been ambassador to France. It later was the home of the Meyer family, publishers of the *Washington Post*. The lower level of both houses are open to the public showing internationally oriented art exhibitions. Metro: Dupont Circle, and then a long walk or S2 or S4 Bus running along 16th St.

Meridian International Center 1630 Crescent Pl. and 1624 Crescent Pl. off 16th St. NW (202) 667-6800 www.meridian.org

Operating in two mansions on Meridian Hill, which were designed by John Russell Pope, this nonprofit educational and cultural institution sponsors a number of programs for international visitors to the United States and for Americans interested in foreign cultures. The center also mounts changing exhibitions of international art and offers lectures and concerts and provides conference services and other programs to promote international understanding. The lovely grounds are open daily 8 a.m.–5 p.m. and tours of the buildings can be arranged by telephone. The exhibitions in the galleries of both buildings are open to the public Wed–Sun 2 p.m.–5 p.m. Admission free. Metro: Dupont Circle, and then a long walk or S2 or S4 Bus running along 16th St. *See also* Meridian House, White-Myer House.

Merriweather Post Pavilion 10475 Little Patuxent Pkwy., Columbia, MD (301) 982-1800 www.mppconcerts.com

This outdoor amphitheater, popular with summer concertgoers, provides more than 5,000 "pavilion seats" and 10,000 lawn seats. Three large video screens are located next to the stage. Veggie wraps, gyros, and similar light fare are available. Tickets are available at (202) 432-SEAT or TicketMaster. Directions. I-95 (about 18 miles from Washington) to Rte. 32 toward Columbia to Rte. 29 W. Take Broken Land Pkwy. (Exit 18B) and then the first right into the Pavilion parking lot.

Meskerem 2434 18th St. NW btw Columbia and Belmont Rds. (202) 462-4100

This Adams Morgan restaurant offers spicy lamb, chicken, beef, fish, and vegetables served with spongy *injera* bread, which is also the implement for scooping up the tasty food. The décor is simple, the staff pleasant, and prices somewhat higher than at other such places, but this spot is considered among the best of the city's Ethiopian dining choices. Open daily for lunch and dinner. Metro: Woodley Park-Zoo, then 90, 91, 92, 93, or 96 Bus; or Dupont Circle, then L2 Bus.

Metro (202) 637-7000 www.wmata.com

The Washington Metropolitan Area Transit Authority, commonly termed Metro, runs the entire D.C. area public transport network providing bus and subway service. The Metrorail is a pleasant and efficient way to travel to and from many of the popular tourist destinations, particularly those in the center of the city, but also out to the Maryland and Virginia suburbs. Metro publishes useful brochures: "Getting There by Metro" and "A Metro Guide to the Nation's Capital," which can be picked up at any station. Station entrances are identified on the street by square columns with a big white M at the top. Trains run Sun–Thurs 5:30 a.m.– midnight; Fri, Sat, and holidays 8 a.m.–2 a.m., with more frequent service during morning and evening rush hours. Fares are based on the time of day and distance traveled and tickets are sold at Farecard machines in the stations. Information about routes and rates is available by phone Mon–Fri 6 a.m.–10:30 p.m. and Sat– Sun 8 a.m.–10:30 p.m., and at the Web site. One-day passes at economical rates can be purchased at many hotels, banks, and supermarkets as well as from the Sales and Information Center on the mezzanine near the 12th and F St. entrance to Metro Center station. Reduced rate Farecards for the disabled and senior citizens are also available here. There are no transfers from buses to the Metro, but there are transfers available at the bus ticket machines on the inside of the Metro stations before the exits. With a transfer the connecting bus fare is sharply reduced. *See also* Georgetown Shuttle Bus, www.commuterpage.com.

Metrobus *see* Buses.

Metro Café 1522 14th St. NW at Church St. (202) 588-9118 www.metrocafe.net

This dance spot features local artists and touring groups performing rock music in a friendly setting. Open nightly with an admission charge that varies with the talent. Information on program schedule and entrance cost by phone or on the Web site. Metro: Dupont Circle.

Metro Center Area

The area around the core station of the Metro system at F St. and 12th and 13th Sts. NW is where many downtown hotels, theaters, and restaurants can be found. It is within walking distance of the Mall's museums, the MCI Center, and the White House. The Hecht Company, the central city's sole surviving department store, is located on G St. between 12th and 13th Sts. and is one of the biggest department stores built in any center city in the country in the last 50 years. It has two direct connections to the Metro Center station.

Metro Center Marriott *see* Marriott at Metro Center.

Metro Rail *see* Metro.

Metropolitan African Methodist Episcopal Church 1518 M St. NW btw 15th and 16th Sts. (202) 331-1426

This large red brick Gothic building was constructed in 1886 and paid for by former slaves. Frederick Douglass was one of its parishioners and the funeral of this orator and statesman took place here. The church still offers its pulpit to leading figures in African-American activism and services are conducted every Sunday. Metro: Farragut North or McPherson Square.

Metropolitan Baptist Church 1225 R St. NW near 12th St. (202) 483-1540 www .metropolitanbaptist.org

This is one of the largest African-American Baptist Churches in the city and is celebrated for the extraordinary renditions of gospel music by its choir at services every Sunday morning. Metro: U St.-Cardozo.

Metropolitan Washington Regional Outings Program (202) 547-2326 (recorded message) www.mwrop.org

MWROP is a regional activity of the Sierra Club offering a variety of activities including rental canoe trips, hikes to Rock Creek Park and other places, social events, and training in outdoor safety and natural history topics. The telephone message provides information on the event newsletter, activities, the rating scale of hikes, and membership information. The site provides a calendar of forthcoming events, driving instructions, and contact information.

Mexicali Blues 2033 Wilson Blvd. at Garfield St., Arlington, VA

This is a colorful, cheery Latin American dining spot with authentic dishes drawn from Mexico and Central America, all at modest prices. Open daily with lunch Mon–Sat, brunch Sun, and dinner daily. Metro: Clarendon.

Mexican Cultural Institute 2829 16th St. NW at Columbia Rd. (202) 728-1628 www.dcmexicancultural.org

Situated in an extraordinary 1912 Italianate structure that was once the Mexican Embassy, this vibrant center sponsors a range of public events like seminars, films, concerts, book readings, and discussions, many of which are open to the public and are free. Exhibitions here showcase the work of Latin American artists and the gallery is open Tues–Sat 11 a.m.–5:30 p.m. with free admission. Details on the current schedule of events and gallery exhibitions by phone or on the Web site. The best way to get here by public transportation is the S2 or S4 Bus along 16th St.

Mexican Restaurants *see* Austin Grill, Banana Café, The Burro, Cactus Cantina, Enriqueta, Mixtec, Rio Grande Café, Santa Fe East, El Tamarindo, Tequila Grill. *See also* www.dcpages.com, www.restaurant.com, www.washingtonpost.com, www.opentable.com.

Mexico Embassy 1911 Pennsylvania Ave. NW (202) 728-1600 www.embassyof mexico.org

Mezza 9 in the Hyatt Arlington btw Fort Myer Dr. and N Nash St., Arlington, VA (703) 276-8999

This unusual hotel restaurant within walking distance over the Key Bridge from Georgetown is open for all three meals daily and always has a good number of Middle Eastern meze to choose from plus well-prepared fish and vegetarian dishes that are served attractively at moderate prices. Metro: Rosslyn.

La Miche 7905 Norfolk Ave. btw St. Elmo and Cordell Aves., Bethesda, MD (301) 986-0707

French country dishes are featured in a gracious setting where flowers and prints enhance the dining experience of hearty Gallic staples at moderately expensive prices. Open for lunch Tues–Fri, dinner Mon–Sat. Metro: Bethesda.

Micronesia Embassy 1725 N St. NW (202) 223-4383 www.fsmembassy.org

Embassy of the Federated States of Micronesia.

Mid-Atlantic Anarchists (Web site) www.infoshop.org

Infoshop.org provides an online clearinghouse "of interest to anarchists, antiauthoritarians, and other activists," and suggest that you "put some anarchy into your life today and learn why anarchists are trying to create a more anarchist society." Examples of local coverage include articles entitled "Closing of the DC Hospital," and "Corporate Takeover of Public Space." It provides links to alternative news sources, archives, and publications related to anarchy and anarchists' approach to present-day issues.

Middle East Market 7006 Carroll Ave. near Laurel Ave. (301) 270-5154

This specialty food store in Takoma Park is an especially good place for finding exotic breads, spices, and coffees. Metro: Takoma.

Middle Eastern Restaurants *see* Bacchus, Beduci, Café Olé, Layalina, Lebanese Taverna, Levantes, Mamma Ayesha's, Mezza 9, Moby Dick House of Kebob, Quick Pita, Rosemary's Thyme, Skewers. *See also* Web sites: ww.dcpages.com, www.restaurant.com, www.washingtonpost.com, www.opentable.com.

Middle-Range Hotels *see* American Inn of Bethesda, Capitol Hill Suites, Carlyle Suites, Courtyard by Marriott, Crystal Gateway Marriott, Days Inn Connecticut Avenue, Doubletree Guest Suites, Doubletree Park Terrace Hotel, Doyle Normandy, Dulles Airport Marriott, Embassy Suites Old Town Alexandria, George

Washington University Inn, Georgetown Inn, Governor's House Hotel, Hamilton Crowne Plaza, Henley Park Hotel, Holiday Inn Arlington at Ballston, Holiday Inn Capitol, Holiday Inn Chevy Chase, Holiday Inn Downtown, Holiday Inn Dulles Airport, Holiday Inn Georgetown, Holiday Inn Old Town, Holiday Inn on the Hill, Holiday Inn Rosslyn Westpark, Hotel Lombardy, Howard Johnson Plaza Hotel and Suites, Jury's Washington Hotel, Key Bridge Marriott, Latham Hotel, Lincoln Suites Downtown, Marriott at Metro Center, Marriott Residence Inn Pentagon City, Monticello Hotel, Morrison House, One Washington Circle, Residence Inn Bethesda–Downtown, River Inn, Savoy Suites, State Plaza Hotel, Tabard Inn, Topaz Hotel, Washington Plaza Hotel, Westin Grand Hotel, Wyndham Bristol Hotel. *See also* www.frommers.com.

Military Museums *see* Fort Myer the Old Guard Museum, Fort Ward Museum and Historic Site, Marine Corps Museum, Museum of the National Guard, National Air and Space Museum, National Museum of American Jewish Military History, National Museum of Health and Medicine, Navy Art Gallery, Navy Museum. *See also* Art and Design Museums, Ethnic and Community Museums, Historical Museums, Major Museums, Media Museums, Museums of Particular Interest to Children, Science and Technology Museums, Smithsonian Institution Museums, Specialized Museums.

Millennium Arts Center 65 I St., SW near 1st St. (202) 479-2572 www.millennium artscenter.org

This recently established nonprofit space is housed in 150,000 square feet spread over seven wings and two inside courtyards. It brings together in one place fine, visual, and performing artists and is designed to be the country's first national arts center of its type. In addition to serving the needs of artists, there are public programs of exhibits, art education, and entertainment. Open Wed–Sat 11 a.m.–5 p.m. or by appointment. Metro: Waterfront-SEU.

Millennium Stage at the Kennedy Center for the Performing Arts *see* Kennedy Center for the Performing Arts Millennium Stage.

Miller Cabin *see* Joaquin Miller Cabin.

Miller Cabin Poetry Series *see* Joaquin Miller Poetry Readings.

Millie and Al's 2440 18th St. NW btw V and U Sts. (202) 387-8131

This neighborhood bar opens from 4 p.m. until late every day but Sunday. It's been here in Adams Morgan since the '60s and you can get a good traditional pizza to go with the fairly priced beers that the casual crowds of patrons are all noisily enjoying. Metro: Woodley Park-Zoo, then 90, 91, 92, 93, or 96 Bus.

Mimi's American Bistro 2120 P St. NW near 21st St. (202) 464-6464

This bustling restaurant/cabaret just east of Dupont Circle has been going since the fall of 2000. It's become a very popular spot, less for the food than for the intimate candlelit ambiance and the cast of talented musical entertainers who serve as the wait staff, punctuating their food delivery with singing for the patrons. Some of this talent is so good that the job here is only a way station to a theatrical career. Metro: Dupont Circle.

Minuteman Sculpture

Located and on display in the building that houses the National Guard Association of the U.S. at 1 Massachusetts Ave. NW at N Capitol St., this monument replicates the Daniel Chester French statue in Concord, Massachusetts. This statue was sculpted by Evanglos Frudakis and corrects some of the historical inaccuracies of French's work, which had the Revolution's citizen-soldier wearing leggings before they had come into popular use. This statue also depicts the correct flintlock musket of the period rather than the percussion-cap gun French shows. The building is open to the public during business hours. Metro: Union Station.

Miss Saigon 3057 M St. NW near 30th St. (202) 333-5545

This modest-priced Georgetown restaurant is pleasantly decorated to complement the well-prepared and seasoned Vietnamese dishes, from zesty and unusual soups to the seafood and noodle fare and vegetarian choices. Open daily for lunch and dinner. Metro: Foggy Bottom-GWU, then 30, 32, 34, 35, or 36 Bus.

Mr. Henry's 601 Pennsylvania Ave. SE at 6th St. (202) 546-8412

This lively place operates on two levels. Downstairs is the food—hamburgers, Reuben sandwiches, and the like, along with the drinks. Upstairs is the jazz spot. The place is open daily from around 11:30 a.m. until midnight. Minimum cover charge required upstairs for the live entertainment. Metro: Eastern Market.

Mr. K's 2121 K St. NW at 21st St. (202) 331-8868

This is one of the city's more elegant Chinese restaurants with an extensive range of innovative selections served stylishly at fairly expensive prices. Open daily for lunch and dinner. Reservations usually a good idea. Metro: Foggy Bottom-GWU.

Mr. Smith's 3104 M St. NW btw 31st St. and Wisconsin Ave. (202) 333-3104 www .mrsmiths.com

This venerable Georgetown saloon and dining spot features standard pub fare at modest prices to go with the drinks and a delightful outdoor patio. The piano bar in the front room is another popular attraction as is the live band music on Friday and Saturday nights at this casual place. Open daily from 11 a.m. or 11:30 a.m. until 2 a.m. or 3 a.m. Metro: Foggy Bottom-GWU, then 30, 32, 34, 35, or 36 Bus.

Mr. Yung's 740 6th St. NW btw G and H Sts. (202) 628-1098

In spite of its dreary décor this popular Chinatown restaurant draws loyal diners for the fine Cantonese food and pleasant service at relatively moderate prices. Open daily for lunch and dinner. Metro: Gallery Pl.-Chinatown.

Mitchellville

This growing community in Maryland's Prince George's County still has undeveloped wooded areas and the flavor of the countryside. Recent years have witnessed an expanding migration from the city of successful African American families who reside in large homes on spacious lots, making the community the most affluent in the county. The area is bounded by Mitchellville Rd. and Northview Dr. on the north, Rte. 301 on the east, Collington Branch Stream Valley Park on the west, and Central Ave. on the south. The nearest Metro station, some 15 minutes by car, is New Carrollton.

Mixtec 1792 Columbia Rd. at 18th St. NW (202) 332-1011

This Adams Morgan restaurant features a wide selection of authentic dishes at modest prices from different regions of Mexico, all made with fresh ingredients that add up to a zesty and filling meal. Open daily for lunch and dinner. Metro: Woodley Park-Zoo, then L2 Bus.

Moby Dick House of Kabob 1070 31st St. NW at M St. (202) 333-4400

There's little more than an order counter and a couple of tables, but the large portions of deliciously seasoned grilled meat and lamb kabobs and the souvlaki pita sandwiches at modest prices draw a growing loyal following of Persian food enthusiasts. Cash only. Open daily 11 a.m.–late at night. Metro: Foggy Bottom-GWU, then 30, 32, 34, 35, or 36 Bus. Other locations at: 7027 Wisconsin Ave., Bethesda, MD (301) 654-1838; and 6854 Old Dominion Dr., McLean, VA (703) 448-8448.

Moldova Embassy 2101 S St. NW (202) 667-1130/31/37 www.moldova.org

Monaco Hotel *see* Hotel Monaco.

Monarch Hotel 2401 M St. NW at 24th St. (202) 429-2400 or (877) 222-2266 www.monarchdc.com

This luxury hotel offers superior service and perhaps the city's most comprehensive fitness facility plus a large indoor pool. There's a beautiful central courtyard and garden and all the upscale amenities one would expect in such an expensive establishment. Metro: Foggy Bottom-GWU.

Mongolia Embassy 2833 M St. NW (202) 333-7117 http://ubpost.mongolnews.mn/virtualmongolia/embassies.htm

Monocle 107 D St. NE btw 1st and 2nd Sts. (202) 546-4488

This traditional Capitol Hill restaurant offers well-prepared American fare and the buzz of lobbyists, congressional staffers, and the occasional congressman or senator. Prices are moderately expensive and the place is much more relaxed when Congress is in recess. Reservations are recommended. Open for lunch and dinner Mon–Fri. Metro: Union Station.

Monroe House *see* Arts Club of Washington.

Montgomery College 51 Mannakee St., Rockville, MD (301) 279-5000 www.montgomerycollege.edu

This is the largest campus of the state's biggest and oldest community college. Some 15,000 students attend a wide range of college and continuing education arts and sciences and technical classes here. The other two campuses are in Germantown and Takoma Park. Beyond the credit courses, Montgomery College offers a large number of classes of popular appeal on topics running from computer programming to public speaking. Metro: Rockville, then 45, 46, or 55 Bus, or Metrobus 22.

Montgomery County Conference and Visitors Bureau (301) 428-9702 www.cvbmontco.com

Office hours are Mon–Fri 9 a.m.–5 p.m. Call or check the Web site to learn about what's available in this big Maryland suburban region.

Montgomery County Farm Women's Market 7155 Wisconsin Ave. near Bethesda Ave., Bethesda, MD (301) 652-2291 www.mda.state.md.us/market/fmd.htm

This is a long-standing market selling fresh fruit, vegetables, cut flowers, baked goods, plants, eggs, and meats. Open year-round Wed and Sat 7 a.m.–3 p.m. Metro: Bethesda.

Montgomery Mall *see* Westfield Shoppingtown Montgomery Mall.

Monticello Hotel 1075 Thomas Jefferson St. off M St. (202) 337-0900 or (800) 388-2410 www.monticellohotel.com

This is a small recently renovated and renamed European-style suites hotel well located near the C&O towpath with 47 accommodations, which include kitchen facilities. It used to be the Georgetown Dutch Inn. There is a health club and swimming pool at a nearby hotel available free to guests and complimentary continental breakfast is provided. Prices are expensive and lowest on weekends. Metro: Foggy Bottom-GWU, then 30, 32, 34, 35, or 36 Bus.

Montpelier Mansion and Cultural Arts Center 12826 Laurel-Bowie Rd., Laurel, MD (301) 953-1993 (Cultural Arts Center) (301) 953-1376 (Montpelier Mansion) www.pgparks.com

The eighteenth-century Georgian Montpelier Mansion is located next to the center and is situated on grounds with beautiful boxwood gardens. Tours of the mansion are available noon–3 p.m. by appointment by calling (301) 953-1376. The Cultural Arts Center is located on the grounds and contains three galleries, a number of artists' studios, and sponsors a performance schedule of musical and dance programs. Visitors to the center are encouraged to watch artists creating their works in a range of media from painting to sculpture to jewelry design. Open daily 9 a.m.–5 p.m. To reach the mansion by car take the Baltimore-Washington Pkwy. to the turnoff at SR 197 (Laurel-Bowie Rd.) and go north 2/10 of a mile to Muirkirk Rd.

Montrose Park www.cr.nps.gov/nr/travel/wash/dc11.htm

This wooded parkland of 16 acres in Georgetown is bounded on the north by Rock Creek Park and on the east by Dumbarton Oaks Park. Along the park's western boundary, a paved lane called Lovers Lane is open only to foot traffic. The park contains a playground, picnic areas, and tennis courts available on a first-come, first-served basis. The park is open year-round from dawn to dusk. Access to the park is through Lovers Lane, which runs off R St. NW to the left just past the intersection of R and 31st Sts. NW.

Monuments and Memorials *see* A. Philip Randolph Statue at Union Station, Adams Memorial, African-American Civil War Memorial, Air Force Memorial, Albert Einstein Memorial, Albert Gallatin Statue, Albert Pike Statue, Alexander Hamilton Statue, Americans at Work Statue, Andrew Jackson Statue, Andrew W. Mellon Memorial Fountain, Artigas Statue, The Awakening, Banneker Circle and Fountain, Benjamin Franklin Statue, Bishop John Carroll Statue, Bishop William Pinckney

Statue, Bolívar Statue, Boy Scout Memorial, Butt-Millet Memorial Fountain, Christ the Light of the World Statue, Columbus Memorial Fountain, Commodore John Barry Statue, Commodore John Paul Jones Monument, Confederate Memorial, Confederate Statue, D.C. War Memorial, Daniel Webster Statue, Dante Statue, Darlington Fountain, Dupont Memorial Fountain, Edmund Burke Memorial, Emancipation Statue, Family Tree of Life Statue, Farragut Sculpture, First Division Monument, Francis Scott Key Memorial, Franklin Delano Roosevelt Memorial, Freedom Forum Journalists Memorial, Freedom Plaza, Freedom Statue, Garfield Memorial, Gen. James B. McPherson Statue, George Washington Masonic National Memorial, George Washington Statue, Grand Army of the Republic Memorial, Grant Memorial, Hahnemann Memorial, Henry Wadsworth Longfellow Statue, James Buchanan Memorial, Jane A. Delano Memorial, Jefferson Memorial, Joan of Arc Statue, John F. Kennedy Bust, Juárez Statue, Justice William O. Douglas Statue, Korean War Veterans Memorial, Kosciuszko Memorial Statue, LBJ Memorial Grove, Lafayette Memorial, Lincoln Memorial, Lincoln Statue, Man Controlling Trade Statue, Marine Corps War Memorial, Martin Luther Statue, Mary McLeod Bethune Memorial, Masaryk Memorial, McClellan Statue, Minuteman Sculpture, Nathanael Greene Statue, National Japanese American Memorial, National Law Enforcement Officers Memorial, Navy and Marine Memorial, Nuns of the Battle-field Statue, Payne Memorial, Peace Monument, Pershing Memorial, Puck Fountain, Pulaski Statue, Pushkin Statue, Pawlins Statue, Robert A. Taft Memorial, Robert Emmett Statue, Rochambeau Statue, Samuel Gompers Memorial, Seabees Memorial, Second Division Memorial, Sheridan Statue, Sir Winston Churchill Statue, Taras Shevchenko Memorial, Temperance Fountain, Theodore Roosevelt Memorial Bridge, Theodore Roosevelt Statue, Thomas Statue, Titanic Memorial, Tomb of the Unknowns, United Spanish War Veterans Memorial, U.S. Navy Memorial and Naval Heritage Center, Vietnam Veterans Memorial, Vietnam Women's Memorial, Von Steuben Memorial, Washington Monument, Washington Equestrian Statue, William Tecumseh Sherman Monument, Winfield Scott Statue, Winfield Scott Hancock Statue, Witherspoon Statue, Women in Military Service for America Memorial, World War II Memorial.

Moore Colonial Farm at Turkey Run *see* Claude Moore Colonial Farm at Turkey Run.

Moore House *see* Clarence Moore House.

Moorland-Springarn Research Center *see* Howard University Moorland-Springarn Research Center.

Mormon Church *see* Temple of the Church of Jesus Christ of Latter-day Saints.

Moroccan Restaurants *see* Marrakesh.

Morocco Embassy 1601 21st St. NW (202) 462-7979

Morrison-Clark Inn 1015 L St. NW at Massachusetts Ave. and 11th St. (202) 898-1200 or (800) 332-7898 www.morrisonclark.com

This Victorian antique-laden 54-room building is one of the city's oldest and offers small but charmingly decorated rooms with all the amenities of a luxury hotel including a fitness center, daily newspaper, and the old-fashioned complimentary shoe shine. There is also a fine restaurant on the premises. Room rates are moderately expensive. Metro: Metro Center.

Morrison-Clark Inn Restaurant 1015 L St. NW at Massachusetts Ave. and 11th St. (202) 898-1200 www.morrisonclark.com

This small dining room is quaint and formal with its white marble fireplaces, chandeliers, and candles, but the food here is decidedly excellent no matter what one selects from interesting Southern-influenced creative food choices. Meals are expensive but it still takes a reservation to assure a table here. Open for lunch Mon–Fri, dinner Sat, and brunch and dinner on Sun. Metro: Metro Center.

Morrison House 116 S Alfred St., Alexandria, VA (703) 838-8000 or (800) 367-0800 www.morrisonhouse.com

This 1985 building in Old Town has recreated the style and elegance of a late eighteenth-century mansion and the 45 rooms are furnished with four-poster beds, fireplaces, and marble baths. All the contemporary amenities complement the romantic flavor of this classy and expensive inn and its Elysium Restaurant is a highly acclaimed dining location. Metro: King Street.

Morton's of Chicago 1050 Connecticut Ave. NW at L St. (202) 955-5997

Part of a legendary national steakhouse chain, this is where huge choice beef slabs are prepared to perfection to satisfy the most voracious appetites, at lofty prices, naturally. There are other choices on the menu, but then why come here if you're not a true carnivore? Open for lunch Mon–Fri, dinner nightly, with reservations recommended. Metro: Farragut North. Other locations at: 3251 Prospect St. NW in Georgetown (202) 342-6258; 8075 Leesburg Pike at Tysons Corner, VA (703) 883-0800.

Mosques *see* Islamic Center.

Mostly Mozart Music Festival www.kennedy-center.org

Every June at the John F. Kennedy Center for the Performing Arts, the works of Wolfgang Amadeus Mozart take center stage to celebrate the composer's musical contributions. Information at (202) 467-4600 or the Web site: www.kennedy-center.org.

Mother's Aides Inc. http://dcparents.com

This reliable agency schedules baby-sitting services at hotels or lodgings in the area. The office is open Mon–Fri 8:30 a.m.–5 p.m. Call (703) 250-0700 or (800) 526-2269 for full details about the arrangements.

Mother's Day Tour

Each May on the Saturday or Sunday of the weekend of Mother's Day, the Capitol Hill Restoration Society arranges for public visits to some of the most attractive Federal row houses and gardens in the neighborhood. There is a charge for participation with complete details available by telephoning (202) 543-0425.

Mount Olivet Lutheran Church 1302 Vermont Ave. NW at 14th St. (202) 462-9776

This historic building that was constructed in the 1880s with R. G. Russell as its architect is open only for religious services. Metro: U St.–Cardozo.

Mount Pleasant Festival www.mtpleasantdc.org/organizations.html

On the first Sunday in June, Mount Pleasant St. NW between Irving St. and Park Rd. is the site of this neighborhood celebration when the street is closed and live music and children's activities take place and the work of local artists and ethnic foods are sold in this widely diverse community. Details at (202) 588-5272.

Mount Pleasant Neighborhood www.mtpleasantdc.org

This is a tree-lined community in northwest D.C. with rows of houses, many with porches. It is principally residential and has a younger population, many living in group houses, which blends into a growing Latino family population plus a somewhat smaller number of Vietnamese who reside mostly in apartments surrounding the main street, Mount Pleasant St. The area is bounded by Rock Creek Park on the north, Howard St. on the south, Adams Mill Rd. on the west, and 16th St. on the east. The nearest Metro station is Columbia Heights.

Mount Rainier

This is a very small primarily residential neighborhood of varied ethnic and racial composition located right across the district line where Prince George's County, Maryland, begins. Many smaller modest homes run off Rte. 1 (Rhode Island Ave.) and are very close to the center of the city some 5 five miles away. Eastern Ave. is at the border of Maryland and D.C. and the apartment dwellings here are occupied by renters. Metro reaches the area with the West Hyattsville station.

Mount Vernon (703) 780-2000 www.mountvernon.org

Located at the south end of the George Washington Memorial Pkwy. overlooking the Potomac River, the lovely plantation home of George and Martha Washington is one of the most visited sites in the country. The mansion and museum still retain much of the family's original furniture. Visitors can explore the estate's workshops, carriage house, gardens, reconstruction of the slave quarters, and burial places of George and Martha. Open daily 8 a.m.–5 p.m. April to August; 9 a.m.–5 p.m. March, September, and October; and the rest of the year 9 a.m.–4 p.m. Admission charge. There are also many special events scheduled here during the year. Call for information or check the Web site. Metro: Huntington then FX101 or FX102 Bus. By car drive on the George Washington Memorial Pkwy. some 14 miles from Washington where the road ends at the gate to the site. *See also* www.commuterpage.com/venues/sightseeing_Va.htm.

Mount Vernon and Alexandria Tour

Gray Line offers this 4-hour morning and afternoon bus tour, which includes a stop at Christ Church in Alexandria (the Washington family's place of worship) before proceeding to the plantation and estate at Mount Vernon. Details and price information at (202) 289-1995.

Mount Vernon College of George Washington University 2100 Foxhall Rd. NW (202) 625-0400 www.mvc.gwu.edu

This college, even though it has been affiliated with George Washington University since 1996, continues its long tradition of educating women at the undergraduate and graduate levels in the liberal arts. Its lovely residential campus is in one of the city's most attractive neighborhoods.

Mount Vernon Farmers Market at Sherwood Regional Library, 2501 Sherwood Hall La., Mount Vernon, VA (703) 941-7987 www.localharvest.org/farms/M1125

This market selling the produce of growers is open 8:30 a.m.–12:30 p.m. on Tuesdays between early May and late November.

Mount Vernon Holiday Tours

Special candlelit evenings are scheduled in December each year when a recreation of the eighteenth-century holiday season brings George Washington's home back to life, and visitors can see the mansion's 3rd floor, which is normally closed to visitors. Information at (703) 780-2000.

Mount Vernon Place United Methodist Church 900 Massachusetts Ave. at Mount Vernon Square (202) 347-9620

This congregation has had a long history in Washington dating from the mid-nineteenth century. It has been at the present location for a very long period and is open only for services. Metro: Mount Vernon Square.

Mount Vernon Recreation Center 2017 Belle View Blvd., Alexandria, VA (703) 768-3222 http://ci.alexandria.va.us/recreation/recreation/mount_vernon.html

This is a year-round indoor ice-skating rink, open to the public, that has a changing schedule based upon other activities on the calendar. Best to call for the weekly program in advance at (703) 768-3222. It is located off Fort Hunt on U.S. Hwy. 1.

Mount Vernon Trail

Along the Potomac River in Virginia this scenic 18½-mile paved path is administered by the U.S. Park Service (703) 289-2502. It is a favorite with walkers, joggers, and bicyclists. The northern section runs about 4 miles starting near the pedestrian crossover to the Theodore Roosevelt Island across the Potomac from the Kennedy Center. The southern section extends from Alexandria to George Washington's estate at Mount Vernon. It all runs parallel to the George Washington Memorial Pkwy. The best place to park a car is at the Theodore Roosevelt Island parking lot near the northern end of the trail. Rather than going over the footbridge to the island, follow the path near the footbridge. This is the Mount Vernon Trail even though there is no sign identifying it.

Mount Vernon Wine Festival

This well-attended annual event takes place on a weekend in May when the wines of Virginia are presented at this wine-tasting celebration at the historic Washington family plantation. Details and ticket information at (703) 799-8604.

Mount Zion Cemetery www.cr.nps.gov/nr/travel/wash/dc10.htm

Located behind 2515–2531 Q St. NW at 27th St. in Georgetown, this burial ground is the oldest predominantly black cemetery in the city. It has suffered from many years of neglect but recent efforts have been started to clear the grounds and restore some of the headstones. Since 1975 it has been on the National Register of

Historic Places. It is open daily from dawn to dark. Metro: Foggy Bottom–GWU, then 30, 32, 34, 35, or 36 Bus.

Mount Zion United Methodist Church 1334 29th St. NW at Dumbarton St. (202) 234-0148

This is the site of the oldest African-American congregation in Washington. The first church burned down in 1880 and during its history had been a stop on the Underground Railroad. Located just around the corner at 2906 O St., the church's Heritage Center is situated in a simple brick cottage built in 1810. It contains the archives of photographs, church records, manuscripts, and other artifacts of its history. Admission to the Heritage Center and viewing of the archives may be arranged by appointment. Call (202) 337-6711 to schedule a visit. Metro: Foggy Bottom–GWU, then 30, 32, 34, 35, or 36 Bus.

Mountjoy Bayly House 122 Maryland Ave. NE

This building near the Capitol is listed in the National Register of Historic Places, dates from the Federal Period, and bears the name of a one-time sergeant at arms of the Senate. In the twentieth century it belonged to Senator Hiram Johnson, who ran for vice president with Theodore Roosevelt on the Bull Moose Party slate. The house became the headquarters in 1947 for the General Commission on Chaplains and Armed Forces Personnel. Metro: Union Station.

Movie Madness 1083 Thomas Jefferson St. NW btw 30th and 31st Sts. (202) 337-7064

Located just below M St. next to Barnes & Noble in Georgetown, this unusual store stocks thousands of old and new movie posters. Open Mon, Wed, Thurs noon–8 p.m.; Fri–Sat noon–9 p.m.; Sun noon–6 p.m. Metro: Foggy Bottom-GWU, then 30, 32, 34, 35, or 36 Bus.

Movie Theaters *see* AMC Courthouse 8, AMC Mazza Gallerie, AMC Union Station, American Film Institute, Avalon Movie Theater, Bethesda Row Cinema, Cinema Arts Theater, Cineplex Odeon Cinema.

Movies *see* Foreign and Independent Films.

Mozambique Embassy 1990 M St. NW, Suite 570 (202) 293-7146 www.embamoc-usa.org

Mudd House 1724 M St. NW near 17th St. (202) 822-8455

This is a good alternative to the ubiquitous Starbucks and specializes in organic blends for coffee addicts. Open Mon–Fri 6:30 a.m.–5:45 p.m. Metro: Farragut North.

Murphy's Irish Pub and Restaurant 2609 24th St. NW btw Connecticut Ave. and Calvert St. (202) 462-7171

This popular place is off the main line on a side street, and the food is good and the drinks inexpensive. There's live Irish musical entertainment nightly and the outdoor terrace is a good gathering point that's kept warm when the weather gets chillier. Open for lunch and dinner, but the music plays on until 2 a.m. or 3 a.m. Metro: Woodley Park-Zoo. There's another location in Alexandria at 713 King St. between N Washington and N Columbus Sts. (703) 548-1717.

Museum of the Americas *see* Art Museum of the Americas.

Museum of the National Guard 1 Massachusetts Ave. NW at N Capitol St. (202) 408-5877 www.nga.us.org

This museum was opened at the end of 2002 with a focus on the contributions of the American militia throughout its history from the Revolutionary War to the present. Exhibits highlight the efforts each state and territory has made by displaying a range of artifacts, weapons, and portraits. Complementing the museum is a research library that features books and documents dealing with militia history. Details on hours and exhibits available by phone or on the Web site. Metro: Union Station.

Museums *see* Art and Design Museums, Ethnic and Community Museums, Historical Museums, Major Museums, Media Museums, Military Museums, Museums of Particular Interest to Children, Science and Technology Museums, Smithsonian Institution Museums, Specialized Museums. *See also* www.commuterpage.com/venues/museums.htm.

Museums of Particular Interest to Children *see* Capital Children's Museum, Children's Concierge, Discovery Creek Children's Museum, National Air and Space Museum, National Geographic Society Explorers Hall, National Museum of Natural History, Washington Dolls' House and Toy Museum. *See also* Art and Design Museums, Ethnic and Community Museums, Historical Museums, Media Museums, Military Museums, Science and Technology Museums, Smithsonian Institution Museums, Specialized Museums, www/commuterpage.com/venues/museums.htm, www.frommers.com, www.washingtonpost.com.

Music Box Center 1920 I St. NW at 19th St. (202) 783-9399

Situated in the lower level of a remodeled townhouse, this unique store has a very extensive inventory of old and new music boxes that can play the melody of your choosing drawn from a range of several hundred tunes. They also make repairs. Open Mon–Fri 10 a.m.–5:30 p.m., Sat 10 a.m.–3 p.m. Metro: Farragut West.

Music Organizations *see* Columbia Flute Choir, Friday Morning Music Club, Levine School of Music, National Chamber Orchestra, Potomac River Jazz Club, Washington Balalaika Society, Woodbridge Flute Choir.

Musical Entertainment *see* Choral Music, Classical Music, www.dcflamenco.com, Folk and Country Music, Jazz Spots, Opera Music, Orchestras, Popular Music, Rock, Alternative, and Ethnic Music. *See also* Music Organizations, www.washingtonpost.com.

My Brother's Place Bar and Grill 237 2nd St. NW at Constitution Ave. (202) 347-1350

The entrance to this place is down a small one-way road, which takes it off the beaten path and keeps the flavor of a neighborhood pub frequented primarily by regulars. Open Mon–Wed 11 a.m.–11 p.m. and Thurs–Fri 11 a.m.–2 a.m. Saturday only open in the evenings until 2 a.m. The big event here is the Saturday night all-you-can-drink special for a modest charge when there's also music for dancing in a big upstairs space. Metro: Judiciary Square.

Myanmar Embassy 2300 S St. NW (202) 332-9044 http://members.aol.com/mewashdc.com

Embassy of the Union of Myanmar. *See also* Burma Embassy.

Mykonos 121 Congressional Lane off Rockville Pike at Congressional Plaza, Rockville, MD (301) 770-5999

This moderate-priced Greek spot attracts patrons as much for the Middle Eastern appetizers as for the main dishes and homemade desserts. Open for lunch Tues–Fri, dinner Tues–Sun. Metro: Twinbrook.

NASA Goddard Visitors Center at Soil Conservation and Greenbelt Rds., Greenbelt, MD (301) 286-8981 or (301) 286-8103 www.nasa.gov

Here's the place to see models of crafts and rockets that have traveled into space, to participate in interactive exhibits, and learn about the history of rocket science. Open Mon–Fri 9 a.m.–4 p.m. Admission free. Tours must be arranged by calling in advance. Traveling by car use the Beltway (I-495/95) and exit at 22A going east a little more than 2 miles and follow the signs, or exit the Baltimore-Washington Pkwy. (I-295) east at 193 (Greenbelt Rd.) and go east about 2 miles.

Nam Viet 1127 N Hudson St. at Wilson Blvd., Arlington, VA (703) 522-7110

This Vietnamese restaurant is close to the Metro and offers excellent soup and fragrant-smelling and tasty meat and fish dishes in a casual atmosphere at inexpensive prices. Open daily for lunch and dinner. Metro: Clarendon. There is another Nam Viet in the city at 3419 Connecticut Ave. NW at Macomb St. (202) 237-1015. Metro: Cleveland Park.

Namibia Embassy 1605 New Hampshire Ave. NW (202) 986-0540

Nanny O'Brien's Irish Pub 3319 Connecticut Ave. btw Macomb and Ordway Sts. (202) 686-9189 www.nannyobriens.com

This small, friendly pub offers Irish stew and burgers and beer, of course. Lively Irish music every night but Tues. Open nightly. Metro: Cleveland Park.

Nathanael Greene Statue

One of the city's finest bronze equestrian statues stands in the center of Stanton Park, located between Massachusetts and Maryland Aves. and C and D Sts. NE. Henry Kirk Brown was the sculptor in 1876 of the monument of General Nathanael Greene of Rhode Island, a hero of the Revolutionary War. Metro: Union Station.

Nathan's 3150 M St. NW at Wisconsin Ave. (202) 338-2000

This Georgetown standby has been around some 35 years. It's a popular watering hole as well as a dining spot. Open for dinner Mon–Fri, Sat–Sun brunch and dinner, and the moderately expensive American food dishes are very good. Reservations are a good idea. On Friday and Saturday nights there's music for dancing with no cover charge, and regular drink prices. Metro: Foggy Bottom-GWU, then 30, 32, 34, 35, or 36 Bus.

Nation Nightclub 1015 Half St. SE btw K and L Sts. (202) 554-1500

This used to be a boiler works before being transformed in 1995 to what was called the Capital Ballroom. It is a huge party place that can accommodate large crowds, featuring live performances of rock, and tech music disc jockeys on different nights. Charges vary based on what's happening. Shows end in time for patrons to get the Metro before it closes for the night. Metro: Navy Yard.

National Academy of Sciences 2101 Constitution Ave. NW at 21st St. (202) 334-2000 www.nas.edu

This organization, which investigates, examines, experiments, and reports on scientific and technical questions through its committees of renowned volunteer scientists and engineers, is housed in this classical marble structure built in 1924 with high window panels depicting the historic progress of science through the centuries. Visitors passing through its ornate bronze doors enter the Great Hall with its 55-foot-high central dome. The art gallery off the Great Hall is open Mon–Fri 9 a.m.–5 p.m. featuring science-related artworks, often using unconventional methods or materials. Free concerts have been scheduled here since 1970 as part of the Arts in the Academy Program, which also sponsors lectures and the art exhibits here. For information about the schedule of special events call (202) 334-2436. Metro: Foggy Bottom-GWU, then a good walk.

National Academy of Sciences Music Programs

Free performances are scheduled through much of the year by the National Academy of Sciences featuring the National Musical Arts Chamber Ensemble and the Marine Corps Chamber Orchestra at the academy building at 2101 Constitution Ave. NW at 21st St. For schedule information call (202) 334-2436.

National Air and Space Museum 7th St. and Independence Ave. SW (202) 357-2700 www.nasm.si.edu

Since opening in 1976 this has been the Smithsonian Institution's and the city's most popular tourist destination. It is centered upon the history and development of air and space technology, and its numerous galleries depict the story from man's first attempt to fly to the present day. IMAX films are shown on the 5-story screen in the Langley Theater, and in the Einstein Planetarium there are multimedia offerings. For schedule and admission prices call (202) 357-1686. Admission to the museum is free. Metro: Smithsonian or L'Enfant Plaza. Because the museum can no longer contain large new items for its collection, a huge new building is under construction on a 176-acre site just south of Dulles Airport in Virginia. This branch will dwarf the National Air and Space Museum on the Mall. For the new facility, more than 200 aircraft are expected to be on display. The scheduled opening in December 2003 is timed to coincide with the centennial of the Wright Brothers first powered flight. *See also* www.commuterpage.com/venues/museums-si.htm.

National Airport *see* Reagan National Airport.

National Aquarium in the Commerce Department Building lower level, 14th St. and Constitution Ave. NW (202) 482-2825 or 482-2826

This is the oldest public aquarium in the country, opened in 1873. It houses more than 1,700 different aquatic animals including fish, invertebrates, reptiles, and amphibians. It is much smaller than many more-heralded institutions, but it does have a "touch tank" where kids can touch a horseshoe crab or have crustaceans crawl over their hands. Open daily 9 a.m.–5 p.m. Modest admission charge. Call in advance to learn the times for the feeding of the piranha and sharks at (202) 482-2825. Metro: Federal Triangle. *See also* www.commuterpage.com/venues/gardens.htm.

National Arboretum 3501 New York Ave. NE at R St. (entrance on R St.) (202) 245-2726

This 446-acre preserve is committed to research, education, and conservation of trees, flowers, shrubs, and other plants. It was begun in 1927. A scenic drive and a network of paths allow visitors to view the thousands of plants from all over the world. There are also horticultural lectures, demonstrations, and exhibits. The grounds are open daily 8 a.m.–5 p.m. Admission free. Call ahead for information on any special events taking place on the day of the planned visit. Metro: Stadium-Armory, then B2 Bus to Bladensburg Rd. and R St. NE. *See also* www.commuterpage.com/venues/gardens.htm.

National Arboretum Walking Trail located in the National Arboretum, 3501 New York Ave. NE at R St. (entrance at R St.) (202) 245-2726

Three miles of walking trails provide one of Washington's most serene and relaxing places for strolling through a lovely scenic setting. It's normally very quiet except in spring when the azaleas bloom and there are hordes of visitors. Metro: Stadium-Armory, then B2 Bus to Bladensburg Rd. and R St. NE.

National Archives Constitution Ave. and 7th St. NW (enter from Constitution Ave.) (202) 501-5000 www.nara.gov

This monumental classical structure designed in 1935 by John Russell Pope is the nation's shrine to its treasured documentary history. The Declaration of Independence, the Constitution, and the Bill of Rights are on display here, as well as temporary theme exhibitions from the vast holdings. The archives sponsors many public programs of lectures, workshops, film showings, and other cultural events. Details are provided on the recorded program update at (202) 501-5000. Free guided tours are offered as well. Call (202) 501-5205 about reservations. Admission free. The National Archives is open daily 10 a.m.–9 p.m. April 1 to Labor Day, and 10 a.m.–5:30 p.m. Labor Day through March. Metro: Archives-Navy Memorial.

National Baptist Memorial Church 1501 Columbia Rd. NW at 16th St. (202) 265-1410

Architect Egerton Swartout modeled this church built in 1926 after the Church of All Souls in London and its most striking feature is its huge tower. It is a splendid example of an urban house of worship adapting to its community by offering services in English and Spanish and permitting a number of neighborhood organizations to conduct their activities here. Accessible by S2 or S4 Bus along 16th St.

National Building Museum 401 F St. NW btw 4th and 5th Sts. (202) 272-2448 www.nbm.org

This museum is located in a lovely building earlier occupied by the Pension Bureau. It was designed in 1881 by Montgomery C. Meigs, an army general. Its great hall is huge, occupying a space 116 feet by 316 feet, and its tall Corinthian columns are extraordinary indoor pillars. The permanent exhibit here is "Washington—Symbol and City," offering the story of the monuments and structures in the nation's capital. The museum features a variety of exhibitions, films, concerts, and lectures about different aspects of buildings and architects and offers free guided tours. Open Mon–Sat 10 a.m.–4 p.m. and until 5 p.m. June to August, noon–4 p.m. on Sun. Metro: Judiciary Square. *See also* www.commuterpage.com/venues/museums.htm.

National Building Museum Tours

The museum sponsors a number of specialized architectural and buildings bus tours throughout the year led by architectural specialists and historians. For details and prices call (202) 272-2448 or check the Web site: www.nbm.org.

National Capital Barbecue Battle

On a Saturday and Sunday in late June each year on Pennsylvania Ave. NW between 9th and 14th Sts. cooking teams compete for prizes, more than twenty bands play on several stages, and food and drink is sold by barbecue restaurants to support a local charity. Information at (202) 828-3099 or check the Web site: www.bbq.usa.com.

National Capital Trolley Museum 1313 Bonifant Rd. btw Layhall Rd. and New Hampshire Ave., Wheaton, MD (301) 384-6088 www.dctrolley.org

There is a unique collection here of fourteen antique, restored American and European trolleys and streetcars and a chance to take a 1½-mile trolley ride through Northwest Branch Park. Admission to the exhibits is free but the trolley ride has a modest charge. Open Sat and Sun noon–5 p.m. Closed during certain periods of the year and open on some holidays. Best to call in advance for schedule details. Metro: Glenmont, then take Ride-On Bus 26 (which operates only on Saturday and Sunday).

National Capital YMCA 1711 Rhode Island Ave. NW at 17th St. (202) 862-9622

Open to members of other YMCAs and guests of some area hotels for a daily fee, this place has a pool; weight and fitness equipment; and basketball, racquetball and squash courts among its range of exercise options. Metro: Farragut North.

National Capitol Station Post Office *see* National Postal Museum.

National Cathedral *see* Washington National Cathedral.

National Chamber Orchestra 850 Avery Rd., Rockville, MD, box office (240) 314-8690 www.nationalchamberorch.org

Music director and conductor Piotr Gajewski leads this highly respected ensemble. It released its first CD in 2002. Particularly committed to introducing classical music to children, the orchestra allows children from 6 to 16 to attend all of the theater concerts free. There are various subscription offerings including variations on six orchestra concerts and three piano recitals or selected chamber music offerings. There are free pre-concert lectures to many concerts. The orchestra performs at the F. Scott Fitzgerald Theatre at the Rockville Civic Center, located in the Rockville Civic Center Park. Box office open Tues–Sat 2 p.m.–7 p.m. and 2 hours prior to performances. By car from Rte. 28 and I-270, proceed east on Rte. 28, cross Rte. 355 and follow Rte. 28 east (turns left at first light beyond Rte. 355). Travel 4 blocks to Baltimore Rd., turn right, go 3 blocks to Edmonston Dr., turn left, and Civic Center Park entrance is immediately on the right.

National City Christian Church 5 Thomas Circle at Massachusetts Ave. and 14th St NW (202) 232-0323

John Russell Pope, the architect of the Jefferson Memorial and other Washington buildings, designed this big Colonial-style church in 1930. With its tall steeple and lofty position on a small hill it is one of the tallest structures in the city. It is also home to one of Washington's largest pipe organs where organ recitals take place during winter months. Visitors can view the sanctuary 9 a.m.–5:30 p.m. but guided tours of the entire structure are available only by appointment. Call for details. Metro: McPherson Square.

National Club *see* Washington Club.

National Colonial Farm *see* Piscataway Park and National Colonial Farm.

National Council for International Visitors 1420 K St. NW off 14th St. (202) 842-1414 www.nciv.org

This is an organization of nonprofit agencies and community programs committed to offering services to those who participate in international exchange activities by fostering internships, cultural opportunities, and hospitality for foreign officials and international students and faculty. Metro: McPherson Square.

National Cryptologic Museum on the grounds of Fort Meade on Colony Seven Rd., Fort Meade, MD (301) 688-5849

Affiliated with the ultra-secret National Security Agency, this small museum focuses on the history of clandestine activity from the sixteenth century to the present. Displays show rare historic cryptographic books, Civil War signal flags, cipher machines from World War II, and much more that will appeal to enthusiasts of secret codes and spy lore. Admission free. Open Mon–Fri 9 a.m.–4 p.m. By car take exit at Rte. 32 East off the Baltimore-Washington Pkwy.

National Firearms Museum 11250 Waples Mill Rd., Fairfax, VA (703) 267-1600 www.nrahq.org/shooting/museum

The National Rifle Association's National Firearms Museum houses one of the most extensive collections of its kind offering visitors the chance to see more than 2,000 historic weapons. Exhibits span the history of handheld firearms from the mid-fourteenth century to modern pistols, shotguns, and rifles. Admission free. Open daily 10 a.m.–4 p.m. Metro: Ballston-MU, then Metrobus 1C toward Fair

Oaks Hospital to the stop at Lee Jackson Memorial Hwy. and Waples Mill Rd. Walk 5 blocks north. *See also* www.commuterpage.com/venues/sightseeing_VA.htm.

National Gallery of Art consists of two buildings—East and West Buildings, btw 3rd and 7th Sts. NW btw the Mall and Constitution Ave. (202) 737-4215 www .nga.gov

The West Building was designed in 1941 in classical style by John Russell Pope. The East Building is a contemporary structure designed by I. M. Pei and constructed in 1978. The two parts are connected by a paved plaza and an underground concourse. The West Building contains European works from the thirteenth century to the present. The East Building features contemporary art by European and American artists. Both wings are open Mon–Sat 10 a.m.–5 p.m., Sun 11 a.m.–6 p.m. Admission free. There are free tours, gallery talks, concerts and film showings. Call for details on current exhibitions and all the other activities or check the Web site. Metro: Archives-Navy Memorial, Judiciary Square, or Smithsonian.

National Gallery of Art Film Showings

Free classic, international, and exhibit-related film screenings are offered in the large auditorium of the east wing's lower level. Quarterly schedules of the movie program are distributed at the gallery and program information is available at (202) 737-4215.

National Gallery of Art Sculpture Garden located btw Constitution Ave. and Madison Dr. NW on the north and south, and btw 7th and 9th Sts. NW on the east and west

Situated between the West Building of the National Gallery of Art and the National Museum of Natural History this outdoor sculpture garden features a lovely fountain in mild weather and an ice-skating rink in winter months. The garden offers trees, shrubs, lawns, and benches as well as the modern sculpture on display. Metro: Smithsonian.

National Genealogical Society Library 4527 17th St. N at Wakefield St., Arlington, VA (703) 525-0050 www.ngsgenealogy.org

This center has a collection of research materials and local histories that is designed for use by its members. Arrangements for use by non-members can be made by calling. Metro: Ballston-MU.

National Geographic Society 17th and M Sts. NW (202) 857-7700 www.national geographic.com

This organization has been supporting worldwide explorations and publishing its monthly magazine since it began more than 100 years ago. In the Grovesnor Auditorium public programs feature lectures by explorers, dance and music programs, storytellers, and video showings. Call for details or check the Web site. Metro: Farragut North.

National Geographic Society Explorers Hall 17th and M Sts. NW (202) 857-7589 www.nationalgeographic.com

The hall contains a great variety of exciting interactive exhibits and learning experiences including seeing the earth from space, touching a tornado, exploring the solar system, and much more. It is located on the ground floor of a 10-story marble and glass structure. It is a popular tourist destination for the science oriented, and it can be compared in a number of ways to the National Air and Space Museum. Admission free. Open daily. Metro: Farragut North.

National Institutes of Health Building 10 on Center Dr. on campus of the NIH, Bethesda, MD (301) 496-1776 www.nih.gov

The center stage for the war against many of the most debilitating diseases is here in the Maryland suburbs, where some 15,000 scientists and medical personnel carry out research in twenty-one institutes in fifty buildings on a 300-acre campus. At the Visitors Center in Building 10, Room BIC 218, at 11 a.m. on Mon, Wed, and Fri tours begin with a video followed by a short lecture by a staff member before the informative tour is led through the center. It is best to call before visiting to make sure there is no change in arrangements. Metro: Medical Center, then take the free shuttle bus to the Visitors Center, Building 10.

National Japanese American Memorial

Facing the Capitol and located some 200 yards south of Union Station in a triangular park bounded by Louisiana and New Jersey Aves. and D St. NW, this memorial commemorates the internment of Japanese Americans and Japanese aliens during World War II. Metro: Union Station.

National Law Enforcement Officers Candlelight Vigil

On May 13 each year this solemn service is conducted at 8 p.m. to honor the nation's law enforcement personnel who have died in the past year and their names are officially inscribed on the memorial wall. It takes place at the site of the National Law Enforcement Officers Memorial at Judiciary Square. Information at (202) 737-3400 or the Web site: www.nleomg.com.

National Law Enforcement Officers Memorial at Judiciary Square btw E and F Sts. and 4th and 5th Sts. NW (202) 737-3400 www.nleom.com

This 3-acre memorial park is dedicated to honoring the memory of American peace officers killed in the line of duty. There are some 15,000 names engraved on the marble wall, the first being U.S. Marshal Robert Forsyth, slain in 1794. Open daily 24 hours. Metro: Judiciary Square. *See also* www.commuterpage.com/venues/memorials.htm.

National Law Enforcement Visitors Center 605 E St. NW (1 1/2 blocks west of the memorial) (202) 737-3400 www.nleomg.com

This center and museum is a companion to the National Law Enforcement Officers Memorial at Judiciary Square. It displays historic exhibits, photos of legendary police officers and lawmen, and features interactive videotape access to biographical details of slain officers. Open Mon–Fri 9 a.m.–5 p.m., Sat 10 a.m.–5 p.m., Sun noon–5 p.m. Admission free. Metro: Gallery Pl.–Chinatown.

National Library of Medicine 8600 Rockville Pike btw Woodmont Ave. and Cedar Lane, Bethesda, MD (301) 594-5983 or (888) 346-3656 www.nlm.nih.gov

This is the world's largest research library in the health field with more than four million volumes on health care, medicine, public health, toxicology, medical technology, and public health. It is located on the campus of the National Institutes of Health at Center Dr. and is open for public use Mon–Wed and Fri 8:30 a.m.–5 p.m., Thurs 8:30 a.m.–9 p.m., Sat 8:30 a.m.–12:30 p.m. Tours are available with no advance reservations required Mon–Fri at 1:30 p.m. beginning in the lobby of the Lister Hill Center (Building 38A). Metro: Medical Center.

National Mall *see* The Mall under M.

National Memorial Park 7400 Lee Hwy. btw S West St., and Hollywood Rd., Falls Church, VA (703) 560-4400

This exceedingly large burial ground is celebrated for its sculptured fountains and gardens. The park's focal point, designed by sculptor Carl Milles, is the Fountain of Faith with more than thirty bronze figures as part of the scene. The cemetery is open from dawn to dark. By car exit the Washington Beltway (I-495) at Exit 50B and take Rte. 29 (Lee Hwy.) a little less than a mile to the entrance.

National Museum of African Art 950 Independence Ave. SW enter from pavilion in the Enid E. Haupt Garden behind the Smithsonian Institution Building (the Castle) (202) 357-2700 www.si.edu/nmfa

This is the only American museum centered exclusively on the traditional arts of Africa south of the Sahara. Except for its entry level, this Smithsonian museum is located on 3 floors below ground. Its collection includes various types of works in wood, ivory, cast metal, bronze, and ceramics. There are exhibitions from the permanent collection and rotating exhibits. Workshops, lectures, and other special events are sponsored by the museum's education department. Guided tours are also available. Open daily 10 a.m.–5:30 p.m. Admission free. Metro: Smithsonian. *See also* www.commuterpage.com/venues/museums-si.htm.

National Museum of American Art 8th and G Sts. NW (entrance on G St.) (202) 357-2700 www.nmaa.si.edu

This Smithsonian museum is located in what was the Old Patent Office Building. It holds the largest collection of American art in the world and features exhibitions drawn from its collection of more than 35,000 works by American artists reflecting the nation's ethnic, geographic, religious, and cultural diversity. The holdings include paintings, sculpture, photographs, and folk art objects. It is connected to the National Portrait Gallery by hallways and a courtyard. The museum was reopened in 2003 after an extensive building renovation that began in January 2000. Metro: Gallery Pl.–Chinatown.

National Museum of American History btw 12th and 14th St. NW, Constitution and the Mall (202) 357-2700 www.si.edu

This is the Smithsonian's comprehensive collection of materials reflecting America's history with exhibitions of politics, science, technology, and culture. The 3 floors are packed with exhibits of national treasures catering to the widest possible range of interests for nostalgia buffs of every stripe as well as intriguing hands-on-rooms for kids. There are guided tours and even a real old-fashioned ice cream parlor on the lower level. Admission free. Open daily 10 a.m.–5:30 p.m. Metro:

Smithsonian or Federal Triangle. *See also* www.commuterpage.com/venues/mu seums-si.htm.

National Museum of American Jewish Military History 1811 R St. NW at 18th St. (202) 265-6280 www.nmajmh.org

This small museum, run under the auspices of the Jewish War Veterans of the United States, presents displays documenting the role of Jewish men and women in the nation's armed forces. It features photos, posters, flags, medals, guns, and other memorabilia from the Revolutionary War to the present as well as changing exhibitions on special themes. Open Mon–Fri 9 a.m.–5 p.m., Sun 1 p.m.–5 p.m. Admission free. Metro: Dupont Circle.

National Museum of Health and Medicine on the grounds of the Walter Reed Medical Center 6900 Georgia Ave. NW at Elder St. (202) 782-2200 www .natmedmuse.afip.org

Located in Building 54 on the grounds of the medical center, this small museum demonstrates medical progress through graphic displays, some of which may be trying for those without strong stomachs. On the other hand, medicine buffs will be fascinated by the renowned collection of brain specimens. Exhibitions on changing topics are rotated regularly. Open daily 10 a.m.–5 p.m. Admission free. Metro: Silver Spring, then 70 or 71 Bus south. *See also* www.commuterpage.com/venues/ museums.htm.

National Museum of Natural History 10th St. and Constitution Ave., entrance on the Mall (Madison Dr.) (202) 357-2700 www.mnh.si.edu

This Smithsonian museum draws visitors for its seemingly endless collection of animals, plants, rocks, and fossils. It also boasts an IMAX theater and a Discovery Room where kids can touch everything. The building holds 300,000 square feet of exhibition space, the famous 45½-carat Hope Diamond, an insect zoo, a dinosaur hall, and artifacts from everywhere in the world. Open daily 10 a.m.–5:30 p.m. Admission free. Metro: Smithsonian. *See also* www.commuterpage.com/venues/mu seums-si.htm.

National Museum of the American Indian

Scheduled to open in September 2004 in the area between 3rd and 4th Sts. SW and Jefferson Dr. and Independence Ave. east of the Air and Space Museum, the nucleus of the collection will be the artifacts assembled over a half century by New York banker George Gustav Heye. The museum is part of the Smithsonian Institution and dedicated to the preservation, study, and exhibition of the historical and contemporary culture of Native Americans. It is expected to include an interactive library and indoor and outdoor spaces for American Indians to use in ceremonial and ritual care of objects in the collection. Until the opening, information is available at (202) 287-2536 or (202) 357-1300 or the Web site: www.americanindian .si.edu. The nearest Metro stop will be L'Enfant Plaza.

National Museum of Women in the Arts 1250 New York Ave. NW at 13th St. (202) 783-5000 www.nmwa.org

Since 1987 America's sole women-artists-only museum has been operating in a beautifully renovated Renaissance Revival building designed by Waddy Wood as a Masonic Temple in 1907. Founded by Wallace and Wilhelmina Holladay to celebrate and exhibit the artistic creations of women, exhibitions here include original theme shows, traveling exhibitions, and also focus on major women's contributions drawn from abroad or from the museum's 2,500-work permanent collection by more than 600 artists from the sixteenth century to the present. Works include paintings, drawings, prints, sculpture, photographs, and ceramics. The museum also regularly sponsors unique exhibitions of books-as-art. There is also a continuing series of musical programs, lectures, and films, all centered on women-oriented subjects or by female artists. Open Mon–Sat 10 a.m.–5 p.m., Sun noon–5 p.m. Suggested donation. Metro: Metro Center. *See also* www.commuterpage.com/venues/museums.htm.

National Museum of Women in the Arts Film Showings 1250 New York Ave. NW at 13th St. (202) 783-5000 www.nmwa.org

This museum sponsors a program throughout the year of film showings of cinematic works by and about women, often introduced or followed by panel discussions by artists or critics. Call for details. Metro: Metro Center.

National Musical Arts Chamber Ensemble *see* National Academy of Sciences Music Programs.

National Organization for Women 733 15th St. NW near H St. (202) 331-0066 www.now.org

This is headquarters for this active national group and the place to find information on a host of issues of concern to women, referrals to counseling services, and rape crisis centers as well as details about upcoming feminist activities and events. Open Mon–Fri during business hours. Metro: McPherson Square.

National Park Service (Web site) www.nps.gov

This site provides a wealth of information related to local parks and historic sites, a detailed map of Rock Creek Park, details about forthcoming events related to the parks and historic sites, and a "for kids" approach to parks and historic sites, allowing parents and teachers to tailor a visit to young visitors. Virtual tours are available for some sites, as are links to cultural and historic information and links to the Parks and History Association, which manages bookstores and other services at local national monuments and historic sites, as well as sells online books related to local historic and park sites.

National Park Service Information Service

Information about events in and around all of the parks, monuments, and memorials in the Washington area is available by calling the helpful staff during business hours at (202) 619-7125.

National Place Shops *see* Shops at National Place.

National Portrait Gallery located in the southern half of the Old Patent Office Building, F St. NW btw 7th and 9th Sts. (202) 357-2920 www.nationalportraitgallery.edu

This Smithsonian museum preserves the images in portraits, sculpture, and other media of those Americans who have distinguished themselves in science, public life, entertainment, industry, scholarship, sports, art, literature, and other important pursuits, frequently mounting exhibitions on particular themes. The Portrait Gallery is linked to the National Museum of American Art through connecting hallways and a common courtyard. The museum was reopened in 2003 after extensive renovation to the building begun in January 2000. Open daily 10 a.m.–5:30 p.m. Admission free. Metro: Gallery Pl.–Chinatown. *See also* www.com muterpage.com/venues/museums-si.htm.

National Postal Museum 2 Massachusetts Ave. NE at 1st St. (202) 357-2700 www .si.edu/postal

This part of the Smithsonian museum complex opened in 1993 on the lower level of what had been Washington's National Capital Station Post Office from 1914 until 1986. This is a hands-on museum, which entertainingly depicts the history of America's mail service and incorporates a huge collection of philatelic material. It starts with an exhibit on the Pony Express and imaginatively goes on from there to all sorts of interesting interactive and visual exhibits to engage old and young alike. Open daily 10 a.m.–5:30 p.m. Admission free. Guided tours are available. Metro: Union Station. *See also* www.commuterpage.com/venues/museums-si .htm.

National Presbyterian Church and Center 4101 Nebraska Ave. NW at 41st St. (202) 537-0800 www.natpresch.org

Located in Tenleytown in upper-northwest D.C., this important worship center offers meeting facilities for all other faiths, lovely stained glass windows depicting themes from the Bible, and the Chapel of the Presidents. It is often the site for concerts and other public events. Open Mon–Fri 9 a.m.–5 p.m. Tours can be arranged by appointment. Metro: Tenleytown.

National Press Club located in the National Press Building, corner of 14th St. NW and F St. (202) 662-7500 www.press.org

This building has been home to the city's greatest concentration of media offices from around the country and the world for almost 100 years. On the top floor American and foreign leaders from diverse fields frequently deliver widely heralded addresses. Metro: Metro Center.

National Race for the Cure

Beginning in 1988 and continuing every year on a weekend in early June, the world's most celebrated run/walk to benefit breast cancer research, education, screening, and treatment programs with thousands participating takes place in Washington. Details at (703) 848-8884 or the Web site: www.nationalraceforthe cure.org.

National Scottish Rite Center *see* Scottish Rite Masonic Temple.

National Shrine of the Immaculate Conception *see* Basilica of the National Shrine of the Immaculate Conception.

National Symphony Orchestra

This distinguished orchestra performs classical works as well as contemporary compositions during its regular season from fall to spring in the Concert Hall of the Kennedy Center. It also schedules free public summer performances at the Carter Barron Amphitheater and plays on the Capitol grounds during celebratory events on Memorial Day, Independence Day, and Labor Day weekends. Information at (202) 416-8100 or the Web site: www.kennedy-center.org/nso.

National Theater 1321 Pennsylvania Ave. NW btw 13th and 14th Sts. (202) 628-6161 www.nationaltheater.org

This is one of Washington's oldest performance centers, established in 1835 and renovated in 1983. It hosts theatrical premieres, pre- and post-Broadway productions, and musicals. It also offers the free and popular "Monday Night at the National" program from fall to spring featuring local performers in dance, music, readings, and plays. Details at (202) 783-3372. "Saturday Morning at the National" is a free regular children's event from October to May when magicians, storytellers, puppeteers, and other entertainers perform for kids. Information at (202) 783-3372. Metro: Federal Triangle on Metro Center. *See also* www.commuterpage.com/venues/venue-en.htm.

National Theater Saturday Morning Program *see* Saturday Morning at the National Theater.

National Trust for Historic Preservation 1785 Massachusetts Ave. NW btw 17th and 18th Sts. (202) 588-6000 www.nthp.org

This organization occupies what is thought to be one of the most elegant Beaux Arts structures in the city—the McCormick Apartments Building. The architect was Jules Henri de Sibour and it was constructed in 1917 containing only six 11,000-square-foot apartments, one on each floor with living space for forty servants. The building was declared a national historic landmark in 1977 and is now the headquarters for the nonprofit body, which is engaged in activities to protect and preserve significant properties across the country, and also owns and operates a number of such sites. The lobby of the building is open to the public during business hours Mon–Fri. Metro: Dupont Circle.

National War College *see* Fort Leslie J. McNair.

National Wildlife Visitor Center (301) 497-5760 www.patuxent.fws.gov

This large museum south of Laurel, Maryland, is operated by the Fish and Wildlife Service of the Interior Department on the 12,750-acre Patuxent Research Refuge. Interactive exhibits center on wildlife habitats, endangered species, bird routes, and global environmental problems. There are also surrounding ponds, wooded areas, and walking paths. Open daily 10 a.m.–5:30 p.m. Admission free. Thirty-minute narrated tram rides with a wildlife interpreter are available for a modest price. To reach the center by car take the Powder Mill Rd. Exit east off the Baltimore-Washington Pkwy. and proceed 2 miles to the entrance.

National Zoo 3001 Connecticut Ave. NW or Howard St. off Beach Dr. (202) 673-4800 www.si.edu/natzoo

The National Zoological Park is one of the world's finest zoos and it is free. It was designed by Frederick Law Olmsted of New York City Central Park fame and is best known for its Asian rhinoceros, lowland gorillas, Sumatran tigers, Komodo dragons, and, of course, its celebrated pandas. It is situated in a 163-acre biological park with several thousand animal species on view indoors and outdoors. The Education Building is the place to learn the day's feeding times, special events, and new animal births. Grounds open daily 6 a.m.–8 p.m. May 1 to September 15, and 6 a.m.–6 p.m. at other times. Buildings open daily 10 a.m.–6 p.m. May 1 to September 15, and 10 a.m.–4:30 p.m. at other times. Metro: Woodley Park-Zoo. *See also* www.commuterpage.com/venues/museums-si.htm.

Naturally Yours 2029 P St. NW btw 20th and 21st Sts. (202) 429-1718

This place features organic groceries, herbs, and other natural products as well as a juice bar. Open Mon–Sat 10 a.m.–8 p.m., Sun 11 a.m.–6 p.m. Metro: Dupont Circle.

Naval Heritage Center 701 Pennsylvania Ave. NW at 7th St. (202) 737-2300 www .lonesailor.org

The entrance hall adjoins the Navy and Marine Memorial. The center has exhibits on Navy traditions and there is an exciting film showing of *At Sea* describing life on a carrier vessel. Visitors can also search a computer database containing the military records of thousands of sailors, Marines, Coast Guardsmen, and Merchant Marines, who have enrolled in the log. Information on special events is available by telephone. Open Tues–Sat 9:30 a.m.–5 p.m. Admission free but movie tickets are priced. Metro: Archives-Navy Memorial. *See also* www.commuterpage.com/venues/memorials.htm.

Naval Historical Center *see* Navy Museum.

Naval Observatory *See* U.S. Naval Observatory.

Navy and Marine Memorial 701 Pennsylvania Ave. NW btw 7th and 8th Sts. (202) 737-2300

This outdoor plaza is the commemorative tribute to those who have served the country on the sea. Two sculpture walls contain bronze reliefs honoring famous Naval events and accomplishments as well as heroic individuals like John Paul Jones and Admiral David G. Farragut. At the base of the monument is a giant granite world map. Call for information on special events scheduled to take place here. Metro: Archives-Navy Memorial.

Navy Art Gallery in the Washington Navy Yard Building 67, 9th and M Sts. SE (202) 433-3815 www.history.navy.mil

This exhibit space features rotating showings of paintings, prints, and drawings of naval events and personnel, many created by service artists during combat on the sea and in the air in World War II. Open Mon–Fri 10 a.m.–4 p.m. Metro: Eastern Market, then walk south about 10 minutes.

Navy Band Summer Concerts

The Navy Band and various specialty groups of the band perform at many different locations in the city and the suburbs and regularly at the Navy and Marine Memorial and on the Mall. Concerts are free to the public. For schedule details call the Navy Band Performance Information number (202) 433-2525.

Navy Memorial and Heritage Center *see* U.S. Navy Memorial and Naval Heritage Center.

Navy Museum in the Washington Navy Yard Building 76, 9th and M Sts. SE (202) 433-6897

Housed in the former Naval Gun Factory, this museum contains exhibits illustrating American naval history from the Revolutionary War to date. There are some 5,000 artifacts and memorabilia displayed, important battles are depicted, and there is an extensive collection of scale model ships. A number of gun mounts in the display can be handled by visitors, as can other hands-on exhibits. Open Mon–Fri 9 a.m.–5 p.m. Admission free. Metro: Eastern Market, then walk south about 10 minutes. *See also* www.commuterpage.com/venues/museums.htm.

Navy Yard *see* Washington Navy Yard.

Needwood Golf Course 6724 Needwood Rd., Rockville, MD (301) 948-1075

This is a popular public 18-hole course operated by the Montgomery County Parks Department, which offers a pro shop, putting green, and driving range. Phone for fee information and other details. By car take Rte. 270 off the Washington Beltway (I-495), travel west to the Shady Grove Exit, turning on to Redland Blvd., and then turning right on Needwood Rd. and continuing to the golf course.

Neiman Marcus in the Mazza Gallerie, 5300 Wisconsin Ave. NW at Western Ave. (202) 966-9700

This local branch of the Dallas chain focused on high quality and service caters to customers prepared to pay steep prices for the high-fashioned clothing, furs, jewelry, and silver pieces sold here. Metro: Friendship Heights.

Le Neon Theatre in the Rosslyn Spectrum, 1611 N Kent St., Rosslyn, VA (703) 243-NEON www.leneon.org

This company stages productions of classic French dramatic works performed in English during its annual fall to spring season. Metro: Rosslyn.

Nepal Embassy 2131 Leroy Pl. NW (202) 667-4550

Royal Nepalese Embassy.

Netherlands Carillon

Located near the Marine Corps War Memorial (Iwo Jima Memorial) in an open 127-foot-tall bell tower, this large instrument consisting of 49 bells, which is played by professional carillonneurs, was given to the United States after World War II by the Dutch government. It is administered by the National Park Service. Carillon concerts are held May to September. During concerts visitors can enter the tower to watch the carillonneur perform and to take advantage of the view of Washington. Information at (703) 285-2598 or check the Web site: www.nps.gov. *See also* Marine Corps War Memorial.

Netherlands Embassy 4200 Linnean Ave. NW (202) 244-5300 www.netherlands -embassy.org

Royal Netherlands Embassy.

New Heights 2317 Calvert St. NW btw Connecticut Ave. and 24th St. (202) 234-4110 www.newheightsrestaurant.com

This lovely dining room surrounded by trees with a view of Rock Creek Park serves innovative American dishes that are beautiful to behold. There's also an outdoor patio and downstairs bar at this expensive restaurant where reservations are recommended. Open Mon–Sat for dinner, Sun brunch and dinner. Metro: Woodley Park-Zoo.

New Morning Farm Markets Sheridan School, 36th St. and Alton Pl. NW (814) 444-3904

Fruit and vegetable growers sell their produce on Saturdays 8 a.m.–1:30 p.m. from early June to mid-March, and on Tuesdays 4:30 p.m.–8 p.m. from early June through September.

New Year's Eve Celebrations

There's no Times Square with a big ball dropping at the stroke of midnight in Washington, but there are various events taking place around town. Activities include a free musical performance in the Kennedy Center's Grand Foyer, outdoor festivities at the Old Post Office Building, as well as celebrations in the suburbs. The newspapers are the best source of details on these events.

New York Avenue Presbyterian Church 1313 New York Ave. btw 13th and 14th Sts. (202) 393-3700 www.nyapc.org

The present Federal-style building was constructed in 1951, but the congregation was first organized in 1803. This has been the church of a number of American presidents, and Abraham Lincoln's family pew is still on view here in the second row. Tours are offered after services. Call for details. Metro: McPherson Square or Metro Center.

New York Times

This nationally read daily newspaper enjoys a very sizable local readership but particularly on Sunday. In spite of the bravado about becoming a city to rival the Big Apple, many Washingtonians continue to take their main cues from the editorial columns and features of America's leading daily. It can be found at most places where newspapers are sold as well as in many street-corner boxes.

New Zealand Embassy 37 Observatory Circle (202) 328-4800 www.nzembassy.org

Newseum www.newseum.org

This interactive museum of news closed its Arlington, Virginia, facility in March 2002. It is preparing to relocate to its new site in 2006 on the corner of Pennsylvania Ave. NW and 6th St. The Freedom Forum's headquarters and conference center will be located in the 555,000-square-foot space, which will also permit the Newseum to double its old size. The new facility will incorporate many of the exhibits, artifacts, and interactive programs of the former site, and expand its audiences. Information on the progress of the project can be found at the Web site: www.newseum.org.

Newspapers and Magazines see *Capital Spotlight, City Paper, The Common Denominator, The Georgetown Newspaper, Georgetowner, The Hill, Hill Rag, New York Times,* Newsroom, *Roll Call, Time Out Washington, Washington Afro-American, Washington Blade, Washington Diplomat, Washington Informer, Washington*

Monthly, Washington Post, Washington Sun Newspaper, Washington Technology, Washington Times, Washington Woman, Washingtonian Magazine.

Newsroom 1803 Connecticut Ave. NW btw S St. and Florida Ave. (202) 332-1489

If you're looking for newspapers and magazines from major American cities and virtually everywhere else around the world, this is the place. You can also find a good selection of language dictionaries and foreign language primers here as well. Metro: Dupont Circle.

Nicaragua Embassy 1627 New Hampshire Ave. NW (202) 939-6570
Embassy of the Republic of Nicaragua.

Niger Embassy 2204 R St. NW (202) 483-4224 www.nigerembassy.usa.org
Embassy of the Republic of Niger.

Nigeria Embassy 1333 16th St. NW (202) 986-8400 www.nigeriaembassy.usa.org
Embassy of the Federal Republic of Nigeria.

Night Clubs *see* Badlands, Black Cat, Bohemian Caverns, Chi-Cha Lounge, Cities, Club Chaos, D.C. Eagle, Hung Jury, JR's, Latin Jazz Alley, 9:30 Club, Republic Gardens, Third Edition, Zanzibar on the Waterfront. *See also* Comedy Clubs, Dance Clubs, Jazz Spots, www.frommers.com, www.washingtonpost.com.

9:30 Club 815 V St. NW at 9th St. (202) 265-0930 www.930.com

At this location since 1996, this legendary spot began in 1980. This space has a balcony on three sides and a large dance floor in front of the stage and is open nightly. It features every type of music in its bookings—punk, alternative, reggae, hip-hop, and whatever else is new to appeal to its young audience. Admission price varies with the talent. Call about schedule and admissions or check the Web site. Metro: U St.-Cardozo. *See also* www.commuterpage.com/venues/venue-en.htm.

Nissan Pavilion at Stone Ridge 7800 Cellar Door Dr., Bristow, VA (703) 754-6400, box office (703) 754-1288 www.nissanpavilion.com

About an hour's drive from Washington, this open-air pavilion is a popular concert site during the summer months. Theater-style reserved seats are available, or festival lawn chairs can be rented. There are two 30-by-40-foot video screens on each side of the stage. Parking is included in the price of the concert ticket. A variety of snacks and beverages, including beer and wine are available. Backpacks, bags, large purses, strollers, alcohol, food, beverages, coolers, lawn chairs, and cameras are prohibited. Tickets to all events are available at the box office and at TicketMaster. Box office hours vary. By car take I-66 to Exit 43B, then follow Pavilion Signs to Rte. 29, left on Wellington Rd to the site.

Nizam's 523 Maple Ave. W at Nutley St., Vienna, VA (703) 938-8948

This has been adjudged by some as the finest authentic Turkish restaurant in the area. It is an elegant setting offering the full range of deliciously prepared Middle Eastern specialties at moderately expensive prices. Open for lunch Tues–Fri, dinner Tues–Sun. Dinner recommendations are suggested. Metro: Vienna-Fairfax GMU, then a 1-mile walk or taxi ride.

Nora 2132 Florida Ave. NW at R St. (202) 462-5143

This is an attractive and sophisticated restaurant situated in a corner townhouse serving American cuisine using only seasonal organic ingredients. The menu changes frequently and attracts a wide following for the imaginatively prepared healthful dishes that genuinely taste as good as they are for you. Moderately expensive. Open for dinner Mon–Sat. Reservations recommended. Metro: Dupont Circle.

Nordstrom

This fashionable national Seattle-based department store chain has branches at four suburban shopping malls—Montgomery Mall in Bethesda, MD (301) 365-4111; Fashion Center at Pentagon City in Arlington, VA (703) 415-1121; Tysons Corner in McLean, VA (703) 761-1121; and Dulles Town Centre in Sterling, VA (571) 434-4000.

Normandy Hotel *see* Doyle Normandy.

Norris House Inn 108 Loudoun St. SW, Leesburg, VA (703) 777-1806 www.norriss house.com

Located 1 hour from downtown D.C. in the heart of Leesburg's historic district, this attractive 1760 stone-house bed-and-breakfast offers guest rooms attractively appointed with antiques and fireplaces. There are lovely comfortable common rooms and a veranda looking out upon a pretty garden. Rates are moderately expensive.

Northern Virginia Community College 4001 Wakefield Chapel Rd., Annandale, VA (703) 323-3000 www.nvcc.edu

This is one of the nation's largest 2-year community colleges with thousands of students enrolled in more than 100 technical, vocational, and college transfer programs. Additional campuses are in Alexandria, Loudoun County, Manassas, and Woodbridge. Numerous not-for-credit courses are offered at campuses and other community locations. To reach the Annandale campus take the Washington Beltway (I-495) and use Exit 52A. It is $1/4$ mile from the exit on the left side of the road.

Northern Virginia Fine Arts Association *see* Athenaeum.

Northwest Park Golf Course 15711 Layhill Rd., Wheaton, MD (301) 598-6100

This beautifully maintained 6,700-yard public course is located about 30 minutes from downtown. Call for fees and starting time. By car drive north on Georgia Ave. (Rte. 97), or take Exit 31 off the Washington Beltway (I-495) going north on Georgia Ave., continue to Wheaton, and 1 block after Randolph Rd. at Layhill Rd. turn right and drive 4 miles to the course.

Norway Embassy 2720 34th St. NW (202) 333-6000 www.norway.org

Royal Norwegian Embassy.

Nottoway Park Farmers Market Nottoway Park, 9601 Courthouse Rd., Vienna, VA (703) 941-7987

From early May until the end of October this growers market offers produce 8:30 a.m.–12:30 p.m. on Wednesdays.

Numark Gallery 406 7th St. NW btw D and E Sts. (202) 628-3810 www.numark gallery.com

Located on the 3rd floor of this building in the heart of the city's art district, this gallery showcases well-known New York artists and up-and-coming local talents. Open Tues–Sat 11 a.m.–6 p.m. Metro: Gallery Pl.-Chinatown or Archives-Navy Memorial.

Nuns of the Battlefield Statue

This bronze monument by sculptor Jerome Connor was designed in 1924 to pay tribute to the nuns who cared for and comforted wounded and diseased Civil War soldiers. It can be found at Rhode Island and M St. NW. Metro: Farragut North.

O Street Market
Located at 7th and O Sts. NW, this is one of the last three remaining nineteenth-century city markets. The other two are Eastern Market and the Georgetown Market (where Dean & DeLuca now operate). The one at O St. has had a troubled history but continues to function daily except Mondays. Metro: Shaw-Howard University.

OAS *see* Organization of American States.

Oak Hill Cemetery 3001 R St. NW btw 28th and 32nd St. (202) 337-2835
Occupying 35 acres in Georgetown and bordered by Rock Creek Park on the north and Montrose Park on the west, this is one of the oldest and most venerable Victorian garden cemeteries in the country. Many Washington notables have been buried here, including Abraham Lincoln's 12-year-old son who died while Lincoln was occupying the White House. The 1840 gatehouse and the Gothic-style stone chapel that stands inside the grounds were designed by James Renwick, architect of the Smithsonian Castle and New York's St. Patrick's Cathedral. Open Mon–Fri 10 a.m.–4 p.m. Admission free. Metro: Foggy Bottom-GWU, then 30, 32, 34, 35, or 36 Bus.

Oatlands 20850 Oatlands Plantation Lane, Leesburg, VA (6 miles south of Leesburg on Rte. 15) (703) 777-3174 www.oatlands.org
This 22-room Greek Revival house was the center of a 3,400-acre plantation 200 years ago. It offers 4 acres of formal gardens and terraces and contains an 1810 greenhouse, the second oldest of its type in the United States. It is now a National Trust Historic site open April through December offering daily guided tours. Open Mon–Sat 10 a.m.–5 p.m., Sun 1 p.m.–5 p.m. Admission charge. By car take I-66 west to Exit 67 (Dulles Airport), then 267 West (toll road) to Leesburg. Exit 1A then take the second right (Rte. 15 South Warrenton). Oatlands' front gate is 5 miles on the left.

Obelisk 2029 P St. NW btw 20th and 21st St. (202) 872-1180
This small elegant Italian restaurant with a large following offers a five-course

prix-fixe menu with traditional as well as innovative dishes using fine seasonal ingredients, which adds up to a memorable dining experience. It's fairly expensive and reservations are essential. Open for dinner Tues–Sat Metro: Dupont Circle.

O'Brien's Pit Barbecue 387 E Gude Dr., Rockville, MD (301) 340-8956 www .obriensbarbecue.com

This spot has been serving favorite barbecue dishes like brisket, spare ribs, chili dogs, and the accompaniments like beans and rice to satisfied customers for a very long time. It is budget priced and open daily for lunch and dinner. By car take Rockville Pike (Rte. 355), driving west and turning left onto E Gude Dr.

Occidental Grill 1475 Pennsylvania Ave. NW btw 14th and 15th Sts. (202) 783-1475 www.occidentaldc.com

Since 1906 this place has attracted the powerful and the power seekers as much for its clubby flavor with walls covered with photos of notables as for the well-prepared regional American cuisine. Open daily for lunch and dinner at fairly expensive prices with reservations recommended. Metro: Metro Center.

The Octagon 1799 New York Ave. NW btw E and 18th Sts. (202) 638-3221 or (202) 638-3105 www.theoctagon.org

In 1996 this museum was restored to its original many-sided appearance. The brick building is one of the city's oldest private mansions, built around 1800 and designed by William Thornton, one of the architects of the Capitol. It is the nation's oldest museum of architecture and design and is open Tues–Sun 10 a.m.–4 p.m. Modest admission charge. Two or three exhibits a year are shown in this Federal-style building owned by the American Architectural Foundation, and guided tours are offered. Call for information about current exhibitions, lectures, and special programs or check the Web site. Metro: Farragut North or Farragut West.

Odyssey Cruises departs from Gangplank Marina, 600 Water St. SW off 6th St. (202) 488-6000 or (800) 946-7245 www.odysseycruises.com

This is Washington's version of the Parisian *bateau-mouche*. A low-slung glass-covered craft designed to negotiate its way under the Potomac bridges, it offers breathtaking views of the Capitol, the Kennedy Center, and other sites along the way. Among the 2-hour or 3-hour options are lunch, dinner, and Sunday jazz brunch cruises with gourmet food, live music, and dancing at expensive prices. Call for details or check the Web site.

Off the Record in the Hay-Adams Hotel, 1 Lafayette Square at 16th and H Sts. NW (202) 942-7599

This recently renovated lounge in one of the city's finest hotels offers the ambiance of a fine men's club where choice drinks and cigars can be enjoyed. It is open daily from 11 a.m. to around 1 a.m. Metro: Farragut West or Farragut North.

Old Adas Israel Synagogue *see* Adas Israel Congregation.

Old Angler's Inn 10801 MacArthur Blvd. btw Brickyard and Falls Rds., Potomac, MD (301) 365-2425 www.oldanglersinn.com

Situated in a charming old-fashioned country house in the woods across from the C&O Canal towpath, this expensive restaurant features a romantic atmosphere and hearty American fare. In winter the fireplace roars and in mild weather outdoor terrace dining is the main treat. Open for lunch and dinner Tues–Sat, Sun brunch and dinner. Reservations are suggested. By car drive straight out from Georgetown along MacArthur Blvd. to Potomac.

Old Central Public Library Building
The Carnegie Public Library building constructed in 1902 in Beaux Arts style between 7th and 9th Sts. NW at Mount Vernon Square just south of the new convention center was transformed in March 2003 into the new City Museum of Washington, D.C. It is operated by the Historical Society of Washington, D.C., and features permanent and changing exhibitions celebrating the city's neighborhoods, its history and its people. Details on hours of opening and other information may be found at the Web sites: www.hswdc.org or www.citymuseumdc.org, or by phone at (202) 785-2068. Metro: Mount Vernon Square-UDC. *See also* City Museum of Washington, D.C.

Old Dominion Brewing Company Brewpub and Brewery, 44633 Guilford Dr., Ashburn, VA (703) 724-9100
This is an actual working brewery (with several prize-winning beers) with a brewpub/restaurant attached. The beer is so good it sells without advertising. Beer aficionados from across the county make pilgrimages to this shrine. Use the map on the Web site to find it. Besides the extensive and tasty pub menu, for lunch try the jumbo tamarind-glazed shrimp with yucca crisps or pan-roasted monkfish with portobello-potato hash and grilled squash from the dinner menu. Inexpensive. No smoking. Free brewery tours: Sat noon and 2 p.m., Sun 2 p.m. Brewpub open Mon–Wed 11:30 a.m.–9 p.m. Thurs, 11:30 a.m.–10 p.m., Sat 11 a.m.–10 p.m., Sun noon–7 p.m. By car from D.C. take I-395 to Toll Rd. (267) west, right on Rte. 28, left on Waxpool (fifth light), right on Loudoun County Pkwy. (third light), left on Beaumead Circle, right on Guilford Dr.

Old Ebbitt Grill 675 15th St. NW btw Pennsylvania Ave. and G St. (202) 347-4801 www.ebbitt.com
This 150-year-old Victorian-style saloon and eating spot starts serving at 8:30 a.m. and stays open until 2 a.m. daily. It's just 2 blocks from the White House and attracts hordes of Washingtonian and tourist diners, so reservations are a must. The food is first rate, the décor is elegant, the atmosphere casual, and the prices are moderate. The hamburgers and Sunday brunch are popular favorites. Metro: Metro Center or McPherson Square.

Old Europe 2434 Wisconsin Ave. NW near Calvert St. (202) 333-7600 www.old-europe.com
If German food like schnitzel, dumplings, wurst, and other robustly filling dishes are your cup of tea, this is the place. It's been around for more than 50 years and enjoys a loyal following of fans of Teutonic fare at this upper Georgetown location. Open for lunch and dinner daily except Monday at moderately expensive prices. Metro: Foggy Bottom-GWU, then 30, 32, 34, 35, or 36 Bus to Wisconsin Ave., then about a 20-minute walk north.

Old Executive Office Building

Recently renamed the Dwight D. Eisenhower Executive Office Building, this ornate 1888 structure is located beside the West Wing of the White House at the southeast corner of Pennsylvania Ave. and 17th St. NW. The baroque Second Empire façade inspires great pleasure or displeasure. The building's interior has been grandly restored and houses a number of key offices of the executive branch of the government and the office of the vice president. Saturday morning tours, which were formerly possible to arrange with an early advance reservation, have been suspended indefinitely since September 11, 2001. You can check on their status by calling (202) 395-5895. Metro: Farragut West.

Old Glory 3139 M St. NW btw 31st and Wisconsin Ave. (202) 337-3406 www .oldglorybbq.com

This lively Georgetown saloon and barbecue place is open daily for lunch until 2 a.m. or so. People come here for the beers, the Southern roadhouse honky-tonk amplified music and ambiance, as well as the upstairs dining room with its fine barbecue, burgers, sandwiches, and savory side dishes. Very inexpensive and very enjoyable. Metro: Foggy Bottom-GWU, then 30, 32, 34, 35, or 36 Bus.

Old Guard Museum Sheridan Ave., Building 249, Fort Myer, VA (703) 696-6670 www.mdw.army.mil/oldguard

Located at historic Fort Myer, which has been the home and headquarters of the 3rd U.S. Infantry (the Old Guard) since 1948, this museum displays the weapons used before and during the Civil War, and in the later wars in which this distinguished unit fought. A movie theater shows slides of the unit's history and its current duties, and knowledgeable soldiers answer questions and offer tours. Open Mon–Sat 9 a.m.–4 p.m., Sun 1–4 p.m. Admission free. Metro: Pentagon then 24P Bus toward Ballston to stop at S Courthouse Rd. and S 6th St. Walk 1 block north on S Courthouse Rd., turn right on 5th St. S, and go 1 block east to Fort Myer's Hatfield gate.

Old Holy Trinity Church *see* Convent of Mercy.

Old Patent Office Building *see* National Museum of American Art, National Portrait Gallery.

Old Post Office Building and Pavilion 1100 Pennsylvania Ave. NW btw 11th and 12th Sts. (202) 289-4224 or (202) 606-8691 www.oldpostofficedc.com

This building was constructed in 1899 in Romanesque style and designed by Willoughby Edbooke. It was scheduled twice in the past for demolition before being rescued by aroused historical architecture-sensitive citizens. The renovated building houses a popular pavilion containing numerous shops, restaurants, and a center for performances, with offices on the upper floors. The 315-foot clock tower can be reached by a glass elevator, and another elevator rises to the 12th-floor observation deck, which has lovely views. The building is open daily 8 a.m.–11 p.m. April to August, and 10 a.m.–6 p.m. September to March. Tower tours are offered daily. Admission free. For clock tower information call (202) 606-8691. Metro: Federal Triangle. *See also* www.commuterpage.com/venues/sightseeing_VA.htm.

Old Presbyterian Meeting House 321 S Fairfax St., Alexandria, VA (703) 549-6670 www.opmh.org

This church's history dates from more than 200 years. It was established in 1772 by Scottish and Scotch-Irish immigrants. In 1835 the original building was destroyed by fire and rebuilt by 1837 in Greek Revival style. A tombstone honoring an unknown soldier of the Revolution is in the cemetery. Open Mon–Fri 9 a.m.–3 p.m., and on Sun for services. Metro: Braddock Rd. then DAT4 DASH Bus toward Hunting Towers to stop at Royal St. and Queen St. Walk 1 block east on Queen St., turn left on Fairfax St., and go 1 block north. *See also* www.commuterpage.com/venues/sightseeing_VA.htm.

Old Stone House 3051 M St. NW btw 30th and 31st Sts. (202) 426-6851 www.nps.gov/rocr/oldstonehouse

This historic cottage in Georgetown is probably the oldest pre-Revolutionary building still surviving in the city. It has been restored and contains Colonial furnishings in its small rooms. The house and its lovely gardens in the rear are maintained by the National Park Service. Open Wed–Sun noon–5 p.m. Admission free. Metro: Foggy Bottom-GWU, then 30, 32, 34, 35, or 36 Bus.

Old Town Alexandria

Alexandria is some 6 miles south of Washington along the banks of the Potomac River. Historic Old Town, its most visible neighborhood, is where the original settlement began. The beautifully restored port town contains striking eighteenth-century buildings, cobblestone streets, restaurants and bars, chic shops, parks, and the celebrated Torpedo Factory Art Center. Old Town is one of Washington's most popular tourist destinations. It can be reached by Metrorail to the King Street station. From the station it is about a 20-minute walk toward the river. Also, it can be reached by taking the local DAT2 DASH or DAT5 DASH Bus that runs down King St. to Fairfax St.

Old Town Arts and Crafts Fair

Each year for two days on a weekend in May the works of local and regional craftspeople and artists are on display in Alexandria's popular tourist locale. Information at (703) 836-2176 or at the Web site: www.alexandriavolunteers.org.

Old Town Christmas Candlelight Tour

For two days in mid-December visitors can view decorated historic houses and an eighteenth-century tavern in Old Town Alexandria. The celebration includes Colonial dancing and varied musical performances. Details and ticket information at (703) 838-4200.

Old Town Experience

A seasoned local guide leads visitors through Alexandria Old Town's celebrated historic district and its most interesting sites. Information at (703) 836-0694 or (703) 836-6553.

Old Town Fairfax Farmers Market *see* Fairfax Farmers Market.

Old Town Ghost Tours

A costumed tour guide carrying a lantern leads this walking tour through Alexandria's Old Town and a historic old cemetery recounting ghostly tales and spooky lore for 1 hour on Friday, Saturday, and Sunday nights from mid-March to mid-November. Details and prices at (703) 838-4200.

Old Town Trolley Tours *see* Washington Old Town Trolley Tours.

Olney Theatre Center for the Arts 2001 Olney-Sandy Spring Rd., Olney, MD (301) 924-3400 www.olneytheatre.org

This is one of the suburbs most celebrated performance sites for professional productions of drama and musical theater. It is about an hour's drive from the city with ample parking available. By car take Connecticut Ave. traveling north. Eight miles beyond the Beltway (I-495), turn left on Georgia Ave. going north. After 5 miles turn right on Rte. 108 and go 1½ miles to the center, which is on the left.

Olsson's Books and Records 1307 19th St. NW btw N St. and Dupont Circle (202) 785-1133 (books) (202) 785-2662 (music) www.olssons.com

This is one of the larger independent local bookstore chains with a number of locations around town and in the suburbs. The staff is well informed and helpful and there is a big inventory of books and a wide selection of all kinds of music in CDs and tapes. Book signings and other book-related events take place here and at the other locations. Open Mon–Wed 10 a.m.–10 p.m., Thurs–Sat 10 a.m.–10:30 p.m., Sun noon–8 p.m. Hours at other stores vary. Metro: Dupont Circle. Other locations at 1200 F St. NW (202) 347-3686 (books), (202) 393-1853 (music); 418 7th St. NW (202) 638-7610 (books), (202) 638-7613 (music); 7647 Old Georgetown Rd., Bethesda, MD (301) 652-3336 (books), (301) 652-6399 (music); 106 S Union St., Old Town Alexandria, VA (703) 684-0077 (books), (703) 684-0030 (music); 2111 Wilson Blvd., Arlington, VA (703) 525-4227 (books), (703) 525-3507 (music).

Oman Embassy 2435 Belmont Rd. NW (202) 387-1980, fax (202) 745-4933
Embassy of the Sultanate of Oman.

Omega 2122 P St. NW off 21st St. (202) 223-4917

This gay bar and disco center has been around longer than some of the customers who frequent it. Mostly men in their 20s and 30s frequent this casual 2-floor spot where the company, the nightly drink specials, and the weekly drag show are the lures. Open nightly until 2 a.m. or 3 a.m. Metro: Dupont Circle.

Omni Shoreham Hotel 2500 Calvert St. NW btw Connecticut Ave. and 28th St. (202) 234-0700 or (800) THE OMNI www.omnihotels.com

This started out as an apartment hotel designed in 1930 by architect Joseph Abel. It has undergone recent renovations and is an immense facility adjacent to Rock Creek Park. There are more than 800 rooms in this hostelry, which has a notable history. It has all the amenities of a luxury hotel from swimming pool to fitness center, steam room, whirlpool, clay tennis courts, and an elegant lobby lounge. Metro: Woodley Park-Zoo.

Once Upon a Time 120 Church St., Vienna, VA (703) 255-3285 www.once.upon atime.com

This is an unusually appealing toy store, which has been going more than 20 years. It sponsors frequent special events for kids and is a delight for children of all ages. Open Mon–Wed and Fri–Sat 10 a.m.–5 p.m., Thurs 10 a.m. –7 p.m., Sun noon–5 p.m. By car take Hwy. 66 W exiting at Nutley St. and head toward Vienna.

One Washington Circle 1 Washington Circle NW overlooking Foggy Bottom Metro stop (202) 872-1680 or (800) 424-9671 www.onewashingtoncirclehotel.com

This all-suites hotel offers a variety of suite sizes with each containing a kitchen, dining area, and some with a terrace. Prices are moderately expensive but the Foggy Bottom location is a distinct plus. Metro: Foggy Bottom-GWU.

Online Sources on Washington, D.C. *see* Web Sites about Washington, D.C.

Oodles Noodles 1120 19th St. NW btw L and M Sts. (202) 293-3138

Prices are very inexpensive at this highly popular Pan-Asian restaurant, which features a variety of exotic noodle dishes, soups, fish, and vegetarian choices. Open for lunch and dinner Mon–Sat. Metro: Dupont Circle or Farragut North. There's a second location in Bethesda at 4907 Cordell Ave. off Norfolk St. (301) 986-8833.

Opera Music *see* Opera Theater of Northern Virginia, Summer Opera Theatre Company, Inc., Washington Opera.

Opera Theater of Northern Virginia

This company performs during its seasons in October, January to February, and May, offering operatic productions sung in English at a community center venue. In December a one-act opera is performed for families and children. Information at (703) 528-1433.

Orchestras *see* Arlington Symphony, Georgetown Symphony Orchestra, Jewish Community Center Symphony Orchestra, McLean Orchestra, McLean Symphony, National Chamber Orchestra, National Symphony Orchestra, Washington Symphony Orchestra.

Organization of American States 17th St. and Constitution Ave. NW (202) 458-3000 www.oas.org

This is the headquarters for the organization begun in 1890 as the International Union of American Republics and later known as the Pan-American Union. The building, designed by combining classical and Latin American elements, was conceived by architects Paul Cret and Albert Kelsey. The interior includes the lush Tropical Patio, palatial staircases, the Art Gallery, and on the 2nd floor the striking Hall of the Americas with busts of statesmen, stained glass windows, and Tiffany chandeliers. Behind the building's west terrace is the idyllic Aztec Garden. Open Mon–Fri 9 a.m.–5:30 p.m. Admission free. Concerts are offered here in fall and spring and information about the series is available at (202) 458-3069. Metro: Farragut West. *See also* Art Museum of the Americas.

Ortanique 730 11th St. NW btw G and H Sts. (202) 393-0975 www.ortaniqueon theweb.com

Now metamorphosed into a new restaurant from the old Bet on Jazz, this spot still features Caribbean cooking but with an added dash of nouvelle Asian cuisine. Open for lunch Mon–Fri, dinner Mon–Sat. Moderately expensive with reservations a good idea particularly on weekend nights. Metro: Metro Center.

Outer Circle Movie House *see* Cineplex Odeon Outer Circle.

Oxon Hill Farm 6411 Oxon Hill Rd., Oxon Hill, MD (301) 839-1177 www.nps .gov/nace/oxh

This farm is operated by the National Park Service and has the flavor of early twentieth-century rural life with its chickens, pigs, cows, horses, vegetables, and demonstrations of farm methods and crafts. It offers children the chance to watch milking by hand and plows drawn by horses and even help with some of the easier chores. Farm workers and guides are around to explain things to visitors. Open daily 8 a.m.–4:30 p.m. Admission free. Located about 10 miles from Washington just west of Indian Head Hwy. By car take the Washington Beltway (I-495) to Exit 3A, Indian Head Hwy. S, to Oxon Hill Rd.

Ozio 1813 M St. NW near 18th St. (202) 822-6000 www.oziodc.com

This spot bills itself as a martini and cigar lounge and that is an apt description for the wide choice of gin and vodka martinis to go with the stogies here. Open Mon–Thurs 5 p.m.–2 a.m., Fri–Sat 5 p.m.–3 a.m. Metro: Farragut West or Farragut North.

P Street NW Bridge P St. NW btw 23rd and 26th Sts.

This 1935 arched stone bridge was designed to harmonize with other bridges spanning Rock Creek Park. The contractor bid and was paid $194,054 for its construction. Unfortunately for him, construction cost $250,000. The site, pre-bridge, served as a fording point for General Lafayette and his Baltimore Light Dragoons. Metro: Dupont Circle.

Paddle Boats at the Tidal Basin *see* Tidal Basin Boathouse.

Pakistan Embassy 2315 Massachusetts Ave. NW (202) 939-6200 www.pakistan-em bassy.com

Embassy of the Islamic Republic of Pakistan.

The Palm 1225 19th St. NW at Jefferson Pl. (202) 293-9091

This is the place noted for its popularity with Washington's movers and shakers in politics, media, and sports with the walls bearing their caricatures to prove it. Celebrated for its fine steaks and lobster at expensive prices. Open for lunch Mon–Fri, dinner nightly. Reservations recommended. Metro: Dupont Circle.

Panama Embassy 2862 McGill Terrace NW (202) 483-1407

Pan-American Union *see* Organization of American States.

Panjshir 924 W Broad St. btw N Spring and N West Sts., Falls Church, VA (703) 536-4566

First-rate Afghan dishes including beef, lamb, and chicken kebabs, and fine meat and vegetarian stews over rice are served at this comfortable and relaxed restaurant. Prices are moderate and it is open for lunch Mon–Sat, dinner nightly. A second location is in Vienna, Virginia, at 224 Maple Ave. W between Courthouse Rd. SW and Pleasant St. SW (703) 281-4183. The Vienna branch is not open on Sunday.

Paolo's 1303 Wisconsin Ave. NW btw N and Dumbarton Sts. (202) 333-7353

This is a very popular Georgetown Italian restaurant/bar serving fine pasta, pizza, salads, and other savory dishes, frequented by locals and tourists for the moderately priced food and good wines. Open daily for lunch and dinner. Metro: Foggy Bottom-GWU, then 30, 32, 34, 35, or 36 Bus. There's a branch in Reston, Virginia, at 11898 Market St. in Reston Town Center (703) 318-8920.

Papua New Guinea Embassy 1779 Massachusetts Ave. NW, Suite 805 (202) 745-3680 www.pngembassy.org

Parades *see* Events in Washington D.C. and Environs, Events in Washington D.C. by Month.

Paraguay Embassy 2400 Massachusetts Ave. NW (202) 483-6960

Park Hyatt Washington 1201 24th St. NW at M St. (202) 789-1234 or (800) 223-1234 www.hyatt.com

This spacious luxury hotel with 224 smartly decorated rooms in the West End 4 blocks from Georgetown offers an elegant atmosphere and the full range of amenities from health club to pool, sauna, steam room, and more. Metro: Foggy Bottom-GWU.

Park Inn International 11410 Rockville Pike, Bethesda, MD (301) 881-5200 www.parkinnwashdc.com

Located near the White Flint Shopping Mall in north Bethesda on the heavily traveled extension of Wisconsin Ave. in the Maryland suburbs, this moderately priced motel has 157 recently renovated rooms and suites. Metro: White Flint.

Parks and History Association 44 Canal Center Plaza, Suite 5, Alexandria, VA (703) 535-1544 www.parksandhistory.org; Book store: Parks and History Association, Attn: Park Store, 4598 MacArthur Blvd. NW, Washington, D.C. 20007 (800) 990-7275, (202) 472-0631; Online bookstore site: www.parkexplorer.org

This nonprofit organization, an official partner to the National Park Service, was founded in 1968 to support the activities of the National Park Service. The association develops original interpretive print and electronic materials related to local parks, monuments, and historic sites, and operates twenty-five bookshops in these sites. Many books and items are specifically selected for school-age visitors. From Ford's Theatre, Arlington National Cemetery, to inside the Washington Monument, these bookstores offer relevant books and other items. The Web site offers around-the-clock book ordering of the same materials found in these special bookshops, lists locations of all the bookstores, and offers free downloadable photos related to the park sites. Central bookstore is open Mon–Fri 10 a.m.–5 p.m.

Parks and Playgrounds *see* Alexandria African American Heritage Park, Algonkian Regional Park, Anacostia Park, Bartholdi Park, Battery-Kemble Park, Black Hill Regional Park, Bull Run Regional Park, Burke Lake Park, Cabin John Regional Park, Cameron Run Regional Park, Capital Crescent Trail, Chesapeake and Ohio Canal National Historical Park, Dumbarton Oaks Park, Dupont Circle Memorial Park, Dyke Marsh, Fort Dupont Park, Fort Stevens, Fort Washington Park, Frances Scott Key Memorial Park, Franklin Park, George Washington Memorial Parkway, Glen Echo Park, Great Falls and Riverbend Parks, Green Spring Gardens Park, Greenbelt Park, Grist Mill Historical State Park, Huntley Meadows Park, John Marshall Park,

Kahlil Gibran Memorial Garden, Kalorama Park, Kenilworth Aquatic Gardens, Kidwell Farm, Kidzone, Lady Bird Johnson Park, Lake Accotink Park, Leesburg Animal Park, Leesylvania State Park, Lincoln Park, The Mall, Manassas National Battlefield Park, Meadowlark Gardens Regional Park, Meridian Hill Park, Montrose Park, National Wildlife Visitor Center, National Zoo, Pershing Park, Piscataway Park and National Colonial Farm, Pohick Bay Regional Park, Prince William Forest Park, Rawlins Park, Reston Zoo, Riverbend Park, Rock Creek Park, Rock Creek Regional Park, Rockville Civic Center Park, Sculpture Gardens Outdoor Rink, Seneca Creek State Park, Six Flags America, Theodore Roosevelt Island, Upton Hill Regional Park, Washington's Grist Mill Historical Park, Watkins Regional Park, West Potomac Park, Wolf Trap Farm Park for the Performing Arts, Woodend. *See also* www.trails.com.

Participatory Sports Activity *see* Active Sports Activity. *See also* Fitness Centers.

Pasta Mia 1790 Columbia Rd. at 18th St. (202) 328-9114
This is the place for an inexpensive Italian meal in Adams Morgan where the only choice is from a big variety of deliciously prepared pasta. Open for dinner Mon–Sat. Metro: Dupont Circle, then L2 Bus or Woodley Park-Zoo, then 90, 91, 92, 93, or 96 Bus.

Patent and Trademark Museum *see* U.S. Patent and Trademark Museum.

Patisserie Poupon 1645 Wisconsin Ave. NW btw Q St. and Reservoir Rd. (202) 342-3248
Some call this authentic Parisian pastry spot in Georgetown the best in the city for lovely tarts, cakes, and chocolate treats. The *salade niçoise*, oversized baguette sandwiches, and fine coffee are other good reasons for stopping in. Open Mon–Sat 8 a.m.–6:30 p.m., Sun 8 a.m.–4 p.m. Metro: Foggy Bottom-GWU, then 30, 32, 34, 35, or 36 Bus.

Patriot Center George Mason University, 4400 University Dr., Fairfax, VA (703) 993-3000 www.patriotcenter.com
This arena on the University campus seats 10,000 spectators at the men's and women's home basketball games but is also the venue for numerous country and popular music concerts and other family event specials throughout the year. For schedule information and other details call or check the Web site.

Patterson House *see* Washington Club.

Paul Garber Preservation, Restoration, and Storage Facility *see* Garber Preservation Restoration and Storage Facility.

Payne Memorial
This monument to John Howard Payne, the songwriter who created the celebrated "Home Sweet Home," is at R and 30th Sts. NW in Georgetown. The 1882 sculpture was the work of Moffet and Doyle. Metro: Foggy Bottom-GWU, then 30, 32, 34, 35, or 36 Bus.

Peace Monument Pennsylvania Ave. at 1st St. NW
This marble memorial was first called the Navy Memorial. The sculptor de-

signed it in 1877 to commemorate the American sailors who lost their lives during the Civil War. It features a number of allegorical figures among which is a female American weeping at the shoulder of the figure of History. The scroll held by History reads "They died that their country might live." Metro: Union Station.

Peking Gourmet Inn 6029 Leesburg Pike at Baileys Crossroads, Falls Church, VA (703) 671-8088

This is said to be the best restaurant in the area for the finest, crisp, fat-free Peking duck and it has long been a favorite. The menu features many other choices as well in this very large brightly lit restaurant where dinner reservations, particularly on weekends, are recommended. Open for lunch and dinner daily. Prices are moderate.

Penderbrook W Ox Rd. off Rte. 50, Fairfax, VA (703) 385-3700

This challenging golf course is a 5,927-yard par 72 course not far from Dulles Airport. By car take Hwy. 66 W to Rte. 50 and then take the first exit, W Ox Rd., toward Reston and turn right after the first traffic light.

Pennsylvania Avenue

If America has a Main Street, Pennsylvania Avenue may well be it. It is the broad thoroughfare from the Capitol to the White House along which triumphal newly inaugurated presidents travel to their new home at 1600 Pennsylvania Ave. For many decades this avenue was in decline but from the 1970s on, strenuous efforts have gone into rejuvenating, rebuilding, and upgrading the path block by block. It now boasts new plazas, hotels, shopping areas, and office buildings along the way so that the main artery of the city's downtown is no longer an eyesore but a source of national pride.

Pennsylvania Avenue NW Bridge Pennsylvania Ave. NW btw 26th and 28th Sts.

Completed at a cost of $121,032 in 1916, this low-arched bridge over Rock Creek covers a nineteenth-century engineering marvel: two 48-inch Washington Aqueduct pipes, now embedded into poured concrete, the largest single-span cast-iron arched structures in the world when put in place pre–Civil War. The present structure simply replaced an 1862 roadbed atop those pipes. Metro: Foggy Bottom-GWU.

The Pentagon I-395 at Washington Blvd., Arlington, VA (703) 695-1776 www .defenselink.mil/pubs/pentagon

This five-sided structure containing 6½ million square feet is the world's largest single-structure office building. It is the headquarters of the Department of Defense and covers 29 acres with a 5-acre courtyard at the center and holds 17½ miles of corridors and more than 20,000 civilian and military personnel. As a consequence of September 11, 2001, tours are restricted to only prearranged educational groups. Call to find out if the policy has been relaxed. Metro: Pentagon. *See also* www.com muterpage.com/venues/sightseeing_VA.htm.

Pentagon Center 1201 S Hayes St. at S 12th St., Arlington, VA (703) 413-8700

This mall across the street from the Fashion Center at Pentagon City is home to a number of superstores and restaurants. Among its occupants is Marshalls, a discount clothing department store, and Best Buy for home electronic products. Metro: Pentagon City.

Pentagon City

This area is located just south of the Pentagon in Arlington, Virginia, off Army-Navy Dr. It is a bedroom community with single-family homes and huge apartment complexes. But its primary claim to fame is the major shopping mall, Fashion Center at Pentagon City, which is located here right at the Pentagon City Metro stop, about half an hour's ride from downtown D.C.

Pentagon City Fashion Center *see* Fashion Center at Pentagon City.

Perry Belmont House *see* International Eastern Star Temple.

Perry's 1811 Columbia Rd. NW at 18th St. (202) 234-6218

There's lots of atmosphere at this Adams Morgan restaurant, which serves Japanese and American-Asian fusion dishes to diners reclining on couches. In mild weather the rooftop terrace is a big attraction. Open for dinner nightly at moderately expensive prices, and a big draw here is the Sunday brunch drag show 10:30 a.m.–2:30 p.m. Reservations for this are essential. Metro: Dupont Circle, then L2 Bus or Woodley Park-Zoo, then 90, 91, 92, 93, or 96 Bus.

Pershing Memorial

Located in Pershing Park on Pennsylvania Ave. between 14th and 15th Sts. NW, on the 14th St. side, this statue celebrates the victorious leader of the American Expeditionary Forces in France during World War I, Gen. John J. Pershing. The sculptor was Robert White. To the right of the statue is a granite wall with a map of Europe and description of the military campaigns. Metro: Metro Center.

Pershing Park

Situated on a small green area surrounded by 14th and 15th Sts. NW and Pennsylvania Ave., this park honors Gen. John J. Pershing. On the 15th St. side of the park there are shaded areas with benches and a large pond. The statue can be found on the 14th St. side. Metro: Metro Center.

Pershing Park Ice Rink Pennsylvania Ave. NW btw 14th and 15th Sts.

With the elegant Willard Hotel just opposite, this is one of the city's most popular ice-skating rinks. It is open only during the winter season. Admission charge. Skates are available for rental. For details on hours of operation call (202) 737-6938. Metro: Metro Center.

Persimmon 7003 Wisconsin Ave. btw Leland and Walsh Sts., Bethesda, MD (301) 654-9860

This is a smart restaurant located nearer Chevy Chase than to the main downtown Bethesda area. It serves an eclectic range of American bistro dishes with a Mediterranean slant in a storefront that has been renovated to appear colorfully exotic. Open for lunch Mon–Fri, dinner Mon–Sat. Metro: Bethesda.

Peru Embassy 1700 Massachusetts Ave. NW (202) 833-9860 www.peruemb.org

Pesce 2016 P St. NW btw 20th and 21st Sts. (202) 466-3474 www.robertodonna .com/pesce

This moderately priced menu-on-a-blackboard seafood specialty restaurant is a casual, busy place that can be counted on for good, fresh-fish dishes based on market availability. Open for lunch Mon–Sat, dinner nightly. Metro: Dupont Circle.

Petersen House 516 10th St. NW btw E and F Sts. (202) 426-6830 www.nps.gov/foth

Located across the street from Ford's Theatre, this is the boardinghouse where Lincoln was brought after being shot and where he died the next morning on April 15, 1865. The house, built in 1850, has been restored with period furniture and its three rooms on the 1st floor are open to the public daily 9 a.m.–5 p.m. Admission free. Metro: Metro Center or Gallery Pl.–Chinatown.

Petra's Skin Spa 3915 Old Lee Hwy., Fairfax, VA (703) 385-6800

Situated in the Old Town area of Fairfax this elegant and expensive center treats women to all sorts of facial therapies in a stylish and welcoming atmosphere. Open Tues and Thurs 10 a.m.–8 p.m., Wed and Fri–Sat 10 a.m. –6 p.m. By car take Little River Turnpike (Rte. 236) into the Fairfax shopping center area at Old Lee Hwy.

Pharmacy Bar 2337 18th St. NW at Belmont Rd. (202) 483-1200

This neighborhood watering hole in Adams Morgan features a wide range of brews at moderate prices and stays open late. The name reflects only the gimmicky tabletop fixtures. Open daily from 5 p.m. to last call. Metro: Woodley Park-Zoo, then 90, 91, 92, 93, or 96 Bus, or Dupont Circle then L2 Bus.

Philippines Embassy 1600 Massachusetts Ave. NW (202) 467-9300 www.philippineembassy-usa.org

Phillips Collection 1600 21st St. NW at Q St. (202) 387-2151 www.phillipscollection.org

Located in the former residential mansion of Duncan Phillips, this is the country's oldest museum of modern art. The main building and the annex, added in the 1980s, houses an extraordinary display of European and American nineteenth- and twentieth-century masterpieces of which Renoir's *Luncheon of the Boating Party* may be the most celebrated. Events sponsored by the museum include lectures, concerts, special exhibitions, symposia, gallery talks, and tours. The museum's Artful Evenings take place Thursdays 5 p.m.–8:30 p.m. featuring live music. Open Tues–Sat 10 a.m.–5 p.m., Sun noon–7 p.m. Suggested donation. Admission charge for special art showings. Metro: Dupont Circle.

Phillips Collection Sunday Chamber Music Concerts 1600 21st St. NW at Q St. (202) 387-2151 www.phillipscollection.org

A series of concerts are held in this museum from September to May on Sunday afternoons. For details call or check the Web site. Metro: Dupont Circle.

Phillips Flagship 900 Water St. SW off Maine Ave. (202) 488-8515 www.phillipsfoods.com

This seafood restaurant is giant sized and overlooks the Yacht Club Marina. It's open daily for lunch and dinner with the brunch buffet being the most popular selection by the crowds that arrive by tour bus for the moderately expensive meals. Metro: L'Enfant Plaza.

Pho 75 1711 Wilson Blvd. btw N Quinn and Rhodes Sts., Arlington, VA (703) 525-7355

This very modest Vietnamese spot serves only different versions of the wonderfully tasteful noodle broth with beef and vegetables that makes a meal. Open daily for lunch and dinner. Very inexpensive, but cash only. Metro: Court House or Rosslyn. Other locations at 3103 Graham Rd., Falls Church, VA (703) 204-1490; 771 Hungerford Dr., Rockville, MD (301) 309-8873.

Phoenix Park Hotel 520 N Capitol St. at Massachusetts Ave. (202) 638-6900 or (800) 824-5419 www.phoenixparkhotel.com

Calling itself the center of Irish hospitality in America, this deluxe hotel with 150 upscale rooms attracts Capitol Hill frequenters as well as tourists. It is home to the popular Dubliner Pub and is conveniently near Union Station and the Capitol. There is a state-of-the-art fitness facility here, too. Metro: Union Station.

Pier 7 650 Water St. SW near 7th St. (202) 554-2500

Located in the Channel Inn Hotel on the waterfront, this restaurant offers panoramic views as well as a selection of fresh seafood, pasta, and meat dishes, including a very good bouillabaisse, at moderate prices. Open for lunch and dinner Mon–Fri, Sat dinner, Sun brunch and dinner. Metro: Waterfront-SEU.

Pierce Mill 2311 Tilden St. NW at Beach Dr. (202) 426-6908 or (202) 895-6070 www.nps.gov/pimi or www.nps/rocr/piercemill

This is a restored 1820 stone building, which is home to a water-powered gristmill, one of eight that lined Rock Creek in the early nineteenth century. It is managed by the National Park Service and is open Wed–Sat noon–5 p.m. Metro: Cleveland Park then walk up Connecticut Ave. to Rodman St. and follow signs to Melvin Hazen Trail down to Rock Creek, and then turn left on West Ridge Trail and walk for a few minutes to the mill.

Pike Statue *see* Albert Pike Statue.

Pimlico Race Course Hayward and Winner Aves., Baltimore, MD (410) 542-9400 www.pimlico.com

This is the second oldest racetrack (from 1743) in the United States, after the one in Saratoga. Baltimore is beyond the bounds of this book, and this entry is included only because of the famous Preakness Stakes thoroughbred race on the third Saturday in May. The racing seasons here are April to June and July to September. Call for information about schedules and tickets or check the Web site. From Washington take Amtrak from Union Station to Baltimore's Penn Station and then take a taxi, or simply drive up by car.

Pines of Rome 4709 Hampton Lane off Wisconsin Ave., Bethesda, MD (301) 657-8775

This is a solid, reliable, and authentic old-fashioned Italian restaurant serving pastas with fine sauces, fish and meat specials, and pizzas, in hearty portions that are well prepared, tasty, and budget priced. It's a great family favorite that's open daily for lunch and dinner. Metro: Bethesda.

Piscataway Park and National Colonial Farm 3400 Bryan Point Rd. at Cactus Hill Rd., Accokeek, MD (301) 283-2115

This is a restoration of an eighteenth-century plantation across the Potomac River on the Maryland side opposite Mount Vernon. The park is open daily from dawn to dusk. The farm, open Tues–Sun 10 a.m.–5 p.m., is operated to portray historical authenticity in methods and equipment used two centuries ago in raising farm animals and growing vegetables and farm crops. There is a visitors center and a display in the barn of the farm tools customarily used by those who worked on the plantation. Modest admission charge. By car take Exit 3A off the Beltway (I-495) and take Rte. 210 south 9.2 miles before turning onto Farmington Rd. and proceeding 4 miles to the park.

Pizzeria Paradiso 2029 P St. NW btw 20th and 21st Sts. (202) 223-1245

Typically, long lines form here for the flavorful crusty and chewy wood-fired pizzas with inventive toppings. They also serve other dishes for dine-in or carry-out. Open daily for lunch and dinner at affordable prices with no reservations accepted. Metro: Dupont Circle.

Pizzerias *see* Coppie's, Faccia Luna, Generous George's Positive Pizza, Julio's, Ledo, Luigi's, Millie and Al's, Pizzeria Paradiso. *See also* Italian Restaurants.

Places of Worship *see* Churches, Mosques, Synagogues.

Places That Appeal to Children and Teens *see* Adventure Theater, Al's Magic Shop, Bureau of Engraving and Printing, Children's Concierge, Children's Theater, Garrett's, Glen Echo Park, Imagination Stage, J. Edgar Hoover FBI Building, A Likely Story, MCI Center, Made By You, National Aquarium, National Geographic Society Explorers Hall, National Zoo, Oxon Hill Farm, Puppet Company Playhouse, Rainbow Company, Reston Zoo, Rock Creek Nature Center and Planetarium, Saturday Morning at the National Theater, Smithsonian Carousel, Smithsonian Discovery Theater, Sportrock I II III, Strathmore Hall Arts Center, Textile Museum, Uncle Beazley, Washington National Cathedral Medieval Arts and Crafts Workshops, Washington Monument, Washington Navy Yard. *See also* Museums of Particular Interest to Children, Parks and Playgrounds, www.frommers.com, Wolf Trap Farm Park for the Performing Arts, YMCA of Metropolitan Washington, YWCA.

Planet Hollywood 1101 Pennsylvania Ave. at 11th St. (202) 783-7827

The food is standard burgers, salads, and pizzas so it has to be the displays of unique Hollywood memorabilia and continuously running film clips on TV screens that draw in the endless stream of tourists. Open daily for lunch and dinner at moderate prices. Metro: Federal Triangle or Metro Center.

Pleasant Valley Golfers Club 4715 Pleasant Valley Rd., Chantilly, VA (703) 631-7902

Located off Rte. 50 south of Dulles Airport, this 6,957-yard 18-hole course is well maintained in a lovely setting with trees, grassy meadows, wildflowers, and water elements. Call for green fees and starting times.

Poetry Readings *see* Book and Poetry Readings.

Pohick Bay Regional Park 6501 Pohick Bay Dr., Lorton, VA (703) 339-6104 www .norpa.org/pohickbay

Located in southeastern Fairfax County and open year-round, this park has attractive water features including an enormous outdoor swimming pool, and sailboat and pedal-boat rentals. There is also miniature golf, an 18-hole golf course, nature and equestrian trails, picnic tables, and campsites. Open daily 8 a.m.–dusk. Admission charge and fees for swimming, golf, and other activities. By car take Hwy. I-95 south to Lorton Exit 163, turn left and go ½ mile to Armistead Rd. Turn right, and at first light at Rte.1, go south. At third light turn left on Gunston Rd. (Rte. 224) and proceed to park.

Pohick Bay Regional Park Golf Course 10301 Gunston Rd. off U.S. Hwy. 1, Lorton, VA (703) 339-8585

This challenging course is run by the Northern Virginia Regional Park Authority. It is a hilly 6,405-yard, par 72, 18-hole course with a driving range and pro shop. Call for tee times and fees. By car take Hwy. I-95 south to Lorton Exit 163, turn left and go ½ mile to Armistead Rd. Turn right, and at first light at Rte.1, go south. At third light turn left onto Gunston Rd. (Rte. 224) and proceed to park and golf course.

Pohick Church 9301 Richmond Hwy. (U.S. Hwy. 1), Lorton, VA (703) 550-9449

Built in 1774 from George Washington's plans, this Episcopal Church has undergone numerous periods of damage and reconstruction since it was the congregating center of the Washington and George Mason families. It remains an active parish. Metro: Pentagon, then Metrobus 9A toward Lorton VRE, stop at Telegraph Rd. and Belvoir Woods Pkwy. Then walk 1 block south on Telegraph Rd., then right 2 blocks on Richmond Hwy.

Poland Embassy 2640 16th St. NW (202) 234-3800 www.polandembassy.org

Political Americana in Union Station, 50 Massachusetts Ave. NE (202) 547-1685

This shop stocks vintage campaign buttons, bumper stickers, and political posters as well as books and gifts for political buffs of every persuasion. Open Mon–Fri 10 a.m.–6 p.m., Sat–Sun 10 a.m.–7 p.m. Metro: Union Station.

Politics and Prose 5015 Connecticut Ave. NW btw Fessenden St. and Nebraska Ave. (202) 364-1919 www.politics-prose.com

This independent bookstore and café features one of the most frequent and popular programs of author appearances and readings in town, sponsors a book club, and distributes a newsletter. It also carries a line of books for children and is a comfortable and hospitable place to browse. Open Mon–Thurs 9 a.m.–10 p.m., Fri–Sat 9 a.m.–11 p.m., Sun 11 a.m.–7 p.m. Metro: Van Ness-UDC, then L1 or L2 Bus.

Politiki 319 Pennsylvania Ave. SE btw 3rd and 4th Sts. (202) 546-1001

There are three bars on different levels here. The basement features a tiki bar, the ground floor has a Polynesian motif, and the floor above that is something that resembles a dance hall lost in a time warp with posters from World War II, sometimes with dancing or game-watching on TV screens. Something's always going on on every floor. Open Mon–Thurs 4 p.m.–1:30 p.m., Fri–Sat 4 p.m.–2:30 a.m. or 3:30 a.m. Call to learn about specials. Metro: Eastern Market or Capitol South.

Polly Esther's 605 12th St. btw F and G Sts. (202) 737-1970

The music at this dance spot draws on the '70s and '80s, bringing disco excitement to D.C., featuring a *Saturday Night Fever* dance floor. Another floor offers the Culture Club—flashing back to the '80s with music and memorabilia. There's even a 3rd-floor '90s club. Open and enthusiastically rocking Thurs 5 p.m.–2 a.m., Fri 5 p.m.–3 a.m., Sat 8 p.m.–3 a.m. Higher cover charge on weekend nights. Metro: Metro Center.

Polo *see* Georgetown Polo Club.

Pomander Way

Located in Georgetown, this miniscule dead-end mews off Volta Pl. between 33rd and 34th Sts. NW comprises ten charming pastel-colored residential row houses, transforming what had been a neglected and decrepit alley as late as the 1950s into a lovely group of dwellings. Metro: Foggy Bottom-GWU, then 30, 32, 34, 35, or 36 Bus.

Pool *see* Atomic Billiards, Babe's Billiards, Bedrock Billiards, Buffalo Billiards, Carpool, Champion Billiards, Dr. Dremo's Tap House, Fast Eddie's.

Pope John Paul II Cultural Center 3900 Harewood Rd. NE off Michigan Ave. (202) 635-5400 www.JP2cc.org

Located opposite Catholic University in a striking recent architectural addition to the Washington scene, this gracious and tranquil center provides a place for visitors to pursue their spiritual paths. The displays include memorabilia of this pope's personal and papal life and interactive computer and audiovisual exhibits help visitors explore and understand better the role of faith in modern life. There are also showings of artistic works from the Vatican's collections. Open Tues–Sat 10 a.m.–6 p.m., Sun noon–5 p.m. Admission charge. Metro: Brookland-CUA. *See also* www.commuterpage.com/venues/museums.htm.

Pope-Leighey House *see* Frank Lloyd Wright's Pope Leighey House.

Popular Music *see* Armed Forces Concerts, Carter Barron Amphitheater, District Curators, MCI Center, Merriweather Post Pavilion, Nisson Pavilion at Stone Ridge, RFK Stadium, Sylvan Theater, Transparent Productions, Washington Performing Arts Society, Wolf Trap Farm Park for the Performing Arts.

Portugal Embassy 2125 Kalorama Rd. NW (202) 328-8610 www.portugalemb.org

Positano 4940 Fairmont Ave. btw Old Georgetown Rd. and Norfolk Ave., Bethesda, MD (301) 654-1717

This popular Italian restaurant located in Bethesda's busy dining neighborhood serves well-prepared dishes in a pleasant ambiance with a front patio open in mild weather. Open daily for lunch and dinner. Prices are moderate. Metro: Bethesda.

Post Office Pavilion *see* Old Post Office Building.

Post Office Tower *see* Old Post Office Building.

Post Pub 1422 L St. NW btw 14th and 15th Sts. (202) 628-2111

Taking its name from its spiritual ties to the *Washington Post* around the corner, this watering hole has the flavor of an English private club with its wooden booths, gold metal ceiling, and clientele in suits. The drinks and bar food are moderately priced, and there is usually a crowd of downtown professionals, journalists, and somewhat younger wannabe's around lunchtime and early evenings. Open Mon–Fri 11 a.m.–midnight, Sat 11 a.m.–8 p.m. Metro: McPherson Square.

Potomac

This is among the most affluent of the city's suburbs. Located close to Rockville, Maryland, this community is noted for the spacious grounds and posh residential dwellings occupied by some of Washington's elite, with fine public and private schools and well-manicured golf courses. It is accessible to the city from the Clara Barton Pkwy., which runs parallel to the Potomac River down into Canal Rd. and Georgetown. Potomac is bounded by Wooten Pkwy. on the north, Seven Locks Rd. on the east, Tuckerman Lane on the south, and the Potomac River on the west.

Potomac Cannons G. Richard Pfitzner Stadium, 7 County Complex Court off Davis Ford Rd., Woodbridge, VA (703) 590-2311 www.potomaccannons.com

This Class-A minor league affiliate of the St. Louis Cardinals plays its home games here in the same Carolina league that includes the Durham Bulls of movie fame. Like most minor-league baseball teams, this one enjoys enthusiastic support and has inexpensively priced games from April to September in its 6,000-seat stadium. For schedule and ticket information call or check the Web site.

Potomac Mills 2700 Potomac Mills Circle, south of Prince William Pkwy., Dale City, VA (703) 643-1770 or (800) VA MILLS www.potomacmills.com

This mile-long shoppers' paradise is located at the Potomac Mills exit off Hwy. I-95 near Woodbridge, Virginia. It is 15 miles south of the Washington Beltway (I-495), and some 30 minutes from downtown D.C. It bills itself as the state's leading tourist attraction, and it contains more than 220 stores, some twenty eateries, and even a multi-screen movie house, and, of course, endless hordes of voracious bargain hunters, especially on weekends. Open every day. *See also* www.commuter page.com/venues/venue-shop.htm.

Potomac Park

This is the city's 722-acre playground along the river and is divided into West Potomac Park and East Potomac Park. West Potomac Park features such attractions as views of the Lincoln and Jefferson Memorials, Constitution Gardens, the Franklin D. Roosevelt Memorial, the Vietnam Veterans Memorial, Vietnam Women's Memorial, Korean War Veterans Memorial, and the Tidal Basin ringed by the 3,000 renowned Japanese cherry trees. There is more room to relax and roam around in the East Potomac Park where the facilities include a golf course, picnic grounds, tennis courts, swimming pool, and biking and hiking trails. The 5-mile loop around East Potomac Park is Washington's most extensive path directly beside the water. To reach the parks by car from downtown, take 14th St. toward the 14th Street Bridge and take the Ohio Dr. Exit, which to the north leads to West Potomac Park, and East Potomac Park to the south. The Potomac River bounds both parks on the west. Constitution Ave. is the northern boundary of West Potomac Park, which merges with the Mall on the east and joins East Potomac Park to the south. The remaining boundaries of East Potomac Park are the Potomac River on the west and the Washington Channel on the east.

Potomac River Jazz Club (703) 698-7752 or (202) 244-6636 www.prjc.org

This group is dedicated to the encouragement and preservation of jazz, ragtime, and blues music. It sponsors its own membership events and helps to publicize and promote jazz concerts and performances in the greater Washington, D.C., area through its newsletter and its Web site. Call for details on upcoming music events or check the Web site.

Potomac Riverboat Company

Between April and October this tour group offers narrated cruises from the dock at the Alexandria City marina behind the Torpedo Factory Art Center at King and Union Sts. in Old Town Alexandria and also from Washington Harbour in Georgetown at 31st and K Sts. NW. For information about schedules and prices phone (703) 548-9000 or (703) 684-0580 or check the Web site: www.potomacriver boatco.com.

Potomac Spirit

The *Potomac Spirit* fleet offers one 2-hour tour to Mount Vernon, while the other features a sailing trip accompanied by live entertainment along the river past the Washington and Old Town Alexandria sights. Both tours start from Pier 4 at 6th and Water Sts. SW in Washington. Information on schedules and prices at (202) 554-8000 or (202) 554-8013 or check the Web site: www.spiritcruises.com.

Prime Rib 2020 K St. NW btw 20th and 21st Sts. (202) 466-8811 www.theprime rib.com

Well-aged prime beef and excellent fresh fish are the attractions here in a clubby environment of wood and leather. The atmosphere is formal, the portions robust, and the prices very expensive. Reservations are recommended and jacket and tie required. Open for lunch Mon–Fri, dinner Mon–Sat. Metro: Foggy Bottom-GWU or Farragut West.

Primi Piatti 2013 I St. NW btw 20th and 21st Sts. (202) 223-3600 www.primipiatti .com

This trendy and busy Italian restaurant in Foggy Bottom specializes in antipasto and pasta choices. It is invariably crowded, so reservations are a good idea. Prices are moderately expensive. Open Mon–Fri for lunch, dinner Mon–Sat. Metro: Foggy Bottom-GWU.

Prince George's Community College 301 Largo Rd., Largo, MD (301) 336-6000 www.pg.cc.md.us

This community educational institution accepts all applicants to its programs in a wide range of study areas. Courses are offered at the main campus and at extension sites to the 40,000 young and older student body enrolled in credit and adult-learning courses.

Prince George's County Conference and Visitors Bureau 9200 Basil Court, Suite 101, Largo, MD (301) 925-8300 www.visitprincegeorges.com

Open Mon–Fri 9 a.m.–5 p.m. with information on county tourism questions available by telephone or at the Web site.

Prince George's County Farmers Market in the parking lot of the Ellen Linson Swimming Pool Complex, 5211 Calvert Rd. btw Kenilworth Ave. and U.S. Hwy. 1, College Park, MD (301) 277-3717

Fruit and vegetables are sold by their producers from May to November on Saturdays 7 a.m.–noon.

Prince George's Plaza 3500 E West Hwy. at Riverdale Rd., Hyattsville, MD (301) 559-8383

This is a large complex of department stores, fashion and jewelry shops, as well as dining and entertainment spots. Metro: Prince George's Plaza. *See also* www .commuterpage.com/venues/venue-shop.htm.

Prince George's Publick Playhouse for the Performing Arts *see* Publick Playhouse.

Prince Royal Gallery 204 S Royal St. at Prince St., Alexandria, VA (703) 548-5151 www.princeroyalgallery.com

This Old Town gallery is located in what was the historic Concordia Hotel built in 1880. The main display gallery is the hotel's former ballroom with enormous windows, fine light, and a handsome tin ceiling. There are six or seven shows a year here, as well as a permanent exhibit of watercolors, etchings, and limited edition prints by P. Buckley Moss. Open Tues–Thurs and Sat 11 a.m.–5 p.m., Fri 11 a.m.–7 p.m., Sun 1 p.m.–5 p.m. Metro: Braddock Road, then DAT34 DASH Bus toward Hunting Towers Loop to S Royal St. and King St. Then walk 1 block south. *See also* www.commuterpage.com/venues/sightseeing_VA.htm.

Prince William Forest Park on Park Headquarters Rd., Triangle, VA (703) 221-7181 www.nps.gov/prwi

This parkland stretches over 18,500 acres of Quantico Creek's watershed containing thick forests of hardwood and pine trees. There are some 35 miles of hiking and biking trails and camping sites as well as cabins. Open daily dawn to dusk with the visitor center open 8:30 a.m.–5 p.m. Small vehicle admission charge. By car take I-95 South to Exit 50W and go a short way to the park entrance on the right.

Princely Bed and Breakfast (800) 470-5588 www.alexandriabandb.com

This rental agency offers a wide range of accommodations in Old Town Alexandria, Virginia, at different price levels. During peak periods a two-day minimum stay may be required.

Professional Soccer *see* Soccer (Spectator Sport).

Progressive Review (Web site) www.prorev.com

This Washington-based Web site provides links to an enormous range of organizations, publications, and other Web sites, and a "DC Daybook" of the day's news events and federal and congressional activities. It also includes a compilation of information on topical issues, such as "Behind the Bushes," "Clinton Legacy," and "Sex and Crime in Washington." Its masthead reads "Inside the Beltway, out of the loop, and ahead of the curve, edited by Sam Smith, since 1964 Washington's most unofficial source."

Prospect House 3508 Prospect St. NW off 35th St.

This Georgetown Federal-style townhouse was built in the late eighteenth century with modifications in the mid-nineteenth century and restoration in the 1930s. The original architect was J. W. Adams. It is not only the fine features of this house but the splendid view of the river from its site that command interest. Not open for visitors. Metro: Foggy Bottom-GWU, then 30, 32, 34, 35, or 36 Bus.

La Provence 144 W Maple Ave., Vienna, VA (703) 242-3777

Situated in a shopping strip about a mile from the Metro this attractive dining place features Provençal dishes as authentic as they are appetizing. Open for lunch Mon–Sat, dinner nightly. Prices are moderately expensive and reservations are suggested. Metro: Vienna/Fairfax-GMU.

Ptak Science Books *see* J. F. Ptak Science Books.

Public Lectures *see* The Women's Center, The Writer's Center. *See also* Book and Poetry Readings.

Public Toilets *see* Rest Rooms.

Public Transportation *see* Buses, Metro.

Publick Playhouse 5445 Landover Rd. near intersection with Rte. 450, Cheverly, MD (301) 277-1710 www.pgparks.com

This theater seats about 450 and is under the umbrella of the Maryland National Capital Park and Planning Commission. The official designation is Prince George's Public Playhouse for the Performing Arts, and it is the venue for concerts, dramatic and musical attractions, and other types of performances. Call for program details or check the Web site. Metro: Cheverly, then F2 Bus, or New Carrollton, then T18 Bus.

Puck Fountain

This 4-foot-marble-statue reminder of the playful Shakespearean character from *A Midsummer Night's Dream* can be found in front of the fountain on the west side of the Folger Shakespeare Library at E Capitol St. and 2nd St NE. Brenda Putnam sculpted it in 1932. Metro: Union Station or Capitol South.

Pulaski Statue

This equestrian monument celebrating the Polish general, Count Casimir Pulaski, who left his home to fight in the American Revolutionary War battles, can be found at Pennsylvania Ave. and 13th St. NW. It was erected in 1910 and its sculptor was Kasimir Chodzinski. Metro: Federal Triangle.

Puppet Company Playhouse Glen Echo Park, 7300 MacArthur Blvd., Glen Echo, MD (301) 320-6668

Featuring hand puppets, rod puppets, marionettes, and shadow puppets, this company presents classic fairy tales and original stories during productions all through the year. It is the only theater in the east completely given over to puppet shows. Performances are normally Wed–Fri at 10 a.m. and 11:30 a.m., and Sat–Sun 11:30 a.m. and 1 p.m. For schedule and ticket information call or check the Web site: www.nps.gov/glec/gepuppet.htm.

Puppet Theaters *see* Discovery Theater, Puppet Company Playhouse, Smithsonian Discovery Theater, Wolf Trap Farm Park for the Performing Arts.

Pushkin Statue

This bronze 10-foot-tall monument honoring one of Russia's most celebrated literary notables, Alexander Pushkin, can be found at the corner of 22nd and H Sts. NW in the George Washington University campus area. The sculptor was Alexander Bourganov and the statue was completed in 2000. It is believed to be the first monument in the country to a Russian writer. Metro: Foggy Bottom-GWU.

Qatar Embassy 4200 Wisconsin Ave. NW, Suite 200 (202) 274-1600

Quality Hotel Courthouse Plaza 1200 N Courthouse Rd. at Wilson St. and U.S. 50, Arlington, VA (703) 524-4000 or (800) 228-5151 www.choicehotels.com
 This is a large, comfortable, near-to-town, moderately priced hotel with good-sized rooms and suites that offers a giant outdoor pool, a sauna, an exercise facility, and free parking. It is a popular place with families and the suites include kitchens. Metro: Court House.

Quality Inn Iwo Jima 1501 Arlington Blvd. (Rte. 50), Arlington, VA (703) 524-5000 or (800) 424-1501
 This budget-priced hotel is within walking distance of the Metro station and the Marine Corps War Memorial from which it takes its name. There are 141 rooms, free parking, an indoor/outdoor heated pool, and a fitness center. Metro: Rosslyn.

Queen Anne Row Houses 638-642 E Capitol St. NE btw 6th and 7th Sts.
 Situated on Capitol Hill, these three handsome houses boast such features as gable roofs and beautiful stained glass transom windows. They were constructed in the late nineteenth century by architect/builder Charles Gessford and are not open to visitors. Metro: Eastern Market.

Queen Bee 3181 Wilson Blvd. btw N Hudson and N Irving Sts., Arlington, VA (703) 527-3444
 This exceedingly popular Vietnamese restaurant serves well-prepared Oriental dishes at budget prices and is 1 block from the Metro station. Open daily for lunch and dinner. Metro: Clarendon.

Queen Isabella I Statue
 Located in front of the entry to the Organization of American States building at 17th St. and Constitution Ave. NW, this memorial to the sponsor of Columbus's journey to the New World was a gift from Spain in 1966. Metro: Farragut West.

Quick Pita 1210 Potomac St. NW btw M and Prospect Sts. (202) 338-7482

There are few places to sit in this miniscule storefront, but the tasty Middle Eastern fare attracts Georgetown strollers seeking a fast bite as much for the savory budget choices as for the fact that it's almost never closed. Open daily from 11 a.m. Closes Sun–Thurs at 3 a.m., and Fri–Sat at 5:30 a.m. Metro: Foggy Bottom-GWU, then 30, 32, 34, 35, or 36 Bus.

R

RFK Stadium 2400 E Capitol St. SE, box office (202) 547-9077 www.dcarmory.com/rfk_stadium

Built in 1961, this former home of the Redskins football team is the venue of athletic events and music concerts and hosts the Washington Freedom and D.C. United, Washington's professional soccer teams. For ticket information, call the box office. Metro: Stadium/Armory. *See also* www.commuterpage.com/venues/venue-sp.htm.

RFK Stadium Farmers Market *see* D.C. Open Air Farmers Market.

Racquetball *see* D.C. Jewish Community Center, National Capital YMCA, Radisson Plaza Hotel, Sheraton Premiere at Tysons Corner.

Radicchio *see* Il Radicchio under I.

Radio Stations in Metropolitan Washington

Stations offering live Internet audio from their Web sites (LIAS) are indicated along with their Web site addresses.

FM Radio Stations

88.1 WMUC University of Maryland–College Park. Student station, mix

88. 5 WAMU American University. With National Public Radio material, talk, news, bluegrass, LIAS www.wamu.org

89.3 WPFW Pacifica Foundation station. Real jazz, talk, news, some BBC, LIAS www.wpfw.net

90.1 WCSP C-SPAN owned. Live coverage of Congress and hearings, press conferences, talk shows, LIAS www.c-span.org

90.9 WETA WETA-TV PBS owned. News, talk, some National Public Radio programs, some BBC, LIAS www.weta.org/fm

91.5 WBJC Baltimore City Community College. Classical music, 50,000 watts; can be heard in D.C. area, LIASwww.bccc.state.md.us/bcccfacilities.html/radio.html

91.9 WGTS Columbia Union College, Takoma Park. Religious, LIAS www.wgts.org

93.9 WKYS Radio One owned. Urban contemporary (hip-hop and soul)

94.7 WARW Stands for "We Always Rock Washington." Infinity-CBS owned. Classic rock

95.5 WPGC Infinity-CBS owned. Urban contemporary

95.9 WWIN Light rock from Glen Burnie, Maryland

96.3 WHUR Howard University owned. Urban contemporary

97.1 WASH Clear Channel owned. Adult contemporary (soft rock), LIAS www.wash-fm.com

98.7 WMZQ Clear Channel owned. Country music, LIAS www.wmzq.com

99.5 WIHT Clear Channel owned. Adult, urban contemporary

100.3 WBIG Clear Channel owned. For "Big" oldies. Old-time rock, LIAS www.oldies100.com

101.1 WWDC Clear Channel owned. Rock

102.3 WMMJ Radio One owned. Urban, adult contemporary

103.5 WGMS Bonneville International owned. Classical, LIAS www.wgms.com

104.1 WWZZ Bonneville International owned. Adult contemporary, LIAS www.thez.com

105.1 WAVA Salem Broadcasting owned. Religious, talk

105.7 WXYV Infinity-CBS owned. Urban contemporary

105.9 WJZW Disney-ABC/WMAL owned. Light jazz, LIAS www.smoothjazz1059.com

106.7 WJFK Infinity-CBS owned. Talk

107.3 WRQX Disney-ABC/WMAL owned. Contemporary, LIAS www.mix1073fm.com

107.7 WTOP WTOP owned. Simulcasts WTOP's AM 1500/820 all-news broadcasts, LIAS www.wtopnews.com and www.federalnewsradio.com

AM Radio Stations

570 WTNT VerStandig Broadcasting owned. Talk and news

630 WMAL ABC-Disney owned. Talk and news

730 WKDL Mega Communications owned. Spanish music and talk

780 WABS Salem Broadcasting owned. Religious and talk, LIAS www.wabs.com

900 WILC ILC Corporation owned. Spanish

930 WFMD AMFM owned. Talk and news

950 WCTN Seven Locks Broadcasting owned. Religious

980 WTEM Clear Channel owned. Sports talk, LIAS www.sportstalk980.com

1050 WPLC Multicultural Broadcasting owned. Spanish talk and music

1120 WUST New World Radio owned. Ethnic multi-lingual, LIAS www.wust1120.com

1150 WMET Beltway Communications owned. Business news, LIAS www.wmet.kivex.com

1220 WFAX Newcomb Broadcasting owned. Religious

1260 WWRC Clear Channel owned. Business news and talk

1310 WDCT Family Radio Owned. Korean

1340 WYCB Radio One owned. Religious

1390 WZHF Multicultural Broadcasting owned. Multi-ethnic

1450 WOL Radio One owned. Talk

1500 WTOP Bonneville International owned. News, sports. Covers U.S. government at www.federalnews radio.com, LIAS

1540 WACA Los Cerezos Television Corp. owned. Spanish

1600 WKDM Mega Communications owned. Spanish

Washington Area Internet Only Radio Stations

www.eradiomet.com From Montgomery College in Rockville, MD. Adult contemporary, oldies

www.wtop2.com Federal News Radio in Washington D.C. World and local news and federal government; news briefings and events

www.planetpopradio.com Zero Population Growth runs this international pop station from Washington.

www.radiodelray.com Radio Del Ray. Eclectic/blues/talk from Alexandria, VA

www.radiomojo.com RadioMojo provides a spectrum of rock from Silver Spring, MD

www.skyfm.com Sky FM offers progressive rock from Alexandria, VA

www.fcas.org/webr/ Web Radio offers local groups access to a microphone via the Fairfax, VA, Public Access (Cable) Corporation.

www.wgmuradio.com George Mason University students operate this station. Provides a wide variety of programs.

www.wmuc.umd.edu Students from University of Maryland-College Park operate this station. Provides a wide range of programs.

Radisson Barcelo Hotel 2121 P St. (202) 293-3100 www.radisson.com

This 301-room hotel's location can't be beat: a block away from Dupont Circle with its restaurants, shops, galleries, bars, and Metro stop, and close to Georgetown and its similar attractions. Two blocks away is Rock Creek Park. The guest rooms are large—the property was once an apartment building—with the usual amenities of the Radisson chain, as well as a business center, sauna, outdoor pool, and fitness center. Nuevo Latino cuisine is served at the Gabriel Restaurant. Moderately expensive. Metro: Dupont Circle.

Radisson Plaza Hotel Mark Center, 5000 Seminary Rd., Alexandria, VA (703) 845-1010 www.radisson.com

This spacious 30-story hotel with 500 rooms is located off I-395 and is 10 minutes by free shuttle from Reagan National Airport. Besides the usual plentiful Radisson amenities, there are indoor and outdoor swimming pools, an exercise room, tennis and racquetball courts, a game room, four restaurants, lounge, barber-shop, and free parking. Moderate rates. Metro: Pentagon with 30-minute shuttles 6 a.m.–11 p.m. daily.

Rainbow Company P.O. Box 12493, Burke, VA 22009 (703) 239-0037 http:// home.earthlink.net/~reciact/

Since 1991, this innovative program, using trained actors and professional storytellers, has been introducing children of all ages to theater and classic children's stories. The performances are "interactive," in that audience members are included in the presentations, and after the show, they can try on costumes and talk to the actors. Performances and a variety of enrichment programs are scheduled in schools and public libraries throughout the greater Washington area. Phone for details or check the Web site.

Rainforest Café Tysons Corner Center, 1961 Chain Bridge Rd., McLean, VA (703) 821-0247 www.rainforestcafe.com

Washington Families Magazine's reader poll lists this institution among the "best restaurants for kids," and for you grown-ups, "best fine dining with kids." It's fun even if you don't bring the kids, has first-rate American cuisine, and a full bar. But this chain's popularity is its rainforest environment, complete with monsoon thunder and periodic showers, trumpeting elephants, talking trees, chest-thumping gorillas, and a live parrot show. Open Mon–Thurs 11 a.m.–10 p.m., Fri 11 a.m.–11 p.m., Sat 10:30 a.m.–11 p.m., Sun 10:30 a.m.–9 p.m. Reservations accepted. There can be a considerable wait. Metro: Rosslyn, then take Metrobus 15K to Tysons Corner, or exit Metro at West Falls Church and take Metrobus 28B to Tysons Corner. By car from I-495 (the Beltway) take Exit 123 (Chain Bridge Rd.), toward Tysons Corner/Vienna. Bear right on Chain Bridge Rd.

Raku—An Asian Diner 1900 Q St. NW (202) 657-7528 and 7240 Woodmont Ave., Bethesda, MD (301) 718-8680

These prototypes for chef-restaurateur Mark Miller's coming-soon chain are founded on the premise that Asian street-stall food trumps American fast food. Fast it is, with Bangkok noodles, yakitori, lemongrass chicken, squid sticks, *mooshi* pancakes, or duck dumplings arriving minutes after ordering. And tasty: witness the lively crowds mostly on stools noshing on salads, noodles, skewers, dumplings, and wraps. Q St. open Sun–Thurs 11:30 a.m.–2:30 p.m. and 5 p.m.–10 p.m., Fri and Sat noon–3 p.m. and 5 p.m.–10:30 p.m., Sun noon–3 p.m. and 5 p.m.–10 p.m. Metro: Dupont Circle; Woodmont Ave.: Sun–Thurs 11:30 a.m.–10 p.m., Fri–Sat 11:30 a.m.–11 p.m. Metro: Bethesda.

Raljon Stadium *see* FedEx Field.

Ramsey House 221 King St., Alexandria, VA (703) 838-4200 www.cybvis.com/alex/ ramsey.htm

Built in 1724, this oldest surviving house in Alexandria was the home of William Ramsey, who entertained his friend George Washington here on inaugural eve. Extensively restored, the building now houses the Alexandria Convention and Visitors Bureau, which provides tourists with brochures and tour information. Open daily

9 a.m.–5 p.m. Closed Thanksgiving Day, Christmas Day, and New Year's Day. Metro: King Street, then a 9-block walk.

Randolph Statue at Union Square *see* A. Philip Randolph Statue at Union Station.

Raspberry Falls Golf and Hunt Club 41601 Raspberry Dr., Leesburg, VA (703) 779-2555 www.raspberryfalls.com

This par 72 course surrounded by rolling hills was designed by Gary Player. There is a pro shop, full grill, practice sand bunkers, a chipping green, and a driving range as well. The Loudoun Hunt West fox-hunting club shares the grounds during the fall, winter, and early spring hunt season. By car it is off Hwy. 15, 3 miles north of Leesburg.

Rawlins Park 18th and E Sts. NW (202) 619-7222 www.dcheritage.org

This small green rectangle offers not only a statue of Maj. Gen. John A. Rawlins, chief of staff to Gen. Ulysses S. Grant and his first secretary of war, but a couple of shallow pools with water lilies, tulip trees, and in spring, an explosion of blooming magnolias. Metro: Foggy Bottom-GWU, then a 10-minute walk.

Rawlins Statue Rawlins Park, E St. btw 18th and 19th Sts. NW

This 8-foot sculpture of Gen. John A. Rawlins by Joseph A. Bailey reportedly is cast from melted cannon, which the general's forces captured in the Civil War. Rawlins rose from being aide-de-camp to General Grant to chief of staff of Union forces, and finally, secretary of war in Grant's first administration. Metro: Foggy Bottom-GWU, then a 10-minute walk.

Reagan Building and International Trade Center *see* Ronald Reagan Building and International Trade Center.

Reagan National Airport George Washington Pkwy., Arlington, VA Information (703) 417-8000, Parking (703) 417-4311 www.mwaa.com

Airline arrival/departure times: www.flightarrivals.com
Nearby hotel information: www.mwaa.com/national/hotels.htm
Parking information: www.mwaa.com/national/parking.htm
Driving directions: www.mwaa.com/national/directions.htm

Formerly called Washington National Airport, the name was changed in 1998 to honor President Ronald Reagan. In 1997, a billion-dollar terminal building opened on 23 acres under a glass and steel domed structure designed by Cesar Pelli, in contrast to the low-slung original terminal, now Terminal A, which was opened in 1941 by President Roosevelt. With the larger Dulles Airport nearby, this airport is restricted to short-haul flights not exceeding 1,250 miles, except for a congressionally mandated exception, and flights to and from Denver, Phoenix, Las Vegas, and Seattle. The airport is about a 10-minute drive to Washington across the Potomac. It is open daily 24 hours and there is a food court, restaurant, and shops. Hourly and long-term parking are available. Shuttles, taxis, and rental cars are available with details provided on their Web sites. The Metropolitan Washington Airport Authority recommends arriving 90 minutes before departure. Metro: National Airport. *See also* Airport Transportation.

Red 1802 Jefferson Pl. NW at 18th St. 202-466-3475

This lively after-hours underground club is for dancing and attracts a diverse clientele—black and white, straight and gay, young and a bit older. Cover charge. Open Wed–Sat 10 p.m.–3 a.m. Metro: Dupont Circle.

Red Apple Market 7645 New Hampshire Ave., Langley Park, MD (301) 434-1810

Providing the needful for your West Indian meals, this long-established market offers, for example, ginger beer and various brands of that unique Jamaican barbecue seasoning, jerk, a succulent blending of Jamaican pimento, cinnamon, nutmeg, hot peppers, and other ingredients. Metro: Fort Totten, then take White Oak Metrobus K6 to New Hampshire Ave. and Holton Lane.

Red Circle of Washington 3900 Tunlaw Rd. NW, Suite 119 (202) 338-1808

These local Baker Street Irregulars, aficionados of Sherlock Holmes stories, meet occasionally throughout the Washington area for dinner and discussion, a theater party, or film showings. Members pay a modest fee to cover the cost of mailings.

Red Cross Square behind Red Cross Headquarters at 403 17th St. NW

This small park is surrounded by National Red Cross buildings. The Red Cross Visitor's Center is at 1730 E St. NW. Metro: Foggy Bottom-GWU, then a 10-minute walk.

Red Cross Waterfront Festival Oronoco Bay Park, Oranoco St., at the waterfront, Alexandria, VA (703) 549-8300

About 60,000 celebrants each year visit this top-rated summer festival, established in the 1980s to raise money for the Alexandria Red Cross. Every year in early June this weekend festival offers more than fifty juried arts-and-crafts booths, a festival wine garden, gyros, crab cakes, roasted corn, barbecue, a health and safety pavilion with medical screening booths, a meet-your-firefighters booth, a petting zoo, amusement rides, river cruises, races, tall ships, and rock, country, and folk music. Entry fee. Metro: King Street or Eisenhower Avenue station, then take free shuttle to the festival.

Red, Hot and Blue Maryland: 16809 Crabbs Branch Way, Gaithersburg, MD (301) 948-7333; 677 Main St., Laurel, MD (301) 953-1943. Virginia: Kingstowne 6482 Landsdown Centre, Alexandria, VA (703) 550-6465; 1600 Wilson Blvd., Arlington, VA (703) 276-7427; Clarendon, 3014 Wilson Blvd., Arlington, VA (703) 243-1510; 4150 Chain Bridge Rd., Fairfax, VA (703) 218-6989; 541 E. Market St., Leesburg, VA (703) 669-4242; 8366 Sudley Rd., Manassas, VA (703) 367-7100

This popular, top-rated national chain offers Memphis pit-style barbecued ribs, pulled pork, chicken, brisket, and fried catfish served with fresh-baked rolls, baked beans, and coleslaw. Try the pulled pig platter while studying posters of blues artists and enjoying a local brew. Blues jukebox. Open daily for lunch and dinner.

Red Roof Inn 500 H St. NW (202) 289-5959 (800) 843-7663

This 10-story, 197-room hotel is only 2 blocks from a Metro stop and the MCI Center, 4 blocks to the Washington Convention Center, and is surrounded by a number of Chinese restaurants. Rooms are large and the rates are reasonable. It offers nonsmoking rooms, valet service, an exercise room, laundry facilities, a coffee shop, and outdoor parking at moderate rates. Children under 18 stay free. Weekend and seasonal rates. Metro: Gallery Pl.-Chinatown.

Red Sage 605 14th St. NW at H St. (202) 638-4444 www.redsage.com

For more than a decade, this restaurant, created by chef-restaurateur Mark Miller, has been popular with patrons nearby from the National Press Club, the White House and Treasury, as well as from farther afield. It continues to collect awards; the street-level Border Café—serving Southwestern cuisine such as chili and tostadas—was named one of Zagat Survey's "America's best meal deals." *Conde-Nast Traveler* and *Esquire* singled out The Grill—the upscale, expensive downstairs section—as one of America's top restaurants offering "modern American cuisine based on traditional influences of the American West." View their seriously rich ranch-home decor as well as their current menu on the Web site. Reservations needed for The Grill, which is open Mon–Sat 11:30 a.m.–11 p.m. Metro: Metro Center.

Red Sea 2463 18th St. NW (202) 483-5000

This Adams Morgan fixture has been offering savory Ethiopian dishes since the 1980s. Spicy lamb, seafood, and beef and vegetable stews are served with *injera*, a pancake-like bread. There is a full vegetarian menu as well. Open daily 11:30 a.m.–11:30 p.m. Metro: Woodley Park-Zoo, then a 10-minute walk.

Redskins *see* FedEx Field.

Reel Affirmations (202) 986-1119 www.reelaffirmations.org

Founded in 1991, this nonprofit organization's mission is to "bring the newest, most-anticipated gay, lesbian, bisexual and transgender films to Washington audiences from around the country and around the world." Today this organization has more than 300 volunteers, an annual 10-day International Gay and Lesbian Film Festival in October—with more than 30,000 attendees making it the third largest of its kind in the United States—and a series of follow-up screenings the rest of the year. Films are usually shown at the Lincoln Theatre, the D.C. Jewish Community Center, or the Goethe-Institut.

Reeves Restaurant and Bakery 1306 G St. NW (202) 628-6350

One of a handful of establishments in the city operating for more than 100 years, it keeps its customers coming—about 1,000 a day—by modest prices, sandwiches made with fresh-baked bread, light fare, homemade pastries, pies—such as strawberry—an all-you-can-eat breakfast and fruit bar, other baked goods, and did we mention their pies? Open Mon–Sat 7 a.m.–6 p.m. Metro: Metro Center.

Reflecting Pool btw the Washington Monument and Lincoln Memorial near Constitution and Henry Bacon Dr. NW

The idea of the reflecting pool, mirroring the Washington Monument and Lincoln Memorial, surfaced with the McMillan Park Commission plan in 1902. The pool was designed by Henry Bacon and Charles McKim, who proposed a cross-shaped design. Along came World War I, however, and the Navy Department built "temporary" structures along Constitution Ave., botching the plan. During World War II, the "temporaries," which were still there, were connected by bridges crossing over the Reflecting Pool. The bridges came down after the war, and with enormous effort by wrecking crews, the well-built temporaries came down in 1971. The 2,000-foot-long, 160-foot-wide reflecting pool can freeze in the winter allowing ice-skating, when the National Park Service okays it. Participants in the 1963 Civil Rights March on Washington gathered around the reflecting pool listening to Martin Luther King's "I Have a Dream" speech. At the eastern end of the pool, the National World War II Monument is under construction. Metro: Foggy Bottom-GWU, or Smithsonian.

Reiters 2021 K St. NW (202) 223-3327 www.reiters.com
Established in 1936, Reiter's—aka Reiter's Scientific and Professional Books—is both a local and national bookshop, offering specialized book ordering online. Their focus is on the scientific and book needs of academics, medical students, health professionals, economists, engineers, computer scientists, political scientists, and law students. For students and health professionals, their online Reiter's Expanded Medical Mall provides current information and reviews of thousands of medical books, as well as an interactive ordering system. The company is associated with Washington Law and Professional Books, a comprehensive source for legal books. Open Mon–Fri 8 a.m.–8 p.m., Sat 9:30 a.m.–6 p.m., Sun noon–5 p.m. Metro: Farragut West or Farragut North.

Renaissance Mayflower Hotel 1127 Connecticut Ave. NW (202) 347-3000 (800) 228-7697 www.renaissancehotels.com
Open in time to host President Coolidge's inaugural ball, and home to president-elect Franklin Delano Roosevelt while waiting for the Hoovers to move, this 660-room hotel remains one of Washington's finest. Warren and Wetmore, the architects who designed New York's Grand Central Station, built this Beaux Arts structure in 1925. A remodeling took place in the 1980s leaving the luxurious rooms even more comfortable. In the heart of the city's business district, close to fine restaurants, good shopping, and three Metro lines within 2 blocks, access to the city is easy. It has all the usual deluxe hotel amenities, an exercise room, sauna, parking (there's a fee), business center, top restaurants and bars, and great service. In the public areas expect polished brass, Italianate murals, silver, crystal, chandeliers, and gilded ceilings. Expensive. Metro: Farragut North.

Renaissance Washington Hotel see Washington Renaissance Hotel.

Renwick Gallery of the National Museum of American Art 17th and Pennsylvania Ave. NW (202) 357-2531 www.si.edu/activity/plansvis/museums/aboutren.htm
Banker William Wilson Corcoran commissioned well-known architect James Renwick to design this Second Empire showcase for Corcoran's growing art collection. Completed in 1859, it was used by the Quartermaster Corps and as Gen. Montgomery Meigs's headquarters during the Civil War, later the U.S. Court of Claims, and in 1972 opened as the Smithsonian's craft museum. While the upstairs grand salon and gallery features paintings and 1860s furnishings, the focus of the collection is American crafts from the nineteenth to twenty-first centuries. Special exhibitions highlight contemporary artists. Admission free. Open daily 10

a.m.–5:30 p.m. Closed Christmas Day. Metro: Farragut West and Farragut North. *See also* www.commuterpage.com/venues/museums-si.htm.

Reprint Bookshop 455 L'Enfant Plaza SW (202) 554-5070

Back in 1955, when the original owner, Jack Cooper, founded the store, real books were hardcover and all others mere "reprints." Hence the name. In 1988 Michael Cooper, who had worked there since the '60s, bought it and continues to run an independent store with a 30,000-book collection—paperbacks and hardcover now—tailored to his (and his two fellow workers') knowledge of the dynamic and eclectic reading community surrounding his shop inside the Plaza shopping arcade. Popular fiction you expect, but Mike offers as well a rich collection of African American literature and computer books and—it has been found—travel books and social science studies that want to follow you home. Don't miss the occasional book event in the store. Open 8 a.m.–6 p.m. weekdays only. Metro: L'Enfant Plaza.

Republic Gardens 1355 U St. NW (202) 232-2710

With exposed brick walls, cut flowers, dark polished wood, and packed dance floors, this upscale club in a Victorian townhouse attracts a loyal following of black professionals. Dress is business casual. There are 3 floors: downstairs an upscale bar pouring top brands and a Caribbean restaurant, upstairs a dance floor and pool tables. If you can't figure out how all this fits together, take a look at the streaming video of the place on www.barseen.com. Music can be disco, hip-hop, house, R&B, reggae, or soul. Wednesday is singles night and also features comedy acts. The club is in the same building that housed the original Republic Gardens club where Charlie Parker sometimes performed. Cover charge. Open Wed 5 p.m.–3 a.m., Fri 5 p.m.–4 a.m., Sat 9:30 p.m.–4 a.m. Metro: U St.-Cardozo.

Residence Inn Bethesda-Downtown 7335 Wisconsin Ave. NW (301) 718-0200 (800) 331-3131 www.residenceinnbethesdahotel.com

This hotel is designed, as it says, for longer-term stays. Each room is actually a suite with a modest dining and living area, a full kitchen, a large bedroom, and a huge bathroom. There are self-service laundry facilities, child care services, a complimentary buffet breakfast, dinner delivery service from local restaurants, as well as voice mail, data ports on the phone, and a work desk with lamp. One block from the Metro. Useful for families, this hotel has a rooftop outdoor pool, a workout room, a public playground around the corner, is 2 blocks from a public library, and across the street from a six-screen theater. Pets are permitted. Rates are midrange. Metro: Bethesda.

Rest Rooms

Because of the number of public buildings and hotels in Washington, there are any number of accessible rest rooms, most of them clean. On the Mall, you will find facilities in the National Air and Space Museum, the National Gallery of Art, National Museum of Natural History, the National Museum of African Art, Hirshhorn Museum, Arthur M. Sackler Gallery, the Smithsonian's Arts and Industries Building, and the Visitor's Center at the Castle. Most of the monuments provide rest rooms. Hotels are a sure bet, and farther afield, don't forget Union Station. There are no rest rooms in Metro stations.

Restaurants *see* Afghan, Asian, Barbecue and Ribs, Cajun, Chili, Chinese, Contemporary, Continental, Delicatessens, Diners, Ethiopian, French, German, Greek, Hamburgers, Indian, Indonesian, Irish, Italian, Japanese, Jewish, Korean, Kosher, Latin American, Malaysian, Mexican, Middle Eastern, Moroccan, Pizzerias, Russian, Seafood and Fish, Senegalese, Southern, Southwestern, Spanish, Steak, Tearooms, Thai, Turkish, Vegetarian, Vietnamese. *See also* www.dcpages.com, www.washingtonpost.com, www.restaurant.com, www.opentable.com.

Reston Fairfax County, VA Reston Greater Chamber of Commerce, 1763 Fountain Dr., Reston, VA (703) 707-9045 www.restonchamber.org

Ranked as one of the foremost planned communities in the United States, this town of more than 58,000 residents grew from the vision (and cash from the sale of Carnegie Hall) of Robert E. Simon Jr. Hence R-E-S ton. In 1961 he bought 11.5 square miles of rolling farmland near Dulles Airport 15 miles from Washington. He convinced Fairfax County to allow close clustering of homes, leaving open spaces for fields and trees; an urban landscape in a rural setting. Now it has lakes, large wooded areas, playing fields, shopping villages, office and professional buildings, theaters, an ice rink, restaurants, a library, golf courses, nature paths, jogging trails, recreation centers, the Reston Town Center, and the Dulles access road for commuters. High-tech firms were attracted to the area, as well as more than 1,400 companies including the headquarters of the U.S. Geological Service.

Reston Farmers Market Lake Anne Plaza off North Shore Dr., Reston, VA (703) 941-7987

Open Saturdays 8 a.m.–noon from mid-May to early November when vegetables and fruits are sold by their growers.

Reston National Golf Course 11875 Sunrise Valley Dr., Reston, VA (703) 620-9333

This par 71 course remains the top-ranked public golf course in the Washington area, with large greens sited on rolling terrain in a park-like setting. The club hosts the Steve Buckhantz/St. Jude's Celebrity Golf Tournament. Reston National includes a driving range, putting green, pitching green with bunker, club rentals, pro shop, and snack bar. Lessons are available. Tee time policy: seven days in advance. By car take Dulles Toll Rd. (Rte. 267) to Exit 12 (Reston Pkwy.), south to Sunrise Valley Dr.

Reston Zoo 1228 Hunter Mill Rd., Vienna, VA (703) 757-6222

This zoo offers a petting area where children can hand-feed goats, bottle-feed baby lambs, and pet other animals. There are ponies to ride as well as "safari wagon rides." There are zebras, emus, donkeys, ostriches, antelope, monkeys, bison, and many small birds. The zoo offers birthday party packages. Hours vary by season. Open daily 9 a.m.–4 p.m. spring and summer. By car take Rte. 7 to Baron Cameron Ave. (Rte. 606) to Hunter Mill Rd.

Results, the Gym 1612 U St. NW (202) 518-0001 and 315 G St. SE (202) 234-5678 www.resultsthegym.com

This exercise and body maintenance facility offers a bright, naturally lit facility popular with the kind of people who look like they don't need to go to a gym. It provides exercise and body maintenance routines to meet your individual goals. Results also provides aerobics classes, cycling, volleyball, spinning, and yoga, as well as massage, tanning, facials, manicures, and pedicures. Their Web site provides a virtual tour. Open Mon–Fri 5 a.m.–11 p.m., Sat–Sun 8 a.m.–9 p.m. Metro: Dupont Circle or U St.-Cardozo; Metro for Capitol Hill: Capitol South or Eastern Market.

Ricchi *see* I Ricchi under I.

El Rincón Español 1826 Columbia Rd. NW at 18th St. (202) 265-4943

This restaurant features Spanish cuisine including three kinds of paellas, spicy shrimp dishes, and yummy salmon steaks. Upstairs (Fri–Sat 11 p.m.–3 a.m.) live Cuban jazz and salsa often. No cover charge. Restaurant open Mon–Thurs 11 a.m.–1 a.m., Fri–Sat 11 a.m.–1 a.m. Metro: Woodley Park-Zoo.

Ringgold-Carroll House 1801 F St. NW Dacor Bacon House Foundation (202) 682-0500 www.dacorbacon.org

It is hard to find key figures in American history who have not visited or lived at this F St. site from today back to 1815, when Tobias Lear, former secretary to George Washington, built a smaller home on the lot. The present Federal-style mansion was built in 1825 by Tench Ringgold, close friend of President James Monroe. Ringgold served as U.S. marshal for the District from Monroe's presidency to the second year of Andrew Jackson's first term. When the British burned Washington, Ringgold rode alongside the fleeing President James Madison. In the 1830s, Chief Justice John Marshall boarded with the Ringgolds, as did Associate Justice Joseph Story, another major player in American law. A daughter of the Ringgolds married Edward D. White, then governor of Louisiana, who served as chief justice of the Supreme Court from 1910 to 1921. In 1936 Ringgold sold the house to Samuel Sprigg, governor of Maryland, who in turn presented it to his daughter Sally when she married the clerk to the Supreme Court, William Carroll. In 1861, the Carrolls' daughter married a Union captain in the house and the wedding was attended by President and Mrs. Lincoln. In 1896, another chief justice bought the house: Melville W. Fuller. Upon Fuller's death in 1910, the house was bought by the sister of Harry K. Thaw, murderer of architect Stanford White in an *affaire d'amour* over a chorus girl. Next came Congressman Robert Bacon renting the home with his wife Virginia Murray Bacon, until they finally bought it in 1925. Mrs. Bacon, one of the "three B's," the grand-dames who drove Washington society, lived in the house until her own death in 1980. As a memorial to Congressman Bacon, the house was given to the Bacon House Foundation, which merged with the DACOR Foundation in 1985. DACOR is an acronym for Diplomatic and Consular Officers Retired, an association of retired U.S. Foreign Service officers promoting the welfare of its members and fostering better understanding of U.S. foreign relations. Thus, to this day the house has been a meeting place for many a former secretary of state, hundreds of retired ambassadors, and other members of the diplomatic community. Metro: Farragut West.

Rio Grande Café 4919 Fairmont Ave., Bethesda, MD (301) 656-2981; 827 Library St., Reston Town Center, Reston, VA (703) 904-0703; 231 Rio Blvd., Gaithersburg, MD (240) 632-2150; 4301 N Fairfax Dr., Arlington, VA (703) 528-3131

This popular chain provides consistently well-prepared tacos, enchiladas, burritos, fajitas, chili rellenos, and other Tex-Mex fare in overflowing plates. Beyond T-M, they offer grilled shrimp and the occasional surprise such as quail and orange roughy. The atmosphere is cantina-funk, the margaritas are frosty and potent, bowls of fresh tortilla chips and salsa keep coming, and the service is fast and accommodating. Large dining areas, somewhat noisy, and usually crowded. Open for lunch Mon–Fri 11 a.m.–3 p.m., dinner Sun–Thurs 3 p.m.–10:30 p.m., Fri 3 p.m.–11:30 p.m., Sat 11:30 a.m.–11:30 p.m. Brunch Sun 11:30 a.m.–3 p.m. Metro: Bethesda; Metro for Arlington: Ballston.

Ritz 919 E St. NW (202) 638-2582

This upscale mainly black night club, near the FBI building, offers assorted rap, hip-hop, funk, and jazz in assorted rooms—some live, some spun by DJs—until the wee hours of the morning. Cover charge. Open Wed 9 p.m.–2 a.m., Fri 9 p.m.–3:30 a.m., Sat 10 p.m.–3:30 a.m., Sun 10 p.m.–2 a.m. Metro: Metro Center or Gallery Pl.-Chinatown.

Ritz-Carlton Pentagon City 1250 South Hayes St., Arlington, VA (703) 415-5000 (800) 241-3333

This 366-room hotel is 5 minutes from National Airport and 10 minutes from downtown Washington, with a Metro stop at its front door. Next door is the Pentagon City shopping mall (Fashion Center) with 150 specialty shops and a cinema complex. Besides the usual amenities, the hotel features large and comfortable meeting facilities, a business center, in-room fax machines and computer access, twice-daily maid service, indoor lap pool, sauna, steam room and massage, an exercise room, valet parking, and 24-hour room service. Expensive. Metro: Pentagon City.

Ritz-Carlton Tysons Corner 1700 Tysons Blvd., McLean, VA (703) 506-4300 www .ritzcarlton.com

Adjacent to Tysons Galleria shopping mall, this hotel is located in the heart of Fairfax County's shop-till-you-drop area, 14 miles from Reagan National Airport and 12 miles from Dulles. Its 399 rooms provide the usual array of superior amenities, including a restaurant, a lobby bar, complimentary self-parking, and 24-hour room service. The beautifully furnished rooms are a plus, as is the complimentary transport service within a 3-mile radius. Metro: West Falls Church, then take Fairfax Connector Bus 425 to Tysons Westpark Loop, exit at Park Run Dr. and Tysons Blvd., about 1½ blocks to hotel. By car from Dulles Airport: Take Dulles Toll Rd. (Rte. 267), take Exit 8, turn right onto Spring Hill Rd., which becomes International Dr., take left at Tysons Blvd. to hotel.

Le Rivage 1000 Water St. SW (202) 488-8111

Appropriately, since it shares parking with a floating fish market, this waterfront café offers particularly fresh seafood dishes as well as classic French cuisine. A loyal following of the nearby Arena Stage takes advantage of the pre-theater specials. In summer, the outdoor deck is popular, particularly with the theater crowd. Reservations suggested. Open Mon–Thurs 11:30 a.m.–2 p.m. and 5:30 p.m.–10:30 p.m., Fri 11:30 a.m.–2 p.m. and 5:30 p.m.–11 p.m., Sat 5:30 p.m.–11 p.m., Sun 5 p.m.–9 p.m. Metro: Waterfront-SEU.

River Farm 7931 East Boulevard Dr., Alexandria, VA (703) 768-5700 (800) 777-7931 www.ahs.org/riverfarm/river.htm

This 27-acre site, formerly part of George Washington's holdings, houses the headquarters of the American Horticultural Society and its lavish gardens, home to 200-year-old walnut trees, 450 tea varieties, and award-winning roses. There are seasonal displays, garden tours, horticultural seminars and workshops, musical events, and even wine tastings, which are listed on the Web site. Open weekdays 9 a.m.–5 p.m., open some Saturdays during the summer. By car from I-495 (the Beltway) exit Rte. 1 North, turn right on Franklin St., go 3 blocks, take a right on Washington St., which becomes the George Washington Pkwy. at the south end of Alexandria. Drive 4 miles and take a left on E Boulevard Dr., then follow signs to River Farm.

River Inn 924 25th St. NW (202) 337-7600 (800) 424-2741 www.theriverinn.com

The proximity to Georgetown, the State Department, and the Kennedy Center makes this 126-unit reasonably priced hotel a favorite of government travelers, as well as musicians and academics. Its Foggy Bottom Café, featured in a Margaret Truman mystery, is open for a full breakfast buffet, as well as lunch and dinner. Bar, business center, laundromat, voice mail. Parking. Metro: Foggy Bottom-GWU.

Riverbend Park 8700 Potomac Hills St., Great Falls, VA (703) 759-9018 www.co .fairfax.va.us/parks/nature.htm

This 400-acre Fairfax County park, upstream of Great Falls, offers Potomac River views, forest and meadow trails, lovely ponds, horse trails, streams, bird watching, and wildflowers. A riverside trail leads to Great Falls. There are picnic tables and a boat ramp. Swimming in the river is prohibited. Programs are conducted from either the visitors' center at the park entrance or the nature center at 8814 Jeffery Rd. A park naturalist is on duty at the visitor center, and there are exhibits, a nature library, and live animals. The park is open year-round 7 a.m.–dusk. Visitor center open Mon and Wed–Fri 9 a.m.–5 p.m., Sat–Sun, noon–5 p.m. Closed Tuesday. By car from I-495 (the Beltway) take Exit 44, Georgetown Pike west, then right on Riverbend Rd., then right on Jeffery Rd. to the park entrance.

Riverdale Park Farmers Market Queensbury Rd. at the MARC Station, Riverdale, MD (301) 927-6381

Producers sell their fruit and vegetables on Thursdays 3 p.m.–7 p.m. from mid-May to early October.

Riverfront

This area is bracketed by Fort McNair along the Washington Channel, and to the east by the Washington Navy Yard, at the confluence of the Potomac and Anacostia rivers, with the U.S. Naval Station and Anacostia Park skirting the southeast bank of the Anacostia River. Metro: Navy Yard.

Robert A. Taft Memorial Constitution Ave. btw New Jersey Ave. and 1st St. NW www.aoc.gov/cc/grounds/art_arch/taft.htm

Completed in 1959, and built by popular subscription, this is the only monument in Washington honoring a senator. It consists of a bell tower and statue sculpted by Wheeler Williams. Senator Taft, "Mr. Republican," represented Ohio in the Senate from 1938 until his death in 1953. His father, William Howard Taft, served as the 27th president of the United States and later as chief justice of the Supreme Court. Metro: Union Station.

Robert Brown Gallery 2030 R St. NW (202) 483-4393 www.robertbrowngallery .com

Focusing on twentieth-century paintings, drawings, sculptures, prints, photography, and Chinese advertising posters from 1912 to 1935, this gallery moved to Washington from New York in 1981. The gallery, as well, publishes print and photographic portfolios. Open Tue–Sat noon–6 p.m. First Friday of every month noon–8 p.m. Metro: Dupont Circle.

Robert E. Lee Birthday Celebration Arlington National Cemetery, Memorial Dr., Arlington, VA (703) 557-0613

On or close to General Lee's birthday, January 19, a celebration takes place at his home, Arlington House, that includes Civil War–era food, music, and displays. A celebration usually takes place at his boyhood home in Alexandria, Virginia, as well.

Robert E. Lee Boyhood Home 607 Oronoco St., Alexandria, VA (703) 548-8454 www.alexandriacity.com/leehome.htm

Gen. Henry "Light Horse Harry" Lee of Revolutionary War fame moved here with his wife, Ann Hill Carter, and their five children, including their 5-year-old son Robert E., in 1812. In 1825 Robert E. Lee left this house to enroll in West Point and later, of course, led the Confederate forces in the Civil War. The house was built in 1795 and remains a showcase of Federal-period architecture. Before the Lees moved here, however, it was occupied by Col. William Fitzhugh, whose daughter, Mary Lee, married Martha Washington's grandson, George Washington Parke Custis, in this house. Custis was to build Arlington House in association with Robert E. Lee. Lee, of course, was to marry the Custis daughter, Mary Anne Randolph Custis. The house, filled with period antiques and Lee memorabilia, is now a museum. Open Mon–Sat 10 a.m.–4 p.m., Sun 1 p.m.–4 p.m. Modest admission charge. Closed Easter, Thanksgiving, some special occasions, and December 15 to January 31. Metro: Braddock Road, exit the station and take Metrobus 10C toward Hunting Towers to the stop at Washington and Princess Sts. Walk 1 block north on Washington St., turn right on Oronoco St., and walk 1 block east. Or take the DAT5 DASH Bus toward Van Dorn Metro to the stop at Fairfax and Oronoco Sts. *See also* www.commuterpage.com/venues/sightseeing_VA.htm.

Robert E. Lee Memorial House *see* Arlington House, the Robert E. Lee Memorial.

Robert Emmett Statue Massachusetts Ave. and S St. NW www.robertemmett.org

This bronze sculpture by Jerome Conner, an Irish immigrant, was given to the Smithsonian Institution in 1917 and in 1966 was placed at its present location, facing the nearby Irish Embassy. In 1803, Emmett, a member of the United Irishman's Party, led an uprising in Dublin against British occupation that was quickly crushed by British troops. At his trial he stated "I wished to procure for my country the guarantee which Washington procured for America." Emmett, convicted of treason, was hanged, possibly beheaded. Metro: Farragut West, then take Farragut Heights Metrobus N4 to Massachusetts and Florida Aves., or exit Dupont Circle Metro and walk 5 blocks.

Robert F. Kennedy Memorial Stadium *see* RFK Stadium.

Rochambeau Bridge *see* 14th Street Bridges.

Rochambeau Statue Lafayette Park, Pennsylvania Ave. btw Jackson and Madison Pl. NW

This replica of a statue of Gen. Jean-Baptiste Donatien de Vimeure, Comte de Rochambeau, leader of the 5,500 French Expeditionary Force in the American Revolution, was dedicated by President Theodore Roosevelt in 1902. The original sculpture by J. J. Fernand Hamar stands in Vendôme, France, the birthplace of Rochambeau. Metro: Farragut Square or McPherson Square.

Rock, Alternative, and Ethnic Music *see* Black Cat, Fadó Irish Pub, Galaxy Hut, Grog and Tankard, Iota Café, Jaxx, Madam's Organ Restaurant and Bar, Metro Café, Nation Nightclub, 9:30 Club, Rumba Café, Songhai, State of the Union, Velvet Lounge. *See also* Radio Stations, www.washingtonpost.com.

Rock Climbing *see* Climbing.

Rock Creek Cemetery Rock Creek Church Rd. and Webster St. NW (202) 829-0585

The oldest cemetery in Washington, dating from 1719, is overseen by St. Paul's Episcopal Church, the city's oldest church. Among the historical personages buried here, and there are many, is Marion Hooper "Clover" Adams, who committed suicide in 1885. A moving memorial to her by Augustus Saint-Gaudens was erected by her husband, historian Henry Adams, who is buried next to his wife. Other notables include Alice Longworth Roosevelt and writer Upton Sinclair. The cemetery is open from dawn to dusk. Metro: Rhode Island, then take Metrobus H8 to Rock Creek Rd. and Upshur St.

Rock Creek Golf Course 1600 Rittenhouse St. NW (202) 882-7332 www.golfdc .com

This public 18-hole course located at 15th and Rittenhouse Sts. NW is open dawn to dusk year-round except for December 25. There is a golf school, golf shop, cart rentals, putting green, and snack bar. Dense woods border the fairways, and small greens plus the rolling terrain provide challenges. Open daily 6:30 a.m.–5:30 p.m. Low cost. Metro: McPherson Square, then take Metrobus S4 to 16th St. and Stevens Dr. NW.

Rock Creek Nature Center and Planetarium 5200 Glover Rd. (202) 895-6070
www.nps.gov/rocr/naturecenter

This facility provides programs, activities, and exhibits related to the park. The aim is to instill "affection for wild places" and to teach the concepts of ecology, as well as to identify local plants and animals. There are 30-minute to 45-minute guided nature hikes led by park rangers, environmental exhibits, trail maps, nature films, a puppet show, live snake and turtle installations, a bookstore, and a natural history "discovery room" for children under 8. A 75-seat planetarium provides regular shows for children 4 and older. Other activities include an "after school planetarium show," a monthly "exploring the sky" program, and many special events. Open daily 9 a.m.–5 p.m. After Labor Day, open Wed–Sun 9 a.m.–5 p.m. Planetarium shows Wed 3:45 p.m., Sat and Sun 1 p.m. and 4 p.m. Admission free. Closed federal holidays. Phone or check the Web site for schedule. Metro. Friendship Heights, then take the E2 or E3 Bus to Military Rd. *See also* www.commuterpage.com/venues/gardens.htm.

Rock Creek Park Visitor Information Center, 5000 Glover Rd. NW

Headquarters: (202) 895-6060, Nature Center (202) 895 6070, Natural Resources (202) 895-6235, Pierce Mill (202) 426-6908, Carter Barron Amphitheater (202) 426-0486, Park Events Recording (202) 895-6239 www.nps.gov/rocr

This park of 1,755 acres—much of it rolling urban forest—was purchased by Congress in 1890. It winds along Rock Creek running from Thompson's Boat Center at Virginia Ave. and Rock Creek Pkwy. past the National Zoo, and crossing into Montgomery County near 16th St. The Maryland sector of the park stretches for 3 miles from Boundary Bridge at the District line to the Beltway. A useful park map is available online at www.parkexplorer.org/parkguide. Following the southern section of the park is Rock Creek Pkwy., still a pleasant drive except during rush hours. Popular park activities include hiking the forest trails, horseback riding, biking—there are paved bike trails—picnicking, educational and interpretive programs, bird watching, cross-country skiing, golf, tennis, exercise trails, running, rollerblading, and jogging. Recreational fields support soccer, football, and field hockey. Other attractions in the park include the water-powered Pierce Mill, with its stone wheel that ground corn and wheat from the 1820s to 1897. Interpretive programs are provided at the mill. The Pierce barn, once the wagon shed, is used for occasional exhibits. Pierce Mill is found at the corner of Tilden St. (same as Park Rd.) NW and Beach Dr. Remnants of Fort De Russey are found near Military and Daniel Rds. In 1864, its ramparts withstood a Confederate raid. *See also* Carter Barron Amphitheater, Rock Creek Golf Course, Rock Creek Nature Center and Planetarium, Rock Creek Park Horse Center, Thompson's Boat Center, Washington Tennis Center. Metros: Foggy Bottom-GWU, Dupont Circle, Woodley Park-Zoo, Cleveland Park, Van Ness-UDC, Silver Spring.

Rock Creek Park Carter Barron Amphitheater *see* Carter Barron Amphitheater.

Rock Creek Park Day Nature Center, Rock Creek Park, 5200 Glover Rd. NW (202) 895-6070 www.nps.gov/rocr

On September 27, 1890, Congress established Rock Creek Park as a "pleasuring ground for the benefit and enjoyment of the people of the United States." Every year, on the Saturday closest to that date, the park throws itself a birthday party. There are exhibits, food, crafts, music, children's events, and, hopefully, cake. Metro. Friendship Heights, then take the E2 or E3 Bus to Military Rd.

Rock Creek Park Golf Course *see* Rock Creek Golf Course.

Rock Creek Park Horse Center 5100 Glover Rd. NW (202) 362-0117
The center offers riding lessons and guided trail rides. There are summer camp programs as well as special classes for the disabled. Children under 12 are not allowed on trail rides. Reservations required with credit card. Office open Tues–Fri noon–6 p.m., Sat and Sun, 9 a.m.–5 p.m. Guided trail rides: Tues–Thurs 3 p.m., Sat–Sun noon, 1:30 p.m., 3 p.m. Metro: Friendship Heights, then take Ivy City Metrobus E3, exit at Military and 27th St., then a 10-minute walk.

Rock Creek Park Tennis Center *see* Washington Tennis Center.

Rock Creek Regional Park 6700 Needwood Rd., Derwood, MD (301) 948-5053
www.mc-mncppc.org/permits/facility/picnic/rock_creek_rgnl_shelter.htm
This 3,000-acre park skirts Needwood Lake. You may launch your own boat (for a small fee) or rent a canoe, paddleboat pontoon, or fishing boat, or embark (Memorial Day to Labor Day) on the *Needwood Queen* for a 20-minute cruise. There are also hiking and bike trails, guided nature walks, a nature center, 18 picnic shelters (which require reservations), an archery range, a snack bar, and the Needwood Golf Course. The Nature Center is open Tues–Sat 9 a.m.–5 p.m. Park open dawn to dusk, closed major holidays in the winter. By car take the Shady Grove exit from I-270 onto Redland Rd. past Rte. 355, then right on Needwood Rd.

Rock Creek Tennis Center *see* Washington Tennis Center.

Rock Creek Trail starts at corner of Pennsylvania Ave. NW ramp and Rock Creek Pkwy. NW http://www.waba.org/new/paths/rcpdc.php
This popular 25-mile bike trail leads from the Lincoln Memorial to Lake Needwood Park in Montgomery County, Maryland. This 8-foot-wide, often crowded trail follows the east bank of the Potomac, runs past the Mall and through Rock Creek Park to Lake Needwood. See Web site for details and entry points. Metro: Foggy Bottom-GWU, then 3 blocks to Pennsylvania and Rock Creek Pkwy. ramp.

Rock Sports Bar and Restaurant 717 6th St. NW (202) 842-7625
Often packed with—you guessed it—sports fans from the nearby MCI Center, the 3 floors of the Rock offer billiards, all possible televised sports at all possible angles, a rooftop tiki bar, and a venue for the young singles crowd. Metro: Judiciary Square.

Rockland's 2418 Wisconsin Ave. NW (202) 333-2558 and 4000 N Fairfax Dr., Arlington, VA (703) 528-9663 www.rocklands.com
Their wondrous real hickory and oak-smoked ribs, pulled pork or chicken sandwiches, and a long listing of other Texas-style barbecued temptations, not to mention baked beans, corn pudding, slaw, and a range of hot sauces, are found in

two very different venues: a small mostly take-out at Wisconsin Ave. and Calvert St., and a huge space in Arlington where at one time you could have parked your car inside. The latter, a converted auto dealership, shares its space with a billiard parlor, the aptly named Carpool. The *Washington Post*'s food critic states, "Few places anywhere make available such satisfying, down-home, from-scratch American cooking at fast-food prices." Wisconsin Ave. open Mon–Fri 11:30 a.m.–10 p.m., Sat 11 a.m.–10 p.m., Sun 11 a.m.–9 p.m.

Rockville www.ci.rockville.md.us

The county seat of Montgomery County since 1776, this city has grown along with Washington, 12 miles away. Post–World War II single-family homes are spread across former farmlands, now augmented by townhouses, office buildings, apartment complexes, a commercial strip, and the popular White Flint Mall. Metro: Rockville, Twinbrook, White Flint.

Rockville Arts Place 100 East Middle Lane, Rockville, MD (301) 309-6900 www.rockvilleartsplace.org

This nonprofit center promotes interest in and access to the visual arts through its three active galleries, art classes for all ages and levels, resident artists, an extensive photography program, a computer graphics lab, various workshops, and gallery talks and seminars. You need not be a county resident to make use of the facility. It provides a summer day camp for students aged 5 to 15, three galleries featuring regional and nationally known artists, more than a dozen artists-in-residence studios on public view, and various internship and volunteer opportunities. The Web site lists forthcoming exhibits and programs. Modest membership fees. Metro: Rockville. By car take Exit 5 from I-270 toward Rockville Town Center. Turn right onto East Middle Lane and proceed for about a mile.

Rockville Civic Center Park Baltimore Rd. and Edmonston Dr., Rockville, MD (240) 314-8660 www.ci.rockville.md.us/facility/ccpark.htm

This 153-acre park serves as the hub of many of Rockville's cultural and social events. The 25-room Glenview Mansion and the F. Scott Fitzgerald Theatre are located here. The park offers a climbing gym, tennis courts, nature trails, and beautiful terraced gardens. By car from Rte. 28 and I-270, proceed east on Rte. 28, cross Rte. 355 and follow Rte. 28 east (turns left at first light beyond Rte. 355). Travel 4 blocks to Baltimore Rd., turn right, go 3 blocks to Edmonston Dr., turn left, and Civic Center Park entrance is immediately on the right.

Rockville Farmers Market Rockville Town Center, East Montgomery Ave., Rockville, MD (301) 309-3330 www.ci.rockville.md.us/recreation/farmmark.htm

Providing not only farm-fresh fruits and vegetables, this market also sells bedding plants, cut flowers, preserves, and baked goods. Wednesdays at East Montgomery Ave., Saturdays Middle Lane Parking Lot. Open Wednesdays June 5 to September 25, 11 a.m.–2 p.m.; Saturdays May 11 to October 26, 9 a.m.–1 p.m. Metro: Rockville.

Rodman's 5100 Wisconsin Ave. NW (202) 363-3466; 4301 Randolph Rd., Wheaton, MD (301) 946-3100; White Flint Plaza, 5148 Nicholson Lane, Rockville, MD (301) 881-6253

These eclectic supermarkets, still family owned, first opened in 1955 as a single drugstore that, well, evolved. Now each of the three is an international marketplace filled with coffees, teas, gourmet cheeses, wines and ales, cookware, kitchen gadgets, cookies, crackers, preserves, herbs, spices, oils, pastas, rice and grains, groceries, produce, ethnic foods, and small kitchen appliances, European soaps, body care products, and other stuff. Wisconsin Ave. store open Mon–Sat 9 a.m.–10 p.m., Sun 10 a.m.–7 p.m. Pharmacy is open Mon–Fri 9 a.m.–9 p.m., Sat 10 a.m.–6 p.m., Sun 10 a.m.–5 p.m. Metro: Friendship Heights; Randolph Rd.: Mon–Sat 9 a.m.–10 p.m., Sun 10 a.m.–7 p.m.; White Flint: Mon–Sat 9 a.m.–9 p.m., Sun 10 a.m.–7 p.m. Metro: White Flint.

Roll Call 50 F St. NW (202) 824-6800 www.rollcall.com

Since 1955, this paper, appearing Monday and Thursday mornings, has been covering Congress, including a daily vote roll call, insider news "heard on the hill," campaign news, election previews, a comprehensive current listing of policy briefings, and opinion pieces from various columnists. The Web site offers much of the same information. Metro: Union Station.

Romania Embassy 1607 23rd St. NW (202) 332-4848 www.roembus.org

This Beaux Arts–style building, constructed in 1907 by the firm of Carrère and Hastings (designers of the Cannon House Office Building on Capitol Hill and the Cosmos Club), was acquired in 1921 by the Embassy of Romania. Metro: Dupont Circle.

Ronald Reagan Building and International Trade Center 1300 Pennsylvania Ave. NW Building management office: (202) 312-1300 www.itcda.com

Completed in 1998 at a cost of $818 million, this mammoth building provides 71 acres of floor space—only the Pentagon is a larger federal building—and offices to more than 5,000 government workers as well as a food court, a government bookstore, several libraries and information centers, the D.C. Visitor Information Center, and various exhibition spaces open to the public. The U.S. Center for World Trade shares the building with a large conference center, many private tele-communications and trade organizations, university programs, and various federal offices including the Environmental Protection Agency and the U.S. Agency for International Development. The complex was designed by the firm of Pei, Cobb, Freed & Partners in association with Ellerbe Beckett. Open Mon–Fri 7 a.m.–7 p.m., Sat 11 a.m.–7 p.m. Food Court open Mon–Fri 7 a.m.–7 p.m., Sat 11 a.m.–6 p.m., Sun (March 1 to August 31 only) noon–5 p.m. Metro: Federal Triangle.

Ronald Reagan National Airport *see* Reagan National Airport.

Roof Terrace Restaurant Kennedy Center New Hampshire Ave. and F St. NW (202) 416-8555 www.kennedy-center.org

Combining a splendid Potomac view atop the Kennedy Center with opulent furnishings, this restaurant attracts patrons not only for a pre-show meal but for its brunch buffet. American Cuisine. Expensive. Open Tues–Sat, 5 p.m.–7:30 p.m., Sun 5 p.m.–7 p.m., Sat brunch 11:30 a.m.–1:30 p.m., Sun brunch 11:20 a.m.–2 p.m.

Reservations recommended. Metro: Foggy Bottom-GWU, then a 7-minute walk via New Hampshire Ave. Or use the free Kennedy Center Show Shuttle (signs are on the left at the bottom of the escalator). It departs every 15 minutes Mon–Fri 9:45 a.m.–midnight, Sat 10 a.m.–midnight, and noon–midnight Sun and holidays.

Roosevelt Birthday Celebration *see* Theodore Roosevelt Birthday.

Roosevelt Island *see* Theodore Roosevelt Island.

Roosevelt Memorial *see* Franklin Delano Roosevelt Memorial.

Roosevelt Memorial Bridge *see* Theodore Roosevelt Memorial Bridge.

Rosecroft Raceway 6336 Rosecroft Dr., Fort Washington, MD (301) 567-4000 www.rosecroft.com

Since 1949, Rosecroft has been offering evening harness racing from February through December. Post time Thurs–Sat 7:20 p.m. Simulcasting of thoroughbred races is also provided. No public transportation. Modest admission fee. Free parking. By car take Exit 4A from the Beltway (I-495/95) in Fort Washington, MD, and follow signs to the track.

Rosemary's Thyme 1801 18th St. NW (202) 332-3200; 5762 Union Mill Rd., Union Mill Shopping Center, Clifton, VA (703) 502-1084

First came the Clifton restaurant, but both provide tempting Middle Eastern dishes. Try their eggplant salad, a shrimp remoulade, a lamb or beef adana kebab, or their lamb shank served with Turkish flat bread. Moderate prices. Open Mon–Fri 11:30 a.m.–11 p.m., Sat 11 a.m.–midnight, Sun 11 a.m.–11 p.m. Metro: Dupont Circle. By car take I-66 W to U.S. Hwy. 50 E, Exit 57A toward Fairfax, take Lee Jackson Hwy., right on Waples Mill Rd., right on Lee Hwy., left on Union Mill Rd.

Rosslyn Arlington County, VA www.smartplace.org/smartplaces/rosslyn.html

Situated in Arlington County, Virginia, directly across the Potomac River from Georgetown and strongly identified with the former *USA Today* high-rise, Rosslyn hosts towering office buildings and many high-rise apartments. It provides easy access to Washington and the farther suburbs via its Metro station and Key and Roosevelt Bridges. Metro: Rosslyn. *See also* Crystal City.

Rotunda *see* Capitol Rotunda.

Round House Theater 7501 Wisconsin Ave, Bethesda, MD (240) 644-1100 www.round-house.org

In 2002 this long-time Montgomery County repertory company opened its five-play season in a new state-of-the-art stage in Bethesda, 1 block from the Metro. The group continues to offer a mix of contemporary works with classics such as *The Cherry Orchard*. Ticket prices are moderate. See their Web site for performance dates. Metro: Bethesda. *See also* www.commuterpage.com/venues/venue-en.htm.

Round Robin Bar Willard Inter-Continental Hotel, 1401 Pennsylvania Ave. NW (202) 628-9100

Complementing the Willard's turn-of-the century décor, this circular bar with its intimate private-club feel boasts attentive barkeeps, heavy crystal glasses, and a rather dressy crowd. Being circular, it tends to encourage conversations between guests. High-end spirits with matching prices. Mon–Sat 3 p.m.–11 p.m. Metro: Metro Center.

Rowboats *see* Boating.

Rumba Café 2443 18th St. NW at Columbia Rd. (202) 588-5501 www.rumbacafe .com

Located in Adams Morgan, the Rumba Café offers live salsa, Brazilian samba, Batucada bossa nova, and Latin jazz four nights a week. Add to that combination tropical drinks and tempting dishes such as sautéed breaded eggplant and *puerco con piña*—sautéed pork loin with fresh sliced pineapple and mojo sauce, and of course, served with black beans and plantain. No cover charge. Open Mon–Thurs 5:30 p.m.–2 a.m., Fri–Sat 5:30 p.m.–3 a.m., Sun 5:30 p.m.–2 a.m. Metro: Woodley Park-Zoo.

Rumors 1900 M St. NW (202) 466-7378 www.rumorsrestaurant.com

Easily recognizable by its glassed California room, Rumors is a popular singles bar and a required stop for young professionals and older college students cruising 19th St. Check the Web site for demographics. Cover charge after 10 p.m. on Fri and Sat. DJ spins dance music. Hamburgers, steaks, pastas, sandwiches. Sun–Thurs 11:30 a.m.–2 a.m., Fri–Sat 11:30 a.m.–3 a.m. Metro: Farragut West or Dupont Circle.

Running (Active Sports Activity) *see* C&O Canal, The Mall, Marine Corps Marathon, Mount Vernon Trail, Rock Creek Park.

Running (Spectator Sport) *see* Marine Corps Marathon.

Rupperts 1017 7th St. NW (202) 783-0699 www.rupperts.com

Opened in 1994 by chef John Cochran, this restaurant quickly became one of Washington's destination restaurants, apparently unhampered by its location in an area devastated by the new convention center construction. Ranked for years running as one of the city's top 50 restaurants, and collecting other awards as well, the menu changes daily, according to what is most tempting from locally grown or raised foods. Try the vegetable soup, the breads—buttermilk or oatmeal or mashed potato—and desserts such as white chocolate mousse. Open for lunch Thurs only 11:30 a.m.–2:30 p.m., dinner Thurs 6 p.m.–10 p.m., dinner Wed and Fri–Sat 6 p.m.–11 p.m. Reservations required. Expensive. Metro: Mount Vernon Square.

Russia Embassy 2650 Wisconsin Ave. NW (202) 298-5700 www.russianem bassy.org

Russia House 790 Station St., Herndon, VA (703) 787-8880

This treasure-trove of true Russian cuisine includes Cornish hen, pickled herring, smoked salmon, roast lamb, beef Stroganoff, and pirozhki. And of course, this place provides a spectrum of special vodkas, and for dessert, try the chocolate mousse. Open for lunch Tues–Fri 11:30 a.m.–2:30 p.m., dinner Mon–Fri 5:30 p.m.–10 p.m., Sat 5:30 p.m.–10:30 p.m., Sun 5 p.m.–9 p.m.

Russian Consulate 2001 Connecticut Ave. NW at 20th St.

This building, constructed early in the twentieth century by architects Hornblower and Marshall, was the palatial home of one of the partners of the Woodward and Lothrop Department Store and was long known as the Lothrop Mansion. It combines elements of Georgian and Beaux Arts styles. It is not open to visitors. Metro: Dupont Circle.

Russian Gourmet 1396 Chain Bridge Rd., McLean, VA (Langley Shopping Center) (703) 760-0680

This unique store provides Russian, Polish, and other European food, wine, beer, and specialty items as well as Russian videos and books and gifts and, of course, it stocks more than five brands of Russian caviar and sturgeon. Mon–Fri 10 a.m.–8:30 p.m., Sat 10 a.m.–7:30 p.m., Sun noon–6:30 p.m. Metro: Ballston-MU, then take 23A Tysons Westpark Bus to Chain Bridge Rd. and Emerson Ave.

Russian Restaurants *see* Maxim, Russia House.

Ruth's Chris Steak House 2231 Crystal Ave., Arlington, VA (703) 979-7275; 7315 Wisconsin Ave, Bethesda, MD (301) 652-7877

The Crystal Ave. site of this 55-restaurant chain offers a lovely sky view of Washington and Reagan National Airport, while the Bethesda branch provides a warm marble and wood-paneled club atmosphere. As serious steak eaters know, we are talking about aged corn-fed Midwestern steaks brought sizzling to the table. Don't overlook the seafood, however, tuna and salmon steaks, and lobsters of varying degrees of enormous size, which also describes the steaks. Good service. Expensive. Bethesda: open Mon–Sat 5 p.m.–10:30 p.m., Sun 5 p.m.–9:30 p.m. Metro: Bethesda; Crystal City: Lunch Mon–Fri 11:30 a.m.–5 p.m. Dinner Sun–Fri 5 p.m.–10:30 p.m., Sat 5 p.m.–11 p.m. Metro: Crystal City, then a 10-minute walk.

Rwanda Embassy 1714 New Hampshire Ave. NW (202) 232-2882 www.rwandemb .org

S

S. C. F. Hahnemann Memorial *see* Hahnemann Memorial.

Sabang 2504 Ennalls Ave., Wheaton, MD (301) 942-7859 or (301) 942-7874
You have a choice of three routes at this restaurant. Route one is the always wondrous many-dished sampler termed *rijsttafel*, concocted by Indonesian cooks in Batavian kitchens. Route two is to sample a series of truly Indonesian appetizers: satays, corn fritters with shrimp, crab meat on lemon grass, or fried squid covered with a peanut/tomato sauce. Route three is to choose among the main dishes, for example, shrimp in chili sauce, or *rendang*, which is spicy beef simmered in a coconut sauce. Inexpensive. Open Sun–Thurs 11 a.m.–10 p.m., Fri–Sat 11 a.m.–11 p.m. Metro: Wheaton.

Sackler Gallery *see* Arthur M. Sackler Gallery.

Saigon Gourmet 2635 Connecticut Ave. NW (202) 265-1360
This accurately named restaurant still carries a French accent in its Vietnamese dishes, and is one of the places you can trust to prepare a whole fish and watch it boned at your table. On the subject of seafood, try the deep-fried soft-shell crabs, or maybe blackened shrimp or perhaps shrimp Saigon, pork and shrimp simmered in a peppery sauce. There are some wonderful grilled pork dishes, as well as the traditional *pho* varieties. And when is the last time you had the courage to order banana flambé served, you must insist, with ginger ice cream? All that and it is listed by *Washingtonian Magazine* as one of the city's 100 top bargain restaurants. Open daily for lunch 11:30 a.m.–3 p.m., dinner 5 p.m.–10:30 p.m. Metro: Woodley Park-Zoo.

Saigon Inn 2828 M St. NW (202) 337-5588
This Vietnamese restaurant gets high marks for its low, low cost, its popular pork dishes, generous portions, and its good service. Open daily for lunch 11 a.m.–3 p.m., dinner daily 5 p.m.–midnight. Metro: Foggy Bottom-GWU.

Saigonnais 2307 18th St. NW (202) 232-5300 www.dcnet.com/saigonnais
This restaurant introduces you to the culinary heritage of Vietnam. Besides the

usual dishes found in a Vietnamese restaurant, this place offers Mekong shrimp from the Delta, curry chicken from Saigon's Indian community, and *nem nuong*— minced pork on a skewer from the central hills. Or try a Saigon's favorite, *bahn uot thit nuong*, slices of tender charbroiled marinated pork served in rice crepes. Open Mon–Sat for lunch 11:30 a.m.–3 p.m., dinner 5 p.m.–11 p.m. Metro: Farragut West, then take Metrobus 42 Mt. Pleasant to Columbia Rd. and 19th St. NW.

St. Aloysius Catholic Church 19 I St. NW (202) 336-7200 www.stalsdc.org

Opened in 1859 with President James Buchanan attending the ceremony, this is the second oldest Catholic Church in Washington. It has been in constant use since that time. The Renaissance Revival building was designed by a Jesuit, Father Benedict Sestini, a mathematics professor at Georgetown University. His friend, Constantine Brumidi, who later painted the Capitol dome frescoes, created the painting over the main altar, including Father Sestini in it. The basement of the church houses the Father McKenna Center, active since 1984 in providing shelter for the homeless and helping them rebuild their lives. Metro: Union Station.

St. Augustine Catholic Church 1425 V St. NW (202) 265-1470 www.saintaugustine-dc.org

This church was founded in 1858 by freed slaves who built a small chapel and school at 15th and L Sts. NW. The school operated for 4 years before free public education for black children was legislated in the District. Fund-raising for a larger building, including a fete on the White House lawn during Lincoln's presidency, finally resulted in the construction of the original St. Augustine Church at 15th and M Sts., completed in 1878. A rectory and parochial school building were added nearby in 1928. When the Archdiocese of Washington sold this building in 1948 to allow for the construction of the *Washington Post* building, the parish found temporary quarters at a nearby Presbyterian church. Later, the St. Augustine Parish, a mostly black parish, united with the nearby mostly white parish of St. Paul at the present church, an 1883 Gothic Revival building. St. Paul's was renamed the Parish of St. Augustine in 1882. Metro: U St.-Cardozo.

St. Augustine's Episcopal Church 600 M St. SW (202) 554-3222 www.edow.org/staugustines

This church, built in 1966, was designed by Alexander Cochran. There is an eleventh-century baptistery inside. Metro: Waterfront-SEU.

St. Dominic Church 630 E St. SW (202) 554-7863

To stretch construction funds, this church, completed in 1875, made use of construction workers in the parish. It replaced an earlier St. Dominic Church established in 1852 by the Dominican Fathers. In 1885 the 10-year-old church was almost lost to fire: the entire interior and roof were destroyed. Still another fire damaged the roof and interior in 1929, but the granite walls from Fort Deposit, Maryland, survived, and the rest was rebuilt. This Victorian Gothic church is known for the beauty of its 57 stained glass windows. The 24 windows along the side of the church and in the chapels date from 1965. Metro: L'Enfant Plaza.

St. Elmo's Coffee Pub 2300 Mount Vernon Ave. at East Del Ray Ave., Alexandria, VA (703) 739-9268 www.radiodelray.com/stelmos

This is more of an empire than a coffee café, with its full schedule of book sign-ings, folk music, live bands, Radio Delray Internet Radio, and poetry readings over-seen by platinum-topped Nora Partlow. There are sidewalk tables as well, and besides the mochas, cappuccinos, and the Daily Roast, try the substantial salads, soups, croissant sandwiches, sinfully good turnovers, several kinds of quiches, fruit smoothies, juices, fruit tarts, cookies, and brownies. Open daily 6 a.m.–10 p.m. Metro: Braddock Rd., then 10E Bus.

St. Gregory Hotel and Suites 2033 M St. NW (202) 223-0200 or (800) 950-1363

This 9-story hotel opened in 2000 with 145 rooms, 100 of which are suites. Be-sides the usual amenities, there is same-day laundry, valet parking, a pool, fitness center, meeting rooms, a café, and coffee bar. There are 3 keyed floors of "club level" suites that allow private access, and special amenities including a personal concierge, complimentary breakfast, evening cocktails in the club lounge, and a business center. Middle-range rates. Metro: Dupont Circle, then a 3-block walk.

St. John's Episcopal Church 1525 H St., NW (202) 347-8766 www.stjohns-dc.org

In 1816, while busy restoring the Capitol from the British burning, Benjamin Latrobe completed this Greek Revival–style church and enrolled as its first organist. A porch was added in 1822 along with other changes, and in 1883 James Renwick added a Palladian window. From James Madison to the present, every president has attended regular or occasional services; thus, it is known as "the church of the presidents." The steeple bell, cast by Paul Revere's son, is from melted British can-non. The parish house next door to the church first served as the British Legation, and it was there that Secretary of State Daniel Webster signed the treaty fixing the border between the New England states and the Canadian provinces. The church offers brochures for a self-guided tour. Admission free. Open weekdays 9 a.m.–3 p.m. Guided tours by appointment. Metro: McPherson Square.

St. Kitts and Nevis Embassy 3216 New Mexico Ave. NW (202) 686-2636 www .stkittsnevis.org

St. Lucia Embassy 3216 New Mexico Ave. NW (202) 364-6792

St. Luke's Episcopal Church 1514 15th St. NW at Church St. NW (202) 667-4394 www.edow.org/stlukesdc

This was the city's first independent African American Episcopal church, founded in 1873 by Reverend Alexander Crummell, who 24 years later founded the African American Negro Academy. The church was designed by Calvin T. S. Brent in early English Gothic style and completed in 1879. Metro: U St.-Cardozo.

St. Luke's Gallery 1715 Q St. NW (202) 328-2424

This gallery, directed by Ellen and Nizar Jawdat, offers European paintings, drawings and extensive prints, mainly from the sixteenth to the eighteenth centu-ries. Often in their delightful townhouse studio there are early Piranesi etchings, David Roberts original lithographs, and etchings by Domenichino and Whistler. Open Sat 11 a.m.–5 p.m., Tues–Fri by appointment. Metro: Dupont Circle.

St. Mark's Episcopal Church 118 Third St. SE (202) 543-0053 www.stmarks.net

This beautiful Romanesque church, located behind the Adams Building of the

Library of Congress, was designed by T. Buckler Ghequier and was under construction from 1888 to 1894. The interior is exposed red brick studded with brilliant stained glass windows, including a Louis Comfort Tiffany window in the north-end baptistery. President Lyndon Johnson was a frequent visitor. Open for services only. Metro: Capitol South or Union Station.

St. Mark's Players 118 Third St. SE (202) 546-9670 www.stmarksplayers.org

Since 1983 this award-winning theater group presents three works each season: a "family-oriented" musical, a dramatic selection, and a major Broadway musical. More than 300 people, many from the church membership, assist with each production. The church provides rehearsal and performance space, but parking in Capitol Hill is, as they say, limited, and thus, public transportation is advised. See the Web site for performances, show times, and ticket ordering. Modest prices. Metro: Capitol South, then walk east on C St. SE, turn left onto 3rd St. SE and continue north to A St. SE; or Union Station Metro, walk southeast on Massachusetts Ave. to 3rd St. NE. Turn right and continue south to A St. SE.

St. Mary Mother of God Catholic Church 725 5th St. NW (202) 289-7770

This Gothic-style church, built by E. F. Baldwin in 1890, uses Potomac bluestone with Ohio sandstone for trim. The stained glass windows were imported from Munich. The building replaced one built in 1846, which was the first Roman Catholic church in Washington. It served the large German community in the area. Masses are no longer offered in German; besides English, customarily in Tridentine Latin and Cantonese. Metro: Gallery Pl.-Chinatown or Judiciary Square.

St. Mary's Catholic Church 300 block of Royal St., Alexandria, VA

St Mary's Church, the first Catholic church in Virginia, was founded in 1795 and its building was erected on this site between 1789 and 1793. George Washington, although not Catholic, contributed to its construction. Only the church graveyard is left, the oldest Catholic cemetery in Virginia. It is located between Royal and Washington Sts., boxed in by St. Mary's School to the north and I-95 and construction for the new Wilson Bridge on the south. There is a gate at the north end at Washington St. Metro: King Street, then DAT7 DASH Bus.

St. Mary's Church Cemetery *see* F. Scott Fitzgerald's Grave Site.

St. Mary's Episcopal Church 730 23rd St. (202) 333-3985

Designed by James Renwick Jr., this Gothic-style church was completed in 1867. It became the first Protestant Episcopal church in Washington for African Americans after the Civil War. The stained glass windows were crafted by the Lorin company of Chartres, France. The previous building on the site was a small chapel that was moved there thanks to the efforts of President Abraham Lincoln's secretary of war, Edwin M. Stanton, who had it dismantled, moved across Washington by cart, and rebuilt. Metro: Foggy Bottom-GWU.

St. Matthew's Cathedral 1725 Rhode Island Ave. NW (202) 347-3215 www.stmatthewscathedral.org

Completed in 1895, this church was designed in Renaissance style by architect C. Grant La Farge and designated a cathedral in 1939 at the time the Archdiocese of Washington was established. It honors Saint Matthew the Apostle, who is the patron saint of civil servants. A major event each year is the Red Mass, focusing on the legal profession, which can include Supreme Court justices, members of Congress, and other government officials. President John F. Kennedy attended this church, and a funeral mass was held for him there. Fine mosaics and large frescoes brighten the interior. A new copper dome was installed in 2000. Metro: Farragut West, then a 10-minute walk.

St. Patrick's Catholic Church 619 10th St. NW (202) 374-2713 http://users.erols .com/saintpat

The original parish of St. Patrick's, dating from 1794, was made up mostly of Irish immigrants employed at the worksite of the Capitol and the White House. They met in a frame chapel. In 1809 a brick church was built based upon a design by James Hoban. British soldiers, taking a break from burning the sites built by the St. Patrick's parishioners, attended mass there in 1814. The present Gothic structure, composed of Potomac bluestone, and completed in 1884, was designed by the firm of Wood, Donn, and Deming. Metro: Metro Center.

St. Patrick's Day Parade Washington: St. Patrick's Day Parade Committee, P.O. Box 11584 (202) 637-2474 www.dcstpatsparade.com; Alexandria: Ballyshaners, Inc., P.O. Box 21595, Alexandria, VA (703) 237-2199 www.ballyshaners.org

The Washington event, held the Sunday before March 17, includes top marching bands, pipe bands, dancers, floats, and fire trucks led by a grand marshal. The assemblage travels down Constitution Ave. from 7th to 17th Sts. and usually starts at noon. The Old Town Alexandria parade is held on a Saturday a week or two before the Washington Parade. It steps off at 12:30 p.m. at King and West Sts. and follows King St. to Fairfax St. Many related events are scheduled. Besides the two parade's Web sites, a useful regional calendar of events related to St. Patrick's Day is maintained at the Irish Embassy Web site: www.irelandemb.org.

St. Paul's Episcopal Church Rock Creek Parish, Church Rd. and Webster St. NW (202) 726-2080 www.rockcreekparish.org

The only surviving Colonial church in Washington, St. Paul's was built in 1775, by a parish founded in 1712. The structure was remodeled in 1864 and restored after a 1921 fire left only the 18-inch brick walls standing. In the 1940s stained glass windows were added. The church is surrounded by the 86-acre Rock Creek Cemetery dating from 1719. Metro: Rhode Island Ave., then take Metrobus H8 to Rock Creek Rd. and Upshur St. *See also* Rock Creek Cemetery.

St. Regis 923 16th St. NW (202) 638-2626 (800) 325-3535 www.starwood.com/ stregis

This grand hotel started life in 1926 as the Carlton, the most fashionable smaller hotel in Washington, with an Italian palazzo exterior and enormous rooms, which in those days included a grand piano. The interior is still Renaissance-plush. During the administrations of President Theodore Roosevelt and President Harry Truman, the hotel served as headquarters for America's diplomatic functions. Roosevelt's secretary of state, Cordell Hull, lived there, and kings, queens, presidents, and prime ministers, as well as singer/actress Cher stayed there. A recent $27-million renovation reinforced the hotel's opulent reputation. It has 179 rooms and 14 suites and is located 2 blocks from the White House, the center of the business district, and galleries and museums. It offers the usual luxury hotel amenities. Parking (there is a fee). Expensive. Metro: McPherson Square.

Saint Sophia Greek Orthodox Cathedral 36th St. and Massachusetts Ave. NW (202) 333-4730 www.saintsophiawashington.org

This Byzantine-style building, designed by Archie Protopappas, was completed in 1984. The spectacular interior mosaics covering the walls and dome were a 20-year project of Dimetrios A. Dukas. Tours by appointment. Metro: Dupont Circle, then take Metrobus N6.

St. Teresa's Catholic Church 13th and V St. SE (202) 678-3709

St. Teresa (of Avila) Church, in Victorian Gothic style, was designed by E. Francis Baldwin and completed in 1879. It is stucco with a large rose window on the front façade. This was the first Catholic church in Anacostia. Open for Masses only. Metro: Anacostia.

St. Thomas Episcopal Church 1772 Church St. NW

This large granite neo-Gothic structure with a central tower and spire was built in 1894 and destroyed by arson in 1970. Only the altar wall still stands, surrounded by a park the parishioners opted to provide, rather than rebuild a church. Eleanor and Franklin Roosevelt worshipped at this church. Metro: Farragut West, then take Metrobus N6 to Friendship Heights and Massachusetts Ave.

St. Vincent and the Grenadines Embassy 3216 New Mexico Ave. NW (202) 364-6730

Saks Fifth Avenue 5555 Wisconsin Ave., Chevy Chase, MD (301) 657-9000; Tysons Galleria, 2051 International Dr., McLean, VA (703) 761-0700

A monument to power shoppers, this department store is not just for Washington's grandes dames, but now younger shoppers are filling the aisles as well. Saks provides top cosmetics and offers leading designer clothing for men, women, and children. Free parking, at least. Chevy Chase: Mon–Wed and Fri 10 a.m.–6 p.m., Thurs 10 a.m.–9 p.m., Sun noon–6 p.m. Metro: Friendship Heights. Tysons Galleria: Mon–Fri 10 a.m.–9 p.m., Sat 10 a.m.–7 p.m., Sun noon–6 p.m. Metro: West Falls Church, then take Fairfax Connector 425 Bus to Tysons Westpark Loop.

Sala Thai 2016 P St. NW (202) 872-1144

This inexpensive Thai restaurant is a neighborhood favorite. The popular dishes include eggplant with black-bean sauce; steamed dumplings stuffed with crab, shrimp, and chicken; or just a fix of pad Thai noodles. The extensive menu is a plus in this fluorescent-lit downstairs eatery. Open daily for lunch 11:30 a.m.–2:30 p.m. and dinner 5 p.m.–10:30 p.m. Metro: Dupont Circle.

Salon (Web site) www.salon.com

Founded in 1995, and now receiving more than 2.7 million hits a year, this prize-winning webzine offers in-depth political coverage of Washington, as well as many other features that have a Washington angle. A San Francisco–based media company, Salon offers downloadable interviews and commentary and includes access to The Well, where its online community of influential observers discuss issues of the day.

Saloun 3239 M St. NW (202) 965-4900

This jazz and blues club has been a part of the Georgetown scene for more than 30 years. Saturday is blues night, jazz the rest of the week. No cover charge before 9 p.m. Open Sun–Thurs 5 p.m.–2 a.m., Fri–Sat 4 p.m.–3 a.m. Metro: Foggy Bottom-GWU, then a 10-minute walk, or take Georgetown M St. Shuttle from Metro stop at Dupont Circle or Rosslyn.

Sam and Harry's 1200 19th St. NW (202) 296-4333; and Tysons Corner 8240 Leesburg Pike, Vienna, VA (703) 448-0088 www.samandharrys.com

Not only do many claim this to be the best steakhouse around, but it oozes a comfortable polished mahogany club atmosphere with a pleasant bar. The portions are gigantic. Besides prime meats, or huge juicy burgers, there are lobsters, crab cakes, and shrimp dishes. The Web site offers lunch and dinner menus and tantalizing shots of dishes. Open Mon–Fri 11:30 a.m.–10:30 p.m., Sat 5:30 p.m.–10:30 p.m. Bar open Mon–Sat until midnight. Tysons Corner: Mon–Fri 11:30 a.m.–10:30 p.m., Sat 5:30 p.m.–10:30 p.m. Bar open until midnight.

Sam Woo 1054 Rockville Pike, Rockville, MD (301) 424-0495

This is one of the area's top-ranked Korean restaurants whose extensive menu also provides many Japanese dishes. Try the *bul gorki*, marinated sliced beef, or *bul kalbi*, grilled short ribs. Some dishes are grilled at your table. Inexpensive. Metro: Grovesnor-Strathmore, then Metrobus 46.

Samuel Gompers Memorial Massachusetts Ave. and 10th St. NW

In 1933, the American Federation of Labor erected this bronze memorial of Samuel Gompers, an immigrant cigar maker from England. He founded the organization in 1881 and was reelected president forty-two times until his death in 1924. Metro: McPherson Square, then a 10-minute walk.

Santa Fe East 110 S Pitt St., Alexandria, VA (703) 548-6900

This restaurant offers contemporary Southwestern cuisine in a Santa Fe hacienda—well, at least in a romantic-enough building dating from 1810—right in the heart of Old Town. Try the white chili, blue cornmeal fried calamari, and don't overlook the poblano peppers stuffed with goat cheese or honey-chipotle glazed salmon. Delicious margaritas made from scratch—no mixes. Moderate prices. Mon–Thurs 11:30 a.m.–10 p.m., Fri–Sat 11:30 a.m.–11 p.m., Sun 11:30 a.m.–10 p.m. Metro: King Street.

Sarah Adams Whittemore House *see* Women's National Democratic Club.

Satay Sarinah 512-A S Van Dorn St., Alexandria, VA (703) 370-4313 www.satay sarinah.com

Formerly the Sarinah Satay House in Georgetown, and now located in the Van Dorn Metro Station plaza, this restaurant has been satisfying patrons with a hankering for authentic Indonesian cuisine since 1985. Try the *udang belado*, peeled jumbo shrimp fried in belado chili sauce; or *lontong rames*, steamed; a rice roll served with chicken in coconut milk; and hot and spicy green beans, satay, and shrimp chips. Check out the extensive menu on the Web site. Inexpensive. Mon–Thurs noon–9 p.m., Fri–Sat noon–10 p.m., Sun 5 p.m.–9 p.m. Metro. Van Dorn Street.

Saturday Morning at the National Theater 1321 Pennsylvania Ave. NW (202) 783-3372 (recorded information) www.nationaltheater.org

Free performances for children 4 and older are held on about twenty Saturdays throughout the year at 9:30 a.m. and 11 a.m. in the National's Helen Hayes Gallery. Events could involve puppets, storytelling, clowning, dance, sport figures, natural history, science, and music. Seating is limited. Tickets are required and are distributed without charge a half hour prior to the performance on a first-come, first-served basis. For a program schedule, check the Web site or send a self-addressed, stamped envelope to Saturday Morning, National Theater, 1321 Pennsylvania Ave. NW, Washington, D.C. 20004. Metro: Metro Center or Federal Triangle.

Saudi Arabia Embassy 601 New Hampshire Ave. NW (202) 337-4076 www.saudi embassy.net

Savoy Suites 2505 Wisconsin Ave. NW (202) 337-9700 or (800) 944-5377 www. savoysuites.com

This 150-room hotel overlooking the Russian Embassy offers comfortable suites, some with Jacuzzis or kitchens. The hotel is located farther up on Wisconsin Ave. between Calvert and Davis Sts. The hotel provides a shuttle service to the Metro station. Besides the usual amenities, the hotel provides free underground parking, multi-line phones with data ports and voice mail, a restaurant and lounge, and an exercise facility. Metro: Woodley Park.

Sawatdee 2250 Clarendon Blvd., Arlington, VA (703) 243-8181

This upscale Thai restaurant with comfortable booths and an accommodating staff provides a flavorful array of Thai dishes. Moderate prices. Mon–Thurs 11:30 a.m.–10 p.m., Fri –Sat 11:30 a.m.–10:30 p.m., Sun noon–9 p.m. Metro: Court House.

Scandal Tours 1602 South Springwood Dr., Silver Spring, MD (202) 783-7212 www.gnpcomedy.com/ScandalTours.html

The long-running Gross National Product improvisational comedy team is the group behind this tour of some of Washington's scandal scenes, which means, alas, many national landmarks. Team members impersonate political figures. The 1½-hour tour runs every Saturday from April to September. The tour bus departs from the Old Post Office Pavilion, 12th and Pennsylvania NW. Phone for reservations. Metro: Archives-Navy Memorial.

Science and Technology Museums *see* Alexandria Archeology Museum, Intelstat, NASA Goddard Visitors Center, National Air and Space Museum, National Building Museum, National Museum of Health and Medicine, National Museum of Natural History. *See also* Art and Design Museums, Ethnic and Community Museums, Historical Museums, Major Museums, Media Museums, Museums of Particular Interest to Children, Smithsonian Institution Museums, Specialized Museums.

sc94.ameslab.gov (Web site) http://sc94.ameslab.gov/
Placed on the Web years ago to assist visitors attending computer conferences, this site provides a map of Washington with hotlinks to some of the major tourist sites and selected hotels.

Scott Circle Massachusetts Ave., Rhode Island Ave., and 16th St. NW
Dominating Scott Circle is Henry Kirk Brown's equestrian statue of General Winfield Scott. Metro: Farragut West, then a 10-minute walk. *See also* Winfield Scott Statue, U.S. Soldiers' and Airmen's Home.

Scott-Grant House 3238 R St. NW
This in-town retreat of President Ulysses S. Grant was built in 1858 for A.V. Scott from Alabama. During the Civil War, Lt. Gen. Henry Hallick rented it, and occasionally President Abraham Lincoln would drop by. Metro: Farragut West, then take Metrobus 35.

Scott Memorial *see* Winfield Scott Statue.

Scottish Christmas Walk Alexandria Convention & Visitors Association, 421 King St., Suite 300, Alexandria, VA (703) 838-4200 or (800) 388-9119 www.funside.com
Alexandria's Old Town was, of course, a Colonial seaport, and seafaring Scots were there aplenty. Celebrating this heritage takes place over a weekend in early December. The parade usually includes tartan-clad bagpiper units, military regiments, highlanders, and marching bands. Included in the weekend festivities are old home tours, children's events, highland dancing, and a Christmas marketplace and crafts fair. Metro: Braddock Road, then take DAT34 DASH Bus to King St.

Scottish Rite Masonic Temple 1733 16th St. NW (202) 232-3579 www.cr.nps.gov/nr/travel/wash/dc54.htm
This remarkable building, designed by John Russell Pope, who also designed the National Archives and the Jefferson Memorial, was completed in 1915. It is patterned after one of the seven wonders of the ancient world, the mausoleum of Halicarnassus in what is now Turkey. The two sphinxes guarding the entrance, sculpted by Alexander Weinman, were each cut from solid blocks of limestone. The building serves as the headquarters for the Supreme Council of the Southern Jurisdiction of the Thirty-Third Degree of the Ancient and Accepted Scottish Rite of Freemasonry. Their library maintains a major collection of books by and about Scottish poet Robert Burns. Tours Mon–Fri 8 a.m. and 2 p.m. Library access by appointment. Metro: Dupont Circle.

Sculpture Gardens Outdoor Rink on the Mall at 7th St. and Constitution Ave. NW (202) 737-6938 www.guestservices.com/skating
The National Gallery of Art Sculpture Garden ice-skating rink's season runs from mid-November to the middle of March, weather permitting. The rink has more than 48,000 skaters a year, who mostly glide across the ice to a state-of-the-art music system. The Pavilion Café, overlooking the remarkable sculpture garden as well as the skaters, serves wraps, sandwiches, pizzas, and salads. Coffee, tea, hot chocolate, wine, and beer are available. Open Mon–Thurs 10 a.m.–11 p.m., Fri–Sat

10 a.m.–midnight, Sun. 11 a.m.–9 p.m. Inexpensive skating fee with season tickets available. Metro: Archives-Navy Memorial.

Seabees Memorial Memorial Dr., Arlington National Cemetery, Arlington, VA (703) 607-8052 www.arlingtoncemetery.org/site_map.html

Commissioned by the Seabees Memorial Association, this memorial honors the U.S. Naval Construction Battalions (CB or Seabee) formed early in World War II. The Seabees' extraordinary feats included building landing strips in tropical Pacific Islands, routinely accomplishing such tasks almost overnight and while under fire. The sculptor of the standing bronze figures, Felix de Weldon, also created the Iwo Jima Memorial. Behind the bronze figure of a bare-chested Seabee holding the hand of a small child is a black granite wall bearing a bronze relief of Seabees working at various construction sites. The memorial was erected in 1974. Arlington National Cemetery is open to the public daily at 8 a.m. From April 1 to September 30 the cemetery closes at 7 p.m.; the other six months it closes at 5 p.m. Metro: Arlington Cemetery.

Sea Catch 1054 31st St., N.W. (202) 337-8855 www.seacatchrestaurant.com

This seafood restaurant overlooks the historic C&O Canal, with a deck just feet from the water. Indoors two fireplaces and stone and brick walls accent the equally historic building constructed in 1840. This early canal warehouse became Herman Hollerith's 1890s factory producing punched-card tabulating machines that evolved into IBM. Besides picking from ten yards of raw seafood from the bar including oysters, clams, shrimp, and lobster, you can choose from an impressive array of seasonal fresh fish and even roast chicken and steaks. Consider taking a virtual tour of the restaurant from the Web site. Moderate prices. Open for lunch Mon–Sat noon–3 p.m., dinner Mon–Thurs 5:30 p.m.–10 p.m., Fri–Sat 5:30 p.m.–10:30 p.m. Metro: Foggy Bottom-GWU, Rosslyn, and Dupont Circle.

Seafood and Fish Restaurants *see* Bethesda Crab House, Crisfield, Dancing Crab, Fish Market, Georgetown Seafood Grill, Grillfish, Hogates, Johnny's Half Shell, Legal Seafoods, McCormick and Schmick's, Melrose, Old Ebbitt Grill, Pesce, Phillips Flagship, Pier 7, Le Rivage, Sea Catch, Sequoia, Tony and Joe's Seafood Place. *See also* www.washingtonpost.com.

Seaport Center Alexandria Seaport Foundation, Alexandria Waterfront, Old Town Alexandria, VA (703) 549-7078 http://alexandria.rezcenter.com/alexandria_seaport_center.shtml

Founded in 1983 to celebrate the Potomac riverfront and Alexandria's maritime history, this organization offers a floating museum, library, boat building and restoration demonstrations, a marine sciences lab, and rental of sailing and rowing boats. Open daily 9 a.m.–4 p.m. Closed national holidays. Metro: King Street.

Season Celebrations *see* Events in Washington D.C., Events in Washington D.C. by Month.

Seasonal Events in Washington, D.C. *see* Events in Washington by Month.

Seasons Four Seasons Hotel, 2800 Pennsylvania Ave. NW at 28th St. (202) 342-0444 www.fourseasons.com/washington/dining/dining.html

This highly ranked restaurant (*Wine Spectator, Gourmet* magazine, AAA) provides imaginative American cuisine amid a bubbling fountain, large windows, lush plants, the occasional celebrity, and people getting engaged. While much of the menu changes daily, a typical entrée could be lamb with Provençale vegetables, Yukon gold potatoes, and cabernet sauce, or maybe mushroom and barley-stuffed quail. Expensive. Breakfast 7 a.m.–11 a.m., lunch Sun–Fri noon–2 p.m., dinner daily 6 p.m.–10:30 p.m. Metro: Foggy Bottom, then a 10-minute walk.

Second Division Memorial Constitution Ave. near 17th St. NW www.nps.gov/whho/Statues/second_division_memorial.htm

Designed by architect John Russell Pope, this memorial honors the 17,669 U.S. Army Second Division soldiers who died in World Wars I and II and the Korean Conflict. The original memorial, honoring the Division's dead in World War I, was dedicated in 1936. The memorial's 18-foot gilded flaming sword was sculpted by James Fraser. Metro: Federal Triangle, then take Metrobus 13B to Constitution Ave. and 17th St.

Second Story Books 2000 P St. NW (202) 659-8884; 4836 Bethesda Ave., Bethesda, MD (301) 656-0170; 12160 Parklawn Dr. (at Wilkins Ave.), Rockville, MD (301) 770-0477 www.secondstorybooks.com

These three stores, all within walking distance of a Red Line Metro stop, are a browser's delight; fresh stock keeps pouring in. They do appraisals, assist in donations to institutions, and buy books from single titles from walk-ins to personal libraries from estates. All in all, you have access to more than a million used books as well as manuscripts, maps, LPs, CDs, ephemera, prints, paintings, and vintage posters. You can browse through their shelves by keyword from home. Check out their Web site for the process. However, only one book in ten is listed online, still reason for personally perusing the stacks, particularly the half-million titles in the Rockville warehouse. Their topical depth is astounding. The Rockville warehouse offers 10,000 collectable mystery and science fiction hardbacks and 35,000 mystery and science fiction paperbacks. P St.: Open daily 10 a.m.–10 p.m. Metro: Dupont Circle; Bethesda: 10 a.m.–10 p.m. Metro: Bethesda; Warehouse: Open Sun–Thurs 10 a.m.–8 p.m., Fri–Sat 10 a.m.–9 p.m. Metro: Twinbrook, then a 10-minute walk.

Senate and House Office Buildings Capitol Hill (202) 224-3121 www.aoc.gov/cc/cc_overview.htm

This congressional complex on Capitol Hill holds the office suites for legislators and their support staff as well as the standing-committee suites and hearing rooms. There are three major office buildings and two annex buildings for the House of Representatives and three major office buildings for the Senate. The Cannon House Office Building is located southeast of the Capitol on a site bounded by Independence Ave., 1st St., New Jersey Ave., and C St. SE. It opened in 1907. Longworth House Office Building, which opened in 1933 and replaced Conrad and McMunn's Boarding House where Thomas Jefferson lived as vice president, is located south of the Capitol on a site bounded by Independence Ave., New Jersey Ave., S Capitol St., and C St. SE. Rayburn House Office Building opened in 1965 and is located south of the Capitol on a site bounded by Independence Ave., New Jersey Ave., S Capitol St., and C St. SE. House annexes include the former Congressional Hotel, located on C St. and renamed for former Speaker Thomas P. O'Neill Jr., and an old FBI building at 2nd and D Sts., renamed for former Minority Leader Gerald R. Ford. The Russell Senate Office Building, which opened in 1909, is located northeast of the Capitol on a site bounded by Constitution Ave., 1st St., Delaware Ave., and C St. NE. The Dirksen Senate Office Building, which opened in 1958, is located northeast of the Capitol, adjoining the Hart Senate Office Building on a site bounded by Constitution Ave., 2nd St., 1st St., and C St. NE. The Hart Senate Office Building, which opened in 1982, is located northeast of the Capitol, adjoining the Dirksen Senate Office Building, on a site bounded by Constitution Ave., 2nd St., 1st St., and C St. NE. These buildings are open 9 a.m.–6 p.m. weekdays and closed on Federal holidays. Metro: Capitol South.

Seneca Creek State Park 11950 Clopper Rd., Gaithersburg, MD (301) 924-2127 www.dnr.state.md.us/publiclands/central/seneca.html

This 7,000-acre park runs 12 miles along its namesake creek on its way to the Potomac. For history buffs, there is a self-guided interpretive walk as well as a restored eighteenth-century log cabin. The 90-acre Clopper Lake provides opportunities for canoeing, kayaking, boating, and fishing. A hand launch site is available for the lake. Private boats are not permitted on weekends and holidays May through September. A concession rents boats from May to September. More than 12 miles of mountain biking and hiking trails are available. There are playgrounds, picnicking areas, and shelters as well as an 18-hole golf course. A visitor center provides interpretive programs throughout the year. Check the Web site for hours. Open year-round. By car take I-270 north toward Frederick, Maryland. Take Exit 10, Clopper Rd. and continue through six traffic lights. *See also* www.commuter page.com/venues/gardens.htm.

Senegal Embassy 2112 Wyoming Ave. NW (202) 234-0540

Senses 3206 Grace St. NW (202) 342-9083

You could hop on one foot from the C&O Canal to this delightful French patisserie or maybe bakery or French restaurant—you decide—if only it was easier to find. It is hidden off Wisconsin Ave. and a block from M St. in Georgetown. The menu is such that it's a favorite stop for breakfast, brunch, lunch, afternoon tea, or dinner. Try the roasted sea bass with butternut squash or an afternoon fix of chocolate torte. Metro: Foggy Bottom-GWU, then a 15-minute walk, or take Georgetown M St. Shuttle from the Metro stop at Dupont Circle or Rosslyn.

Sequoia 3000 K St. NW at 30th St. at Washington Harbour (202) 944-4200

This large restaurant, named after President Richard M. Nixon's yacht, offers terraced seating behind enormous windows or outside on the large terraced patio. While both offer glorious Potomac views, it seems more fun to lounge out on the patio and watch the river as well as the 20-somethings swarm. The cuisine is contemporary American and includes sandwiches, pastas, and seafood. Fairly expensive. Metro: Foggy Bottom-GWU, then a 10-minute walk, or take Georgetown M St. Shuttle from the Metro stop at Dupont Circle or Rosslyn.

Service for Disabled *see* Disabled Services.

Sesto Sento 1214 18th St. NW (202) 785-9525

This restaurant does a great job providing authentic Italian meals during lunch and dinner. Then about 11:30 onward on Friday and Saturday a youngish crowd dressed in dark clothes dance, with a DJ usually providing music. There are large mirrors, large chandeliers, and the comforting fragrance of *penne arrabiata, linguini di mare*, pizza, and spicy tomato sauces. Open for lunch Mon–Fri 11:30 a.m.–3 p.m., dinner Mon–Sat 5:30 p.m.–11 p.m. Club open Wed–Sat 11 p.m.–3 a.m. Metro: Dupont Circle.

701 Pennsylvania Avenue 701 Pennsylvania Ave. NW (202) 393-0701 www.701 restaurant.com/

Overlooking Pennsylvania Ave. and the Navy Memorial fountain, this spacious, comfortably elegant restaurant offers an eclectic international cuisine, from chick-pea-encrusted diver scallops to coriander-crusted pork chops. Check the current menu on the Web site, along with "what the critics are saying." The clubby Caviar Lounge serves Russian and domestic caviar and twenty different kinds of chilled vodka. The restaurant is close to the Shakespeare Theatre, attracting a lively pre-theater crowd. Moderate prices. Open Sun–Thurs 5:30 p.m.–10:30 p.m., Fri–Sat 5:30 p.m.–11 p.m. Metro: Archives-Navy Memorial.

1789 Restaurant 1226 36th St. NW (202) 965-1789 http://1789restaurant.com

Opened in 1962, wondrous American cuisine is being served in this Georgetown Federal-era townhouse with 3 floors and 5 dining rooms, each with its own theme. With the working fireplaces, the Limoges china, burnished American antiques, and hand-colored English prints, as *Washingtonian Magazine* suggests, this is a great "special occasions" restaurant. If there were such a cuisine as haut comfort food, that could describe award-winning chef Ris Locoste's classic seafood stew, rack of lamb in merlot sauce, or roast lobster. Expensive. Open Mon–Thurs 6 p.m.–10 p.m., Fri 6 p.m.–11 p.m., Sat 5:30 p.m.–11 p.m., Sun 5:30 p.m.–10 p.m. Metro: Foggy Bottom-GWU.

Seventh-Day Adventist World Headquarters 12501 Old Columbia Pike, Silver Spring, MD (301) 680-6310 www.adventist.org/visitgc

Tour leaders relate the history of the Adventist Church from its beginnings in the early 1800s, to today's 11-million-member worldwide church, and introduce you to its programs, including their health care institutions located around the globe. After the tour, you are welcome to stay for lunch in their vegetarian cafeteria, which is open Mon–Thurs 11:30 a.m.–1 p.m., and Friday 11:30 a.m.–12:30 p.m. Tours of about an hour take place Mon–Thurs 10:30 and 1:30, and Fri at 10 a.m. Closed on major holidays. Metro: Glenmont, then take Metrobus 10 toward Hillandale.

Sewall-Belmont House 144 Constitution Ave. NE (202) 546-3839 www.cr.nps.gov/ nr/travel/wash/dc82.htm

One of the oldest houses in Washington, this Federal/Queen Anne–style house has seen more history than the Discovery Channel. To cite a few instances, King

Charles II gave the land to Lord Baltimore in 1632. Robert Sewall built the present structure in 1800, incorporating an existing carriage house dating from 1680. Albert Gallatin, secretary of the treasury to Presidents James Madison and Thomas Jefferson, arranged the financing of the Louisiana Purchase here in 1803. In 1814 pot shots from behind the house by retreating Yankee soldiers killed an invading British soldier as well as the horse carrying the British commanding general. In retaliation, troops torched the house. It was rebuilt and in 1929 sold to the National Women's Party, to which the wealthy Alva Belmont was a major benefactor. Alice Paul, founder of the National Women's Party and author of the Constitution's original Equal Rights Amendment, lived here from 1929 to 1972. The mansion remains NWP headquarters. It also serves as a museum, with photos and portraits and artifacts of women involved in the suffrage and equal rights movements. These include Susan B. Anthony's desk and a banner raised across from the White House during the first U.S. protests demanding women's enfranchisement. Open Tues–Fri 9 a.m.–5 p.m., Sat noon–4 p.m. Daily docent-led tours at 11 a.m., noon, and 1 p.m. Closed New Year's Day, Thanksgiving Day, and Christmas Day. Metro: Eastern Market.

Shady Grove Metro Station Sommerville Dr., Rockville, MD www.wmata.com

The Shady Grove Metro station in northern Rockville is the end of the Red line. Inexpensive all-day parking fees make this a favorite of day-trippers. By car from I-270 near Gaithersburg, take Exit 9, Sam Eig Hwy./Metro Station.

Shakespeare Theatre 450 7th St. NW (202) 547-1122 (877) 487-8849 http://shakespearedc.org

Founded in 1970, the theater moved in 1992 from its location with rock-hard chairs in the Folger Shakespeare Library to a comfortable, as well as state-of-the-art, 450-seat stage in the former Lansburgh Department Store. Artistic Director Michael Kahn together with the theater's artists and much behind-the-scenes physical and financial support (7,500 individuals and 300 corporations) contributed to make it (in the words of the *Wall Street Journal* "the nation's foremost Shakespeare Company." More than forty Helen Hayes Awards have come their way to this theater since 1987. Each season the theater presents five plays by Shakespeare and other classical playwrights. It offers, as well, free Shakespeare at the Carter Barron Amphitheater every summer. The active educational programs include a curriculum enrichment program working with local public school teachers, many activities involving local students, master acting classes for both teens and adults, and professional internships. The shows often sell out. Thus, it is best to book one of the assorted annual offerings, which have a considerable price range and are explained on the Web site. Metro: Gallery Pl.-Chinatown or Archives. *See also* www.commuterpage.com/venues/venue-en.htm

Shakespeare Theatre in the Park Carter Barron Amphitheatre, 16th St. and Colorado Ave. NW (202) 547-3230

Since 1991, for two weeks in June, Washington's Shakespeare Theatre Company offers admission-free Shakespearian productions (Shakespeare Free for All) in the

Carter Barron Amphitheatre. This popular event, attracting more than 2,500 theatergoers each evening, makes Shakespeare available to nontraditional audiences. The stage is covered but the audience is under the stars. Metro: Metro Center, then take Metrobus S4 to 16th St. and Colorado.

Shakespeare's Birthday *see* William Shakespeare's Birthday.

Shamash: the Jewish Network (Web site) www.shamash.org

This site maintains a worldwide annotated listing of kosher, and to a lesser degree, vegetarian restaurants, including sixteen in the metropolitan Washington area. The search engine allows brief to more-than-you-want-to-know information about each restaurant.

Shaw Neighborhood btw N Capitol and 16th Sts. on the east and west, Florida Ave. and M St. on north and south www.dcheritage.org/information2550/

This neighborhood includes the U Street Corridor, Howard University, and the neighboring area around Logan Circle. The neighborhood's name came from Shaw Junior High School, which in turn was named for Col. Robert Shaw, leader of the African American 54th Massachusetts Regiment in the Civil War. Following the Civil War, black professionals built homes here, erecting handsome Victorian, mostly row houses, largely built and financed by the black community and now being rebuilt and restored. Shaw's central role in all aspects of the city's black community continues. In the 1920s and 1930s, the U Street Corridor became "the Great Black Way" with the Lincoln Theatre, lively clubs, and name entertainers. The recent resurgence of clubs and restaurants, related in part to the recently opened U Street Metro stop, has put an end to the neighborhood's decline that started in the middle 1950s. It is recovering, as well, from the devastation brought about by the riots in 1968 following the assassination of Martin Luther King Jr. Shaw residents have been active in supporting civil rights. In the late 1930s Shaw activists picketed local businesses to end discriminatory practices. A court injunction banning such picketing went all the way to the Supreme Court. The court's 1938 landmark decision *New Negro Alliance v. Sanitary Grocery* supported the Shaw activists and their use of consumer pressure to right civil-right wrongs; a major stepping-stone furthering equality. In the 1950s, the work of the neighborhood's Committee for School Desegregation led to what was to be known as the Supreme Court decision *Brown v. Board of Education* mandating school desegregation. Metro: Shaw-Howard University.

Sheraton National 900 South Orme St., Arlington Blvd., Arlington, VA (703) 521-1900 (800) 468-9090 www.sheratonnationalhotel.com

This 408-room hotel is convenient to Washington, D.C., and Reagan National Airport. Complimentary shuttle transportation is available to and from Reagan National Airport as well as to the Pentagon City Metro station and shopping mall. A $25-million renovation included an upgrade of its meeting and exhibit facilities. The usual Sheraton amenities are provided. Besides the lounge area café open for breakfast, lunch, and dinner, there is a rooftop restaurant for evening dining. Metro: Pentagon City.

Sheraton Premiere at Tysons Corner 8661 Leesburg Pike, Vienna, VA (703) 448-1234 (800) 950-1363 www.starwood.com/sheraton

This contemporary 437-room luxury hotel has spacious guestrooms and the usual array of amenities, as well as indoor and outdoor pools, a fitness center, racquetball courts, tennis courts, golf privileges, hair salon, free parking, bar, restaurants, spa, and free breakfast. Near northern Virginia's major shopping malls. Pets are allowed. The hotel offers a shuttle to nearby Dulles Airport, about 15 minutes away, and a free shuttle to the nearest Metro stop. Expensive. Metro: Dunn Loring-Merrifield.

Sheraton Suites Alexandria 801 N Asaph St., Alexandria, VA (703) 836-4700 www.starwood.com/sheraton

Located in Old Town Alexandria, with its nearby restaurants, galleries, and shops, this 247-suite hotel offers easy access to and from Reagan National Airport. Besides the usual Sheraton amenities, the hotel offers a restaurant, pool and health club, and self-pay parking. Free Reagan National Airport/Metro shuttle as well as to King St. in Old Town. Shuttle runs 6 a.m.–11 p.m. Metro: Reagan National Airport.

Sheridan Circle Massachusetts Ave. and 23rd St. NW www.dcheritage.org/dch_tourism2556

Dominating the circle is the bronze equestrian sculpture of Civil War general, Philip H. Sheridan. Sheridan's death in 1888 led to the renaming of the circle—it was originally named after Commodore Stephen Decatur—and the subsequent statue erected in his honor. Sheridan's widow, 24 years younger than the general, was so taken with the circle that she moved to 2211 Massachusetts Ave. overlooking the sculpture and lived there until her death in 1938. Her home is now part of the Greek Embassy. A small medallion marker on the circle notes a 1976 political assassination at the site. A remote-controlled bomb blew apart a car in which former Chilean Ambassador Orlando Letelier and aide Ronni Karpen Moffitt were riding, killing Letelier and wounding Moffitt's husband who was in the backseat. The crime, traced to Chilean agents working for Gen. Augusto Pinochet, resulted in several convictions. Metro: Dupont Circle. *See also* Sheridan Statue.

Sheridan Statue Sheridan Circle, Massachusetts Ave. and 23rd Sts. NW

This bronze sculpture of Gen. Philip H. Sheridan on his favorite horse was sculpted by Gutzon Borglum of Mount Rushmore fame. It was dedicated in 1908 in what was originally known as Decatur Circle. Sheridan rose from an obscure captain at the beginning of the Civil War to command of the Union cavalry at the end of the war. He was regarded as one of the Union's top three commanders. Metro: Dupont Circle.

Sherman Monument *see* William Tecumseh Sherman Monument.

Shevchenko Memorial *see* Taras Shevchenko Monument.

Shiloh Baptist Church 1500 9th St. NW (202) 232-4200 www.shilohbaptist.org

In 1854 in Fredericksburg, Virginia, a black church group bought a building for $500 from a white congregation and named it Shiloh Baptist Church. By 1861, at the onset of the Civil War, the Shiloh congregation grew to 750 members; most were slaves, the rest free blacks. The following year Union troops used the church as a hospital and offered safe passage to Washington, allowing the congregation to move there. Their first permanent home in Washington was built on the present site in 1924. The present building has been rebuilt after several fires. It is one of Washington's most active churches, with a number of choirs and services filling its 800-seat auditorium to capacity. Metro: Federal Triangle, then take Metrobus 66 at Pennsylvania Ave. and E St. to 11th St.

Shipman House Bed and Breakfast 1310 Q St. NW (877) 893-3233 www.bbonline .com/dc/thereeds

This 1887 Victorian home has been lovingly restored by its present owners, Charles and Jackie Reed. Features such as original wood paneling, stained glass windows, a player piano, authentic Victorian decorations and antique furnishings have placed this B&B in various top-ranked guide books and national publications. After an evening in one of their six guest rooms, descend to a home-cooked breakfast of German pancakes or gourmet omelettes. Centrally located in the Logan Circle Historic District, the Shipman House is just 6 blocks to Dupont Circle. Inexpensive. Metro: Shaw-Howard University.

Shopping Malls *See* Ballston Common, Beltway Plaza, Chevy Chase Pavilion, City Place Mall, Crystal City Underground Shopping Center, Dulles Town Center, Fair Oaks Mall, Fashion Center at Pentagon City, Foxhall Square Mall, Galleria at Tysons II, Lakeforest Mall, Mazza Gallerie, Old Post Office Building and Pavilion, Pentagon Center, Potomac Mills, Prince George's Plaza, Shops at Georgetown Park, Shops at National Place, Springfield Mall Shopping Center, Tysons Corner Center, Tysons Galleria, Union Station Shops, Watergate Shops, Westfield Shoppingtown Montgomery Mall, Westfield Shoppingtown Wheaton, White Flint Mall. *See also* Department Stores, Discount Stores and Factory Outlets.

Shops at Georgetown Park 3222 M St. NW (202) 298-5577 www.shopsatgeorge townpark.com

Built in 1981 and backing on the historic C&O Canal, this 100-store shopping mall occupies an entire block and 4 stories of upscale shops in a beautifully designed atmosphere: a Federalist façade, huge skylights, a food court, Abercrombie & Fitch, Dean & DeLuca, Victoria's Secret, Ann Taylor, FAO Schwartz, and lots more. Discounted parking available with moderate mall purchase. An interactive shopping guide from the Web site helps. Open Mon–Sat 10 a.m.–9 p.m., Sun noon–6 p.m. Metro: Foggy Bottom-GWU, then take 30, 32, 34, 35, or 36 Bus. *See also* www.commuterpage.com/venues/venue-shop.htm.

Shops at National Place 1331 Pennsylvania Ave. NW (202) 662-1250

This mall, connected to both the J. W. Marriott Hotel and National Press Building, offers three levels with more than eighty shops, a food court, and several restaurants. Find out-of-town papers and Washington souvenirs here as well. Open Mon–Sat 10 a.m.–7 p.m., Sun noon–5 p.m. Metro: Metro Center. *See also* www .commuterpage.com/venues/venue-shop.htm.

Shops at Union Station *see* Union Station Shops.

Shops at Watergate *see* Watergate Shops.

Shore Shot Cruises Washington Harbour, 31st and K Sts. (202) 554-6500 www .shoreshot.com

The cruise of the 53-foot *Shore Shot* lasts about 50 minutes, departing from Washington Harbour, and traveling about 10 miles along the Potomac, allowing a river's-eye view of the major sights between Georgetown and Reagan National Airport, including the Lincoln and Jefferson Memorials, Arlington Cemetery, Georgetown, the Pentagon, and Kennedy Center. The boat holds up to ninety-nine passengers. Very moderate cost. Tours depart at 11:40 a.m., 12:40 p.m., 1:40 p.m., 2:40 p.m., 3:40 p.m., 4:40 p.m., 5:40 p.m., 6:40 p.m., 7:40 p.m., and from Memorial Day to Labor Day there is an 8:40 p.m. tour. From April 13 to April 30 tours offered only Sat and Sun. From May 1 to Sept. 29 tours offered every day. From October 1 to October 12 tours are offered only Sat and Sun. Metro: Farragut West, then take Metrobus 38B to 31st and K Sts.

Shoreham Omni *see* Omni Shoreham.

Shrine of the Immaculate Conception *see* Basilica of the National Shrine of the Immaculate Conception.

Shrine of the Sacred Heart 16th St. and Park Rd. NW (202) 234-8000 www.paris hes.org/sacredheartdc.html

This Catholic shrine, designed by the firm of Murphy and Olmstead, opened in 1922. The elaborate mosaics inside include John J. Earley's depictions of the lives of the saints. The original parishioners were mostly Irish and German. Now the parish is home to people from sixty countries and, thus, mass is celebrated each weekend in English, Vietnamese, Spanish, and Haitian Creole. Sacred Heart offers a variety of social services to its parish, providing emergency food and meals for the homeless, and cooperates with other service agencies in the neighborhood, including the support systems of the Spanish Catholic Center. Metro: Metro Center, then Metrobus S2 toward Silver Spring.

Sierra Club Mid-Atlantic Field Office, 200 N Glebe Rd., Suite 905, Arlington, VA (703) 312-0533; Washington, D.C. Chapter, 408 C St. NE www.sierraclub.org; District: www.dc.sierraclub.org; Maryland: http://maryland.sierraclub.org; Virginia: www.sierraclub.org/va/

These chapters of the Sierra Club offer opportunities to participate in local outings and chapter activities, as well as volunteer to support local environmental issues. District issues in which they are involved include city recycling programs, transportation and air quality, and many environmental topics. Members receive *Sierra* and a newsletter of local events, forthcoming outings, and campaigns. Among their Washington, D.C., programs is Inner City Outings providing D.C. youth outdoor adventures in natural settings. Their national Web site has links to local chapters in the District, Montgomery County, Prince George's County, Great Falls, Vienna, and Alexandria.

Sierra Leone Embassy 1701 19th St. NW (202) 939-9261

Sights and Entertainment for Children *see* Amusement Parks, Museums of Particular Interest to Children, Places That Appeal to Children.

Sightseeing Tours *see* Boat Tours, Bus Tours, Special Interest Tours, Walking Tours.

Sign of the Whale 1825 M St. NW (202) 785-1110 and 7279 Arlington Blvd., Falls Church, VA (703) 573-1616 www.signofthewhale.com

There are two sites of this popular watering hole, the M St. site, looking inside and out like an après-ski Swiss pub, while the Virginia site is just another space in a Falls Church strip mall. The M St. saloon has a college neighborhood bar feel and the Virginia site is more like an informal neighborhood pub. Evenings, a DJ plays requests. Both serve up A+ hamburgers. The Captain Ahab includes bacon, bleu cheese, and mushroom gravy. The daily specials, from prime rib to seafood gumbo, are always tasty. Inexpensive to moderate. M St. open Sun–Thurs 11:30 a.m.–2 a.m., Fri–Sat 11:30 a.m.–3 a.m. Metro: Farragut North; Falls Church open Mon–Sun 11 a.m.–2 a.m. Metro: Dunn Loring-Merrifield, then take Ballston Metrobus 1B to Arlington Blvd. and Westmoreland Rd.

Signal 66 926 N St. NW (202) 842-3436 www.signal66.com

There should be zither music and cobblestones: walk down Blagden Alley and finally find the buzzer—there is no sign—which speakeasy-like—opens the door with your buzz. Inside is your not-typical-for-Washington exhibit space, a warehouse party atmosphere, and shows of innovative artists. There are evenings of video and music, a "Media That Matters" film festival, sculpture, paintings, photographs, and drinks. Half club, half gallery. Open Thurs 1 p.m.–5 p.m., Fri 5 p.m.–8:30 p.m., Sat noon–6 p.m. Check Web site for new shows. Metro: Mount Vernon Square-UDC.

Signature Theatre 3806 S Four Mile Run Dr., Arlington, VA, box office (703) 218-6500 Administration: (703) 218-6500 www.sig-online.org

This group does amazing things in its 136-seat black box theater. Founded in 1989, the theater offers a five-play season featuring contemporary theater with a special emphasis on musical theater. Ambitious always, the productions have garnered 28 Helen Hayes Awards and 100 nominations in the past 10 years. Productions of Stephen Sondheim musicals are the theater's signature dish, but the menu includes, occasionally, world premieres of new plays. The troupe offers readings of plays in development and an annual all-student production as part of its Signature in the Schools program. Modest prices. Free parking. Metro: Pentagon, then take Ballston Metrobus 25A to S Quincy St. and S Arlington Mill Dr., then a 10-minute walk. By car take I-395 South to Exit 7-Shirlington/Glebe Rd. and remain in the left lane of the exit. The overhead sign is marked "Shirlington," then after passing under the overpass, bear to the right to exit into Shirlington. At the end of the exit at the traffic light turn right. Then go ½ block and turn left onto Four Mile Run Dr. *See also* www.commuterpage.com/venues/venue-en.htm.

Silver Spring Montgomery County, MD

Bordered by Washington, D.C., to the south, Prince George's County to the east, and Howard County to the north, this city was a major shopping center in the '50s and '60s. It now has a population over 200,000. Its revitalization efforts involve renovations and new construction of more than $400 million in private and government investment. The downtown area consists of a mix of office buildings including the National Oceanic and Atmospheric Administration, small businesses, ethnic restaurants, and a 22-acre area attracting some big name retailers. Farther afield, clusters of apartment buildings are surrounded by tree-lined streets of mostly World War II to 1950s-vintage detached houses, colonials, split-levels, and ramblers. Lovely Sligo Creek Park runs through the city, a sort of miniature Rock Creek. Silver Spring's search for a unique identity may be ending. Media organizations have discovered the city with the arrival of Discovery Communications and the American Film Institute. The city is blessed with excellent mass transit service from Metro, Amtrak, MARC commuter rail, and Ride-On, as well as easy access to Annapolis; Washington, D.C.; Baltimore; northern Virginia; and I-95 to points north and south. Metro: Silver Spring.

Silver Spring Farmers Market Fenton St. Village Parking Lot 3, Silver Spring, MD (301) 590-2923 www.farmerlink.com

Rain or shine, this active market offers farm fresh produce and more. Parking at the lot at corner of Fenton St. and Thayer Ave. Open Saturdays, June to October 7 a.m.–1 p.m.

Sim Lee Building 3001–3009 M St. NW www.nps.gov/rocr/oldstonehouse/walk .htm

This large Federalist-era building runs 120 feet along M St. and 240 feet up 30th St. In the 1940s, local citizens saved it from demolition, and their action prompted the Congressional Historic Georgetown Act, making the entire community a protected historic district. The property was the one-time home of Thomas Sim Lee, who twice served as governor of Maryland. He was a close friend to George Washington, active in the American Revolution, and his home served as headquarters of the Federal Party. It was renovated several times and most recently made into several shops, but the building's integrity was protected by both exterior and interior historic easements. Metro: Foggy Bottom-GWU, then 30, 32, 34, 35, or 36 Bus.

Singapore Embassy 3501 International Place (202) 537-3100 www.gov.sg/mfa /washington

Sir Winston Churchill Statue British Embassy, 3100 Massachusetts Ave. NW

This sculpture of a striding Churchill is positioned with his left foot on British soil—the British Embassy—and his right foot in America. Metro: Farragut West, then take Friendship Heights Metrobus N4.

Sirius Coffee Company 4250 Connecticut Ave. NW (202) 364-2600

While serious about their freshly roasted coffee or cappuccino or espresso or whatever, you can also move on to non-caffeine drinks such as beer. Occasional live music. Open Mon–Wed 7:30 a.m.–9 p.m., Thurs–Fri 7:30 a.m.–11 p.m., Sat 8 a.m.–11 p.m., Sun 9 a.m.–7 p.m. Metro: Van Ness-UDC.

Sisterspace and Books 1515 U St. NW (202) 332-3433 www.sisterspace.com

This bookstore specializes in books by and about African American women. In that capacity, it offers book signings, workshops, seminars, and related events throughout the community. Books may be ordered online through the Web site. Metro: U St.-Cardozo.

Site Seeing Tours, Inc. 412 E Melbourne Ave., Silver Spring, MD (301) 445-2098 www.siteseeingtoursinc.com

Founded in 1994 and a member of the DC Heritage Tourism Coalition, the company offers a variety of 4-hour and 8-hour tours. The 8-hour museum tour includes the National Gallery of Art, Air and Space Museum, National Museum of American History, National Museum of Natural History, Freer Gallery of Art, Sackler Gallery of Art, and Hirshhorn Museum. The company offers a wide spectrum of tours, including Washington at Night, several well-designed African American tours, neighborhood 2-hour walking tours such as the heritage tour of U St., and customized tours for school groups and other visitors. Call or check the Web site for planning and arranging pickup.

Six Flags America 13710 Central Ave., Largo, MD (301) 249-1500 www.sixflags .com/america/

This amusement park, formerly Adventure World and Wild World, offers various roller-coaster rides, a wave pool, lots of chutes and flumes, shows, and concessions. Hours vary by month and day of week. Phone or check Web site for hours. Moderate prices. By car from I-495 (the Beltway) take Exit 15A, Rte. 214 East and proceed 5 miles to park. *See also* www.commuterpage.com/venues/gardens.htm.

16th Street Bridge 16th St NW btw Arkansas Ave. and Spring Rd.

Guarded by four tigers sculpted by Alexander Phimister Procter, this unreinforced poured-concrete structure opened for traffic in 1910. The tea-kettle-top curve of its single arch resembles a sister bridge that makes use of a parabolic arch, the world-famous Bixby Creek Bridge on Hwy. 1 in California. However, the 16th Street Bridge has its own claim to fame, being the first parabolic arch bridge in the United States. Metro: Columbia Heights.

16th Street Corridor www.dcheritage.org

Briefly renamed "Avenue of the Presidents" from 1913 to 1914, this street runs north–south from the White House. In city designer Pierre L'Enfant's plan, 16th St. was the city's northerly grand entrance terminating in the "President's Park," now Lafayette Park. Its growth spurt of elegant homes and stately buildings was due in large measure to Mary Henderson, "Queen of 16th Street," whose husband, Senator John Brooks Henderson, drafted the 13th Amendment and whose nay vote on the impeachment of President Andrew Johnson cost him reelection. Mary Henderson lived the rest of her life in litigious splendor at her turreted castle at Florida Ave. and 16th St., built in 1888 and razed in 1949. Working with architect George Oakley Totten, she salted 16th St. with mansions suitable for embassies and the very rich. The Warder-Totten House is one of their buildings, as is 2801 16th St., which she built and tried to give to Uncle Sam for the vice president's residence. Like an architectural display case, the street offers Queen Anne, Italianate, Richardsonian, Romanesque, and Beaux Arts–style buildings. The Web site of University of Virginia School of Architecture provides a block-by-block analysis—with historical photos—of the corridor: http://arch.virginia.edu/dcplaces/16thstreet.html.

Skating *see* Ice-skating.

Skewers 1633 P St. NW (202) 387-7400 www.skewers-cafeluna.com

You guessed it, Skewers is deeply into kebabs, with more than twenty choices, which are served with almond-flaked rice or pasta. Don't overlook the *baba gannouj* to spread over your warm pita bread. Skewers is located directly over Café Luna, and the two share a Web site. Open Mon–Thurs 11 a.m.–11 p.m., Fri–Sat 11 a.m.–1 a.m., Sun 11:30 a.m.–11p.m. Moderate prices. Metro: Dupont Circle.

Sky Terrace 515 15th St. NW at Pennsylvania Ave.

This seasonal outdoor bar atop the Hotel Washington provides good views of the Mall, monuments, and the White House. Lines are common. Light fare. Seasonal. Open May to September daily 11 a.m.–1 a.m. Metro: Metro Center.

Slate (Web site) http://slate.msn.com

This award-winning interactive online magazine has lots to say about Washington, particularly in the "news and politics," "art and life," and "people in the news" departments.

Sligo Creek Pkwy. (301) 650-2600 www.mc-mncppc.org/trails

This road follows Sligo Creek Park through Takoma Park and Silver Spring. Some of the sections of Sligo Creek Pkwy. are closed to auto traffic on Sundays, allowing joggers, skateboarders, and bikers more access. There are hiking trails and 10.6 miles of asphalt bike trail. Local residents are fighting speeding cars on the Pkwy. In 2002, a cyclist was killed by a speeder on the parkway resulting in an ongoing highway safety campaign sponsored by the Washington Area Bicyclist Association.

Slovakia Embassy 3523 International Court NW (202) 237-1054 fax: (202) 237-6438 www.slovakembassy-us.org

Slovenia Embassy 1525 New Hampshire Ave. NW (202) 667-5363 www.embassy.org/slovenia

Small Jewish Museum *see* Lillian and Albert Small Jewish Museum.

Smartraveler.com (Web site) (202) 863-1313 www.smartraveler.com

This is an online or phone traffic report for the Washington, D.C., metropolitan area, a project using resources of various organizations and the *Washington Post*. It provides on-demand real-time traffic reports from 5:30 a.m. to 7 p.m. Monday through Friday, as well as during Redskins home games, major special events (including storms), and holidays. Current traffic information from commuters is updated from spotter planes, cameras, commuters, and other sources. It provides as well Metrorail and Metrobus conditions and schedules, special events and holiday schedules, and schedules of the various regional commuter rails: MARC, VRE, and AMTRAK.

Smith & Wollensky 1112 19th St. NW btw L and M Sts. (202) 466-1110 www .smithandwollensky.com/washington.htm

This latest edition to the Smith & Wollensky steakhouse chain offers a turn-of-the-century New York steakhouse experience in Washington. All beef is prime and dry-aged. This is the place to try a rib eye, filet mignon, and seafood as well. Grilled fish and lobster are also offered. The prize-winning wine collection is still another reason to stop by. Expensive. Open Mon–Fri 11:30 a.m.–4 p.m., 5 p.m.–11 p.m., Sat–Sun 5 p.m.–11 p.m. Upstairs Grill Room open daily 11:30 a.m.–2 a.m. Metro: Farragut West.

Smith Center for the Performing Arts *see* University of Maryland Clarice Smith Center for the Performing Arts.

Smith Row 3255–3267 N St. NW http://www.cr.nps.gov/nr/travel/wash/dc15.htm

These fine examples of brick Federal-style homes are known as Smith Row. They were built in 1815 by Clement Smith and his brother, Walter, as investments. Clement was a cashier and eventually became the president of the Farmers and Mechanics Bank. The interiors, which are oval and circular, with freestanding stairs, are reportedly little changed since the day they were built. Down the block at 3307 N St., was the home of president-elect John F. Kennedy, who sometimes would appear on the porch in 1961 to announce cabinet appointments. Not open to the public. Metro: Rosslyn, then Georgetown Shuttle.

Smith's Bar *see* B. Smith's.

Smithsonian Annual Kite Festival Washington Monument Grounds, 15th St. and Constitution Ave. NW (202) 357-3030 http://kitefestival.org/contact.htm

This annual kite festival for people of all ages includes kite-making workshops, displays by national kite organizations, and you guessed it—kite flying. Kite-flying masters demonstrate their skills, and there is usually a traditional rokkaku kite battle. Competitions for all ages. This day-long event takes place in late March. Metro: Smithsonian.

Smithsonian Asian Pacific American Heritage Month Contact: Smithsonian Center for Education and Museum Studies, Arts and Industries Building, 1000 Jefferson Dr. Various venues at the Smithsonian's museums (202) 357-2700 http:// educate.si.edu/heritage

Celebrating the history of Asian Pacific Americans and how they have contributed so much to the nation's heritage and culture, the Smithsonian sponsors a month-long series of events each May including children's programs, lectures, films, dance exhibitions, and dramatic readings at various sites. Admission free. Metro: Smithsonian.

The Smithsonian Associates Visitor's Information Center, 1000 Jefferson Dr. SW (202) 357-3030 http://residentassociates.org

The Smithsonian Associates provides the world's largest museum-based continuing education and study-tour program. There is a modest annual fee for joining the associates and additional fees for the individual course, project, or tour. Besides various tours in and around Washington, the group sponsors half-day to full-day tours focused on historical neighborhoods, with commentary on their history, art, and architecture. Further, there are national and international tours to the world's museums, cruises, and specialized study tours and seminars. For Washington area residents, the Resident Associates program offers an enormous variety of continuing education activities, hundreds of courses, lectures, and seminars led by some of the world's leading experts. Studio arts classes are also offered. Courses take place on a quarterly basis. Fall classes are announced in the August *Associate* publication, winter classes in the November issue, spring in the March issue, and summer classes are announced in the May issue. Recently, the Smithsonian Associates instituted weekend activities for children and families. These are day-long "Weekend Camp" Saturday or Sunday programs designed for children. Professional instructors introduce Smithsonian treasures through activities, projects, and various museum visits. Topics include current museum exhibitions to the sciences, world cultures, art, and music. Metro: Smithsonian.

Smithsonian Carousel 1000 Jefferson Dr. SW (202) 357-2700 www.si.edu/resource/faq/nmah/carousel.htm

This popular carousel rotates before the Smithsonian Castle. The carousel was built in the 1940s by Allan Herschel and continues to delight children and their parents. Open daily, weather permitting, 10 a.m.–5 p.m. on weekdays, 10 a.m.–6 p.m. weekends. Small fee. Metro: Smithsonian.

Smithsonian Craft Show National Building Museum, 401 F St. NW (202) 357-2700 www.smithsoniancraftshow.org/fact.htm

Since the 1980s, in late April, the Smithsonian has sponsored the nation's premier juried exhibition and sale of contemporary American crafts. It is held at the National Building Museum. About 120 artists from across the states display their remarkable creations in basketry, ceramics, decorative fiber, furniture, glass, jewelry, leather, metal, mixed media, paper, wearable art, and wood. Besides sales at the show, there is an online auction. Moderate admission fee. Museum open Mon–Sat 10 a.m.–5 p.m., Sun 11 a.m.–5 p.m. Metro: Judiciary Square.

Smithsonian Discovery Theater Arts and Industries Building, West Entrance, 900 Jefferson Dr. SW (202) 357-1500 www.discoverytheater.org

This innovative program provides young people the opportunity to see age-graded productions featuring puppets, storytellers, actors, musicians, and mimes. Often the shows are interactive. Performers present stories for children, folktales, historical episodes, and a variety of events. Recent events include puppets with a Russian folktale or Hopi legends, and a call and response program in the Twi language from Ghana. The Web site provides a listing of performances and appropriate ages. The theater sponsors special events such as a Halloween program and workshops for teachers. Hours vary, but show times are usually at 10 a.m. and 11:30 weekdays. Moderate ticket prices. Ticket office is open Mon–Fri 8:30 a.m.–4 p.m. Individual tickets (202) 357-3030, Group sales (202) 357-1500. Metro: Smithsonian.

Smithsonian Folklife Festival The Mall, btw 7th and 14th Sts. (202) 357-2700
http://www.folklife.si.edu/CFCH/folklife.htm

Founded in 1967, this annual event attracts about a million visitors during its
two-week run. It is held outdoors on the Mall in circus tents and demonstration
booths from late June to early July. There is a theme to each festival with daily and
evening demonstrations of crafts, music, song, dance, storytelling, experts, and
living "national treasures" providing show-and-tell. Visitors are encouraged to participate: sample the traditional foods, chat with the presenters. All the performances—and there may be as many as 350 artists, performers, and experts from
around the states or around the world—are framed with a scholarly presentation.
The Web site provides dates, topics, virtual festivals, curricular materials, publications, and recordings related to the festival. Paradoxically, rare and unique offerings
are commonplace. Admission free. Metro: Smithsonian.

Smithsonian Institution Smithsonian Castle, 1100 Jefferson Dr. SW (202) 357-
2700 24-hour recorded announcement (202) 357-2020 www.si.edu

Established in 1846, the Smithsonian Institution is the largest museum complex
in the world, as well as a zookeeper, publisher, research institution, school, federal
library, concert and festival giver, and national closet. Its mammoth scientific, cultural, and artistic resources require special attention to take advantage of its diverse
programs, services, and activities. The fourteen museums and galleries and the National Zoo in the Washington area are free. A thirty-six-page Visitors Booklet is
available to print from the Web site. The Web site also provides a calendar of events
and topical access to the collections, as well as suggestions for visits for groups,
"kids and families," visitors with disabilities, tours, museum stores, maps, and dining. Many of the museums have a concert series, and there is an IMAX theater in
the National Air and Space Museum. The three-level underground complex near
the Castle houses the S. Dillon Ripley Center, including the International Gallery
and classrooms used in lecture programs. The first Smithsonian building, now the
Visitors Information Center—and recommended as a first orientation stop—is a
James Renwick building, completed in 1855. The Smithsonian Associates Program
provides a lecture series and various courses and study tours. Phone (202) 357-
3030. Hours at most sites Mon–Fri 9 a.m.–5 p.m., Sat and Sun 10 a.m.–4 p.m.
Metro: Smithsonian, Federal Triangle, L'Enfant Plaza. *See* Arthur M. Sackler Gal-
lery, Arts and Industries Building, Freer Gallery of Art, Hirshhorn Museum and
Sculpture Garden, National Air and Space Museum, National Museum of African
Art, National Museum of American History, National Museum of Natural History,
and Smithsonian Institution Building (The Castle). *See also* entries on sites away
from the central complex: Anacostia Museum and Center for African American
History and Culture, National Museum of American Art, National Portrait Gallery,
National Postal Museum, National Zoological Park, and Renwick Gallery.

Smithsonian Institution Building (The Castle) 1000 Jefferson Dr. SW (202) 357-
2700 www.si.edu/visit

This building, housing administrative offices and the Visitors Information Center, is easily recognizable by its red-turreted Romanesque Revival exterior. It was

designed by James Renwick and completed in 1855. Popularly known as The Castle, it houses the crypt of James Smithson, a wealthy Oxford scientist whose donation, along with the support of a president-turned-congressman, John Quincy Adams, brought about the birth of the institution. The information center serves as a central orientation site for the institution's fourteen-plus museums in the area. Orientation activities include a 20-minute video, which repeats all day long, interactive video programs, and information specialists responding to your queries. The Visitor Information Center Web site offers suggestions regarding visits for kids and families, visitors with disabilities, dining facilities, maps and directions, tour, and various membership opportunities. Admission free. Open daily 9 a.m.–5:30 p.m. Closed Christmas Day. Metro: Smithsonian.

Smithsonian Institution Museums *See* Anacostia Museum and Center for African American History and Culture, Arthur M. Sackler Gallery, Arts and Industry Building, Freer Gallery of Art, Garber Preservation Restoration and Storage Facility, National Air and Space Museum, National Museum of African Art, National Museum of American Art, National Museum of American History, National Museum of the American Indian, National Museum of Natural History, National Portrait Gallery, National Postal Museum, National Zoo, Smithsonian Institution Building. *See also* www.commuterpage.com/venues/museums-si.htm.

Smithsonian Institution Visitors Information Center *see* Smithsonian Institution Building (The Castle).

Soap Box Derby Constitution Ave. NW btw New Jersey and Louisiana Aves. NW (301) 670-1110 www.dcsoapboxderby.org

Between forty and fifty children between the ages of 9 and 16 roll down the hill in this "Gravity Grand Prix" held in mid-July. This is part of a national competition of so-called soap box cars, but nowadays, mostly sleek racers. Metro: Union Station, then a 10-minute walk.

Soccer (Spectator Sport) *see* D.C. United, RFK Stadium.

Society of the Cincinnati at Anderson House 2118 Massachusetts Ave. NW (202) 785-2040

This palatial mansion, designed by Arthur Little and Herbert Brown, was completed in 1905 for its owner, career Foreign Service officer Larz Anderson III, who briefly served (1912–1913) as ambassador to Japan. Larz had the good fortune on his first overseas posting to meet Isabel Weld, a debutante on her world tour, who had, at age 5, inherited $17 million. They married and spent the rest of their lives collecting cars, antiques, tapestries, and paintings, and of course, built this mansion with its marble staircases, inlaid wood, and 600-foot ballroom, one of Washington's most opulent. In accordance with Anderson's will, in 1937 the building became the headquarters of the Society of the Cincinnati, the oldest patriotic organization in the states, formed by some of the officers who served under George Washington in the Continental Army and Navy in 1783. It is open to the public and offers tours, lectures, and a concert series at 1:30 p.m. on most Wednesdays and Saturdays. The 1st floor contains Revolutionary War memorabilia and paintings by John Trumbull and Gilbert Stuart. Upstairs are the various Anderson acqui-sitions. The society maintains a 42,000-title collection related to eighteenth-century warfare and the Society of the Cincinnati. Admission free. Open Tues–Sat 1 p.m.–4 p.m. Closed federal holidays. Metro: Dupont Circle.

Sofitel Hotel *see* Hotel Sofitel.

SoHo Tea and Coffee 2150 P St. NW (202) 463-7646
     This independent coffeehouse, elbowing neighboring gay bars, offers the usual coffee concoctions and the like as well as an occasional live music session and the popular Wednesday open-mike night for poets, songwriters, and other scribes. Sometimes smoky. Outdoor seating, weather permitting. Open Tues–Sat 7:30 a.m.–5 a.m., Sun–Mon 7:30 a.m.–3 a.m. Metro: Dupont Circle.

Soldiers' and Airmen's Home *see* U.S. Soldiers' and Airmen's Home National Cemetery.

Songhai 1211 U St. NW (202) 232-1965
     This restaurant and dance spot serves up mostly West African cuisine and DJ music providing *soca*, reggae, and other beats. The music starts about 11 a.m. Cover charge. Open Sun–Thurs noon–11 p.m., Fri–Sat noon–3 p.m. Metro: U St.-Cardozo.

Source Theatre Company 1835 14th St. NW (202) 462-1073 www.source theatre.com
     Celebrating its twenty-fifth anniversary in 2002, the Source Theatre Company, known for its fine acting, offers a mix of new and contemporary plays and riveting interpretations of classics. Source offers five productions a year plus its Liaisons Co-production Series. Each summer, Source offers a Washington Theater Festival, a four-week showcase of new plays in its 107-seat theater. Purchase tickets online as well. Metro: U St.-Cardozo. *See also* www.commuterpage.com/venues/venue en.htm.

Sousa Bridge *see* John Philip Sousa Bridge.

South Africa Embassy 3051 Massachusetts Ave. NW (202) 232-4400 www.usaem bassy.southafrica.net

South Austin Grill *see* Austin Grill.

South Korea Embassy 2450 Massachusetts Ave. NW (202) 939-5600 www.emb .dsdn.net/english/frame.htm
     The Republic of Korea Embassy.

South Riding Visitors Center, Stonewall Pond St., South Riding, VA (703) 327-3600 www.southriding.com
     Just 10 miles from Dulles Airport, this planned community is sited on what was 2,000 acres of rolling Loudoun County farmland. When completed the community will include about 6,000 houses, apartments, townhouses, several schools, churches, shopping centers, pools, and a golf course. Presently more than 3,000 families live in South Riding. In place is the town hall, pools, tennis courts, schools, medical offices, a bank, a day care center, a fire station, and several restaurants. The

Visitors Center is open daily 11 a.m.–6 p.m. By car from I-495 (the Beltway) take I-66 West to Rte. 50 West. South Riding is 4 miles past Rte. 28. Turn left onto South Riding Blvd. to first left at Stonewall Pond St. to the visitors center.

Southeast Washington btw E Capitol St. and S Capitol St. to Maryland

This historic section of the city drops south of the Capitol, and a section of Capitol Hill, incorporates the area known as Anacostia, and follows E Capitol St. past RFK Stadium to the Maryland border. It includes such landmarks as the Navy Yard, RKF Stadium, Congressional Cemetery, and the area known as Anacostia applied to the area east of the Anacostia River. The Anacostia sector is the site of Cedar Hill, home of abolitionist Frederick Douglass; St. Elizabeth's Hospital; and the Smithsonian's Museum of African-American History. Anacostia has the city's highest percentage of low-income residents and public housing units. However, recent police statistics show that the area is below the citywide average for violent crimes. Metro: Eastern Market, and several Green Line stops. *See also* Anacostia.

Southeastern University 501 I St. SW (202) 488-8162 www.seu.edu

This small, private university founded in 1879 by the YMCA offers certificate, undergraduate, and graduate degrees in a variety of areas, including computer science and information systems, accounting, liberal studies, business management, and marketing and public administration, including nonprofit organizational management. Metro: Waterfront-SEU.

Southern Restaurants *see* B. Smiths, Ben's Chili Bowl, Florida Avenue Grill, Georgia Brown's, Hitching Post, Vidalia. *See also* Barbecue and Ribs Restaurants, Cajun Restaurants, www.washingtonpost.com.

Southwest Washington www.swdc.org

This area is bordered by Independence Ave. on the north, S Capitol St. to the east, the confluence of the Potomac and Anacostia Rivers to the south, and 14th St. on the west. It includes Wheat Row built in the 1790s, Fort Leslie J. McNair strategically placed at 4th and P Sts. by city designer Pierre L'Enfant, making it America's oldest military installation, as well as its first prison, and now the site of the National Defense University. Much like the other side of the tracks, an 1815 canal cut the area off from the more fashionable part of the city and, thus, it was settled by a diverse population of low-income residents, mostly immigrants and African Americans. In the 1960s, the area was redeveloped by urban renewal projects. However, it is also an area heavily populated with federal structures, including the National Gallery of Art, the Smithsonian Institution, Holocaust Museum, and the Air and Space Museum. A number of restaurants and marinas line the waterfront with Arena Stage just across the street. Metro: L'Enfant Plaza, Federal Center SW, and Waterfront-SEU.

Southwest Waterfront

This area follows the Washington Channel parallel to Maine Ave. and Water St. SW from about 6th St. to 11th Sts. SW. At the northwestern end of Water St. several barges have been made into an open-air seafood market. Next door is Le Rivage Restaurant with its deck overlooking a yacht-filled marina, and farther along, a strip of restaurants and a hotel. Up one street, Maine at 6th, is the Arena Stage complex. This area, flattened in the 1960s in the name of urban development, held railroad yards and warehouses from the time when this was a commercial waterfront for the city. Metro: Waterfront-SEU.

Southwestern Restaurants *see* Cottonwood Café, Florida Avenue Grill, Red Sage, Santa Fe East, Thunder Grill.

Spain Embassy 2375 Pennsylvania Ave. NW (202) 452-0100 www.spainemb .org/ingles/indexing.htm

S/p/alon 1605 17th St. NW (202) 462-9000
   This day-spa and salon offers haircutting, highlighting, coloring, facials, manicures, pedicures, as well as massages and various body treatments. About an equal number of clients between men and women. Moderately expensive. Metro: Dupont Circle.

Spanish Restaurants *see* Andalucia, Jaleo, Mar de Plata, El Rincón Español, Taberna del Alabardero. *See also* www.washingtonpost.com.

Spas *see* Beauty Spas and Salons, Fitness Centers.

Special Events in Washington, D.C. *see* Events in Washington D.C., Events in Washington D.C. by Month.

Special Interest Tours *see* African American Heritage Tour, Capitol Entertainment Services, Celebrity Washington Tours, D.C. Preservation League, Duke Ellington's D.C. Tour, Embassy Annual Goodwill Tour, Old Town Christmas Candlelight Tour, Old Town Ghost Tours, Scandal Tours, Site Seeing Tours, Inc., Washington Post Tour. *See also* Bus Tours, Walking Tours.

Specialized Museums *see* Alexandria Archeology Museum, American Red Cross Museum, Bead Museum and Learning Center, Black Fashion Museum, College Park Aviation Museum, Drug Enforcement Administration Museum and Visitors Bureau, Dumbarton Oaks Research Library and Collections, Fonda del Sol Visual Arts Center, Frederick Douglass Museum and Hall of Fame for Caring Americans, Freeman House Museum, Gadsby's Tavern Museum, Hillwood Museum and Gardens, House of the Temple Library/Museum, International Spy Museum, Kiplinger Collection, Kreeger Museum, Lillian and Albert Small Jewish Museum, Meridian International Center, National Building Museum, National Cryptologic Museum, National Firearms Museum, National Museum of American Jewish Military History, National Museum of Health and Medicine, National Museum of Women in the Arts, National Portrait Gallery, National Postal Museum, The Octagon, Pope John Paul II Cultural Center, Renwick Gallery of the National Museum of American Art, Seaport Center, Society of the Cincinnati at Anderson House, Stabler-LeadbeaterApothecary Shop, Textile Museum, U.S. Chess Hall of Fame and Museum, U.S. Patent and Trademark Museum, Washington Doll's House and Toy Museum. *See also* Art and Design Museums, Ethnic and Community Museums, Historical Museums, Military Museums, Museums of Special Interest to Children, Science and Technology Museums, Smithsonian Institution Museums.

Specialty Food Stores and Bakeries *see* Addisu Gebeya Americana Market, Asian Foods, Bread and Chocolate, Breads Unlimited, Corner Bakery Café, Da Hua Market, Daruma, Dean & DeLuca, Eden Supermarket, Eko Food Market, Firehook Bakery and Coffeehouse, Fresh Fields Whole Foods Market, German Gourmet, Heidelberg Pastry Shop, Hellers, Indian Spices and Gifts, Litteri's, Manuel's Grocery, Marvelous Market, Maxim Gourmet Oriental Market, Mediterranean Bakery, Middle East Market, Naturally Yours, Red Apple Market, Russian Gourmet, Sutton Place Gourmet, Trader Joe's, Vace, Yekta Market, Yes! Natural Gourmet, Yes! Organic Market.

Specialty Stores *see* Addisu Gebeya, Artifactory, The Artisans, Counter Spy Shop, Distinctive Bookbinding and Stationery, Fahrney's Pens, Indian Craft Shop, Movie Madness, Music Box Center, Naval Heritage Center, Political Americana, Tennis Factory, Tiny Jewel Box.

Spectator Sports *see* Ballooning, Baseball, Basketball, Bird Watching, Football, Golf, Horse Racing, Ice Hockey, Polo, Running, Soccer, Tennis. *See also* www.com muterpage.com/venues/venue-sp.htm.

Spectrum Gallery 1132 29th St. NW (202) 333-0954 http://spectrumgallery.org/
Since 1966 this gallery has been offering abstract as well as representational art by nationally known artists in its Georgetown studio. There is usually a mix of original prints, sculpture, photography, painting, and drawings. Major one-artist exhibition monthly. Open Tues–Sat noon–6 p.m., Sun noon–5 p.m. Metro: Rosslyn, then Georgetown Shuttle.

Spices 3333-A Connecticut Ave. NW
This popular Cleveland Park restaurant offers sushi and a variety of other delights from countries bordering the South China Sea. Besides the sushi, try the ginger chicken, tangerine peel beef, or one of the stir-fried noodle dishes. Open weekdays for lunch 11:30 a.m.–3 p.m., dinner 5 p.m.–11 p.m., Sat lunch and dinner 11:30 a.m.–11 p.m., and Sun dinner only 5:30 p.m.–10:30 p.m. Metro: Cleveland Park.

Spirit Cruises *see* Potomac Spirit.

Spirit of Freedom Memorial *see* African American Civil War Memorial.

Spoken Word *see* Book and Poetry Readings, Public Lectures.

Sportrock Climbing Centers *see* Sportrock I, II, III.

Sportrock I 14708 Southlawn Lane, Rockville, MD (301) 762-5111 www.sport rock.com
Open since 1994, this is the first of the Sportrock Climbing Centers. It offers 30-foot walls, with a vertical terrain large enough to accommodate seventy-five climbers. Classes are provided for beginners. The gym is reserved for members only. On Friday from 6:30 p.m. to 8 p.m. the area is set aside for children between the ages of 6 and 14. Overseen by instructors, the children climb throughout the facility. Sportrock offers various sessions for children's teams, where they advance through various skill levels and are taught both safety skills and climbing tech-

niques. Equipment may be purchased or rented. Both gym members and non-members can participate with varying fees. Open Mon, Tue, Thurs 3 p.m.–11 p.m., Wed and Fri noon–11 p.m., Sat 11 a.m.–8 p.m., Sun noon–8 p.m. By car from I-270 north of Rockville, exit at Shady Grove Rd. E. Turn right onto Rte. 355, Frederick Rd. Left onto E Gude and right onto Southlawn.

Sportrock II 5308 Eisenhower Ave., Alexandria, VA (703) 212-7625 www.sportrock.com

Opened in 1996, this Sportrock Climbing Center features 40-foot walls with slabs, steep walls, arches, roofs, towers, and a boulder cave. This location offers an extensive selection of classes for novice to advanced climber. Other information and hours are the same as Sportrock I. Metro: Van Dorn.

Sportrock III 45935 Maries Rd., Sterling, VA (703) 212-7625 www.sportrock.com

Opened in 2001, this Sportrock Climbing Center features 40-foot walls with 30-foot overhangs, as well as a cave. There is a separate teaching and party area. Other information the same as Sportrock I. By car from Rte. 7 take Cascades Pkwy. S approximately ½ mile. Turn right on Maries Rd., left into Cascades Business Park. Sportrock III is at the back of the park.

Sports *see* Active Sports Activity, Fitness Centers, Spectator Sports.

Spout Run Bridge 24th St., Arlington, VA, over Spout Run near George Washington Memorial Pkwy.

This handsome reinforced concrete structure best viewed from Virginia's George Washington Memorial Pkwy. was constructed in the late 1950s. Its soaring arches spanning Spout Run resemble the work of Robert Maillart. Metro: Rosslyn.

Spring Antiques Show *see* D.C. Armory Antiques Fair.

Springfield Mall Shopping Center 6500 Springfield Mall, Springfield, VA (703) 971-3000 www.springfieldmall.com

This mall houses more than 230 stores including JC Penney, Gap, Target, and Macy's, and provides 8,000 parking spaces. It is located at the intersection of I-95 and the Washington Beltway (I-495) with direct access to the new Fairfax County Pkwy. Open Mon–Sat 10 a.m.–9:30 p.m., Sun noon–5 p.m. Metro: Franconia-Springfield, with a complimentary shuttle every 15 minutes. *See also* www.commuterpage.com/venues/venue-shop.htm.

Springriver 5606 Randolph Rd., Rockville, MD (301) 881-5694; 2757 Summerfield Rd., Falls Church, VA (703) 241-2818

Since 1972, Springriver has been a leading provider of fitness equipment and paddling merchandise. The store offers a variety of kayaks and canoes for sale, and daily and weekend rentals. Rockville store open Mon and Wed 10 a.m.–8 p.m., Tues, Thurs, Sat 10 a.m.–5 p.m., Fri 10 a.m.–7 p.m., Sun noon–4 p.m. By car From Rte. 270, take the Montrose Rd. Exit. Go east on Montrose Rd. to Randolph Rd. Falls Church: Mon, Wed 10 a.m.–8 p.m.; Tues, Thurs, Sat 10 a.m.–5 p.m.; Fri 10 a.m.–7 p.m. By car From the Washington Beltway (I-495), take exit 8A, Arlington Blvd. (Rte. 50) east toward Arlington. Go 2 miles. Turn left onto Graham Rd. and right on Lee Hwy. and right onto Summerfield Rd.

Squash *see* D.C. Jewish Community Center, National Capital YMCA.

Sri Lanka Embassy 2148 Wyoming Ave. NW (202) 483-4025 www.slembassy.org

Stabler-Leadbeater Apothecary Shop 105 S Fairfax St. btw Prince and King Sts., Alexandria, VA (703) 836-3713 www.apothecary.org

From 1792 when it opened until 1933, this drugstore remained in the Stabler family. When it closed it was the second oldest such shop in America. The shop and its contents, last remodeled in the 1850s, stayed as they were until 1939, when this remarkable time capsule reopened as a museum. Exhibits include old account books, early medical instruments, and a major collection of eighteenth- and nineteenth-century apothecary bottles. The shop supplied the entire region, including downriver to Martha Washington who bought her castor oil there, and Robert E. Lee, Henry Clay, James Monroe, Union troops, and even Confederate POWs. Open Mon–Sat 10 a.m.–4 p.m., Sun 1 p.m.–5 p.m. Modest fee. Metro: King Street. *See also* www.commuterpage.com/venues/sightseeing_VA.htm.

Star of Siam 1113 19th St. NW (202) 785-2839

This highly regarded inexpensive Thai restaurant offers an enormous menu— about eighty dishes as well as chalkboard specials. The curries are particularly popular; try the country-style curry with beef and chicken. Also popular are the noodle stir-fry dishes. Metro: Dupont Circle or Farragut North.

Star Spangled Banner Monument *see* Francis Scott Key Memorial.

Starbucks www.starbucks.com

Since its arrival in the 1990s, Starbucks has grown to more than 240 outlets in the metropolitan Washington area. While often lacking the ambiance of its independently owned competitors, Starbucks knows consistency and location, location, location. There are outlets in some of the historic buildings in Washington, such as the 1882 Fireman's Insurance Company Building at 7th St. and Indiana Ave., as well as at university sites, and seemingly, every shopping mall. Check the Web site for locations.

State Department 2201 C St. NW Tour reservations (202) 647-3241 www.state .gov/www/about_state/diprooms

The State Department moved into this building in 1947, which was extended in 1961. It is closed to the public except for tours of the diplomatic reception rooms, heavily used for functions hosted by the secretary of state and other officials. These rooms are open for prearranged 45-minute tours of an outstanding collection of eighteenth-century American furniture, paintings, and decorative arts. Included is a writing table used by Thomas Jefferson; George Washington's dinner service; and the desk where the Treaty of Paris was signed, ending the Revolutionary War. Reservations should be made about a month in advance. Reservations for children under the age of 12 are discouraged. Tour hours are Mon–Fri 9:30 a.m., 10:30 a.m., and 2:45 p.m. Free. Metro: Foggy Bottom-GWU.

State Department Diplomatic Reception Rooms *see* State Department.

State of the Union 1357 U St. NW at 14th St. (202) 588-8810

This club, located amid many U St. hot spots, offers live bands five nights a week playing jazz, house, hip-hop, and Latin. At 11:30 p.m. DJs take over the two rooms. The dance floors can get packed. "Union" refers to the Soviet Union—the place is covered floor to ceiling with Russian flags, posters, Lenin paintings, and May Day equipage. Superior vodka and beer selections. Modest cover charge. Open Mon–Thurs 5 p.m.–2 a.m., Fri–Sun 5 p.m.–3 a.m., Sun 6 p.m.–2 a.m. Metro: U St.-Cardozo.

State Plaza Hotel 2117 E St. NW (202) 861-8200 (800) 424-2859 www.stateplaza.com

This 225-suite hotel offers fully equipped kitchens, a small fitness center, a sun deck, and garage parking. The Garden Café serves three meals a day. Views of various rooms are on the Web site. First-class hotel rates. Metro: Foggy Bottom-GWU.

Statuary Hall *see* Capitol Statuary Hall.

Statues *see* Monuments and Memorials.

Steak Restaurants *see* Blackie's House of Beef, Bobby Van's Steak House, Capital Grille, Les Halles, Morton's of Chicago, The Palm, Prime Rib, Ruth's Chris Steak House, Sam and Harry's, Smith and Wollensky. *See also* www.washingtonpost.com.

Stoddert House 3400 Prospect St NW at 34th St.

This house, completed in 1787, was the home of Benjamin Stoddert, a wealthy shipping magnate who became America's first secretary of the Navy. He later served as secretary to the War Board. He was less successful as a real estate developer albeit he represented George Washington in the negotiations to acquire the district land-holdings. At a later date, a tunnel into the basement, part of the Underground Railroad, was used by escaped slaves. More recently, extensive changes were made to the property, but the north side and garden—designed by Stoddert's friend Pierre L'Enfant—remain almost as they were 200 years ago. Metro: Rosslyn, then Georgetown Shuttle.

Stoney's 1307 L St. NW (202) 347-9163

This neighborhood bar and grill has a loyal following, including many a Secret Service agent from a neighboring building. There are no ferns; this is basic dingy. But Stoneyburgers are succulent, as well as the chili, homemade fries, buffalo wings, Philly cheese steak, and cheap beer by the pitcher. Outdoor seating. Inexpensive. Metro: McPherson Square.

Straits of Malaya 1836 18th St. NW btw Swann and T Sts. (202) 483-1483

This popular restaurant's specialty, as the name implies, offers the cuisine of the straits: Chinese, Thai, Malayan, Indian, and Singaporean. Try the rooftop and dig into *udang goring*—shrimp in coconut milk—curried eggplant, curry puffs, and chicken satay. Moderate prices. Mon–Fri noon–2 p.m. 5:30 p.m.–11 p.m., Sat 5:30 p.m.–11 p.m., Sun 5:30 p.m.–10:30 p.m. Metro: Dupont Circle.

Strathmore Hall Arts Center 10701 Rockville Pike, North Bethesda, MD (301) 530-0540 www.strathmore.org

This nonprofit cultural arts center, located in a 1902 mansion, has been providing a venue for art exhibitions, lectures, and performing arts programs since 1981.

Activities include twelve major art exhibitions each year; classical, jazz, and pop music programs; family festivals; children's events; theater performances; tea musicales; and literary lunches. A 2,000-seat concert hall and music education center opens in 2004, at which time the Baltimore Symphony Orchestra, the National Chamber Orchestra, the Masterworks Chorus and Orchestra, the Montgomery County Youth Orchestras, and the Levine School of Music will become residents. A pedestrian bridge connecting the music center to the future Metro garage station is being built. Events are listed on the Web site. Members receive a newsletter and discounts. Moderate fees for performances. Gallery open Mon–Tues and Thurs–Fri 10 a.m.–4 p.m., Wed 10 a.m.–9 p.m., Sat 10 a.m.–3 p.m. Metro: Grovesnor-Strathmore.

Strayer University 1025 15th St. NW (202) 408-2400 www.strayer.edu

This private, independent college, founded in 1892, offers associate's, bachelor's, and master's degree programs in a variety of areas. Its enrollment of more than 10,000 includes many working adults who take advantage of Strayer's diverse sites and classes offered on weekends and evenings and online. Some degree programs are offered completely online. Besides its 15th St. campus, the college offers classes in Takoma Park, Arlington, Alexandria, Ashburn, Suitland, Germantown, Millersville, Ashburn, and Owings Mills. Metro: McPherson Square.

Street Markets *see* Flea Markets, Markets.

Studio Theatre 1333 P St. NW (202) 332-3300 www.studiotheatre.org

This theater, founded in 1975, has long been providing quality productions on its two stages—the larger seating 200—training more than 6,000 actors and directors in the process. Its mission is, in fact, to offer the best in contemporary theater, while providing opportunities and training for emerging artists. There are usually five productions a year with the small Secondstage, which seats 50, offering more experimental works. Plays by Edward Albee, Peter Nichols, Neil Labute, Javon Johnson, Edward Kleban, Steven Berkoff, and Ruben Santiago-Hudson have been offered recently. Its well-respected Acting Conservatory offers a range of acting classes for adults and young people (10 and up). The 2001 purchase of a nearby building will provide a larger home for its Secondstage, as well as additional conservatory space when renovations are completed. Moderate ticket prices. See the Web site for production schedule and conservatory classes. Tickets may be purchased through the Web site. Metro: Dupont Circle. *See also* www.commuterpage.com/venues/venue-en.htm.

Subway *see* Metro.

Sudan Embassy 2210 Massachusetts Ave. NW (202) 338-8565 www.sudanembassyus.org

Sugarloaf Crafts Festival Sugarloaf Mountain Works, Inc., 200 Orchard Ridge Dr., Suite 215, Gaithersburg, MD (301) 990-1400 (800) 210-9900 www.sugarloafcrafts.com

In 1975 two Gaithersburg friends founded a festival of contemporary crafts and fine art—not "country craft." It has grown to an event with 15 shows annually throughout the East Coast, and a staff of twenty still headquartered in Gaithersburg. Spring, fall, and winter shows take place in the metropolitan Washington area. Each year, 15,000 artisans throughout the states send in color slides for juried selection for the 300 to 600 spaces available per show. All work is handmade, and you can watch artisans at their booths demonstrating their crafts: wood turning, potting, furniture making, and the like. There are live musical performances as well. Check out the Web site for venues and dates. The Web site offers, as well, American Crafts Online—the Internet version of these craft festivals where hundreds of artisans offer their wares. Spring festivals: April in Gaithersburg, May in Chantilly. Fall festivals: September in Manassas, October and November in Gaithersburg. Winter festivals: Gaithersburg and Chantilly. Locations: Prince William County Fairgrounds, 10624 Dumfries Rd., Manassas, VA; Montgomery County Fairgrounds, 16 Chestnut St., Gaithersburg, MD; Dulles Expo Center, 4320 Chantilly Place Center, Chantilly, VA.

Sulgrave Club Wadsworth House, 1801 Massachusetts Ave. NW (202) 462-5800

This large residence, a Beaux-Arts eclectic, was designed by architect Frederick H. Brooke and was built for Henry Wadsworth and his socialite wife, Martha. It was completed in 1900. In 1932 it was purchased for a women's social club, Sulgrave. Not open to the public.

Sully Historic Site 3601 Sully Rd. off VA-28, Chantilly, VA (703) 437-1794 www.co .fairfax.va.us/parks/sully/index.htm

This Georgian plantation-style mansion was built in 1794 for Richard Bland and Elizabeth Collins Lee. Richard Bland Lee, uncle of Robert E. Lee, served in America's first Congress. The house is furnished with Federal-period antiques and replicas of items commonly used in a working plantation's kitchen, laundry, smokehouse, dairy, and living quarters. The gardens have been restored as well. Tours on the hour. Modest charge for guided tour; grounds are free. Open 11 a.m.–4 p.m., 11 a.m. – 3 p.m. January to February. By car it is off VA 28, ¾ mile north of U.S. Rte. 50, and 4 miles south of the Dulles Toll Rd.

Summer Opera Theatre Company, Inc. 620 Michigan Ave. NE (202) 526-1669, box office (202) 319-4000 www.summeropera.org

Founded in 1978, this independent troupe offers two operas a season in June and July. They perform at Catholic University's 590-seat Hartke Theatre. Memberships offer additional benefits such as trips to other opera companies and participation in theater activities. The troupe performs at Hartke Theater, 3801 Harewood Rd. NE. Metro: Brookland-CUA.

Sumner School *see* Charles Sumner School Museum and Archives.

Supreme Court 1st St. and Maryland Ave. NE (202) 479-3000 www.supremecourt us.gov

The Supreme Court moved from the Capitol Building into this imposing structure in 1934. The neoclassical Vermont marble structure was designed by Cass Gilbert. The nine justices on the court hear oral arguments for cases from October through April, usually about 100 out of the 6,000-some requests they receive. Cases are heard 10 a.m.–2 p.m. on Mondays through Wednesdays in 2-week intervals.

For each case, the oral arguments usually take 1 hour, $^1/_2$ hour each for pro and con. Visitors are welcome to hear these oral arguments. You may watch about 5 minutes of the proceedings from a gallery or sit and watch an entire session. Tickets are on a first-come, first-served basis. Thus, there are two lines, the gallery short-timers, or the entire oral argument line—about a 1-hour session. Seating begins at 9:30 a.m. so you need to get there long before that to get a ticket. A public lecture on the court is provided every hour on the half hour from 9:30 a.m.–3:30 p.m. on the days the court is not is session. An excellent 20-minute film on the court is shown throughout the day and there is a small museum as well. The main hall contains a statue of John Marshall, the court's most influential chief justice. There is a cafeteria in the building, a snack bar, and a gift shop. The building is open Mon–Fri 9 a.m.–4:30 p.m. Closed Federal holidays. Metro: Union Station or Capitol South.

Suriname Embassy 4301 Connecticut Ave. NW, Suite 460 (202) 244-7488

Surratt House Museum P.O. Box 427, 9118 Brandywine Rd., Clinton, MD (301) 868-1121 www.surratt.org

Docents in Victorian garb show visitors about the Surratt House, home of Mary Surratt, who was hung as one of the Lincoln assassination conspirators. The house was Surratt's home from 1852 to 1864, but she moved to Washington in 1862 where her boardinghouse came into play in the assassination plotting. The focus of the museum is not on the assassination plot, although that is presented as well, but on providing an insight into mid-nineteenth-century Victorian life and culture. Open for public tours January to mid-December Thurs–Fri 11 a.m.–3 p.m., Sat–Sun noon–4 p.m. Small admission fee. Last tour begins $^1/_2$ hour before closing. Closed Fourth of July and Easter Sunday. By car from (I-95), take Exit 7A, Branch Ave. S (MD Rte. 5). Turn right onto Woodyard Rd. (Rte. 223W) to the second light, and turn left onto Brandywine Rd.

Susan Conway Gallery 1214 30th St. NW (202) 333-6343 www.artnet.com

Founded in 1987, this gallery offers an enormous collection of contemporary and modern paintings, drawings, sculpture, and prints. Artists such as Will Barnet, Mary Ellen Doyle, Leonard Baskin, and Gleb Bogomolov are represented. Susan Conway offers, as well, an extensive collection of political cartoonist Pat Oliphant's sculpture, paintings, and drawings. Open Thurs–Sat 10 a.m.–6 p.m. Metro: Foggy Bottom-GWU.

Susan G. Komen Race for the Cure *see* National Race for the Cure.

Sushi-ko 2309 Wisconsin Ave. NW (202) 333-4187

This restaurant opened on Wisconsin Ave. in the early 1980s. It continues to be the kind of place other sushi restaurants are measured against. Besides extensive and always fresh sushi and sashimi offerings, you may want to try the tempura or smoked monkfish or grilled baby octopus. Open for lunch Tues–Fri noon–2:30 p.m.; dinner Mon–Thurs 6 p.m.–10:30 p.m., Fri 6 p.m.–11 p.m., Sat 5:30 p.m.–11 p.m., and Sun 5:30 p.m.–10 p.m. Moderately expensive. Metro: Foggy Bottom-GWU, then Wisconsin Ave. Shuttle.

Sushi Taro 1503 17th St. NW (202) 462-8999 www.sushitaro.com

This restaurant is known for its long sushi bar offering more than thirty kinds of fish and shellfish. Plus, there is an authentic Japanese feel to it. It is a light, pleasant place with seating at tables, the long sushi bar, or on traditional Japanese-style straw mats. Besides its extensive sushi bar there are tempting yakitori and tempura dishes. Open Mon–Thurs 11:30 a.m.–2 p.m., 5 p.m.–10 p.m.; Fri 11:30 a.m.–2 p.m., 5:30 p.m.–10:30 p.m.; Sat 5:30 p.m.–10:30 p.m.; Sun 5:30 p.m.–10 p.m. Metro: Dupont Circle.

Sutton Place Gourmet 3201 New Mexico Ave. NW (202) 363-5800; 10323 Old Georgetown Rd., Bethesda, MD (301) 564-3100; 600 Franklin St., Alexandria, VA (703) 549-6611; 6655 Old Dominion Dr., McLean, VA 22101 (703) 448-3828; 11860 Spectrum Center, Reston, VA 20190 (703) 787-4888

These gourmet and specialty-food department stores first opened in Washington in 1980. If you can't find that special cheese, bread, coffee, fresh-baked pastry, oil, wine, meat, or fish you are looking for here, you might have to go to Balducci's in New York, which, by the way, has merged with Sutton Place Gourmet. Washington: open Mon–Sat 8 a.m.–9 p.m., Sun 8 a.m.–8 p.m.; McLean: Mon–Fri 8 a.m.–9 p.m., Sat–Sun 9 a.m.–8 p.m.; Reston: Mon–Sat 8 a.m.–9 p.m., Sun 9 a.m.–8 p.m.; Alexandria: Mon–Sat 8 a.m.–9 p.m., Sun 8 a.m.–8 p.m.

Swain's Lock Boat House 10700 Swain's Lock Rd., Potomac, MD (301) 299-9006

For generations, this boathouse on Lock 21 of the C&O Canal has been renting canoes, kayaks, and rowboats for use on the canal only. Bike rentals are also available. There are picnic tables and a refreshment stand. Cash and checks only. Open March to November. Tue–Wed and Fri 10 a.m.–5 p.m., Thurs 10 a.m.–8 p.m., Sat–Sun 10 a.m.–6 p.m. Closed Mon. By car from the Beltway (I-495) take Exit 39 MD 190/River Rd. toward Washington/Potomac, merge onto MD-190 W, right on Swain's Lock Rd.

Swann House 1808 New Hampshire Ave. NW at 18th St. (202) 265-4414 www .swannhouse.com

This top-ranked bed-and-breakfast in an 1883 Richardson-arched red brick mansion offers high ceilings, turret windows, working fireplaces in many rooms, a small pool, sunroom, continental breakfast, Jacuzzis in many rooms, cable TV, VCRs, voice mail and data port, conference facilities, a garden, and parking. Moderate prices. Metro: Dupont Circle.

Swaziland Embassy 3400 International Dr. NW (202) 362-6683

Sweden Embassy 1501 M St. NW (202) 467-2600 www.swedish-embassy.org

Sweetwater Tavern 3066 Gatehouse Plaza, Falls Church, VA (703) 645-8100; 14250 Sweetwater Lane, Centreville, VA (703) 449-1108; 45980 Waterview Plaza, Sterling, VA (571) 434-6500 www.greatamericanrestaurants.com

There are now three Sweetwater Tavern brewpubs in northern Virginia: in Merrifield, Centreville, and Sterling. All are located in newly constructed buildings seating about 200 with a beautifully crafted Southwestern décor including cattle-drive murals, wrought iron hanging lamps, and etched-glass Western scenes. Their food is Southwestern, and features seafood, Angus beef prime ribs and steaks. Try their baby back ribs with fries and coleslaw and wash it down with a Snake River Pale Ale or a Giddyup Stout made on the premises. Falls Church and Sterling open Mon–Thurs 11 a.m.–11 p.m., Fri 11 a.m.–midnight, Sat 11:30 a.m.–midnight, Sun 11:30 a.m.–11 p.m. By car to Falls Church: From I-495 (the Beltway) Exit 8 Arlington Blvd. to Rte. 50 W, Arlington Blvd./Fairfax. Take the Gallows Rd./Merrifield Exit. Left on Gatehouse Rd. onto Gatehouse Plaza. By car to Sterling: 28 N, then take Rte. 7 E/Leesburg Pike, right onto Loudoun Tech Dr., and right into parking lot. Centreville: Tues–Thurs 11:30 a.m.–11 p.m., Fri–Sat 11:30 a.m.–midnight, Sun–Mon 11:30 a.m.–10 p.m. By car to Centreville: Rte. 66 W, Exit 53 toward Centreville on Rte. 28 S. Turn right onto Machen Rd., left onto Multiplex Dr.

Swimming *see* Anacostia Park, Bull Run Regional Park, Capitol East Natatorium, East Potomac Park, Frances Pool, Georgetown Pool, Jewish Community Center of the District of Columbia, Jewish Community Center of Northern Virginia, Pohick Bay Regional Park, WYCA, YMCA of Metropolitan Washington. *See also* D.C. Department of Parks and Recreation Aquatic Division.

Swiss Inn 1204 Massachusetts Ave. NW (202) 371-1816 (800) 955-7947 www.the swissinn.com

Billing itself as the smallest hotel in Washington, this 7-room, family-owned, 4-story turn-of-the-century brownstone was, until 1982, an efficiency apartment building. Each room has high ceilings, large windows, and a fully equipped kitchenette. Allows pets. Parking with modest fee weekdays, free weekends. Easy to spot with its Frederick Douglass mural covering the west wall. Budget prices. Metro: Metro Center, then a 4-block walk.

Swissôtel Washington–The Watergate 2650 Virginia Ave. NW (202) 298-4490 (800) 424-2736 www.swissotel.com

This 250-room hotel, many with balconies overlooking the Potomac, was formerly the Watergate Hotel, and is part of that complex. This deluxe hotel has the usual amenities plus a health club, sauna, hairdresser, business center, pool, concierge and baby-sitting services, and several restaurants and lounges. There is a complimentary shuttle service to downtown 7 a.m.–10 a.m. weekdays. Close by is the Kennedy Center, the State Department, and Georgetown. Expensive. Metro: Foggy Bottom-GWU.

Switzerland Embassy 2900 Cathedral Ave. NW (202) 745-7900 www.eda.admin.ch

Sylvan Theater 15th St. SW and Independence Ave. Monument grounds (202) 426-6841

During the summer months and on Washington's Birthday in February this outdoor stage on the Washington Monument offers free concerts from military bands stationed nearby. There are occasionally big-band and pop concerts there as well. Metro: Smithsonian.

Synagogues *see* Adas Israel Congregation, Kesher Israel Congregation–Georgetown Synagogue, Washington Hebrew Congregation.

Syria Embassy 2215 Wyoming Ave. NW (202) 232-6313 www.syrianembassy.org

T

Tabard Inn 1739 N St. NW Hotel: (202) 785-1277 Restaurant: (202) 833-2668
www.tabardinn.com

This 42-room hotel, 25 rooms with bath, sits among three Victorian town-houses. There is an Agatha Christie/Miss Marples quality about the hotel; partly the fireplaces and sofas and partly the characters—some stopping by from a neighboring science publisher—some cognoscenti drawn by the hotel, bar, or restaurant. The hotel rooms are different in size, décor, and facilities and thus their prices vary from room to room. It is best to look at each one on the Web site. Free continental breakfast. About the restaurant: Concentrate on the award-winning contemporary American cuisine. Try a pan-seared striped bass or roasted Cornish hen or duck leg, served over smothered onions, and finish it off with homemade ice cream. Open Sun 8 a.m.–10 a.m., 11 a.m.–2:30 p.m., 6 p.m.–10 p.m.; Mon 7 a.m.–10 a.m., 11:30 a.m.–2:30 p.m.; Tues–Fri 7 a.m.–10 a.m., 11:30 a.m.–2:30 p.m., 6 p.m.–10:30 p.m.; Sat 8 a.m.–10 a.m., 11 a.m.–2:30 p.m., 6 p.m.–10:30 p.m. Metro: Dupont Circle.

Taberna del Alabardero 1776 I St. NW (entrance on 18th St. between H and I Sts.) (202) 429-2200

This top-rated Spanish restaurant combines European-class service, an elegant setting—arches frame the exhibition kitchen—with a sumptuous selection of the various cuisines of Spain. Start with the *tapas*, and then try the rabbit, lamb or tuna and potato stew, roast duck, suckling pig, sweetbreads, paella or one of the seafood specials. Expensive. Open Mon–Fri 11:30 a.m.–2:30 p.m., 5:30 p.m.–10:30 p.m. Metro: Farragut North.

Tachibana 6715 Lowell Ave., McLean, VA (703) 847-1771 www.j-netusa.com/com/tachibana/

Opened in Arlington in 1982 before moving to its present location, Tachibana is an upscale Japanese restaurant offering an extensive sushi bar as well as its popular yakitori, tempura, *shumai* (deep-fried dumplings) and sukiyaki. Moderately expensive. Open for lunch Mon–Fri 11 a.m.–2 p.m., Sat noon–2:30 p.m., Sun 12:30 p.m.–3 p.m., dinner Mon–Thurs 5 p.m.–10 p.m., Fri–Sat 5 p.m.–10:30 p.m., Sun 5 p.m.–9–p.m. Metro: Pentagon, then take Metrobus 23B or C.

Taft Bridge Connecticut Ave. and Calvert St. NW over Rock Creek Park
    Connecticut Avenue crosses over Rock Creek on Washington's first great masonry bridge, built between 1897 and 1907. When completed, this much-photographed bridge, the work of architects George S. Morrison and Edward Pearce Casey, ranked as one of the world's first and largest poured-in-place, unreinforced concrete structures. Nicknamed the Million Dollar Bridge due to its long and costly construction, in 1931 it was renamed for William Howard Taft, who lived nearby. Four concrete lions guard both ends of the bridge, the work of sculptor R. Hinton Perry, and restored by sculptor Renato Lucchetti in 1965. Metro: Woodley Park-National Zoo.

Taft Bridge Inn 2007 Wyoming Ave. NW btw 20th St. and Connecticut Ave. (202) 387-2007 www.taftbridgeinn.com
    This Georgian-style bed-and-breakfast offers 13 guest rooms decorated with antiques; 4 have private baths, and 6 rooms have fireplaces. Phone/voice/modem line. There is a porch, garden, and parking (for a fee). Complimentary full breakfast. Moderate prices. Metro: Dupont Circle or Woodley Park-Zoo, then a 15-minute walk.

Taft Memorial *see* Robert A. Taft Memorial.

Tahoga 2815 M St. NW (202) 338-5380
    This restaurant offers variations on modern (sort of) American cuisine in a bright, airy space with an inviting garden setting as well. The cuisine selects from various regional dishes, but the regions sometimes stray across international borders. Try the braised lamb shank, roast chicken, or bourbon-glazed pork chops or maybe duck lasagna. Expensive. Open for lunch Mon–Fri 11:30 a.m.–2 p.m., dinner Sun–Thurs 5:30 p.m.–10 p.m., Fri–Sat 5:30 p.m.–11 p.m. Metro: Foggy Bottom-GWU, then 30, 32, 34, 35, or 36 Bus.

Taj Mahal 1327 Connecticut Ave. NW (202) 659-1544; 7239 Commerce St., Springfield, VA (703) 644-2875
    The Washington Taj Mahal opened in 1965, making it one of the oldest authentic Indian restaurants in the city. Now there is a sister restaurant in Springfield; both offer northern Indian cuisine including Mogul and tandoori dishes, but have modified their recipes with low-cholesterol, low-fat cooking methods. The Springfield branch offers cooking classes, so you, too, can attempt mulligatawny soup or *aloo matar* (potatoes and peas). Try the fish *tikka marsala* or chicken vindaloo. Washington open for lunch with buffet Mon–Sat 11:30 a.m.–2:30 p.m., dinner daily 5:30–10 p.m. Metro: Dupont Circle; Springfield open for lunch with buffet Mon–Sat 11:30 a.m.–2:30 p.m., Sun noon–2:30 p.m. buffet, dinner Mon–Sat 5:30 p.m.–10 p.m. By car from the Beltway (I-395/95) south, take VA-644 W Old Keene Mill Rd. Exit toward Springfield, right on Commerce St.

Tako Grill 7756 Wisconsin Ave., Bethesda, MD (301) 652-7030 www.takogrill.com
In a subdued room with clear wooden tables that could be found in a typical Sapporo restaurant, diners may select from a variety of fresh sushi and sashimi, but beyond that, there is also grilled whole red snapper, grilled fresh vegetables, and glazed grilled eel. And of course, teriyaki and tempura. The take-home menu is online. Very educational as well as pleasant zen-like sake bar offering possibly the best sake selection in the area. Open for lunch Mon–Fri 11:30 a.m.–2 p.m.; dinner Mon–Thurs 5:30 p.m.–10 p.m., Fri–Sat 5:30–10:30 p.m., Sun 5 p.m.–9:30 p.m. Metro: Bethesda.

Takoma Park Montgomery County, MD, borders the upper northwest/northeast boundary of Washington, D.C. www.cityoftakomapark.org
Less than 5 miles from the center of D.C., this community's 18,000 residents are diverse in age, ethnicity, primary language, economic condition, and length of residence. Since the 1980s, there has been an influx of immigrants from Central America and south and Southeast Asia. It was founded in 1833 as a real estate venture on farmland along the Baltimore & Ohio Railroad tracks, and its hilly winding streets are bordered by some gigantic Victorians, smaller brick Colonials, and increasingly, apartment complexes. Its political activism and mix of citizenry prompts a comparison with Berkeley; lots of writers, musicians, academics, and government researchers. The Seventh-Day Adventist Church's Columbia Union College (see entry), which supplies physicians throughout the world, and the Washington Adventist Hospital are located here. Metro: Takoma.

Takoma Park Farmers Market Laurel Ave. btw Carroll and Easter Aves., Takoma Park, MD (301) 422-0097 www.cityoftakomapark.org/ecd/documents/farmers .html
Open from the third Sunday in April to the third Sunday in December, the market offers "producer only" fruits, vegetables, baked goods, herbs, bedding plants, honey, eggs, and cider that come from the sellers' own garden, farm, or kitchen. Farms must be 125 miles or less from the city. No crafts or nonagricultural products are allowed. Metro: Takoma.

Takoma Park Folk Festival Takoma Park Middle School, 7611 Piney Branch Rd., Takoma Park, MD (301) 589-3717 www.tpff.org
Founded in 1977 and held on a Sunday in mid-September, this benefit festival offers dancing, an enormous range of folk music, blues, and ethnic music throughout Takoma Park on seven stages, as well as a juried craft sale, international foods, and for children, folk singing, interactive musical games, clowns, and storytelling. Many performances are sign-language interpreted. Free parking at Montgomery College. Admission free. Metro: Takoma, then free festival shuttle bus.

Takoma Park JazzFest Jenquie Park, Fenton St. and Takoma Ave., Takoma Park, MD (301) 589-4433 www.cityoftakomapark.org
This annual May outdoor festival runs from Friday evening through Saturday and includes events at the Takoma Theater as well as at Jenquie Park. There are jam sessions, performances by local and nationally known bands, community ta-

bles, crafts, food, a jazz flea market, and a Takoma Artists Guild children's art contest. Metro: Takoma. By car parking is free at Montgomery College garage. From the Beltway (I-495) go south on George Ave. (Rte. 97). Turn left on Sligo Ave. to Fenton St., and turn right. The parking garage is on the right and the campus is on the left.

Takoma Park Old Town Carroll and Laurel Aves., Takoma Park, MD

This commercial district with brick sidewalks, a Victorian-style gazebo, and small 1920-era stores is anchored by the remarkable House of Musical Traditions at 7040 Carroll with its exotic acoustic instruments from around the world, a wall of used accordions, books, and recordings. Other shops offer antiques, collectibles, ethnic food, and the work of local artists. An Old Town Street Fair is held the first Sunday in October. Metro: Takoma.

Takoma Park Presbyterian Church 310 Tulip Ave., Takoma Park, MD (301) 270-5550 www.takomaparkpc.org

The land on which this church was built has been used for religious services since the nineteenth century. Originally, there was a tent, followed by a simple frame structure built in 1888. In 1893 the land was purchased by the Presbyterians and a sanctuary was completed in 1923. This was followed by a 3-story education building in 1950, which houses church activities and the Takoma Park Child Development Center. A fellowship hall, completed in 1962, provides church offices and is used by various community groups, including Casa de Maryland, a Central American social service and advocacy group. Metro: Takoma.

Takoma Park Seventh-Day Adventist Church 6810 Eastern Ave. (202) 829-4800

Actually located in Washington, D.C., across the line from Takoma Park, this Gothic Revival–style fieldstone church was completed in 1953. However, the Takoma Park Seventh-Day Adventist Church dates from 1904, when the general conference headquarters building and Columbia Union College were built. The Washington Sanitarium followed in 1907, but was demolished in 1982 to be replaced by the Washington Adventist Hospital. The Adventists' presence in the area developed a family-oriented community. Other areas of the Adventist life style—no dancing, no drinking, and a vegetarian diet—also had an impact on the community. But times have changed. Now alcohol is sold within the city limits, and even the city sponsors dances. Metro: Takoma.

Takoma Station 6914 4th St. NW (202) 829-1937 www.takomastation.com

This popular family-owned tavern has been providing the Takoma Park area with Latin, traditional, and progressive jazz and blues since 1984. Located on the District line just 2 blocks from the Takoma Metro Station, the tavern has exposed brick walls, a pressed-tin ceiling, and ten TVs. The food is Southern: chicken, seafood, meat loaf, and ribs. This is one of the top jazz clubs in the area and while offering mostly local acts, biggies such as Stevie Wonder, Wynton Marsalis, and Gil Scott Heron have performed here. Live music five nights a week, with early (6:30 p.m.) sets sometimes on Thursdays and Fridays. Monday is comedy night. Sunday features reggae. No sneakers, no athletic wear. Cover charge varies. Open Mon–Sun 4 p.m.–2 a.m. Metro: Takoma.

El Tamarindo 1785 Florida Ave. NW btw U St. and California Ave. (202) 328-3660; 7331 Georgia Ave. NW (202) 291-0525

There are now two El Tamarindos, both well known to locals, that offer delicious, authentic, low-priced Salvadoran and Mexican dishes such as grilled shrimp, rice and beans, or chicken fajitas. Wash it down with cold Mexican beers, sangria by the pitcher, or margaritas. Florida Ave. open Mon–Thurs 11 a.m.–3 a.m., Fri–Sun 11 a.m.–5 a.m. Metro: U. St.-Cardozo; Georgia Ave. open daily, 11 a.m.–11 p.m. Metro: Takoma, then a 10-minute walk.

Tanzania Embassy 2139 R St. NW (202) 939-6125 www.tanzaniaembassy-us.org

Tara Thai 226 Maple Ave. W, Vienna, VA (703) 255-2467; 4828 Bethesda Ave., Bethesda, MD (301) 657-0488; 7501 Leesburg Pike, Falls Church, VA (703) 506-9788; 4001 N Fairfax Dr., Arlington, VA (703) 908-4999; 12071 Rockville Pike, Rockville, MD (301) 231-9899

This small chain of Thai restaurants collects awards almost as fast as it collects loyal patrons. Friendly, attentive service, low prices, and consistently delectable dishes, particularly fresh seafood, is the hallmark of these restaurants. This is authentic Thai cuisine, the creation of chef Nick Srisawat who got into Thai cookery at age 8 in his homeland. Delightful undersea décor. Reservations suggested. Open Mon–Thurs 11:30 a.m.–3 p.m., 5 p.m.–10 p.m.; Fri 11:30 a.m.–3 p.m., 5 p.m.–11 p.m.; Sat noon–3:30 p.m., 5 p.m.–11 p.m.; Sun noon–3:30 p.m., and 5 p.m.–10 p.m. Metro to Vienna: Rosslyn, then Metrobus 404 to Maple and Lawyers Rds.; Bethesda Metro: Bethesda, and then a 10-minute walk; Falls Church Metro: West Falls Church, then Metrobus 28A to Leesburg Turnpike and Pimmit Dr.; Arlington Metro: Ballston; Rockville Metro: Twinbrook, then Ride-On Bus 46 to Rockville Pike and Montrose Rd.

Taras Shevchenko Memorial P St. btw 22nd and 23rd Sts. NW

This 24-foot bronze and granite monument was unveiled in 1964 by President Dwight D. Eisenhower. Taras Shevchenko (1814–1861) is considered the Ukraine's greatest poet whose nationalist Ukrainian writings caused Czar Nicholas I to exile him to Siberia for 10 years. Radoslav Zuk, a Ukrainian-born architect teaching at McGill University in Canada designed the monument. Leo Mol, born in Polonne, Ukraine, and moving to Canada in 1948, sculpted the piece. The Leo Mol Sculpture Garden in Winnipeg's Assiniboine Park displays more than 300 works of this now world-renowned artist. Metro: Dupont Circle.

Tartt Gallery 2017 Q St. NW (202) 332-5652

This gallery offers nineteenth-century, twentieth-century, and contemporary photographs. Leading historical figures and major photographers are included. The collections include news photos of the past, providing fascinating visual sociological, anthropological, and historical commentary. Larger collections include the expansion of the American West, the Civil War, and major new events. Open Fri–Sat 11 a.m.–5 p.m. Metro: Dupont Circle.

Taste of Arlington Ballston Common Mall, N Glebe Rd. and Wilson Blvd., Arlington, VA (703) 841-7768 www.tasteofarlington.com

This annual May street festival, established in 1987, offers local entertainment, children's activities, and samplings of foods from local restaurants. There is, as well, a juried antique arts and crafts show. Kids will enjoy the Taste of Science Tent and Activities sponsored by the National Science Foundation. Local restaurants represent Asian, Tex-Mex, Indian, Lebanese, Italian, French, and Southern cuisines. The event supports Community Residences, a local nonprofit agency that provides essential community services. Tickets are good for samples at the various booths. Metro: Ballston.

Taste of Bethesda Fairmont, Norfolk, and St. Elmo Sts., Bethesda, MD (301) 215-6660 www.bethesda.org/specialevents/specialevents.htm
This street festival held the first Saturday in October offers food samples from more than fifty local restaurants, a music festival, kids' activities, and prizes. Admission free, food samples have modest fees. Metro: Bethesda.

Taste of D.C. Pennsylvania Ave. NW btw 7th and 14th Sts. (202) 789-7002 www.washington.org/taste
This annual festival takes place three days during the Columbus Day weekend. Stands offer samples from more than forty Washington restaurants. Tickets are traded for food at the booths. There are, as well, free concerts, cooking demonstrations, crafts exhibits, and kids' activities. Proceeds go to various charities. Metro: Archives-Navy Memorial.

Taste of Saigon 410 Hungerford Dr. at Beall Ave., Rockville, MD (301) 424-7222; 8201 Greensboro Dr., McLean, VA (703) 790-0700
These top-rated, inexpensive sister restaurants offer a pleasing ambiance and an extensive variety of Vietnamese dishes. They offer, as well, some French dishes from their long-ago restaurant days in Saigon. Try the steamed whole rockfish in black-bean sauce, grilled pork meatballs, or a lamb shank covered with a spicy sauce. Inexpensive. Open Mon–Thurs 11 a.m.–10 p.m., Fri–Sat 11 a.m.–11 p.m., Sun 11 a.m.–9:30 p.m. Metro: Rockville or Rosslyn, then take the Metrobus 15K toward George Mason University to the Tysons Corner Shopping Center stop. Or exit at West Falls Church station and take the Metrobus 28B. Driving to McLean: Taste of Saigon is directly off Gallows Rd. and located across the street from the Tysons Corner II Mall.

Taste of the Nation Share Our Strength, 735 15th St. NW, Suite 640 (202) 478-6525 www.strength.org/see/taste/events.asp
Since 1988, Taste of the Nation events throughout the states have raised $46 million supporting more than 450 organizations working to end hunger and poverty in the United States and abroad. In Washington, this prestigious annual April event raises more than $4 million by offering tastings from some of Washington's finest chefs and their restaurants. Participating restaurants often include Equinox, Bis, Butterfield, Galileo, Kinkead's, Ortanique, Tosca, Ten Penh, and Vidalia. Expensive. Check Web site for location.

Taste of Wheaton Grandview and Ennalls Aves., Wheaton, MD. (240) 777-8115
This annual May street festival, established in 1995, offers local entertainment,

children's activities, and foods from local restaurants. Participating restaurants offer samples of their dishes in exchange for tickets that support local charities. Live musical entertainment and children's activities include face painting. The Wheaton Volunteer Rescue Squad demonstrates equipment, offers free blood screenings, and displays their specialized vehicles. Metro: Wheaton.

Tastee Diner 7731 Woodmont Ave., Bethesda, MD (301) 652-3970; 8601 Cameron St., Silver Spring, MD (301) 589-8171; 118 Washington Blvd., Laurel, MD (301) 725-1503

Three Edward Hopper–like diners have been owned since 1988 by Gene Wilkes, but their history is much older. The Silver Spring diner first opened in 1935 on Georgia Ave. and Wayne where it served its 'murican classics of pie, meat loaf, sandwiches, and coffee until June 2000 when it was moved to the present location—and enlarged. The three diners offer a traditional caloric values menu and the same hours—open daily 24 hours. Local filmmaker Sujewa Ekanayake (www .wilddiner.com) shot a 70-minute chronicle of life in the Silver Spring eatery, *Wild Diner*, which is screened occasionally at local film houses. Metro: Bethesda, Silver Spring.

Taverna the Greek Islands 307 Pennsylvania Ave. SE (202) 547-8360

This restaurant is likely a major purveyor of Greek take-out to congressional staff; it's 2 blocks east of the Capitol. Try the Greek-style sandwiches such as chicken souvlaki, or for sit-down meals, char-grilled lamb shish kebab, *kalamarakia* (baby squid pan fried to a golden crisp), or the moussaka. Moderate prices. Open Mon–Sat 11 a.m.–11 p.m., Sun 5 p.m.–11 p.m. Metro: Capitol South.

Taxis http://dcpages.ari.net/Travel/Reviews/taxi.shtml

Taxicabs in Washington are plentiful and may be hailed from the street. They have no meters. To calculate your fare, you need to understand the zone system they use. The city is divided into eight zones and a number of subzones. There are fixed fees per zone. If you stay in one zone you pay the one-zone fee. That is less expensive than crossing into another zone. A zone map and fare chart should be facing you when you get into the cab, but you may want to simply ask the driver to confirm the fare to your destination. There are various surcharges and special fees that might apply. These include modest fees for rush hour (Mon–Fri 7 a.m.–9:30 a.m., 4 p.m.–6:30 p.m.), each additional passenger, and more than one piece of luggage. Dispatched cabs, responding to your phone call, add another surcharge. Taxis in Maryland and Virginia use meters. The Web site provides explanations of fees, zones, phone numbers, and useful taxi travel tips. Reliable, radio-dispatched D.C. cabs include Diamond Cab (202) 387-6200 and Yellow Cab (202) 544-1212.

Tea Cosy 119 S Royal St., Alexandria, VA (703) 836-8181 http://alexandriacity .com/food/teacosy.htm

This authentic British tearoom offers breakfast, lunch, and afternoon teas. There are important decisions to be made involving crumpets, scones, tea sandwiches, and what the British insist on calling biscuits. For lunch, the options include shepherd's pie, steak and kidney pie, bangers, and mash. Find a British magazine or paper available for reading, and make sure to browse their mustards, teapots, teas, and other imports. Open Tues–Sun 10 a.m.–6 p.m., Fri 10 a.m.–7 p.m. Metro: Braddock Rd., then take DAT5 DASH Bus toward Van Dorn St.

Teaism 800 Connecticut Ave. NW (202) 835-2233; 2009 R St. NW (202) 667-3827; 400 8th St. NW (202) 638-6010 www.teaism.com

These tea bar and Asian restaurants offer various oolongs, white teas, green teas, and herbals. For breakfast, their dishes include Irish oatmeal with mango and raisins, scrambled tofu, ginger scones, and fresh hot nan. Lunch and dinner dishes are equally Asian eclectic, including a fish bento box with baked teriyaki salmon, cucumber-ginger salad, lamb *korma* with brown rice, or a simple grilled ostrich burger on a brioche. Highlighted by *Tea Magazine, Bon Appetit,* www.economist .com, and others. Inexpensive. Connecticut Ave. open Mon–Fri 7:30 a.m.–5:30 p.m. Metro: Farragut West; R St: Mon–Thurs 8 a.m.–10 p.m., Fri 8 a.m.–11 p.m., Sat 9 a.m.–11 p.m., Sun 9 a.m.–10 p.m., Brunch Sat–Sun 9 a.m.–2:30 p.m. Metro: Dupont Circle; 8th St: Mon–Thurs 7:30 a.m.–9:30 p.m., Fri 7:30 a.m.–10 p.m., Sat 9:30 a.m.–10 p.m., Sun 9:30 a.m.–9:30 p.m., Brunch Sat–Sun 9:30 a.m. to 2:30 p.m. Metro: Archives-Navy Memorial.

Tearooms *see* Ching Ching Cha, Coeur de Lion, Melrose, Seasons, Tea Cosy, Teaism, Washington National Cathedral. *See also* Cafés, Coffee and Cakes.

Teens in Washington, D.C. *see* Museums of Particular Interest to Children, Places That Appeal to Children.

Temperance Fountain Pennsylvania Ave. and 7th St. NW www.geocities.com/ Colosseum/Park/8386/cogswell.htm

This heron-topped Victorian monument is one of fifteen fountains presented to cities throughout the states by Dr. Henry Cogswell, who made his fortune filling Gold Rush miners' teeth, and then investing in prime California property. The monument celebrates temperance. Congress accepted the donation in 1882. In 1990 the city turned off the fountain's water. While some cities have been able to remove their Cogswell fountains on artistic grounds, this one is protected by the Cogswell Society, a secret fraternity founded in 1983. The society protects the monument but not the concept of temperance. Metro: Archives-Navy Memorial.

Temperance Row Farmers and Artists Market 12th and U Sts. NW (202) 232-2915

From 3 p.m. to 7 p.m. on Wednesdays between early June and the end of October, producers sell their vegetables and fruit here.

Temple of the Church of Jesus Christ of Latter-day Saints 9900 Stoneybrook Rd. off Capitol View Ave., Kensington, MD (301) 587-0144

This massive structure, designed by Wilcox, Marham, Beecher, and Fetzer, was completed in 1974, at a cost of $15 million. The white marble 16-story building is topped by six gold-plated spires, easily seen from the Washington Beltway. The temple is closed to non-members of the Church of Jesus Christ of Latter-day Saints. A visitor center, however, is open to all. It offers various multimedia presentations on the church's beliefs and the temple itself. Visitor Center Open daily 10 a.m.–9 p.m. Admission free. By car from I-495 (the Beltway) take Exit 33 to Beach Dr., going east then north on Stoneybrook Dr.

Tempo 4231 Duke St., Alexandria, VA (703) 370-7900 www.temporestaurant.com
This high-ceiling restaurant with large glass windows offers a light, open feeling. The cuisine, mostly northern Italian and French, emphasizes seafood. House specialties include *linguini vongole*, sole amandine, lamb chops, and veal scallopini. Open for lunch Sun–Fri 11:30 a.m.–2:30 p.m.; dinner Sat 5:30 p.m.–10 p.m. and Sun 5:30 p.m.–9 p.m. Metro: King Street, then DAT8 DASH Bus to Duke and Gordon Sts.

Tennis (Active Sports Activity) *see* Cabin John Regional Park, D.C. Department of Parks and Recreation, East Potomac Tennis Center, Montrose Park, Potomac Park, Rock Creek Park, Rockville Civic Center Park, South Riding, Washington Tennis and Education Foundation, Washington Tennis Center, Watkins Regional Park.

Tennis (Spectator Sport) *see* D.C. Department of Parks and Recreation, East Potomac Tennis Center, Hains Point, Pierce Mill, Washington Tennis Center. *See also* Washington Tennis and Education Foundation, Legg Mason Tennis Classic, Washington Tennis Classic.

Tennis Factory 2500 Wilson Blvd., Suite 100, Arlington, VA (703) 522-2700 www.tennisfactory.com
Founded in 1976, this store offers a complete collection of tennis products, services, and tennis garb for men, women, and children, as well as a full range of court equipment, ball machines, nets, and services such as racquet restringing. Open Sun noon–5 p.m., Mon–Wed 10 a.m.–7 p.m., Thurs 10 a.m.–8 p.m., Fri 10 a.m.–7 p.m., Sat 10 a.m.–6 p.m. Metro: Court House.

Tequila Grill 1990 K St. NW (202) 833-3640
With a 60-foot bar, Tex-Mex décor, including a series of painted cattle skulls, this has a popular following of after-work margarita lovers, not to mention the Long Star and Corona crowd. Tex-Mex prevails: tacos, enchiladas, cheese chile rellenos. Moderate prices. Open Mon–Fri 11:30 a.m.–2:30 p.m., Mon–Thurs 5:30 p.m.–10:30 p.m., Fri–Sat 5:30–11 p.m. Metro: Farragut West.

Terrace Theater *see* Kennedy Center for the Performing Arts Terrace Theater.

Tex-Mex Restaurants *see* Mexican Restaurants.

Textile Museum 2320 S St. NW (202) 667-0441 www.textilemuseum.org
George Hewitt Myers, of the Bristol-Myers fortune, opened this museum in 1925, allowing the public to see his remarkable collection of the textile traditions of non-Western cultures. This private museum in two buildings has grown to include more than 17,000 objects dating from 3,000 B.C. The world-class collection of pre-Colombian Peruvian, Islamic, and Coptic textiles, as well as the oriental carpet collection, draws more than 30,000 visitors a year. A research library, open to the public, offers unparalleled holdings of literature and visual materials related to the textile arts. The Museum shop sells textile-related books, and can be accessed on-

line. In addition to the ever-changing exhibits, the hands-on textile learning center and the online interactive collections database can enrich your visit. Docent-led tours may be reserved by phone. The building where visitors enter the museum was built in 1913 by John Russell Pope for the Myers residence. The adjacent house, 2320 S St., built in 1908 by Waddy B. Wood, was purchased by the Myers to house and display their ever-expanding collection. Admission free. Suggested donation of $5. The museum is open Mon–Sat 10 a.m.–2 p.m., Sun 1 p.m.–5 p.m. Docent-led tours: First Mon of the month at 1 p.m., and every Sat and Sun at 1:30 p.m. Special exhibition tours may be scheduled at least three weeks in advance by telephone, ext. 64. The library is open Wed–Fri 10 a.m.–2 p.m., Sat 10 a.m.–4 p.m., or phone for an appointment, ext. 31. Metro: Dupont Circle, then a 10-minute walk. *See also* www.commuterpage.com/venues/museums.htm.

Thai Kingdom 2021 K St. btw 20th and 21st Sts. NW (202) 835-1700

This popular Thai restaurant offers a spectrum of traditional dishes at very moderate prices. Try the pad Thai or scallops wrapped in chicken. Open for lunch Mon–Fri 11:30 a.m.–3 p.m.; dinner Mon–Thurs 5 p.m.–10:30 p.m., Fri 5 p.m.–11 p.m.; Sat noon–11 p.m.; Sun noon–10 p.m. Metro: Farragut West.

Thai Restaurants *see* Bangkok Bistro, Bangkok Garden, Basil Thai, Benjarong, Bua, Busara, Duangrats, Haad Thai, Ivy's Place, Jandara, Sala Thai, Sawatdee, Tara Thai, Thai Kingdom, Thai Square. *See also* www.washingtonpost.com.

Thai Square 3217 Columbia Pike, btw S Highland St. and S Glebe Rd., Arlington, VA (703) 685-7040

This popular, albeit small, restaurant offers authentic Thai cuisine, including spicy grilled catfish, crispy squid with basil, and crispy pork with Chinese broccoli. For dessert try mango sticky rice. Open Mon–Thurs 11:30 a.m.–10:30 p.m., Fri 11:30 a.m.–11 p.m., Sat noon–11 p.m., Sun noon–10:30. Metro. Pentagon, then take 16B Culmore Bus to Columbia Pike and Walter Reed Dr.

Thailand Embassy 1024 Wisconsin Ave. NW (202) 944-3600 www.thaiembdc.org

Theater Lab *see* Kennedy Center for the Performing Arts Theater Lab.

Theater Tickets *see* TicketMaster, TICKETplace.

Theaters *see* Adventure Theater, American Century Theater, American University Department of Performing Art, Arena Stage, The Barns at Wolf Trap, Carter Barron Amphitheater, Church Street Theater, District of Columbia Arts Center, F. Scott Fitzgerald Theatre, Ford's Theatre and Lincoln Museum, Gala Hispanic Theater, George Mason University Center for the Arts, Hartke Theater at Catholic University, Howard Theater, Kennedy Center for the Performing Arts Concert Hall, Kennedy Center for the Performing Arts Eisenhower Theater, Kennedy Center for the Performing Arts Opera House, Kennedy Center for the Performing Arts Terrace Theater, Kennedy Center for the Performing Arts Theater Lab, Kreeger Theater, Lincoln Theatre, Lisner Auditorium of George Washington University, Little Theater of Alexandria, Merriweather Post Pavilion, National Theater, Le Neon Theater, Nissan Pavilion at Stone Ridge, Olney Theatre Center for the Arts, Publick Playhouse, Round House Theater, St. Marks Players, Shakespeare Theatre, Signature

Theater, Source Theatre Company, Studio Theater, University of Maryland Clarice Smith Center for the Performing Arts, Warner Theatre, Washington Stage Guild, Woolly Mammoth Theater Company. *See also* Concerts, Theater Tickets.

Theodore Roosevelt Birthday Theodore Roosevelt Island, George Washington Memorial Pkwy., Arlington, VA (703) 289-2530

Late in October, Theodore Roosevelt's birthday is celebrated at his monument on Theodore Roosevelt Island. There are island tours, activities for kids, exhibits, and family activities. Sometimes a Theodore Roosevelt look-alike appears.

Theodore Roosevelt Island Potomac River near Georgetown (202) 289-2500 www.nps.gov/this/pphtml/activities.html

This ½-mile-long Potomac island, purchased in 1931 to be dedicated as a memorial to President Theodore Roosevelt, is administered by the National Park Service. A monument and statue were erected on the island in 1967. The wilderness area offers a haven for wildlife, with more than fifty species of trees and 200 varieties of wildflowers. Several trails wind across the 88-acre island. The island is reached by a footbridge leading from a parking lot off the George Washington Memorial Pkwy. north of the Theodore Roosevelt Bridge. Open 8 a.m.–dusk.

Theodore Roosevelt Island Hiking Path Potomac River near Georgetown (202) 289-2500 www.nps.gov/this/pphtml/activities.html

The 2½ miles of nature trails in this nature preserve offer a variety of terrains: woodlands, rocky beaches, and swampy marshlands. The trails are well marked and during the summer months, National Park Service rangers lead interpretive hikes along the trails. A comfort station is closed in the winter. The island is reached by a footbridge leading from a parking lot off the George Washington Memorial Pkwy. north of the Theodore Roosevelt Bridge. Open 8 a.m.–dusk.

Theodore Roosevelt Memorial Bridge Constitution Ave. crossing the Potomac into Virginia

Completed in 1960 at a cost of $24.5 million, this shallow-arched multiple-span structure was built contrary to the recommendations of various groups including the Commission on Fine Arts of the National Park Service, since it intrudes into the sanctuary of Theodore Roosevelt Island. A tunnel was suggested as an alternative. Metro: Rosslyn.

Theodore Roosevelt Statue Roosevelt Island, Potomac River, adjacent to the George Washington Memorial Pkwy. (202) 289-2500

This memorial to Theodore Roosevelt includes a 17-foot bronze statue by Paul Manship, which was dedicated in 1967. While the Theodore Roosevelt Memorial Association purchased the island in 1931, Congress did not fund the erection of a memorial until 1960. On both sides of the sculpture granite monoliths are inscribed with quotations from Roosevelt about preserving the environment. Known as America's environmental president, it seems fitting to place the memorial in this natural setting. It is accessible only from the Virginia side via a footbridge. By car access to the island is available only from the northbound lane of the George Washington Memorial Pkwy.

Third Edition 1218 Wisconsin Ave. NW (202) 333-3700

This Georgetown institution, seen in the film *St. Elmo's Fire*, has been packing in college students and the slightly older for almost three decades. Food is inexpensive bar fare. Upstairs, a dance club with a DJ gets popular from about 9 p.m. onward. Open Sun–Thurs 11 a.m.–2 a.m., Fri–Sat 11 a.m.–3 a.m. Cover charge after 10 p.m. Metro: Foggy Bottom-GWU or Rosslyn, then Georgetown Shuttle.

THOMAS–Legislative Information on the Internet (Web site) http://thomas .loc.gov

This Library of Congress electronic publication—updated hourly—first appeared in 1995, and now is definitely on the charts—ranked in the "top 100" most useful Web sites. Thomas's powerful search engine leads you to requested parts of all U.S. House and Senate legislation, the Congressional Record and Index, e-mail and snail mail addresses for lawmakers, member directories, voting records, committee Web sites, and historic documents, as well as links to related resources. For example, you can check to see what measures are expected to be considered on the House floor this week.

Thomas Circle Massachusetts Ave. and 14th St. NW

Northwest of the circle the impressive National City Christian Church is another Washington landmark by architect John Russell Pope. On the opposite side of 14th St. is the Luther Place Memorial Church and standing before it, facing the circle, is a statue of Martin Luther. The circle's namesake, a bronze equestrian statue of Maj. Gen. George H. Thomas, was erected in 1879, and marked an experimental Washington first: electric lights were used in the ceremony. Metro: McPherson Square.

Thomas House *see* Alma Thomas House.

Thomas Jefferson Community Children's Theater *see* Children's Theater.

Thomas Jefferson Memorial *see* Jefferson Memorial.

Thomas Law House 1252 6th St. SW (202) 554-4844 www.tiberisland.com/tiberis land/law.html

Built in 1795 by William Lovering, this Federal-style mansion was the site of the short-lived marriage between a well-connected British land speculator, Thomas Law, then 39, and Eliza Park Custis, 19, the granddaughter of Martha Washington. They spent their honeymoon here, thus the nickname "Honeymoon House." President John Adams and King Louis Philippe of France were dinner guests here. In 1816 the house was purchased by Richard Bland Lee (see Sully Historic Site). The house is now owned by the Tiber Island apartment compex, and is rented out for receptions. There are some period antiques in the building. Private tours may be arranged by phoning the Tiber Island offices at 461 N St. SW, at the number above. Metro: Waterfront-SEU.

Thomas Masaryk Memorial T. G. Masaryk Memorial Park, 22nd St. and Massachussetts Ave. NW

This monument honors Tomas Garrigue Masaryk, the first president of Czechoslovakia. While in exile in Washington in 1918, he drafted the Czechoslovakian

Declaration of Independence ending the Hungarian Empire's rule of the Czech and Slovak people. The 12-foot sculpture was created by Czech artist Vincenc Makovsky in 1937, the year Masaryk died, but the statue was never cast; honors to this leader were forbidden under the Nazi occupation and later under Communism. It was finally cast in bronze in 1968, but hidden from public view until post-Communism reform in 1992. The monument was unveiled in Washington on September 19, 2002, by Vaclav Havel in what is now designated the T. G. Masaryk Memorial Park. The remarkable Havel, of course, is a writer and dramatist, a leader in the Velvet Revolution of 1989, last president of Czechoslovakia, and the first president of the Czech Republic. Metro: Dupont Circle.

Thomas-Siegler House and Gardens corner of Tulip and Cedar Aves., Takoma Park, MD (301) 270-2831 Administration: Historic Takoma, Inc., P.O. Box 5781, Takoma Park, MD www.historictakoma.org

Horace and Amanda Thomas built their home and carriage house in 1884, the first house in the city. Horace Thomas was not only the Baltimore & Ohio Railroad stationmaster for Takoma Park, but its postmaster and a local merchant as well. He died 5 years after the completion of the house. Amanda Thomas sold the house to Franklin and Catherine Siegler in 1919. The Trust for Public Land bought the property and resold it in 1985 to the City of Takoma Park. Historic Takoma, Inc., administers what is now the Thomas-Siegler Carriage House Museum. Hours vary, but usually, the home is open May through August on Sundays 1 p.m.–4 p.m. The gardens, which contain rare azaleas, are open daily dawn to dusk. Metro: Takoma.

Thomas Sim Lee Corner *see* Sim Lee Building.

Thomas Statue Thomas Circle, Massachusetts Ave. and 14th St. NW www.dcheritage.org

In 1879, the Society of the Army of the Cumberland, colleagues of Maj. Gen. George H. Thomas, unveiled this bronze equestrian statue of their Civil War leader. John Quincy Adams Ward, one of the finest artists of his day, sculpted the piece. "Pap" Thomas was loved by his troops and was a brilliant and heroic figure in the Civil War. While Virginia born, when the war broke out, this West Pointer stayed loyal to the Union causing his family to disown him, never to reconcile, and the State of Virginia to seize his property. Metro: McPherson Square, then a 10-minute walk.

Thompson-Markwood Hall 235 2nd St. NE at C St. (202) 546-3255

Often recommended to summer interns working on Capitol Hill, this boarding facility is open to women only from 18 to 34 who will be working or studying in Washington. A minimum stay is two weeks, and there is a moderate summer reservation fee. There are one to two interns per room. Rooms have air-conditioning, a phone and a shared bath, and breakfast and dinner are included. No alcohol, smoking, or male guests above the lobby common area. Inexpensive. Metro: Union Station.

Thompson's Boat Center 2900 Virginia Ave. NW at Rock Creek Pkwy. (202) 333-9543 www.guestservices.com/tbc

Run by Guest Services, Inc., for the National Park Service, the center rents bikes, boats, and offers rowing lessons. Thompson's has many regattas each year and Georgetown University and George Washington University store their sculls there. You can rent kayaks, canoes, and rowing shells, including single and double kayaks, single recreational shells, and single and double racing shells. Boat rentals are on a first-come, first-served basis. You must be certified to rent shells, but the center offers various kinds of lessons. Bicycle rentals are offered from March through November. Boat rentals are available from April to November. Rentals: Mon–Sat 7 a.m.–6 p.m., Sun 8 a.m.–5 p.m. By car take Wisconsin Ave. south to K St. NW, also known at that point as Water St. A commercial parking lot is directly ahead next to the river. Metro: Foggy Bottom-GWU.

Thunder Grill 50 Massachusetts Ave., inside Union Station (202) 898-0051

This new arrival to Union Station offers Southwest offerings such as fajitas, enchiladas, and quesadillas enhanced by an attractive modern Tex-Mex décor. For those in a hurry—after all, it is a train station—there are salads and sandwiches (try the vegetarian burrito) and, of course, tangy margaritas to wash it all down. Moderate prices. Open daily 11:30 a.m.–10 p.m. Metro: Union Station.

The Thurgood Marshall Center for Service and Heritage 1816 12th St. NW (202) 462-8314 http://hswdc.org

This was originally the 12th Street YMCA, then in 1972, the Anthony Bowen YMCA. In 2000 it was rebuilt and renamed for a frequent visitor to the original Y, attorney Thurgood Marshall, later appointed to the Supreme Court. The original building was designed by W. Sidney Pittman, one of America's first African-American architects and son-in-law of Booker T. Washington. President Theodore Roosevelt laid the cornerstone in 1908. This YMCA was founded by educator—and former slave—Anthony Bowen, and offered, in segregated Washington, lodging, sports, and a venue for social events. The Thurgood Marshall Center serves as the home for several community organizations as well as providing the Heritage Room, artifacts, photos, and historical items related to the history of African-Americans in the Shaw/U Street community. Open weekdays 8:30 a.m.–5:30 p.m. Closed federal holidays. Metro: U St.-Cardozo.

Thurgood Marshall Federal Judiciary Building 1 Columbus Circle NE (202) 502-4000 www.fjc.gov

This building, designed by noted architect Edward Larabee Barnes, opened in 1992. It was named for Thurgood Marshall, whose 1954 presentation before the Supreme Court in *Brown v. Board of Education* led to the desegregation of America's schools. He later, of course, became a Supreme Court justice himself. An indoor bamboo garden is lighted by a 5-story atrium in the building. Metro: Union Station.

Thyme Square 4735 Bethesda Ave., Bethesda, MD (301) 657-9077

With its vegetable and fruit façade, this restaurant is hard to miss, and its American cuisine, echoing its mural, offers any number of healthy low-fat food options—and no meat. There are pasta dishes and seafood offerings as well as imaginative wraps. Try the wood-fired pizza sprinkled with spinach, mushrooms, and potatoes, or a Caesar salad and then reward yourself with a slice of berry pie. Moderate prices. Open Mon–Thurs 11 a.m.–10 p.m., Fri –Sat 11 a.m.–11 p.m., Sun 3 p.m.–10 p.m. Metro: Bethesda.

TicketMaster (202) 432-7328 www.TicketMaster.com

TicketMaster sells tickets to most of the area's concerts, family attractions, sporting events, and arts and theatrical offerings. TicketMaster takes phone charges, or you can purchase TicketMaster tickets in person at Hecht's, Tower Records, Record & Tape Traders, D.C. Visitors Information Center, MCI Center, Old Post Office Pavilion, or other sites. Charge-by-phone orders are available Mon–Fri 9 a.m.–9 p.m., Sat 9 a.m.–7 p.m., Sun 9 a.m.–6 p.m. You can also buy tickets online at any time day or night, 365 days a year. The TicketMaster Web site offers any number of ways to scan for local events you may be interested in seeing, as well as seating charts, directions, and parking information.

TICKETplace inside Pavilion at the Old Post Office, 1100 Pennsylvania Ave. NW (202) 842-5387 or (202) TICKETS for recorded information about the day's available tickets www.cultural-alliance.org/tickets/today.html

This service, sponsored by the Cultural Alliance of Greater Washington, is Washington's only half-price, day-of-show ticket outlet. It offers tickets to performances in Maryland, Virginia, and the District of Columbia. The sixty-plus organizations they represent include Arena Stage, Ford's Theatre, George Mason University Center for the Arts, Kennedy Center, National Geographic, National Theatre, Shakespeare Theatre, National Theatre Signature Theatre, Olney Theatre, Source Theatre Company, and Washington Opera. You may buy tickets on the day of the show for half price plus a small service charge. The service charge is equal to 10 percent of the full face value of the ticket. For example, a $20 ticket costs $12 at TICKETplace. Tickets are sold in person only, on a first-come, first-served basis. The Web site carries, as well, a few special half-price advance sale offerings, as well as information on free offerings such as CNN's *Crossfire*, arts festivals, and Smithsonian events. TICKETplace is, as well, an outlet for full-price TicketMaster tickets. Open Tues–Sat 11 a.m.–6 p.m. Open Sat when there are tickets available. Closed Sun and Mon. Metro: Federal Triangle.

Tidal Basin near Independence Ave. and East Basin Dr. www.nps.gov/nacc/cherry

In 1882 the Army Corps of Engineers created this placid pond hoping to eradicate malaria and yellow fever associated with these river lowlands. Three years later, travel writer Eliza Ruhamah Scidmore began planting cherry trees along its barren banks and agitating for what is there now. By 1912, thanks in large part to Scidmore, the basin was ringed with Japanese cherry trees, mostly a gift from the Japanese people, creating an annual spring experience—a basin seemingly bordered in whipped cream. This explosion of blossoms takes place in late March or early April and is celebrated with Washington's Cherry Blossom Festival. Rented paddleboats provide splendid views of the blossoms as well as the beautifully sited Jefferson Memorial—landscaped by Frederic Law Olmsted during World War II. Metro: Smithsonian, then a 10-minute walk.

Tidal Basin Boathouse at Jefferson Memorial, 1401 Maine Ave. SW (202) 479-2426

Foot-powered paddleboats, available in two-seater and four-seater models, allow you to paddle, water-bug fashion, about the Tidal Basin. Open from March to September daily, 10 a.m.–7 p.m. Metro: Smithsonian, then a 10-minute walk.

Tiffin Unilang Shopping Center, 1341 University Blvd. E, Langley Park, MD (301) 434-9200

This Langley Park Indian restaurant provides a dazzling luncheon buffet, with even more temptations on the weekends. The tandoor provides fresh-baked nan and succulent chicken *tikka*, and not to be overlooked, lamb *palak*, chickpea and potato curry, or Bengali fish curry. Inexpensive. Open for lunch with buffet daily 11:30 a.m.–3 p.m., dinner 5 p.m.–10 p.m. Metro: Fort Totten, then take Metrobus K6 to New Hampshire Ave. and University Blvd. By car from I-495 north take 29B Exit, E University Blvd., toward Langley Park, merge onto MD-193 E/University Blvd. E.

Tilden Gardens 3000 Tilden St. NW www.dcheritage.org

This 200-unit complex was built between 1927 and 1930. Innovations included better access to air and light and professional landscaping across the 5-acre site that incorporated fountains, terraces, and pools. Not open to the public. Metro: Cleveland Park.

Time Out Washington (guidebook and Web site) www.timeout.com

This Web site, based on the guidebook of the same name, is part of a series of guides of major cities, printed and online, written by resident journalists. The information provided on restaurants, sightseeing, shopping, accommodations, local events of the month, bars, shops, and services appears both current and knowing. Pull-down menus allow you to pinpoint an area for pub crawling, or offer a sampling of Asian restaurants, film developers, or fish markets.

Tiny Jewel Box 1147 Connecticut Ave. NW (202) 393-2747

This not-so-tiny store—it has 3 floors—is well known for its modern designer and antique jewelry. Here you can browse through bracelets, brooches, rings, and necklaces from the Victorian era, as well as Art Nouveau, Edwardian, and Art Deco. The store also offers fine crystal, scarves, and other fashion accessories. Open Mon–Sat 10 a.m.–5:30 p.m. Metro: Farragut North.

Tipping

For taxi drivers, bartenders, and waiters, 15 percent is standard, 20 percent for exceptionally good service. Bellhops and airport baggage handlers should be given $1 or $2 per bag. Hairdressers get 10 percent. Hotel maids get $1 to $2 per day. Checkroom attendants get $1 per garment.

Al Tiramisu 2014 P St. NW (202) 467-4466 www.altiramisu.com

Consistently ranked by *Washingtonian Magazine* as one of the city's 100 best restaurants, this small, friendly, white-walled restaurant offers a daily special of fresh fish and homemade pasta. The catch of the day is presented on a platter by your waiter or award-winning chef Luigi Diotaiuti. Besides the popular *linguini alle vongole*, meat dishes include beef tenderloin with wine sauce and veal scallopini with Parma ham. Don't overlook the namesake dessert—one among many glories. Saturday cooking classes are explained on the Web site. Kid friendly as well. Open Mon–Fri noon–2:30 p.m. and 5 p.m.–11 p.m., Sat–Sun 5 p.m.–11 p.m. Metro: Dupont Circle.

Titanic Memorial 4th and P St. SW

Presently located in Washington Channel Park, this memorial to the men who died in the Titanic disaster—giving up their space in lifeboats for women and children—was dedicated by Mrs. William Howard Taft in 1931 at a site now covered by the Kennedy Center. The sculptor, Gertrude Vanderbilt Whitney, one of America's richest women, cast the sculpture in 1915. Her own brother died at sea the same year, a victim of the Lusitania torpedoing by a German submarine. The stone bench below the sculpture was designed by Henry Bacon of Lincoln Memorial fame. The funds for the memorial were raised by the Women's Titanic Memorial Association through society balls, a White House fund-raiser, and, among other things, a memorial poster by Charles Dana Gibson (of Gibson Girl fame) depicting a "young, deep-chested woman." Metro: Waterfront-SEU.

Tobago *see* Trinidad and Tobago Embassy.

Togo Embassy 2208 Massachusetts Ave. NW (202) 234-4212

Toilet Facilities *see* Rest Rooms.

Tom Sarris' Orleans House 1213 Wilson Blvd., Arlington, VA (703) 524-2929

This Rosslyn pioneer is known for its delicious, hefty portions of prime rib as well as its salad bar as big as the Ritz. This is a good place for a luncheon burger combined with the more-than-it's-possible-to-eat salad bar. Moderate prices. Open for lunch Mon–Fri 11:30 a.m.–3:30 p.m., dinner Mon–Sat 4 p.m.–11 p.m. and Sun 4 p.m.–10 p.m. Metro: Rosslyn.

Tomb of the Unknowns Arlington National Cemetery, Memorial Dr., Arlington, VA (703) 695-3250 www.arlingtoncemetery.org

Formerly the Tomb of the Unknown Soldier, this memorial was sculpted from a massive block of Colorado marble by Thomas Hudson Jones. It was dedicated in 1931. The remains of unknown American soldiers from World Wars I and II, the Korean Conflict, and until 1998, the Vietnam War lie in a sarcophagus under the tomb. The remains of the Vietnam unknown were later identified and reburied elsewhere. Soldiers from the Third U.S. Infantry Division guard the tomb. Since dedication in 1931, the tomb has been under 24-hour guard, night and day. During daylight hours, from April through September, the guard changes every half hour, involving an elaborate routine of rifle inspection and saluting. Otherwise, during daylight, the guard changes hourly and every 2 hours at night. West of the tomb is the Memorial Amphitheater, used in ceremonies on Easter, Memorial Day, and Veterans Day. The Easter service begins at 6 a.m. Memorial Day, and Veterans Day services always begin at 11 a.m. Open daily at 8 a.m. From April 1 to September 30 the cemetery closes at 7 p.m.; the other six months it closes at 5 p.m. Metro: Arlington National Cemetery.

Tono Sushi Japanese and Asian Cuisine 2605 Connecticut Ave. NW (202) 332-7300 www.tonosushi.com

This Woodley Park favorite, often selected among *Washingtonian Magazine*'s "100 best bargain restaurants" offers outdoor seating, weather permitting, and authentic Thai and Asian stir-fry entrees as well as fresh sushi, sashimi, and a variety of noodle soups, teriyakis, and yakitori. Take-out and delivery available. Open for lunch Mon–Fri 11:30 a.m.–2:30 p.m., Sat–Sun noon–3 p.m.; dinner Mon–Thurs 5 p.m.–10:30 p.m., Fri–Sat 5 p.m.–11 p.m., Sun 5 p.m.–10 p.m. Metro: Woodley Park-Zoo.

Tony and Joe's Seafood Place Georgetown Washington Harbour, 3000 K St. NW (202) 944-4545 www.tonyandjoes.com

This moderately priced restaurant overlooking the Potomac at the Washington Harbour complex offers a light airy setting, inside or outdoor seating, and any number of delightful seafood selections. Browse the ever-changing lunch or dinner menu online. Consider the popular crab cakes or a fillet of sole or flounder, or maybe the scallops. Open daily 11 a.m.–10 p.m. Metro: Foggy Bottom-GWU, then a 10-minute walk, or take Georgetown M St. Shuttle from Metro stop at Dupont Circle or Rosslyn.

Tony Cheng's 619 H St. btw 6th and 7th Sts. (202) 842-8669

This popular Chinatown establishment offers two choices: Mongolian hot pot or Mongolian barbecue. With the barbecue, you select fresh meats, vegetables, and oils, and then pass your collection over to a chef who grills the ingredients before your eyes and returns it to you. The hot pot allows you to place seafood, meats, vegetables, and noodles in boiling stock at your table for a sort of fondue, except you end up with a delicious soup broth as well. Inexpensive and fun. Upstairs is still another Tony Cheng's. Open Sun–Thurs 11 a.m.–11 p.m., Fri–Sat 11 a.m.–midnight. Metro: Gallery Pl.-Chinatown.

Topaz Hotel 1733 N St. NW btw 17th and 18th Sts. (202) 393-3000 (800) 775-1202 www.topazhotel.com

Formerly the Canterbury, this hotel offers good-sized comfortable rooms at moderately expensive rates with the full range of hotel services and a restaurant as well as free access to the facilities of the nearby YMCA. It is located on a quiet street near the Massachusetts Ave. embassies and Dupont Circle. Metro: Dupont Circle.

Torpedo Factory Art Center 105 N Union St., Alexandria, VA (703) 838-4565 www.torpedofactory.org

Opened in 1918 as, not surprisingly, a torpedo factory, later a munitions plant, and back to a furious 24/7 torpedo-making schedule during World War II, this waterfront building was converted into the Torpedo Factory Art Center in 1974. The interior was redesigned in 1983 by Washington architects Keyes, Condon, and Florance. The building now holds one of America's most dynamic arts centers, with eighty-four working studios, eight group studios, and six co-op galleries. The local artists' co-op, The Art League, offers juried monthly shows, enrolls 2,500 students a semester in its school, and offers various workshops. There are 3 floors of potters, photographers, jewelry makers, artists working in stained glass and wearable art, printmakers, sculptors, and painters. You can often watch a painting in progress, a print being pulled, or a pot being thrown. The 3rd floor houses a working lab of the Alexandria Archeology Museum. Good shopping for fine art as well as inexpensive, unique gifts. Open daily 10 a.m.–5 p.m. Metro: King Street, then a 15-minute walk. *See also* The Art League.

Tortilla Coast 400 1st St. SE (202) 546-6768 www.tortillacoast.com

This busy Capitol Hill restaurant and bar has been packing in Tex-Mex aficionados since 1988. There are any number of tequilas available, sangria, margaritas of course, pots of its homemade salsas, and a fine selection of beers. This is not just a bar, however. There are delicious fish tacos, wraps, and sandwiches, barbecue chicken fajitas, burritos, enchiladas, and sour cream flautas. Moderate prices. Hours Mon–Thurs 11:30 a.m.–10 p.m., Fri–Sat 11:30 a.m.–11 p.m. Metro: Capitol South.

Touchstone Gallery 406 7th St. NW (202) 347-2787

This longtime 7th St. co-op gallery offers minimalist paintings, one-artist and topical shows, as well as photography. Open Wed–Fri 11 a.m.–5 p.m., Sat–Sun noon–5 p.m. Metro: Gallery Pl.-Chinatown.

Tour DC 1912 Glen Ross Rd., Silver Spring, MD (301) 588-8999 www.tourdc.com

Led by Mary Kay Ricks, a writer, nationally recognized guide, and "recovering lawyer," her walking tours offer fascinating, historically accurate insights into bygone Washington. Her topics include—but are not limited to—Civil War days, Black Georgetown, the Historic C&O Canal, the Kennedys, Spies and Scandals, Embassy Row, and Federalist and Victorian architecture. Modest charge. The tours are about 2 miles long, and Ricks suggests these walks for ages over 12. Call for reservations. No walks in July and August. Usually, the walks take place on either Sat or Sun at 10:30 a.m. or 2 p.m. Call or check the Web site for future tours.

Tourist Information *see* Alexandria Convention and Visitor Association, Arlington Convention and Visitors Service, D.C. Chamber of Commerce Visitor Information Center, Fairfax County Convention and Visitors Bureau, Fairfax Museum and Visitor Center, Georgetown Information Center, Loudoun Tourism Council, Meridian International Center, Montgomery County Conference and Visitors Bureau, National Park Service Information Office, Prince George's County Conference and Visitors Bureau, Smithsonian Institution Building, Travelers Aid Society, Washington Convention and Tourism Corporation, Washington Metropolitan Area Transit Authority, White While House Visitors Center. *See also* Web Sites about Washington D.C., particularly www.commuterpage.com.

Tourmobile Sightseeing, Inc. 1000 Ohio Dr. SW (202) 554-5100 www.tourmobile .com

This organization provides narrated tours in its familiar red, white, and blue open-air articulated buses. Tours include a full-day tour of Washington, D.C., and Arlington National Cemetery with twenty-four stops, a 2-hour Arlington National Cemetery, a 4-hour Mount Vernon Estate and Gardens, and a 3-hour Frederick

Douglass National Historic Site tour. The full-day tour allows riders to get on and reboard at any stop on their route. Tourmobiles run on about a 20-minute schedule, 9:30 a.m.–4:30 p.m. year-round. Final reboarding is at 3:30 p.m. A 3-hour seasonal night tour includes 35-minute stops at the Jefferson Memorial, Lincoln Memorial, and the Franklin Delano Roosevelt Memorial. Tickets may be purchased from the driver at any stop. Various combinations of tour tickets are available, and can be purchased from TicketMaster, the Tourmobile Office at Arlington National Cemetery, or from ticket kiosks during the summer months at major sites including the Lincoln Memorial, the White House Pavilion, the Washington Monument, the main hall of Union Station, the Air and Space Museum, and the Smithsonian Arts and Industries Building. Moderate prices. Free all-day parking is available at West Potomac Park, south of the Jefferson Memorial.

Tours *see* Bike the Sites Tours, Boat Tours, Bus Tours, Limousine Tours, Special Interest Tours, Walking Tours.

Townsend House *see* Cosmos Club.

Trader Joe's 5847 Leesburg Pike, Falls Church, VA (703) 379-5883; 12268H Rockville Pike (in Federal Plaza), Rockville, MD (301) 468-6656; 9464 Main St. (in Pickett Shopping Center), Fairfax, VA (703) 764-8550; 6831 Wisconsin Ave. (in Shops of Wisconsin), Bethesda, MD (301)907-0982; 18270 Contour Rd., Gaithersburg, MD (301) 947-5953; 7514 Leesburg Pike (in the Tysons Station Shopping Center), Vienna, VA (703) 288-0566 www.traderjoes.com

This California-based specialty food chain offers any number of unique products including low-cost wines; health foods; extensive frozen seafood; ready-to-eat frozen specialty items; low-fat, fat-free products; and an extensive line of soy products, including soy "ice cream" and soy milk. Open daily 9 a.m.–9 p.m.

Tragara 4935 Cordell Ave., Bethesda, MD (301) 951-4935

This restaurant in downtown Bethesda features northern Italian cuisine and offers a lovely setting for a special occasion. Try the oysters Florentine, homemade pasta, veal scallopini with wild mushrooms, or a braised red snapper. Open Mon–Fri 11 a.m.–2:30 p.m., 5:30 p.m.–10 p.m., Fri–Sat 5:30–10:30 p.m., Sun 5 p.m.–9 p.m. Expensive. Metro: Bethesda.

Transparent Productions (703) 243-3787 www.pressroom.com/~lartis/transparent

This small nonprofit, volunteer organization (transparently) produces creative improvised music concerts in the Washington, D.C., area. There is no fixed venue, but the group cooperates with several clubs and universities in the area, maximizing the benefit for the artists by giving them 100 percent of all proceeds. Check the Web site for a listing of their productions of jazz, improv, and new music.

Transportation in Washington, D.C. *see* Airport Transportation, Buses, Metro, Taxis.

Trattoria Alberto 506 8th St. SE (202) 544-2007

Located near Eastern Market, this unpretentious, small, two-level restaurant, offers inexpensive wines, a variety of homemade pastas, and veal dishes. The upstairs bar can get smoky. Their meat and seafood entrees, such as filet mignon and salmon, are served with pasta side dishes. Open Mon–Sat 5:30 p.m.–10:30 p.m. Metro: Eastern Market

Travelers Aid Society Union Station, 50 Massachusetts Ave. NE (202) 371-1937; Reagan National Airport, Terminal A (703) 417-3972, Terminal B-Baggage (703) 417-3974; Dulles Airport, Main Terminal Baggage Level (703) 572-8296 www .travelersaid.org/ta/dc.htm

Trained volunteers provide travelers with airport and airline information, directions, and social service referrals. Dulles open Mon–Fri 8 a.m.–9 p.m., Sat–Sun 8 a.m.–7 p.m.; Reagan: Mon–Fri 9 a.m.–9 p.m., Sat–Sun 9 a.m.–6 p.m. Metro: National Airport; Union Station: Mon–Sat 9:30 a.m.–5:30 p.m., Sun 12:30 p.m.–5:30 p.m. Metro: Union Station. Closed Thanksgiving Day, Christmas Day, and New Year's Day.

Travelodge Cherry Blossom Motel 3030 Columbia Pike, Arlington, VA (703) 521-5570 www.travelodge.com

This 76-room motel offers a fitness center, laundry facilities, free on-site parking, and free local phone calls. It is located less than 2 miles from the Pentagon and the shops, restaurants, and cinemas of Shirlington Village and the Fashion Center at Pentagon City. The Rincome Restaurant, a Thai restaurant, is located at the motel. Inexpensive. Metro: Clarendon then take Metrobus 24M to Columbia Pike and Walter Reed Rd. By car from U.S. 50, take W Arlington Blvd., George Washington Pkwy. Exit, merge onto Arlington Blvd., turn left on S Fillmore St., which becomes S Walter Reed Dr., and turn right onto VA 244-Columbia Pike.

Treasury Department *see* U.S. Treasury Department.

Tree Lighting Ceremony *see* Christmas Tree Lighting.

Tree of Life Statue *see* Family Tree of Life Statue.

Trinidad and Tobago Embassy 1708 Massachusetts Ave. NW (202) 467-6490

Trinity College 125 N Michigan Ave. NE (202) 884-9000 www.trinitydc.edu

Opened in 1900 by the Sisters of Notre Dame as one of the nation's first Roman Catholic liberal arts colleges for women, the school has grown to include graduate programs, of which some are co-ed. More than 1,500 full-time students are enrolled in the undergraduate programs and more than 500 in graduate studies. The college offers a Weekend College, and other continuing education programs. The limestone Notre Dame Chapel with its stained glass windows provides a fine example of Byzantine architecture. Metro: Brookland-CUA.

Trotters Glen Family Golf Center 16501 Bachellors Forest Rd., Olney, MD (301) 570-4951

This 6,300-yard 18-hole course, opened in 1991, was designed by Ed Ault. Bentgrass grows in the greens, and bluegrass in the fairways. There are practice bunkers, a putting green, and a grass diving range.

Trover Books 221 Pennsylvania Ave. SE (202) 547-2665

This bookstore's 60,000-book collection is certain to have the hot, new books by and about its neighboring Capitol Hill politicos and office workers, often signed first editions. In any aspect of political science you will discover the key backgrounders as well as the buzz books on today's issues, or the evergreen issues of fund-raising, lobbying, and electioneering. Also, you can pick up a copy of an out-of-town newspaper and one of those magazines policy wonks read. Metro: Capitol South. Other locations: 1031 Connecticut Ave. NW, and 1706 G St. NW.

Troyer Gallery 1710 Connecticut Ave. NW (202) 328-7189 www.troyergallery.com
Founded in 1983 as a gallery exclusively devoted to photography, it has also included prints, paintings, and sculpture since 1990. Corporate and residential art consulting are also provided. Open 11 a.m.–5 p.m. Tues–Fri, Sat noon–5 p.m. Metro: Dupont Circle.

True Family Education Center *see* Unification Church.

Tryst 2459 18th St. NW (202) 232-5500
Picture a San Francisco pensioners hotel, with urban hipsters sunk in over-stuffed chairs and couches, sipping excellent coffee, observing the passing Adams Morgan fauna through large windows while drafting entries in personal notebooks, and you get the idea of Tryst. It turns into a popular bar in the evenings serving wine, beer, mixed drinks, snacks, soup, and sandwiches to mostly 20-somethings. Open Mon–Thurs 7 a.m.–1 a.m., Fri 8 a.m.–3 a.m., Sat 8 a.m.–midnight. Metro: Woodley Park-Zoo, then 90, 91, 92, 93, or 96 Bus.

Tudor Place 1644 31st St. NW (202) 965-0400 www.tudorplace.org
In 1805, using an $8,000 inheritance from George Washington, Martha Custis Peter and husband, Scotsman Thomas Peter, purchased the land and the twin houses built in 1794. They hired architect William Thornton, designer of the Capitol, to construct Tudor Place by connecting the extant "wings" to a main house. This structure, completed in 1816, was to remain in the Peter family for the next 180 years. It then opened as a museum. Tudor Place, with its gardens, collections, and archives, provides an insight into long-vanished Washington life as well as a large collection of Asian objects collected by the Peter family through the years. Docent-led tours are provided. No reservations are needed for groups of ten or less. House tours are available every hour Sun noon–3 p.m., Tues–Fri 10 a.m.–3 p.m., Sat 10 a.m.–4 p.m. Admission charge. The gardens are open Mon–Sat 10 a.m. to 4 p.m. A self-guided garden tour is available for a small fee. Metro: Dupont Circle, then a 20-minute walk. Street parking is available.

Tune Inn 331 Pennsylvania Ave. NW (202) 543-2725
To understand this establishment you need to know that it is a Capitol Hill hangout, and that pretense stops at the door. This is a bar. It could qualify as a dive. Drinks are served poured from a bottle or straight from a tap; blender orders attract attention. They also serve breakfast, lunch, and dinner: try the cheeseburgers or wings washed down with a pitcher of beer. Inexpensive. Open Fri–Sat 8 a.m.–3 a.m., Sun–Thurs 8 a.m.–2 a.m. Metro: South Capitol.

Tunisia Embassy 1515 Massachusetts Ave. NW (202) 862-1850

Turkey Embassy 2525 Massachusetts Ave. NW (202) 612-6700 www.turkey.org
The Turkish Ambassador's residence at 1606 23rd St. NW was designed by George Oakley Totten Jr. and built in 1915 for industrialist Edward H. Everett,

inventor of the crimped bottle cap. The residence was purchased by Turkey, along with its magnificent furnishings, in 1935. Metro: Farragut West, then take Metrobus N6 Friendship Heights.

Turkish Restaurants *see* Anatolia Turkish Café, Kazan, Levantes, Nizam's. *See also* Middle Eastern Restaurants, www.washingtonpost.com.

Turkmenistan Embassy 2207 Massachusetts Ave. NW (202) 588-1500 www.turk menistanembassy.org

Turner Memorial A. M. E. Church 600 1st St. NW (202) 638-2343

This red-tiled, flat-domed building, incorporating Byzantine, Roman, and Moorish elements, was designed by Baltimore architect Lewis Levi. Completed in 1908, it was built as a synagogue for the Adas Israel Congregation. Since 1951 the Turner Memorial A. M. E. Church has occupied the structure. Metro: Gallery Pl.-Chinatown, then a 10-minute walk. *See also* Adas Israel Congregation.

Tuscana West 1350 I St. NW btw 13th and 14th Sts. (202) 289-7300 www.tuscana west.net

Be it ravioli filled with roast chicken or herbs and vegetables, a hearty risotto, or a mushroom-coated linguini, this popular Tuscan-style Italian restaurant provides a variety of delightful and beautifully presented dishes—all prepared in a what-you-see-is-what-you-get open-air kitchen. Moderate prices, notably good service. Open Mon–Fri for lunch and dinner, Sat dinner. Metro: McPherson Square.

Twilight Tattoo (202) 685-2888 www.mdw.army.mil/tlt/tlt.htm

Members of the Third U.S. Infantry (the Old Guard), the U.S. Army Band, the Fife and Drum Corps, and the U.S. Army Drill Team provide a sunset military pageant on Wednesday evenings from mid-April through July. The hour-long presentation includes 100 Old Guard soldiers dressed in period uniforms. Call or check the Web site for locations: either the White House Ellipse or the south side of the Washington Monument.

Twins Jazz 1344 U St. NW, 2nd floor (202) 234-0072 www.twinsjazz.com

Live jazz is heard every evening at this intimate club, which is really owned by twin sisters. On weeknights local artists appear, with out-of-towners appearing on weekends. Doors open at 6 p.m. for Happy Hour and dinner, which includes Creole, Italian, and Caribbean dishes. Live jazz Tues–Thurs at 8 p.m., Fri–Sat 9 p.m.; open jazz jam sessions Sun and Wed at 8 p.m. Usually two performances a night on weekends at 9 p.m. and 11 p.m. Minimum charge weeknights and a variable cover charge and a minimum on weekends. Tickets may be purchased for performances through the Web site. Metro: U St.-Cardozo.

Two Quail 320 Massachusetts Ave. NE (202) 543-8030

It all looks so normal from the façade of this Capitol Hill row house but the interior walls reveal an eBay collector's fantasy, or possibly, nightmare. Yet this restaurant is rated as one of Washington's most romantic restaurants as well as a hangout for congressional staffers. The eclectic menu offers pecan-stuffed chicken, spicy seafood pasta, and other temptations. Open Mon–Thurs 11:30 a.m.–10 p.m., Fri 11:30 a.m.–11 p.m., Sat noon–11 p.m., Sun 4 p.m.–10 p.m. Metro: Union Station.

Two-Nineteen Restaurant 219 King St., Old Town Alexandria, VA (703) 549-1141
Gourmet magazine reports "219 serves some of the best Creole food to be found anywhere in the country." This restored 1890 Victorian underscores the New Orleans feel with an elegant dining room, an informal bayou room, and an outdoor terrace. Open for lunch Mon–Sat 11:30 a.m.–5 p.m., dinner Sun–Thurs 5 p.m.–10:30 p.m. and Fri and Sat 5 p.m.–11 p.m., Sun brunch 10 a.m.–4 p.m. Metro: King Street, then DAT5 DASH Bus toward Braddock St.

Tysons Corner in Virginia next to I-495 (the Beltway) btw Rtes. 7 and 123
Located in Fairfax County, with its high-tech economy and the highest median household income in the country, it is not surprising that one of the nation's premier shopping malls would develop here. Tysons Corner offers a mix of almost 400 department and specialty stores and restaurants. These include Nordstrom, Bloomingdale's, Lord & Taylor, L.L. Bean, Eddie Bauer, Banana Republic, Rainforest Café, Legal Seafood, Ann Taylor, Restoration Hardware, and The Disney Store. Metro: Rosslyn, then take the Metrobus 15K toward George Mason University to the Tysons Corner Shopping Center stop. Or exit at West Falls Church station and take the Metrobus 28B toward Tysons Corner to the Tysons Corner Shopping Center Stop. By car from I-495 (the Beltway) take Rte. 123 Exit (Chain Bridge Rd.) toward Tysons Corner/Vienna. Bear right on Chain Bridge Rd.

Tysons Corner Center next to I-495 (the Beltway) at intersection of Rtes. 7 and 123, Vienna, VA (703) 892-2787 www.shoptysons.com
Opened in 1968, this is the original Tysons Corner mall, offering more than 250 specialty stores and restaurants, including Bloomingdale's, Coach, AJX Armani Exchange, Brooks Brothers, Rainforest Café, Williams-Sonoma Grande Cuisine, Discovery Channel Stores, Victoria's Secret, and Banana Republic. Find the complete listing on the Web site. Metro: Rosslyn, then take the Metrobus 15K toward George Mason University to the Tysons Corner Shopping Center stop. Or exit Metro at West Falls Church and take the Metrobus 28B toward Tysons Corner to the Tysons Corner Shopping Center stop. By car from I-495 (the Beltway) take Rte. 123 Exit (Chain Bridge Rd.) toward Tysons Corner/Vienna. Bear right on Chain Bridge Rd. *See also* www.commuterpage.com/venues/venue-shop.htm.

Tysons Galleria 2001 International Dr., McLean, VA (703) 827-7730 www.tysons-galleria.com
One of Washington's most upscale shopping malls, this 100-store complex includes Macy's, Saks Fifth Avenue, Neiman Marcus, FAO Schwartz, Hugo Boss, Elan Salon and Day Spa, and several first-rate restaurants. Metro: West Falls Church, then take the FX427 FX Bus toward Loop to the stop at International and Greensboro Drs. By car from I-495 (the Beltway) take Rte. 123 Exit (Chain Bridge Rd.) toward Tysons Corner/Vienna, bear right on Chain Bridge Rd., and right on International Dr. *See also* www.commuterpage.com/venues/venue-shop.htm.

U

U Street Corridor

Once a center of African-American night life akin to Harlem, this area stretches from 10th St. to 15th St. along U Street. Washington's own Duke Ellington, as well as Count Basie, Billie Holiday, Nat King Cole, and Ella Fitzgerald performed here. The riots of the 1960s following the assassination of Martin Luther King Jr. devastated the neighborhood. The boarded windows are long gone, however, replaced with restaurants, galleries, night spots, and shops reflecting its mix of African-American, Hispanic, and Asian residents. Rock, jazz, and blues can be heard in a variety of clubs. Check out "Historic U St. Jazz" with locations, photos of clubs, musician bios, and club locations at www.gwu.edu/~jazz/. Metro: U-St.-Cardozo and Shaw-Howard University.

Udupi Palace 1329 University Blvd. E, Langley Park, MD (301) 434-1531 www
.udupipalace.com

Ranked in the top 100 best bargain restaurants by *Washingtonian Magazine*, the popular Udupi Palace provides authentic southern Indian totally vegetarian cuisine. Besides dozens of curries, you might want to try the featured dish: huge, thin-crusted *dosas* filled with seasoned vegetables. Open daily 11:30 a.m.–9:30 p.m. The Web site provides driving directions. Metro: Takoma.

Uganda Embassy 5911 16th St. NW (202) 726-7100 www.ugandaembassy.com

Ukraine Embassy 3350 M St. NW (202) 333-0606 www.ukremb.com

Purchased by the Ukraine Government in 1992, the structure dates from 1788, and is the site of the discussion leading to the purchase of the land needed to establish the city of Washington. The meeting was hosted by Uriah Forrest, aide-de-camp to George Washington, who met there with Washington and local landowners over dinner on March 29, 1791. In 1800 William Marbury purchased the house, enhancing its historic value by losing one of America's most significant court cases involving last-day-in-office commissions signed by outgoing President John Adams, which were not honored by incoming President Thomas Jefferson. The chief justice of the Supreme Court, John Marshall, established, with this case, the right of the Supreme Court to rule on the constitutionality of laws passed by Congress as well as the right of judicial review. The embassy's Web site provides a history of the building and these events. Metro: Rosslyn, then Georgetown Shuttle.

Ulysses S. Grant Memorial *see* Grant Memorial.

Uncle Beasley 3000 block of Connecticut Ave. NW (202) 357-2700

A life-size fiberglass triceratops named Uncle Beasley hangs out at the National Zoo. The 25-foot dinosaur, the brainchild of Oliver Butterworth in his children's book, *The Enormous Egg,* allows kids to climb on his back. Metro: Woodley Park-Zoo.

UNIFEST UNIFEST Foundation, 1247 W St. SE (202) 678-9152 www.unifestfoundation.com

For the past 20 years, the UNIFEST foundation has been highlighting "the culture, diversity and rich history of African-Americans" particularly in the Anacostia area. It is now Washington's largest community festival promoting African culture. During two days in early June the festival features a parade, live entertainment, health promotion activities, athletic events, carnival rides and games, a marketplace, international foods, and children's activities. UNIFEST was founded by Union Temple Baptist Church, which continues its involvement in the event. The festival is held at Good Hope Rd. and Martin Luther King Jr. Ave. SE. Metro: Anacostia.

Unification Church (Washington, D.C., Family Church) 16th and Harvard Sts. NW (202) 462-5700 www.unification.net

The Salt Lake City architectural firm of Young and Hansen designed this handsome structure for the Church of Jesus Christ of Latter-day Saints. Architect Don Carlos Young was the grandson of Brigham Young. The church's golden angel, Moroni, who topped its narrow spire when the church was completed in 1933, has been removed. For more than 20 years the church has been occupied by the True Family Education Center, a branch of the Unification Church of Reverend Sun Myung Moon. Metro: Metro Center, Metrobus S2 or S4 toward Silver Spring, or Metrobus 42 toward Mt. Pleasant.

Union Burial Society of Georgetown Cemetery 2616 Chain Bridge Rd.

A chain-link fence with, usually, an unlocked gate surrounds a 2-acre cemetery of former slaves and their descendents, evidence of the small black community that once lived in this area. The long-ago shuttered 2-story school building of this community, mostly obscured by a tall fence, is a short walk farther up the hill at 2820 Chain Bridge Rd. The cemetery is maintained by a descendent of one of the families buried there. Metro: Metro Center, then take Sibley Hospital Metrobus D6 to MacArthur and Nebraska Aves.

Union Market (Florida Avenue Market) 5th St. and Neal Pl. NE, Florida Ave. NE between 5th St. and 4th St. (202) 547-3142

Truck farmers with just-picked fruits and vegetables, fishmongers, butchers, and West African and Asian importers offer their goods from small stalls stretching across several wholesale warehouses in a bazaar of different languages and fragrances. Open year-round Tues–Thurs 7 a.m.–5:30 p.m., Fri–Sat, 7 a.m.–6:30 p.m., Sun 7 a.m.–2 p.m. Closed Mondays. Metro: Union Station.

Union Station 40 Massachusetts Ave. NE btw 1st and 2nd Sts. www.unionstationdc.com

Designed by architects Daniel Burnham and Pierce Anderson to serve as a gateway to Washington, the mammoth Beaux Arts structure, the largest terminal in the world when it opened in 1908, has looked down on countless historic events. After a $160-million restoration it has taken on new life as an elegant shopping mall and entertainment center, far beyond its function as the city's railroad station. Modeled in scale and design after Rome's Baths of Caracalla, its colossal columns and soaring ceilings surround one of Washington's most vibrant sites, awash with millions of visitors a year. Metro: Union Station.

Union Station A. Philip Randolph Statue *see* A. Philip Randolph Statue at Union Station.

Union Station Shops 40 Massachusetts Ave. NE btw 1st and 2nd Sts. www.unionstationdc.com

Besides Amtrak and Metro commuters, the building provides a dynamic retail mall with more than 100 stores, including shops devoted to National Zoo–related items, crafts, railroading, and political collectibles, a nine-screen movie complex, several well-known restaurants, a large food court offering a variety of cuisines, currency exchange, ample and low-cost parking for cars and RVs, car rental agencies, several sightseeing companies, and of course, Amtrak ticketing and baggage handling. It boasts a central Capitol Hill location, 2 blocks from the Capitol, 4 blocks from the Library of Congress, 6 blocks from the Folger Shakespeare Library, 1 block from the Capital Children's Museum, and across the street from the National Postal Museum. Stores open Mon–Sat 10 a.m.–9 p.m., Sun noon–6 p.m. Metro: Union Station. *See also* www.commuterpage.com/venues/venue-shop.htm.

Unique Stores *see* Specialty stores.

United Arab Emirates Embassy 3522 International Court NW off Van Ness (202) 243-2400 http://travel.state.gov/uae.html

Embassy of the United Arab Emirates. Metro: Van Ness-UDC.

United Church (Die Vereinigte Kirche) 1920 G St. NW (202) 331-1495 www.theunitedchurch.org

A more imposing structure replaced the original in 1892—the work of architects Paul Schultz and Albert Goenner. The present United Church, formed in 1975 with the merger of the Concordia United Church of Christ and the neighboring United Methodist Church, continues to offer two services a month in German on the first and third Sundays. Metro: Foggy Bottom-GWU and Farragut West.

United Kingdom Embassy 3100 Massachusetts Ave. NW (202) 462-1340 www.britainusa.com

The embassy of the United Kingdom of Great Britain and Northern Ireland. This stately embassy complex, completed in 1931, was designed by Sir Edwin Lutyens. The embassy's extensive Web site includes a virtual tour of the building. In front of the building is William McVey's sculpture of Winston Churchill, frequent visitor to Washington during World War II. Metro: Woodley Park-Zoo.

United Spanish War Veterans Memorial along Memorial Dr. approaching Arlington National Cemetery

The 8-foot bronze sculpture of an American veteran wearing his Spanish-American War uniform honors the 450,000 veterans of the Spanish-American War. Commonly called "The Hiker," sculpted by Theodora Alice Ruggles Kitson, the memorial was erected by United Spanish War Veterans in 1965. You may have seen the sculpture elsewhere: more than fifty bronze replica casts were erected in various municipalities throughout the United States between 1921 and 1965. Metro: Arlington Cemetery.

U.S. Air Force Band Summer Concerts *see* Air Force Band Summer Concerts.

U.S. Arboretum *see* National Arboretum.

U.S. Army Band Summer Concerts *see* Army Band Summer Concerts.

U.S. Botanic Garden 2000 Independence Ave. SW (202) 225-8333 Program and Tour Reservations (202) 226-4082 Special Events (202) 226-7674 www.usbg.gov

A living plant museum, located at the foot of Capitol Hill, the garden's vast collections are housed in a building resembling London's iron and glass Crystal Palace. Newly renovated, exhibits include plant discoveries, carnivorous plants, endangered species, the influence of plants on civilization, a Jurassic landscape, desert plants, and jungle settings. A 3-acre National Garden is located west of the conservatory. The Web site provides detailed information about visiting the garden and about the garden's history, functions, facilities, exhibits, events, and services, as well as a virtual tour and educational offerings for adults to preschoolers. Open 9 a.m.–5 p.m. daily. Admission free. Metro: Federal Center SW. *See also* www.commuter page.com/venues/gardens.htm.

U.S. Bureau of Engraving and Printing *see* Bureau of Engraving and Printing.

U.S. Capitol 1st St. NW btw Independence and Constitution Aves. (202) 225-6827 www.aoc.gov

The Capitol is the tallest, most recognizable building in Washington. George Washington laid its cornerstone in 1793, Congress moved in 1800, and the British tried to burn it down in 1814. Not only the meeting place of the nation's Legislature, it serves also as an art and history museum and a major tourist destination. The Capitol is open to the public for guided tours only, 9 a.m.–4:30 p.m. Mon–Sat. Closed on Thanksgiving Day and Christmas Day. Tour tickets are free and issued at a southside screening facility. An overview of the building, how the location was chosen, construction milestones, historic spaces, and a discussion of the art in the Capitol, as well as visitor information may be found on the Web site. A massive underground $385 million Capitol Visitor Center complex on the east side is scheduled for completion in 2006. Metro: Capitol South or Union Station.

U.S. Capitol Historical Society 200 Maryland Ave. NE (202) 543-8919 (800) 887-9318 www.uschs.org

This nonprofit organization, founded in 1962, celebrates the history and heritage of the Capitol and Congress through a variety of programs, products, and services for both the casual visitor to the Capitol and specialists. These include educational programs for both elementary and secondary students, production and sales of publications related to the Capitol, sales of memorabilia, scholarly conferences and fellowships, and special tours and exhibitions. Its extensive Web site provides a calendar of events, educational resources, online exhibits, a virtual tour, an online gift shop, a site map, and also publications and videotapes available for purchase online or at the Capitol kiosk. Metro: Union Station.

U.S. Capitol Rotunda *see* Capitol Rotunda.

U.S. Chess Center 1501 M St. NW (202) 857-4922

Washington area kids are learning chess, and much of the credit goes to this nonprofit organization, whose chess enthusiasts offer Saturday classes (K–6), tournaments, Sunday chess for teenagers, and sponsor chess leagues in schools and summer camps, volunteer opportunities, and a tournament primer for parents. Photos and posters of chess champions line the walls of the center, and there is a gift shop—also accessible through the Web site. Open Mon–Thurs 6 p.m.–9 p.m. (sometimes later), Sat–Sun noon–6 p.m. Metro: McPherson Square or Farragut North.

U.S. Department of Agriculture Visitor's Center 12th St. and Jefferson Dr. SW, Room 103 (202) 720-4197

The Visitor's Center is a 700-square-foot space, soon to be renovated, providing a sampling of publications from USDA departments on topics as diverse as backyard conservation, nutrition, and rural development. Exhibits and "discovery drawers" provide nutritional guidelines, conservation information, and illustrate programs of the department. Open Mon–Fri 9 a.m.–3 p.m. Closed federal holidays. The USDA building, completed in 1930, was first scheduled to be constructed in the middle of the Mall. President Theodore Roosevelt stopped that from happening. Metro: Smithsonian.

U.S. Department of Commerce *see* Commerce Department.

U.S. Department of Commerce Library *see* Commerce Department Library.

U.S. Department of Housing and Urban Development *see* Department of Housing and Urban Development.

U.S. Department of the Interior Museum *see* Department of the Interior Museum.

U.S. Department of State *see* State Department.

U.S. Department of the Treasury *see* U.S. Treasury Department.

U.S. Drug Enforcement Administration Museum *see* Drug Enforcement Administration Museum and Visitors Bureau.

U.S. Federal Bureau of Investigation *see* J. Edgar Hoover FBI Building.

U.S. Federal Reserve *see* Federal Reserve Board.

U.S. Federal Trade Commission *see* Apex Building.

U.S. Holocaust Memorial Museum 100 Raoul Wallenberg Pl. SW (202) 488-0400

A compelling, moving museum for the documentation, study, and interpretation of Holocaust history, and serving as America's memorial to the 11 million Jews, gypsies, Jehovah's Witnesses, homosexuals, political prisoners, and others murdered by the Nazis between 1933 and 1945. The exhibit can take up to several hours to tour. Smaller special exhibitions take less time. Timed passes are necessary for visiting the Permanent Exhibition. They may be obtained at the museum on the day of your visit or in advance by calling tickets.com at (800) 400-9373. Open 10 a.m.–5:30 p.m. daily. Closed on Yom Kippur and Christmas Day. Museum stays open until 8 p.m. from April 11 to June 13. Metro: Smithsonian. *See also* www .commuterpage.com/venues/museums.htm.

United States Marine Band Marine Barracks, 8th and I Sts. SE Concert Information: (202) 433-5809 www.marineband.usmc.mil

On July 11, 1798, President John Adams officially brought the United States Marine Band into existence. It is America's oldest professional musical organization. Thomas Jefferson heard the band play at his inauguration and gave them the title they still go by, "The President's Own." The band has been playing in the White House ever since, which is its primary mission. However, another honored tradition is its annual tour initiated by the band's seventeenth director, John Philip Sousa, in 1891. (You can hear Sousa's "Stars and Strips Forever" on the Web site.) Besides this fifty-day tour, the musicians average about 200 White House performances a year. That does not include state dinners and diplomatic receptions. The group can perform as a chamber orchestra, a dance band, or a full concert band. It also participates seasonally in Friday evening parades at the Marine Barracks or the Marine Corps War Memorial, and offers concerts at local venues. The concert information line or the Web site provides program and concert schedules. The Web site offers an e-mail service to notify subscribers of future activities. *See also* National Academy of Sciences Music Programs, Marine Band Summer Concerts.

U.S. Marine Band Summer Concerts *see* Marine Band Summer Concerts.

U.S. Marines Chamber Ensemble *see* National Academy of Sciences Music Programs.

U.S. National Arboretum *see* National Arboretum.

U.S. National Archives *see* National Archives.

U.S. National Institutes of Health *see* National Institutes of Health.

U. S. Naval Observatory 3450 Massachusetts Ave. NW at 34th St. (202) 762-1467 www.usno.navy.mil

Noted architect Richard Morris Hunt designed the main buildings, which were completed in 1893 in their new "secluded" location, away from the bright lights of Foggy Bottom. Established in 1830, the observatory became America's first scientific agency, continuing even today measuring the earth's rotation for navigational astronomy and serving as the nation's alarm clock, setting standard time. Also on the observatory grounds is the vice president's residence. The only way to visit the observatory is through a scheduled reservations-only tour, available on most Monday evenings from 8:30 p.m.–10 p.m. Tours must be reserved 4–6 weeks prior to the visit. You may submit tour requests by phone or through the Web site. Entry will be permitted only with a tour pass for the visit. A photo ID must be presented at the time of entry. Visitors must pass through a security-screening device. Metro: Farragut West, then Metrobus N4.

U.S. Navy Band Summer Concerts *see* Navy Band Summer Concerts.

U.S. Navy Birthday Navy Memorial, 701 Pennsylvania Ave. NW, Suite 123 (202) 737-2300 www.lonesailor.org

Tracing its origins to the Continental Congress, the U.S. Navy claims October 13, 1775, as its birthday. The Navy celebrates the occasion with a wreath-laying ceremony at the memorial. Metro: Archives-Navy Memorial.

U.S. Navy Memorial and Naval Heritage Center 701 Pennsylvania Ave. NW (202) 737-2300 www.lonesailor.org

Conklin Rossard designed this plaza. It features a 100-foot granite inlay world map, fountains, and at eye level, the pea-jacketed *Lone Sailor* bronze sculpture by Stanley Bleifeld. Low sculptured walls of historic naval events define the space. In the summer months the U.S. Navy Band, other military bands, and even visiting high school bands provide concerts. The Web site has the schedules. The nearby subterranean Naval Heritage Center contains interactive displays, a gift shop, and has continuous screenings of its 70-mm, 35-minute film, *At Sea*, about life on a carrier, on a 52-foot-high screen. The center is open Mon–Sat 9:30 a.m.–5 p.m. Metro: Archives-Navy Memorial.

U.S. Office Building *see* Senate and House Office Buildings.

U.S. Patent and Trademark Museum 2121 Crystal Dr., Suite 0100, off 23rd St., Crystal City, Arlington, VA (703) 305-8341 www.uspto.gov/web/offices/ac/ahrpa/opa/museum

Besides its permanent exhibit of famous patents and inventors' first attempts at mechanized refrigerators, sewing machines, washing machines, and, of course, Edison's lightbulb, this museum provides rotating topical exhibits of patent models and trademarks as diverse as ice cream trademarks to Goodyear's rubber tire design. The museum includes a gift shop you can visit online at www.invent.org. The museum is open Mon–Fri 8:30 a.m.–4:30 p.m. Closed on federal holidays. Metro: Crystal City.

U.S. Senate Office Building *see* Senate and House Office Buildings.

U.S. Soldiers' and Airmen's Home Rock Creek Church Rd. and Upshur St. (202) 730-3556

Following the Mexican War, in 1851, Lt. Gen. Winfield B. Scott founded the home with funds he received from General Santa Ana for not ransacking Mexico City. Scott's statue now shares a site on its 300 acres with century-old buildings, a golf course, natural woodlands, and historic Anderson Cottage. George W. Riggs, founder of Riggs National Bank, built the cottage. Now closed for renovation until 2004, it became the summer White House for several U.S. presidents, most notably Abraham Lincoln who wrote the final draft of the Emancipation Proclamation there. Nearly 1,300 vets still call it home. Visits by appointment only. Metro: Brookland-CUA.

U.S. Soldiers' and Airmen's Home National Cemetery 21 Harewood Rd. NW (202) 829-1829

This cemetery, opened during the Civil War, predates the only other national cemetery overseen by the U.S. Army: Arlington National Cemetery. Arlington was created, in part, because this cemetery was filled. It was used only for those who resided at the home. Open 8 a.m.–5 p.m. daily. Metro: Rhode Island, then Metrobus M8 to Rock Creek Church Rd. and Upshur.

U.S. State Department Diplomatic Reception Rooms *see* State Department.

U.S. Treasury Department 1500 Pennsylvania Ave. NW (202) 622-0896 www .ustreas.gov/opc/opc0006.html

Look on the back of a $10 bill for an etching of this huge Greek Revival building, the third oldest federally occupied building in Washington. Begun in 1836 and designed by Robert Mills, whose portfolio includes the Washington Monument, the building was not completed until 1869. The statue on the building's south side is that of Alexander Hamilton, the first secretary of the treasury. Looking out from the north side is Albert Gallatin, secretary of the treasury to Presidents Thomas Jefferson and James Madison. After September 11, 2001, all tours were suspended, but the Treasury's Web site provides a virtual tour of the interior. Metro: McPherson Square or Metro Center.

The Universalist National Memorial Church 1810 16th St. NW at S St. (202) 387-3411 www.unmc.org

Completed in 1930, noted architect Charles Collins designed a massive Romanesque "cathedral church" to represent the denomination of Universalism in the nation's capital. Its stone tower is dedicated to the cause of peace and international justice. The parish's earlier site was the 1861 Church of Our Father whose members included the founder of the Red Cross, Clara Barton. Sunday worship starts at 11 am. Metro: Dupont Circle.

Universities and Colleges *see* American University, Bowie State University, Capitol College, Catholic University of America, Columbia Union College, Corcoran School of Art, Gallaudet University, George Mason University, George Washington University, Georgetown University, Howard University, Maryland College of Art and Design, Marymount University, Montgomery College, Mount Vernon College of George Washington University, Northern Virginia Community College, Prince George's Community College, Southeastern University, Strayer University, Trinity College, University of Maryland-College Park, University of the District of Columbia.

University of Maryland Clarice Smith Center for the Performing Arts Stadium Dr., University of Maryland Campus, College Park, MD. (301) 405-ARTS www .claricesmithcenter.umd.edu/cs/about_vis.html

The Clarice Smith Center, a 17-acre, 318,000-square-foot performing arts center located on the university campus, features six performance halls and houses, as well as the School of Music, the Department of Theatre, the Department of Dance, and the Performing Arts Library. Performance halls include an 1,100-seat Concert

Hall, the 650-seat Ina and Jack Kay Theatre, the 300-seat Joseph and Alma Gilden-horn Recital Hall, the 200-seat Robert and Arlene Kogod Theatre, a 180-seat Dance Theatre, and a 100-seat black box theater. The Web site provides a listing of forth-coming performances, a map, and driving instructions. Parking is available next to the center. The ticket office in the main lobby provides tickets for all events, or call the number above or purchase tickets online through the Web site. Ticket office hours are Mon–Sat 11 a.m.–9 p.m. and Sun 11 a.m.–9 p.m. Metro: College Park, then shuttle bus to campus.

University of Maryland-College Park U.S. Hwy. 1 (Baltimore Ave.), College Park, MD (301) 405-1000 www.umcp.umd.edu

The flagship of the university system of Maryland, this state-supported co-educational institution was established when the original University of Maryland (1820) merged with the Maryland Agricultural College in 1856. The university offers degrees in 111 majors in thirteen colleges and schools to its 25,000 undergraduate students and 9,000 graduate students. Metro: College Park, then shuttle bus to campus.

University of Maryland-College Park Libraries College Park Campus, College Park, MD (301) 405-0800 www.lib.umd.edu

The university's main library, Theodore R. McKeldin Library, holds more than two million items. Besides the McKeldin Library, there are department and special-ized libraries including the Architecture Library (301) 405-6317, the Art Library (301) 405-9061, East Asia Collection (301) 405-9133, Engineering and Physical Sci-ences Library (301) 405-9157, Library of American Broadcasting (301) 405-9160, National Public Broadcasting Archives (301) 405-9988, Performing Arts Library (301) 405-9217, and the Wasserman Library of the College of Information Studies (301) 405-2066. Days and hours vary. Hours for all libraries at (301) 405-0800. Metro: College Park, then shuttle bus to campus.

University of Maryland Football University of Maryland, College Park, MD (310) 314-7070 http://umterps.fansonly.com/sports/m-footbl/md-m-footbl-body.html

University of Maryland's Terrapins play their home games at Byrd Stadium on the College Park Campus. Tickets can be ordered in advance by phone (301) 314-7070 or www.umterps.com. Metro: College Park.

University of Maryland Terrapins University of Maryland, College Park, MD (301) 314-7070 www.umcp.umd.edu

The University of Maryland's Terrapins basketball team, national champions in 2002, plays home games at Comcast Center, and Terrapins football is played at Byrd Stadium on the College Park Campus. The Terrapins compete in the Atlantic Coast Conference. Tickets for either sport can be ordered in advance by phone (301) 314-7070 or at www.umterps.com. The 17,100-seat Comcast Center replaces the Terps former home, Cole Field House. Comcast's $20 million naming gift matched the largest corporate naming gift ever for a newly built collegiate facility. Comcast gave an additional $5 million for naming rights to the floor. Metro: College Park.

University of the District of Columbia 4200 Connecticut Ave. NW (202) 274-5000 www.udc.edu

Established in 1977, this is the only urban land-grant institution in the United States. Its purpose is to allow access to higher education at affordable tuition rates to all high school graduates residing in Washington. The university was formed from three public colleges in the District: District of Columbia Teachers' College, Washington Technical Institute, and Federal City College. The university has had a law school since 1995, when it took over the former Antioch Law School. Present enrollment in credit courses is around 5,300 with more than 15,000 students taking noncredit courses through its Division of Community Outreach and Extension Services. Over 450 degrees are awarded annually. Metro: Van Ness-UDC.

University Park Prince George's County, MD

This is a small independent municipality of less than 1,000 families located adjacent to the University of Maryland's College Park campus. It is a residential nesting ground for local academics and others in search of tree-lined streets, a small-town atmosphere, good schools, and walking distance to the university and its amenities. Metro: College Park-University of Maryland.

Upper Northwest

The neighborhoods of upper-northwest D.C. flow upward along Connecticut, Wisconsin, and Massachusetts Aves. Dozens of imposing embassies line Massachusetts Ave. Woodley Park, home of the National Zoo, boasts quiet streets lined with stately apartment buildings. In the Cleveland Park area large single-family frame houses rise stolidly amid tree-lined streets along with the occasional apartment building, house, or restaurant. The Spring Valley area, site of American University, runs just beyond the National Cathedral along the Foxhall Road Corridor, and is one of the city's most prestigious areas, studded with mansions belonging to the city's rich and powerful. Sibley Hospital in Tenleytown is surrounded by mostly owner-occupied homes sitting squarely on their lots, along with, increasingly, townhouses. Friendship Heights, close to Chevy Chase and Bethesda, provides a canyon of ritzy stores running along Wisconsin Ave. into Maryland. Metro: Woodley Park-Zoo, Cleveland Park, Van Ness–UDC, Tenleytown-AU.

Upton Hill Regional Park 6060 Wilson Blvd., Arlington, VA (703) 352-5900 www.nvrpa.org/uptonhill.html

This wooded urban park, open all year, provides walking trails, and from mid-March through October, a bocce ball court, a batting cage, and miniature golf. The outdoor pool remains open from Memorial Day through Labor Day. Located at the intersection of Patrick Henry Dr. and Wilson Blvd. Metro: Ballston, then IB Dunn Loring Bus to Wilson Blvd.

Uptown Theater *see* Cineplex Odeon Uptown Theater.

Uruguay Embassy 1913 I St. NW (202) 331-1313 www.embassy.org/uruguay
Embassy of Uruguay. Metro: Farragut West.

U-Topia 1418 U St. NW (202) 483-7669

A friendly, inexpensive restaurant nightly serving up good blues or jazz and with no drink minimums or cover charges. Even an occasional poetry reading. Sound like your favorite hangout on a back street in New Orleans? You are not too far off the mark; besides bar nibblings, there are gumbos and chicken jambalaya, steaks, of course, and Sunday brunch as well. Open Mon–Fri 11 a.m.–2 a.m., Sat–4:30 p.m.–3 a.m., Sun 11 a.m.–2 a.m. Metro: U St.-Cardozo.

Uzbekistan Embassy 1746 Massachusetts Ave. NW (202) 887-5300 www.uzbekis tan.org

Vace 4705 Miller Ave., Bethesda, MD (301) 654-6367 and 3515 Connecticut Ave. NW (202) 363-1999

Truly Italian, this deli offers thin-crusted Neapolitan pizza by the slice, home-made pastas and sauces, salamis, and olive oils served up with a genuine Italian accent. Bethesda open Mon–Tues 9 a.m.–8 p.m., Wed–Fri 9 a.m.–9 p.m., Sat–9 a.m.–8 p.m. Closed Sunday. Metro: Bethesda. Cleveland Park: Mon–Fri 9 a.m.–9 p.m., Sat 9 a.m.–8 p.m., Sun 10 a.m.–5 p.m. Metro: Cleveland Park.

Van Ness Connecticut Ave., north of Cleveland Park, south of Nebraska

This neighborhood, running north of Cleveland Park along Connecticut Ave., boasts both Howard University Law School and the University of the District of Columbia. Across from UDC is a free-floating spur of Rock Creek Park known as Soapstone Valley, fringed with mansions. On Connecticut itself, there are apartment buildings and pockets of shops and restaurants. Metro: Van Ness-UDC.

Vatican Embassy *see* Holy See Embassy.

Vegetable Garden 116 Rockville Pike, White Flint Station Shopping Mall, Rockville, MD (301) 468-9301 www.thevegetablegarden.com

Serving a healthy cuisine with no animal products, little or no oil, and low sodium, this restaurant has a national reputation as a top vegetarian restaurant. Savor the *kung pao* tofu with peanuts and green peppers or the hot-pot mock duck with vegetables. Open 11:30 a.m.–10 p.m. daily, including major holidays. Metro: White Flint. From I-495 (the Beltway), exit Rockville Pike (355 N), pass White Flint Mall on right, restaurant is on the left, across from the Metro stop.

Vegetarian Restaurants *see* Amma Vegetarian Kitchen, Delights of the Garden, Red Sea, Thyme Square, Udipi Palace, Vegetable Garden, Woodlands. *See also* www.washingtonpost.com.

Velvet Lounge 915 U St. NW (202) 462-3213

This small space with lots of candles, red velvet, and couches, hosts touring bands playing alternative rock, hard rock, heavy metal, punk, and ska. Cover charge. Open Sun–Thurs 8 p.m.–2 a.m., Fri–Sat 8 p.m.–3 a.m. Metro: U St.-Cardozo.

Venezuela Embassy 1099 30th St. NW (202) 342-2214 www.embavenez-us.org

Vermont Avenue Baptist Church 1630 Vermont Ave. NW (202) 667-1078 www
.vabc.org

Seven former slaves established the Fifth Baptist Church in 1866. The present brick structure dates from 1872. In 1890 the church underwent extensive renovations and changed its name to Vermont Avenue Baptist Church. Further structures were added to the site, including a Family Life Center completed in 1992. Metro: McPherson Square, then Metrobus 52 to 14th and Q Sts.

Vertigo Books 7346 Baltimore Ave., College Park, MD (301) 779-9300

Recently moved to its College Park location from years at Dupont Circle, this bookstore is noted for its frequent literary events; in-depth coverage of literature, politics, and contemporary issues; and its knowledgeable staff. E-mailing list. Open Mon–Fri 10 a.m.–7 p.m., Sat 10 a.m.–7 p.m., Sun noon–5 p.m. Metro: College Park.

Veterans Day Ceremonies Arlington National Cemetery (202) 619-7222

A solemn ceremony with thousands of spectators takes place on Veterans Day at the memorial amphitheater near the Tomb of the Unknowns. A color guard representing all military services executes "Present Arms" at the tomb at 11 a.m. on November 11. Traditionally on Veterans Day, the president lays a wreath at the tomb while a bugler plays "Taps." Also, ceremonies are held at the Vietnam Veterans Memorial (202) 619-7222, the U.S. Navy Memorial on Pennsylvania Ave. (202) 737-2300, and Mount Vernon (703) 780-2000. Metro: Arlington Cemetery.

Veterans of Foreign Wars Building 200 Maryland Ave. NE (202) 543-2239

On February 8, 1960, President Dwight D. Eisenhower spoke at the opening of this building. It serves as the VFW headquarters and as a memorial to soldiers who died in foreign wars. Call to arrange a visit. Wheelchair accessible. Metro: Union Station.

Victorian Lyric Opera Company F. Scott Fitzgerald Theatre, Rockville Civic Center Park, Baltimore Rd. at Edmonston Rd., Rockville, MD, box office (240) 314-8690 www.srbnet.com/vloc

This volunteer semiprofessional theater company is best known for its Gilbert and Sullivan productions, but occasionally performs other pieces of the Victorian era. Performances are at the F. Scott Fitzgerald Theatre at the Rockville Civic Center located in the Rockville Civic Center Park. The box office is open Tues–Sat 2 p.m.–7 p.m., and 2 hours prior to performances. By car from Rte. 28 and I-270, proceed east on Rte. 28, cross Rte. 355, and follow Rte. 28 (turns left at first light beyond Rte. 355). Travel 4 blocks to Baltimore Rd., turn right, go 3 blocks to Edmonston Dr., turn left, and Civic Center Park entrance is immediately on the right.

Victoria's Day Spa 1926 I St. NW (202) 254-0442

Provides pedicures, linen herbal or seaweed body wraps, massages, and paraffin manicures in a relaxing atmosphere at comparatively moderate prices. No credit cards. Open Mon–Fri 11 a.m.–7 p.m., Sat 11 a.m.–6 p.m. Metro: Farragut West.

Vidalia 1990 M St. NW (202) 659-1990

Sophisticated, creative, and Southern cooking at its best are terms often applied to this popular, albeit somewhat expensive, restaurant. Flavorful crab cakes, roasted monkfish, a basket of cornbread, lamb steak with artichokes, and did we mention grits? Open for lunch Mon–Fri 11:30 a.m.–2:30 p.m.; dinner Mon–Thurs 5:30 p.m.–10 p.m., Fri–Sat 5:30 p.m.–10:30 p.m., Sun 5 p.m.–10 p.m. Metro: Dupont Circle.

Vienna Farmers Market 127 Center St. behind Vienna Town Hall, Vienna, VA (703) 243-4145

At this market producers sell their fruits and vegetables from early May to late October on Saturday 8 a.m.–noon.

Vienna Halloween Parade Branch and Maple Aves., Vienna, VA (703) 281-1333

Join the several thousand costumed paraders as they skulk down Main St., a tradition going back to the 1940s. Metro: Vienna/Fairfax-GWU.

Vietnam Embassy 1233 20th St. NW, Suite 400 (202) 861-0737 www.vietnam embassy-usa.org

Vietnam Georgetown 2934 M St. NW (202) 337-4536

For more than a quarter century, this moderate-priced, but highly rated restaurant has been placing fragrant beef noodle soups and other South Asian plates before appreciative locals indoors or out on the patio. Lunch buffet weekdays. Open Mon–Thurs and Sun 11 a.m.–11 p.m., Fri–Sat 11:30 a.m.–11:30 p.m. Metro: Foggy Bottom-GWU, then a 10-minute walk.

Vietnam Veterans Memorial on the Mall, 21st St. and Constitution Ave. NW www.nps.gov/vive/

Opened in 1982, this monument honors the sacrifice of American military personnel in the Vietnam War. Now it is the most visited monument in the city: more than 1.7 million annually. This simple, black marble wall displaying the names of 58,196 Americans who died in Vietnam was the inspiration of a Yale architecture student, Maya Ying Lin. Placed nearby are two figurative sculptures, one of which, *Three Servicemen* by Frederick Hart, was added in 1984. The other, the Vietnam Women's Memorial by Glenna Goodacre, was dedicated in 1993. Open daily 24 hours. Metro: Foggy Bottom-GWU, then a 10-minute walk. *See also* www.com muterpage.com/venues/memorials.htm

Vietnam Women's Memorial on the Mall, 21st and Constitution Ave. NW www .nps.gov/vive/memorial/women.htm

This bronze sculpture, designed by Glenna Goodacre and erected in 1993, honors the women who served in uniform in the Vietnam War. It depicts three servicewomen and a wounded soldier. Always open. Metro: Foggy Bottom–GWU, then a 10-minute walk. *See also* www.commuterpage.com/venues/memorials.htm.

Vietnamese Restaurants *see* Café Dalat, Café Saigon, Little Viet Garden, Miss Saigon, Nam Viet, Pho 75, Queen Bee, Saigon Gourmet, Saigon Inn, Saigonnais, Star of Siam, Taste of Saigon, Vietnam Georgetown. *See also* www.washingtonpost.com.

Le Vieux Logis 7925 Old Georgetown Rd., Bethesda, MD (301) 652-6816

In a room of polished copper pots and fresh cut flowers, behold the beautifully presented French and Scandinavian dishes. Try the roast rack of lamb, or pan-seared veal chop with calvados sauce, or leek and potato soup. Great breads and pastries. Somewhat expensive. Open Mon–Fri 5:30 p.m.–8 p.m., Sat 5:30 p.m.–8:30 p.m. Reservations suggested. Metro: Bethesda.

Vigilant Fire Department Building 1066 Wisconsin Ave. NW

The Paparazzi Restaurant occupies this building, the oldest extant firehouse in the city, built in 1844, and renovated in 1994. Metro: Foggy Bottom, then 7-block walk, or from Foggy Bottom take 32, 34, 35, or 36 Bus toward Friendship Heights on Pennsylvania Ave.

Village Bistro 1723 Wilson Blvd., Arlington, VA (703) 522-0284

Noted for its long listing of daily specials, this restaurant is loved as well for its good service, splendid offerings, and low prices. Lots of seafood dishes, or for winter comfort food, try the roast goose. Open for lunch Mon–Fri 11:30 a.m.–2:30 p.m.; dinner, Mon–Thurs 5 p.m.–10 p.m., Fri–Sat 5 p.m.–11 p.m. Metro: Court House.

Virginia Scottish Games 3901 W Braddock Rd., Alexandria, VA (703) 912-1943 www.cascottishgames.org

Caber tossing, highland dancing, bagpipery, and a heptathalon competition are part of this two-day Celtic festival held in late July each year at Episcopal High School. Admission fee.

Visions Cinema Bistro Lounge 1927 Florida Ave. NW (202) 667-0090 www.visionsdc.com

This unique theater offers independent, art, and foreign films as well as a bistro lounge providing a full bar, wraps, pizzas, salads, *tapas*, empanadas, and coffee, espresso, tea, and sodas. Metro: Dupont Circle.

Visitor Information *see* Tourist Information.

Visual Arts *see* Art Galleries.

Vocal Arts Society 1818 24th St. NW (202) 265-8177 www.vocalartssociety.com

At varied locations, the society sponsors master classes, programs in Spanish, education programs at local high schools, and concerts featuring established vocal artists, as well as young promising singers, at the Terrace Theater in the Kennedy Center for the Performing Arts. Eight-concert subscription or single event tickets. Metro: Foggy Bottom-GWU.

Voice of America *see* International Broadcasting Bureau.

Volta Bureau *see* Alexander Graham Bell Association for the Deaf.

Von Steuben Memorial Lafayette Park northwest corner, Pennsylvania Ave. btw Jackson and Madison Pl. NW www.nps.gov/whho/statues

Sculpted by Albert Jaegers and unveiled by President Howard Taft's daughter, Helen, in 1910, this memorial portrays Gen. Friedrich (Baron) Wilhelm Von Steuben in the uniform of a major general in Washington's Continental Army. Von Steuben, who trained troops under Frederick the Great, repeated the process under General Washington at Valley Forge. Metro: McPherson Square.

W & OD Trail *see* Washington and Old Dominion Railroad Regional Park.

WPA/Corcoran *see* Washington Project for the Arts.

Wadsworth House *see* Sulgrave Club.

Walking Tours *see* African-American Heritage Tours, Anecdotal History Walks, Capitol Entertainment Services, Celebrity Washington Tours, D.C. Heritage Walking Tours, D.C. Preservation League, Doorways to Old Virginia, Downtown Civil War Tour, Georgetown Walking Tours, Historic Downtown D.C. Walking Tours, Historic Georgetown Tour, National Building Museum Tours, Old Town Christmas Candlelight Tour, Old Town Experience, Old Town Ghost Tours, Tour DC, Washington Walks. *See also* Hiking, Special Interest Tours.

Walsh-McLean House *see* Indonesia Embassy.

Walter Reed Army Medical Center 6900 Georgia Ave. NW (202) 782-3501 www .wramc.amedd.army.mil

First opening its doors to patients in 1909, and rapidly expanding during the First and Second World Wars and the wars in Korea and Vietnam, this is now the Army's leading medical facility. The center is named for the Army physician renowned for his work fighting yellow fever, cholera, and dysentery. Also on the site is the Walter Reed Institute for Research, Armed Forces Institute of Pathology, the Army Physical Disability Agency, and the National Museum of Health and Medicine. The Institute of Pathology Building, built in the 1940s, was designed to withstand an atomic blast—but not, alas, that of an H-bomb. Visitors to the museum enter the campus through the Georgia Ave. and Elder St. gate. If you drive onto the campus, your car may be stopped for inspection. Visitors must present a valid motor vehicle driver's license or other picture ID card and tell the guard that the museum is the destination. Metro: Takoma, then a 10-minute walk *See also* National Museum of Health and Medicine.

Warder-Totten House 2633 16th St. NW

Washington's only example of a Henry Hobson Richardson arch—actually, the only (sort of) extant Richardson-designed house in Washington—continues its *Perils of Pauline* existence. Manufacturer Benjamin H. Warder built it at 1415 F St. in 1865. Architect George Oakley Totten, who studied under Richardson, bought the stone façade and some of the interior of the house from a wrecking company in 1902, and in 1925, rebuilt it for his own home at its present location. Rescued again, it had been listed as a "most endangered" architectural landmark as late as 1998. Metro: Columbia Heights, then a 10-minute walk.

Wardman Park Marriott *see* Marriott Wardman-Park Hotel.

Wardman Tower *see* Marriott Wardman-Park Hotel.

The Warehouse Bar and Grill 214 King St., Alexandria, VA (703) 683-6868 www .warehousebarandgrill.com

Order the shellfish and penne pasta salad, or shrimp-stuffed ravioli, or maybe all-lump crab cakes, or show up for Sunday brunch and enjoy the atmosphere in this lively restaurant in the heart of Old Town Alexandria. Open daily Mon–Thurs 11 a.m.–4 p.m., 5 p.m.–10:30 p.m.; Fri 4 p.m.–11 p.m.; Sat breakfast 8 a.m.–10:30 a.m., lunch 11 a.m.–4 p.m.; Sun brunch 10 a.m.–4 p.m., dinner 5 p.m.–9:30 p.m. Metro: Braddock Rd., then a 9-block walk, or take DAT34 DASH Bus (Hunting Towers) to King St. and Royal St.

Warner Theatre 13th and E Sts. NW (202) 783-4000 www.warnertheatre.com

This Art Deco grand dame of a theater, born in 1924 as the Earle, her gilt and crystal ablaze again after a recent facelift, has a show-biz scrapbook that includes vaudeville, silent films, a ballroom below and a rooftop restaurant above, the dancing Roxyettes, *Ben Hur*, porno films, the Rolling Stones, touring Broadway shows, Mikhail Baryshnikov, Frank Sinatra, and stand-up comedians. The box office is open 10 a.m.–4 p.m. when dark, or noon–7 p.m. when a show is running. Tickets online at www.TicketMaster.com. Metro: Metro Center, Federal Triangle. *See also* www.commuterpage.com/venues/venue-en.htm.

Washington Afro-American 1612 14th St. NW (202) 332-0080 www.afroam.org

Containing news and features of interest to Washington's black community, this paper is published every Thursday. Founded in 1892, it is one of Washington's oldest newspapers. Metro: U St.-Cardozo.

Washington and Old Dominion Railroad Regional Park (W & OD) from Shirlington near I-395 to Purcellville in Loudon County. Park Office: 21293 Smiths Switch Rd., Ashburn, VA (202) 729-0596 www.nvpa.org.wod.html

A 45-mile paved trail for walking, running, bicycling, and skating, and 32 miles of adjacent trails for horseback riding, run along the 100-foot-wide bed of the defunct railroad. Park office hours Mon–Fri 8 a.m.–4:30 p.m. Trails are open dawn to dusk. Metro: Arlington Cemetery, then proceed to Arlington Memorial Bridge area.

Washington Antiques Show Omni Shoreham Hotel, 2500 Calvert St. NW (202) 965-0640 www.washingtonantiques.org

For close to 50 years, this show in early January hosts nationally known dealers and a themed exhibit displaying quality pieces from some of America's great collections. Admission charge. Metro: Woodley Park-Adams Morgan.

Washington Arboretum *see* National Arboretum.

Washington Area Bicyclist Association 733 15th St. NW, Suite 1030 (202) 628-2500 www.waba.org

Founded in 1972, this active organization has a solid list of accomplishments, including instigation of the Mount Vernon, Washington and Old Dominion, and Capital Crescent trails; allowing bikes on Metrorail and Metrobus; providing bicycling information; and urging the use of bikes for commuting. The Web site provides membership information. Metro: McPherson Square or Metro Center.

Washington/Arlington National Cemetery Tour Arlington National Cemetery Visitor Center, Arlington, VA (202) 554-5100 www.tourmobile.com

Tourmobile Sightseeing, Inc., offers several narrated sightseeing tours of Washington and environs. Tours from 1½ hours to 2 days are available. The Arlington Cemetery Tour includes the Tomb of the Unknowns, Arlington House, the Robert E. Lee Memorial, and the Kennedy grave sites. For the shorter tours, there are continuous departures daily April to September 8:30 a.m.–6:30 p.m., October to March 8:30 a.m.–4:30 p.m. Last tour begins 30 minutes before cemetery closes. Closed Christmas Day. Tickets available at the Arlington National Cemetery Visitor Center. Metro: Arlington Cemetery. *See also* Tourmobile Sightseeing, Inc.

Washington Balalaika Society 400 Madison St., Suite 2103, Alexandria, VA www.balalaika.org

Forty musicians share their love of Russia's folk music at concerts throughout the year. Weekly rehearsals in Arlington gather together these players of balalaikas, *domras*, and *bayans*. You can, as well, learn how to play these instruments. Nonmusicians are welcome to join the society. Moderate annual membership fee. Metro: Braddock Road, then DAT5 DASH Van Dorn Bus to Madison and Royal Sts.

Washington Ballet 3515 Wisconsin Ave. NW (202) 362-3606 www.washington ballet.org

Performing a diversified repertoire of classical and contemporary ballets, the company performs at the Kennedy Center, the Warner Theater, and George Mason University Center for the Arts. The Washington Ballet's affiliated school, the Washington School of Ballet, provides dance training. Metro: Tenleytown-AU.

Washington Blade 1408 U St. NW, 2nd floor (202) 797-7000

This free newspaper with a weekly circulation of 45,000 and an estimated readership of 100,000 provides news and events of particular interest to the gay and lesbian population. For the past 30 years it has been dropped each Friday at bookstores, libraries, and business sites throughout metropolitan Washington. The publisher also prints a glossy quarterly, *Window Magazine*.

Washington Boat Show 6017 Tower Court, Alexandria, VA (703) 823-7960 www.washingtonboatshow.com

On a snowy February day, what could be more diverting than this annual event at the Washington Convention Center, featuring all kinds of pleasure craft, from cruisers to yachts to catamarans? Or maybe you can find just the right accessory for your fishing dinghy. More than 300 boat dealers participate. Metro: Metro Center.

Washington Capitals MCI Center, 601 F St. NW (202) 432-SEAT www.washing toncaps.com

From October through May the Washington Capitals, a National Hockey League team, draws fans to its new home at the MCI Center. The Web site provides a virtual tour of the Caps locker room and the training facility in Piney Orchard, the schedule, and statistics. Phone-in ticket sales are available 10 a.m.–9 p.m. daily, or anytime through www.TicketMaster.com. Metro: Gallery Pl.-Chinatown.

Washington Chamber Symphony 1099 22nd St., Suite 602 (202) 452-1321 www .wcsymphony.org

For more than 25 years, the ensemble has been performing at the Kennedy Center Terrace Theater, as well as giving occasional Saturday recitals at the Corcoran Gallery of Art. Its series of concerts for young people "guarantees that your child will find classical music fun and interesting." A sell-out each December is the Holiday Sing-Along featuring the orchestra, a chorus of 300, and children's choirs and bell-ringers. Metro: Foggy Bottom-GWU.

Washington Channel Promenade end of Water St. on the waterfront

Walking along the marina past the Channel Inn Hotel and the Government Pier to Waterside Park, a sculpture Gertrude Vanderbilt Whitney completed in 1931 memorializes those lost when the Titanic struck an iceberg in 1912. Metro: Waterfront-SEU. *See also* Titanic Memorial.

Washington Chorus

In addition to its own subscription concerts at the Kennedy Center, this 180-person vocal company (formerly known as the Oratorio Society of Washington) makes frequent appearances with the National Symphony Orchestra singing traditional and modern music. Details and program information at (202) 342-6221 or at www.thewashingtonchorus.org.

Washington Circle Pennsylvania Ave. NW intersecting New Hampshire Ave., K St., and 23rd St.

Washingtonian Clark Mills's sculpture of a uniformed George Washington on a horse stands in the center of the circle. Jefferson had wanted to put the Capitol building at this location, which was then known as Camp Hill. City designer Pierre L'Enfant, who sited the circle and Washington, thought otherwise. The George Washington University Hospital on 23rd St. is where President Ronald Reagan and Press Secretary James Brady were rushed after being shot. Metro Foggy Bottom-GWU.

Washington *City Paper* see *City Paper*.

Washington Civic Symphony *see* Washington Symphony Orchestra.

Washington Club 15 Dupont Circle NW btw P St. and New Hampshire Ave. (202) 483-9200

Since 1951 this white marble and terra cotta Italian palazzo-style mansion has been home to one of the oldest women's literary and educational clubs in the country, founded in 1891. It was built in 1903 for "Cissy" Patterson, a well-known socialite and owner of the *Washington Times-Herald*. Its famous architect was Stanford White from New York. The building is not open to the public. Metro: Dupont Circle.

Washington Consumers' Checkbook Center for the Study of Services, 733 15th St. NW, Suite 820 (202) 347-7283 www.checkbook.org

Since 1974 this independent nonprofit has been providing Washington area consumers with information to help them get quality services and products at the best possible prices. Its subscription publication *Washington Consumers' Checkbook* evaluates the quality and prices of local service firms, stores, hospitals, health plans, and health care providers through in-depth articles and survey-based ratings. The organization also provides services for buying or leasing a car. Its biweekly newsletter, *CarDeals*, outlines the latest in car rebates and incentives. A product price guide "BARGAINS" locates local retailer's prices for 2,000 products. The group's *Guide to Washington Area Restaurants* is another survey-based publication. Metro: McPherson Square.

Washington Convention and Tourism Corporation 1212 New York Ave. NW (202) 789-7000 www.washington.org

As the city's tourism marketers for people planning to come to Washington, this group is geared to respond to queries prior to your arrival in Washington by phone or through its Web site, which offers a gold mine of information. You can request print or electronic versions of the Gay and Lesbian Traveler's Guide to Washington, Official Visitors Guide, and the American Heritage and Multicultural Guide. The Web site has vacation planning information, suggests where to shop, what to see, where to eat, and provides a survey of D.C. neighborhoods. Metro: Metro Center.

Washington Convention Center 900 9th St. NW (202) 789-1600 www.dcconvention.com

Since its opening in 1983, the center has been the venue for exhibitions, trade shows, and historic events such as South Africa's Nelson Mandela's first public address in Washington. A new, enlarged supplemental center, to open in 2003, will be 2 blocks away on N St. between 7th St. and 9th St. NW. Metro: Gallery Pl.-Chinatown or Metro Center.

Washington Court Hotel 525 New Jersey Ave. NW (202) 628-2100

This modern luxury hotel has glass elevators, polished granite, and a glass-ceiling atrium that brightens the place even on the gloomiest of days. The bathrooms are decorated with marble and many rooms have full kitchens. The hotel offers a café/grill, fitness center, valet parking, and business services. Lots of the guests are dealing with Congress (2 blocks away from the Capitol) or the Department of Education (almost next door). Close to Union Station. Metro: Union Station.

Washington Courtyard by Marriott *see* Courtyard by Marriott.

Washington Craft Show Washington Convention Center, 900 9th St. NW (202) 789-1600 www.craftsamericashows.com/washington.htm

Every November, this juried show presents work by nationally recognized artists who showcase and sell their work in furniture, glass, jewelry, leather, metal, mixed media, paper, wood, and even wearables. Metro: Gallery Pl.-Chinatown or Metro Center.

Washington D.C. Chamber of Commerce Visitor Information Center *see* D.C. Chamber of Commerce Visitor Information Center.

Washington D.C. Convention and Tourism Corporation *see* Washington Convention and Tourism Corporation.

Washington D.C. Newspapers and Magazines *see* Newspapers and Magazines.

Washington D.C. Radio Stations *see* Radio Stations.

Washington Diplomat P. O. Box 1345, Wheaton, MD (301) 933-3552 www.washingtondiplomat.com

This monthly magazine covers the comings and goings of members of Washington's diplomatic corps, their social life and cultural events, and includes profiles of leading members. The magazine also lists film showings at the various embassies, as well as international art shows. Some of this information is contained in the Web site, but not the film showings and cultural events. You may subscribe to the publication or pick up a free copy at drop points around Washington at embassies, the World Bank, OAS, State Department, and other "points of influence."

Washington Dolls' House and Toy Museum 5236 44th St. NW (202) 244-0024 www.dollshousemuseum.com

Founded in 1975, this small museum displays unusual and antique dollhouses, miniature toys, and a variety of dolls. There are dollhouse kits and dollhouses for sale. Can be booked for tea parties and birthdays. Small admission fee. Open Tues–Sat 10 a.m.–5 p.m., Sun noon–5 p.m. Metro: Friendship Heights. *See also* www.commuterpage.com/venues/museums.htm.

Washington Embassy Row and Arlington National Cemetery Tours Union Station, 40 Massachusetts Ave. NE btw 1st and 2nd Sts. (202) 289-1995

This 4-hour tour includes the Lincoln, Vietnam, and Marine Corps Memorials, and the Arlington National Cemetery where a tram brings you past the Kennedy grave sites, and includes the Changing of the Guard Ceremony at the Tomb of the Unknowns. From the coach you can view the Capitol, Library of Congress, Supreme Court, House and Senate Office Buildings, FBI building, White House, Embassy Row, Georgetown, the U.S. Navy Memorial, and the Corcoran Galley of Art. Hotel pickup. Daily tours at 8:30 a.m., 2:30 p.m. No tours on Thanksgiving Day, Christmas Day, or New Year's Day.

Washington Equestrian Statue Washington Circle, Pennsylvania Ave., intersected by New Hampshire Ave., 23rd and K Sts. NW

This sculpture of George Washington astride his horse was cast in bronze by local artist Clark Mills and dedicated in 1859. Washington's face was modeled from Houdon's famous bust, and the dress uniform was copied from one actually worn by Washington. Metro: Foggy Bottom-GWU.

Washington Families (magazine and Web site) 462 Herndon Pkwy., Suite 206, Herndon, VA (703) 318-1385 www.familiesmagazines.com

Founded in 1992, this free monthly parenting publication can be found in bookstores, toy stores, and hundreds of other sites throughout metropolitan Washington. It is a fine source of information on all aspects of family life. Its monthly calendar of events and "Going Places" column are the area's most comprehensive listing of family and home-related activities. Its Web site provides these same resources and more. Check the "Places To Go" and the museum guide.

Washington Harbour 31st and K Sts. NW

Transformed from a cement factory to a million-square-foot postmodern-style office and residential development, Washington Harbour provides a river promenade, including bike lanes, indoor and outdoor shops and lively restaurants, and one of Washington's best river vistas. The development, designed by Arthur Cotton Moore Associates, includes innovative river-walk pylons with expandable floodgates, protecting the plaza areas during Potomac floods. Bronze human figures scattered about the complex by sculptor J. Seward Johnson Jr. produce double takes. Metro: Foggy Bottom, then a 10-minute walk, or Farragut West, and take 38B Bus to 31st and M Sts. NW.

Washington Hebrew Congregation 3935 Macomb St. NW (formerly 816 8th St. NW) (202) 362-7100 www.whctemple.org

A Hebrew Congregation formed in Washington in 1852 purchased the Methodist Episcopal Church at 8th and I Sts. in 1863, which eventually was razed to build a new temple on the site. This striking Romanesque building was completed in 1897, with President William McKinley laying the cornerstone. A new temple was built in 1955 on Macomb St., the present site, with President Harry S. Truman laying the cornerstone, and President Dwight D. Eisenhower officially dedicating it in 1955. Services: Fri 5:45 p.m., 8:30 p.m., Sat 10:30 a.m. The Greater New Hope Baptist Church now worships at the 8th St. building. Metro: Dupont Circle, then take the Metrobus N6 to Macomb St. and Massachusetts Ave.

Washington Hilton and Towers 1919 Connecticut Ave. NW (202) 483-3000 (800) 445-8667, fax (202) 232-0438 www.hilton.com

This moderately expensive 1,100-room hotel indeed towers over Connecticut Ave. at T St. Its many amenities, including an Olympic-size outdoor pool, jogging paths, business center, shops, lighted tennis courts, exercise rooms, restaurants, and bars, attracts many attending conferences and conventions. Close to Adams Morgan. This was where John Hinkley shot President Ronald Reagan in 1981. Metro: Dupont Circle, then a 5-block walk.

Washington Home and Garden Show Washington Convention Center, 900 9th St. NW (703) 823-7960

Join the 60,000 visitors each March who browse through almost 3 acres of blossoming gardens, demonstrations, lectures, and 600 booths and exhibits—everything from roofing to kitchen and bath concepts to landscape design. Metro: Gallery Pl.-Chinatown or Metro Center.

Washington Hotel *see* Hotel Washington.

Washington Informer 3117 Martin Luther King Jr. Ave. SE (202) 561-4100

Founded in 1964 and appearing every Friday, this newspaper provides particularly strong coverage of the African-American metropolitan community. Metro: Anacostia.

The Washington Institute for Skin Care 2311 M St. NW, Suite 200 (202) 785-8855 www.skinlaser.com

Associated with a celebrity author-physician, the institute provides skin care consultation with scanner evaluation, customized medical cleansing facials, specialty treatments for face and body, as well as a wide variety of skin care products. Metro: Foggy Bottom-GWU, then a 10-minute walk.

Washington International Horse Show Administration: 9070 Shady Grove Court, Gaithersburg, MD (301) 840-0281 Venue: MCI Center, 601 F St. NW. www.wihs.org

For more than 40 years, this October charity event has been bringing together some of the world's top equestrian teams for competitions in jumping, dressage, and exhibition. Tickets go on sale September 1, but are also available at the door. Tickets may be purchased at TicketMaster (202) 432-SEAT. Hours to purchase by phone are 10 a.m.–9 p.m. daily. Metro: Gallery Pl.-Chinatown.

Washington International Youth Hostel *see* Hostelling International-AYH Hostel.

The Washington Kantorei 1011 Hillwood Ave., Falls Church, VA (703) 533-1169 www.washingtonkantorei.org

Founded in 1994, this respected choral group specializes in performing unpublished manuscripts, particularly sacred music of the German baroque, but performs as well modern choral repertory, particularly from Europe. Dr. Dale Voelker leads the group, whose repertoire includes compositions by J. S. Bach, G. P. Telemann, H. Schütz, and other pillars of the baroque. The chorale performs at various churches in the area, as well as at the German embassy. For concert information, call or check the Web site.

Washington Mall *see* The Mall.

Washington Masonic National Memorial *see* George Washington Masonic National Memorial.

Washington Metropolitan Area Transit Authority 600 5th St. NW (202) 637-7000 www.wmata.com

This organization provides bus and subway service to the metropolitan Washington area. Phone for Metrobus and Metrorail schedule information. The extensive Web site provides a number of services: sites offering maps; guides and tickets; passes; senior discount cards; a map of the system; schedules; and the "Ride Guide," allowing interactive location of routes to take you to a specific location.

The Metro Center Sales Office at 12th St. and F St. is one of the sites selling Metro fare cards and passes.

Washington Monarch Hotel *see* Monarch Hotel.

Washington Monthly 733 15th St. NW, Suite 1000 (202) 393-5155 www.washing tonmonthly.com

Specializing in "helping you understand how to make our system of politics work," this general interest magazine, read by journalists, academics, and those involved in government, has kick-started the careers of many of today's top journalists and political reporters. The most-read page is "Memo of the Month," which celebrates real-life bureaucratese. Metro: McPherson Square.

Washington Monument Constitution Ave. and 15th St. NW (800) 967-2283 (National Park Service Reservation Service)

Exterior repairs to the marble and masonry exterior and elevator upgrades were completed in 1997 for this national icon. It evolved from a monument first voted on by Congress while there were still surrendered British troops waiting for homebound ships. Funding was problematic until Senator Henry Clay bullied Congress into supplementing private contributions. Ground breaking finally took place on July 4, 1848. In a freezing gale on December 6, 1884, the aluminum capstone was attached, completing what was then the tallest man-made structure in the world. At 555 feet, it remains the world's tallest masonry construction. An elevator takes visitors to the observation room at the 500-foot level. Open daily 9 a.m. to 4:45 p.m. Closed Christmas Day. Tickets are required and can be reserved from 24 hours up to 5 months in advance. Reservations may be made by telephone or at http://reservations.nps.gov. Those making advance reservations will be charged $1.50 per ticket, plus a 50-cent service charge per order. Free tickets are distributed for each day's visit from a kiosk on the Washington Monument grounds at 15th St. and Madison Dr. on a first-come, first-served basis. Hours for the ticket kiosk are 8 a.m. to 4:50 p.m. Tickets are usually distributed for the day during the morning hours, thus it is important to be at the kiosk early. No food, drinks, or large bags allowed in the monument. Metro: Federal Triangle, then a 10-minute walk. *See also* www.commuterpage.com/venues/memorials.htm.

Washington Monument Reflecting Pool *see* Reflecting Pool.

Washington Mystics MCI Center, 601 F St. NW (202) 661-5000, or for ticket information (202) 661-5050 www.wnba.com/mystics

Established in 1998, the Women's National Basketball Association's Washington Mystics hopes to develop a championship team under newly appointed coach, Marianne Stanley. The season runs from June to August. Tickets are available by phone or through the Web site. Metro: Gallery Pl.-Chinatown, Metro Center, or Archives-Navy Memorial.

Washington National Airport *see* Reagan National Airport.

Washington National Cathedral Massachusetts and Wisconsin Aves. NW (202) 537-6200 www.cathedral.org

Since President Theodore Roosevelt laid the cornerstone in 1907 until its completion in 1990, this towering Gothic-style church has overseen great historic events: the funerals of Presidents Dwight D. Eisenhower and Woodrow Wilson, services for the American soldiers who died in Vietnam, funerals of Generals Omar Bradley and Douglas MacArthur, and the last Sunday sermon of Martin Luther King Jr. Information and a virtual tour are available at the Web site or by telephone. The second largest cathedral in the United States, and the sixth largest in the world, it serves as the chief mission church of the Episcopal Diocese of Washington. It is open to all faiths and denominations. Besides daily worship services, the active calendar includes tours, evensong, choral groups, recitals, and various observances. Several architects had their hands in its creation, but Philip Hubert Frohman is considered to be the principal architect. The cathedral is open to the public weekdays 10 a.m.–5 p.m. and Saturdays 10 a.m.–4:30 p.m. On Sunday mornings, the cathedral is open for worship only until the conclusion of the 11 a.m. service (about 12:45 p.m.). On weeknights during the summer (May 1 through Labor Day), the nave (main) level remains open to the public until 9 p.m. Gardens are open daily until dusk. Available tours include a docent-led group highlights tour, or an audio tour. Metro: Tenleytown-AU, then 30, 32, 34, or 36 Bus going south on Wisconsin Ave. to the cathedral; about a 1 1/2-mile ride.

Washington National Cathedral Choral Society Washington National Cathedral, Massachusetts and Wisconsin Ave. NW (202) 537-6200 www.cathedralchoralso ciety.org

Founded in 1941, this distinguished 180-voice chorus is the oldest choral group in Washington. Through the years, it has performed twenty world premiers, many commissioned for the society. Internationally acclaimed artists, as well as promising newcomers, routinely appear as guest soloists. The group participates in the Washington Performing Arts Society at the Kennedy Center and at the Cathedral's Summer Festival, the Fall Open House, and the free summer community concerts. Details on the Web site. The society receives no direct funding from the Washington National Cathedral and stages various fund-raisers and sponsors many educational and community events. Metro: Tenleytown–AU station, then 30, 32, 34, or 36 Bus going south on Wisconsin Ave. to the cathedral; about a 1 1/2-mile ride.

Washington National Cathedral Christmas Celebration Washington National Cathedral, Massachusetts and Wisconsin Aves. NW (202) 537-6200 www.cathedral .org

From early December onward, the cathedral's seasonal decorations frame bagpipers, choral sing-alongs, pageants, and choral performances. Christmas Eve services require tickets—the 3,400 seats are usually spoken for in November. The services are at 6 p.m. and 10 p.m. On Christmas Day there are services at 9 a.m., noon, and 4 p.m., none of which need tickets. Details of festival services are available on the Web site. Metro: Tenleytown-AU, then 30, 32, 34, or 36 Bus going south on Wisconsin Ave. to the cathedral; about a 1 1/2-mile ride.

Washington National Cathedral Flower Mart Washington National Cathedral, Massachusetts and Wisconsin Aves. NW (202) 537-3185 www.cathedral.org/cathe dral/flowermart

The Flower Mart, styled after a medieval springtime festival, is usually held in early May, and has been a cathedral tradition since 1939, with stands and displays encircling the church. The festival is sponsored annually by the All Hallows Guild (www.revelsdc.org) to benefit the cathedral's extensive gardens, grounds, and woodlands. Each year, a different country is featured. Besides maypole dancing, and other programs, visitors can browse through stalls that sell antiques, used books, and collectibles. Metro: Tenleytown-AU station, then 30, 32, 34, or 36 Bus going south on Wisconsin Ave. to the cathedral; about a 1 1/2-mile ride. For the Mart there is a shuttle service from the Tenleytown Metro.

Washington National Cathedral Medieval Arts and Crafts Workshops Washington National Cathedral, Massachusetts and Wisconsin Aves. NW (202) 537-2934

Children 5 and above can participate in the cathedral arts and crafts workshops held every Saturday. They learn about the life, culture, and skills of people in the Middle Ages through hands-on activities. Reservations are not required except for groups of ten or more. Modest participation fee. Activities take about 1 hour to 90 minutes. Open 10 a.m.–2 p.m., except in July when hours are 1 p.m.–4 p.m. Metro: Tenleytown-AU, then 30, 32, 34, or 36 Bus going south on Wisconsin Ave. to the cathedral; about a 1 1/2-mile ride.

Washington National Cathedral Open House Washington National Cathedral, Massachusetts and Wisconsin Aves. NW (202) 537-6200 www.cathedral.org

Commemorating the 1907 laying of the foundation stone by President Theodore Roosevelt, this late September festival includes carillon and organ playing, cathedral construction exhibits, crafts, choir performances, food, and an opportunity to climb the cathedral tower and get a close-up view of the bells and see Washington from its highest point. Metro: Tenleytown-AU station, then 30, 32, 34, or 36 Bus going south on Wisconsin Ave. to the cathedral.

Washington National Cathedral Summer Music Festival Washington National Cathedral, Massachusetts and Wisconsin Aves. NW Schedule: (202) 537-6200 www.cathedral.org/cathedral/programs

This annual free festival of music features a variety of performers including the 180-voice Cathedral Choral Society. Concerts held in June and July and are free and open to the public. Metro: Tenleytown-AU station, then 30, 32, 34, or 36 Bus going south on Wisconsin Ave. to the cathedral.

Washington National Zoological Park *see* National Zoo.

Washington Navy Yard 9th and M Sts. NW (202) 433-4882 www.history.navy.mil

This site, the Navy's oldest shore facility, was acquired in 1800, first building 50 gunboats ordered up by Thomas Jefferson's administration, and later large warships, both sail and steam, and later still becoming a testing site and ordnance plant, producing 16-inch guns for World War II battleships. All this ceased in 1964, and the U.S. Naval Gun Factory, with up to 25,000 workers, became the U.S. Navy Yard. The former factories converted to their present functions. These include the Navy Museum; the U.S. Navy Combat Art Center; the Marine Corps Museum; the USS *Barry*, a decommissioned Navy destroyer; and the Navy Historical Library.

The Navy Museum, supported by the next-door Naval Historical Center, displays but a small part of its historical artifacts from World War II. There are anti-aircraft guns you can climb onto and a replica of the gun deck of the frigate *Constitution*, which you can also board. The Marine Museum displays a flag raised on Mt. Suribachi during the taking of Iwo Jima in World War II. Visitors are also welcome to visit the USS *Barry* and a Vietnam-era PCF Swift Boat. Because of increased security at the Navy Yard, to visit the Navy Museum, Marine Corps Museum, or the USS *Barry* you must first make a telephone reservation to enter the Navy Yard. The only exception is if you possess a military or Department of Defense ID. Otherwise, call the number above to make a reservation through the recorded message system. You will require a picture ID to enter. Navy Museum open Mon–Fri 9 a.m.–4 p.m. Closed weekends, Thanksgiving Day, Christmas Eve, Christmas Day, New Year's Day, and federal holidays. The USS *Barry* is open Mon–Fri 10 a.m.–4 p.m. Once on the Navy Yard grounds, you may also visit the Marine Corps Museum (202) 433-3534. No separate appointment is necessary. Open Mon–Fri 9 a.m.–4 p.m., closed weekends and federal holidays. Metro: Navy Yard.

Washington Old Town Trolley Tours Union Station, 40 Massachusetts Ave. NE btw 1st and 2nd Sts. (202) 832-9800 www.trolleytours.com

These narrated tours, which use a motorized board-at-will Victorian streetcar replica, cover about 100 points of interest throughout Washington, including the National Cathedral and Georgetown, both well beyond Metro access. The trolley stops at many hotels, as well as at Union Station. Tours depart every 30 minutes from seventeen sites, allowing you to stop, shop, dine, and reboard as needed. Stops include the Capitol and Library of Congress, Lincoln Memorial, National Geographic Society, Arlington Cemetery, and the Smithsonian. Tours last around 2 hours and 15 minutes. Open daily 9 a.m.–5 p.m. Memorial Day to Labor Day, 9 a.m.–4 p.m. rest of year. Closed Thanksgiving Day and Christmas Day. Lower fares for children 4-12. Metro: Union Station.

Washington Opera Administrative offices: 2600 Virginia Ave. NW, Suite 104 Ticket Office: (202) 295-2400 or (800) 876-7372

Artistic Director Placido Domingo leads one of the country's finest resident opera companies. Tickets often sell out well in advance. There are various subscription packages, however, from which three or more operas may be selected; the full season offers seven or eight operas. Standing-room tickets may be available. The opera season opens in September and runs through March. Tickets are available from the Washington Opera ticket office number above or (800) 876-7372 and via the Web site, which also provides the company history and the schedule of the season's operas. The ticket office during off-season is open weekdays 10 a.m.–5 p.m. Ticket office hours during the opera season is open weekdays 10 a.m.–7 p.m. or 90 minutes prior to curtain if there is a performance, Saturdays: noon–5:30 p.m. (No office visits after 2 p.m.—phone service only.) Sundays with a matinee 11:30 a.m.–12:30 p.m.

Washington Parent 4701 Sangamore Rd., Bethesda, MD (301) 239-0247 www.wash ingtonparent.com

This award-winning free monthly publication has been covering all aspects of parenting since 1982. Geared toward families, it covers infants to teens, health and fitness, activities for children, and parent resources. Its calendar of events, in print and online, is particularly useful in locating activities for 3-year-olds to 12-year-olds. Typical events are introductions to artists at various art museums, storytelling at public libraries, children-oriented events at the national museums, puppet shows, children's book discussion groups, toy store events, "family friendly" music and dance performances, and preschooler story times. Events are evenly divided between downtown Washington and the Maryland and Virginia suburbs. Parent resources provide a similar listing of events of interest to parents: vaccination schedules, La Leche League meetings, Mocha Moms, Parents without Partners, and Coping with Divorce seminars. The magazine distributes 75,000 copies through Toys R Us, Zany Brainy, Fresh Fields, public libraries, and specialty bookstores.

Washington Performing Arts Society Ticket Office: 2000 L St. NW, Suite 510 (202) 833-9800 www.wpas.org

WPAS is a nonprofit "impresario" organization offering Washington a cornucopia of performing artists. Established in 1965, WPAS has not a hall to call its own, but instead brings emerging and internationally acclaimed artists to facilities throughout Washington with more than 100 public engagements and arts education activities each year. Be it modern or traditional dance, jazz, classical music, or contemporary performance work, there is likely a subscription series intersecting with your interests. The educational outreach programs annually offer free performances in more than 300 area public and parochial schools. All programs are supported by both corporate contributors, an active volunteer group, and 7,000 plus members. Tickets can be purchased at (202) 785-WPAS (9727) Mon–Fri 9 a.m.–5 p.m. Tickets may also be purchased daily 24 hours through the Web site, which also provides theater seating diagrams and travel and parking information.

Washington Places (Web site) http://urban.arch.virginia.edu/dcplaces/

This Web site, developed by University of Virginia School of Architecture students, provides neighborhood silhouette maps, photos, and historical and "architectural" comments about Washington. You can take neighborhood tours along Massachusetts Ave., Pennsylvania Ave., 16th St., and the Mall. Particularly noteworthy are the virtual era-by-era maps, showing, for example, the history of the Mall. An innovative and unique virtual resource.

Washington Plaza Hotel 10 Thomas Circle NW (202) 842-1300 (800) 424-1140

Just 3 blocks from the Metro and 5 blocks from the White House or the Convention Center, this hotel offers room service, cable TV, and coffee makers. There is an exercise room, gift shop, restaurant, bar, and seasonal outdoor pool. Moderate pricing. Metro: McPherson Square.

Washington Post 1150 15th St. NW (202) 334-6000

Read daily by more than 1.6 million and even more than 2 million on Sundays, the *Post*'s 850-member news staff routinely collects Pulitzer Prizes. Besides the bustle of the Washington newsroom, which visitors can see on a *Post* tour, staffers work out of offices in seven states and twenty foreign countries. Robert Redford played a *Post* reporter in *All the President's Men*, based on the book by young *Post* employees Bob Woodward and Carl Bernstein. The late publisher, Katharine Graham, published a prize-winning best-seller about her life and the *Post*. With the seat of government as its beat, this newspaper provides coverage of policy issues and politics, at home and abroad, like no other paper. Its Friday tabloid, *Weekend*, offers coverage of "whazzup." A "Post-Haste" phone freebee (202) 334-9000 allows callers to punch in codes for late-breaking news, the latest basketball scores, or the amount of snow pack on the slopes. The paper includes the *Sunday Magazine*, *TV Week*, and *Book World* supplemental sections. Its extensive classified ad and job sections are also online. Metro: McPherson Square, Farragut West.

Washington Post Tours 1150 15th St. NW (202) 334-7969

Guided group tours, taking about an hour and surveying the history and production of the *Post* are offered on Mondays. Reservations are required at least two weeks in advance and no more than six weeks in advance. A picture ID is required. Tour members must be 11 years or older and children must be accompanied by an adult. Detailed instructions for reserving tours are available at the Community Relations section of the *Post* Web site: www.washingtonpost.com/community/you/tours.shtml. Tours Mon at 10 a.m., 11 a.m., 1 p.m., 2 p.m., 3 p.m. Metro: McPherson Square, Farragut West.

Washington Post (Web site) www.washingtonpost.com

You can read, free and online, the entire output of the *Post* for the past two weeks, but you must pay a fee to access older news articles. Check out the "Visitor's Guide" and related tourist information. There you can find traffic reports, driving directions, airport information, travel tips, the travel "deal of the week," suggested visits and tours, hotel bookings, listings of current art and museum exhibits, and information on the monuments and memorials and other important landmarks. The interactive entertainment guide provides a near comprehensive listing of restaurants, often with reviews, of theaters, dance, movies, bars, clubs, and much more.

Washington Printmakers Gallery 1732 Connecticut Ave. NW (202) 332-7757

Founded in 1985, the gallery features monthly shows of member artists as well as invitational exhibits and traveling shows. Only original, contemporary, hand-pulled lithographs, etchings, and drypoint graphics are displayed. Open Tues–Thurs noon–6 p.m., Fri noon–9 p.m., Sat–Sun noon–5 p.m. Metro: Dupont Circle.

Washington Project for the Arts Corcoran Gallery of Art, 17th St. and New York Ave. NW (202) 639-1828

In 1996, the Corcoran Gallery of Art became the home of the formerly independent nonprofit Washington Project for the Arts, an organization that has been promoting contemporary art in the region through exhibitions and educational programs for more than 20 years. Its broad range of projects includes exhibits such as the biennial exhibition of regional artists, a regional artist directory, and exhibits at other venues in Washington. Its membership, open to all, provides invitations to exhibits and other benefits. Metro: Dupont Circle.

Washington Redskins FedEx Field, Arena Dr., Landover, MD (301) 276-6050
www.redskins.com

In 1937, the Redskins moved here from Boston, and President Franklin Delano
Roosevelt returned for his second term. There may be someone in Washington who
ranks the latter event as more important, but from the preseason games on, August
through December, the city is obsessed. In 1997, the team moved to Jack Kent
Cooke Stadium, which for $200 million was renamed FedEx Field. Its 80,000 seats
are held by season ticket holders and few if any seats are available. But the ticket
office number is provided, and you may be able to locate a preseason ticket or two
or ask to be on the waiting list for season tickets. In 1999, the team was sold for
$800 million to a partnership headed by Daniel Snyder, then 34. Parking is pro-
vided at the stadium, but the traffic can be intense. Metro: Cheverly, Landover, or
Addison Road-Seat Pleasant, then take a shuttle bus directly to FedEx Field. Buses
go to and from the stadium every 15 minutes. During regular season games, buses
begin 3 hours before game time and end 1 hour after the game. For Monday night
games, the shuttle runs from 5 p.m. until 1 a.m. *See also* FedEx Field.

Washington Renaissance Hotel 999 9th St. NW (202) 898-9000 www.marriott
.com

This 800-room hotel, opposite the Washington Convention Center and 4 blocks
from the MCI Center, is within walking distance of the Smithsonian museums. It
has spacious rooms with all the amenities, including data ports. There is a fitness
center on the premises, a 60-foot indoor pool, a food court and restaurants, shops,
and even a post office. Metro: Gallery Pl.-Chinatown.

Washington Sailing Marina 1 Marina Dr. off George Washington Memorial
Pkwy., Alexandria, VA (703) 548-9027 www.guestservices.com/wsm/slips.html

A concession of the National Park Service offers sailboat rentals by the hour
and a weekend sailing school. This is the homeport for the Potomac River Sailing
Association, Daingerfield Island Cruising Fleet, Sailing Club of Washington,
Georgetown Sailing Team, and the National Yacht Club. Boat rentals, by reservation only, 11 a.m.–4 p.m. daily during the season. Bring your sailing certificate or
take a test at the marina. Year-round you may rent a bike at the marina, which is
on the Mount Vernon Bike Trail. Bike rentals 9 a.m.–4 p.m. daily. No Metro service
to this area.

The Washington Sängerbund Administration: 5817 Runford Dr., New Carrollton,
MD (301) 577-3505 Events hotline: (202) 310-4691 www.geocities.com/saenger
bund/

Founded in 1851 and still going strong, this German singing society performs
concerts of German music, usually at three large annual events: Fasching (Mardi
Gras), Oktoberfest, and Christkindlmarkt. The venues are listed on the Web site
and on the hotline.

Washington Sports Clubs 214 D St. SE (202) 547-2255 www.washingtonsports
.com

Now operating from 16 sites in Washington or nearby, the Washington Sports Clubs offer a wide range of exercise and fitness programs. Check out their Web site for locations, hours, and services. Operating for more than 27 years, some branches offer, as well, massage, steam rooms and saunas, Sports Clubs for Kids, and fitness assessments. Month to month memberships are available. Capitol Hill open Mon–Thurs 6 a.m.–11 p.m., Fri 6 a.m.–10 p.m., Sat–Sun 8:30 a.m.–8:30 p.m. Hours vary at other locations.

Washington Stage Guild Source Theatre, 1835 14th St. NW (240) 582-0050

This organization, presently using the Source Theatre for its productions, performs the classics including many a play by George Bernard Shaw.

Washington Statue *see* George Washington Statue.

Washington Studio School 4505 Stanford St., Chevy Chase, MD (301) 718-7210 www.washingtonstudioschool.org

This highly regarded school offers day and evening classes in drawing and painting for adults and older teens.

Washington Suites Hotel 100 Reynolds St. at Duke St., Alexandria, VA (703) 370-9600 www.washingtonsuiteshotel.com

Formerly the Doubletree Guest Quarters, this expensive hostelry offers 225 suites with fully equipped kitchens, a restaurant, outdoor pool, exercise room, and complimentary continental breakfast. It is a 5-minute drive from Old Town. Metro: Van Dorn, then phone hotel for free shuttle, which runs 6:30 a.m.–10:15 p.m. daily.

Washington Sun Newspaper 830 Kennedy St. NW (202) 882-1021

This small metropolitan weekly, published on Thursdays, provides a mix of national and community news and events.

Washington Symphony Orchestra Administration: 4200 Wisconsin Ave. NW #106-125 (703) 203-5325 www.washingtonsymphony.org Tickets: (202) 374-7474 or through the Web site

Founded in 1934 as the Washington Civic Symphony, it grew to 130 members by the late 1930s, usually performing at the DAR's Constitution Hall. World War II reduced the orchestra to performing concerts at Roosevelt High School. In 1964, budget cuts pushed the orchestra to recast itself to chamber size and was renamed the Baroque Arts Orchestra. In the 1970s, it changed its name to D.C. Community Orchestra, followed briefly in the 1990s to Washington Civic Symphony again, and in 1993 it adopted the title of "official symphony orchestra of Washington, D.C." and the name, Washington Symphony Orchestra. The orchestra's four-concert season runs from October to May, and during the renovations at Constitution Hall, it is performing at the Lincoln Theatre at 1215 U St. NW. Metro: U St.-Cardozo.

Washington Technology corporate offices of Post Newsweek Tech Media, 10 G St. NW (202) 772-2500 www.washingtontechnology.com

Published bimonthly since 1986, this free 40,000-circulation newspaper covers information technology (IT) in government, including new services, government initiatives, contracts, case studies, exhibits, information fairs, and training. Coverage also includes emerging technology, a calendar of events, IT and the law, doing business with various offices and departments, homeland defense, Capitol Hill, and company profiles. The Web site provides online access to the current and archived issues of the paper and links to related resources, Webcast access, and online chat transcripts. The publication sponsors several IT events each year. Metro: Union Station.

Washington Tennis and Education Foundation William H. G. Fitzgerald Tennis Center, 16th and Kennedy Sts. NW (202) 291-9888 www.wtef.org

This foundation partners with a number of organizations presenting tennis-related activities and offers a variety of after school and weekend tennis programs for children. Metro: McPherson Square, then S4 Bus.

Washington Tennis Center Rock Creek Park at 16th and Kennedy Sts. NW (202) 722-5949

This public tennis club is part of the Rock Creek recreational facility and is associated with the Washington Tennis and Educational Foundation and the William H. G. Fitzgerald Tennis Center. The Washington Tennis Center is known as well as the Rock Creek Tennis Center—the phone is answered either way. There are fifteen clay courts and ten lighted courts plus ten hard courts. Five courts are under a bubble. Open year-round 7 a.m. to 11 p.m. The next-door foundation offers a spectrum of programs for children. Moderate court rental fees. Metro: McPherson Square, then S4 Bus.

Washington Tennis Classic William H. G. Fitzgerald Tennis Center, 16th and Kennedy Sts. NW (202) 722-5949

Attracting top-ranked players, this showcase event is held annually the second week in August. Metro: McPherson Square, then S4 Bus.

Washington Theatre Festival Source Theatre, 1835 14th St. NW btw S and T Sts. (202) 462-1073 http://users.starpower.net/sourcetheatre

This award-winning event, almost 20 years old, annually showcases more than sixty new scripts in staged reading events, workshops, and 10-minute play competitions, running between mid-July and mid-August. The performances are spread at locations across the city, including the Source Theatre, as well as the Kennedy Center, the National Museum for Women in the Arts, and other venues. Metro: U St.-Cardozo, then a 2-block walk.

Washington Times 3600 New York Ave. NE (202) 636-3333 www.washtimes.com

The *Washington Times*, the other daily in Washington, celebrated its 20th birthday in 2002. It is owned by Reverend Sun Myung Moon's New World Communications, which has poured, to date, more than $1 billion into the paper to keep it afloat. In paying birthday respects to the *Times*, the *Washington Post* said "It is now a must-read for conservatives in town. Even many liberals have come to respect it for aggressive reporting and provocative editorials." Its daily circulation is about 110,000 and about half that on Sunday. Every Thursday, the paper issues its weekend insert. Metro: Brookland-CUA, then Metrobus H6 Ft. Lincoln/Brookland to 33rd Pl. and S Dakota Ave., and a 5-minute walk.

Washington University Inn *see* George Washington University Inn.

Washington Walks (202) 484-1565 www.washingtonwalks.com

Licensed, knowledgeable guides provide a spectrum of regularly scheduled Washington walks, rain or shine. No reservations are necessary, simply show up. Each walk lasts about 2 hours. Most walks embark from outside a Metro station. Moderate prices. Walks include Foggy Bottom, Embassy Row, Capital Hauntings, I've Got a Secret, the White House (from the outside), and the Washington Waterfront. Details and times are available on the Web site or by phone.

Washington Wizards MCI Center, 601 F St. NW (202) 661-5000 Tickets (202) 432-7328 www.nba.com/wizards

This National Basketball Association team moved into its new home, the MCI Center, and changed its name from the (non-PC) Bullets to the Wizards in 1997. The season, with or without Michael Jordan playing, runs November through April. Metro: Gallery Pl.-Chinatown.

Washington Woman 4701 Sangamore Rd. N-270, Bethesda, MD (301) 239-0247 www.washingtonwoman.com

Targeting women between 28 and 55, this free monthly newspaper hits all the hot topics: fashion, travel, home and garden, fitness, finance, food, and finance. A typical issue has articles on "Looking Your Best," "Eldercare Is Coming to a Generation Near You" and "Do It Yourself Design." Its calendar of events provides an astounding number of cultural events, meetings, and lectures. Some events are listed on the Web site. Fifty thousand copies of the magazine are distributed through libraries, Metro stops, and "800 other drops where women shop, live and work."

Washington Zoo *see* National Zoo.

Washingtonian Magazine 1828 L St. NW Editorial: (202) 296-3600 Subscriptions: (202) 331-0715 www.washingtonian.com

This glossy magazine tells what's happening, where to dine, and what to do. Besides its restaurant and gallery coverage and shots of celebrity homes, it provides profiles of Washington-based movers and shakers and absorbing feature stories. Its Web site tells you where you can park and ride into the city, and provides information on city tours, links to "dining that's real cheap and real good," "100 best restaurants," "100 bargain restaurants," "museum eating," "the ultimate museum guide," and the "best theater, music, dance, art, and special events" in the city. Metro: Farragut North, Farragut West.

Washington's Grist Mill Historical State Park 5514 Mt. Vernon Memorial Hwy., Alexandria, VA (703) 550-0960 www.dcr.state.va.us/parks/georgewa.htm

Located 3 miles west of Mount Vernon, George Washington's grist mill is powered by the waters of Dogue Run. Used for grinding wheat and corn into flour and meal, the mill passed through various owners and eventually fell into ruin. Restorers in the 1930s made use of machinery from another eighteenth-century mill. The mill is being renovated again and is not open to the public. By car take Mount

Vernon Hwy., Rte. 235, ¼ mile south from U.S. Hwy. 1, or 3 miles west of the Mount Vernon estate.

Water Events *see* Washington Boat Show.

Waterfront *see* Southwest Waterfront.

Watergate Virginia Ave. and 27th Sts. NW
   In 1972, this serpentine, walled riverfront complex was mostly posh apartments whose residents included, then and now, much of establishment Washington. Across the street on June 17, a break-in on the 6th floor of the (then) Howard Johnson Motor Lodge in the national offices of the headquarters of the Democratic National Committee was detected, and in the growing scandal President Richard Nixon resigned and more than thirty officials were convicted. The Watergate complex now includes the upscale Swissôtel Washington-The Watergate, some boutiques, and offices. Metro: Foggy Bottom.

Watergate Hotel *see* Swissôtel Washington-The Watergate.

Watergate Salon 2532 Virginia Ave. NW (202) 333-3488
   This shop pampers clients with hour-plus facials followed by manicures. Metro: Foggy Bottom.

Watergate Shops 2650 Virginia Ave. NW
   These high-ticket stores cater to the rich and famous living in the nearby apartments. Metro: Foggy Bottom.

The Watergate Swissôtel Washington *see* Swissôtel Washington–The Watergate.

Watkins Regional Park 301 Watkins Park Dr., Upper Marlboro, MD (301) 218-6700
   Explore this 850-acre wooded parkland through miles of hiking and biking trails. The park is also home to a nature center, an antique carousel, a farm, train rides, miniature golf, sports fields, indoor and outdoor tennis courts, a snack bar, campsites, playgrounds, and picnic facilities. Phone for hours or reservations. Driving directions: I-495/I-95 (the Beltway) to Exit 15 (Central Ave./Rte. 214) east. Proceed 4 miles to Watkins Park Dr. (Rte. 193), and turn right. Proceed 1 mile to park entrance.

Web sites about Washington, D.C. *see* City Paper, www.dcflamenco.com, D.C. Heritage Tourism Coalition, www.dcpages.com, www.dcregistry.com, District of Columbia Government, Georgetown DC, Mid-Atlantic Anarchists, Progressive Review, Salon, sc94.ameslab.gov, Slate, Legislative Information on the Internet, *Washington Families*, Washington Places, *Washington Post*, *Washingtonian Magazine*, White House, www.thecommondenominator.com, www.commuterpage.com and various entries under www).

Webster Statue *see* Daniel Webster Statue.

Weekend Camp *see* Smithsonian Associates.

West End Café Washington Circle Hotel, 1 Washington Circle (202) 293-5390
   A pleasant room decorated with photographer Yousuf Karsh's celebrity photos. A mix of cuisines from smoked salmon to pizza. Open for breakfast and pre- or

post-theater dining Mon–Fri 7 a.m.–10 a.m., 11:30 a.m.–2:30 p.m., 5:30 p.m.–10 p.m. Fri and Sat until 11 p.m. Sunday brunch. Metro: Foggy Bottom-GWU.

West Potomac Park Basin Dr. and Ohio Dr. off Independence Ave. NW

This area between the Potomac River and the Tidal Basin is home to 1,678 flowering Japanese cherry trees, a 1909 gift from Japan, and now the backdrop for the Jefferson Memorial, the D.C. War Memorial, and the recently completed Franklin Delano Roosevelt Memorial. Metro: Smithsonian, then a 15-minute walk.

Westfield Marriott 14750 Conference Center Dr., Chantilly, VA (703) 818-0300, fax (703) 818-3655 Reservations: (800) 635-5666

This 335-room hotel, located on 1,100 rolling acres, is a popular corporate retreat site, with its distraction-free environment and state-of-the-art technological capabilities, not to mention its elegant accommodations, business center, indoor heated pool, health club, tennis courts, and its Palm Court restaurant. Expensive. Seven miles from Dulles Airport. Metro: Vienna/Fairfax-GMU, and a 20-minute taxi ride or, with reservations, free hotel pickup daily from 5:30 a.m.–midnight.

Westfield Shoppingtown Montgomery Mall 7101 Democracy Blvd., Bethesda, MD www.westfield.com

This mall includes almost 200 specialty stores, P&G movie theaters, a food court, and three restaurants including Legal Seafood. Not only does it encourage senior mall walkers, it provides free senior movie mornings. Metro: Medical Center, then J1, J2, or J3 Bus. *See also* www.commuterpage.com/venues/venue-shop .htm.

Westfield Shoppingtown Wheaton 11160 Viers Mill Rd., Wheaton, MD (301) 942-3200

Formerly called Wheaton Plaza, the major attractions at this mall are the more than 130 specialty stores, a food court, five restaurants, and an 11-screen movie theater. Metro: Silver Spring, then Q2, Y8, or Y6 Bus.

Westin Fairfax 2100 Massachusetts Ave. NW (202) 293-2100, fax (202) 466-9867

This Embassy Row landmark opened in 1924 as an apartment building, purchased in 1937 by Senator Albert Gore and, thus, the childhood residence of former Vice President Al Gore. Formerly the Ritz Carlton, the hotel is the home of the famous Jockey Club, as well as one of Washington's coziest watering spots, the Fairfax Bar, with its working fireplace. The hotel's 206 well-appointed rooms were renovated in 1990. In-room data ports, in-room safes, minibars, 24-hour room service, sauna, exercise room. Expensive. Metro: Dupont Circle.

Westin Grand Hotel 2350 M St. NW (202) 429-0100 www.westin.com

This 263-room hotel located between 23rd and 24th Streets is within easy walking distance of Georgetown and the Kennedy Center. It was designed in 1984 by Skidmore, Owings and Merrill and recently renovated. Known for its large guestrooms and marble bathrooms, there is also a fitness center, a heated outdoor pool, and a variety of dining choices. Middle Range. Metro: Foggy Bottom.

The Wharf 119 King St., Old Town Alexandria, VA (703) 836-2836 www.wharf restaurant.com

The restaurant building was built around 1800, and transformed in 1970 from a feed and grain warehouse to a restaurant. You can still see some of the original beams. Try the Maryland-style crab soup or the steamed littleneck clams bordelaise at this casual seafood restaurant. Open daily for lunch and dinner. Moderate prices. Metro: Braddock Rd., then take 10B Hunting Towers bus to Washington and King Sts.

Wheat Row 1315–1321 4th St. SW

This row of federal-era townhouses is one of the best examples of Federal style in the District. They were built in 1794 on four of the original 3,000 lots President Washington's administration thankfully unloaded onto speculator James Greenleaf, who shelled out $66.50 each for the lots and then built Wheat Row. John Wheat was the resident of number 1315. Metro: Waterfront-SEU.

Wheaton Montgomery County, MD

This residential area with its moderately priced homes is named after General (and John Barrymore look-alike) Frank Wheaton, who saw service on the Indian frontier, and commanded the Union troops in the Modoc Indian war, not to mention fighting against his high-ranking father-in-law in the Civil War. This diverse community hosts many ethnic restaurants, small shops, and the Wheaton Plaza Shopping Mall. Metro: Wheaton.

Wheaton Farmers Market Blue Ridge Rd. and Elkins St., Wheaton, MD (301) 217-8122

This open air seasonal market appears every Sunday from mid-June through late October one block off Georgia Ave. Open 8 a.m. to 1 p.m. Metro: Wheaton.

Wheaton Park Stables 1101 Glenallan Ave., Wheaton, MD (301) 622-2424 www.wheatonparkstables.com

This Montgomery County stable offers horseback riding for the whole family, from newcomers to advanced riders. All lessons and trail rides are done in the English style of riding. Children must be at least 8 years old to ride. Open Sun 8 a.m.–4 p.m., Mon–Tues 9 a.m.–8 p.m., Wed–Fri 9 a.m.–9 p.m., Sat 8 a.m.–5 p.m. Directions: From the Beltway (I-495) get off at Exit 31A, take Georgia Ave. N toward Wheaton, right on Glenallan Ave.

Wheaton Plaza Westfield Shoppingtown *See* Westfield Shoppingtown Wheaton.

Wheaton Regional Park 2000 Shorefield Rd., Wheaton, MD (301) 746-7033 www.mc-mcppc.org

This Montgomery County park includes picnic areas, play structures with bridges for climbing, giant slide tunnels, an enormous climb-through sand castle, a carousel, a miniature riding train, sports fields, hiking and biking trails, a 5-acre stocked lake for fishing, an ice-skating rink (open October through March), and an adjacent nature center. Open daily dawn to dusk. Closed Thanksgiving, Christmas, and New Year's Day. By car North Capitol St. becomes Blair Rd., right on U.S. 29 Georgia Ave., which becomes MD-97, right onto Shorefield Rd.

White Flint Mall 11301 Rockville Pike, North Bethesda, MD (301) 231-7467

This 800,000-square-foot, enclosed mall has free shuttle service from the nearby

Metro stop. Stores include Bloomingdale's, Borders Books & Music, Gap, Banana Republic, Lord & Taylor, and about 125 other stores and restaurants including a food court and a 5-screen theater complex. The mall was built in 1977 with a 60,000-square-foot Dave and Buster's food and entertainment center added in 1996. By car take Wisconsin Ave. north, which becomes Rockville Pike. White Flint is about 1½ miles after you cross under the Beltway (I-495). Metro: White Flint. *See also* www.commuterpage.com/venues/venue-shop.htm.

White House 1600 Pennsylvania Ave. NW (202) 456-7041 www.whitehouse.gov
This fine example of eighteenth-century British colonial architecture was designed by Irish immigrant, and Yank artillery captain, James Hoban, who also supervised the construction. George Washington and Hoban laid the cornerstone on September 13, 1793. President John Adams moved into the almost completed mansion on November 1, 1800, and all presidents since then have lived there. British troops sacked and burned it in 1814. Hoban, working on the Capitol, supervised its reconstruction, lasting until 1829. It was gutted and rebuilt in the 1950s, with President Truman moving across the street to Blair House. Since September 11, 2001, only "organized veteran groups" and school groups are allowed visits. City designer Pierre L'Enfant selected the site in his original planning document for the city. See the Virtual Tour of the White House and the White House for Kids on the Web site, both well done. Metro: McPherson Square.

White House Easter Egg Roll The White House, 1600 Pennsylvania Ave. NW, South Lawn (202) 456-7041 www.whitehouse.gov/history/tours/special_events.html
This annual event originally took place on the Capitol grounds but was moved to the White House grounds in 1878 by President Rutherford B. Hayes. Rolling a hard-boiled egg across the lawn is still the main event in a program that includes Cabinet members, musicians, celebrities, and the official White House Easter Bunny. Tickets are now required for this event that takes place on the Ellipse and the South Lawn of the White House. It is planned for children 6 and under. Metro: McPherson Square.

White House Fall House and Garden Tour White House, 1600 Pennsylvania Ave. NW, Ellipse (202) 456-7041 www.whitehouse.gov/history/tours/special_events .html
The tour, held in October and open to the public, includes the Jacqueline Kennedy Garden, the Rose Garden, and the Children's Garden on the White House grounds. Military bands perform on the balcony. A ticket is required for all attendees, including children. They are distributed free by the National Park Service at the White House Visitor Center located at 15th and E Sts. Check the Web site or phone for details. Metro: McPherson Square.

White House Nannies, Inc. 7200 Wisconsin Ave. NW, Suite 409, Bethesda, MD (301) 654-1242, and 332 Commerce St., Alexandria, VA (703) 838-2100 www.white housenannies.com
Founded in 1985, this organization provides full-time, temporary, and emergency child care. See Web site for an application.

White House Spring Garden and Grounds Tour White House, 1600 Pennsylvania Ave. NW, Ellipse (202) 456-7041 www.whitehouse.gov/history/tours/special_events .html

The event, held in April, is open to the public and includes the Jacqueline Kennedy Garden, the Rose Garden, and the Children's Garden on the White House grounds. Military bands perform on the balcony. A ticket is required for all attendees, including children. They are distributed free by the National Park Service at the White House Visitor Center located at 15th and E Sts. Check the Web site or phone for details. Metro: McPherson Square.

White House Visitors Center 1450 Pennsylvania Ave. NW (202) 208-1631 www .whitehouse.gov

This small exhibit space, maintained by the National Park Service, is formerly where visitors picked up tickets to tour the White House. Currently, White House tours are restricted to veterans groups and school groups. The center has a gift shop operated by the White House Historical Center. Metro: McPherson Square.

White House (Web site) www.whitehouse.gov

Provides Executive Office talking points on issues, news from the White House by month, briefings (updated daily), letters, pictures, a kid's page, the President's Cabinet (with background information on each secretary), and a history of the White House including a virtual tour and a schematic diagram of the building. Metro: McPherson Square.

White-Meyer House 1624 Crescent Pl. NW (202) 667-6800 www.meridian.org

John Russell Pope, who designed the Jefferson Memorial, the National Archives, and the National Gallery of Art, designed this mansion. Eugene Meyer, owner of the *Washington Post*, purchased it in 1910 from diplomat Henry White, and in 1934 the *Post*'s later owner, Katharine Graham, grew up in the house. In 1987 it was purchased by Meridian International Center. Metro: Dupont Circle, then a 25-minute walk.

White's Ferry 24801 White's Ferry Rd., Dickerson, MD (301) 349-5200

About 30 miles from Washington, this is the only ferry still operating on the Potomac River. It runs daily 5 a.m. to 11 p.m., unless high water or ice shuts it down. Moderate fees for cars and pedestrians. The Maryland side provides picnic benches, canoe and boat rentals, and remnants of the C&O Canal.

Whitehurst Freeway

This elevated roadway blocking the sun from K Street strollers in Georgetown was completed in 1947. Its designer was Archibald Alphoso Alexander, the first Republican territorial governor of the U.S. Virgin Islands.

Whitey's 2761 Washington Blvd., Arlington, VA (703) 525-9825

This neighborhood restaurant and watering hole provides good eats, neighborhood tavern friendliness, and becomes a blues and jazz roadhouse on weekends. Open for inexpensive breakfasts, followed by home-style dinners or sandwiches and bar food. Open Mon–Wed 11 a.m.–midnight, Thurs–Fri 11 a.m.–2 a.m., Sat 8 a.m.–2 a.m. Moderate cover charge. Metro: Rosslyn, then transfer to Metrobus 4B, exit at N Pershing Dr. and Washington Blvd.

Whitney M. Young Jr. Memorial Bridge East Capitol St. over the Anacostia River
Formerly known as the East Capitol Street Bridge, this low-lying steel plate girder structure spanning the Anacostia River was completed in 1955. Metro: Stadium-Armory.

Wilderness Society 900 17th St. NW (202) 833-2300
The society maintains a remarkable collection of more than seventy Ansel Adams photographs on permanent display in its gallery. Open 9 a.m.–5 p.m. weekdays. Metro: Farragut West.

Wilkins House *See* Peru Embassy.

Willard Inter-Continental Hotel 1401 Pennsylvania Ave. NW (202) 628-9100, fax (202) 637- 7326 http://washington.interconti.com
The current building, designed by Henry Janeway Hardenbergh, dates from 1901 and was renovated in 1986. It offers 341 rooms, the Willard Room Restaurant, Café 1401, the Round Robin Bar, and a business and fitness center. It is located in the heart of Washington, just 2 blocks from the White House, and it was here that Martin Luther King Jr. drafted his "I Have a Dream" speech. An earlier building that stood on the site claims such guests as Ulysses S. Grant, Abraham Lincoln, and Julia Ward Howe. Expensive. Metro: Metro Center.

Willard Room Willard Inter-Continental Hotel, 1401 Pennsylvania Ave. NW (202) 637-7440
This elaborate reproduction of a turn-of-the-century grand dining salon features high ceilings, oak-paneled walls, sparkling chandeliers, and a rich cuisine of seafood, steak, game, and pasta. Breakfast, lunch, dinner. Reservations suggested. Mon–Fri 7:30 a.m.–10 a.m., 11:30 a.m.–2 p.m., 6 p.m.–10 p.m., Sat 6 p.m.–10 p.m. Closed Sun. Metro: Metro Center.

William H. G. Fitzgerald Tennis Center *see* Washington Tennis Center.

William Henry Scheutze Memorial
This statue titled *Serenity* is found in the northwest corner of Meridian Hill (Malcolm X) Park. It celebrates the memory of Lt. Col. William Henry Scheutze, the navigator of the USS *Iowa* during the Spanish-American War and who also fought at the battle of Santiago. The park is located on Connecticut Ave. between 15th and 16th Sts. NW with Euclid St. on its north end. It is easiest to get there by taking Bus S2 or Bus S4 along 16th St.

William Howard Taft Bridge *see* Taft Bridge.

William O. Douglas Statue *see* Justice William O. Douglas Statue.

William Petersen House *see* Petersen House.

William Shakespeare's Birthday at the Folger Shakespeare Library, 201 E Capitol St. SE (202) 544-4600
This annual mid-April birthday celebration, for both kids and adults, features jugglers, staged combat demonstrations, actors, music, food, children's events, special exhibits, and provides a chance to gain access to the Reading Room and its

treasures, usually open only to scholars and graduate students. Metro: Union Station.

William Tecumseh Sherman Monument 15th St., Pennsylvania Ave., and Treasure Pl. NW www.nps.gov/whho/statues/sherman.htm

This elaborate monument to the major general commanding the Union "Army of Tennessee" (whose vets contributed to its construction) was dedicated in 1903 by President Theodore Roosevelt. It consists of a bronze equestrian statue atop a marble platform upon which are mounted various scenarios and brass medallions of subordinate generals to Sherman. The site is supposedly where Sherman stood, reviewing his Union troops returning from their march through Georgia. Most bizarre is the group titled War, showing a woman with her hands bound standing on a dead soldier, while vultures feed on his body. A bronze soldier guards each corner of the monument. The work is by sculptor Carl Rohl-Smith, who died during its execution, and was thus completed by a "group of Danish sculptors."

Wilson House *see* Woodrow Wilson House.

Wilson Memorial Bridge *see* Woodrow Wilson Memorial Bridge.

Windsor Inn 1842 16th St. NW (202) 667-0300 or (800) 423-9111, fax (202) 667-4503

This small hotel offers 45 rooms, some of which are spacious suites. It was built in 1922 as an apartment building and first emerged as a hotel in 1929. The present owners bought the property in 1986 and have renovated it. It offers a complimentary "expanded continental breakfast" and evening coffee, sherry, and snacks served in the lobby. Inexpensive. Metro: McPherson Square, then a 12-block walk, or take Metrobus S2, exiting at 16th and Swann Sts. NW.

Windsor Park Hotel 2116 Kalorama Rd. NW (202) 483-7700 or (800) 247-3064, fax (202) 332-4547 www.windsorparkhotel.com

This 43-room hotel just off Connecticut Ave., calling itself a "bed-and-breakfast" hotel, provides a free continental breakfast buffet. Rooms are clean with Queen Anne and Chippendale-style furnishings, and all come with a minibar, the usual amenities, direct-dial phones, voice mail, and modem-ready jacks. Inexpensive and close to Adams Morgan night life and the National Zoo. Metro: Woodley Park-Zoo, then a 15-minute walk.

Winfield Scott Statue 2nd and Upshur Sts. NW

This is one of two statues in the District of Lt. Gen. Winfield B. Scott, who in his career served every president from Jefferson to Lincoln, was instrumental in ending two wars, helped to keep the country from involvement in others, and founded the nearby Soldiers' and Airmen's Home using $100,000 of ransom money received from General Santa Ana during the Mexican War. This bronze statue, executed in 1873, was sculpted by Launt Thompson. Metro: Fort Totten, then Metrobus 60.

Winfield Scott Statue Scott Circle (Massachusetts Ave., Rhode Island Ave., and 16th St. NW)

This equestrian statue of a portly Gen. Winfield B. Scott—he was tall as well, 6 foot 5—is by Henry Kirke Brown and was erected in 1874. Scott's descendents took issue with his mount, forcing the sculptor to transform the animal from a mare to a more fitting stallion: never mind that the general preferred riding mares. He led the U.S. Army in its victory against Mexico in 1848, and in 1852 ran unsuccessfully for president against Franklin Pierce. Metro: Farragut North, then a 10-minute walk.

Winfield Scott Hancock Statue 7th St. and Pennsylvania Ave. NW

This bronze equestrian statue mounted on a red granite base honors Maj. Gen. Winfield Scott Hancock, whose tactical sense as well as what Gen. Ulysses Grant termed his "personal courage and his presence with his command" was responsible for holding firm the center of the Union line against Gen. George Pickett during the Battle of Gettysburg. He was the Democratic Party candidate for president in 1880; Garfield won in a close election. Sculpted by Henry Jackson Ellicott and erected in 1898. Metro: Gallery Pl.-Chinatown.

Winston Churchill Statue *see* Sir Winston Churchill Statue.

Wisconsin Avenue Bridge Wisconsin Ave. btw Grace and Canal Sts.

Of the many bridges in Georgetown over the C&O Canal, all but the Wisconsin Ave. span were destroyed in the 1860s to allow a wider canal clearance. This low arched Aquia Creek sandstone structure was completed in 1831. Metro: Foggy Bottom-GWU, then a 15-minute walk.

Witherspoon Statue Connecticut Ave. and N St. NW

This bronze sculpture of John Witherspoon, erected in 1909, is the work of sculptor William Couper. Witherspoon, the only clergyman to sign the Declaration of Independence, was an active man: a member of Congress, president of what is now Princeton University, and at 68 married a 24-year-old widow. Two daughters followed. Metro: Dupont Circle.

Wolf Trap Farm Park for the Performing Arts 1551 Trap Rd., Vienna, VA (703) 255-1860 www.wolftrap.org

More than 500,000 people a year enjoy opera, symphony, dance, jazz, musicals, country, folk, traveling bands, and blues performers in America's only national park devoted to the performing arts. The striking Filene Center operating late May to early September seats about 3,500 people under cover with another 3,000 seated on the sloping lawn looking down on the stage. You may picnic on the lawn, and food is available for purchase. Nearby, the "Barns of Wolf Trap"—renovated eighteenth-century barns—provide a weatherproof year-round center for the performing arts and educational programs. Some performances are filmed for Web casting for on-demand viewing from the Web site. Every summer, Wolf Trap presents a series of performances for children 3 and up that includes storytelling, mimes, puppetry, and dance performances at the open-air Theater-in-the-Woods at (703) 255-1800 or www.nps.gov/wotr/titw.html. Tickets are required. Workshops-in-the-Arts provides free workshops giving children 5 and older hands-on experiences in puppetry, music, dance, and creative drama. Workshop reservations at (703) 255-1824. Parents and teachers should check out a by-product of the workshop programs:

Artsplay Online (www.artsplay.org), an interactive resource with examples of artist-developed activities and other resources. Tickets at (703) 218-6500 or online or in person at the Wolf Trap box office, which is open Mon–Fri 10 a.m.–6 p.m., Sat–Sun and holidays noon–6 p.m., and performance nights until 9 p.m. Metro: West Falls Church. On Filene Center performance nights Metro operates a shuttle service from the Metro station running every 20 minutes starting 2 hours before each performance. The last shuttle leaves the station at show time. Round-trip fare is $4 per person (exact change required). The shuttle bus is wheelchair accessible. The shuttle departs Wolf Trap 20 minutes after the performance ends (no later than 11 p.m. Sun–Thurs). The last train for downtown leaves the West Falls Church station at 11:32 p.m. Sun–Thurs, and at 1:32 a.m. Fri and Sat. By car take I-66 W to Exit 20, turn right on Rte. 267 (a toll road). The second exit after the toll is the Wolf Trap parking lot. *See also* www.commuterpage.com/venues/venue-en.htm.

Women in Military Service for America Memorial Main Entrance, Arlington National Cemetery, Arlington, VA (703) 892-2606 (800) 222–2284 www.womens memorial.org

The memorial opened in 1997, making use of a 1932 granite-faced curved wall at the ceremonial entrance to the main gate. There is also a fountain and reflecting pool. Inside the exhibit area alcoves provide displays of women's contributions to the military from the Revolutionary War to the present day. Film showings and seminars are held in the small theater at the site. A database provides military histories of more than 130,000 registered servicewomen. Metro: Arlington Cemetery. *See also* www.commuterpage.com/venues/memorials.htm.

The Women's Center 133 Park St., Vienna, VA (703) 281-2657 www.thewomens center.org

Operating from sites throughout the Washington area for more than 20 years, the nonprofit Women's Center has been providing an array of personal, professional, legal, and financial services to women and their families. One-day to several-week workshops are offered either at the Georgetown University Women's Center; the Centreville, Virginia, site; or other locations. The Center's Information and Career Advisory Net (ICAN) provides career counseling. Services, special events, forthcoming courses, hyperlinks to helpful sites related to careers, finance, health, and women's issues, as well as information on the annual leadership conference may be found on the Web site. Open Mon–Thurs 9 a.m.–8 p.m., Fri 9 a.m.–5 p.m., Sat 9 a.m.–4 p.m. Metro: Vienna/Fairfax-GMU.

Women's Information Network 1800 R St. NW, Suite C-4 (202) 347-2827 www .winonline.org

Self-described as an "all-volunteer organization for young, pro-choice, Democratic women in the Washington D.C. metropolitan area" it offers monthly programs related mostly to career development and an online job bank where members may post jobs and search job postings. Metro: Dupont Circle.

Women's National Democratic Club Whittemore House, 1526 New Hampshire Ave. NW (202) 232-7363

Architect Harvey Page built this turreted brick mansion in 1892 for socialite Sarah Adams Whittemore, cousin of historian Henry Adams. Later John C. Weeks moved here. He served as congressman, senator, and secretary of war under Presidents Warren Harding and Calvin Coolidge. In 1927 it was purchased by the WNDC. A self-guided tour booklet allows visitors to learn more about the handsome and historic objects as well as the presidents, first ladies, and notables of all kinds who have participated in the group's forums and programs. There are twice-weekly speaker luncheons and "Ambassadorial Evenings," public policy seminars, and a variety of programs for members. Both men and women are eligible. Open Mon, Wed, Fri 9 a.m.–2 p.m.; Tues and Thurs 2 p.m.–5 p.m.

Women's Services in Washington, D.C. *see* Commission for Women Counseling and Career Center, National Organization for Women, Women's Center, Women's Information Network.

Women's Titanic Memorial *see* Titanic Memorial.

Woo Lae Oak 1500 South Joyce St., Arlington, VA (703) 521-3706
With a décor of traditional rice-paper panels and each table with its own barbecue grill, this well-established local favorite provides consistently highly ranked Korean food and service. Try the spicy beef stew or *gun man doo*, fried pork dumplings, or make use of the grill on your table and savor the boneless short ribs or spicy pork. Metro: Pentagon City.

Woodbridge Flute Choir (703) 244-6732 www.pwcweb.com/woodbridgeflutechoir
This flute ensemble, founded in 1996, performs at flute festivals, various charitable events, and in a concert series. It is the largest ensemble of its type in northern Virginia. The group has appeared at the Kennedy Center and the White House.

Woodend 8940 Jones Mill Rd., Chevy Chase, MD (301) 652-8107
Architect Russell Pope built this Georgian Revival mansion in the 1920s on a 40-acre estate, whose pedigree dates to a 1699 colonial land grant. Since 1967 it has served as the national headquarters of the Audubon Naturalist Society and as a venue for weddings, receptions, an annual nature fair, and the Audubon holiday nature crafts fair. A bookshop (301) 652-3606 features environmental and natural history books and bird feeders. In the mansion are several original Audubon prints. Open 9 a.m.–5 p.m. weekdays. By car from Connecticut Ave., turn left on Manor Rd., right on Jones Bridge Rd., and left on Jones Mill Rd. *See also* www.commuter page.com/venues/gardens.htm.

Woodlands 8046 New Hampshire Ave., Langley Park, MD (301) 434-4202; 18216 Contour Rd., Gaithersburg, MD (301) 963-4466; 4078 Germantown Rd., Fairfax, VA (703) 385-1996
These no-frills restaurants found amid suburban malls serve a single purpose: to provide authentic, pure vegetarian, southern Indian cuisine. They are hugely popular with the local Indian community, certifying their authenticity. Try their many delightful eggplant dishes, or a savory *Mysore masala dosa*, thin rice crepes with a layer of hot chutney filled with potatoes and onions. Lunch buffet until 3 p.m. Inexpensive. Sun–Thurs 11:30 a.m.–9:30 p.m., Fri–Sat 11:30 a.m. to 10 p.m.

Woodlawn Cemetery 4611 Benning Rd. NE

Established in 1885, this is one of the few predominantly black cemeteries in Washington. In the 1990s it was added to the District of Columbia's Register of Historic Sites and the National Register of Historic Places. Notable internments include Senator Blanche K. Bruce, James F. Bundy, W. Bruce Evans, and John Mercer Langdon. It is not regularly open to the public. Metro: Benning Road.

Woodlawn Plantation 9000 Richmond Highway at Mount Vernon Memorial Pkwy., Mount Vernon, VA (703) 780-4000 www.nationaltrust.org

This lovely Georgian estate, now the property of the National Trust for Historic Preservation, is much less frequented than Mount Vernon even though it is equally impressive and only 3 miles from Mount Vernon. Some of the house furnishings are original pieces. The house sits on 2,000 acres, which visitors can wander about to view the lovely lawns and gardens. On the same estate is the Pope-Leighey House built by Frank Lloyd Wright (*see* Frank Lloyd Wright Pope-Leighey House). Woodlawn is open daily 10 a.m.–5 p.m., and there are guided tours with the last one starting at 4:30 p.m. Admission charge. By car take the George Washington Memorial Pkwy. to Mount Vernon, continue 3 miles west on Rte. 235 to the signs for Woodlawn. *See also* www.commuterpage.com/venues/sightseeing_VA.htm.

Woodley Park Historic District north along Connecticut Ave. from Calvert St. NW and Rock Creek Park

A streetcar line inaugurated in 1892 contributed to the development of this area where "summer homes" were built. Now, besides the many stately homes, the area boasts the National Zoo, several large hotels, a number of restaurants, and sidewalk cafés near the Metro stop. Metro: Woodley Park-Zoo.

Woodrow Wilson House 2340 S St. NW (202) 387-4062 www.woodrowwilson house.com

Designed in 1915 by Waddy B. Wood, who also designed the Department of the Interior and the building now occupied by the National Museum of Women in the Arts, this brick Georgian Revival townhouse was the post-presidential residence of Woodrow Wilson, the 28th president. Wilson lived here upon completion of his second term in office in 1921 until his death in 1924. His second wife, Edith, continued to live here until her death in 1961, when the house and its furnishings became a museum, the only museum of a former president in Washington. There is a 45-minute tour and a 25-minute video about Wilson. Special topical tours and school programs with curricular guides are available. Check the Web site. Modest fee. Open Tues–Sun, 10 a.m.–4 p.m. Closed federal holidays, Thanksgiving Day, Christmas Day, and New Year's Day. Metro: Dupont Circle, then a 5-block walk. *See also* www.commuterpage.com/venues/museums.htm.

Woodrow Wilson Memorial Bridge crosses the Potomac River on I-495 (the Beltway) www.wilsonbridge.com

Over a mile long, the structure cuts across the Potomac to Maryland from Alexandria, Virginia. Opened in 1961, it has deteriorated from the constant pounding of heavy traffic, and its replacement is under way. Its drawspan's occasional openings often back up traffic for a mile or more on this heavily traveled north–south route.

Woodward Apartments 2311 Connecticut Ave. NW (202) 232-2312

This Spanish Colonial–style apartment building constructed in 1913 by the owner of Washington's first department store, S. Walter Woodward, was converted to condos in 1973. The firm of Harding and Upman designed it. Not open to the public. Metro: Woodley Park-Zoo.

Woolly Mammoth Theater Company Administration: 917 M St. Temporary Theater: AFI Theater, Kennedy Center, 2700 F St. NW (202) 393-3939 www.woolly mammoth.net

What the *New York Times* calls "Washington's most daring theater company," now in its 20s, has a national reputation for its development of new plays. A new 250-seat theater is being built at its former site, 7th and D Sts. NW. Until 2005 the troupe is performing at the Kennedy Center and other area venues. Woolly Mammoth's outreach programs provide workshops and performances in neighborhoods and schools throughout Washington, and it also offers a variety of acting classes. Metro: Foggy Bottom-GWU, then a 10-minute walk. *See also* www.com muterpage.com/venues/venue-en.htm.

World War II Memorial off Henry Bacon Dr. and 23rd St. NW (800) 639-4992 www.wwiimemorial.com

This monument of raised granite slabs denoting epochal events during the conflict is dedicated to all who served in the U.S. Armed Forces and Merchant Marine during World War II and acknowledges the commitment and achievement of the entire nation. Its location at the east end of the Reflecting Pool between the Lincoln Memorial and the Washington Monument has caused controversy. Designed by Friedrich St. Florian, it was dedicated by President Bill Clinton in 1995 and is scheduled for completion in 2004. Metro: Smithsonian.

World Wide Web Sites about Washington D.C. *see* Web Sites about Washington D.C.

World's Largest Chair V St. and Martin Luther King Jr. Ave. SE www.roadsideam erica.com

Well, maybe not the largest any more, but it is 19½ feet tall and made of solid mahogany. Built in 1939 by the Bassett Furniture Co. to honor the long-gone Curtis Brothers furniture company, it now stands on a plot of land maintained by the Anacostia Garden Club. Metro: Anacostia, then Metrobus U2 to Martin Luther King Jr. Ave. and W St. Walk north to V St.

The Writer's Center 4508 Walsh St., Bethesda, MD (301) 654-8664 www.writer .org

For more than 25 years, this dynamic nonprofit has been an epicenter of literary activities in Bethesda. Recently, it has expanded its role with programs in nearby areas (see the Web site for venues). Its membership of more than 2,200 writers, editors, small-press publishers, and graphic artists celebrate the creation, distribution, and enjoyment of literature and the graphic arts through a stuffed in-basket of programs: workshops, publications, readings, visiting writers, staged readings, conferences, and an annual book fair. Also, there is a storytelling theater, "conversations about ideas" of interest to writers by authors of new nonfiction books, plays in progress, film showings, an improv theater, a gallery of local literary magazines, a newsletter, and on and on. Many events are free. Modest membership fee. Metro: Bethesda.

www.thecommondenominator.com (Web site)

This Web site, published by the biweekly *Common Denominator* newspaper, offers excellent D.C. public affairs coverage, as well as coverage of neighborhoods and wards, the local labor scene, and allows archival access to the past year's stories from the organization's biweekly newspaper. Its elections page provides, in cooperation with the League of Women Voters, online transcripts of local candidate forums as well as election-related stories. Also useful are the public events column, common interests forum, and the classified section in the print version. *See also The Common Denominator.*

www.commuterpage.com (Web site)

This prize-winning site offers a delightful array of services facilitating your leaving the car at home and increasing your reliance on public transportation in the metropolitan Washington area. It provides, as well, links to related sites. This site includes traffic, transit, and commuting information. Sports, entertainment, shopping, museums, galleries, sightseeing destinations are all annotated with detailed public transportation directions. You are told which rail line to take, which station, which exit, which bus, and then you get detailed walking directions to your destination. You may buy transit fares on the site. It discusses using taxis, resources for hikers and bikers, resources for out-of-town visitors, and offers transportation news and online maps and guides. Commuter services include a "ride home program," current schedules, timetables and route maps, information for disabled and senior services, and current traffic conditions. You can learn about telecommuting, commuter rail, air quality concerns, car/van pools, electric vehicles, local commuter buses, and transportation advocacy groups. Links are offered to Metro's Ride Guide, for finding point-to-point directions from wherever you are to wherever you want to go using Metro bus and rail. The site is complex and it's sometimes difficult to find all the information it contains, but the following specific addresses should get you on your way.

www.commuterpage.com/venues/gardens.htm

This section of commuterpage.com provides profiles of seventeen parks and gardens in the metropolitan Washington area and detailed directions to them by public transportation.

www.commuterpage.com/venues/memorials.htm

This section of commuterpage.com provides profiles of thirteen memorials and monuments in D.C. and detailed directions to them by public transportation.

www.commuterpage.com/venues/museums.htm

This section of commuterpage.com provides profiles of twenty-six museums in the Washington area, with detailed directions to them using public transportation.

www.commuterpage.com/venues/museums-si.htm

This section of commuterpage.com provides profiles of sixteen Smithsonian Institution museums and detailed directions to them by public transportation.

www.commuterpage.com/venues/sightseeing_VA.htm

This section of commuterpage.com provides profiles of forty-three historic sites, museums, and galleries in Virginia and detailed directions to them by public transportation.

www.commuterpage.com/venues/venue-en.htm

This section of commuterpage.com provides profiles of thirty-five theaters and other entertainment sites in the metropolitan Washington area, and detailed directions to them by public transportation.

www.commuterpage.com/venues/venue-shop.htm

This section of commuterpage.com provides profiles of thirty-two D.C. area shopping malls including Potomac Mills and detailed directions to them by public transportation.

www.commuterpage.com/venues/venue-sp.htm

This section of commuterpage.com provides profiles of twelve sports arenas, including local college stadiums, FedEx Field, MCI Center, Oriole Park at Camden Yards, PSINET Stadium, and RFK Memorial Stadium. Detailed directions to them by public transportation are provided.

www.frommers.com

Once you locate Washington, D.C., in this worldwide interactive guide, you can find useful and delightfully subjective suggestions on where to find the best business lunch, the best American or Chinese meal in the city, the bar scene, accommodations ranked by cost or location or "best bets," attractions especially for kids, suggested itineraries, "active pursuit" suggestions, and walking tours. Particularly noteworthy is the "favorite experiences" section pinpointing memorable activities. There are also helpful downloadable maps of the city keyed to this guide's recommendations.

www.hostels.com

This site provides listings of hostel accommodations throughout the world, including ten in the metropolitan Washington area. Rooms are usually dormitory style, and facilities are shared with other guests. Families and persons of all ages who travel inexpensively make use of hostels. The site offers useful information about hostelling under FAQs.

www.opentable.com

This unique site provides a listing of hundreds of restaurants in the metropolitan Washington area, includes hours, a short summary of the restaurant, links to further reviews, and pull-down windows allowing you to locate a restaurant by cuisine, price range, neighborhood, cost, or all of the above. Once you find a restaurant, a simple online process allows you to book a table online day or night. If no table is available, the site suggests an alternative time. Weak in suburban listings but useful for locating downtown D.C. restaurants.

www.shop.viator.com

This site allows you to locate under Washington, D.C., or other major cities, a summary of most of the sightseeing tour offerings, with details, prices, and booking information. It also lists the various airport shuttle services and their costs.

www.smokefreeworld.com

This site allows you to find listings by city of smoke-free restaurants. There are about two dozen listings for smoke-free D.C. restaurants, with the various suburban cities adding to that count. The listed restaurants carry varying amounts of information about the cuisine, hours, et cetera. There are links to other smoke-free venues, for example, dance, jazz.

www.trails.com

This site provides overviews of the Washington area, as well as other North American locations, on hiking and walking trails, campgrounds, biking paths, mountain bike trails, canoe sites, and related information. Once you find an interesting trail (for example, a 9-mile bike trail past monuments on the Mall), you can purchase more detailed information that you download from the Web.

www.zagat.com

Besides the annual *Zagat Survey* publication of Washington, D.C., and Baltimore restaurants, there is also a Web site, allowing you to locate local restaurants by seventy categories of cuisine from Afghan to Vietnamese. It also lists new restaurants, locates restaurants by neighborhood, and ranks them by several criteria. However, without subscribing (about $15) all you get from your customized search is the address and phone number of the restaurant you have located and a chance to participate in the surveys.

Wyndham Bristol Hotel 2430 Pennsylvania Ave. NW (202) 955-6400, fax (202) 955-5765 www.wyndham.com

Close to Georgetown, this 8-floor 239-room hotel offers a fitness center, room service, parking, restaurants, safety deposit service, and complimentary newspapers. All rooms have hair dryers and coffee machines. Moderate prices. Metro: Foggy Bottom-GMU.

Wyndham City Center 1143 New Hampshire Ave. NW (202) 775-0800 www .wyndham.com/CityCenter

This 352-room, 16-suite hotel, formerly the Sheraton City Centre, is located at M St. and New Hampshire Ave., a few blocks from three Metro stops in the central part of Washington. Rooms provide a work desk and besides the usual amenities, the hotel offers a restaurant, lounge, and a health club. Mid-range prices. Metro: Foggy Bottom-GWU.

Wyndham Washington Hotel 1400 M St. NW (202) 429-1700 www.wyndham .com/Washington_DC/

Formerly the Washington Vista as well as the Westin Washington, this bright, modern hotel with its 5-story atrium, located near Thomas Circle, provides well-appointed rooms (including data ports, irons, and ironing boards) with 24-hour room service, and a sauna and fitness center. The Veranda Restaurant serves breakfast, lunch, and dinner. Moderately expensive. Metro: McPherson Square, then a 3-block walk.

Xando Cosi www.xando.com

The coffee bar chain Xando (kisses XXX and hugs OOO) recently merged with Cosi, also a coffee bar. These are cozy coffeehouses by day, but drop by in the evening and patronize a full liquor bar and try your favorite cocktail or a liquor-spiked coffee. Highly rated sandwich fare. Walls display local art. Hours vary. The fifteen outlets are listed on the Web site.

YMCA of Metropolitan Washington Administrative Office: 1112 16th St NW, 7th floor (202) 232-6700 www.ymcawashdc.org

YMCA facilities are scattered throughout the metropolitan area, offering a variety of programs and services. Its mission is to "foster the spiritual, mental and physical development of individuals, families and communities according to the ideals of inclusiveness, equality and mutual respect for all." The programs vary from site to site but are centered on community services, health and fitness, child care, and camps. Activities include literacy programs, food banks, seniors programs, individual and group counseling, physical fitness programs including seniors and children, before and after school and school programs for children, and traditional and specialty camps. Most locations provide swimming lessons and a gym with a variety of fitness classes. Program fee or membership fees. Branch locations: 1325 W St. NW (202) 462-1054; 1711 Rhode Island Ave. NW (202) 862-9622; 1906 Allison St. NE (202) 526-4233; 1301 L'Enfant Square SE (202) 575-2670; 5650 Oakmont Ave., Bethesda, MD (301) 530-8500; 9401 Old Georgetown Rd., Bethesda, MD (301) 530-3725; 7425 MacArthur Blvd., Cabin John, MD (301) 229-1347; 3501 Moylan Dr., Bowie, MD (301) 262-4342; 9800 Hastings Dr., Silver Spring, MD (301) 585-2120; 1102 Forest Glen Rd., Silver Spring, MD (301) 593-1160; 10011 Stedwick Rd., Montgomery Village, MD (301) 948-9622; Camp Letts, P.O. Box 21037 (410) 919-1400; 420 E Monroe Ave., Alexandria, VA (703) 838-8085; 3422 N 13th St., Arlington, VA (703) 525-5420; 12196 Sunset Hills Rd., Reston, VA (703) 742-8800 www.restonymca.org; 3440 South 22nd St., Arlington, VA (703) 892-2044. *See also* National Capital YMCA, YWCA.

YWCA 619 9th St. NW (202) 626-0700 www.ywca.org

The YWCA of the National Capital Area was founded in 1905. This is a women's membership program that "creates opportunities for growth, leadership, and power through career education, health, fitness and aquatics programs, and child development centers." Unique programs include Nontraditional Employment for Women, the Harrison Center for Career Education that provides nursing education, various Child Development Centers, and youth mentoring programs. Program fee or membership fees. A fitness and aquatics center is located at 629 9th St. NW (202) 626-0710, as is the Harrison Center for Career Education (202) 628-5672. Child Development Centers are located at 1441 K St. NW (202) 626-6708; 8101 Wolftrap Rd., Vienna, VA (703) 560-1111; St. Thomas Episcopal Church, 8991 Brook Rd., McLean, VA (703) 442-9718; Westmoreland Community Church, 1988 Kirby Rd., McLean, VA (703) 532-3235.

Yacht Club 8111 Woodmont Ave., Bethesda, MD (202) 654-2396

Crowded with the over-30 singles (men in jackets and ties except on theme nights), who inhabit the upscale warrens of Bethesda, this is known as a primo matchmaking site, claiming a marriage a month. Also, lots of dates, not just singles. Dancing and pool. Sometimes live music or, more likely, a DJ. Bar food and a crowded bar. Moderate cover charge some nights. Open Tues–Thurs 5 p.m.–1 a.m., Fri 5 p.m.–2 a.m., Sat 7 p.m.–2 a.m. Metro: Bethesda.

Yanni's Greek Taverna 3500 Connecticut Ave. NW (202) 362-8871

This restaurant provides authentic Greek cuisine, including spanakopita (spinach pie), gyros, charbroiled shrimp, and *octapoda* (not squid, guess again). Save room for some dolmas and allow yourself the temptation of the baklava. Daily 11:30 a.m.–11 p.m. Metro: Cleveland Park.

Yanyu 3433 Connecticut Ave. NW (202) 686-6968

The same person who developed the popular Oodles Noodles restaurants brings this recently opened Pan-Asian restaurant featuring offerings from throughout Asia for your enjoyment. Try the steamed Chilean sea bass with ginger medallions or the crabmeat soup. Open Mon–Sat 5:30 p.m.–11 p.m., Sun until 10:30 p.m. Metro: Cleveland Park.

Yawa Books and Gifts 2206 18th St. NW (202) 483-6805

This bookshop offers unique woven bags and other items from Africa, as well as a selection of cards and, of course, books (fiction, nonfiction, and children's books) by African and African-American authors. Open Mon–Fri 11 a.m.–8 p.m., Sat noon–6 p.m. Metro: Woodley Park-Zoo, then 90, 91, 92, 93, or 96 Bus.

Yekta Market 1488A Rockville Pike, Rockville, MD (301) 984-1190

Pick up some salted pistachios at one of the area's oldest Persian markets, but also look over the preserves, meats, breads, and other Persian foods. Open Mon–Sat 10 a.m.–9 p.m., Sun 11 a.m.–6 p.m. Metro: Twinbrook.

Yemen Embassy 2600 Virginia Ave. NW, Suite 705 (202) 965-4760 www.yemenembassy.org

Yes! Natural Gourmet 1825 Columbia Rd. NW (202) 462-5150

"Your one-stop health food store." Conveniently located in the Adams Morgan area, near Woodley Park Metro station. For a healthier you the store offers vitamins, herbs, produce, bulk foods, oils, ginseng products, diet foods, books, cosmetics, sports supplements, sandwiches, soups, and salads-to-go. Open Mon–Fri 9 a.m.–7:30 p.m., Sat 9 a.m.–7 p.m. Closed Sun. Metro: Woodley Park-Zoo.

Yes! Organic Market 3425 Connecticut Ave. NW (202) 363-1559; 658 Pennsylvania Ave. NW (202) 546-9580

Sisters to Yes! Natural Gourmet, these stores provide juices, bulk foods, cosmetics, grocery items, salads, organic produce, soy drinks, vitamins, herbs, and a deli. They offer a complete line of bodybuilding and weight loss supplements. Their online catalog lists all of these items, as well as clothes. Connecticut Ave.: open Mon–Sat 9 a.m.–9 p.m., Sun 10 a.m.–8 p.m. Metro: Cleveland Park. Pennsylvania Ave.: open Mon–Sat 8 a.m.–9 p.m., Sun 9 a.m.–7 p.m. Metro: Eastern Market.

Youth Hostels *see* Hostels.

Yugoslavia Embassy 2134 Kalorama Rd. NW (202) 332-03333 www.yuembusa.org

Z

Zambia Embassy 2419 Massachusetts Ave. NW (202) 265-9717

Zanzibar on the Waterfront 700 Water St. (202) 554-9100 www.zanzibar-otw.com
Named by *Washingtonian Magazine* as the city's "best place for dancing" and "best happy hour," Zanzibar on the Waterfront offers a "tropical and romantic supper club" with great views of the Potomac marina, and, weather permitting, patio dining, good music, and 2 crowded dance floors. Friday's 5 p.m.–7 p.m. Happy Hour has live jazz and a raw seafood bar. Weekend cover charge. Closed Mon. Restaurant open Tues–Fri 11:30 a.m.–2:30 p.m., 5 p.m.–10 p.m.; Sat 5 p.m.–10 p.m.; Sun brunch 11 a.m.–4 p.m., 5 p.m.–10 p.m. Metro: Waterfront-SEU.

Zed's Ethiopian Cuisine 1201 28th St. NW (202) 333-4710
Tear off a piece of *injera* bread to sop up *doro wat*—chicken stew in red-pepper sauce—using the bread, no silverware is provided, or try the pungent lamb, chicken, seafood, and vegetarian meals. Open daily for lunch and dinner 11 a.m.–11 p.m. Metro: Foggy Bottom or Rosslyn, then Georgetown Shuttle.

Zenith Gallery 413 7th St. NW (202) 783-2963 www.zenithgallery.com
An important and long-standing Washington gallery, Zenith offers ten major exhibits a year. Particularly strong in three-dimensional mixed media works, Zenith provides one of America's preeminent annual shows of neon artists. Exhibits include tapestries, fine crafts, "fine art furniture," papier-mâché, sculptures, as well as wearable art, prints, lithographs, and abstract and realistic paintings. Located in "Gallery-Row," an award-winning building. Open Tues–Fri 11 a.m.–6 p.m., Sat noon–7 p.m., Sun noon–5 p.m. Metro: Archives-Navy Memorial.

Ziegfeld's 1345 Half St. SE (202) 554-5141 www.ziegfelds.com
Billing itself "Washington's premier club of female impersonators," the club offers drag shows and male strippers. Thurs–Sun 9 p.m. to closing. Metro: Navy Yard, then a 4-block walk.

Zimbabwe Embassy 1608 New Hampshire Ave. NW (202) 332-7100 www.zimem bassy-usa.org

Zoos see National Zoo, Reston Zoo.

Zorba's Cafe 1612 20th St. NW at Connecticut Ave. (202) 387-8555 www.zorbas cafe.com

It's smart to relax at this long-established Greek restaurant whose genial atmosphere has been attracting Mensa members for years. Try the chicken souvlaki, the moussaka, or maybe a gyro and a beer at low, low prices. Self-service. Eat indoors or out. Metro: Dupont Circle.